W9-CCT-213

WORLD PREHISTORY IN NEW PERSPECTIVE

WORLD PREHISTORY

IN NEW PERSPECTIVE

AN ILLUSTRATED THIRD EDITION

GRAHAME CLARK

MASTER OF PETERHOUSE, CAMBRIDGE

CAMBRIDGE UNIVERSITY PRESS

CAMBRIDGE

LONDON · NEW YORK · MELBOURNE

Published by the Syndics of the Cambridge University Press
The Pitt Building, Trumpington Street, Cambridge CB2 1RP
Bentley House, 200 Euston Road, London NW1 2DB
32 East 57th Street, New York, NY 10022, USA
296 Beaconsfield Parade, Middle Park, Melbourne 3206, Australia

This edition © Cambridge University Press 1977

First edition 1961
Reprinted 1962 (twice), 1965
Second edition 1969
Reprinted 1969, 1971, 1972
Third edition 1977

Printed in Great Britain at the
University Press, Cambridge

Library of Congress Cataloguing in Publication Data

Clark, John Grahame Douglas.
World prehistory.

Includes index.
1. Man, Prehistoric. I. Title.
GN740.C55 1977 930'.1 76-51318

ISBN 0 521 21506 4 hard covers
ISBN 0 521 29178 X paperback

(Second edition
ISBN 0 521 07334 0 hard covers
ISBN 0 521 09564 6 paperback)

TO THE DIVERSITY OF MEN

CONTENTS

TABLES

ACKNOWLEDGEMENTS

Acknowledgement is due to the following for their permission to reproduce the photographs indicated:

3 Cambridge Museum of Archaeology and Ethnology. **6** National Geographical Society; photo Baron Hugo van Lawick. **9** Courtesy of the Trustees of the British Museum (Natural History). **20** Jericho Excavation Fund. **21** Jericho Excavation Fund. **29** Iraq Museum, Baghdad. **31** Courtesy of the Oriental Institute, University of Chicago. **32** (*above*) Department of Antiquities, Ashmolean Museum; (*below*) Vorderasiatisches Museum, Berlin. **35** (*top*) Hirmer Fotoarchiv München; (*lower two*) Courtesy of the Oriental Institute, University of Chicago. **42** O. N. Bader, Moscow. **44** Musée des Antiquités Nationales, Paris. **46** P. Graziosi, *L'Arte dell'Antica Eta della Pietra* (Florence 1956), tav. 95. **47** S. Giedion, *The Eternal Present: The Beginnings of Art.* Bollingen Series xxv.6.1. The A. W. Mellon Lectures in the Fine Arts. © 1962 by the Trustees of the National Gallery of Art, Washington D.C. Plate 177 (photo Weider), reproduced by permission of Princeton University Press. **48** Ibid. Plate 267 (photo Herdeg and Weider). **61** V. G. Childe. **62** Courtesy of the Trustees of the British Museum. **65** Commissioners of Public Works, Ireland. **67** Alan Sorrell. **71** National Museum of Finland. **82** A. Evans, *The Palace of Minos* III, 66–7, pl. XVIII. **85** Heraklion Museum. **89** Hirmer Fotoarchiv München. **93** A. W. Persson, *The Royal Tombs at Dendra, near Midea* (Lund 1931), pl. IV. **95** G. W. G. Allen. **96** Montelius, *Meisterstücke im Museum Vaterländischer Altertümer zu Stockholm* (Stockholm 1913), Heft I, Taf. 3–5. **97** Aerofilms Ltd. **98** Museo Nazionale Tarquiniense. **102** Committee for Aerial Photography, University of Cambridge. **105** National Museum, Copenhagen. **107** Hermitage Museum, Leningrad. **111** State Historical Museum, Stockholm. **112** J. Desmond Clark. **119** Alex Willcox. **124** Henri Lohte in *Simposio International de Arte Rupestre,* ed. E. Ripoll Parello (Barcelona 1968). **127** Cairo Museum. **131** Cairo Museum. **133** Jos Museum, Nigeria. **135** David Attenborough. **136** Courtesy of the Trustees of the British Museum. **137** Cambridge Museum of Archaeology and Ethnology. **145** (*above*) Sir John Marshall, ed., *Mohenjo-Daro and the Indus Civilization* vol. I (Arthur Probsthaim 1931), pl. xc. Copyright Government of India. By permission of Arthur Probsthaim; (*below*) Ibid. vol. II, pl. CIV n.36. **146** (*left*) Ibid. vol. II, pl. XCVIII.3. (*right*) Ibid. vol. II, pl. XCIV.6. **147** Ibid. vol. I, pl. xc. **150** Ibid. vol. II, pl. CLIV.10, 11. **166** The Wen Wu Press, Peking. **172** The China Friendship Society. **173** The Wen Wu Press, Peking. **176** Courtesy of the Trustees of the British Museum. **177** Courtesy of the Smithsonian Institution, Freer Gallery of Art, Washington, D.C. **178** The Wen Wu Press, Peking. **180** Li Chi, *The Beginnings of Chinese Civilization* (Univ. Washington Press, Far Eastern & Russian Institute Publications on Asia, 1968), pl. XXIII. **182** The Wen Wu Press, Peking. **188** J. E. Kidder. **193** J. E. Kidder, *Japan before Buddhism* (Thames & Hudson 1966), fig. 62. **194** Tokyo National Museum. **207** Denver Museum of Natural History. **209** Robert S. Peabody Foundation for Archaeology. **212** Courtesy of the Trustees of the British Museum. **214** University Museum, University of Pennsylvania. **217** The Peabody Museum, Harvard University. **220** Center for Pre-Columbian Studies, Dumbarton Oaks, Washington, D.C. **223** The Peabody Museum, Harvard University. **225** The Field Museum of Natural

History, Chicago. **231** United States Department of the Interior, National Park Service, Washington, D.C. **233** United States Department of the Interior, National Park Service, Washington, D.C. **236** Ohio Historical Society. **240** W. G. Haag, ed. *Early Indian Farmers and Villages and Communities.* U.S. National Survey of Historic Sites and Buildings. Themes II and III (1963), fig. 69. **252** Courtesy of the American Museum of Natural History. **256** Junius B. Bird. **258** Cambridge Museum of Archaeology and Ethnology. **259** (*above*) The Peabody Museum, Harvard University; (*below*) Courtesy of the American Museum of Natural History. **260** Reproduced by permission of the American Geographical Society. **261** Courtesy of the American Museum of Natural History. **262** G. Reichel-Dolmatoff. **263** Center for Columbian Studies, Dumbarton Oaks, Washington, D.C. **264** Professor Irving Rouse. **266** Courtesy of the American Museum of Natural History. **277** Casey. **280** Donald Thomson. **282** Rhys Jones. **283** Aboriginal Arts Board, Sydney. **284** J. D. Mulvaney. **286** Permission of Charles Scribners' Sons; photo: Richard A. Gould. **287** John Oxley. **288** Bryan Cranstone. **289** Axel Steensberg. **292** National Museum of Victoria, Melbourne; photo: W. Ambrose. **296** Department of Anthropology, Bernice P. Bishop Museum. **302** Folding plate opposite p. 463 of John Hawkesworth's ed. of *An Account of Voyages...Discoveries in the Southern Hemisphere* vol. III (London 1773). **303** Cambridge Museum of Archaeology and Ethnology. **304** Cambridge Museum of Archaeology and Ethnology. **305** Cambridge Museum of Archaeology and Ethnology.

The following publications have served as sources for the drawings indicated. Thanks are due to the authors and publishers listed for their permission to use these drawings.

2 W. Le Gros Clark, *The Fossil Evidence for Human Evolution* (Univ. Chicago Press 2nd ed. 1964), figs. 13, 14. **4** W. Le Gros Clark, *History of the Primates* (British Museum 1970), fig. 40, reproduced by courtesy of the Trustees of the British Museum, and *The Fossil Evidence for Human Evolution* (Univ. Chicago Press 2nd ed. 1964), fig. 4. **5** K. Oakley, *Frameworks for Dating Fossil Man* (Weidenfeld & Nicolson 1964), fig. 4. **14** R. G. Klein, 'The Mousterian of European Russia', *Proc. Prehist. Soc.* XXXV (1969), fig. 2. **15** D. A. E. Garrod & D. M. Bate, *The Stone Age of Mount Carmel,* vol. I (Oxford Univ. Press 1937), pl. LII. **17** R. J. Braidwood, *The Near East and the Foundations for Civilization* (Condon Lectures, Oregon State System of Higher Education), figs. 5, 10. **23** *Jnl Near Eastern Studs.* 4–5 (1945–6), figs. 34, 36 (upper). **24** Ibid. figs. 2, 3, 4; 19, 21, 22. **25** M. E. L. Mallowan & J. Cruikshank Rose, *Prehistoric Assyria: the excavations at Tell Arpachiyah 1933,* figs. 53.1, 60.6, 62.5, 65.3, 4. **26** J. Mellaart, 'Excavations at Çatal Hüyük', *Anatolian Studs.* XIII (1963), fig. 6. **28** J. Mellaart, 'Excavations at Çatal Hüyük 1963, 3rd Prelim. Rep.', *Anatolian Studs.* XIV (1964), fig. 22. **30** V. G. Childe, *New Light on the Most Ancient East* (Routledge & Kegan Paul 1952), fig. 63. **33** Ibid. fig. 86. **54** R. R. Rodden, 'Excavations at the Early Neolithic Site at Nea Nikomedeia, Greek Macedonia (1961 season)', *Proc. Prehist. Soc.* XXVIII (1962), fig. 9; D. R. Theocharis, *Neolithic Greece* (National Bank of Greece 1973), pls. IV, VI, IX.2. **58** P. Modderman, 'Elsloo, a Neolithic farming community in the Netherlands', *Recent Archaeological Excavations in Europe* ed. R. Bruce-Mitford (Routledge & Kegan Paul 1975), fig. 86. **63** G. & V. Leisner, *Die Megalithgräber der Iberischen Halbinsel,* vols. I and II (Madrid 1943, 1959). **64** T. G. E. Powell, 'The Passage Graves of Ireland', *Proc. Prehist. Soc.* n.s. IV, 2 (1938), fig. 3. **66** M. Almagro Basch, *Manual de Historia Universal,* Tomo I *Prehistoria* (Espasa Calpe, S. A. Madrid 1958), fig. 702. **69** S. Piggott, 'The earliest wheeled vehicles and the Caucasian evidence', *Proc. Prehist. Soc.* XXXIV (1968), fig. 6. **72** Y. A. Savvateev, *Zalavrouga* (Leningrad 1970), fig. 25. **76** V. G. Childe, *The Danube in Prehistory* (Oxford Univ. Press 1929), figs. 112, 113. **78** R. W. Hutchinson, *Prehistoric Crete* (Penguin 1962). **79** Ibid. fig. 57. **81** The Evans Trustees. **86** A. J. B. Wace, *Mycenae, an archaeological history and guide* (Hafner Publishing Co. 1964), fig. 22 (by G. Dexter after Piet de Jong). **91** C. Renfrew, *The Emergence of Civilization: The Cyclades and the Aegean in the Third Millennium B.C.* (Methuen 1972), fig. 18.13 (2, 5). **92** Lord William Taylour, *The Mycenaeans* (Thames & Hudson 1964), fig. 29. **101** A. M. Snodgrass, *The Dark Age of Greece* (Edinburgh Univ. Press 1971). **104** J. Brailsford, *Early Celtic Masterpieces from Britain in the British Museum* (British Museum), fig. 91; reproduced by courtesy of the Trustees of the British Museum. **110** R. Bruce-Mitford, *The Sutton Hoo Ship-burial* (British Museum 1972), figs. 8, 29*b*; reproduced by courtesy of the Trustees of the British Museum. **113** J. D. Clark, *The Prehistory of Africa*

(Thames & Hudson 1970), fig. 19. **115** Ibid. fig. 39. **117** Ibid. fig. 54. **120** Ibid. fig. 33. **121** G. Caton-Thompson, 'The Aterian Industry: Its Place and Significance in the Palaeolithic World', *Jnl Roy. Anthrop. Inst.* LXXVI, part II (1946). **125** H. Frankfort, *The Birth of Civilization in the Near East* (Ernest Benn 1951), pl. III. **128** I. E. S. Edwards, *The Pyramids of Egypt* (rev. ed. Penguin 1961), fig. 56. **129** Ibid. fig. 5. **130** Ibid. fig. 27. **139** V. N. Misra, 'Bagor – a late mesolithic settlement in north-west India', *World Archaeology* 1973, fig. 22. **140** R. Thapar, *A History of India,* vol. I (Penguin 1966), fig. 12. **143** Sir Mortimer Wheeler, *The Indus Civilization* (Cambridge Univ. Press 3rd ed. 1968), fig. 13. **148** Ibid. fig. 10. **149** Ibid. fig. 7. **152** B. & R. Allchin, *The Birth of Indian Civilization* (Penguin 1968), fig. 46. **153** H. D. Sankalia et al. *From History to Prehistory at Nevasa (1954–56)* (Poona 1960), figs. 86, 87, 90. **154** F. R. Allchin, *Neolithic Cattle-keepers of South India* (Cambridge Univ. Press 1963), fig. 22. **155** B. B. Lal, 'Excavations at Hastinapura and other explorations in the Upper Ganga and Sutlej Basins, 1950–2', *Ancient India* nos. 10–11 (1954–5). **156** Ibid. **158** Ibid. **160** Kwang-chih Chang, *The Archaeology of Ancient China* (Yale Univ. Press 1971), fig. 14. **161** Ibid. fig. 20. **164** Ibid. fig. 40. **167** Ibid. fig. 30. **168** Ibid. fig. 56. **169** Ibid. fig. 69. **170** Ibid. fig. 81. **181** Li Chi, *The Beginnings of Chinese Civilization* (Univ. Washington Press 1957), fig. 5. **189** J. E. Kidder, *Japan before Buddhism* (Thames & Hudson 1966), fig. 3. **191** Ibid. fig. 29. **196** H. R. van Heekeren & E. Knuth, *Archaeological Excavations in Thailand,* vol. I (Copenhagen 1967), figs. 18, 20. **199** P. Sørensen, *Archaeological Excavations in Thailand,* vol. II (Copenhagen 1967), pls. 13, 35. **201** H. R. van Heekeren, *The Bronze-Iron Age of Indonesia* (Martinus Nijhoff 1958), fig. 3–1320. **202** Ibid. 8A. **211** G. R. Willey, *An Introduction to American Archaeology,* vol. I *North and Middle America* (Prentice Hall 1966), fig. 3–21. **215** Dr F. Rainey. **219** G. R. Willey, op. cit. fig. 3–46. **221** I. Bernal, *Mexico before Cortez* (Doubleday), pl. XVI. **232** G. R. Willey, op. cit. fig. 4–27. **238** J. B. Griffin, ed. *Archaeology of the Eastern United States* (Univ. Chicago Press 1952), fig. 107A, B. **247** S. A. Arutyonov et al. 'Ancient burials on the Chukchi peninsula', *The Archaeology and Geomorphology of Northern Asia: Selected Works,* ed. Henry N. Michael (Univ. Toronto Press for the Arctic Institute of North America 1964), 343, fig. 4. **249** G. R. Willey, *An Introduction to American Archaeology,* vol. I *North and Middle America* (Prentice Hall 1966), fig. 7–12 (*left*). **250** J. L. Giddings, *Ancient Men of the Arctic* (Alfred A. Knopf 1967), figs. 40*c*, 41*a*, *b*. **251** H. G. Bandi, *Eskimo Prehistory* (Univ. Alaska Press 1967), fig. 47, copyright Gustav Fischer Verlag, Stuttgart. **257** G. R. Willey, *An Introduction to American Archaeology,* vol. 2 *South America* (Prentice Hall 1971), fig. 3–35. **270** D. J. Mulvaney et al. 'Archaeological excavation of rock shelter 6, Fromm's Landing, S.A.', *Proc. Roy. Soc. Vic.* 77 (1964), 479–516. **275** F. D. McCarthy, *Australian Aboriginal Stone Implements* (Australian Museum, Sydney 1967). **276** Brough Smyth, *The Aborigines of Victoria* (Melbourne 1878). **279** G. F. Angas, *South Australia Illustrated* (London 1847), **281** D. F. Thomson, 'The seasonal factor in human culture', *Proc. Prehist. Soc.* V (1939). **285** Dr Isabel McBryde. **298** W. Shawcross, 'The Cambridge University Collection of Maori artefacts made on Captain Cook's first voyage', *Jnl Polynesian Soc.* 9, no. 3 (Sep. 1970), 313, pl. II. **301** E. Best, *The Maori Canoe* (Wellington 1925).

Every reasonable effort has been made to identify and acknowledge the copyright owners of the illustrations in this work, but if further acknowledgement seems appropriate this will be made at the earliest opportunity.

PREFACE TO THIRD EDITION

When the second edition of this work appeared in 1969 it was offered as 'virtually a new book'. This is even truer of the present one. It is substantially longer and is much more fully illustrated. It has benefited from another decade of research. And it has been written in a world in which some of the trends noted in the last edition have become more pronounced. It is now even more appropriate that we should view the archaeology, that is the material embodiment of the culture of each territory, as something worthy of study on its own merits. The notion of a single and implicitly western stereotype no longer survives in any conscious sense. Interest is focused on the adaptive capacity and inventiveness of men and every pattern of culture is assumed to have its own validity. Diffusion and migration can hardly be ignored, but can no longer be accepted as blanket explanations of change. Where they can be proved to have operated they are seen not as replacing so much as enriching the endowments of societies whose main characteristic has been their capacity to survive.

If even greater efforts have been made to avoid viewing prehistory from a Europocentric point of view or from the vantage point of the present, it would be absurd to allocate space on a neutral time-space grid. The rate of change has speeded up progressively with the multiplication of variables brought about by the expansion of human settlement and the growth in social and cultural complexity and diversity. More has happened during the last two hundred than during the previous fifty thousand years and more in the last fifty thousand than during the preceding two million years. Nothing can compare in importance with the process by which the earliest men emerged from the world of non-human primates. From a biological point of view the rest of the book might be put into an appendix. From a historical standpoint on the other hand it is not unreasonable to compress this vital stage into an opening chapter and to allocate ten to the fifty thousand years during which men have inherited the earth adapting to a plenitude of environments beyond those to which their predecessors were confined, multiplied enormously in numbers, created an intricate series of socio-cultural mechanisms and developed abstract thought to the point at which they can increasingly understand and control their physical environment and at the same time gain an awareness of their entire history.

Other problems are posed by how much space to allot to different territories. At a technical level there is the fact that archaeological research has been unevenly applied. In a work about prehistory this may present fewer problems than it would do in a descriptive handbook of archaeology, but it does mean a compression in the better studied areas that will irritate specialists, whereas in others of great potential importance the meagre facts presently to hand are frequently ambiguous and serve more to define areas of research than provide material for the exposition of prehistory. More fundamentally the problem remains of emphasis. The treatment of prehistory in which the world was equated largely with western Europe, its present and former colonies and its current zones of interest, although it persisted until remarkably recently in the works of some European authors, is now universally regarded as an anachronism. Again it is no longer the case that we regard the only prehistory worth writing as that of the great literate civilizations of mankind. This does not mean that we have to treat the prehistory of every region as of equal interest. Prehistory, like history itself, is about what happened and very little happened in communities cocooned in the state designated by Soviet prehistorians, ironically one might think, 'primitive communism'. As to the relative amount of space due to the various great traditions of mankind no two prehistorians are likely to agree. If Europe receives two out of eleven chapters in this book (it would probably have been given ten only thirty or forty years ago), the question may still be asked, why two instead of one? This is not the place to offer an apology for western civilization. Let it only be said that Europe created the one world that called for a world prehistory as well as developing the very concept and working methods of prehistory. The formulation of theoretical laws governing the universe and of the concept of history are fields to which other civilizations and even so-called primitive peoples have made their contributions; they are nevertheless ones in which the European tradition from the time of the classical Greeks has been massive. Again it was European technology, European capitalism and, let it be admitted, European imperialism, which in their day created and opened up the world economy and created the net-work of communications that willy-nilly has knit together the peoples of the world. To say so much is not to lessen the contributions made by other civilizations or the peoples who have only lately emerged from traditional societies to share in the economy, the experience and the imagination of the world at large.

When should a book about world prehistory begin and where should it end? To a thorough-going evolutionist there can be no logical point of departure. There is however an empirical one, the appearance in the archaeological record of implements and tools made to standard patterns, the beginning of a continuous development which not merely leads to modern technology but more significantly symbolizes the world of Man in which cultural increasingly outweighed genetic inheritance as a controlling factor. In this book the cultural apparatus is consistently viewed in the context of ecology, but the ecosystems inhabited by men are viewed as unique, the product to an increasing degree of socio-cultural, that is in essence of historical, factors. Those primarily interested in the biolo-
48–50, 56 gical antecedents of man are referred to works on the palaeontology
of the Primates. Again, research on Primate behaviour, increasingly
fruitful since it has been carried on in the wild as well as in the
35–40, 42–3 confines of zoos or laboratories, has recently been the subject of an
exceptionally well-written literature.

Where to end a work on prehistory is equally a matter of convention. The term prehistoric, while it serves a useful purpose in designating a period for which written records are available only for the concluding phase, is in some respects unfortunate. The roll of history is nothing if not continuous. It is only that different parts of it have to be read by different means. Prehistory is not merely an antecedant of history. In a broader sense it forms a part, indeed much the larger part of the story of man's past. From a temporal, though not from an existential point of view, almost the whole of human history is prehistoric in the technical sense that it has to be reconstructed without the aid of written records. Only some five thousand out of two million years are documented in this way and then only for a minute area. Conversely vast territories remained 'prehistoric' until 'discovered' by western man in recent centuries. Indeed the remoter parts of territories like Australia, New Guinea or Brazil remained outside the range of recorded history until our own generation.

18, 21–3, 30 As a work of synthesis this book is not directly concerned with the analytical techniques employed in research or with tracing the diverse lines of approach to the raw data of prehistory. Yet it is essential to appreciate that the value of any attempt to describe, let alone account for what happened in prehistory must depend for its success on the quality of the data themselves and of the insights brought to bear upon them. At the present time these vary very greatly from one territory to another. In extensive tracts only now being opened up to archaeology the preliminary task of establishing a bare chronological sequence often remains incomplete. Even in the territories most intensively worked archaeology still needs to be pursued at several levels, not to mention from several directions, at the same time. In a field as dark as prehistory there is a need to project beams from as many directions and by as many means as possible.

19 Since archaeology has emerged from its museological phase when its main concern was with the temporal and cultural classification of objects, many new fields of study have been opened up. One of the broadest of these is bioarchaeology, the study of archaeological and associated biological data as sources of information about the way men have adapted to and survived in diverse and changing eco-systems. Among the many facets of bioarchaeology to receive special
20, 26–7, 33–4 study have been prehistoric demography, economy and technology, not to mention the palaeontological aspects made important by the depth of time spanned by the data. Another field coming into
32 increasing prominence is social archaeology which stems from a realization that men have survived not as individuals or in random crowds, but as members of organized communities constituted by sharing common traditions. Social archaeology illuminates not merely the synchronic patterns which define communities and classes but also the processes of diachronic change which account for the unfolding sequence of prehistory and no less for the emergence of the literate societies for whom alone the concept of prehistory is relevant or meaningful. Social archaeology, like bioarchaeology, with which it needs to be pursued in the closest conjunction, presents many facets, among them art historical, intellectual, political and religious. It is by deploying techniques and concepts directed from many angles, rather than by espousing a single line of enquiry or adopting a particular standpoint, that a better understanding of

prehistory as of history itself is most likely to be reached. Whatever the field of research greater precision is sought in the handling of data. In the case of archaeology this has been achieved both by
16–17 bringing to bear the techniques of natural science and by extending
24, 28 mathematical control through measurement and statistics.

Although a work of this kind is not concerned with the minutiae of chronology, the enterprise of world prehistory is founded on the availability of a system of worldwide validity. For measuring the earliest phases of human evolution a dating method with a wide chronological range of application is needed. For this the potassium–argon (K–Ar) method has proved of some value in territories with the necessary volcanic rocks. The rate of change was so slow for most of human prehistory that even a scale calibrated in decimal points of millions of years has proved useful (see Table 17). For the period since modern man (*Homo sapiens sapiens*) speeded up the rate of change so dramatically a more precise chronological grid is necessary.
1–15 Prehistorians are fortunate that W. F. Libby's radiocarbon method spans more or less precisely the period that witnessed a dramatic expansion both in the area of human settlement and in the dynamism and diversity of human culture.

The prime value of radiocarbon dating continues to lie in its ability to synchronize sequences established in widely separated ter-
2: 7–10, 47–55 ritories. This is in no way lessened by the fact that radiocarbon dates
12–15 underwent wide divergencies from solar ones. This has been made apparent by taking the radiocarbon ages of individual annual growth rings from timbers of bristle-cone pine (*Pinus aristata*) that grew in California over a total span of over seven millennia. Previous to the first millennium A.D., for which radiocarbon dates are rather older than the solar chronology registered by tree growth rings, the divergence goes the other way and radiocarbon dates become progressively younger until during the middle of the fifth millennium the discrepancy is as much as seven centuries. In certain contexts, more particularly in interpreting the relations between early literate and surrounding prehistoric societies, discrepancies even of a few centuries can be crucial. The recalibration of radiocarbon in terms of solar dates is, therefore, much to be desired, but not premature recalibration from smoothed curves. The Californian results badly need checking from different environments and independent sequences are already in prospect in both Germany and Britain. The shorter and often sharp fluctuations which distort the curve of determinations made from the bristlecone pine samples by the lab-

oratories of the universities of Arizona, California and Pennsylvania call urgently for research and elucidation. In the present as in the last edition C 14 dates will be cited in terms of Libby's original half-life of 5,568 years, unless otherwise indicated. The practice followed by some authors of quoting dates calculated from the half-life of 5,730 years has only led to the confusion anticipated at the Cambridge radiocarbon conference when the decision was taken to continue with the practice followed by *Radiocarbon* of using the original half-life. Since radiocarbon dates are now recognized as being only relative and since also there is no reason to suppose that the 5,700 half-life is definitive, the case for maintaining a conservative stance is all the stronger. Dates based on the original half-life can readily be converted into ones calculated from the new half-life by the simple process of multiplying by 1·03.

Another promising method depends on quite a different circumstance, the fact that the degree of thermoluminescence given out by a sample of pottery or stone under heat is proportional to the amount of radiation accumulated since the sample was last fired. The thermoluminescent method is still in the experimental stage and has yet to be applied on anything like as wide a scale as radiocarbon dating. On the other hand it is encouraging that a fair amount of agreement has been noted where both methods have been employed.
8 A particularly well-controlled test is that carried out on a stone boiling tank from Orkney, Scotland, dating from early in the first millennium B.C. For what it is worth the eleven thermoluminescent dates agree much more closely with straight rather than with recalibrated radiocarbon determinations.

In closing this Preface I wish to acknowledge the immense debt I owe to my wife for enduring and assisting the writing of this book as well as to all those at the Cambridge University Press who in their various capacities have been responsible for its production.

Cambridge
July 1976

Grahame Clark

In the margins of this book, italic numbers refer the reader to items in the list of further reading (pp. 510ff.), upright numbers refer to illustrations.

1

Early prehistory

As we confront our origins we face a major paradox. The being, who through the power of his mind and imagination has come near to mastery over the forces of external nature as they confront him on this planet, and who has already begun to extend his dominion over parts of outer space, is himself an animal. As primitive man has always known, as some even of the higher religions have taught explicitly and as Charles Darwin and others have expressed it in scientific terms, human beings form an integral part of the web of life. Individual men are subject to the same processes of birth, growth, maturity and death as other organisms even if they alone are conscious of their fate. If we seek to understand the process by which man has emerged to civilization through his capacity to adjust to almost every environment encountered on earth and even momentarily on the moon, we need to take some account of his evolution as an organism and to recognize that both his biological and his social evolution have been accomplished in the context of a changing physical setting.

The evolution of man as an organism

If all existing organisms have emerged by imperceptible degrees from antecedent ones, it follows that one can hardly expect to be able to identify the first men merely by examining a succession of skeletal remains. This would be so even if the record were complete. As it is fossils are scarce, as a rule fragmentary and only rarely datable with precision. The position has not been improved by the exuberance of some writers in human palaeontology in respect of nomen-
44–57 clature. The literature is studded with generic and specific terms which enshrine views about the course of Primate evolution based on frequently ill-documented and incomplete fossils. In compiling

the highly simplified Tables 1–3 some of the better known obsolete terms are shown alongside their more recent equivalents in order to serve as a guide to the earlier literature.

The Primates

In zoological terms man falls within the hierarchy of the order Primates. Of the two sub-orders we need only concern ourselves with that appropriately termed *Anthropoidea*, leaving on one side for inspection in zoos man's exceedingly remote relatives the miniature and engaging *Prosimii*. Similarly, of the three super-families of the *Anthropoidea* we may ignore those comprising monkeys (*Ceboidea* and *Cercopithecoides*) and concentrate on the *Hominoidea* comprising the anthropoid apes (*Pongidae*) and the hominids (*Hominidae*).

The physical similarities between men and anthropoid apes have long been appreciated. They are indeed so close as to leave no reasonable doubt about their affinity. Similarities appear whether one considers the general structure of the skeleton, muscular anatomy or the disposition of visceral organs, the evidence of serological reactions and metabolic processes, or even the structure of the brain

1 Growth of the brain in course of Primate evolution.

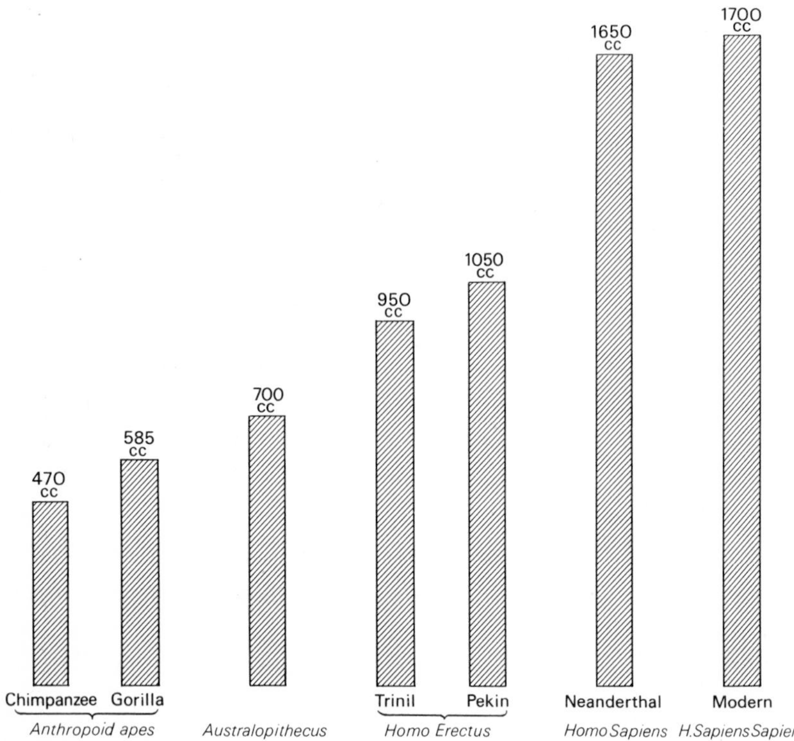

itself. The differences are no less pronounced. No competent zoologist would hesitate in attributing particular parts of the skeleton to man or ape. Even the layman cannot help but be impressed by the obvious differences in dentition, limb proportions and size of brain. It follows that the hominids must have diverged from the apes a very long time ago.

The hominid fossils so far available in adequate samples are generally divided into two genera. Each displays characteristics implying that they held themselves upright and walked on two legs. Both share a number of features in respect of the skull, including the height above the orbits, the contour of the forehead and the conformation of the mastoid process. Their dentition also shows points of resemblance. The teeth are comparatively small and are arranged in evenly curved parabolic arcades. The canines are spatulate and there are no diastemic gaps. Yet there is one difference of overwhelming significance for behaviour. Whereas the brains of some Australopithecines were scarcely larger than those of the great apes, those of man were invariably larger and in most species much larger. It was this and all the manifold consequences that flowed from

Table 1. *Some of the main occurrences of Australopithecine fossils showing some obsolete nomenclature*

Locations	Age	Obsolete nomenclature
Australopithecus africanus		
Chad		
Koro Toro (Yayo)	EMP	*Tchadanthropus uxoris*
South Africa		
Makapansgat	LP	*Australopithecus prometheus*
Sterkfontein	LP	*Pleisanthropus transvaalensis*
Swartkrans	EMP	
Taung	LP	
Tanzania		
Garusi, L. Eyasi	LP	*Meganthropus africanus*
Olduvai FLK.NN I	LP	*Homo habilis/A. africanus*
Australopithecus robustus		
Ethiopia: Lower Omo	UPlio	
Indonesia: Sangiran	Djetis	*Meganthropus palaeojavanicus*
Kenya: Kanopoi, L. Rudolph	UPlio	
South Africa		
Kromdraai	EMP	*Paranthropus robustus*
Swartkrans	EMP	*Paranthropus robustus*
Tanzania		
Olduvai FLK I	LP	*Zinjanthropus boisei*
Peninj	LP	*Paranthropus* cf. *boisei*

UPlio = Upper Pliocene. LP = Lower Pleistocene. EMP = Early Middle Pleistocene.

it that in the opinion of most authorities calls for the recognition of *Australopithecus* and *Homo* as distinct genera. Having said this it is important to recognize that systems of classification are mainly valuable as a generally accepted code for identification. While such codes serve for the majority of fossils, they are liable to break down precisely for those which from an evolutionary point of view are most important. If for instance the genus *Homo* stemmed from the same roots as *Australopithecus*, one could hardly expect fossils dating from the crucial intermediate stage to fall unambiguously into one or the other category.

The Australopithecines

Table 1 Fossils of the Australopithecines have so far been found in several parts of Africa, in the contiguous zone of south-west Asia and in Indonesia. They range in date from Late Pliocene to early Middle Pleistocene with some emphasis on the Early Pleistocene, whereas fossils certainly classifiable as human are at present almost entirely confined to the Middle and Upper Pleistocene. Although there may well have been some chronological overlap, the two genera thus appeared in a broad sense successively in time.

47: ch. 4 As fossils of Australopithecine character came to light they were
endowed with a variety of names most of which have since been
discarded. Only two species are now generally recognized, *Australo-*
2 *pithecus robustus* having a rather heavier jaw adapted to a herbivorous
diet, and *A. africanus* rather closer to man and having a lighter jaw possibly related to an omnivorous diet including meat. Reference should be made at this point to fossils from locus FLK. NN I at Olduvai (bed I) to which the name *Homo habilis* was applied by its discoverers on account of its inferred ability to make tools. Since the ability to make tools to standard patterns implies a form of life

2 *Australopithecus*: skulls of the more gracile *A. africanus* (*left*) and of the heavier *A. robustus* (*right*).

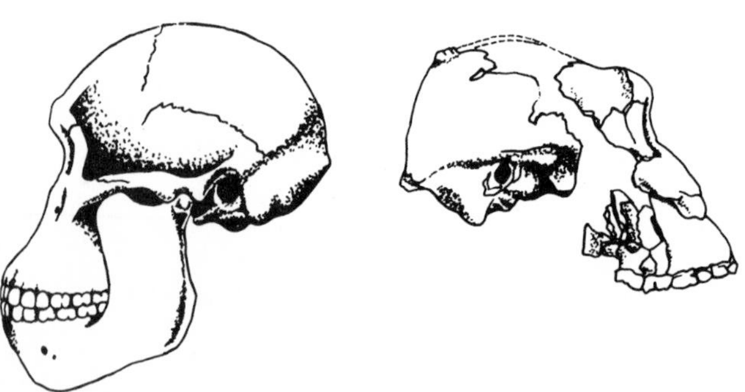

radically different from that of other animals and one which underlies the subsequent history of man, it is logical that this characteristic should be given due weight in nomenclature. Whether we adopt this classification or whether we follow the alternative course and include these fossils in the species *A. africanus* would in this case depend on whether or not the hominid in question manufactured the implements with which he was associated (see p. 22).

The genus Homo

It has for some years been accepted that all hominids other than
47:86–7 Australopithecines are best classified under the single genus *Homo.* This means that the numerous fossils from localities in Africa, Europe, North China and Indonesia formerly grouped within the genus '*Pithecanthropus*' or even accorded separate generic status have now been transferred to form a new species of man, *Homo erectus.* Another concept to be discarded is that Neanderthal and other more or less closely related forms showing characteristics that mark them off from the living races of men qualify as a distinct species. The modern view is rather that they form sub-specific varieties of *Homo sapiens,* such as *Homo sapiens neanderthalensis* or *soloensis,* and that modern man *Homo sapiens sapiens* is merely the sub-species that happens to have been living during the last thirty thousand years or so.

Table 2. *Present and former designation of the main groups of fossil hominids*

	Modern designation		Former designation
Pleistocene	*Homo sapiens*	*sapiens*	*Homo sapiens*
Upper	*Homo sapiens*	*neanderthalensis*	*Homo neanderthalensis*
		rhodesiensis	*Homo rhodesiensis*
		soloensis	*Homo soloensis*
		steinheimensis	
Middle	*Homo erectus*	*africanus*	*Pithecanthropus africanus* or *Atlanthropus*
		heidelbergensis	*Pithecanthropus heidelbergensis*
		javanensis	*Pithecanthropus erectus* or *javanensis*
		pekinensis	*Pithecanthropus pekinensis* or *Sinanthropus*
Lower	*Homo habilis?*		
	Australopithecus	*africanus*	
		robustus	*Paranthropus*
		boisei	*Zinjanthropus*

Homo erectus

47: ch. 3 Since fossils of what was then known as *Pithecanthropus erectus* were first found in the Trinil beds in Java, the island has yielded further specimens and there can be no doubt that the species was living there during the Middle Pleistocene. The largest assemblage of fossils is undoubtedly that from Middle Pleistocene beds filling the rock-
57 fissures at Choukoutien near Peking, a discovery all the more important because traces of fire, together with stone implements and utilized animal bones came from the same deposits. More recently traces of the same species (needlessly termed *Atlanthropus mauritanicus*) have come to light in Pleistocene deposits exposed in a sand-pit at Ternifine near Palikao, Algeria. The northern margin of the range is completed by the old find of a mandible from Mauer near Heidelberg, also of Middle Pleistocene age. Morphologically these fossils show as a group a notable increase in the size of the brain: the mean of three crania from Java gave a capacity of 860 cubic centimetres and that of four from Choukoutien 1,075 cubic centimetres, placing the group more or less intermediate between *Australopithecus* and *Homo sapiens*. On the other hand they show a number of characteristics that mark them off decisively from *Homo sapiens*. Thus the skull has a low vault and frontal flattening, a marked ridge at the junction of the two main side bones, and thick walls; the mastoid process is smaller; the palate is enormous and there is marked alveolar prognathism, the lower part of the face projecting noticeably; the mandible is massive and although the teeth are human in general arrangement, in the case of the Java fossils the canines have a tendency to overlap and for a diastematic gap to appear between these and the incisors; and the weight of the mandible is matched by a correspondingly massive development of the supraorbital and occipital brow-ridges, which, together with the flattened forehead, would probably strike us most forcibly were we to meet an individual in the flesh.

Homo sapiens

Homo sapiens can be presumed to have developed from the old *Homo erectus* stock. One of the few fossils of *Homo sapiens* type known for certain to date from the Middle Pleistocene is the incomplete cranium
53, 55 from Swanscombe in the lower Thames basin. It is particularly unfortunate that the frontal part is absent, but since the surviving portion agrees more or less closely with a more complete cranium from Steinheim dating from an interstadial of the Riss glaciation, it

is on the whole likely that it shared the massive brow-ridges of the German fossil, a feature that usually goes with large teeth and heavy jaws.

Much the most numerous fossils belonging to this stage in human
52 evolution are those named after the original discovery at Neanderthal in the Rhineland. It is important, if a false impression is not to be formed of the characteristics of this group, that it should be realized that the descriptions found in the early literature are based on what now appears to be an aberrant form, that represented by the early French finds at La Ferrassie and La Chapelle-aux-Saints. This classic west European form, which dates from the first onset of the Würm glaciation, is now commonly regarded as a genetic variation in a territory marginal to and to some extent isolated by ice-sheets; and, indeed, in individual cases pathological deformation has to be taken into account. The leading features of this form of the Neanderthal sub-species include, as is well known, a short stocky build, a flat-vaulted head with pronounced brow-ridges set rather forward on the vertical column, and massive chinless jaws set with

3 Skull and mandible of *Homo erectus pekinensis* from cast based on Weidenreich's reconstruction.

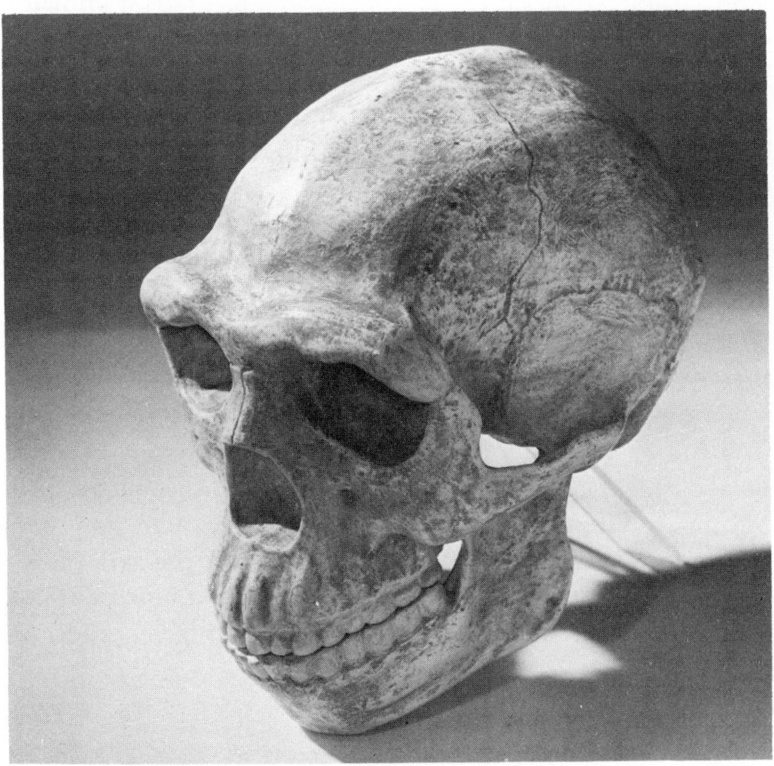

large teeth. The Neanderthaloid fossils from more remote territories like those from North Africa, the Levant, Iraq and Uzbekistan and those from such European localities as Ehringsdorf in Germany and Saccopastore in Italy that date from the interglacial preceding the Würm glaciation share these characteristics but to a less pronounced degree.

Although they show a clear continuity of development from the preceding stage, this whole early *sapiens* group, including the aberrant Westerners, exhibit an outstanding advance in respect of size of brain; the cranial capacity of the Neanderthalers was well up to that of the average for modern man. There can hardly be any question, if we leave aside the aberrant form, that this group of fossils marks a significant stage in human evolution. A point which will no doubt be further underlined as discovery proceeds is that this evolution was not by any means confined to Europe or contiguous parts of Africa and Asia. The occurrence of analogous forms as far afield as Broken Hill in Rhodesia and Ngandong on the River Solo in Java has already made this plain.

Homo sapiens sapiens

The earliest exemplars of *Homo sapiens sapiens* so far known are those recovered from cave deposits at Cromagnon and elsewhere in the Dordogne, France, and from other sites with mode 4 Palaeolithic equipment scattered over a territory extending from western Europe to Iran and the Soviet Union, all dating from a fairly advanced phase
4 of the last major glaciation. Men of this species were more lightly built than Neanderthal man and his cousins; they stood fully upright; their skulls were free from strong muscle attachments; the forehead was steep and well-rounded; the brow-ridges were only moderately developed and never continuous; the teeth were relatively small; and the chin prominent. This modern type, to which all existing races belong, was associated in the sub-tropical and temperate zones with flint industries in mode 4 and other components of an advanced Palaeolithic technology, as well as with a conceptual endowment far beyond anything available to Neanderthal man and his cousins. Indeed one can assume from his art and the complexity of his technology that the mentality of Cromagnon man can hardly have differed substantially from that of the existing races of man.

When and where did the various races of man emerge in their existing form? The first question is particularly hard to answer, since so many of the criteria by which racial differences are characterized, such as pigmentation and hair form, can hardly be inferred from skeletal remains. Attempts have been made to infer racial attributes from certain fossils – for instance skeletons from the Grimaldi caves near Mentone have been variously interpreted as Mediterranean or Negroid and one from Chancelade in the Dordogne as Eskimo – but the danger of drawing any such conclusions from miniscule samples of skeletal evidence is clear. It is wisest to recognize that almost everything remains to be discovered in this field. One suggestion might be that racial differences were an outcome of genetic variations linked with the widespread colonization of new territories towards the end of the Pleistocene.

Early types of man were confined to the warmer parts of the world: their remains, cultural and physical, are confined to Africa, to Europe as far north as southern Britain and central Germany, to south western Asia, to India and to south-east Asia as far as the Makassar

4 Skeletons and skulls of (*a*) *Homo sapiens neanderthalensis* and (*b*) *Homo sapiens sapiens.*

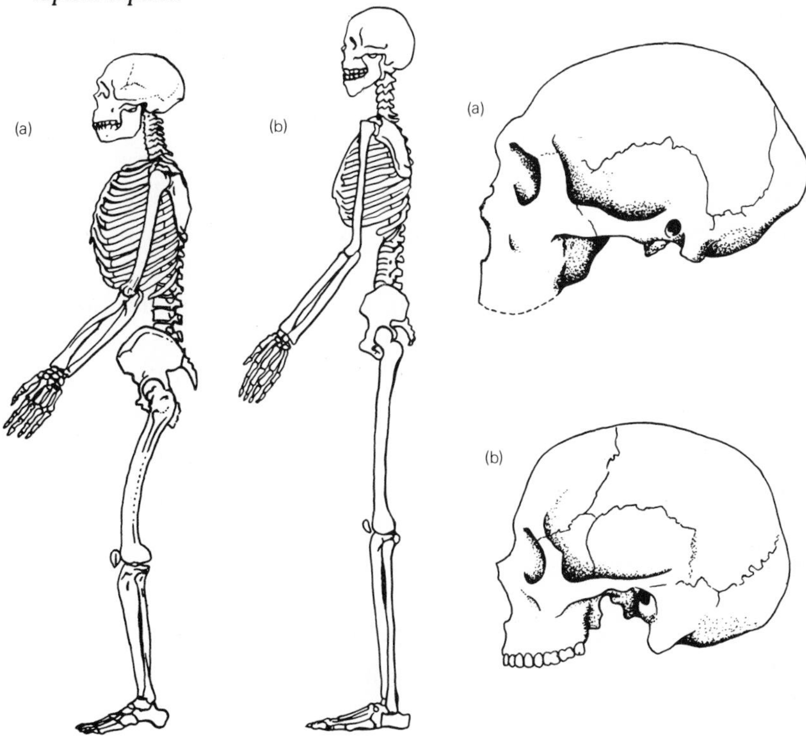

Strait, the major palaeontological divide first recognized by Darwin's collaborator A. R. Wallace. Significant extensions of the zone of settlement were made in a northerly direction, notably in the Soviet Union, by Neanderthal man, but it was left to modern man to colonize the New World and the remainder of the Old, including Australia and the Pacific islands.

The degree of correlation between certain criteria of race and existing environments is sufficiently close to suggest that they were to some extent adaptive. The extent of ethnic movement during recent millennia helps to explain evident exceptions, but at the same time makes more striking the extent to which pigmentation and the width of nasal aperture accord with climate. Thus in the Old World blond fair-skinned people go with the cool, cloudy habitat of the north temperate zone; brunettes with the Mediterranean zone; yellow-skinned crinkly haired people with the tropical rain-forest; and the darkest skins with the hottest, non-forested African savannah. Again, the fact that the Eskimo and north Europeans have narrow nostrils, the Mediterraneans medium ones and the Negroes broad ones suggests a high degree of correlation between this feature and climate, something hardly surprising when one remembers that one function of the nose is to regulate the temperature of the air breathed into the lungs.

58–62 Environmental change

Subdivision of the Pleistocene

The Pleistocene or Quaternary epoch has the supreme interest for human beings that it spanned crucial stages in their physical and social evolution. It can hardly be a coincidence that it was a time of repeated ecological change. The extension and contraction of ice-sheets, the rise and fall of land and sea levels and extensive shifts in the distribution of animals and plants in response to climatic change, all these combined to alter more or less radically the physical conditions to which early communities had to accommodate themselves. And the cycle of change was many times repeated during the course of the Pleistocene.

On palaeontological grounds this epoch is commonly divided into three temporal phases. Deposits of Lower Pleistocene age are consistently marked by faunal assemblages of the kind first recognized at Villefranche-sur-Mer, including such well defined forms as *Dinotherium, Stylohipparion, Sivatherium* and *Elephas* (*Archidiskodon*) *meridionalis.* By the Middle Pleistocene these archaic forms had disappeared and new ones had arrived including a new genus of elephant, *Elephas* (*Palaeoloxodon*) *antiquus*. The emergence of a developed form of *Elephas* (*Mammuthus*) *primigenius* was one of the distinguishing marks of the Upper Pleistocene. On the other hand the Recent or Holocene epoch, during which the environment as a whole assumed its present character, witnessed the disappearance of this as of other species now extinct.

If we accept the latest findings of potassium–argon analysis, the transition from the Lower to the Middle Pleistocene occurred some seven hundred thousand years ago. Although least is known about the Lower Pleistocene, the period in the course of which the most vital steps must have been taken in the process of hominization, it is known to have lasted about twice as long as the rest of the epoch. Precisely when the Upper Pleistocene began has not yet been determined, but protoactinium–thorium analysis indicates an age of around 108,000 years for the peak of the glaciation that introduced it. Radiocarbon dates are available only for the last fifty or sixty thousand years and only for the last thirty do they fall within an acceptable range of probability. Nevertheless it seems likely that the last major glaciation (Weichsel/Würm of Europe) began within a few

5 Geography of Europe at the peak of the last Pleistocene glaciation.

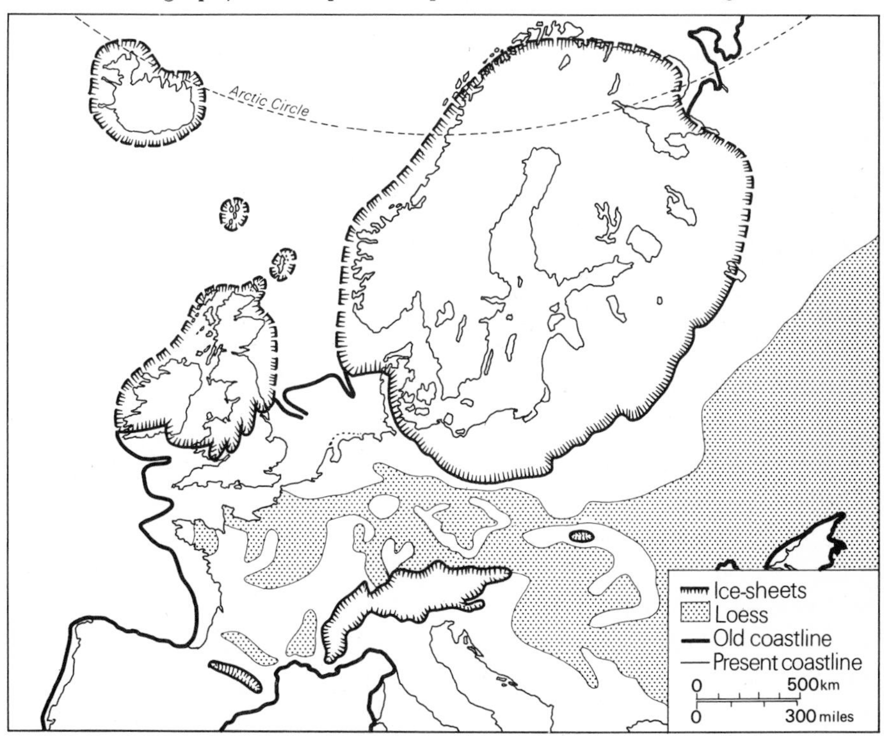

thousand years of 65,000 before the present and that within this glaciation the first major interstadial (Laufen/Göttweig) fell within the period 40/50,000 years ago.

When we apostrophize the Pleistocene as the Ice Age, we no longer imply that the expansion of ice-sheets was a once-and-for-all phenomenon. On the contrary the Pleistocene witnessed a whole series of glaciations interrupted by interglacial periods during which temperatures rose above those prevailing in recent times. In the present temperate zone and at higher altitudes even in the tropics, there were, if we may judge from the evidence obtained from cores taken from ocean beds, some fifteen major phases of increased glaciation during the Quaternary period. It is this recurrence of glacial and interglacial episodes that offers the best possibilities of subdividing the main chapters of the Pleistocene. Once again, it is important to emphasize that so far as the Lower Pleistocene is concerned the geological record is woefully incomplete on dry land where alone it can be related directly to the archaeological record. This is understandable when we consider the destructive effect of the repeated glaciations of which geological traces survive.

In western Europe, where Quaternary Research was first developed, knowledge of Pleistocene stratigraphy still relates only to its later stages. It is solely in East Africa and more particularly in Olduvai Gorge, where the need to date the remarkable series of fossil hominids brought to light during recent decades has provided a powerful stimulus to geologists and palaeontologists, that we have Table 18 much detail about the stratigraphy of the Lower Pleistocene, a period which, nevertheless, lasted twice as long as the Middle and Upper put together. Even for the Middle Pleistocene only the major phases can be defined in Europe. It is for the Upper Pleistocene Tables 3, 4 and Holocene geological periods alone that the course of environmental change can be plotted with any precision and then only in Europe and territories within reach.

If, as is commonly thought, the episodes of the Ice Age were an outcome of changes in solar radiation there is promise of being able to discern a world-wide pattern. On the other hand it would be quite wrong at this stage to seek to apply European results to other parts of the world. What is required is that local sequences should first be worked out in each particular territory, as they have been in East Africa. Only so can prehistoric communities be assessed in the context of their local environments on the appropriate temporal plane. As more local sequences become available the opportunity

Table 3. *Main Pleistocene sequences in parts of Europe*

	Glacial and *interglacial* stages		Marine transgressions:	Potassium–Argon
	North-west Europe	Alps	Mediterranean	years B.P.
Pleistocene				
Upper	South Pomeranian (Weichsel III)	Main Würm III		
	Brandenburg/ Frankfurt-Posen (Weichsel II)	Main Würm II		
		Laufen/ Göttweig	*Late Monastirian (Tyrrhenian III)*	*c.* 40/50,000
	Stettin (Weichsel I)	Early Würm I		
	Eemian/Ipswichian	*Riss/Würm*	*Main Monastirian (Tyrrhenian II)*	
	Warthe	Riss II		
	Saale	Riss I		*c.* 65,000
Middle	*Hoxnian*	*Mindel/Riss*	*Tyrrhenian I*	
	Elster	Mindel II	*Sicilian II*	
		Mindel I		
	Cromerian	*Günz/Mindel*	*Sicilian I*	
Lower	Weybourne	Günz		*c.* 700,000
	Tiglian	*Donau-Günz*	*Calabrian*	
	Red Crag	Donau		
	Sequence not yet known			*c.* 2,000,000
Pliocene				

Table 4. *Periodization of the Late-glacial and Postglacial in north-west Europe*

Radiocarbon dates B.C.	Pollen zones	Climate
Postglacial		
500–	VIII	Subatlantic
3000– 500	VII *b*	Sub-boreal
5500– 3000	VII *a*	Atlantic
7000– 5500	VI	Late Boreal
7700– 7000	V	Early Boreal
8300– 7700	IV	Preboreal
Late-glacial		
8800– 8300	III	Younger Dryas
10000– 8800	II	Allerød oscillation
10500–10000	I *c*	Older Dryas
11500–10500	I *b*	Bølling oscillation
15000–11500	1 *a*	Oldest Dryas

will present itself of attempting to synchronize them by means of radiocarbon and other geophysical methods. Progress is already being made in this direction but Quaternary Research has still a very long way to go.

The question of pluvial periods

In the tropical and equatorial regions remote from glaciation, except at the highest altitudes, there are indications of periods of increased rainfall during the Pleistocene; and much discussion has centred on how so-called pluvial periods could be synchronized with the glacial sequence. Recent research on the other hand has called into question the status of pluvial periods as chronological markers on anything approaching even a continental scale. Evidence for variations in rainfall certainly exists in strand-lines around lakes, fossil-springs and the nature of certain widespread deposits like laterite. This means that they offer possibilities for establishing local sequences. When more of these have been worked out, when radiocarbon and other methods of dating have been applied to them and above all when greater understanding has been reached about the explanation of their causes it may be possible to incorporate them in a world-wide framework of geochronology. What is beyond cavil is that in so far as major changes in precipitation occurred in these regions they must have affected more or less profoundly the circumstances of life for prehistoric communities.

Geographical and biological changes in the Ice Age

58, 60, 62 The fluctuations of climate dramatically symbolized by the expansion and contraction of ice-sheets transformed the setting of early man across its whole range. For instance, the alternate locking-up and release of vast quantities of water as ice-sheets all over the world alternately expanded and contracted – and one has to remember that the largest ice-sheets might be hundreds of metres thick – affected ocean-levels, not merely in glaciated areas but over the whole world. Periods of glaciation were in general marked by the eustatic lowering of ocean-levels and interglacials by their corresponding rise. Although in regions central to the formation of major ice-sheets this might be offset or even surpassed by local isostatic depression of the land under the weight of ice and its alternate recovery, the effect over the world as a whole was to alter, sometimes quite drastically, the shape of land-masses. For instance during glacial phases in areas immediately outside isostatic depressions continents were more

extensive: most of Indonesia was joined to south-east Asia by the
159 Sunda shelf; New Guinea and Tasmania were both attached to Australia; north-east Siberia was linked by a broad land-bridge to Alaska; and to mention an example on a smaller scale Britain was
5 joined on a wide front to the European continent. It goes without saying that if climatic change was sufficiently pronounced during the Pleistocene to alter the basic geography of the world it can also be expected to have had the most profound influence on living things, on man himself and on the animals and plants on which directly or indirectly he sustained life.

59, 61 The fluctuations of climate implied by the succession of glacial and interglacial episodes involved corresponding shifts in vegetational and faunal distributions. For example, when ice-sheets and periglacial conditions encroached on formerly temperate zones, as must have happened with every glacial advance, this meant that forests had to give place to open vegetation and that in the animal world sylvan species were replaced by ones adapted to steppe or tundra; and, conversely, during interglacial or interstadial phases, as well as during the Recent period following the last retreat of the ice, the situation was reversed. Further, it need hardly be emphasized that ecological displacement was by no means confined to territories immediately adjacent to the ice-sheets. During glacial periods it was not merely the temperate zones that were displaced, but to some degree the sub-tropical arid zones shifted nearer the equator. At such times also the equatorial rain forests must in turn have undergone some contraction. Conversely during interglacial and interstadial periods, not forgetting the Recent period, the equatorial rain-forest expanded, the sub-tropical arid zone moved further away and the forest spread again over territory formerly occupied by open vegetation.

The impact of such changes on early man can only be fully imagined when it is remembered how closely his life was linked with that of the animals and plants on which he depended for subsistence. Men, no less than other species, must needs live in ecosystems. They have to establish some kind of relationship to the habitat (soil and climate) and biome (vegetation and animal life) in which they exist and being men they have to evolve definite transmissible patterns by which these relations are structured. The cultural apparatus of which archaeologists study the surviving traces embodies the patterns developed by particular communities for coping with particular ecological situations. It follows that any drastic change, whether this occurs in the sphere of the habitat or biome or for that matter in the sphere of culture, must have involved readjustment, either through migration or cultural innovation, as the only alternative to decline and ultimate extinction; for natural selection in however roundabout a way applies no less to human societies than to any other societies of living organisms.

Until a much more complete picture of ecological change has been built up in different parts of the world it follows that our understanding of the underlying causes of the movements and cultural changes of which prehistory is composed must remain imperfect.

The Holocene

The ultimate status of the Recent or Holocene period in which we live will only appear in the fullness of geological time. Whether it proves to coincide with an interstadial or even an interglacial episode or whether it turns out to mark a definitive end of the Pleistocene Ice Age is for us an academic question. What is important in our present context is that it equates with a period during which our familiar climate, geography and animal and plant life made their appearance and one moreover during which human societies developed agriculture and a settled basis of life.

Not all geologists are convinced of the need for distinguishing the last 10/12,000 years as a distinct period. Yet, whatever may be the case for extensive parts of the world where Quaternary Research is still in its infancy, no doubt of the utility of the concept need be entertained for territories strongly affected by the contraction of ice-sheets. Even so there may be room for debate about where the line is most appropriately drawn. In Scandinavia the original convention was to begin the Postglacial at the time when the contracting ice-sheet broke into two. Today the boundary between Late-glacial and Postglacial is drawn in this region at the moment when the ice-sheet began what from our point of view may be accepted as its final withdrawal from the Fennoscandian moraines. In areas remote from the sensitive ice-margin it is possible that the onset of the last warm oscillation of the Late-glacial, that first defined at the Danish locality of Allerød, may prove more useful for defining the beginning of Neothermal time.

The contraction and in some cases complete disappearance of ice-sheets affected human settlement in two obvious ways. For one thing it opened up new areas for occupation by the mere process of uncovering them. In this way much of the Scandinavian peninsula was first laid open to human settlement during the Holocene. Again, in some areas the removal or parting of ice-sheets opened up the way to migration and the settlement of new territories. The way in which the separation of the Cordilleran and Laurentide ice-sheets gave access to the High Plains of North America and so to most of the rest of the New World is only one, though the most dramatic example. The contraction of ice-sheets also affected the possibilities of human settlement through its effect locally on crustal movements and more extensively through eustatic rises of sea-level, the combined effect of which on geography was sometimes profound. The insulation of Britain or the history of the Baltic are two well-studied examples on a relatively miniature scale. The drowning of extensive areas of the south-east Asian peninsula and the insulation of Sumatra, Java and the many smaller islands of Indonesia, not to mention the separation of New Guinea and Tasmania from Australia, illustrate on a grander scale the geographical implications of the close of the Ice Age.

But the contraction of ice-sheets was only the most dramatic outcome of what was in essence from a terrestial point of view a change of climate. The onset of Neothermal conditions had a profound influence on the distribution of the animal and plant species on which man depended for subsistence and for many of the raw materials he needed for his industry. During what is sometimes termed an initial Anathermal phase, corresponding to the Preboreal of temperate Europe, temperatures rose from the low levels of the Late-glacial until during the ensuing Altithermal they reached a peak during which they exceeded those prevailing today; thereafter they declined and during the Medithermal, corresponding to the Subatlantic of temperate Europe, they fell temporarily slightly below those of the present. So far as man was concerned the most important feature of Neothermal climate was its effect on vegetation and consequently on the herbivorous animals on which he depended to a significant extent, either as hunter-forager or as farmer. Information obtained from temperate Europe has already thrown significant light on the history of human settlement during the important period when hunter-forager economies were beginning in favourable areas to give way to those based on different forms of farming. This only emphasizes the need to extend the analysis of pollen and of larger plant remains on a more intensive scale to crucial areas of the Near and Middle East, where a promising beginning is now being made with reconstructing the ecological context of animal and plant domestication in the western part of the Old World. Investigation of climatic and biological changes in remaining parts of the world is no less important as a key to the understanding of the emergence of the societies known to history.

Palaeolithic hunters and foragers

Cultural criteria of humanity

Although most palaeontologists agree that the assumption of an upright posture was sufficiently important to justify separating the hominids from the great apes, few would maintain that it is possible to distinguish on purely zoological grounds between those hominids that remained prehuman and those that had attained the status of man. To qualify as human, a hominid has, so to say, to justify himself by works: the criteria are no longer biological so much as cultural. Yet it remains true that a close interrelationship must exist between cultural achievement and biological endowment. The adoption of an erect posture, which may well have been a response to the thinning of forest and the consequent need to cross open country between one area of woodland and another, in itself facilitated the acquisition of culture; the freeing of the hands from locomotion made them available for tool-using and ultimately for tool-making; and these activities stimulated the development of the brain. At the same time they facilitated it by modifying the architecture of the skull: the diminishing role of the teeth for eating and manipulating had the effect of reducing their size, the weight of the jaw and the strength of the brow-ridges and muscular attachments. On the other hand the two-footed stance had its dangers, and ultimately only those hominids survived who made an intelligent use of tools and weapons. Indeed the ability to acquire culture, including the intangible but decisive aid of articulate speech, was evidently of adaptive value in the sense that the strains most capable of doing so were those whose genotypes were propagated most abundantly in the course of natural selection. This may well explain why the increase in the size of the brain that permitted ever greater advances in culture developed so rapidly in the course of Pleistocene times. Even the biological evolution of the most advanced hominids was thus in large measure an outcome of developments in culture.

Subsistence, food-sharing and the home-base

If the systematic manufacture of implements as an aid to manipulating the environment was a characteristic of the earliest men, so also was the form of their economy. To judge from the biological materials recovered from his settlements in different parts of Europe, Africa and Asia Palaeolithic man enjoyed even from the remotest periods a diet far more nearly omnivorous than that of any of the surviving non-human primates. In particular early man was a meat-eater. Whereas the great apes, though not averse to an occasional taste of animal food, are predominantly vegetarian, the earliest men whose food debris is known to us were evidently able to secure a wide range of animal meat. There seems no doubt that man found himself and emerged as a dominant species first and foremost as a hunter. One result of enlarging the range of his diet was in the long run to make it possible for him to explore a much wider range of environment, something in which he was greatly helped as time went on by the development of his material equipment. Another was to initiate the sub-division of labour that was to prove one of the mainsprings of human progress: whereas men pursued game and when necessary fought one another, their mates concentrated on nurturing the family and gathering plants and small items of animal foods such as eggs and insects. Food-sharing in a formalized manner was at least as characteristic of early man as opposed to non-human hominids as was the transport of materials or the manufacture of tools to standard patterns.

It was the economic partnership of the sexes that more than anything else underlay the human family, an institution which grew in importance with every increase in the scope and range of the culture which each generation had to acquire in infancy. The importance of nurture is reflected in the growing importance of the home base. Palaeolithic man remained predatory: he bred no animals and grew no plants but depended on what he could catch or collect from wild nature. It follows that he needed extensive areas for his support. This meant that he had to live in small widely dispersed groups, comprising at most enough adults to man the hunt. Even so it would generally be necessary for him to move, sometimes over extensive territories, in the course of the year exploiting natural sources of food as these ripened and matured. Yet the most primitive man needed a home-base far more permanent and substantial than the nightly nests of chimpanzees. The longer the young needed for protection and education the more equipment was needed in daily life, the more important cooking became, the more vital it was to secure a base close to game and water and congenial for living where essential tasks could be performed.

PALAEOLITHIC HUNTERS AND FORAGERS

It can be assumed, even if the surviving evidence is necessarily slight, that early man must have owed his domination of the animal world to qualities much less tangible than his technology or mode of subsistence. In particular he must have owed much to his ability to understand his environment, accumulate and pass on his experience and ensure the proper functioning of the artificially defined societies in which he lived. One of the principal ways in which he classified his surroundings, pooled and transmitted his experiences and developed traditional modes of behaviour was of course articulate speech.

Students of the great apes are agreed that one of their greatest drawbacks is the lack of speech, which alone is sufficient to prevent them acquiring the elements of culture. It is true that chimpanzees have a wider 'register of emotional expression' than most humans and that they are able to communicate to one another not only their
37 emotional states but also definite desires and urges; yet, as Köhler has emphasized, 'their gamut of phonetics is entirely "subjective", and can only express emotions, never designate or describe objects'. In this connection it is interesting that in their famous enterprise of bringing up the chimpanzee Viki from the age of three days to three
35 years, Dr and Mrs Hayes found it possible to train her to certain commands, but failed after eighteen months of intensive tuition to get her 'to identify her nose, eyes, hands and feet'. Until hominids had developed words as symbols, the possibility of transmitting, and
41 so accumulating, culture hardly existed. Again, as Thorpe has remarked, man's prelinguistic counting ability is only of about the same order as that of birds or squirrels: serious mathematics, with all the immense advances in control of the environment that it portends, first became possible with the development of symbols. Speech, involving the use of symbols, must have been one of the first indications of humanity. Its only drawback as a criterion for the prehistorian is that there is no hope of being able to verify its existence directly for the remotest ages of man. Despite suggestions to the contrary, the best palaeontological opinion is against the notion that articulate speech can be inferred either from the conformation of the mandible or from study of casts taken of the inner surfaces of skulls. Probably the best clue is the appearance of tools of standardized and recognizable form, since it is hard to see how these can have been popularized and transmitted without the use of verbal symbols.

Palpable evidence of increasing self-awareness first appears from a comparatively late stage of prehistory. It is not until the Upper Pleistocene that we get the first evidence for systematic burial of the dead by Middle Palaeolithic man. And it is only towards the end, at a time of rapid technical innovation, that we first encounter evidence for self-adornment and the practice of art, in each case in the context of *H. sapiens sapiens*.

Tool-making

It is generally accepted by primatologists that not merely the hominids, but also gibbons, monkeys and the great apes are capable of a certain level of implemental activity. This has been observed among captive animals and more convincingly in the wild. Indeed if tool-using implies no more than the active manipulation of some external object by an organism in furtherance of its aim, then a sea-otter bringing boulders from the bottom to crack molluscs qualifies as a tool-user. And so do many other organisms of a much lowlier character. But there is a vital distinction between using objects as tools and shaping them in such a way as to make them more effective. The problem

6 Chimpanzee extracting termites from a mound by poking in a blade of grass.

of defining artefacts is a difficult one. On the evolutionary hypothesis no sharp break should be anticipated between utilized objects and those shaped by artificial means. The distinction is necessarily arbitrary, though none the less real. When we ask ourselves what degree of modification qualifies for description as an artefact, one answer might be when materials are shaped to forms standardized by virtue of sharing cultural traditions. The mere fact of having been shaped is not in itself sufficient to qualify an object as an artefact since natural forces are capable under certain conditions of fracturing flint or stone, or if it comes to that bone, and the resultant forms may sometimes closely resemble implements known to have been made by man. This only goes to emphasize the importance of context. It is only when objects are found under conditions where the relevant natural forces can be excluded on sites where man is attested by his own physical remains or by other circumstances that anything approaching certainty is possible when it comes to judging the earliest essays in craftsmanship.

Much discussion has centred on the question at what stage in hominid evolution tool-making to standard patterns began? In particular what was the status in this regard of the Australopithecines? Present indications suggest that the claims of *Australopithecus robustus* can be discounted. Fossils of this species were admittedly found with stone implements in bed I (FLK I) at Olduvai, but the situation changed radically when traces of a more advanced hominid were found at the same level at FLK . NN I. *A. robustus* was then reduced to being a victim of a more advanced hominid. Since the latter was credited by his discoverers with fabricating the stone implements from bed I, it was logical to accept him as representing a new species of man, *Homo habilis.* Yet it can hardly be excluded that further researches at Olduvai may yield traces of a yet more advanced hominid in bed I, who in turn might be accepted as knapper and overlord. In this case there would be no problem from a palaeontological point of view in downgrading *H. habilis* to a variety of *A. africanus.*

Because of their durability and widespread occurrence flint and stone artefacts are bound to attract most attention. Yet sticks and animal bones are likely to have been readily at hand and are liable to have been among the first objects used as implements. There are indeed strong indications from the cave of Makapansgat in South Africa that representatives of *A. africanus* made use of selected animal bones. On the other hand it is significant that there are no signs that these were shaped to purposive, standard designs: they had merely been broken into convenient pieces. As we shall see, the sophisticated utilization of antler and bone as materials for implements and weapons developed surprisingly late in prehistory.

The evolution of flint- and stone-working

63–8 The abundance, persistence and well-nigh universality of flint or stone industries has already been remarked. Other reasons why they played so important a part in the early history of technology is that they could be worked by a number of techniques into a great variety of forms and that being hard and sharp they were in effect dominant materials controlling the use of a wide range of organic substances. Viewed over long periods of time it is hardly surprising that they should display evidence of evolutionary development.

The mere fact that technology was concerned with sustaining and facilitating the process of living ensures that it was subject in the long run to selection in the same way as organisms: by and large techniques which provided a more effective form of livelihood were likely to replace those which were less effective. The trend was for obsolete technology to drop out in favour of innovations acquired by the transmitting generation. Progress was thus built into the system. Yet, as prehistory shows, it proceeded slowly enough even in regions most productive of innovation since it was inevitably opposed by the conservative forces whose essential role was to ensure transmission of the cultural heritage which alone distinguished men from the other animals. It is hardly surprising that these forces were strongest where the social inheritance was most exiguous. That is why progress was so extremely slow during the earlier phases of prehistory.

Yet it is possible to observe a clear progression during the Palaeolithic Age in the technology of working flint and stone. As is only to be expected of the product of an evolutionary process, the discernible stages are rarely clear-cut. It is not so much that one form of technology gave place to another as that technical possibilities were

Table 5. *Lithic technology during the Old Stone Age in Europe*

Dominant lithic technologies	Temporal divisions
Mode 5: microlithic components of composite artefacts	Mesolithic
Mode 4: punch-struck blades with steep retouch	Upper Palaeolithic
Mode 3: flake tools from prepared cores	Middle Palaeolithic
Mode 2: bifacially flaked hand-axes	Lower Palaeolithic
Mode 1: chopper-tools and flakes	

enlarged by the adoption of new processes. The degree of overlap argues that the changes on which prehistorians rely for periodization were as a rule brought about by the spread of ideas rather than as a result of actual movements of people. Again, more often than not particular industries are seen to combine techniques from more than one stage of development. Among the factors that caused peoples living on the same time-plane to retain or discard old forms while adopting new ones were of course variations in the environment to which they had to adapt. Before listing the major stages in lithic technology during the Old Stone Age it needs to be emphasized with some vigour that, although they formed a homotaxial sequence in the sense that however incomplete the succession the order was invariably the same, they were only on rare occasions and as it were by chance synchronous in different territories. In the preceding table the succession of stone technologies is equated broadly with the major phases of the older Stone Age as these are commonly conceived of in Europe and contiguous parts of Africa and Asia.

A point that needs emphasis is that although these modes were homotaxial they were by no means universal. For one thing the territories occupied by early man tended to increase in the course of prehistory as cultures were adapted to an ever-widening range of environments. For another the competition, which in the long run ensured technological advance, only applied to regions accessible to the spread of new ideas. In territories relatively remote from those in which innovations first appeared old forms of technology might survive from the mere fact that they remained without challenge. Industries in mode 1, which must have been practised over an immensely long period of time, are found over the whole territory occupied by early man. Mode 2 industries on the other hand failed to reach south-east Asia or China. Mode 3 industries still did not penetrate these regions in the Far East, but on the other hand extended northwards into European Russia and Inner Asia. This makes it less of a surprise that when for example men first spread into Australia by way of Indonesia they should have carried with them a lithic tradition in mode 1. When men first spread into more northerly parts of Europe and Eurasia they brought with them industries of modes 4 or 5 and these were carried successively into the New World.

Men of *H. erectus* stock, like the Australopithecines and the great apes, were confined to the continent of Africa and the frost-free zones of Asia and Europe. Over the whole of these territories their technology was based on the production of flint and stone industries of an extremely elementary kind. Basically their tools comprised chopper-like forms dressed by percussion from one or both sides and commonly made from pebbles, together with the flakes which resulted from this process. Industries of this kind appeared both in east and north Africa alongside a Villefranchian fauna, but persisted well into the Middle Pleistocene even in these areas where they in due course gave place to ones featuring hand-axes.

Recent discoveries have shown that they occupied territories in the west as far north as central Europe, where well-defined chopper and
8 flake tools made from pebbles of chert and quartzite have been recovered with animal bones of Middle Pleistocene age in a travertine quarry at Vértesszöllös in Hungary. Indeed, if we accept the flint industries named after Clacton as belonging to the same tradition,

7 Extent of settlement during the Middle Pleistocene.

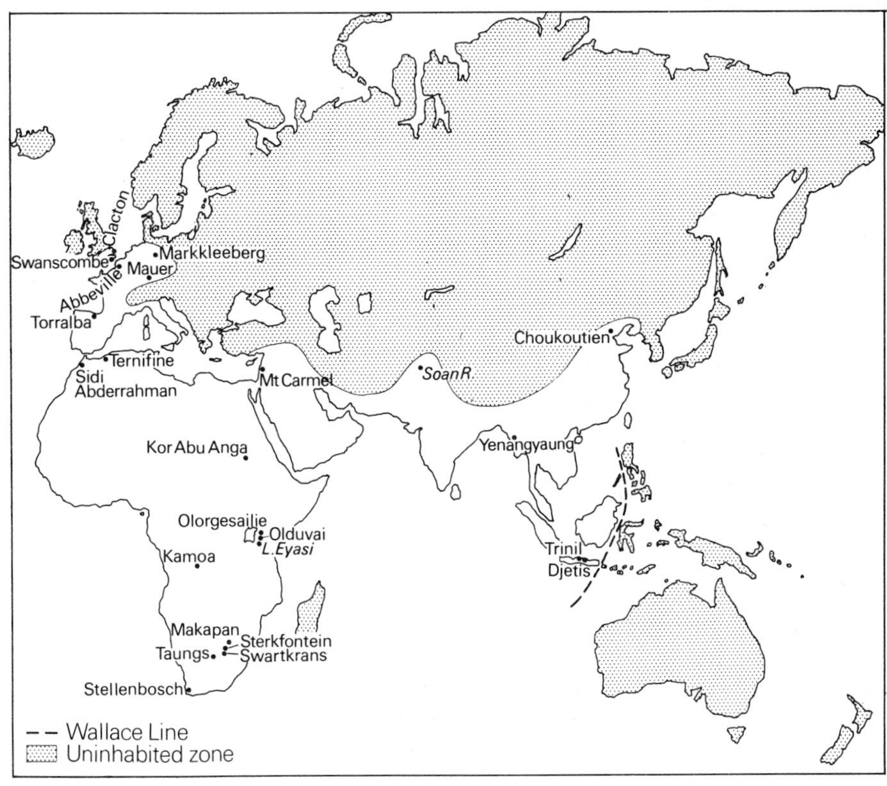

we can say that they extended as far as the western part of the North European Plain. To the east their range also extends from the Tropics to the Temperate zone. The Soan industries from Middle Pleistocene deposits in the north-west of the Indian sub-continent were among the first of their kind to be recognized, outside those of the North China Plain. South-east Asia has shown a variety of industries made from differing and sometimes intractable material, but conforming to the same basic pattern, notably the Anyathian of Burma, the Tampanian of Malaya and the Pajitanian of Indonesia.

Very little is known about the life of the makers of such industries other than what can be inferred from their own skeletal remains and those of their food animals. This is especially true of Africa. The investigation of bed I at Olduvai has however revealed two important things. Analysis of the animal remains suggests that significant steps had already been taken towards an omnivorous diet in which meat played an important part. The dominant hominid was apparently eating birds, fish and small game and had access to the meat of large mammals either as scavenger or hunter. Traces of stone settings also suggest that he sheltered in structures made of wooden branches held in position by heavy stones round the perimeter. A notable absentee from the living area was any indication of the use of fire, a lack confirmed at other African sites of the period.

By contrast *H. erectus* was certainly employing this resource, so valuable for heating, cooking, hunting and hardening wooden equipment, in more northerly territories. Animal bones associated with him at Vértesszöllös show signs of having been charred, and far away to the east in north China there are plentiful indications of this from the caves and rock-fissures at Choukoutien, a locality which has

8 Pebble chopper tools in mode 1 from Olduvai Gorge (bed I), East Africa.

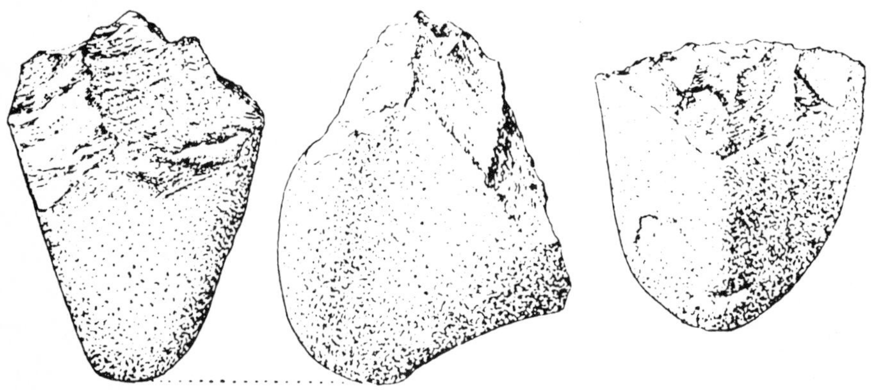

yielded far and away the most complete evidence about *H. erectus* and his way of life. The earliest deposits, those at locus 13 dating from early in the Middle Pleistocene, yielded a typical chopping tool made by removing alternate flakes in either direction from a chert pebble, resulting in a sinuous working edge. The main fissure (locus 1), dating from rather later in the Middle Pleistocene and the source of remains of upwards of forty representatives of Peking man, has produced a wealth of stone artefacts made from intractable materials like green-stone, coarse chert and quartz. It must be admitted that many of these were so crudely fashioned that they would hardly have been recognized as human if recovered from an ordinary geological deposit. Nevertheless the industry, much of the material of which was brought to the site and which was intimately associated with traces of fire and other human activity, has certain well-defined characteristics: there are no tools comparable to the hand-axes of Africa and parts of Europe and south-west Asia; pebbles and flakes were employed as materials for tools and the flakes had sometimes been formed by crushing nodules between two boulders, resulting in signs of percussion at either end; secondary retouch was scarce and irregular; and the leading tools were intended for chopping and scraping, the former generally made from pebbles, from which a few flakes had been struck to form irregular working-edges, and the latter by trimming lumps or flakes to form smooth edges. With this rudimentary stone equipment, supplemented by such tools as he was able to shape by its aid, Peking man succeeded in living largely on the flesh of his competitors in the animal world.

To judge from the animal remains associated with him, Peking man depended largely on venison, since two-thirds of them belong to two species of deer, namely *Euryceros pachyosteus* and *Pseudaxis grayi*. His victims also included elephants, two kinds of rhinoceros, bison, water-buffaloes, horses, camels, wild boars, roebucks, antelopes and sheep, not to mention such carnivores as sabre-toothed tigers, leopards, cave bears and a huge hyena. How he managed to secure this varied selection of game we can only speculate. No specialized projectile-heads have survived in the archaeological record, but to judge from evidence from elsewhere he would have had available wooden spears with the tip hardened in fire and it seems likely in view of the character of some of his victims that he would have used primitive pit-traps. The meagreness of his material equipment only emphasizes the important part that team-work, based on articulate speech and on a conscious network of social relations, must have played even at this early stage of development, when groups were so small and so sparsely scattered. Equally we should recognize the immense courage of these primitive men, who in the face of powerful and largely unknown forces made their way – and our way – in the final resort by their prowess as hunters, by confronting and vanquishing animals larger, faster and stronger than themselves.

One of their most important aids was fire and it was in layers discoloured by burning and mixed with ash and charcoal that most of their discarded refuse was found. Fire would have been of value for keeping wild beasts at bay, for warming the cave, for hardening wooden weapons and of course for roasting meat. In addition to meat, wild animals provided skins and, in their bones, teeth and antlers, potential raw materials for making tools and weapons. There seems no doubt that Peking man utilized certain of these, though not to the extent that has sometimes been claimed. Deer antlers were certainly detached from their frontlets, the beams were sometimes cut into sections and the tines removed, no doubt for use. Again, flakes from the long bones of various animals have the appearance of having been used and even trimmed by flaking. On the other hand there is no sign that Peking man fabricated well-made artefacts from these materials.

9 Skulls from which brains have been extracted through an enlargement of the *foramen magnum* at the base. *Left, Homo sapiens neanderthalensis,* Monte Circeo near Rome; *right,* modern Melanesian.

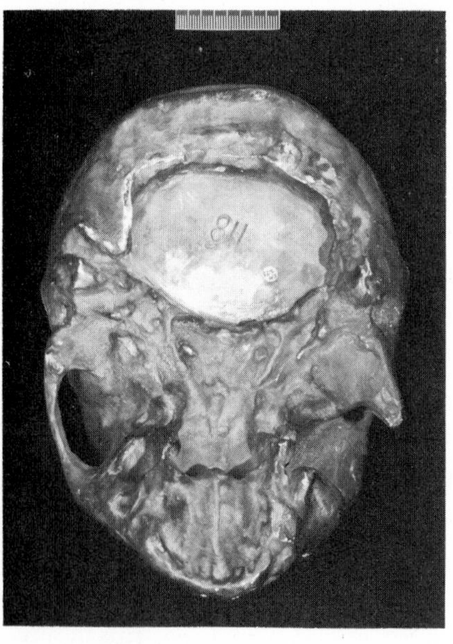

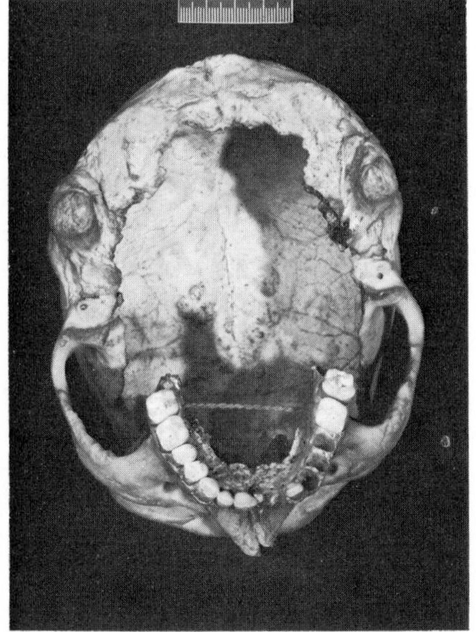

The mode in which his own skeletal remains occurred as well as their condition are important for what they can tell of other aspects of his life. The bones of Peking man were scattered in the culture layers in the same way as the bones of food animals. Clearly there was no question of burial. Indeed, the fact that despite the most careful search of thousands of cubic metres of deposit no trace of any other hominid was found argues that Peking man was not only the hunter of the other animals found, but also practised cannibalism. His long bones were broken in the same way as animal bones for the extraction of marrow and the aperture at the base of the skull was
9 frequently enlarged in the same way as happened recently in Melanesia among people who extracted the brain for eating.

Hand-axe (mode 2) industries

The most striking technical innovation to appear during the Middle
10 Pleistocene was the hand-axe, a tool flaked over part or the whole of both faces in such a way as to produce a working-edge round the greater part of its perimeter and apparently intended to be gripped in the hand. There seems no doubt in the face of stratigraphical sequences like those studied in Morocco or Tanzania that the earliest and most primitive hand-axes, resembling those from the French locality of Abbeville in the Somme Valley, developed from evolved forms of pebble-tool having two-way flaking. All that was involved was the extension of secondary flaking from the edge to the surface of the tool. As time went on the knappers learned to remove shal-

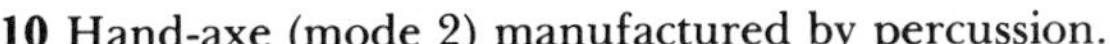

10 Hand-axe (mode 2) manufactured by percussion.

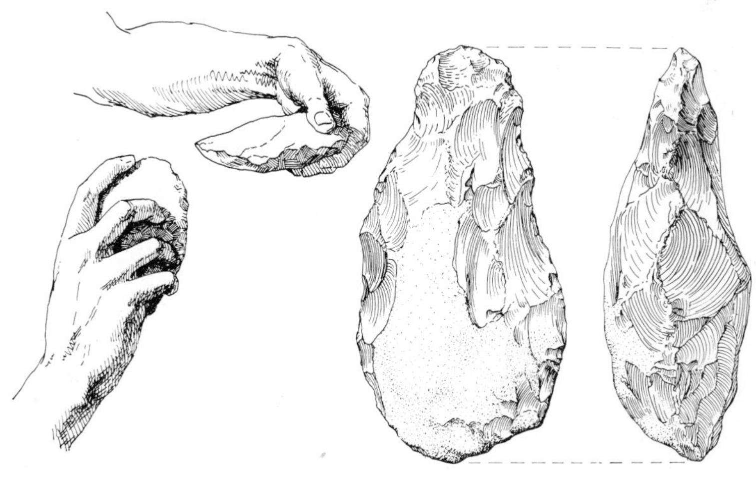

lower flakes and turn out hand-axes which, like those from St-Acheul in France, were thinner, had a more regular working-edge, were easier to handle with precision and needed a smaller quantity of raw material. Evolution thus proceeded in the direction of greater effectiveness and lower requirement of material. It was adaptive in the sense that whoever made or adopted such improvements benefited in relation to those who failed to do so. This may also help to explain the remarkable degree of uniformity to be observed in the production of hand-axes whatever sources of raw material happened to be available in particular localities. To ask where the hand-axe was invented and what regions witnessed the first appearance of different stages in its evolution is not particularly meaningful; nor would it be sensible to interpret the growth of technical innovation over long periods of time with the movements of particular groups of people. One is faced, not with a series of events to be accounted for in terms of human movements, but rather with processes which transformed lithic technology by insensible gradations over extensive territories.

Although hand-axes are the most noteworthy elements of the stone industries in which they occur, they are by no means the only ones. The point has first to be made that chopper-tools, although for some purposes rendered out of date, had not suddenly lost all utility; indeed in territories as far removed from one another as central India and Morocco it has been remarked that they continued to be made throughout the period during which hand-axes were in use. Again, the mere production of hand-axes must have yielded numerous flakes and there is evidence, where this has been observed with care, that some of these were shaped, or if not in all cases shaped at least used as implements on their own account. Furthermore, and more particularly during the more evolved stages of cultures of Acheulian type, the tool-kit was further enriched by narrow pick-like forms, steep core-scrapers and cleavers, the broad, sharp working-edges of which were formed by the intersection of two or more flake-scars.

Geographically the hand-axe industries in mode 2 never extended over the whole territory of those in mode 1. They prevailed extensively over Africa and southern Europe, but in Asia only in restricted areas of the south-west. From Egypt the hand-axe territory extended into the Levant and Mesopotamia and thence to the Indian subcontinent southward from the Narmada basin. Further east over much of China and south-east Asia, not to mention Japan and Australia, industries in mode 1 flourished well into the Upper Pleistocene and indeed locally down to modern times. Within their own territories the makers of hand-axes were by no means undiscriminating in their choice of hunting-grounds. In Africa where their distribution has been closely studied in relation to palaeo-ecology it seems plain that they preferred savannah country and at least to begin with eschewed the dense forest.

Like their predecessors, the hand-axe makers were adept at big-game hunting. For this reason it is no surprise to find that they concentrated in the valleys of rivers like the Thames and the Somme, the Nile, the Vaal, the Zambezi or the Narmada or, again, by the margins of what were then lakes at Olorgesailie in East Africa, at Karar in Algeria, Torralba in Spain or Hoxne in England. The animal bones recovered from their sites show plainly enough their interest in meat. The Olorgesailie people for example killed and ate giant baboon, giant pig and large kinds of horse and hippopotamus; at Karar remains were found of elephant, rhinoceros, hippopotamus, buffalo, zebra, giraffe, warthog and gazelle; and at Torralba straight-tusked elephant, rhinoceros, wild ox, stag and horse. Although, as with the hunters of Choukoutien, their methods of hunting must remain to a large extent a matter of conjecture, we have at least one piece of evidence that they used wooden spears hardened in the fire, namely a broken but more or less complete specimen of yew wood nearly 2·5 metres long found among the rib-bones of a straight-tusked elephant, at Lehringen, near Verden in Lower Saxony, Germany, and dating from the Riss-Würm interglacial. In this connection it is interesting to note that the pygmies of the Cameroons have been accustomed to stalk elephant with a wooden spear no more than two metres long, which they thrust into the animal's body with both hands; as the animal tries to escape the spear works in more deeply and the trail of blood allows the hunters to keep on his track. When a kill of a large beast is made among such people it is customary for folk to collect from far and near to feast off the meat. During the Stone Age, when implements were easily made and expendable, it is likely that these would often be worn out and discarded at the site of a kill and it seems easiest to explain in this way finds like that at site HK in bed IV at Olduvai, which yielded no less than 459 hand-axes and cleavers blunted by use and lying amid the disarticulated skeleton of a hippopotamus.

Evidence for the type of men responsible for hand-axe industries is still scarce, but the indications point to some variety of *H. sapiens*. Bed IV at Olduvai is one case in point. Another is the well-researched discovery at Swanscombe in the lower Thames basin. Although the cranium found at the same horizon as hand-axes lacked the frontal region, the capacity of the skull was probably of the order of 1325cc.

Prepared core and flake (mode 3) industries

As we have already noted, the production of flakes was an inevitable concomitant of the manufacture both of chopper-tools and of hand-axes; and there are indications that their use for making ancillary tools was well understood. A new stage in technology is signalled when the flint- or stone-worker appears to aim first and foremost at producing flake tools, and to this end goes to particular trouble to prepare cores from which they could be struck in a finished state. One of the prehistorian's difficulties is that the intention of the prehistoric knapper may not always be apparent. It may well be indeed that at an early stage a certain ambivalence may have existed. The controversy between those who interpret the large lumps from Clactonian industries in south-east England as cores and those who see them as chopper-tools may well be unreal.

The position is much clearer during the early part of the Upper Pleistocene when we have industries like that first recognized at Levallois, a suburb of Paris, in which flake tools are found together
11 with the tortoise-shaped cores from which they were struck. Here there can be no doubt that the primary object of the knapper was to produce flake tools, the form of which was accurately determined by preparatory work on the core. The technique was one that was developed on the northern margins of the hand-axe province, and may well indicate a response to temperate and sub-tropical conditions which tropical and equatorial ones failed to elicit. Middle Palaeolithic industries based primarily on the Levallois technique are found in

11 Levallois technique (mode 3) with flake removed from prepared tortoise core and replaced.

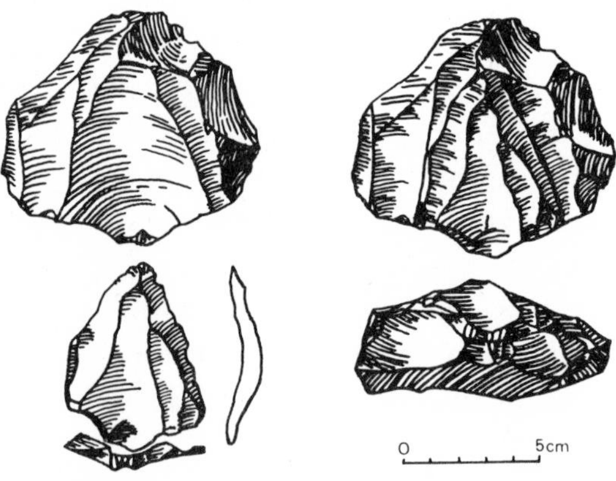

relatively pure form round the southern and eastern shores of the Mediterranean from North Africa to the Levant, extending by way of Iraq and Iran into western Asia. Further north the culture named after the rock-shelter of Le Moustier in the Dordogne also made
12 prominent use of flake tools, though these were commonly made from smaller disc-like cores and were often trimmed into points or side-scrapers by a special technique that led to step- or resolved-flaking. Many variations exist in the Mousterian industries which extend from the Atlantic seaboard to the area north of the Black Sea and Inner Asia. In western Europe for example Middle Palaeolithic industries normally included elements in mode 2, including hand-axes of small triangular or heart-shaped forms, whereas further south these declined greatly in importance. Over much of this territory from the south of France and Italy to central Europe, the Crimea, the Don–Donetz region and the coastal zone of the west Caucasus the loss or minor importance of the hand-axe was compensated by a great variety of flake tools, which then included hand-awls and steeply flaked ribbon-flakes; again, and especially in the east from Greece to South Russia, the inventory included points having shallow flaking on either face and either leaf-shaped or sub-triangular in form with concave base.

12 Mousterian tool-kit: point, bone anvil and sidescraper.

Although the technique of producing flake tools from prepared cores flourished best in the temperate and sub-tropical zones, it was also practised widely in Africa. For instance flakes struck from prepared cores form a significant component alongside hand-axes and cleavers of the Fauresmith culture adapted to the savannah and high grasslands of South Africa, Kenya, South Abyssinia and the Horn. In the complementary Sangoan that flourished to begin with on the fringes of the equatorial rain-forest the flake struck from a prepared core did not become obtrusive until the late or Lupemban stage when for the first time man began effective penetration of the rain-forest. Even so the leading artefacts of the Sangoan continued to be bifacial, including core-axes, picks and narrow lanceolate forms.

Owing to their habit of occupying caves, we have reasonably full information about the animals on which the Neanderthal and Neanderthaloid peoples mainly depended for food, about the use they made of bone and related materials and the way in which they disposed of their dead. As hunters these people show no sign of having been in any way more advanced than their immediate predecessors. Where, as in certain of the Mount Carmel caves in Palestine, Levalloiso-Mousterian levels overlie ones dating from early stages of the Palaeolithic, there is no indication that an extended range of animals was hunted. Equally, there is no sign of any marked improvement in the methods of hunting; reliance evidently continued to be placed on proved methods like wooden spears, stone balls

13 Chart of radiocarbon dates in millennia B.C. for Mousterian and allied sites.

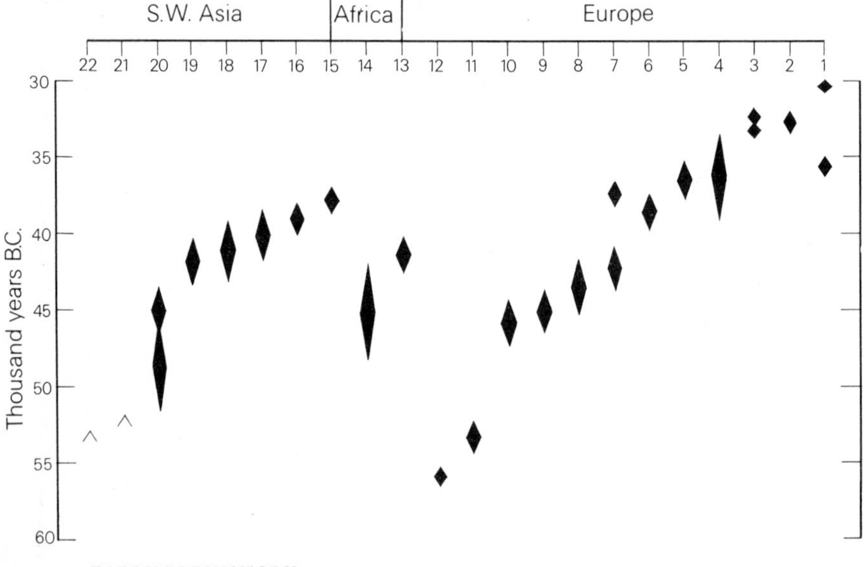

(probably used as bolas stones) and presumably on primitive pit-traps; and there is a notable absence of specialized projectile-heads. Again, exceedingly limited use was made of bone and related materials which, as we know from later practice by Stone Age hunters, were capable of providing a variety of spear-, harpoon- and arrowheads, as well as fish-hooks and pointed fish-gorges, a variety of tools and many kinds of personal ornament: pieces of dense bone, including phalanges, or toe-bones, were used as anvils for working flint, but there is no evidence that bone or antler was worked to make well-defined implements or weapons of any description. Another and possibly more significant limitation is the absence of any indication

Table 6. *Radiocarbon determinations for the Mousterian and allied cultures: site numbers refer to upper register of fig. 13*

	EUROPE		B.C.
1	Les Cottés, Vienne, France	GrN 4334	30,350 ± 400
		GrN 4421	35,650 ± 700
2	Grotte du Renne, Arcy-sur-Cure, Yonne, France	GrN 4217	32,650 ± 850
3	La Quina, Charente, France	GrN 4494	32,150 ± 700
		GrN 2526	33,300 ± 530
4	Radošiná, Czechoslovakia	GrN 2438	36,450 + 2800 − 2100
5	Nietoperzowa, Poland	GrN 2181	36,550 ± 1240
6	Broion Cave, nr Vicenza, Italy	GrN 4638	38,650 ± 1200
7	Érd, Hungary	GrN 4711	37,400 ± 830
		GrN 4444	42,350 ± 1400
8	Regourdou, Dordogne, France	GrN 4308	43,550 ± 1800
9	La Cotte de St Brelade, Jersey	GrN 2649	45,050 ± 1500
10	Gibraltar (Gorham's Cave G)	GrN 1473	45,750 ± 1500
11	Lebenstedt, Germany	GrN 2083	53,290 ± 1010
12	Mussolini Canal, Italy	GrN 2572	55,950 ± 500
	NORTH AFRICA		
13	Haua Fteah, Cyrenaica (level XXVIII)	GrN 2564	41,450 ± 1300
14	Haua Fteah, Cyrenaica (level XXXIII)	GrN 2023	45,050 ± 3200
	SOUTH-WEST ASIA		
15	Tabun B, Israel	GrN 2534	37,750 ± 800
16	el Kebāra, Israel	GrN 2561	39,050 ± 1000
17	Geulah Cave A, Israel	GrN 4121	40,050 ± 1700
18	Jerf Ajla, Syria	NZ 76	41,050 ± 2000
19	Ksâr 'Akil, Lebanon	GrN 2579	41,800 ± 1500
20	Shanidar, Iraq (level D, top)	GrN 2527	44,950 ± 1500
		GrN 1495	48,650 ± 3000
21	Ras el-Kelb, Lebanon	GrN 2556	> 52,000
22	Al Ghab, Syria	GrN 2640	> 53,000

NOTE. It is likely that these cultures first appeared at a period beyond the present useful range of radiocarbon determination.

of a developed aesthetic sense: Middle Palaeolithic man was capable of producing a limited range of tools with an astonishing economy of effort, and the perfection of form and degree of standardization that they achieved, often over great areas and despite wide variations in the qualities of the raw materials used, bear witness to firmness of intention and a definite sense of style; but as far as we know he practised no art – no sign of carving or engraving for example has been found among all the wealth of bone and antler from Mousterian and kindred sites; nor is there evidence of even so much as a single bored tooth to suggest that he fabricated ornaments to adorn his person.

In two significant ways however Neanderthal man made important advances. For one thing he extended the range of settlement well to the north of the frost-free zone to which earlier men had confined themselves and this at a time of glacial intensity. Precisely how far he reached has still to be settled in detail, but there are indications that he colonized parts of Siberia for the first time, though probably not as early as Würm I times, and even reached as far as China. The presence of well-made flint scrapers as an important element in his standard equipment suggests that he found it necessary in his northerly habitat to wear animal skins, at least out of doors. Another sign that Neanderthal man had adapted to relatively cold conditions
14 is provided by excavations at Molodova in the Dnestr Valley. These
164 revealed an oval setting of heavy mammoth bones resembling those from Advanced Palaeolithic sites elsewhere in the Ukraine where they have been interpreted as having served to weight the perimeters of skin-covered dwellings, or even in some instances to indicate remains of structures built entirely from heavy bones. The Molodova I structure evidently had an internal diameter of *c.* 8×5 m. It was associated with numerous hearths, animal bones and Mousterian flints. The presence of collared lemming and the mollusc *Vallonia tenuilabris* suggest a relatively severe climate, and this is confirmed by the fillings of Crimean caves and their contained fauna dating from the same period.

The other marked advance shown by Neanderthal man was in his treatment of the dead. Certain discoveries from the closing phase of the last interglacial seem indeed to indicate the continuance of cannibalism, notably the Neanderthal skull from Monte Circeo, Italy, with the base broken open for the extraction of the brain, and the mass find at Krapina in Yugoslavia, where remains of upwards of a dozen individuals, male and female, young and old, were discovered mixed up in the cultural deposit with wild animal bones and treated in the same way, having been broken up for the extraction of marrow, partly burnt in the fire and so on. On the other hand the Mousterian deposit at La Chapelle-aux-Saints was found to overlie a grave, cut into the rock floor and containing the crouched skeleton of a Neanderthal man; similar burials have been found at La Ferrassie, likewise in the Dordogne, and also at Kiik-Koba in the Crimea. Even more significant evidence was uncovered at the

14 Plan of Mousterian dwelling, Molodova I, Dnestr valley, South Russia.

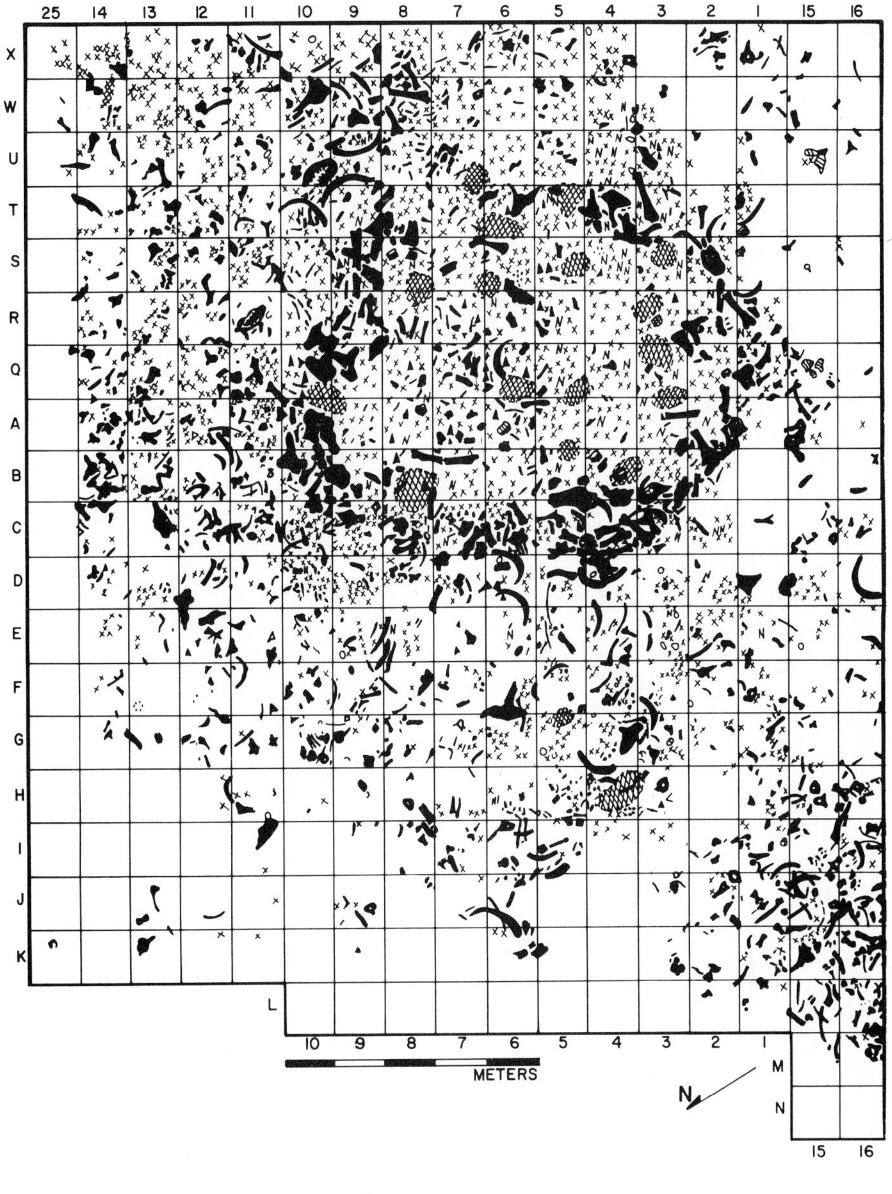

Mugharet es-Skhūl, Mount Carmel, in the form of a veritable cem-
133:97–107 etery of ten graves with remains ranging from a girl of three and a boy of four to a man over fifty years of age. As at La Chapelle-aux-Saints the graves were only just big enough to accommodate bodies with the arms and legs flexed. No red ochre or personal ornaments were found, but the jaw-bones of a large wild boar were
15 seen to be clasped in the arms of the old man. A more recent discovery of exceptional interest is that of a Neanderthaloid child
67 in the cave of Teshik-Tash, Uzbekistan, the head surrounded by six pairs of horns of the Siberian mountain goat, which had evidently been stood upright in a circle while still attached to the frontal bones. Quite clearly men of the Neanderthaloid type had developed concepts well beyond what one might have expected from their lowly material culture.

15 Neanderthal burial in Mugharet-es-Skhūl, Mt Carmel, Palestine.

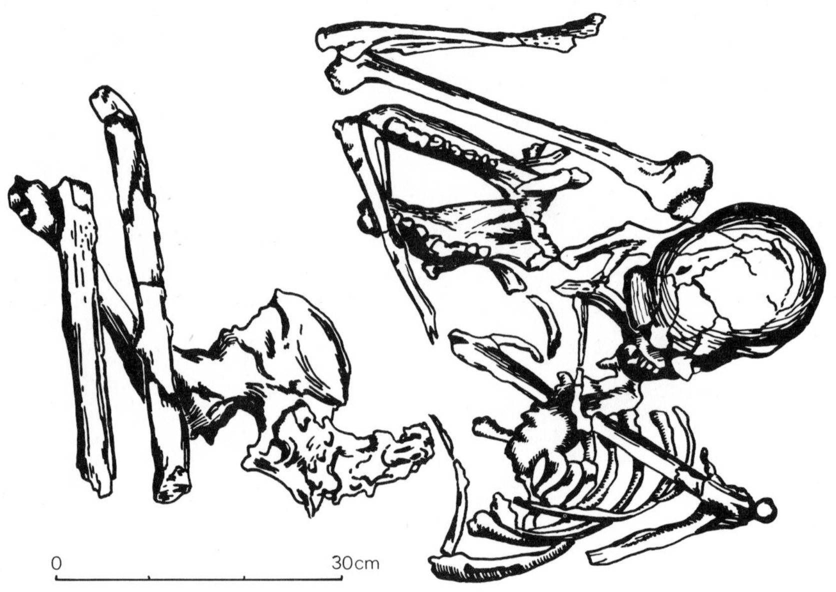

2

Beginnings of civilization in south-west Asia

Background

Limitations of hunter-forager economies

During the Pleistocene Ice Age, that is throughout almost the whole of his history from a temporal point of view, man has lived by appropriating the natural products available to him in the different environments to which he was able to adapt through the medium of his culture. Subsistence during this enormously long period was based on two complementary sources of food: on the fruits, seeds, roots and other plant foods which, together with insects, eggs, shell-fish and various small game, were gathered in the main by women and the children for whom they cared; and on the larger game animals, fish and wild-fowl hunted by men. It is common form to designate these ways of gaining a living as parasitic and by implication inferior to those centred on the production of food by means of various types of farming or manufacture, but it is perhaps worth emphasizing that their successful pursuit in the wide range of environments into which men had penetrated by the end of the Pleistocene implied a detailed knowledge of the whereabouts and habits of a much greater variety of animal and plant species than farmers had to concern themselves with; moreover, as the cave art so well illustrates, under favourable ecological conditions, hunting was capable of sustaining an interesting, exciting and in some measure leisured life. The Garden of Eden had its own, very definite attractions.

Yet the possibilities open to communities exclusively dependent on hunting and foraging were limited. Individual groups like the Late-glacial reindeer hunters of Europe or the recent salmon-catching Indians of the north-west Pacific coast of North America might indeed be able, because of particularly favourable circumstances, to enjoy a certain leisure and indulge in a number of activities beyond those narrowly tied to subsistence. Yet no community whose livelihood was based exclusively on hunting, fishing or gathering has been able to share in the historical possibilities open to those whose subsistence was securely based on farming.

Precisely what were the constraints which limited the possibilities of societies who lived in this way? In descriptive terms their members had to live at least for much of the year in small groups widely spaced over extensive territories, change their settlements with the seasons, make do with a simple if as a rule well adapted and effective technology and operate without structured hierarchies. When considered as aspects of a working system these and other characteristics fall readily and logically in place. The demographic limits are understandably set by the exigencies of the food quest. Because wild food resources had to be harvested or caught wherever and whenever they were available in nature, and because there was no way of ensuring their continued availability except by restrictive cropping, hunter-foragers were compelled to move in small groups over extensive territories. So long as they could only move over land on their feet and lived in communities which were self-sufficient in respect of food, men were under the necessity of obtaining the basis of their subsistence within an hour or two of their home bases. Under exceptional conditions, as with the salmon runs of the Pacific coast of North America or the winter cod fisheries of northern Norway, concentrations of storable food might make it possible to stay for a large part of the year at the same home bases, but in general men had to move with the seasons. This restricted the quantity of gear and meant that for much of the year people lived in light, easily assembled dwellings or in natural shelters. Larger social groupings might for certain purposes be recognized but for most of the time and as a general rule hunter-foragers operated – to judge from recent examples – in single biological families or more often in micro-bands of three or four such units comprising perhaps 15–20 persons. This imposed narrow limits on the sub-division of labour and on the differentiation of social roles. There was a minimal scope or incentive for technological advance and a complete absence of social hierarchy other than the biological ones of age and sex: in the phrase of Soviet archaeologists these people were primitive communists, though in this case by necessity rather than by choice. People subject to such limitations had no hope of an ampler life until the system in which they were caught up was itself replaced by others with different and less oppressive constraints.

BEGINNINGS OF CIVILIZATION IN SOUTH-WEST ASIA

The basic requirement for systems permitting greater densities of population, larger aggregations, more permanent settlements, more complex and dynamic technologies and more elaborate social systems with structured hierarchies and the kind of inequalities of wealth, by and through which civilization itself emerged, was a more effective basis of subsistence, one capable that is of producing greater and more assured concentrations of food from more restricted areas of land. The best way of achieving this was through the domestication of animals and plants and the practice of farming. In every part of the world farming of some kind has preceded and formed so to speak the platform on which civilizations have had to build. It was with this in mind that Gordon Childe formulated the concept of a Neolithic Revolution comparable in importance with the Industrial and Scientific Revolutions.

The use of the term 'Neolithic' in this connection in itself poses a problem. If stadial terms are rarely used in contemporary archaeological discourse, it seems all the more important to be clear about their meaning. It is a sound lexicographical practice to consider the historical circumstances under which words were originally coined. In 1865 when the terms Palaeolithic and Neolithic were first devised they were intended to denote evolutionary stages in the Stone Age. They therefore had a temporal as well as a cultural connotation. They were intended to reflect a dichotomy between:

(a) a period during which Pleistocene animals now extinct were still living and when men lived solely by hunting and foraging and depended on flaked stone tools;
(b) one in which only recent animals and plants existed and men practised farming and a number of new industrial arts, including polishing flint axes, weaving and potting.

This dichotomy was enhanced by the concomitant notion that Europe experienced a hiatus of settlement, a hypothesis which carried with it the implication that continuity must have been maintained elsewhere.

The progress of research since then has shown that in reality settlement was continuous. It was clear already at the beginning of the twentieth century that there was good evidence for continuity of settlement in several different parts of Europe. This at once raised the question how the new finds intermediate in age between the Late Pleistocene Ice Age and the introduction of farming economy were to be labelled. They could hardly be termed Palaeolithic since the associated fauna was exclusively Recent. Still less could they be ascribed to the Neolithic since they yielded no evidence for farming, weaving or potting. One alternative was to stretch the old dichotomous terminology and divide the new finds arbitrarily between Epi-Palaeolithic and Proto-Neolithic. A more radical solution was to interpose a new Mesolithic age. Apart from its consistency this course took account of the fact that the new finds display distinctive and genuinely transitional characteristics. In Europe the Mesolithic witnessed the adaptation of communities with a Palaeolithic background to the changed Neothermal environment and in certain ways prepared the way for the spread and adoption of farming economy.

The spread of prehistoric research in its scientific form to south-west Asia, more particularly since it concerned itself specifically with the period immediately preceding the formation of tells, has documented the continuity of settlement which even the framers of the hiatus hypothesis had always envisaged for this part of the world. In respect of artefacts and of at least one ritual practice relating to the dead the early Postglacial archaeological assemblages of Europe and south-west Asia show a large measure of agreement. Both feature lithic assemblages in mode 5 as well as slotted equipment, fish-hooks and barbed points of antler or bone and in each there is evidence for the burial of detached skulls. Regarding subsistence the inhabitants of both regions engaged at this time in hunting, fishing and gathering, but a notable feature of south-west Asia was the special emphasis laid on harvesting the wild prototypes of cultivated cereals. Beyond this there is evidence from several parts of this region for the domestication of cereals and also of sheep or goat by people who had not yet adopted the Neolithic art of potting. Assemblages of this latter kind have sometimes been categorized as 'pre-pottery Neolithic'. It might be better, if one has to use this stadial terminology, to recognize them as completing the Mesolithic bridge that links the Palaeolithic and Neolithic and restores the continuity of the prehistoric record in this region so crucial to the development of civilization. The change in the relationship between men, animals and plants that precipitated the transformation of social systems was accomplished not by Neolithic but by Mesolithic communities. It was precisely as an outcome of this process that men became Neolithic.

20: 9–10 If the process of transformation was Mesolithic rather than Neolithic, in what sense, if at all, was it a Revolution? That it was revolutionary in its implications for human society admits of no doubt from the standpoint adopted in this book. Was it revolutionary in the sense of being sudden? Here it is important to distinguish between the process as a whole and its ultimate outcome. Modern thinking emphasizes the continuity as much as the dichotomy between so-called 'parasitic' and 'productive' modes of subsistence. However their economy is described, men necessarily live by appropriating some part of the energy taken up by plants through the process of photosynthesis. They do so directly by harvesting plants or indirectly at one or two removes by killing and eating animals. At this level it hardly signifies whether these were 'wild' or 'domesticated'. What matters is that men have the knowledge and skill to exploit these resources. This does not alter the fact that the relationships established between men, animals and plants affect profoundly the size and density of human populations and the nature and potentialities of human societies. It is above all changes in these relationships that are presently under discussion. Their very subtlety suggests that changes would be gradual rather than catastrophic. Indeed, where, as in the Valley of Mexico, it is possible to measure the rate and tempo of change by analysing palaeontological data from a succession of well-dated deposits it can be shown that changes in the intake of plant foods were in fact extremely gradual. Domesticated species were for long in a minority and contributed only to a minor degree to the supply of food. It was only when as an outcome of long experimentation certain species had emerged as sufficiently productive to provide a main source of food that the risk could be taken of settling down and concentrating on cultivation. When this happened decisively in any territory it might be expected to do so in the context of wholesale changes in the entire system.

Viewed from the opposite direction socio-cultural systems have a marked capacity to adjust to changes in any particular sub-system, whether concerned with subsistence, technology, beliefs or any other aspect of social life. Yet there is a limit to the contradictions that any system can tolerate. When a certain threshold is passed the cost of containing and resolving the contradictions implied by change exceeds that of scrapping the system as a whole and replacing it. This is the point at which change may indeed occur at a revolutionary tempo. There is nothing incompatible in the notion that the process of transformation in modes of subsistence was so slow as to be barely discernible throughout most of its history, yet so sudden in the outcome as to merit the designation revolutionary.

The irregularly crescentic zone within which village communities
based on the cultivation of cereals and the domestication of livestock
76, 133 first developed had been occupied by man since a remote period.
Indeed the sequence established for the western arm of the crescent
143 from Palestine to Syria challenges comparison with that obtained for
western Europe. For Anatolia the evidence is still tantalizingly
incomplete, but enough to show that the Mediterranean zone at least
was occupied at the crucial period. The eastern arm of the crescent
123 extending from the Taurus to the Zagros formed part of a key
territory of Neanderthal man during the earlier part of the Upper
Pleistocene. During the latter part there are signs that the mode 4
lithic assemblages found in either arm had begun to diverge. Whereas
the Antelian assemblages of the Levant compared rather closely with
99: 150–65 the Aurignacian of Europe, the Baradostian assemblages of the
Zagros were rather more generalized. Again the Zagros region can show nothing to compare with the highly characterized Atlitian and Kebaran. Indeed at present there is a gap in our knowledge of the Zagros sequence between the Baradostian and the Zarzian assemblages of the Sulaimani district of south Kurdistan. The signs are nevertheless that there was continuity between the two.

Ecological setting

Since early man, whether as hunter-forager or farmer, cropped the

Table 7. *Stratigraphic sequence of lithic assemblages in the Levant calibrated against the sequence in the Mugharet el-Wad, Mt Carmel*

PALESTINE Lithic modes	Lithic assemblages	El-Wād	Naḥal Ōren	Jericho	Syria Jabrud
	Tahunian (Ouady Tahounah)	—	—	PP 'B'	—
			4		
5		B 1		PP 'A'	—
				Proto-neo	
	Natufian (Wādi en-Naṭūf)	B 2	3	Natufian	Natufian
4/5	Kebaran	—	2	Nebekian	Nebekian
4	Atlitian (Athlit)	C	1	—	Skiftian
	Antelian (Antilyās)	D			
		E			
3/4	Emiran ('Emīreh)	F 1			
3	Levalloiso-Mousterian	F 2			
		G			
		Et-Tabun			
2	Acheulean	E b/d			

BEGINNINGS OF CIVILIZATION IN SOUTH-WEST ASIA

resources of particular environments, an accurate knowledge of the palaeo-ecology of the key zones of south-west Asia is of crucial importance. Although a beginning has been made in applying the proved methods of Quaternary Research in this area, far less has yet been ascertained than in temperate Europe, a territory of quite marginal importance in this context. Certain things may be said.
128 Pollen analysis at Lakes Zeribar and Mirabad has shown that during the latter part of the Upper Pleistocene the southern flanks of the middle and south Zagros carried an *Artemesia* steppe vegetation. With the transition to Neothermal climate which apparently began by the twelfth millennium B.C. in this part of the world, deciduous forest began at first very gradually to modify and replace the steppe. Much the same thing happened in the coastal zone of the Levant and southern Anatolia. This was highly significant for early man. Whereas for hunters the *Artemesia* zone offered excellent opportunities the oak-pistachio savannah must have provided an even more attractive environment, all the more so that it favoured the cereals which in domesticated form supported first peasant and later urban life as well as a variety of herbivorous animals.

The animals and plants on which settled farmers depended were necessarily derived from wild prototypes. Since it was the cultivation of crops rather than livestock that first called for settled life, it is logical to begin with plants. From an early stage men reduced the risks of failure by cultivating a number of different plants, including in this area protein-rich legumes and oil-rich seed crops, but the most important sources of plant food in this part of the world were
77 cereals. These were at home in the wild state precisely in the savannah land on the flanks of the mountain zone where traces of many of the earliest communities of farmers occur. The most important species cultivated in early times in south-west Asia and contiguous regions were barley, emmer and einkorn. To judge from the present distribution of wild species and from traces recovered from early archaeological sites, it looks much as if the process of domestication went forward at more than one centre in this as in other regions. The best stands of wild einkorn (*Triticum boeoticum* var. *thaudor*) from which the two-grained cultivated form derives occur in south-east Turkey. Wild emmer (*Triticum dicoccoides*) grows most vigorously in the Upper Jordan Valley and this may have been the centre of domestication rather than Turkey, Iraq, Iran and proximate parts of the USSR where it grows more sporadically. The two-row wild barley (*Hordeum spontaneum*), almost certainly the ancestor of all

varieties of cultivated barley, occurs in several races. The most important are those which formed on the one hand a natural component of the oak forest belt of the Upper Jordan Valley, Jordan, south-west Syria and northern Israel, and on the other hand the oak savannah of the Zagros region. The signs are that sedentary farming

16 Key sites in south-west Asia.

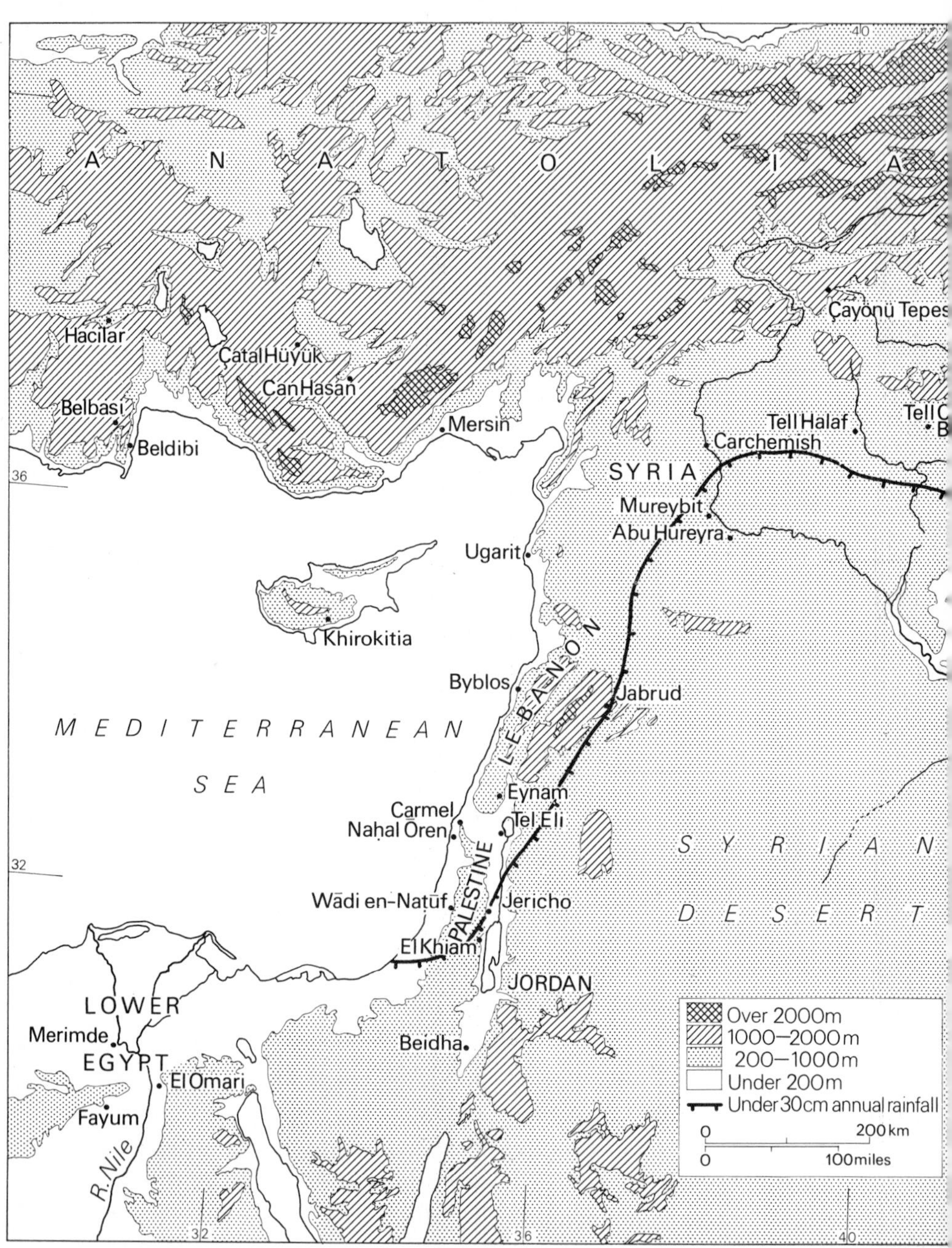

was linked primarily with the cultivation of cereals and that the adoption of this form of economy was marked at least initially by a pronounced change from a meat- to a plant-dominated diet. The changing roles of different animals in subsistence will be reviewed for successive periods both in the Levant and the Zagros.

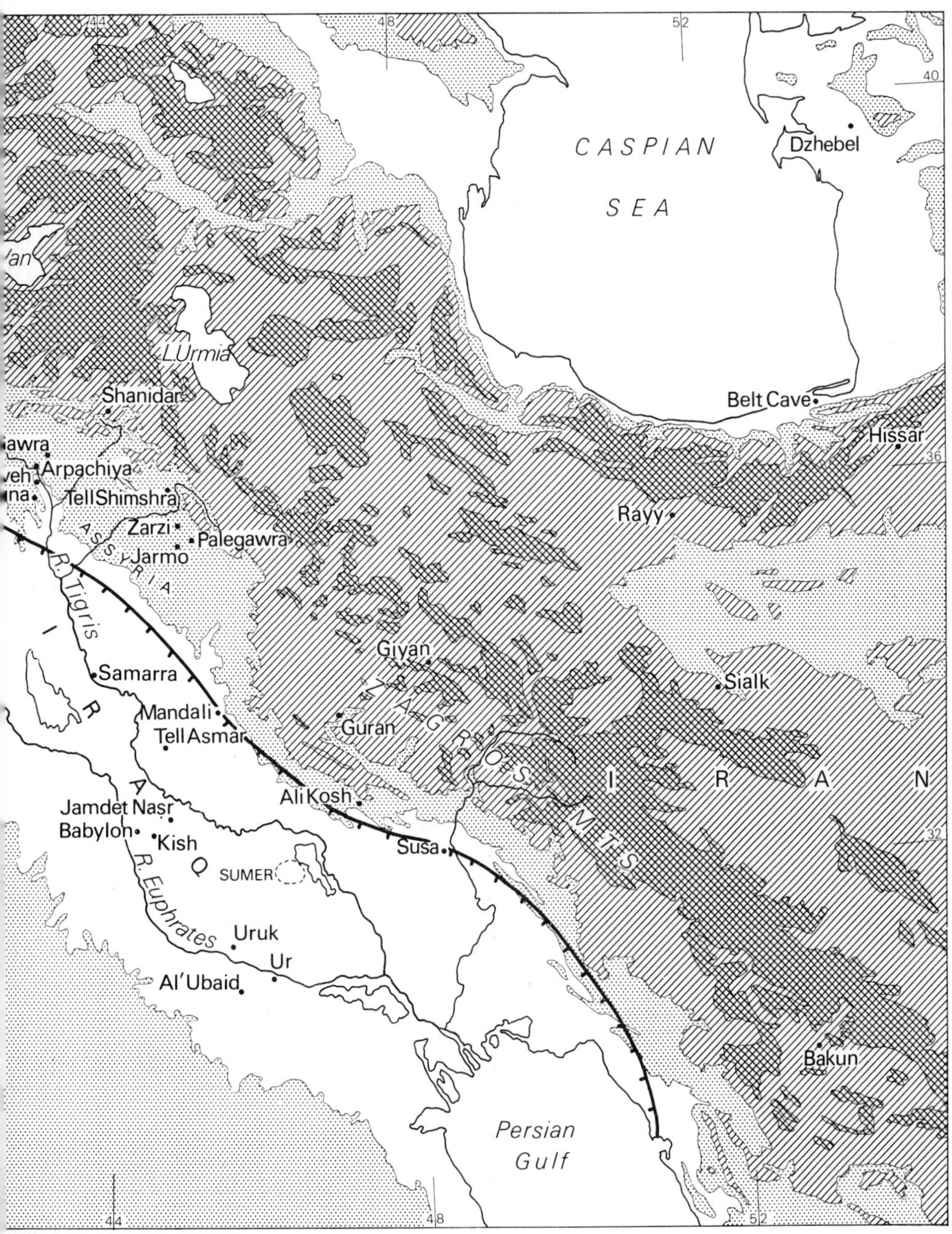

The Levant

The transitional (or Mesolithic) phase from the onset of Neothermal conditions to the appearance of established farming communities based on mixed farming with domesticated animals and plants differentiated morphologically from their wild prototypes and accustomed to the manufacture of pottery is well documented in the Levant except for a period between the mid-sixth and mid-fifth
Table 8 millennium B.C. This can best be seen in tabular form.
131, 132, 133 Natufian assemblages are defined by lithic assemblages in mode
17 5 with microliths, burins, borers, scrapers, blades backed and squared
to fit into the handles of reaping knives and a small component of
picks, to which was added in Natufian II a few notched arrowheads
135 like those from the earlier Pre-pottery Neolithic (PPN A) at Jericho.
Although a few triangles and in Natufian II a few trapezes occur, the overwhelming proportion of microliths are of crescentic form. Of these about one quarter in phase I and over one half in phase II have been backed by flaking from two directions. Flint crescents exhibiting this bipolar retouch were first observed at Heluan in the Nile Valley which probably marks the southern limit of Natufian influence during phase II, just as the appearance of a few examples
82 at Belbasi and Beldibi on the Antalya plain in south Anatolia indicates
its northernmost reach. The main area of characterization was undoubtedly the coastal tract of Palestine, the Rift Valley from
137, 139, 140, 142 Eynam (Ain Alallaha) to Beidha and the Judaean desert. Here the
flint work is supplemented on a number of sites by a rich component of antler and bone artefacts. These include slotted reaping-knife handles, fish-hooks, delicate points barbed on one edge, pins or awls

Table 8. *Stratigraphy of the transitional period in the Levant*

		Caves		Open sites					
B.C.		El-Wād	El Khiam	Jericho	Beidha	Naḥal Ōren	Tell Eli	Horvat Minha	Munhata
4500	Neolithic	—	Neo. B A	—	—	—	1–2	2	2
6000									
	Meso. III	—	Tahunian	PPN B	I–III	4	3–4	3–6	3–6
7000									
	Meso. II	Natufian II B1	Nat. II	PPN A	IV–VI				
8000									
	Meso. I	Natufian I B2		Proto. Natufian		3			

BEGINNINGS OF CIVILIZATION IN SOUTH-WEST ASIA

and a variety of beads including pairs of butterfly form. A significant feature is the presence of art. This comprises incised decoration on beads, carvings of animal heads at the terminals of reaping-knife handles and a series of stone carvings including a limestone cervid and a human head and erotic figures in calcite.

Although the Natufians almost certainly moved seasonally so as to exploit most effectively the animal and plant resources within their annual territories, it is not yet possible to plot the cycle of their movements. One of the few certain conclusions seems to be that certain sites – ones in the open as well as caves – served as base camps to which returns were made over periods of years and at which longish stays may have been made at certain phases in the food cycle. One indication of this is the number of burials. Cemeteries of 87 and 45 burials were found in the caves of el-Wād and Shuqba and of 82
145 and *c.* 50 at the open encampments of Eynam and Naḥal Ōren, numbers all the more impressive in the light of the small size of the communities concerned. The presence of stone pestles and mortars, some cut out of the solid rock, argues for periods of activity at the time of plant harvests. The importance of foraging is confirmed by the abundance of reaping-knife blades which it is worth noting were almost as common *vis-à-vis* lunates, the most numerous flint forms, in the lower (*c.* 1:7) as in the upper (*c.* 1:6) Natufian at the el-Wād cave. As to the nature of the plants harvested we have as yet no direct clue from Natufian levels in Palestine or Jordan. On the other hand

17 Natufian artefacts.

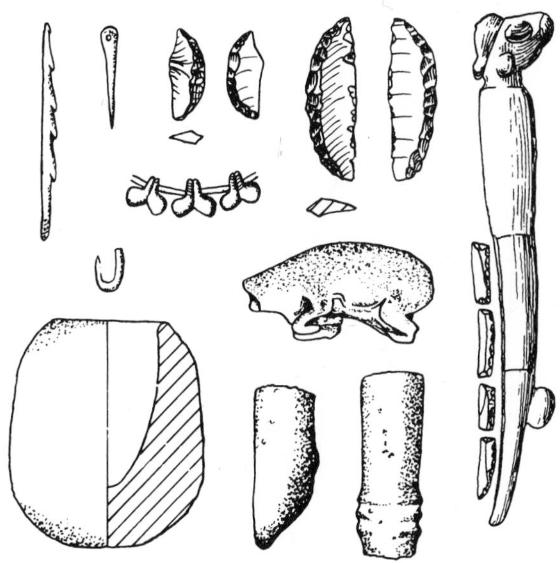

it is significant that barley (*Hordeum spontaneum*) and einkorn of two varieties (*Triticum boeoticum* var. *aegilopoides* and var. *thaudor*), none of them showing morphological features certainly indicative of domestication, were both being harvested about this time on the banks of the Euphrates due east of Aleppo at Mureybit, a site well furnished with reaping-knife blades. In this connection recent experiments have shown that it is possible to harvest wild einkorn with flint-edged reaping-knives and that where adequate stands are available three weeks' work can produce enough cereal food for a family for a year. The only difficulty is that in wild cereals the glume clings so closely to the grain that the ears need pounding to effect its release. In this respect the pestles and rock-cut mortars on Natufian sites are surely suggestive. Meanwhile one can only hope that more effective and systematic attempts are made to extract adequate samples of seeds and other plant residues from Natufian deposits.

The evidence for meat diet is better documented. Of the main animals available – fallow deer, cattle, swine, gazelle and goat – one or other of the last two generally contributed the main share. This concentration on gazelle in the case of el-Wād, Eynam, Naḥal Ōren and the Natufian level at Jericho and on goat at Beidha (76% in the Natufian, 86% in the PPN level) is one reason for suggesting that there was close herding of particular species. Another reason is that where adequate tests have been made it has been found that over

18 Beidha, Jordan: curvilinear and rectangular house plans.

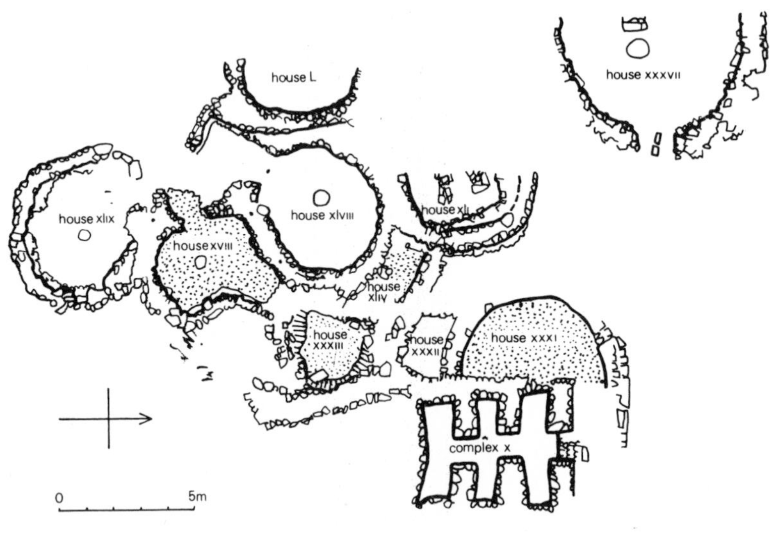

half the goats and gazelles represented were immature, something hardly likely to have occurred as an outcome of normal hunting but fully consistent with purposive herd management. On the other hand there was no suggestion of morphological changes of the kind associated with effective domestication. Even the canid remains from el-Wād, once interpreted as domestic dog, have since been determined to relate to a small variety of Asiatic wolf.

Phases II and III of the Mesolithic period in the Levant, commonly termed 'Pre-pottery Neolithic A and B' in the literature, although sharing a similar subsistence base, are differentiated in the archaeological record in respect of architecture and lithic equipment. The
18 houses in the lower levels at Beidha (IV–VI), like the Natufian ones at Eynam, were curvilinear and constructed from earth and dry stones, but at Tell es-Sultan (Jericho), an exceptional site by any standards, they were built from clay bricks of hog's back form, having crescentic indents on the convex upper face to secure the clay mortar.
19 The Tahunian lithic component shows marked continuity, but one notable innovation in the form of flake arrows with side-notches, prolific at El Khiam and present both in the Natufian II at el-Wād and in the contemporary levels at Beidha. In the Pre-pottery Neolithic B at Jericho, as in the upper levels at Beidha, we find on the other hand rectangular structures with plastered walls and floors, which may in some cases have carried timber superstructures. Among innovations in the continuing lithic tradition to appear in assemblages of this period were polished flint axes associated perhaps with the carpentry involved in more sophisticated dwellings, and daggers and tanged arrowheads made from regular blades and finished by shallow surface flaking.

Quite another aspect of this phase of settlement in Palestine was

19 Tahunian flint artefacts.

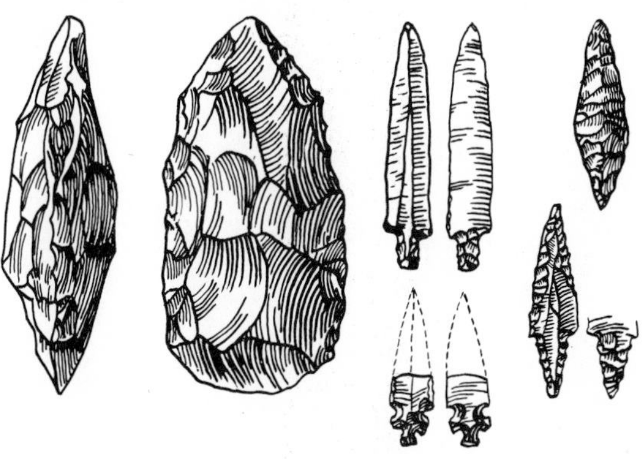

brought into focus by the discovery of a nest of human skulls in the
20 Pre-pottery B level at Tell es-Sultan. The faces were finely modelled in plaster and the eyes indicated by pairs of bivalve shells and in one case by cowries. Numerous individuals, buried without their crania but retaining their lower jaws, from under a house floor at the same site confirms the practice of detaching skulls. Burials from the contemporary level at Beidha confirm this practice and one is inevitably reminded of the Mesolithic skull burials at Ofnet and Kaufertsberg in Bavaria. Fired clay figurines from Beidha, including an ibex and a stylized woman, recall that in Palestine, as much earlier in central Europe, modelling in clay long preceded potting.

As regards subsistence the situation in respect of meat was much as it had been. Available food animals were hunted and there was

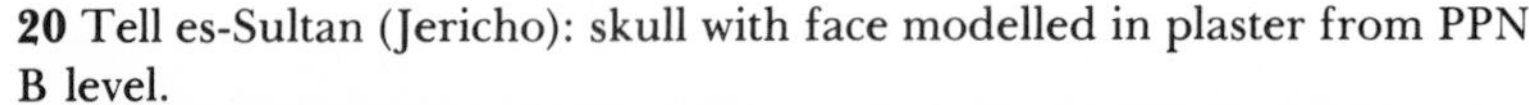
20 Tell es-Sultan (Jericho): skull with face modelled in plaster from PPN B level.

21 Tell es-Sultan (Jericho): section through defences. The lowermost man stands on the floor of the rock-cut ditch.

probably close herding of goats, but no good evidence for the domestication of the livestock basic to later farming, that is cattle, swine and sheep, appeared in the Levant until the appearance of pottery in the mid-fifth millennium B.C. after what appears to have been a break in the archaeological record. The evidence for plant food on the other hand provides some evidence for the morphological changes which occurred in the course of domestication. Both levels at Jericho yielded traces of certainly domesticated emmer (*Triticum dicoccum*) and two-rowed barley (*Hordeum distichum*) and the B level in addition domesticated einkorn (*T. monococcum*) and legumes (peas, lentils and horse-beans). The materials from Beidha again gave evidence of pulse crops and domesticated emmer, but in this case barley, the commoner cereal, had still to display clear morphological differences from the wild form. Wild grasses and a large basket of pistachio (*Pistacia atlantica*) nuts, a significant source of oil in the diet, helped to round off the picture.

It remains to discuss what has been described as the township dating from the 'Pre-pottery Neolithic A' phase of the occupation
21 of Tell es-Sultan, the prehistoric forerunner of Jericho. The stone wall over half a mile in circumference, strengthened by at least one bastion tower and an external ditch 9 metres wide at the top and cut 3 metres into the rock, implies a formidable input of labour and the area it encloses is estimated to have been capable of holding a population of some two thousand people, something quite outside the range of the caves and encampments previously discussed. This is very far from implying a social entity in any way equivalent to an urban centre. A more likely hypothesis is that the site was a focus of an extensive social territory. Its immediate surroundings had no great food potential apart from the spring. This may conceivably have been used to irrigate small plots, though there is no proof that this indeed happened. More likely the permanent population was comparatively small but reinforced seasonally by migrant groups. If, as has been suggested, the inhabitants extracted salt from the Dead Sea, this would have been a powerful attraction for seasonally nomadic groups from a wide surrounding area as well as entering into even more far-reaching exchange networks. Whatever the explanation may prove to be, there is no indication whatever that Tell es-Sultan played a key role in the process of urbanization. Indeed little is known about what went forward in Palestine for over a thousand years before established communities based on mixed farming were established in the region by the middle of the fifth millennium. The

Table 9. *Some key radiocarbon dates for early farming settlements in south-west Asia*

		B.C.
IRAN		
Belt Cave	P 26	5840 ± 330
	Av. of P 19, 19A, 19B	5330 ± 260
Bus Mordeh phase	Hole and Flannery	*c.* 7500–6750
Ali Kosh phase	Hole and Flannery	*c.* 6750–6000
Mohammad Jaffar phase	Hole and Flannery	*c.* 6000–5600
Tepe Guran (U)	K 1006	6460 ± 200
(H)	K 879	5810 ± 150
Tepe Sarab (S 5)	P 466	6006 ± 98
IRAQ		
Jarmo	Estimated (Braidwood)	*c.* 6750
Zawi Chemi Shanidar	W 681	8920 ± 300
Matarrah (middle)	W 623	5620 ± 250
ANATOLIA		
Cayönü Tepesi	MI 610	6620 ± 250
	MI 609	6840 ± 250
Mersin (base)	W 617	6000 ± 250
Çatal Hüyük (X)	P 782	6142 ± 98
SYRIA		
Bouqras		
I	GrN 4852	6290 ± 100
III	GrN 4820	5990 ± 60
Ras Shamra		
VC	P 459	6192 ± 100
	P 460	6414 ± 101
VB	P 458	5736 ± 112
Ramad		
II	GrN 4426	6260 ± 50
III	GrN 4823	5930 ± 55
PALESTINE		
Jericho		
Pottery	Estimated (Kenyon)	*c.* 5000
PPN/B	Av. of GL 28, 38 and GR 963	*c.* 6310
PPN/A	F 40	6775 ± 210
Natufian	F 72	7850 ± 210
Beidha (IV)	BM 111	6830 ± 200

ongoing history of urbanism was enacted not in the Levant, but in a territory extending from Syria and southern Anatolia to the Zagros.

Syria

The site of Mureybit has already been mentioned. Of greater impor-
138 tance because covering three main phases is that of Abu Hureyra a little further down the Euphrates. The bottom metre or so of deposit covered an encampment with hollows and stone pestles and mortars resembling in general the Mesolithic I level at the base of Tell es-Sultan, Jericho. The flint industry was also broadly similar with quantities of lunate microliths, though these lack the bipolar flaking diagnostic of Natufian assemblages proper. Signs of weathering suggest a period of abandonment before the accumulation of the eight-metre thick deposits described as 'aceramic Neolithic'. These appear from their contents to be equivalent to the Mesolithic III phase in the Levant. Thus the houses are rectangular in plan, although in this area built of mud-brick. Prominent in the lithic industry are the tanged arrowheads made on blades and partly finished by a shallow retouch recalling those from Mureybit, from Mesolithic III deposits in Palestine and Jordan and, further afield, from early levels of the Anatolian site of Hacilar. Similar, sometimes more finely finished pieces occurred in the thin pottery Neolithic layer at Abu Hureyra, as also extensively in early Neolithic deposits from Anatolia to northern Iraq.

The evolution in the pattern of subsistence agrees rather with that noted for the Levant. In the basal Mesolithic I phase the plant component combined wild cereals with a main emphasis on einkorn, wild legumes, including lentil and vetch, and the edible seeds of a number of plants of value as sources of fat or starch. In the case of meat there was a marked emphasis on gazelle which accounted for approximately two-thirds of the animal bones, a concentration paralleled in the Levant where it was associated with the culling of young animals and indicated some kind of close herding. By contrast the overlying deposits yielded domesticated cereals, including einkorn, emmer and hulled and naked six-rowed barley, as well as a variety of legumes including domesticated lentils. The most striking change in respect of animals was a swing-over from heavy emphasis on gazelle to sheep and goat, comparable with that noted in Palestine, most markedly between Mesolithic II/III.

Anatolia

Relatively little is yet established about late Pleistocene and early Neothermal settlement in Anatolia. As we have noted lithic assemblages in the Antalya area containing lunates with bipolar flaking suggest occupation in Mesolithic I. Evidence for Mesolithic III occupation comes from two main sites. Materials from the aceramic levels at Hacilar some distance to the north-west of Antalya exhibit a number of traits comparable with sites of similar age as far afield as Beidha in Jordan. These include rectangular dwellings with plaster floors, sickle flints and tanged arrowheads made on blades and sometimes finished by shallow surface flaking. No less striking is the evidence for some form of skull-cult implied by the occurrence of detached skulls on a house floor. Indications that cereals and sheep and goat were domesticated round off the picture.

Further east, significant insights into the nature of settlement during the seventh millennium B.C. on the southern flanks of the Taurus near the headwaters of the Tigris are being gained during
83 the course of ongoing excavations at Çayönü Tepesi. Although the inhabitants still made do without pottery, they were sufficiently sedentary to construct substantial buildings with stone foundations and at several levels. These were rectangular in form and some at least of the superstructures were built of mud-bricks. Grid-like structures with slots between parallel foundations of drystone build were evidently designed to allow the circulation of air and to carry a certain weight. Their resemblance in plan to Roman granaries is suggestive. Technology was based on flint and obsidian blade industries, but native copper was hammered to make such small objects as awls or reamers. The biological materials recovered from successive levels reflect a certain trend from wild species to ones showing the morphological changes that accompany, though not necessarily to begin with, cultivation and domestication. The lower levels are marked by red and fallow deer and wild cattle, swine, sheep and goat together with unmodified cereals (einkorn, emmer), nuts (almond and pistachio) and legumes (wild vetch). On the other hand some at least of the swine, sheep and goat remains from the upper levels show signs of genetic modification and there is also evidence for cultivated emmer, peas, lentils and vetch.

The Zagros

The best clues to the nature of the human settlement of the Zagros during a late stage of the Upper Pleistocene is that from the district

of Sulimaniyah in north-west Iraq. The cave of Palegawra has yielded
110: 57–9, 126 a well-studied fauna associated with a Zarzian assemblage marked
by trapeziform, as well as crescentic, triangular and rectangular microliths, backed blades, drills and scrapers and dating from around 12,000 B.C. It is interesting to see that the adoption of a mode 5 industry and its associated wooden hafts or mounts coincided with the beginning of the change from a steppe to a forest savannah environment. In this respect the presence of oak, tamarisk, poplar and conifer charcoal confirms the evidence from pollen-analysis taken from lake Zeribar in west-central Iran. A clear insight into the animal food eaten by the cave-dwellers is given by a model study summarized in Table 10.

The Palegawra people also ate tortoise and snails as well as clams and crabs from the stream below, but these resources were insignificant by comparison with the meat of herbivorous animals which was brought to the cave in the form of fore- and hind-quarters. By far the most important in terms of weight was onager, but red deer and to a slightly less degree cattle also contributed substantially. Since these animals are represented almost entirely by mature adults, it can be assumed that they were hunted. The only animal to show anatomical signs of domestication was a single dog.

The first signs of domesticated herbivores occurred in the context
of later manifestations of the Zarzian tradition further north. The
123 evidence comes from the village site of Zawi Chemi Shanidar and
the B I level of the cave of Shanidar, both dating from the first half of the ninth millennium B.C. and most probably used by the same people. Among the animal bones were those of sheep which, to judge

Table 10. *Proportions of the various animals contributing to the Zarzian meat supply, Palegawra Cave, N.E. Iraq (after Turnbull & Reed)*

Species	Min. no. individuals	Meat (kg)
Onager (*Equus hemionus*)	27	4,050
Red deer (*Cervus elaphus*)	12	1,200
Sheep (*Ovis orientalis*)	10	350
Goat (*Capra hircus aegagrus*)	8	280
Gazelle (*Gazella subgutturosa*)	7	140
Pig (*Sus scrofa*)	3	105
Cattle (*Bos primigenius*)	2	700
Others: lesser mole rat, red fox, hare, marten, badger, dog and polecat	27	31·6
Totals	96	6,856·6

from the high proportion of immature individuals, may well indicate some form of close herding. Indications that the same people were harvesting cereals is given by slotted bone reaping-knife handles inset with stone blades, as well as by grinding and pounding equipment.

A later and more advanced phase is associated with what may be termed epi-Zarzian lithic industries at the village site of Jarmo in
22 the Palegawran area and further south in Khuzistan and Luristan.
110: 38–50 The site of Jarmo, dating from the first half of the seventh millennium B.C. and situated on a promontory in the Kurdish hills, can hardly, to judge from the thinness of its deposits, have lasted for more than a very few centuries. It probably consisted of about twenty-five houses huddled together, each having an open alley or small court on two sides. The houses themselves, which had several small rectangular rooms each, were constructed of packed mud built up course by course, each being allowed to dry in the sun before the next one was added. Clay ovens and the bases for silos were built into each house and marks on the floors showed that these were covered by plaited mats. The villagers lived only to a slight extent by hunting – the bones of wild animals account for about 5 per cent of the whole – and depended mainly on mixed farming: two-rowed barley, emmer, spelt and peas were certainly cultivated and sheep and goats were herded and maintained. A Palegawra-like array of microliths reflect the continuance of hunting and whole blades showing the tell-tale gloss that came from friction with corn stalks, as well as milling-stones, confirm the importance of cereals. Since mats were made it is likely that baskets were as well. Pottery was confined to the top third of the deposit, even though figurines of animals and women were being modelled in clay throughout. It is

22 Jarmo lithic artefacts.

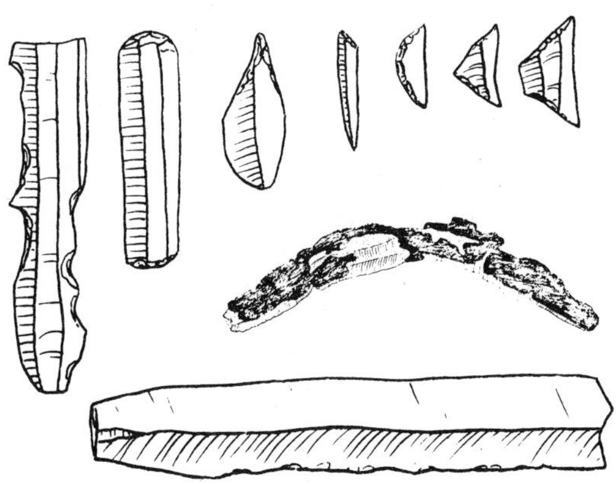

a fair assumption that throughout most of the period of settlement containers other than pottery were used, but that we have here the final phase of farming preceding the appearance of potting.

Three classes of settlement bearing on the early phases in the evolution of farming have been investigated in Khuzistan and Luristan: permanent villages occupied by upwards of a hundred persons;
99 seasonal camps lacking permanent buildings; and caves. In respect of villages two phases can be noted prior to the appearance of pottery round about 6000 B.C. The initial Bus Mordeh phase witnessed the systematic collection of seeds, including those of wild alfalfa, spring milk vetch, wild oats and other wild cereal grasses and the fruit of wild capers. Indeed, wild seeds often of very small size, of a kind that must have been shaken into a fine basket or tray, made up over nine-tenths of those recovered in carbonized form. The remaining fraction included grains of emmer wheat and two-rowed barley which can be presumed on account of their size to have been planted. The fact that seeds of the sea club-rush occurred mixed with cultivated cereal grains suggests that crops must have been grown and harvested in close proximity to marshy ground; and it may be significant in this regard that carp, water-turtle, mussel and water-birds were included in the diet. Hunting remained important, gazelle being the principal quarry along with onager, wild ox and wild boar, but livestock were also maintained. Goats were presumably introduced from the near-by mountains and were herded on a considerable scale. Sheep had hardly begun to appear in any number. The flint-work reflects the economic base of Bus Mordeh society: microliths point to hunting; and blades for insertion into reaping knives to reaping.

During the succeeding Ali Kosh phase cereal cultivation greatly increased at the expense of plant-gathering and emmer and two-rowed barley accounted for two-fifths of carbonized seeds. Goat still outnumbered sheep. Increased prosperity based on higher production of cereals was reflected in larger houses that were now built of sun-dried bricks held together by mud mortar and often plastered over with mud on either face. Mats were used on the floors and the villagers also made twined baskets some of which they apparently waterproofed with pitch. Stone bowls became more numerous and diverse in form. Personal ornaments now included a tubular bead made from cold-hammered native copper. Pottery on the other hand was not brought into use until the onset of the ensuing Mohammad Jaffar phase around *c.* 6000 B.C.

Yet another territory to be considered in connection with the transition from specialized hunting and foraging is that extending from the south-west corner of the Caspian to northern Iran and Turkmenia. The lithic assemblage relating to the earliest phase of settled,
103 pottery-using farmers at Djeitun on the margin of the Kara-kum desert is suggestive for two reasons. For one thing its composition – blades, some set in bone reaping-knives, scrapers, awls on the end of blades and microliths of triangular and trapeziform shape – resembles in general terms that of Jarmo the other side of the Iranian plateau. For another it carries forward a tradition well exemplified in the mesolithic assemblages from the cave of Dzhebel near Krasnovodsk and again from the Belt Cave near Behshahr at
96 the south-east corner of the Caspian. The fauna from the Belt Cave is of outstanding interest because it shows the same swing away from gazelle to caprine dependence so frequently documented in the Palestine sequence (p. 56). Although several links in the chain need to be documented, it is already possible to suggest that the origins
107 of the Djeitun and successive phases of settlement in Turkestan, as in the other parts of south-west Asia already reviewed, stemmed from the indigenous mesolithic of the region. Behind this in turn, as the
101 material from the Ali Tappeh cave, adjacent to Belt Cave, indicates, lies the same Zarzian root which nourished the whole Zagros sequence.

Neolithic/Chalcolithic settlement

Adoption of pottery-making

In terms of narrative it is a fact established by radiocarbon dating that evidence for pottery first appeared within a century or two of 6000 B.C. over a territory extending from the Zagros to the east Mediterranean basin. It appeared among communities which since 9000 to 12000 or so B.C. had been gaining practice in the manipulation of animals and plants and finding it increasingly convenient to occupy year-round settlements over periods of generations. As we have seen such people had enjoyed a long experience of manipulating clay and plaster for figurines and the finishing of house structures. Yet, although potting as a craft was better adapted to a sedentary than to a migratory existence and although pots were of particular use for cereal foods, it would be wrong to argue that the adoption of potting was necessitated either by a sedentary existence or by the practice of farming: agriculture was by no means the only basis of

sedentarism, not all potters were peasants and not all peasants used pottery containers. None of this alters the empirical observation that
69–72, 80 as a matter of historical fact potting first developed in south-west Asia among agricultural communities of a sedentary habit. Such people had advanced so far beyond the experimental stage that they were already cultivating basically the same cereals and maintaining the same species of livestock as their peasant successors over much of the Near East and Europe have done down to recent times. Yet their technology was and for long remained based primarily on stone tools, among them polished stone axe-blades. They were thus formally Neolithic in the sense in which this convenient label was defined over a hundred years ago. The use of native copper for ornaments had already appeared in Mesolithic III contexts, but copper metallurgy and the manufacture of metal-working tools did not begin until the fifth millennium and even then only to supplement a basically lithic technology.

It is important not to exaggerate the scale of the new communities. Whereas the Natufians of Mesolithic I were probably still spending most of the year in groups of three or four households and the seventh millennium inhabitants of Jarmo occupied villages of twenty to twenty-five households, the Neolithic communities of south-west Asia were of the size of villages or at most small towns with populations numbered in hundreds rather than thousands. Again, one should not be misled by the inflation of language popularized by the media into supposing that settlements at this stage had the character or organization of cities. They housed communities of peasants, closely knit in space and time, building their houses in successive generations almost precisely one above the other. Although there are signs of some degree of specialization at the level of craftsmanship, there was no marked social differentiation, let alone stratification. The houses conformed fairly closely in size and lay-out. There is no sign at this stage of anything approaching palatial structures. One has much more the impression of peasant kin sheltering close together in a series of almost contiguous cells. One of the few signs of more complex structuring are the buttressed walls which at the Samarran site of Choga Mami appear to enclose groups of houses as if defining extended families. One of the few signs of buildings transcending the ordinary family unit was the large complex of fourteen rooms found at an early level at Tell es-Sawwan near Samarra. Its size, the fact that it immediately overlay a cemetery and the presence in several rooms of alabaster idols suggest the possibility of a small temple. On the other hand cults and shrines were generally of a domestic kind. Again burials were often made, as most notably at Çatal Hüyük, in actual dwellings.

Within this general description there was room for much variation. A factor common to dwellings is that they were built of mud and re-built, to judge from recent custom, each generation, a practice that led to the formation in the course of centuries of the settlement
78 mounds or tells. On the other hand, it is of interest that, whereas in Assyria the walls were to begin with habitually built of packed mud or *tauf*, further south at Tell es-Sawwan and far away to the west at Çatal Hüyük they were constructed of rectangular mud-bricks shaped in moulds. Again there was a marked difference in the lithic industries. In the Zagros, on the Iranian plateau and in Turkestan

23 Tell Hassuna, north Iraq. (*Upper*) reconstruction of house and yard; (*lower*) section with several building levels.

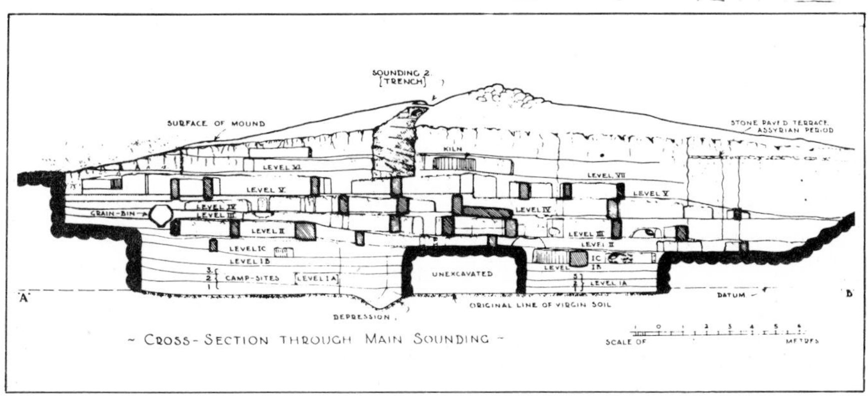

NEOLITHIC/CHALCOLITHIC SETTLEMENT

these were of epi-Zarzian character with microliths, whereas from Hassuna to Çatal they continued the heavy blade tradition with tanged projectile heads and daggers finished in part by flat flaking of the kind noted already in Mesolithic III. The most sensitive medium was pottery. Because of the plasticity of clay and the fact that much pottery was home-made by people tied to the soil by agriculture, ceramic products are unrivalled for defining regional groupings and contrariwise for indicating interaction between groupings whether by exchange or the passage of fashions or ideas. To complicate the picture one should remember that in the course of centuries the extent of social territories and the relations between them underwent change. Moreover it is important to grasp that even a key site like Tell Hassuna was in the nature of things marginal to the areas in which certain of the wares stratified in its deposits were themselves characterized. In reviewing the situation in different regions it will be convenient to begin with Assyria, linked on the one hand with Syro-Cilicia and Anatolia and on the other with the alluvial zone of south Mesopotamia that gave birth to the Sumerian and some later civilizations of the region.

North Mesopotamia, Syria and Cilicia

Whereas in the Sumerian south agriculture was only practicable on any scale with the aid of elaborate irrigation, the zone of northern Mesopotamia later to be identified with the centre of Assyrian power had sufficient rainfall to permit an efficient dry agriculture. Between these zones there is evidence, for instance in the district of Mandali near the foothills of the Zagros, that the cultivation of cereal crops
118, 119 could be carried on with the aid of quite minor and indeed primitive irrigation.

114 Northern Iraq is a classical area for tells. The site of Tell Hassuna has proved particularly useful to archaeology. Together with Nineveh and Yarim Tepe it has provided a sequence of building levels
23, 24 and pottery styles for the period extending from *c.* 6000 to 4500 B.C.

The cultural affinities of the Hassuna A pottery from the basal level I*a* lay with Syria and Anatolia rather than with Kurdistan or Iran. Thus the dark burnished pottery which accompanied the coarse, straw-tempered wares of Hassuna A compares with that from the
85, 144 earliest pottery levels at sites like Mersin, Cilicia, or Ras Shamra and Byblos in Syria, where the vessels were sometimes hole-mouthed and characteristically decorated by shell impressions. The pottery, which
92 occurred along with wooden containers down to the earliest levels

at Çatal Hüyük in southern Anatolia, though differing in many respects, being ovoid in form and provided with lugs or bucket-like handles, was similarly monochrome. The flint technology pointed in the same direction. Instead of an epi-Zarzian industry with microliths we find arrow or javelin heads made on heavy blades and often finished by skilled shallow surface-retouch similar to that from the Syrian sites and Çatal Hüyük and, what is even more interesting, to the Mesolithic III flint assemblages as far south as Beidha. On the other hand polished stone axes and reaping-knife blades were common to a much wider techno-territory.

Painted decoration first appeared in this region in the Hassuna B stage (levels I*b*–II) in the form of multichevron and simple linear patterns. Similar archaic painted ware appeared over an extensive territory from north Mesopotamia (Nineveh I) to Cilicia (Mersin XX–XXIV) and in slightly more complex form in south Anatolia
84, 90 (Can Hasan and Hacilar). At Hassuna the same level saw the beginning of the local Hassuna standard ware comprising bowls and globular necked jars decorated by geometric designs in incision, paint or both.

24 Tell Hassuna stone tools and standard incised and painted pottery.

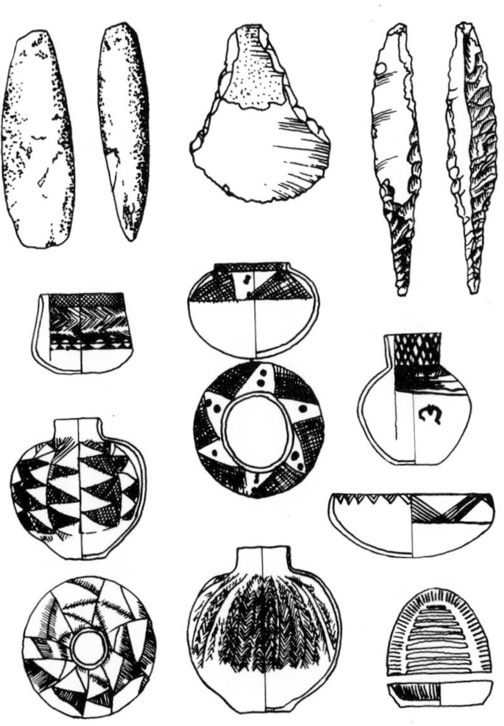

In levels III–V at Hassuna this standard ware was supplemented by Samarra ware from further south. Recent excavations at Yarim Tepe I, a Hassuna settlement dating from the period of Samarra imports, have given a good idea of the scale and nature of settlements at this time. Since the mound was about 100 metres in diameter and twelve houses were found in the 1,440 square metres excavated, it looks as though the number of households occupying the site at any one time might have been of the order of sixty or seventy, implying a population of say four hundred. The houses which were fairly uniform in size and character had evidently been arranged more or less parallel with passages and yards, but as the site filled up at any particular level the gaps tended to be built over. The houses were constructed from clay blocks to a standard rectangular plan. Each had a main living area with an oven in one corner and close at hand

Table 11. *Archaeological stratigraphy of north and south Mesopotamia: 5900–2370* B.C.

	NORTH		SOUTH	
B.C.	Hassuna	Gawra	Uruk	General
2370	....	....	....	....
				Early Dynastic III
2600	....	....	....	....
		VII	I	Early Dynastic II Early Dynastic I
2900	....	....	....	....
		VIII–IX	II–V	Jamdet Naṣr
3100	....	....	....	....
		X–XII	VI–XIV	Uruk
3500	....	....	....	....
		XIII–XIX	XV–XVIII	Al' Ubaid
4300	....	....	....	....
	VI–XI Halafian	XX		
5000	....	....	....	....
	III–V Hassuna C			
5400	....	....	....	....
	I*b*–II Hassuna B			
5600	....	....	....	....
	I*a* Hassuna A			
5900	....	....	....	....

a stone mortar set into the floor. The fact that each one also had a
nest of small storage compartments confirms that we are dealing with
a village of peasants rather than a city with a complex redistribution
system. Interesting details include the way in which door-sills were
protected by large potsherds, and the presence of at least one
sleeping bench. The presence of two-storey kilns helps to explain the
117 high standard of potting and there is evidence from Tell Shimshara
for textiles. Subsistence was based primarily on the growing of
cereals including wheat (*Triticum aestivum* and *T. spelta*) and the
maintenance of the standard livestock of western Asia and Europe
other than horses, each species of which displayed evidence of the
morphological changes which arise under domestication. Hunting
added what was now only a subsidiary source of animal protein.

The Samarran pottery which probably reached Iraq as an import
had developed further south in the middle Tigris and Euphrates
region on the fringes of the alluvium of south Mesopotamia. There
are indeed signs that elementary irrigation was carried out in this
119 marginal area, notably at Choga Mami where channels were evidently cut to redistribute water carried down from the flanks of the
Zagros. How far this type of exploitation extended into Sumer is
still unknown on account of the ancient surface being covered by
deep alluvium deposited by the twin rivers. Samarran ware, most
fully known in context perhaps from Tell es-Sawwan immediately
below the name site, is distinguished by the richness of its painted
designs. These include a variety of shaded bands and among other
geometric patterns a notable number of stepped lines. The fact that
Samarra ware overlay Hassuna B pottery at Tell es-Sawwan itself
confirms that it was largely contemporary with Hassuna C.

Levels VI–XI at Hassuna were marked by the appearance of the
25 brilliant and easily recognizable painted ware named after Tell Halaf,
the mound in south-east Syria where it was first recognized. Halafian
pottery is outstanding on account of the variety of its forms and above
all of its painted decoration and because of the excellence of its firing;
but it was still hand-made, and there is no reason to think it was
necessarily or even probably made by whole-time potters. In addition
to dishes and flasks the forms included bowls with sharp-shouldered
bodies and flaring necks and bowls and flasks on hollow stands. The
decoration comprised geometric patterns like triangles, chevrons,
lozenges, chequers, stars, Maltese crosses, quatrefoils and rosettes;
stipples, including egg and dot; and stylized representations of men
and animals, including designs based on the bull's head. It was

25 Tell Halaf ware from Arpachiyah: (*upper*) painted vessels; (*lower*) bull's head (*bukranium*) designs.

applied to a buff or cream slip by glaze paint. At the climax of the industry the decoration was polychrome; red, orange, yellow and black paints being used, sometimes highlighted by white spots. The pottery was apparently fired to temperatures up to 1200 °C in great domed kilns with rectangular annexes, like those preserved at Carchemish, with walls and ceilings of clay on stone footings.

For some time Halafian technology continued to be based on obsidian, flint and other kinds of stone tool with copper being used only for small things like beads. The Halafians were particularly skilled at working hard stones, which they made into button seals, beads, amulets and small vessels, and they were accustomed to draw raw materials from a considerable range of territory. At its greatest extent Halafian pottery extended as far west as the Syro-Cilician region where it occurred at Mersin (XVII–XIX) and Ras Shamra (III), as far east as Tepe Gawra (XX), as far north as Lake Van and as far south as Babylon. Over this extensive territory it displayed similarities not merely in material equipment but also in evidence of cult. As at Çatal we find on the one hand female figurines and on the other symbols of masculinity such as bulls, whose horned heads were in this case painted on pots and carved in the form of amulets. In addition double-axe amulets and representations on pottery betray the existence of a respect for thunder if not indeed for a thunder-god.

South Anatolia

The possibilities opened up by an assured supply of food are brilliantly displayed at Çatal Hüyük on the Konya Plain, the earliest pottery Neolithic site yet explored in southern Anatolia. The very extent of the mound covering some 13 hectares and the manner in which the houses are packed together in the excavated area argue for a sizeable community amounting to perhaps five thousand souls. On the other hand Çatal Hüyük betrayed none of the architectural or social characteristics of a city in the accepted meaning of that term.

Subsistence rested to a significant degree on the cultivation and harvesting of cereal crops, including bread wheat as well as einkorn, emmer and barley. Sheep and goats were kept, in addition to dogs, but hunting made a big contribution to the supply of meat. Wild ox, wild pig and red deer were the most important game. The people lived in rectangular houses built contiguously but interspersed at
26 intervals by courtyards. The walls were built of large sun-dried bricks held together by thick layers of mortar containing ash and bones.

The buildings were one-storey with flat roofs that were doubtless used during the summer for many purposes other than serving as a means of circulation. The absence of doorways indeed suggests that access to the dwellings was gained through holes in the roofs from which stepped timbers against one wall led down to the ground floor. Indoor ovens were built into the walls so as to help retain heat, but open fireplaces were set near the middle of the floors. Features of the houses were the carefully plastered benches used for sitting and sleeping and not least as receptacles for the family dead. The skeletons, up to thirty or more in a simple bench, appear to have been exposed some while before being buried, but some of them have been laid to rest in fairly good anatomical order. The twelve constructional phases noted by the excavators show that houses were frequently rebuilt and the remarkable evidence for continuity of tradition in successive levels suggests that rebuilding took place at frequent intervals.

Although pottery was made from the very beginning, the good conditions of preservation encountered in some levels allow us to
27 observe that wooden vessels and coiled baskets played an important

26 Çatal Hüyük, Anatolia: tentative reconstruction of houses, level VI.

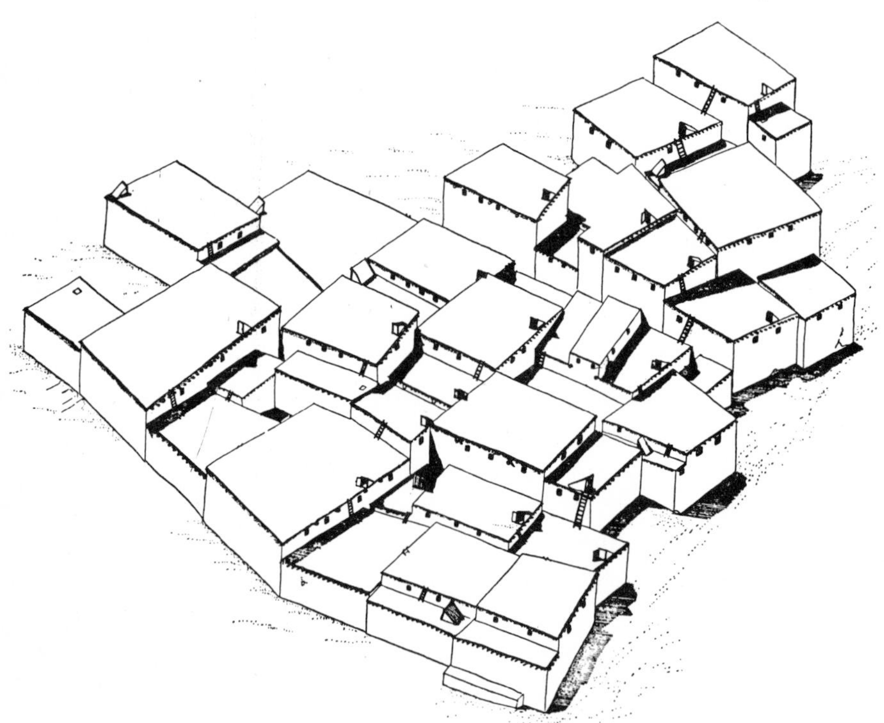

part as containers. The fact that copper and lead were used for beads and trinkets in no wise alters the fact that technology was basically Neolithic. Flint and obsidian provided materials for lanceheads, dagger-blades and blades for setting in the slots of antler reaping-knife handles.

The blades of the axes and adzes needed for felling and shaping timber were made from hard greenstone polished to a sharp edge. Blocks of obsidian were split and polished with the utmost skill to provide mirrors for the women, who used a variety of cosmetics. Antler and bone were worked to provide a wide range of artefacts, including spoons and ladles, needles, belt-fasteners and handles of various kinds. Animal skins were prepared for garments. Woollen textiles were used both for clothing and – to judge from certain wall-paintings – for rugs or hangings. It is impressive to note the wide area from which these early Neolithic people drew their raw
79 materials, and no less to observe the extremely high standard reached in a variety of crafts. The absence of waste materials from the dwellings so far explored argues that separate workshops existed elsewhere on the site and it would seem likely that craft specialization

27 Çatal Hüyük, Anatolia: vessels of pottery (1–3), stone (4) and wood (5–8).

had gone much further than one is accustomed to expect of a Neolithic community.

Richness in material goods was more than matched in the sphere of art and cult. Reliefs and paintings were applied to the plastered
28 walls of certain rooms so richly as to denote their use as shrines, but the number and small size of these argues for domestic family cults: public temples manned by whole-time priests were still something for the future. The iconography of the wall art, as of the numerous small plastic figurines and stone carvings, argues that worship centred round the generative forces of nature. No emphasis was laid on the organs of sex, but the figures shown on the walls were either women or animals such as bulls or rams symbolic of male potency. These last were sometimes represented only by heads and horns, as in scenes showing women giving birth to bulls. Men and boys were sometimes represented in the figurines and one stone carving shows two pairs in embrace, on one side a goddess and her partner and on the other a goddess and her son. Conversely the theme of death is symbolized by leopards, counterparts of the jaguars of Meso-american iconography: opposed leopards are shown in wall reliefs and among figurines there is one of a woman in childbirth supported on either side by leopards and another of a goddess holding a leopard on either arm.

28 Çatal Hüyük, Anatolia: reconstruction of east and part of north wall of shrine VII at level VI.

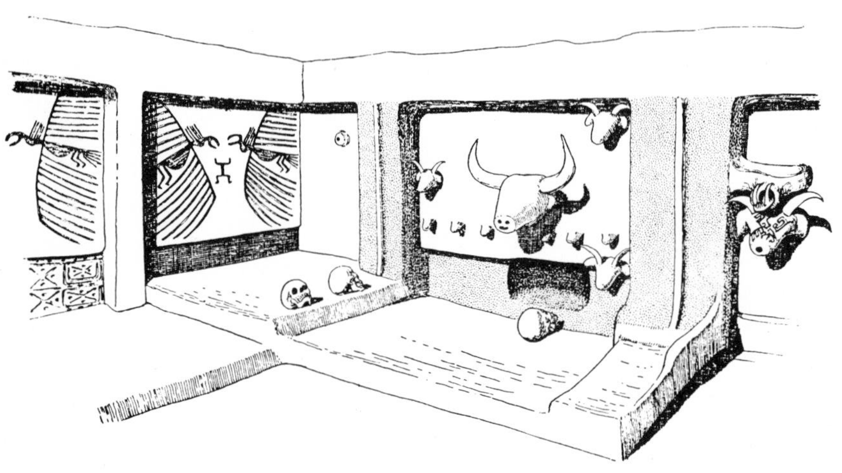

The Neolithic communities of the southern margin of Turkmenia
98 (e.g. Djeitun), the south slopes of the Elburz facing the inner desert
103 zone of the Iranian plateau (e.g. Sialk) and the western slope of the
97, 99, 104 Zagros from Kurdistan and Kermanshah to Fars (e.g. Ali Kosh,
Bakun, Guran), although differing in their pottery styles, were united by the basically epi-Zarzian nature of their flint-work. The normal dwelling was rectangular in form and built of either mud or sun-dried brick. At Djeitun it could be seen that the village was made up of a concentration of about thirty households and there is no evidence at this stage or indeed for another few thousand years of large urban settlements in this part of the world. The animal bones show that antelope and goat contributed significantly to subsistence and no doubt the continued manufacture of microliths and notably of trapezes was related to this. On the other hand the cultivation of cereals involved the manufacture of equipment for reaping. It is extremely interesting to see how at Djeitun and Sialk I flint-blades continued to be inset into slotted bone handles as they had been since Mesolithic times. Much of the pottery made at sites like Djeitun and Sialk was plain but some of it was painted with simple geometric designs; at the former vertical arrangements of wavy lines sometimes broken by horizontal straight ones were favoured, whereas at the latter it was chequer patterns and shaded triangles. Clay figurines of animals and women were a recurrent feature.

There is comparable evidence for farmers settling down and starting to make pottery containers and cooking vessels from many localities along the western slopes of the Zagros from Kermanshah to Fars and on to Baluchistan. Long sustained systematic excavation
99 in Khuzistan has brought to light particularly impressive evidence
for a gradual evolution of farming and the appearance around 6000 B.C. of fully formed Neolithic culture. The earliest pottery, that of the Mohammad Jaffar stage, included some red-slipped burnished vessels, but for the most part it was buff in colour, mostly plain, but sometimes painted with simple geometric designs. It is significant that alongside reaping-knife flakes and other forms related to farming the microlithic component continued down to the ensuing Sabz phase of the second half of the sixth millennium.

Emergence of civilization in south Mesopotamia

Implications of civilization

Although, as we have seen, settled life developed over a tract of high ground extending from the Iranian plateau to Anatolia and the Levant which enjoyed rainfall sufficient for dry farming, civilization first grew up on the alluvial lands of the Tigris and Euphrates with an annual rainfall of less than 25 cm. This would only seem a paradox if we left out of account the unique quality of human societies. It was indeed the very defects in the natural environment of Sumer that led to the emergence there of literate polities. In addition to an arid climate Sumer was conspicuously lacking in many of the materials most needed for the technologies and structures of advanced societies. It had reeds, palm stems and mud, but it lacked good building-stone, most kinds of timber and above all minerals. Yet it was a land of opportunities for those able to develop the institutions needed for effective irrigation and the import of adequate supplies of the missing raw materials. The price of occupying this land by settled communities as opposed to mere swamp dwellers and fishermen was no less than the attainment of civilization. Its full possibilities could only be realized by civilized societies, that is societies with political as distinct from merely familial or social institutions, institutions which ensured the discharge by individuals of increasingly specialized roles. The soil was potentially fertile and the water was there for irrigation; given the level of technology that had already been reached over extensive tracts of south-west Asia

29 Tell al'Ubaid, Sumer: frieze from façade of temple showing dairying scenes.

and above all given the possibility of public works on an adequate scale, it was capable of producing food enough to support societies at increasing levels of complexity; moreover, the great rivers that gave the possibility of exercising political control also facilitated access to sources of raw materials in the distant highlands. To anyone capable of profiting from these conditions the potentialities were immense.

Ubaid

When the alluvial lands were first occupied is still uncertain. The first inhabitants well known to us are those named after Al'Ubaid, a humble village set on a low mound or island of river silt in the Euphrates Valley. These people first appear in the archaeological record in the latter part of the fifth millennium at a time when the Halafian culture had for some centuries been flourishing in the north. The huts of the name-site were built of the most abundant raw materials of the area; some had a flat roof, the walls formed of reed mats suspended between palm-stems and plastered with mud, and others a rounded one formed by bending bundles of reed over from one side to another, creating a structure like a Nissen hut. The peasants lived by farming: cereal crops were harvested by reaping-knives or sickles set with flint teeth, like those used on the highlands and in the Syro-Cilician region, or alternatively by sickles made of baked clay. The use of dung as plaster and the manufacture of animal figurines suggest that domestic livestock were kept. Even more
29 decisive evidence is provided by iconography. The well-known frieze of bronze, stone and bitumen from Al'Ubaid shows a wide range of

dairying activities. There is some evidence also for hunting and fishing in the marshes and rivers. To judge from a clay model with upturned ends, it would appear that they were already using boats made from bundles of reeds like the modern *bellum* to navigate the rivers. Potting was still mainly done by hand during the early stage of the culture, but already the foot-rings added to certain vessels before firing were being shaped on a slow-moving wheel or tournette turned by the potter's hand. The finer wares, of a light buff colour which turned when over-fired to a greenish hue, were decorated by painting with a smooth ferruginous paint having a matt surface, generally blackish but sometimes reddish in colour. The patterns were made up predominantly of relatively simple geometrical designs, such as zigzag lines, triangles, lozenges and cross-hatching, but very occasionally animal motifs, like those used more freely in the highlands, were employed.

The picture of village life given by the exploration of Al'Ubaid has been corrected by later work on a number of town sites. Excavation
112 of Tell Shahrain (the ancient Eridu) and Ur in the south and of Tepe
124, 125 Gawra (XII–XIX) in the north has shown that the Ubaid people also lived in towns and erected their buildings from sun-dried bricks. Another sign of their relative advance over predecessors in Mesopotamia was that they practised metallurgy. In the south few copper objects have been recovered from Ubaid deposits, but at Tepe Gawra
116, 122 and Arpachiya and further afield at Tell Halaf a number of cast copper axes and other tools have been found; even at Al'Ubaid the peasants made baked clay copies of copper tools, notably shaft-hole axes with expanded blades. The most striking monuments of the Ubaid people, not only on account of their physical size but even more because of what they imply in social organization, are their temples. At Abu Shahrain no less than thirteen, the two bottom ones known only from a few walls, were found in the Ubaid levels underlying structures dating from the Third Dynasty of Ur. The earliest temple of which a plan could be recovered (level XVI) was a small, nearly square room with a door near one corner, two short screens suggesting a division of the inner space, an altar in a niche in the rear wall and an offering-place showing signs of burning in the middle; by level VIII, on the other hand, the tripartite plan with a central cella flanked on either side by rows of small rooms had been evolved. This latter type occurred again in the two lower-most Ubaid layers (XVIII–XIX) at Tepe Gawra in the north and was to recur throughout the succeeding Warka and Protoliterate stages of

southern Iraq. The construction and above all the frequent reconstruction of temples, which might be of very substantial size, go to show that the Ubaid people had already so to speak created the characteristic form of early civilization in Mesopotamia, the sacred city whose economic, social and religious life was centred on the temple and its priests. Quite apart from the effect of cults and social rituals the very size of cities and the splendour of their public buildings in Sumerian as in other urban civilizations gave reassurance to citizens bereft of the verities of subsistence farming. The cities and their buildings symbolized the collective institutions on which their very lives depended.

Warka

On the Ubaid foundation Sumerian civilization developed comparatively rapidly in the south, where its progress can most conveniently be followed in the sequence of deposits found in the precinct of the Eanna Temple at Warka (= Sumerian Uruk, Semitic Erech). Here the Warka stage proper is represented by the bottom six layers (XIV–IX), the succeeding six (VIII–III) being assigned to the Protoliterate stage. The Warka stage is marked by the spread of a new kind of pottery which first coexisted with evolved forms of Ubaid

30 Erech, Sumer: plan and elevation of White Temple.

31 Tell Asmar, Iraq: limestone votive figure, Protoliterate phase.

ware and then replaced it. Culturally this pottery is interesting because it belongs to a ware at home in Anatolia and suggests an enrichment of Mespotamia by impulses from the north. Economically its main significance is that it was turned on a free-spinning wheel, generally a sign that its manufacture had ceased to be a domestic craft and was in the hands of whole-time potters. No architectural remains of outstanding interest were found in the levels of this phase at the Eanna site, but in another part a succession of temples was erected at this time to the god Anu. The earliest of these, represented only by a ramp, may have been earlier than Eanna XIV, but those whose plans have been recovered were probably contemporary with Eanna XI–VIII. The culminating structure of the
30 Warka phase was the White Temple, built on the traditional threefold plan and having on the central axis of the cella a rectangular pedestal with a low semicircular step bearing traces of burning, presumably in connection with offerings or incense. The White Temple measured 22·3×17·5 metres and it was set on a great platform 70 metres long, 66 metres broad and 13 metres high, built of rectangular mud-bricks. The size of the temples erected during the Warka phase and above all, perhaps, the frequency with which they were rebuilt go to emphasize their importance in the social structure of the day. Another feature to appear at this time, destined to be of even greater importance in Sumerian society, was the cylinder seal, which first occurred between two underlying building phases most probably of Eanna X–IX age.

Protoliterate Sumer

The Protoliterate phase at Warka was marked by a renewed activity in the construction of temples. On the Anu site a true ziggurat or stepped platform was erected for the first time in Eanna VIII; on the Eanna site a tripartite temple was raised on a limestone footing during period V and above it in period IV a building with great free-standing columns; and on another part of the site a temple was built directly on the level soil, the surface being decorated by vast numbers of small cones of variously coloured stones pressed into gypsum plaster, that gave the effect of a vast mosaic covering not only the building itself but also the wall round the court. The phase further witnessed a number of innovations, including the use of vessels of copper and silver, monumental sculpture and pictographic writing. The uppermost Protoliterate level at Warka (Eanna III) yielded an almost lifesize human head of marble and a number of

large sculptures of animal heads. Again, from a hole beside an altar
31 at Tell Asmar we have a series of human figures carved from yellow limestone with the eyes inlaid with shell, figures which are thought to represent in most instances individual devotees of the god whose temple they originally helped to furnish. It is significant, in view of the central role of the temple and its priests in Protoliterate society, that the earliest traces of writing and numeration belonged to the temple accounts. So far from bearing witness to priestly exploitation of the toiling masses these accounts bear witness to the efficiency of the redistributive system operating in these ancient cities. Adequate rations had to be assured to the large numbers of persons – administrators, scribes, soldiers, artificers and merchants, as well as priests – who performed specialized services on behalf of the community but who were divorced from the production of food. No less important, the large storage installations which feature in the archaeological record of such cities were an insurance against times of dearth. Writing first appeared in the guise of pictographic signs
32 on limestone and clay tablets. The numerical system associated with these primitive scripts combined features of the decimal and sexage-

32 Early pictographic writing from Sumer: (*above*) limestone tablet, Kish; (*below*) clay tablet, Erech.

simal systems and emphasizes the way in which economic activities were controlled from the centre by the temple community. That means of transport over land as well as on rivers had been developed at this time is shown by the occurrence among the pictographic signs of representations of wheeled vehicles and of boats with upturned ends.

The Early Dynastic period

113, 120 The Early Dynastic phase of Sumerian civilization, which began somewhere around 3000 B.C. was marked from a material point of view by an overall increase in wealth rather than by any notable innovations in the sphere of technology. Many of its basic traits were already present in the Ubaid culture and, as we have seen, the use of the wheel for potting and for transport, monumental sculpture, cylinder seals and pictographic writing were all added during the ensuing Protoliterate phases. Among the most potent signs of increased wealth should be mentioned the greater abundance and elaboration of metal tools, weapons, ornaments and vessels, among which forms were evolved that spread in time to Syria, Anatolia, the Aegean, the Caucasus, central Europe and vast tracts of Russia. By the end of Early Dynastic times the Sumerian smiths were riveting and soldering, as well as casting, and were making bronze with a content of from 6 to 10 per cent of tin. Quantities of gold and silver were used for ornaments and vessels, as well as a wide range of more or less hard stones. Representations on painted pottery, models and remains from tombs give us more detailed information about the wheeled transport available at this time: chariots and waggons were evidently mounted on solid wheels, made from three pieces of wood held together by cross-pieces and bound by tyres held in place by copper nails, and drawn by Asiatic asses (onagers) or oxen harnessed by collars and yokes. From this time also engravings on cylinder seals indicate that animal traction was being applied to light wooden ploughs for cultivating the soil.

The rise in material well-being was accompanied by major changes in social structure, the most notable of which was the emergence of kings or officials of comparable status, at first as temporary war leaders, but in due course as established rulers of the city states. The immediate cause of this was undoubtedly the rise of warfare as an institution and this itself was linked with the increase in wealth already noted: thus, the growing affluence of the cities only served to increase their attraction to marauding pastoralists of the highland

and the desert; the citizens needed to secure raw materials in increasing variety and volume from more or less remote territories inhabited by poorer and more barbarous peoples; and, even more to the point, rivalry between the cities grew as the opportunities for enrichment increased and this occurred at a time when armament was becoming more effective and the inhabitants found themselves able to support warriors. Whatever the factors responsible there can be no doubt that war had by this time become a well-organized institution: on the
33 so-called 'Royal Standard' of Ur we see depicted not only the royal chariot with prisoners under guard, but three distinct grades of combat troops, namely ass-drawn chariots riding men down, a phalanx of heavy troops helmeted and cloaked, and light skirmishers in contact with the enemy. Eloquent insight into the status achieved by
127 the Sumerian rulers during Early Dynastic III times is given by the
34 Royal Tombs at Ur. These show that a whole procession of grooms, guards, courtiers and women, together with the oxen drawing the funeral car, were slaughtered to accompany the royal personage to the next world.

Akkadians and Babylonians

Although the Sumerians had developed polities sufficiently effective to ensure irrigation and the acquisition of raw materials from a wide range of more or less distant sources, the level of organization was still that of city states. At least eleven of these, including Ur, Erech, Larsa, Kish and Nippur, at one time supported independent and sometimes warring dynasties. It was not until *c.* 2370 when Sargon and his Semitic-speaking followers founded the city of Agade only a short distance south-west of Babylon that we enter on an ampler stage of history. Although the paucity of information surviving from

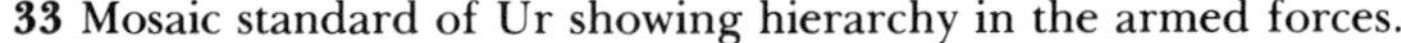

33 Mosaic standard of Ur showing hierarchy in the armed forces.

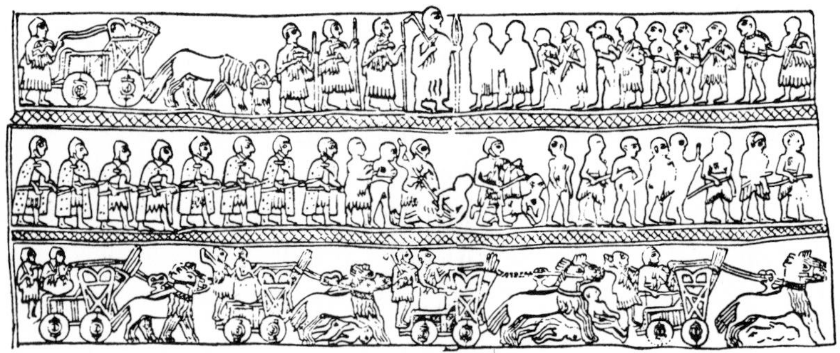

contemporary documents and the opaqueness of subsequent legend have between them made it difficult to establish more than dim outlines of his reign, it seems clear that Sargon and his successors exercised a hegemony not only over Sumer itself, but over the northern part of Mesopotamia later known as Assyria, as well as over Elam, and that their influence extended over north Syria and probably even into Anatolia. The extent of Akkadian influence and

34 Plan of a royal tomb at Ur dating from the Early Dynastic III period. The positions of funerary vehicles and of the 59 people accompanying the king, including grooms, men at arms, musicians and women, are shown in the passage and antechamber. A silver boat was found on the left of the entrance to the tomb itself.

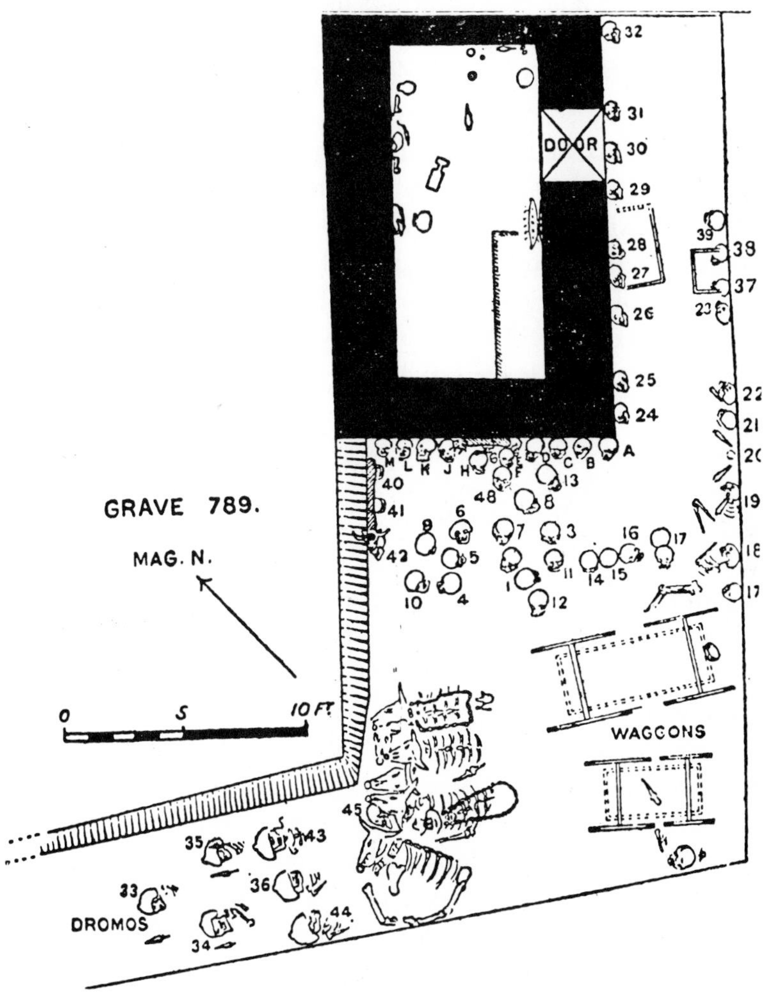

the fact that it lasted for several reigns suggests that it was founded on far more than mere crude military force.

When the Akkadian dynasty was nevertheless overturned by an incursion of Guti highlanders from the Zagros, the way was open for a revival of Ur which under its Third Dynasty enjoyed what from many points of view was its most splendid period. Further waves of rough folk from without, Amorites from the west and Elamites from the east, by toppling the dynasty at Ur opened a period of some confusion, from which the land of Mesopotamia and ultimately large tracts of south-west Asia were in due course to benefit through the founding about 1990 B.C. of the First Dynasty of Babylon. The succession of Hammurabi about 1800 B.C. brought into a position of power an individual as commanding in his way as Sargon of Agade and one about whose reign more details are known. Under his leadership Babylon rose supreme not only over the riverine zone of Mesopotamia but also over the uplands of Assyria, the Zagros and Elam. The benefits of Babylonian law and commerce spread even more widely. During Hammurabi's reign the use of cuneiform writing and Akkadian speech for commerce brought extensive tracts of south-west Asia into fruitful and peaceful contact. This meant that the overthrow of the First Dynasty of Babylon by the Hittites who sacked the capital in *c.* 1595 B.C. and by the Kassites from the east, who in turn set up their own dynasty, was not so serious a disaster from the point of view of civilization in general as it might have been.

Civilizations of the highlands

Assyria

The vast upland regions from Iran to Anatolia and the Levant that gave birth to farming were at once too extensive and too broken to encourage the early growth of centralized authority or of the higher civilization which this makes possible. Yet the mere fact that they were endowed with traditions based on thousands of years of settled life as agriculturalists meant that the upland peoples were capable of absorbing new elements and even leaders speaking new languages without losing their own essential characters.

The land and people of Assyria had a chequered history, the outcome of their situation between a number of competing empires. As we have seen Assyria was brought into the sphere of civilization as a direct outcome of military conquest and political domination from south Mesopotamia. Throughout its earlier vicissitudes the core of Assyrian power was focused on the city of Assur. It was under Shamshi-Adad I, who ruled during much of the second half of the eighteenth century B.C., that Assyria achieved its first imperial expansion, reaching from the Zagros to the Mediterranean. Although the initial phase of empire lasted only a brief time, the Assyrians were a perpetual threat to the wider balance of power. During the New Kingdom of Egypt the pharaohs sought to check the Hittites and Assyrians alike by supporting the Mitanni, and as an extra insurance against the Assyrians they formed an alliance with the Babylonians. When the Hittites succeeded in crushing the Mitanni, they came into direct conflict with the Assyrians over control of the east–west trade route across Syria, and sought to exert pressure by exerting diplomatic leverage on Egypt and Babylonia. As a result the Assyrian power contracted once again to its core territory, only to re-emerge during the New Empire established by Ashur-Nars-Pal II (883–859 B.C.). Under Sennacherib the empire not merely extended from the Zagros to Lake Van and the Levant, but incorporated Egypt itself. Another twist in the struggle and the main cities of Assyria proper were incorporated in the New Babylonian Empire (625–539 B.C.), which in turn fell to Persia and Alexander the Great.

Anatolia and the Hittites

The antiquity of settled life in southern Anatolia has been stressed earlier in this chapter. No attempt will be made here to set out details of the cultural history of this extensive region, still less to distinguish the differences exhibited by each of its several provinces, differences which contributed richness and texture to the pattern as a whole. It will be sufficient to make a few general points. The first is that until trading posts manned with Assyrians were set up in central Anatolia there was no rapid acceleration in the tempo of cultural development. This can be seen in the length of time it took before metal tools began to take the place of stone ones. Copper, as we have noted, was used in its native form for beads and other trinkets from a very early stage in the development of farming economy. The metallurgical treatment of copper ores and the casting of metal in moulds for the production of weapons and implements did not come until the fifth millennium; and the production of standard bronze based on the addition of tin alloy did not begin until *c.* 3000 B.C. and then only in favoured localities.

The next point to observe is that some of the most striking features of Hittite civilization made their appearance already during the Early

Bronze Age (*c.* 3000–2000 B.C.) and that some were even older. Evidence for the concentration of wealth and power that reached its climax under Hittite rule is to be seen first of all in the great walled
81 fortresses at Troy II and Kültepe (the ancient Kadesh) dating from Early Bronze Age II; and it may be noted that the megaron type of public assembly hall, comprising a rectangular structure with inner hall having a central fireplace and outer porch, enclosed by these citadels also appeared in earlier and more modest surroundings at Troy I. Then, again, we have the evidence for concentrated wealth
87 in the great treasures from the royal tombs of Alaca Hüyük (level VII) and in the so-called Priam's treasure of Troy II: it is not merely the value of the metal locked up in these that calls for remark, but still more the high standard of smithing and jewellery, and the evidence for social rank embodied in the personal ornaments, metal utensils and weapons of display. If the Early Bronze Age metal-work itself is scrutinized more closely, we find evidence of the love of polychromatic effects contrived by inlaying, overlaying and incrusting silver, electrum or even semi-precious stones on a bronze base displayed in work of the Hittite period; and conversely the predilection for bulls and stags exhibited in Hittite and Early Bronze Age metal-work alike goes back to the lowermost level at Çatal Hüyük, if not in all probability beyond.

The Middle Bronze Age of Anatolia (*c.* 1950–1700 B.C.) was marked most significantly by the arrival of Assyrian merchants. One of their trading posts was situated in the suburbs formed round the citadel
94 of Kadesh (Kültepe), by now a town covering some 50·6 hectares. The object of these posts was to regulate traffic in raw materials to the south, notably copper and the then extremely rare and precious iron, in exchange for manufactures of which textiles were the most important. Merchandise was carried on the backs of donkeys organized in caravans and we know from business records not merely that silver in the form of rings and bars was used as a standard of value but even the equivalents in terms of silver shekels of most goods common at the time in Central Anatolia. The records themselves were written in Akkadian by an Assyrian cuneiform script on clay tablets and signed by impressing cylinder seals. In other words central Anatolia was brought within the sphere of literacy, at least so far as commerce was concerned, by virtue of direct contact with Assyria. It is significant that when the Hittite rulers wished to record their triumphs and conduct their correspondence they did so in Assyrian cuneiform script, even if their language was Indo-European.

Hittite names began to appear first in mercantile records from 87
86 the closing phases of the Middle Bronze Age. Much controversy surrounds the arrival of Indo-European speakers in Anatolia and the directions from which they came, but the consensus is that some spread into the south-west by way of the Bosphorus, whereas others penetrated central Anatolia from the north-east by way of Armenia. At a stage of social development when only comparatively few people monopolized power and authority it required no mass invasion to infiltrate, seize power and establish a reigning dynasty, and it is likely that the Hittites who eventually took over were comparatively few in number. They were evidently able people and they realized the political possibilities inherent in the natural wealth of their country. Although they established themselves at the head of affairs during the seventeenth century B.C. it was not until the fourteenth century that their power had attained the imperial status symbolized in their great capital city of Boghazköy.

Despite its size – the circuit of the walls was some four miles – the powerfully defended city was founded on a long-standing tradition. The great stores of archives which now included a wide range of state documents including diplomatic correspondence have proved particularly enlightening. Although the language was by this time Indo-European, the script impressed on the clay was still cuneiform, though cylinder seals had given place to stamp ones of a more ancient and local tradition. The leading divinities of the Hittites comprised a weather god, whose attributes the bull and the axe both go back to the Halafian culture, and a sun goddess, a version of the great mother goddess of long-standing antiquity. Their art, hieratic in style, took a monumental form in reliefs cut on natural exposures of rock-surface or again in figures standing guard at gateways.

In history the Hittites took advantage of their situation at the head of the Fertile Crescent to keep at arm's length the two great empires into which the world at that time was divided. Although they sought as far as possible to gain their ends by diplomacy, they were effective warriors. We have already noted that it was a Hittite army that sacked Babylon and helped to topple its First Dynasty. Centuries later at the height of their power they administered a punishing defeat to Ramesses II before their strong city of Kadesh. Yet early in the twelfth century B.C. the Hittite Empire crumbled in a veritable power tremor that brought down the Mycenaeans and Troy VIIA and before long the New Kingdom of Egypt. Phrygians issuing from Thrace overran Anatolia and destroyed the centres of Hittite power.

Hittite culture lived on only as the heritage of a number of small states in northern Syria set up by refugees, states which only preserved their independence precariously at the height of the Assyrian Empire. Ironically, the end of Neo-Hittite culture only came when the Assyrian Empire itself fell a victim (612–610 B.C.) to a combination of Babylonians, Scythians and Medes. Anatolia, having nourished Assyrians, Babylonians and Sumerians, as well as Hittites, on its mineral wealth, was engulfed successively in the empires of Persia, Alexander, Rome, Byzantium and the Ottoman Turks. It was indeed a rich prize. Yet in its heyday it had been able to stand up to the two great powers of the time. It is only in the light of its long prehistory that we can appreciate how this was possible. The Hittites owed much to the strength of a long cultural tradition in Anatolia, much to its mineral and agricultural wealth and much also to the ability of their Indo-European-speaking rulers.

Palestine and the Phoenicians

For much of later prehistoric times Syria shared fully in the cultural development of Cilicia and Mesopotamia. Palestine on the other hand after playing a leading role in the eighth and seventh millennia relapsed into provincial insignificance. Pottery did not appear until *c.* 4500 B.C. and when copper-working reached Palestine nearly a thousand years later it did so as part of a provincial version of the richer culture of northern Syria. Again, at the beginning of the Early Bronze Age Syria and Palestine profited from the cultural influences that radiated from Mesopotamia to Egypt and contributed so notably to the rise of civilization in that country immediately preceding the First Dynasty. Similarly, the change in pottery styles that marked the beginning of Early Bronze Age I in Palestine towards the end of
136 the third millennium was inspired from Syro-Mesopotamia during the expansive Sargonid era. The country did not begin to be drawn within the sphere of literacy until around 2000 B.C. and it is significant and entirely consistent that the clay tablets from sites like Byblos and Ugarit should have been written in cuneiform script of ultimately Mesopotamian origin in the same way that the pottery tradition of Middle Bronze Age Canaan was of Syro-Mesopotamian derivation. Early Bronze Age II was marked by renewed northern influence, this time in the guise of a warrior aristocracy rendered mobile and formidable by their horse-drawn chariots and possessed also of advanced knowledge of the technique of fortification, including the use of earthen ramparts with stone revetment as a base for defensive

walls. It was no doubt a prolongation of this thrust that carried the Hyksos into Egypt (*c.* 1680 B.C.) during the intermediate period that followed the Middle Kingdom. Having established themselves the Hyksos maintained their own rule there for over a century down to the time when Ahmosis I succeeded in expelling them (*c.* 1573 B.C.) and establishing the New Kingdom.

During its Late Bronze Age Palestine formed part of the Egyptian realm, and culture remained eclectic and provincial drawing elements from Syria, Egypt and the East Mediterranean without creating any well-defined image of its own. The fact that the country was subservient to Egypt prevented the rise of any central authority, and the military skills and techniques brought in by the Hyksos strengthened the hands of the rulers of individual cities. Again, it is important to remember that those who sheltered in defended cities were encompassed by semi-nomadic peoples. The tension between the two has after all been a recurrent theme in the history of the life of the region.

It is very easy when depending on archaeological evidence to over-stress the role of settled and urban peoples and under-estimate that of peoples less productive of material debris and bric-à -brac. Yet it is vital to remember that, just as the Fertile Crescent was backed and on the east flanked by mountains, so it enclosed in its wide arc a vast zone of arid land passing on the south into desert. Although this was incapable of supporting settled communities it was well adapted to nomadic or semi-nomadic life with a strong bias to pastoral economy. Yet it remained marginal over large areas even for pastoralists. When pressure on grazing exerted by variations in rainfall weighed too heavily the nomads had an obvious way out of their difficulties in pillaging, infiltrating or even dominating their richer neighbours settled on productive ground. Since the nomads were fitted by selection to withstand hardship and adapted by their economy to be mobile, it is no surprise that they were able to play a role in history disproportionate to their numbers or wealth.

In the archaeological record they made themselves felt indirectly through dislocating the ordered progress of more settled societies, whether as hill-men from the Zagros or as nomads from the Syrian desert moving east into the Euphrates basin or west and south into the Nile Valley. The most positive information about them comes from their own traditions enshrined in the Old Testament scriptures. Here we see patriarchal societies responding to famine by moving their tents into new and sometimes distant lands, pitting themselves if need be, like the modern Beduin, against the peoples settled on richer land. Correlation between the Bible stories and the evidence of archaeology and historical records is unfortunately rarely possible because the sources seldom overlap. One can only say for instance that the traditional trek of Abraham and his people from Mesopotamia to the land of Israel would fit quite well into the context of Early Bronze Age I. Again, the story of Jacob's migration to Egypt to escape famine may well accord with the movements of people that included the Hyksos' irruption into Egypt.

By the same token there is no evident reflection in the Late Bronze Age culture of Palestine of stylistic features attributable to the arrival of the Israelites, dramatized in the story of the Exodus from Egypt under the leadership of Moses. The movement did not begin until the thirteenth century B.C. and is best thought of as an infiltration by Beduin-like folk rather than as a set military invasion. It looks as though fortified cities and townships were only very gradually reduced. And early in the twelfth century B.C., before the process has been completed, the incursion of iron-using raiders from the north Mediterranean, raiders who came to be known when they settled down as Philistines, started Palestine on its Early Iron Age. From a technological point of view Palestine was in this respect several centuries in advance of Egypt, though for some time the Philistines kept the use of the metal to themselves in their coastal tract. From a material point of view the Israelites were relatively poor, but their sense of identity helped them to triumph over the Philistines under the leadership of David (1013–973 B.C.) and enter on a few brief centuries of independent nationhood. Palestine was soon overshadowed again by a greater power, this time the Assyrian Empire. Kings continued to rule in Jerusalem after the Assyrian invasion of 721 B.C., but only as tributaries of Egypt, Assyria and Babylon; and in 587/6 B.C. Nebuchadnezzar destroyed the temple of Solomon and carried off the leading men of Israel into captivity at Babylon.

From a worldly point of view it was the coastal branch of the Canaanites, named Phoenicians by Mycenaean traders, who turned the difficulties of their environment to most profit. They did so by looking to the sea and earning by commerce the wealth denied them by the rich but narrow strip of fertile land between the mountains of the Jebel Libnan and the Mediterranean. Their situation between Egypt and Mesopotamia was turned to good account during the Bronze Age as we know from the wealth of cities like Byblos and Ugarit, but it was not until the fall of Mycenaean power that the

Phoenicians were able to profit from trade with Cyprus and the Aegean. Local products like cedarwood and purple dye had long been staples of their commerce and from early times they had acted as middlemen in the interchange of goods manufactured at the main centres of civilization. The opening up of the Mediterranean brought them access to the sometimes remote sources of important metals like copper and tin.

134 It was as an outcome of their zeal for commerce that the Phoenicians contributed most to world history. The importance of maintaining clear business records provided at least the context in which they developed an alphabetic script that had been brought to a standard form by the tenth century B.C. When Greek traders in the Levant came into contact with this script they were sufficiently impressed to improve it further by introducing letter forms for vowel sounds. Yet much of the credit for the alphabet on which the literature of the western world has ever since been based must rest with the aesthetically unattractive businessmen of Phoenicia. The other great achievement that followed as they entered upon their Mycenaean inheritance was the establishment of colonies along their trade routes, colonies sufficiently vigorous to enter into rivalry with the Classical Greeks and in respect of Carthage to engage in mortal conflict with Rome. Yet the Phoenicians could not in the end escape in their homeland the effects of Assyrian and finally of Babylonian power. Phoenicia passed under the same succession of empires from Babylonian to Ottoman as did the rest of Palestine.

In the end it is worth reflecting that the history of mankind was changed not by Tyre or Sidon but by Jerusalem, not by a merchant or a king so much as by the son of a carpenter in a village set in what appeared to be an insignificant province of the Roman Empire. The limitations of archaeology are pointed up again by the fact that, when the men of large parts of Asia and Africa wish to pray, they mostly turn to Mecca in an oasis of Arabia rather than to the rich cities of Egypt or Mesopotamia.

Iran and Turkmenia

Certain parts of the Iranian plateau and its neighbourhood shared as we have seen (pp. 60f.) in the early history of farming, notably the upland valleys in the south-western Zagros, the western rim of the great inner desert zone, the Caspian shore and the southern margin
35 of Turkmenia. The painted wares from Iranian village sites contemporary with the Early Dynastic period in Sumer display geometric

and stylized anthropomorphic and animal forms that anticipate in
100, 102 a curious way designs on rugs woven thousands of years later. Yet the natural heart of the plateau was desert, and localities favourable to early farmers were not necessarily well adapted to the early emergence of politically more potent units. The most likely territory from this point of view was the low-lying region between the lower Euphrates and the Zagros which in fact provided a setting for the kingdom of Elam, the first unit of its kind to emerge in the whole region. Already in prehistoric times the site of Susa testified both to the natural wealth of the province and to the advantage that came from bordering the Mesopotamian focus of higher civilization. Throughout levels A to D the inhabitants of Susa continued to decorate their pots by painting in the manner of the Neolithic societies discussed previously. Copper metallurgy had already been adopted by Susa A and the inhabitants of Susa B had appropriated the potter's wheel. Both spread far and wide among the makers of
95, 98, 108 painted pottery, appearing for example at Sialk III and Hissar I on the western and northern fringes of the central desert zone. The appearance of cylinder seals at Susa C – the earlier inhabitants had used stamp seals – and their spread as far afield as Hissar III bear further witness to the cultural impact of Mesopotamia on Elam.

Susa and the province of which it was the capital was the earliest centre of highly integrated political authority in Iran. To begin with the Elamite kings were dominated by the Akkadians and in due course by the Third Dynasty of Ur, but around 2000 B.C. they were strong enough to attack and destroy Ur itself. For nearly a thousand years Elam was to enjoy some measure of political independence. Yet, if the development of an Elamite script and of a distinctive style of seal-engraving bear witness to a certain degree of self-expression, the fact remains that texts were frequently written in Akkadian or Sumerian; and it is significant that the earliest large-scale monument in Elam at Tchoga Zanbil took the form of a ziggurat. Even this modest degree of independence was broken when Nebuchadrezzar I invaded the country towards the close of the twelfth century B.C.

When the Assyrians were campaigning to secure their eastern frontier late in the ninth century B.C. they left the first records of the names of the Iranian peoples whose union was to destroy their own Empire, namely the Medes to the north and the Persians to the east-south-east of Elam. The arrival of Iranian-speaking peoples on the plateau is still something about which little is known. What is certain is that, as with the Hittites, another group speaking an Indo-

35 Iranian painted pottery from the village site of Bakun.

European language, the Iranians demonstrated in a signal way what could be achieved by energy and leadership even when geographical conditions were not particularly favourable. The transformation wrought by the Achaemenid Dynasty in the ancient world as a whole was as rapid as it was sweeping. The Empire was founded on the defeat by Cyrus of Persia of his grandfather Astyages king of the Medes in *c.* 550 B.C. Within a single generation the Medes and the Persians engulfed Babylonia, Lydia and Egypt. Their expansion was only checked in the west by the Greeks who, by their victories on land at Marathon (490 B.C.) and Plataea (479 B.C.), and on sea at Salamis (480 B.C.), made possible the development of a distinctively European civilization.

3

Foundations of European civilization: the stone age

During by far the greater part of prehistory the role of Europe was subsidiary to that of Africa. Whereas the record of tool-making goes back in parts of East Africa to the beginnings of the Lower Pleistocene two million years or more ago, the earliest flint or stone tools and for that matter the earliest physical remains of man himself from Europe are no earlier than the Günz–Mindel interglacial stage of the Middle Pleistocene, hardly more than 300,000–500,000 years ago. The industries marked by bifacial hand-axes in mode 2 found over much of southern Europe conform to patterns evolved long previously in Africa. Again, the shift to an emphasis on flakes struck from prepared cores (mode 3) was common to much of Africa and south-west Asia. On the other hand the occurrence in European Russia of Mousterian industries in this mode as far north as the Desna and upper Oka rivers documents a notable expansion in the range of human settlement. The superior degree of adaptability which this implies presages the efflorescence of culture which was especially marked in the territory between Iberia and the Urals during the later part of the Upper Pleistocene, an event which for the first time and only temporarily put Europe in the van of human progress.

Upper Palaeolithic hunters and artists

The vitality of the peoples inhabiting Europe between *c.* 32,000 and 8,000 B.C. is reflected in several ways in the archaeological record. The rate of change proceeded at an unprecedented pace, technology was more diverse and specialized and above all there were notable advances in the psychic field.

It is hardly surprising that attention should have focused first on caves and rock-shelters as sources of information about this stage in European history, since these were particularly abundant and rich

in France, the country where the study of prehistory first developed
on a substantial scale. The expansion of intensive research into other
parts of Europe and the development of excavation techniques that
made it possible to gain significant information from open sites like
those found in the loess of central Europe or along the great rivers
162, 168, 170, 173 of south and central Russia have since put French prehistory in a
new perspective. Yet the sequence first worked out in France still
270 forms a useful frame of reference against which the new discoveries
in central and east Europe can to some extent be calibrated as a result
of radiocarbon dating.

Table 12. *The Upper Palaeolithic sequence in different parts of Europe. Strong vertical lines indicate dates validated by radiocarbon analysis.*

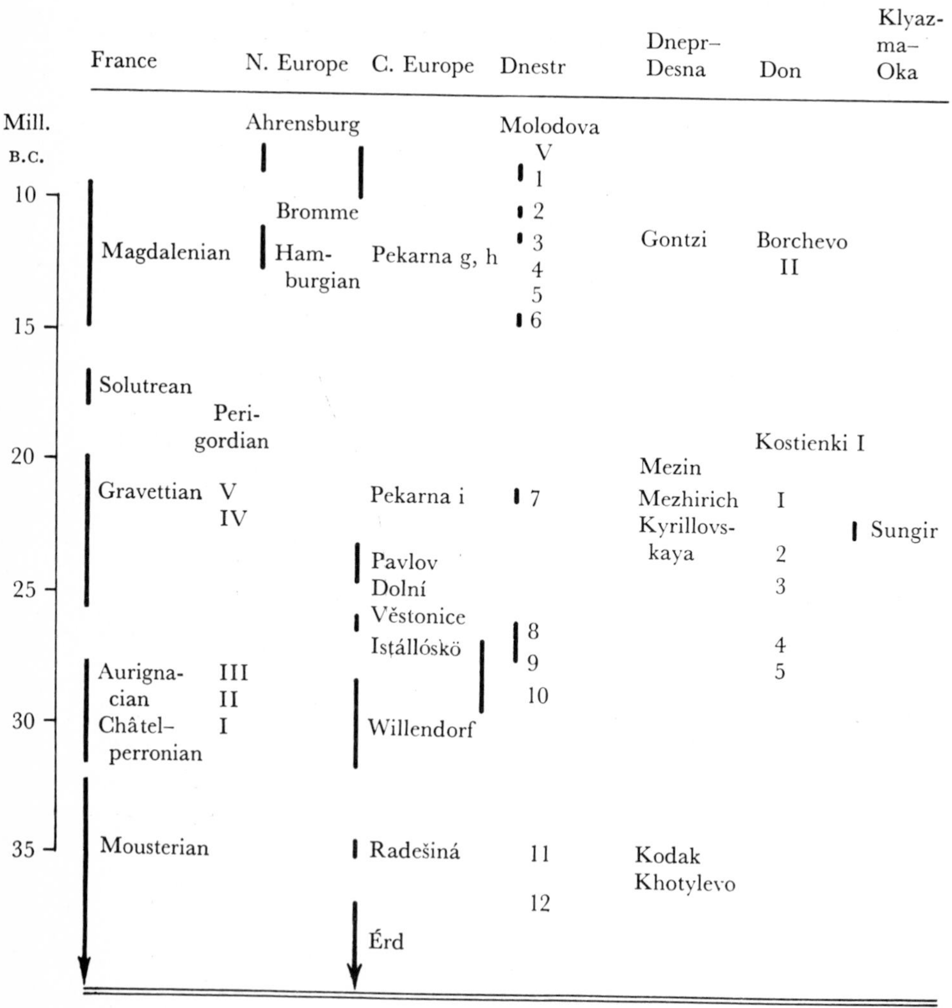

Mill. B.C.	France	N. Europe	C. Europe	Dnestr	Dnepr–Desna	Don	Klyaz-ma–Oka
		Ahrensburg		Molodova V			
				1			
10		Bromme		2			
	Magdalenian	Ham-burgian	Pekarna g, h	3	Gontzi	Borchevo II	
				4			
				5			
15				6			
	Solutrean						
	Peri-gordian						
20						Kostienki I	
					Mezin		
	Gravettian	V	Pekarna i	7	Mezhirich	I	
		IV			Kyrillovs-kaya		Sungir
			Pavlov			2	
25			Dolní			3	
			Věstonice				
			Isťállóskö	8		4	
	Aurigna-cian	III		9		5	
		II		10			
30	Châtel-perronian	I	Willendorf				
35	Mousterian		Radešiná	11	Kodak Khotylevo		
				12			
			Érd				

Table 13. *Some radiocarbon dates for Upper Palaeolithic sites in Europe*

	Lab. no.		B.C.
ITALY			
Romanelli (level A)	R	58	9,850 ± 600
	R	56	9,980 ± 520
Fucino			10,670 ± 410
Palidoro	R	83	11,050 ± 700
Grotta La Punta	Pi	152	12,538 ± 800
Romito III (level XXXIV)	R	297	16,800 ± 350
GREECE			
Kastritsa, Epirus, Greece (hearth-1 m)	I	1960	11,450 ± 210
Kastritsa, Epirus, Greece (hearth in beach)	I	2468	18,250 ± 480
	I	2466	18,850 ± 810
Asprochaliko, Epirus, Greece	I	1965	24,150 ± 900
CENTRAL AND EASTERN EUROPE			
Arka, Hungary	GrN	4218	11,280 ± 85
Ságvar, Hungary	GrN	1959	15,810 ± 150
	GrN	1783	16,950 ± 100
Nitra-Čermáň, Czechoslovakia	GrN	2449	21,050 ± 330
Pavlov, Czechoslovakia	GrN	1325	23,070 ± 150
	GrN	1272	24,780 ± 250
Aggsbach, Austria	GrN	2513	24,850 ± 200
Krems-Wachtberg, Austria	GrN	3011	25,450 ± 300
Nemšova, Czechoslovakia	GrN	2470	26,620 ± 1300
Dolní Vestonice, Czechoslovakia	GrN	2902	26,390 ± 390
Istállóskö, Hungary	GrN	2598	27,170 ± 312
Istállóskö, Hungary	GrN	1935	28,950 ± 600
	GrN	1501	29,590 ± 600
Willendorf, Austria (level I)	GrN	1287	28,580 ± 250
Willendorf, Austria (level IV)	GrN	1273	30,110 ± 250
Willendorf, Austria (level V)	H246/231		32,000 ± 3000
USSR			
Molodova V*			
Level 1	—		8,640 + 230
Level 2	—		9,950 + 230
Level 3	—		11,420 + 540
Level 6	—		*c.* 14,050
Level 7	Mo.	11	21,050 ± 800
	—		21,750 + 320
Level 9–10	—		26,150 + 1000
			27,700 + 1320
Sungir, Vladimir	GrN	5446	22,480 + 400
	GrN	5425	23,550 + 200

* Determinations mainly quoted from Ivanova, 1969, fig. 17.

Whatever their origin the earliest flint and stone industries in Europe
made in mode 4 show signs of continuity with those of the preceding
mode. The tool-kit associated with the earliest Upper Palaeolithic
settlement in France named after Châtelperron combined blades,
burins and steeply retouched knife-blades with flakes and scrapers
of Levallois and Mousterian character. Again, the earliest blade and
burin industries in central Europe, those with split base bone-points
of the kind first noted from the Aurignacian phase of the French
sequence include bifacially flaked points like those found in Mous-
197 terian assemblages in Greece and east Europe. They also occur
185 at Istállóskö and other sites in Hungary, where they are often named
after Szeleta in the Bukk mountains, and also in the Mamutowa
Cave, Wierzchowie, southern Poland where they are accompanied
by lozenge-shaped bone points. Again it is significant that the
164 earliest mode 4 levels at Molodova V and Kostienki I in south Russia
each yielded bifacially flaked points recalling those of the Caucasian
Mousterian.

The geography of Europe was profoundly different at the height of the Würm glaciation. The whole of Scandinavia and much of the British Isles, north Germany, Poland and north-west Russia were covered by the Scandinavian ice-sheet. Similarly sea-levels were so much lower that Britain was still joined to the continent, the Black Sea was a lake and Italy incorporated Sicily and the head of the Adriatic. Outside the glaciated zone was a zone of permanent or at least occasional permafrost. This was occupied by man from France and Britain as far north as Creswell to the Ukraine and beyond the east margin of the ice-sheet as far as Bizovaya, well north of the Arctic Circle. Parts of this carried vegetation notably richer than that of the modern tundra and one which nourished a relatively high bio-mass. In addition to herds of reindeer and smaller game like arctic hare, lemming, voles and birds, including geese and snowy partridge, proper to the tundra, it carried herds of woolly mammoth, bison and wild horse, as well as smaller numbers of woolly rhinoceros, extinct giant elk and saiga antelope. The carnivores which preyed on these animals contributed furs, notably those of arctic fox, wolf and ermine. That these animals were in fact hunted is known from the quantities of bones recovered both from cave deposits and from open stations together with the equipment used to obtain them. Further south and notably in the Iberian peninsula and in the Balkans more temperate forest conditions supported what was presumably a substantially lower biomass than that available in the tundra zone. Among the more important game animals would have been aurochs, red deer and wild boar.

It is hardly surprising that the richest cultural developments of this time should have been achieved by those who preyed on animals of the tundra zone. Their material equipment displayed a much greater degree of cultural diversity and functional specialization than that of their predecessors. The flint blades, punched from elongated cores prepared by side flaking, were converted into tools and weapon armatures by a variety of mode 4 techniques. One such was the use of a steep, abrupt retouch to blunt the backs of knives for the finger. Another was the technique used to make the burins needed among other things for cutting antler and bone. The chisel-like working edge was formed by punching small flakes into the main axis of the blade either on its edge or in the middle, a process easily repeated as the tool got blunt in use. In addition a flat bifacial technique was sometimes used, as in the industries named after Solutré in eastern France but extending from Spain to central Europe as well as in those

36 Upper Palaeolithic Europe with ice-sheets and sea-levels at maxima for the Late Pleistocene.

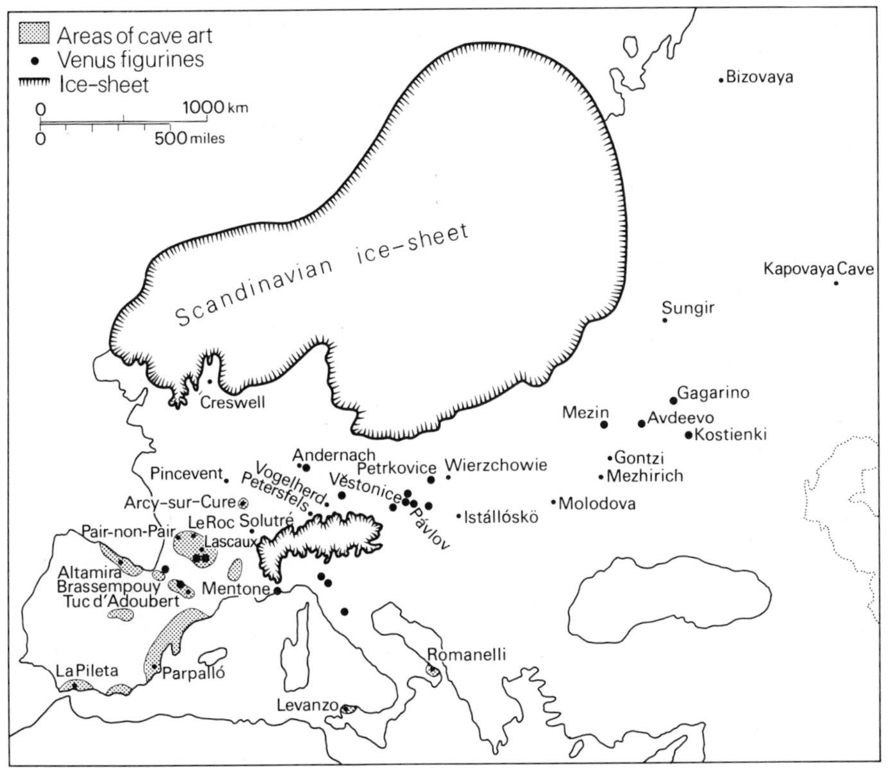

already mentioned in south Russia. In addition to tools used for cutting and engraving, convex and concave scrapers might be made
37 from blades as well as different forms of awl and projectile head.

Another feature of technology among these people was the ex-
38 tensive and varied use of antler, bone and ivory, materials which they reduced to manageable form by cutting with flint burins and which they frequently finished by rubbing and polishing. From these they made a variety of spear and harpoon armatures, shaft-straighteners,

37 Upper Palaeolithic equipment made from flint blades and designed for cutting and penetrating. (1–3) knives (Châtelperron, Gravette and Krems); (4–11) projectile heads (Fort Robert, Solutrean single-shouldered and laurel-leaf, Hamburg, Ahrensburg, Lyngby, Swidry and Chwalibogowice); (12–13) burins (polyhedric and angle); (14) pronged tool (*Zinken*).

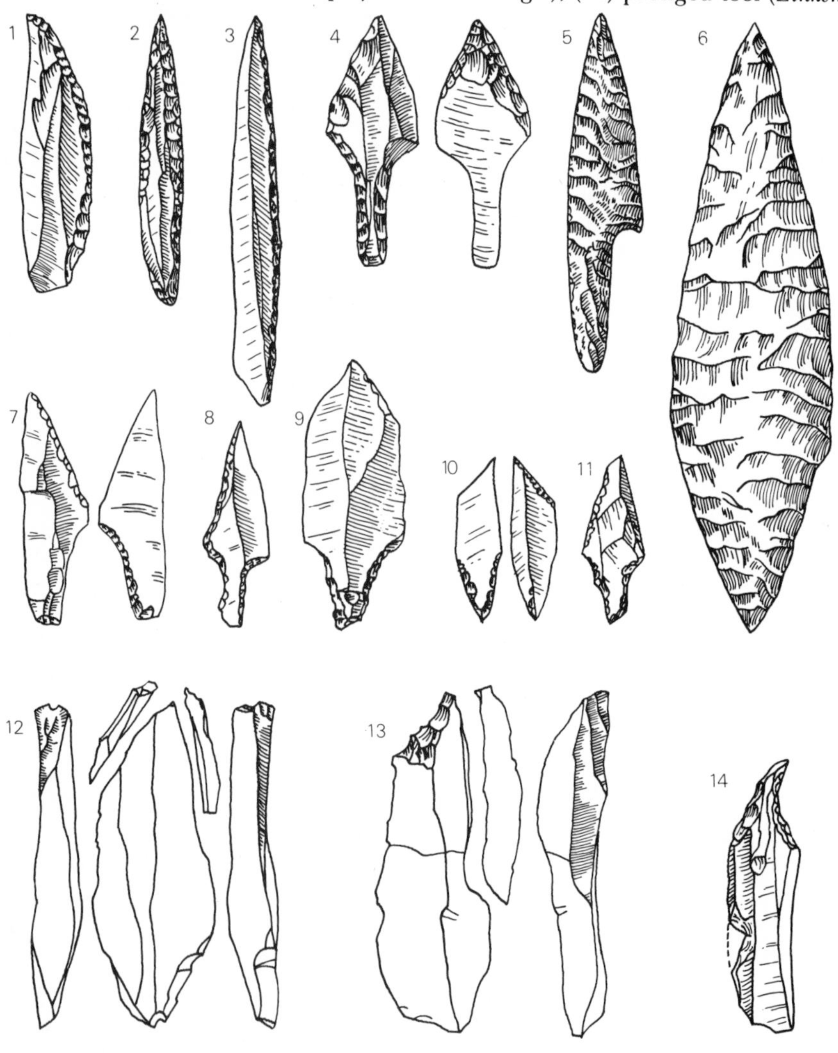

spear-throwers, clubs, leather-working tools, awls, spoons and eyed
39 needles, as well as figurines and personal ornaments.

The artefacts made from flint and organic materials reflect very
clearly the activities of people among whom hunting and the utilization of animal materials played a key role. Indications that skin
clothing was worn is afforded by the abundance of skin-working
equipment, the presence of fine needles, the disposition of orna-
415:30–1 ments in burials and the occurrence, notably at Buret in Siberia, of
40 figurines wearing skin clothing. This in turn reflects the manner
in which Upper Palaeolithic man adapted to arctic and sub-arctic
conditions. Another way in which he conditioned himself for life in
a cold climate was by the construction of suitable artificial dwellings.
Animal skins again played a key part, together with the bones, tusks
and antlers of large game animals. The traces of tent-like structures
so far recognized in western and northern Europe, like those at
269 Pincevent, Seine-et-Oise, or Borneck and Poggenwisch in Schleswig-
Holstein, are presumably only among the first to be noted of what

38 Upper Palaeolithic antler and bone projectile heads: (1–2) single and double bevelled points; (3) split-base; (4) forked base; (5) lozenge-shaped point; (6–7) barbed harpoonhead (bi- and uni-serial).

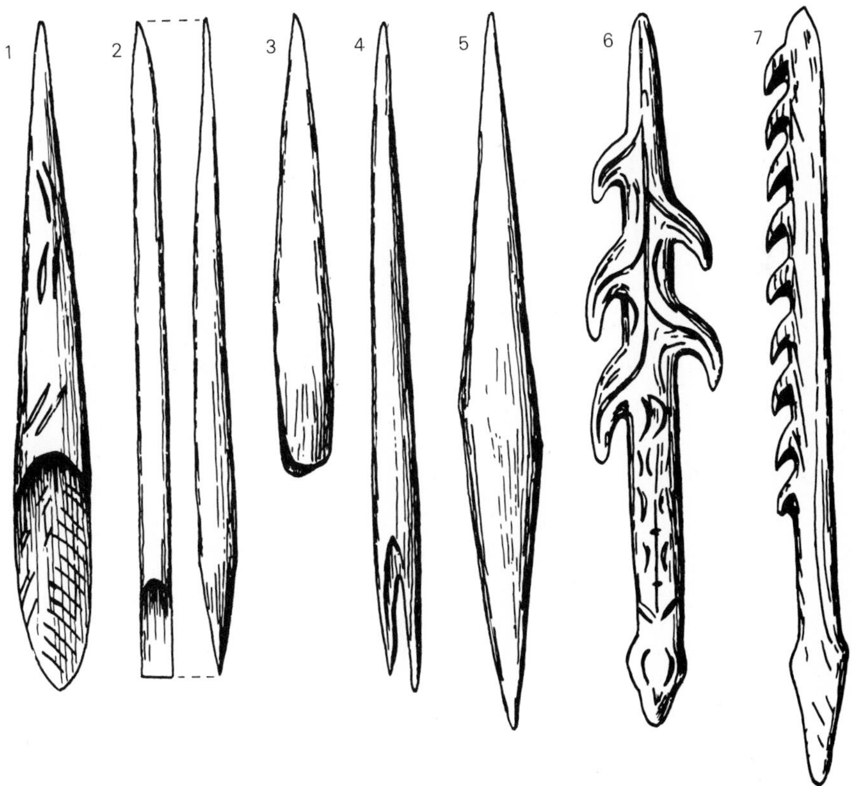

must have been an extremely common class of structure in Late-glacial western Europe.

Traces of what may have been more permanent structures are
41 known from central and eastern Europe. At sites like Pavlov in
Moravia or Gagarino in the Don Valley the hut floors were hollowed
out of the sub-soil. In no case has evidence been found for timber
frame construction, something which could hardly be expected in
the absence of any sign of heavy tree-felling or wood-working equipment. The occasional upright posts of which signs were found in
171, 172 the form of post-holes at Dolní Věstonice served merely to support
a light roof. Structures were curvilinear in plan. In a particularly well
179 preserved example at Mezhirich the foundation wall was built of
mammoth jaws and long bones, capped by skulls and roofed presumably by tree branches overlaid by tusks. The use of parts of

39 Upper Palaeolithic personal ornaments, Europe.

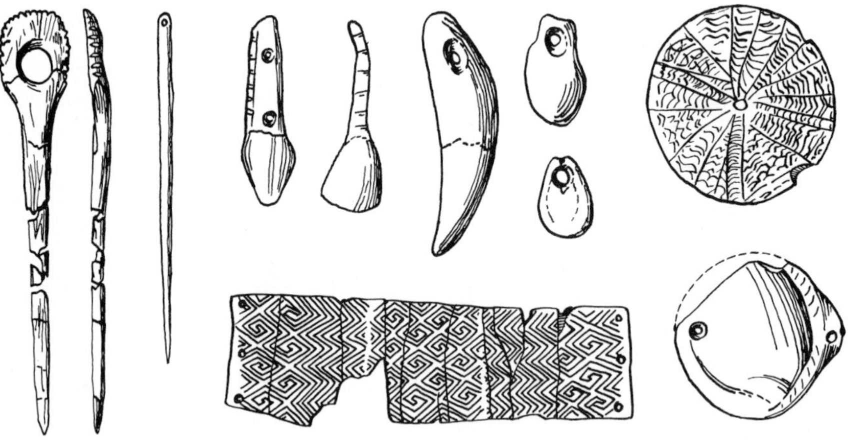

40 Ivory figurine of hooded and fur-clad individual, Buret, Siberia.

mammoth skeletons in the construction of dwellings only emphasizes the importance of this animal in the food-quest, something illustrated by the numbers of individuals represented at Mezhirich (95) and comparable sites in south Russia, notably Dobranichivka (18), Gontzi (25), Kyrillovskaya (70) and Mezin (116). On the other hand the structures can hardly be explained solely in terms of seasonal mammoth hunts. At Mezin for instance remains were also found of the following numbers of individuals of a wide range of species:

3 rhinoceros	112 arctic fox
63 horse	60 wolf (incl. 1 domesticated)
17 musk-ox	5 wolverine
5 bison	11 hare
1 giant deer	4 marmot
83 reindeer	7 snowy partridge
7 bear	

41 Round hut emplacement with mammoth tusks under loess, Pavlov, Czechoslovakia.

The fact that all the main species available in this environment had been hunted and the solidity of the structures themselves argues that they served as bases at least for some time. On the other hand the range of social contacts and interaction was far-ranging. The Mezhirich site yielded beads of amber of unidentified origin as well as fossil mollusc shells from Miocene deposits in the Zaporozhie district between 350/500 km to the east. Again, the designs painted in red ochre on one of the mammoth skulls from Mezhirich is closely paralleled by designs on the lower jaw, pelvic and thigh bones from Mezin, nearly 300 km east-north-east.

A significant outcome of improvements in technology, notably in respect of weaponry, clothing and housing, is that they permitted and went hand in hand with a northward expansion of settlement even beyond the advances made by Neanderthal man. In this respect it is particularly worthy of note that sites as far north as Sungir and Bizovaya to the east of the ice-sheet were occupied at a time of intensely glacial climate.

Ceremonial burial

Even so most striking innovations of this period lay in the psychic sphere. Careful burial as we have seen had already been widely

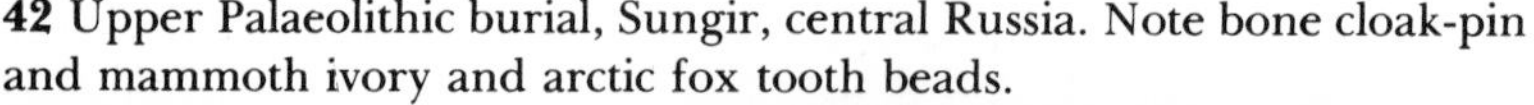

42 Upper Palaeolithic burial, Sungir, central Russia. Note bone cloak-pin and mammoth ivory and arctic fox tooth beads.

practised during an earlier phase of the Upper Pleistocene. What was
distinctive of Upper Palaeolithic practice was the burial of the dead
173 clothed and wearing personal ornaments. One of the most carefully
42 explored finds of this kind is that from Sungir, near Vladimir east-
north-east of Moscow. A man of around sixty and two boys buried
head to head were each extended on their backs and powdered
with red ochre. The disposition of the 3,000 beads accompanying the
man suggests that they were in many cases attached to clothing. The
boys appear to have been wearing upper garments, trousers, headgear and shoes. It is worth noting that the ornaments, as well as
perforated animal teeth and stone pebbles, included artificially
shaped beads of mammoth ivory. There was also a perforated
roundel and an animal form both cut from bone and decorated by
drilled pits. In other parts of Europe fish vertebrae and snail shells
as well as animal teeth were perforated for use as ornaments,
but a variety of beads, pendants, pins and bracelets were made
from other substances. Some of these were themselves decorated
with more or less complex incised patterns like the chevrons and
39 meanders on the well-known ivory bracelet from Mezin.

Art

An even more striking and significant innovation was the appearance
154, 156, 159 for the first time of graphic art. This is found both on loose objects
and on the walls or ceilings of caves or rock-shelters. Although Aurignacian deposits have yielded engraved and painted slabs at La Ferrassie in the Dordogne and ivory animal figures at Vogelherd in south Germany, the main flowering of the art began in Gravettian contexts and persisted down to the end of the Magdalenian, a span of around fifteen millennia. A particularly striking manifestation of the loose or chattel art is to be found in the figurines of women which occur widely between the Pyrenees and the Don Valley with a southward extension to north Italy. Although a few specimens date from the Magdalenian, the majority are Gravettian in age. They suggest that a broad community existed in the psychic as well as the technical fields between eastern and western Europe. The figurines themselves, only a few inches long, were mostly carved from ivory, coal or a variety of stones (calcite, haematite, oolite, serpentine, soapstone and steatite), but an example from Dolní Věstonice, Moravia, was modelled from a clay-like material and fired to a hard consistency. Unlike a few from Siberia, those from Europe are shown naked except for one with a girdle and another with a fringe at the

rear from Kostienki and Lespugue respectively. The heads were generally shown as mere knobs, with the hair rendered conventionally, if at all, the arms puny and the legs commonly without feet. Attention is focused on generous breasts, thighs and buttocks, in short on the attributes and symbols of maternity. In some cases indeed, as in certain ivories from Mezin in the Ukraine or in coal
43 pendants from Petersfels, West Germany, the female form is carried
44 to extreme stylization. Others, like the ivory head from Brassempouy

43 Upper Palaeolithic female figurines from Middle Europe: (*left*) stylized coal pendants, Petersfels, south Germany; (*right*) haematite torso, Ostrava-Petrkovice, Czechoslovakia.

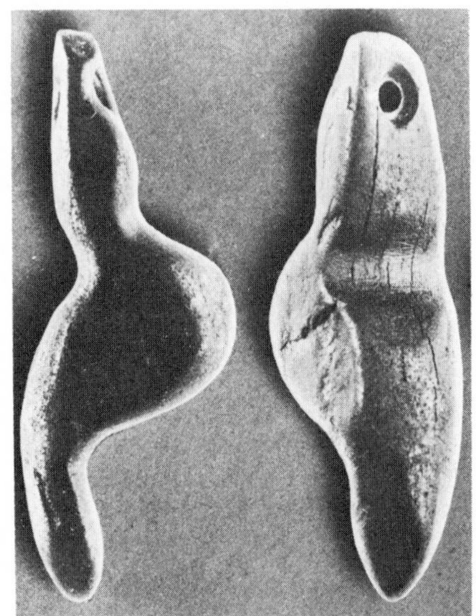

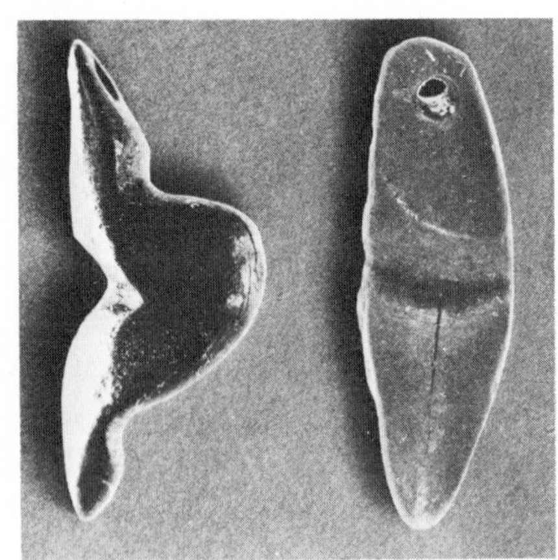

44 Head of ivory figurine of woman, Brassempouy, France.

45 Bison modelled in clay, Tuc d'Adoubert, France.

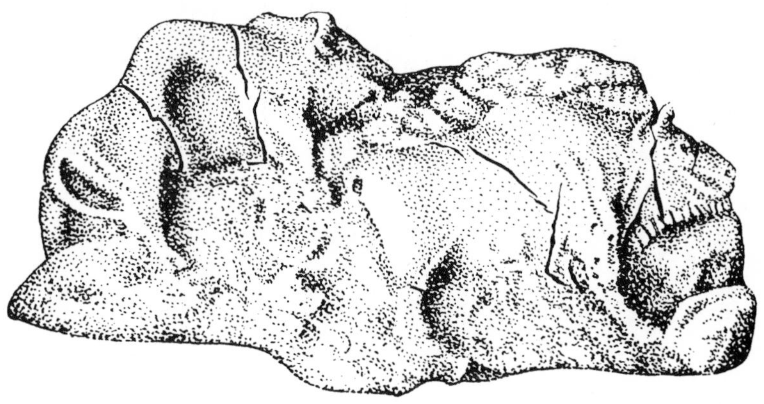

or the haematite torso from Ostrava-Petrkovice, display the tender-
43 ness associated with individual persons. The west Europeans at this
time were also skilled at animal sculpture, as we are reminded by the
limestone reliefs of bison, horse and ibex at Le Roc de Sers or the
45 clay models of bison at Tuc d'Adoubert. Carved and modelled animal
figurines are also known from south Russia and central Europe. Crude mammoth carvings were found at Ardeevo and Kostienki I and ivory profiles of mammoth and cave lion occurred at Pavlov on the Moravian loess. The same site along with Dolní Věstonice yielded numerous miniature clay models of a variety of animals. These include representations of most of the food mammals and their predators available at the time, including a mammoth, rhinoceros, bison, horse and reindeer, not to mention lion or tiger, wolf and lynx, shaped in many cases casually as though by men seated round the fire.

Geometric designs as well as naturalistic representations were used
46 to decorate antler and bone artefacts more particularly during the
Magdalenian phase in the west. These include rods of enigmatic purpose like those from Late Magdalenian layers at Arudy, Lespugue, Lourdes or Isturitz, but also lance and harpoon heads and perforated antler staves. Relief carvings of common food-animals, such as bison horse, ibex, mammoth and reindeer, as well as felines, fish and birds, on Magdalenian spear-throwers commonly achieve a high standard of realism and sometimes display an acute if primitive sense of humour.

46 Geometric designs, including spirals, engraved on Late Magdalenian antler rod, Isturitz, France.

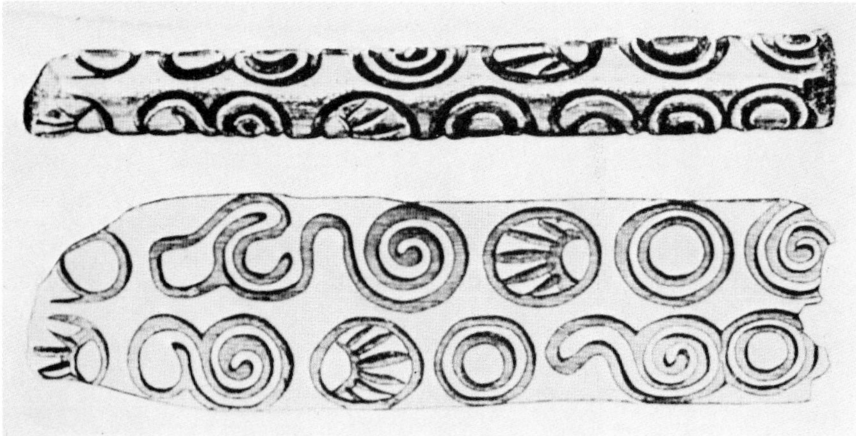

The distribution of art engraved, painted or carved on rock surfaces extends from southern Spain to the mid-Urals. Within this wide range its occurrence is discontinuous since it is restricted to regions provided by nature with caves. The densest occurrence of cave art is still concentrated in the Franco-Cantabric region, where it was first
267 recognized at Altamira, and in the Dordogne at Lascaux and many other sites. The only part of western Europe where it occurs north of this zone is the territory round Arcy-sur-Cure. In the Mediterranean zone on the other hand there are many occurrences from the south of Spain, where the occurrence at La Pileta is especially notable, to the lower Rhône basin and the southern extremities of Italy from Levanzo to Romanelli. The recent discovery of an
160 extensive series of cave paintings in the cave of Kapovaya on the southern bend of the Bielaya river in the south Ural region shows that cave art resembling in many respects that of the Dordogne was practised over 3,000 km to the east. The community of the Upper Palaeolithic world over the whole extent of Europe could hardly be more strikingly confirmed.

In the west there are signs that the cave art formed part of a

47 Wall painting with bulls, horse and stags, Lascaux, France.

continuing tradition that cut across the cultural phases distinguished by archaeologists on the basis of changes in implement and weapon types. From the symbolic signs and elementary outlines of the Aurignacian phase, the art went on to a period of great development during the Gravettian and early Solutrean phases in the Dordogne when engravings were made of the quality of those at Pair-non-Pair in which special emphasis was laid on the back-lines of the animals depicted. During the late Solutrean and Early Magdalenian the artists ceased to engrave limbs as though they were hanging from their back-bones and particularly notable advances were made in
47 painting, as one can see at Lascaux. This third phase also witnessed the first appearance of sculptures carved in relief on the limestone walls as at Le Roc de Sers where the bison was shown in a forceful but still archaic style. The climax of the cave art was reached during the last four or five thousand years of the Pleistocene during the middle and late phases of the Magdalenian. Engravings and also relief sculptures, well seen at Cap Blanc, show a greater degree of naturalism in the representation of animals. Outstanding advances were made in painting, which at Font de Gaume, Altamira and other

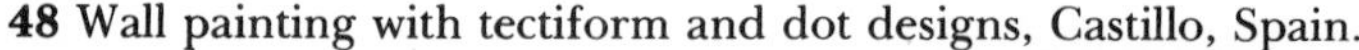

48 Wall painting with tectiform and dot designs, Castillo, Spain.

contemporary sites shows a more developed sense of modelling. The final phase of the Magdalenian displayed at sites like Limeuil, Le Portel and Isturitz an even more notable degree of naturalism in the representation in line and paint of individual animals. It was during this last stage, also, that the carving and engraving of small movable objects reached its climax.

The impression given by the products of Late Magdalenian culture is of a population living primarily by hunting reindeer under highly favourable ecological conditions. This impression is reinforced by the sudden disappearance of the art at the very time when Late-glacial gave way to Neothermal climate at the close of the Pleistocene towards the end of the ninth millennium. One of the few things we can say for certain is that it was produced by hunters well adapted to an environment rich in game animals. No one can contemplate this art without being aware of the outstanding powers of observation which it implies, powers which must have strongly reinforced skill in the hunt. Again, the art has important implications for the mentality of its creators. The advanced Palaeolithic men of Europe evidently had the imagination needed to depict in an increasingly life-like manner the animals on which they depended and with which they identified themselves in an extraordinarily intense manner. Representational and symbolic art, like the concern with personal decoration with which it was associated, was the outcome of a marked intensification of awareness, both of self-awareness and of awareness of the environment in relation to self and the social group. Beyond this there is evidence that the art served as a medium of communication at a conceptual level. In addition to the intricate notation revealed by enlargement of markings on the surfaces of engraved objects, a notation which has been plausibly linked with concern with the passage of time, the caves themselves display enigmatic designs
48 that must have been meaningful to those who painted them on ceilings and walls.

Mesolithic hunter-fishers

Within the territory of the Advanced Palaeolithic inhabitants of Europe the transition from Late-glacial to early Neothermal times was marked by environmental changes which varied widely in character and were notably more accentuated near the borders of the old ice-sheets than further south. When these ice-sheets began their final retreat rather more than ten thousand years ago they opened up new territories for human settlement in the northern parts of the British

49 Mesolithic bows and arrows from northern Europe.

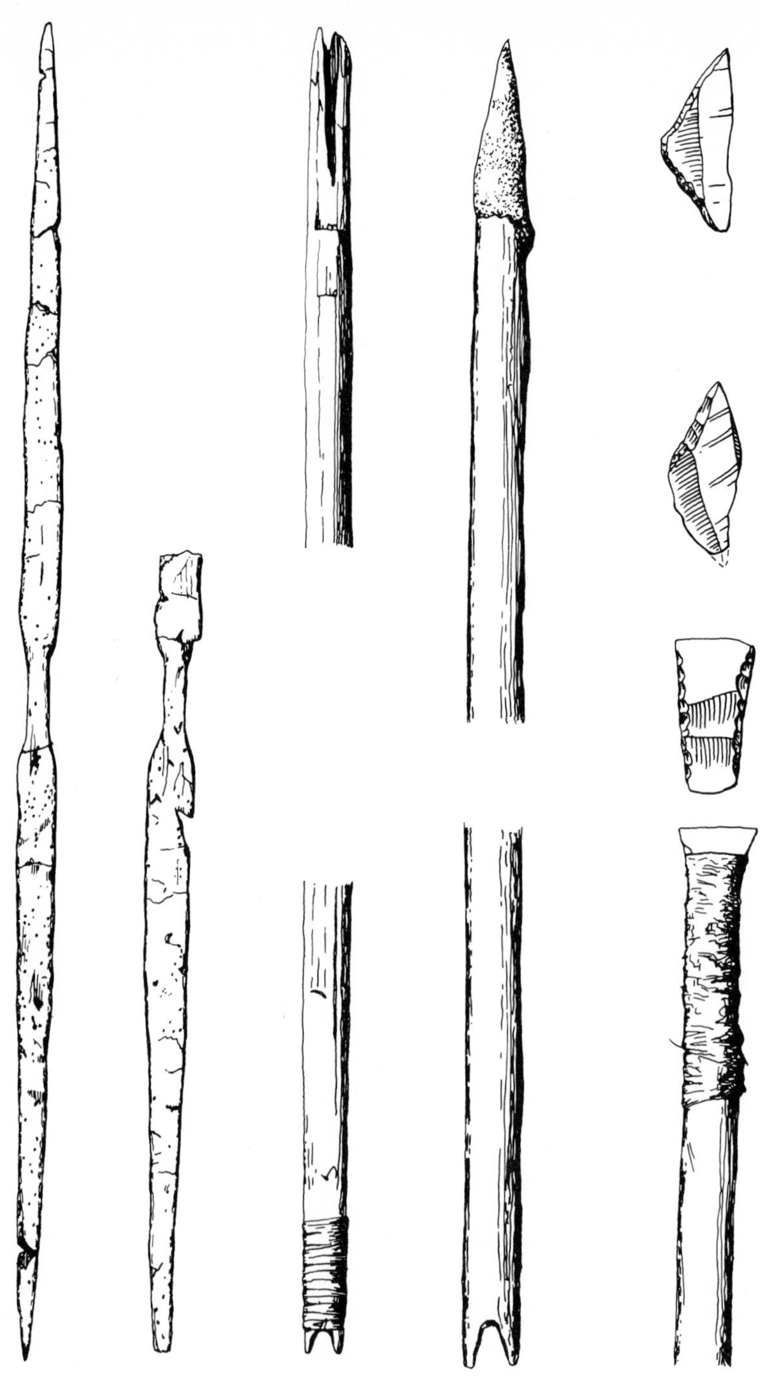

Isles and Scandinavia. On the other hand the replacement of park
222 tundra by forest, which accompanied the onset of temperate conditions, impaired the prospects for people based on a hunting economy by diminishing the available biomass. The pastures available to herbivorous animals were reduced to forest glades, river courses and the margins of lakes and sea coasts. Europe from being in the van of human progress and innovation reverted in a brief period to a marginal role on the stage of world prehistory.

Thanks to favourable conditions for the survival of organic materials provided by the bogs, lake margins and rivers of the area, a good deal is known about the subsistence and technology of the Maglemosian people who occupied much of the north European plain from Britain to south Scandinavia and north-west Russia between *c.* 8000 and 5600 B.C. During the earlier part of this time in particular elk and aurochs were prominent among food animals, but these declined as the deciduous forest established itself. Red and roe deer were always important and these were strongly reinforced by wild pig as the forests responded to higher temperatures. Beaver, fox, marten, wild cat and bear were among the main fur-bearing animals to be trapped. Water-birds were taken and there was extensive fishing for pike and smaller fresh-water fish. Little is known in detail about the nature of settlements at this time. Where there is a fairly marked relief there is evidence for seasonal change. The
248 encampment at Star Carr in northern England, for example, which dates from the middle of the eighth millennium B.C., has been shown to have been occupied mainly during the winter when the red deer, the main food animal, was sheltering in the Vale of Pickering. When the deer moved to upland summer pastures, their predators may be assumed to have done the same.

222: 109–11 The bow and arrow were the main weapons. Actual bows and
49 arrowshafts have survived only from northern Europe, but the microlithic barbs and tips made from microblades struck from conical or double-ended cores and shaped by a steep retouch, which more than any other artefact mark this period over Europe as a whole, show that their use was widespread. During the first phase the emphasis lay on penetrating arrows, but there was later a wide-spread shift to heads with oblique or transverse chisel ends which depended for their effectiveness primarily on their cutting power. Other hunting equipment included barbed spear- and harpoon-heads made from antler or bone. The importance of fishing is signalled by the variety of devices developed at this time including fish-hooks, basket

traps, seine nets, dug-out boats and paddles. The extent to which coastal resources were exploited is difficult to estimate precisely because in many parts of Europe the ancient coasts are submerged. What is certain is that line fisheries for cod and related sea-fish were already established off the east coast of Scotland and the west coast of Sweden by the sixth millennium B.C. and it is likely that this was conducted from skin boats. Shell mounds round the Atlantic coasts in the Tagus estuary, on the Breton coast, on the coasts of Ireland and Scotland and in the West Baltic area emphasize that molluscs were gathered on the sea-shore. Although not important in absolute terms relative to other food resources, shell-fish provided a useful stand-by in times of dearth: they were always there and easily gathered.

Much of the basic technology of Mesolithic Europe stemmed from local or nearby Upper Palaeolithic sources, notably burins and the sophisticated utilization of antler and bone, the use of the steep flint retouch and even the idea of the microlith. One of the main innovations and that only in northern Europe was the introduction of equipment for breaking the ground and for felling and utilizing timber. Where flint was available the blades of axes and adzes were made from thick flakes or nodules by bifacial flaking and sharpened by striking burin-like blows transversely to the axis of the tool, a process which could be repeated until the blade was too short for further use. Where only stone was to hand this was either flaked or

50 Mesolithic flint and polished stone adzes from northern Europe.

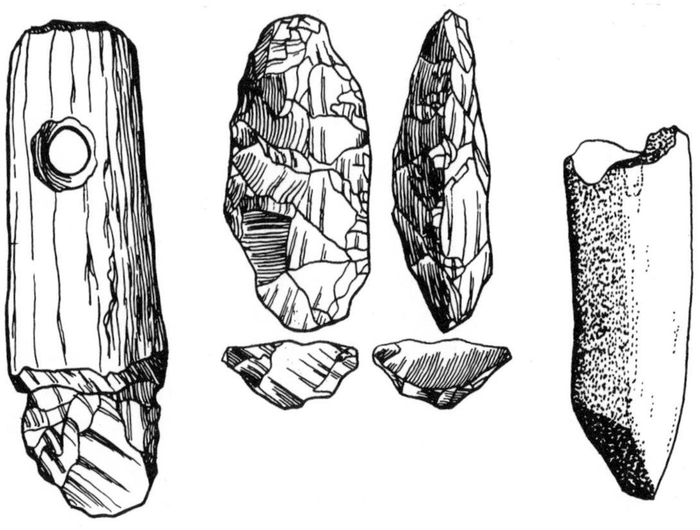

pecked into shape according to its nature and then ground and
50 polished to a smooth working edge. The wood obtained by the use of these tools, supplemented no doubt by wedging, splitting and the use of fire, was used to make dug-out boats, paddles, hafts, handles, bows, arrows, spear-shafts, hut-floors and a great many other things.

Like their predecessors Mesolithic hunter-fishers adorned themselves with ornaments though at a notably lower order of complexity, making do with perforated animal teeth, shale pebbles, amber lumps and the like. Their range of artistic endeavour was also more limited. Even when they occupied the same caves there is no evidence that they executed works of art to anything like the same standard.

51 Mesolithic art: stylized anthropomorphic representations on Maglemosian artefacts, Denmark.

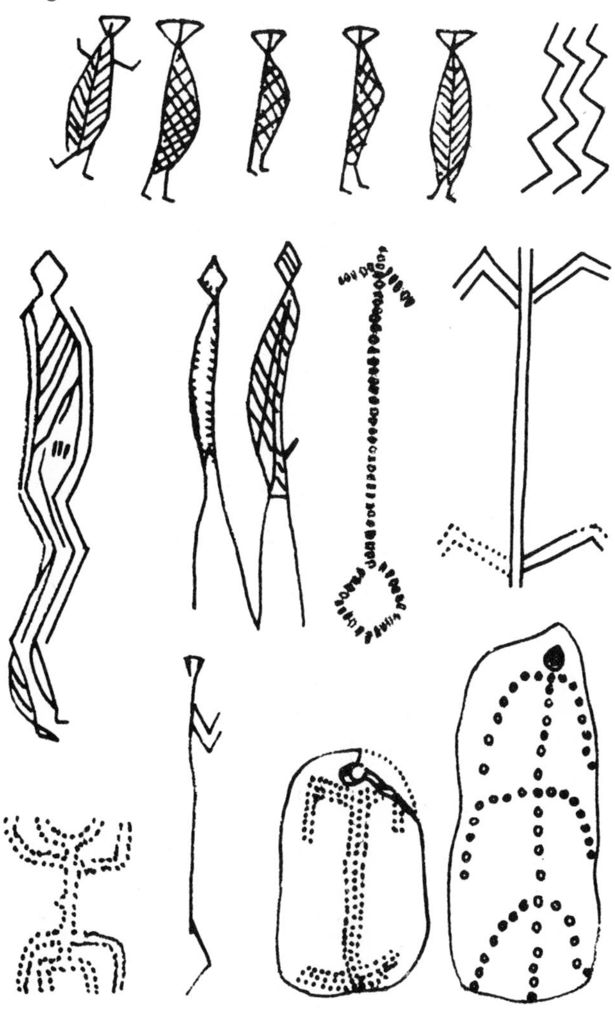

Similarly the small objects they decorated no longer display vivid representations of animal forms. Instead such art as they practised was abstract in character composed in the main of geometrical designs, many of them traceable to Palaeolithic sources. Animal and
222: 147–59 anthropoid forms where they occur are highly stylized as one can
51 see from those engraved or drilled on bone from the Maglemosian territory and painted on pebbles in the Franco-Cantabric region at
277: pl. 23 Mas-d'Azil and other sites. Yet one should beware of treating abstract as in any way inferior to representational art. It is more useful to look upon Maglemosian art as anticipating many of the designs which served for ornamenting middle Neolithic pottery in the northern province.

Late Stone Age farmers

As we have seen it was Mesolithic hunter-fishers who colonized the northern parts of Europe vacated by the melting of the ice-sheets and it was such people who first exploited the Neothermal environment over the continent as a whole. Yet the possibility of living a settled life in larger groups with all that this implied in terms of social and cultural development depended on changing from an economy based on hunting and foraging to one largely resting on farming. This can hardly have been achieved by the Europeans entirely on their own initiative since many of the plants and animals involved were introduced from Asia. Apart from the small-seeded einkorn (*Triticum monococcum aegilopoides*) Europe was lacking in prototypes for the cereals known to have been harvested in Neolithic times. And it is significant that the European farmers used the same kind of reaping-knife and quern for harvesting and milling as their Asiatic predecessors. It is much the same story with livestock. Cattle and swine were certainly available in their wild form in early Neothermal Europe. On the other hand the sheep and goat predominating among the earliest livestock maintained by European farmers had no wild predecessors there and must have been introduced in their domesticated form.

This is not to imply that the adoption of farming was by any means a simple matter for the Europeans. They were faced with the task of introducing exotic animal and plant species into new environments and with the need to adapt farming practices to new conditions. The ecological problems encountered by the pioneers varied widely in difficulty. Whereas conditions in the east Mediterranean were not so different from those of parts of south-west Asia, temperate Europe was another matter. As the zone of farming expanded north its pioneers were faced by conditions of climate, soil and vegetation that differed ever more profoundly from those to which they were accustomed. In particular they had to form their fields and pastures by clearing the forest which at that time covered the lower ground broken only by lakes, rivers and mountains rising above the tree line. Some measure of the struggles endured by the pioneers is given by the fact that it took around three millennia to advance the zone of farming from Greece to Denmark and a fourth to reach the Bothian coastal zone in the Swedish province of Norrland. The concepts

52 Expansion of agricultural economies in Europe.

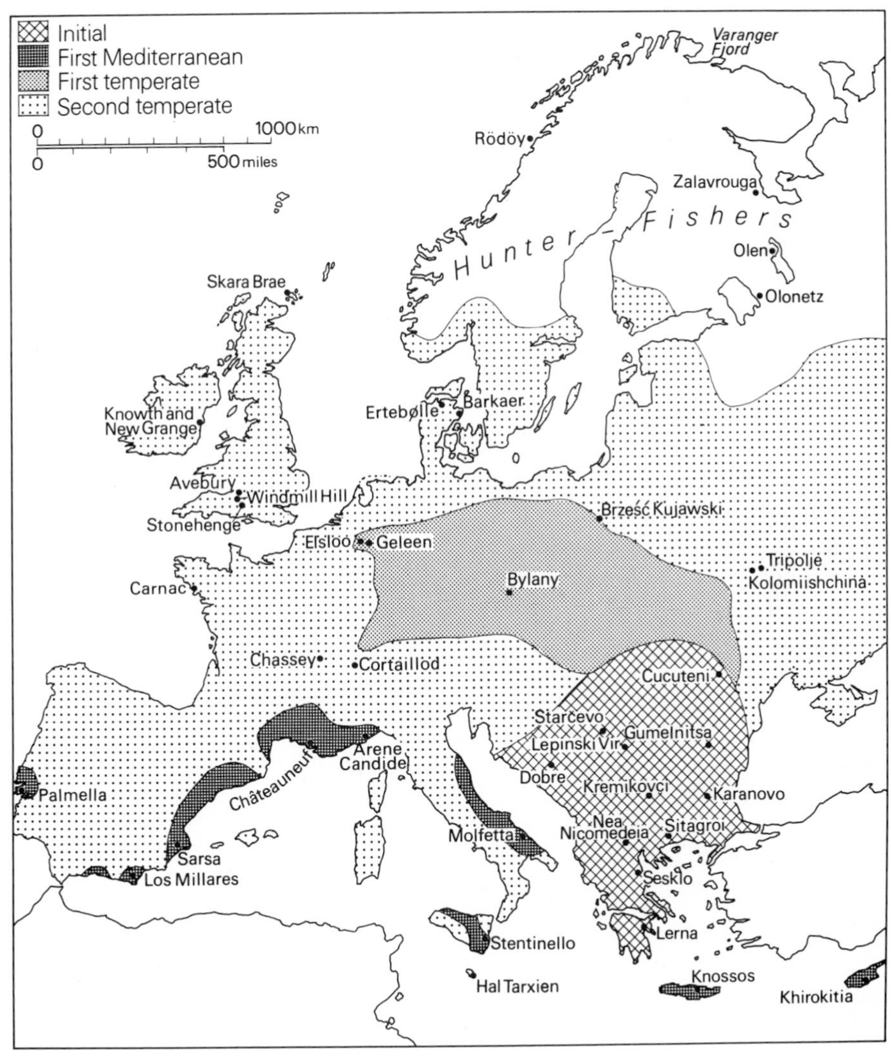

underlying the new economy reached Europe by three main routes. By far the most important was by way of Greece and the south Balkans into central, south, south-eastern and northern Europe. Secondary routes include those spreading across south Russia from inner Asia and that provided by the Mediterranean sea.

Three main stages can be distinguished in the advance of peasant farming economy from the Aegean to the Baltic. The initial phase, dated in conventional radiocarbon terms broadly to the sixth mil-
202 lennium B.C., was confined to Greece and the south Balkans and marked by settlement mounds or tells. As in south-west Asia these implied an agricultural regime sufficiently advanced to permit fixed settlement over prolonged periods of time and a climate sufficiently sunny to make it possible to construct dwellings with walls of sun-dried mud. The first expansion beyond this initial zone occurred during the fifth millennium and occupied two main territories. One comprised discontinuous coastal zones of the Mediterranean basin. The other centred on the loess lands of Middle Europe and affected a territory from the Middle Danube to the Rhine, the Vistula and the Dnestr. Finally during the second phase of expansion agriculture was carried over the rest of the temperate zone as far as the northern

Table 14. *Sequence of early peasant cultures in parts of Europe down to c. 1200 B.C.*

South Britain	Denmark	Danube	Greece	South-east Balkans	Ukraine
		VI			Black burnished
Bronze Age (Wessex)	Bronze Age	V	Late Helladic (Mycenaean)	Karanovo	
Secondary Neolithic	Late Neolithic	IV	Middle Helladic (Minyan)		Tripolje
	Middle Neolithic	III			
Primary Neolithic	Early Neolithic	II	Early Helladic	Gumelnitsa	
			Late Neolithic (Dhimini)		Izvoare
		I		Boian	
		(Spiral-meander ware)	Middle Neolithic (Sesklo)		
			Early Neolithic (Impressed; Otzaki)	Starčevo	
			Proto-Neolithic		

Table 15. *Some radiocarbon dates for the earliest peasant cultures of different zones of Europe*

		B.C.
SECOND EXPANSION		
Northern Europe, funnel-neck beaker ware		
Muldbjerg, Denmark	av. K 123–9; 131–2	2620 ± 80
Konens Høj, Denmark	K 919	2900 ± 100
	K 923	3310 ± 100
Heidmoor, N. Germany	H 30–145	3070 ± 105
	H 29–146	3190 ± 115
Sarnowo, Poland	GrN 5035	3620 ± 60
Western Europe		
Fussell's Lodge, England	BM 134	3230 ± 150
Windmill Hill: enclosure	BM 74	2570 ± 150
pre-enclosure	BM 73	2960 ± 150
Hembury, England	BM 130	3150 ± 150
	BM 138	3330 ± 150
Egolzwil 4, Switzerland	H 227/228	3090 ± 100
	KN 21	3420 ± 160
Mont St Michel, France (megalith)	Sa 96	3770 ± 300
Kercado, France (megalith)	Sa 95	3890 ± 300
FIRST EXPANSION		
Mediterranean impressed ware		
Roucadour, France	Gsy 36a	3990 ± 150
Arene Candide, Italy		
Level 25	Pi 27b	4537 ± 175
Levels 25/6	R 101	4270 ± 70
Penne di Pescara, Italy	Pi 101	4628 ± 135
Grotta della Madonna, Italy	R 285	5605 ± 85
Middle European linear ware*		
Elsloo, Limburg, Netherlands	GrN 2884	4105 ± 80
	GrN 2160	4200 ± 70
	GrN 2164	4320 ± 85
	GrN 2159	4370 ± 90
	GrN 2311	4560 ± 100
Bylany, Czechoslovakia	GrN 4752	4220 ± 45
	M 1897	4370 ± 230
INITIAL		
Tell Azmak I.I (Karanovo I), Bulgaria	Bln 294	4818 ± 100
	Bln 292	4928 ± 100
	Bln 291	5208 ± 150
	Bln 293	5353 ± 150
Nea Nikomedeia, Greece	P 1203a	5331 ± 74
	P 1202	5607 ± 91
	GX 679	5830 ± 270
	Q 655	6230 ± 150
Argissa XXVIII *b*, Greece	GrN 4145	5550 ± 90
Knossos (level X), Crete	BM 436	5790 ± 140
	BM 124	6100 ± 180

* Of the 45 dates available in 1969, 40 fell between 4560 and 3840 B.C.

limit of the deciduous forest. Beyond this hunting, fishing and foraging continued to prevail as the main bases of subsistence.

Initial zone of European agriculture: Greece and the south Balkans

The initial European farmers, whether they lived on Crete, on the Greek mainland or in the southern Balkans, shared the same basic characteristics. They all practised a mixed farming economy in which hunting and foraging merely supplemented cultivation and the maintenance of livestock. There are hints from Knossos and elsewhere that when they first occupied a new territory they made do with temporary camps. On the other hand they very soon became efficient enough to settle permanently. This and the fact that their houses were largely made from sun-dried brick or pisé, structures which required frequent renewal, meant that their settlements came in course of time to form mounds like the tells of western Asia. At
194 Knossos the Neolithic mound accumulated to a thickness of at least
147:45–100 seven metres and that at the Bulgarian site of Karanovo attained
more than twelve metres before it was abandoned during the local
53 Early Bronze Age. In plan the houses over the whole territory were rectangular and over most of Greece and the Balkans they had gabled roofs to cope with heavy rainfall, something made possible by abundant timber and adequate axes and adzes. The Neolithic peasants grew emmer, barley and einkorn and on Crete also bread wheat, as well as lentils and beans. Sheep and goat composed anything from

53 Section through the tell at Karanovo, Bulgaria. Scale in half metres.

three-quarters to four-fifths of their livestock with swine accounting for a sizeable part of the remainder. Cattle played only a comparatively minor role in respect of numbers.

Technology was elementary and gave no sign of advanced craft specialization or the systematic exchange of fabricated objects. Regular blades of the type used to inset the antler or wooden handles of reaping-knives were made from chert and obsidian. It is also of interest to note trapezes and microliths on some of the mainland Greece sites. Considerable skill was shown in the shaping and polishing of stone. Axe- and adze-blades speak of tree-felling and woodwork. Polished stone was also used for personal ornaments including what may have been nose-plugs, as well as for figurines. Occasionally also it was shaped to form bowls, a reminder that at the more or less contemporary site of Khirokitia in Cyprus vessels of this kind were used to the exclusion of pottery. A number of tools used in other crafts, such as potting, leather-work and basketry, were made from animal bone, including awls, eyed needles and spoons of a type found both in Greece and in the south Balkans.

In many respects the most revealing manufactures were pots,
stamp seals and figurines made from fired clay. The hand-made pots
were of simple shapes, mainly hemispherical or globular vessels with
round, disc-flattened or ring-footed bases, varied at Starčevo sites by
ones with high feet, and in the Körös valley by lopsided flasks with
perforated lugs. Rims were as a rule merely tapered, and there were
no spouts or indeed handles other than lugs. The earliest pottery
12, 213, 215 from Greece, from sites like Sesklo, Otzaki and Argissa in Thessaly
or Lerna in the Peloponnese or Knossos on Crete, was monochrome,
217 though painted decoration began early in western Macedonia and
the south Balkans. Painted pottery was also, as we have seen, an early
feature in a territory extending from Syria to Iran, but there is no
reason to think there was any direct link. The style of the earliest
European manifestations was already distinct. Indeed two main
groups may be distinguished; whereas the early inhabitants of Greece
54 favoured triangles, wavy lines and block designs in red paint on a
pale slip, the earliest potters of the Starčevo group in the Middle
Danube–Morava zone and of Bulgaria, as seen at Kremikovci and
Karanovo, went in for linear designs in black or white on a red
55 ground. Clay stamps from Nea Nikomedeia recall stone ones from
Thessaly and clay ones from both Çatal Hüyük in Anatolia and the
Morava valley to the north. The same two-directional analogies
pointing on the one hand to Asia and on the other to the south

54 Neolithic painted pottery, Greece: (1–2) Dhimini; (3–7) Sesklo; (8–11) Nea Nikomedeia.

Balkans are presented by another basic trait, the painted clay figu-
56 rine. A feature of those from Nea Nikomedeia, the way they were
207 sometimes made from several pieces, head, arms and lower limbs
being pegged to the trunk, recalls the method used about the same time as far off as the Zagros. The curious coffee-bean eyes have many parallels in south-west Asia and even remind one of the cowrie-shells inset in the plastered skulls from Jericho. Other features, notably figurines with rod-like heads, serve to link mainland Greece with the Starčevo group by way of the Vardar–Morava valleys.

The Neolithic mode of life persisted both in Greece and the south Balkans for between two and three thousand years without fundamental innovations. The changes in styles of artefacts, notably in pottery, recognized by archaeologists indicate hardly more than changing fashions. During the middle or Sesklo stage in Greece more sophisticated forms came into use including mugs with concave handles and necked jars with strap handles, and at the same time painting became much more important as a mode of decoration. Again the IIIrd and IVth levels at Karanovo are marked by the appearance of Veselinovo I pottery in which wooden prototypes influenced the forms of vessels and painted decoration gave place

55 Designs on stamp seals from Anatolia, Greece and the south Balkans: (1) Starčevo-Körös culture, Hungary; (2) Tsani, Thessaly; (3–5) Nea Nikomedeia, Macedonia; (6–9) Çatal Hüyük.

56 Clay figurine with rod-shaped head and coffee-bean eyes, Nea Nikomedeia, West Macedonia, Greece, with heads in similar style from Starčevo, Yugoslavia.

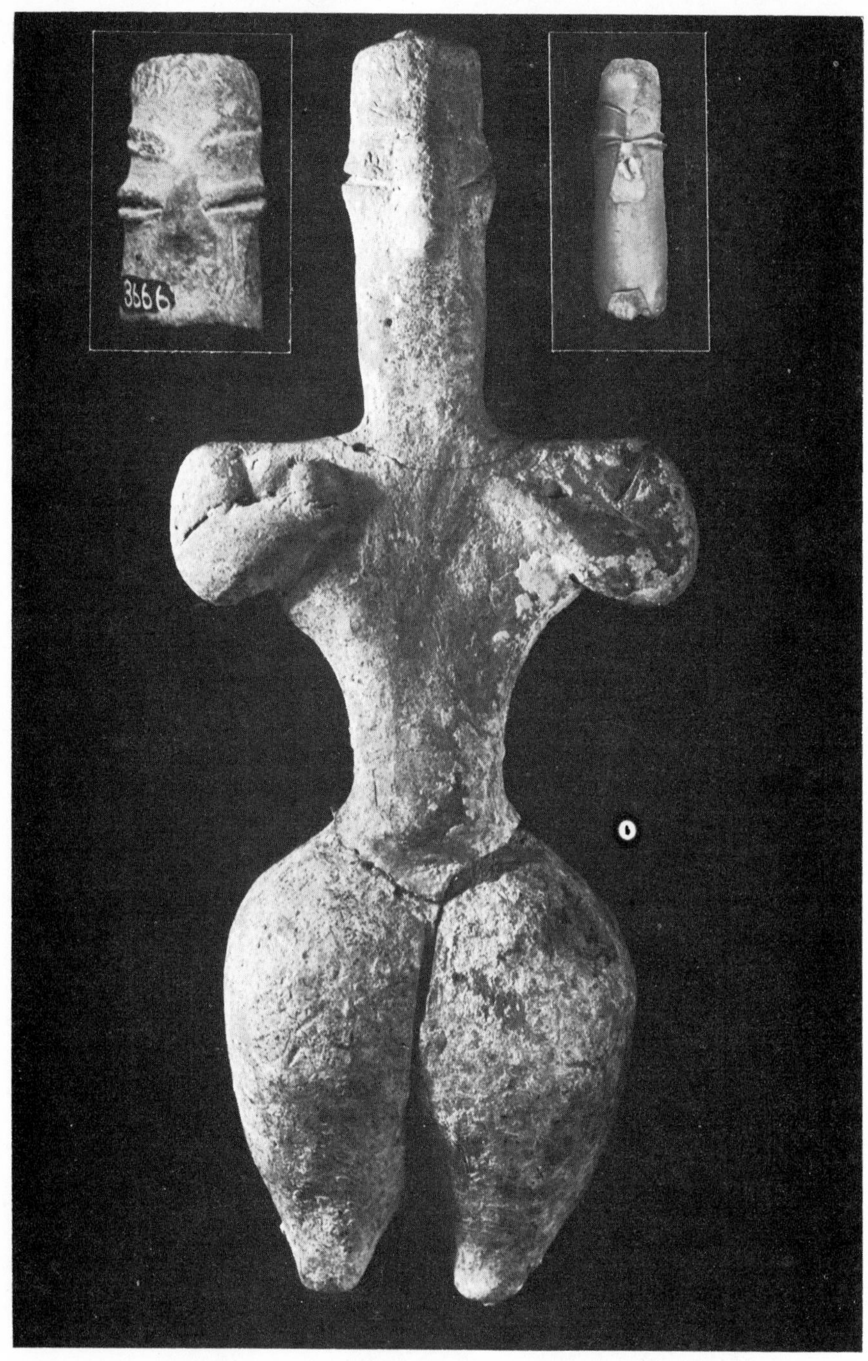

to excised and plastic ornament. The Late Neolithic or Dhimini stage in Thessaly showed notable changes in the forms and decoration of pottery, free-standing handles giving place to pierced lugs and chequer, spiral and meander designs appearing among the motifs which were now rendered in dark paint on a pale ground, sometimes as in the fashionable open dishes applied to the inside as well as the outside of the vessel. In due course Veselinovo wares gave place to Gumelnitsa pottery in Vth and Vith levels at Karanovo. Changes in ceramic styles have equally been recognized in successive levels at Knossos. Yet from an economic and social point of view successive levels in settlements which significantly remained on the same sites give the impression of continuity rather than change. The only common factor is a progressive increase in the size of communities occupying the same sites. Whereas at Knossos the original encampment on the Kephala hill covered only a quarter of a hectare and the first hamlet of mud-brick houses only half a hectare, by the close of Early Neolithic I the settlement, by then consisting of houses with pisé walls on stone foundations, was *c.* 2 hectares in extent; by the end of Early Neolithic II it had grown to 3 and by the close of the Late Neolithic to *c.* 4½ hectares. Similarly the settlement of Sesklo which to begin with had comprised no more than 30/50 buildings perched on a small hill grew to be a township covering 20/25 acres, in which the site of the original settlement served as an acropolis. The growth in size of individual settlements was only one sign of increasing population. Another was the expansion of the farming base into adjacent lands.

First expansion

Middle Europe. The first expansion into temperate Europe is marked by Danubian I pottery. Vessel forms were elementary comprising hemispherical bowls and gourd-like flasks with round bases, tapered
57 rims and lug handles. Decoration took the distinctive form of incised bands that might take the shape of spirals or meanders and, rather later, of discontinuous stroke ornament in the form of chevrons.
6, 272–3, 286 Female figurines are notably absent. Danubian I wares extended from Hungary almost to the estuary of the Oder and from north France, Limburg and the Rhineland to the Ukraine, a tract roughly 1,000×1,600 kms in extent. The succession of ceramic and house styles was notably similar in areas as far apart as Limburg and Moravia, suggesting that movement was sustained as well as rapid. The Danubian peasants lived together in hamlets or small villages

comprising houses built of timber and plaster. The regime of slash and burn, involving the shift of cultivation every few years and the clearance of new patches of forest, inevitably implied the temporary abandonment of settlements when the whole surrounding area had been exploited and a return when the regeneration of forest made possible a new cycle. The pioneer farmers were able to concentrate on the rich easily worked soils formed on loess formations. The discontinuity of these soils in itself contributed to the speed at which the colonization proceeded. The ready availability of land and lack of competition – the scanty population of hunter-foragers could take refuge on other formations – meant that there was no problem for younger generations in budding off to form new communities. It also explains why the colonizers were able to occupy such extensive tracts without seemingly having to modify their way of life. Everywhere we find peasants living in hamlets or villages like Bylany in Moravia,
58 Köln-Lindenthal in the Rhineland and Elsloo in Limburg. In tem-

57 First temperate Danubian pottery and stone adze blades: (1–4) spiral meander pots (1–3 Elsloo I–III; 4 Danube basin); (5) stroke-ornamented ware of Hinkelstein type; (6–7) shoe-last adze blades.

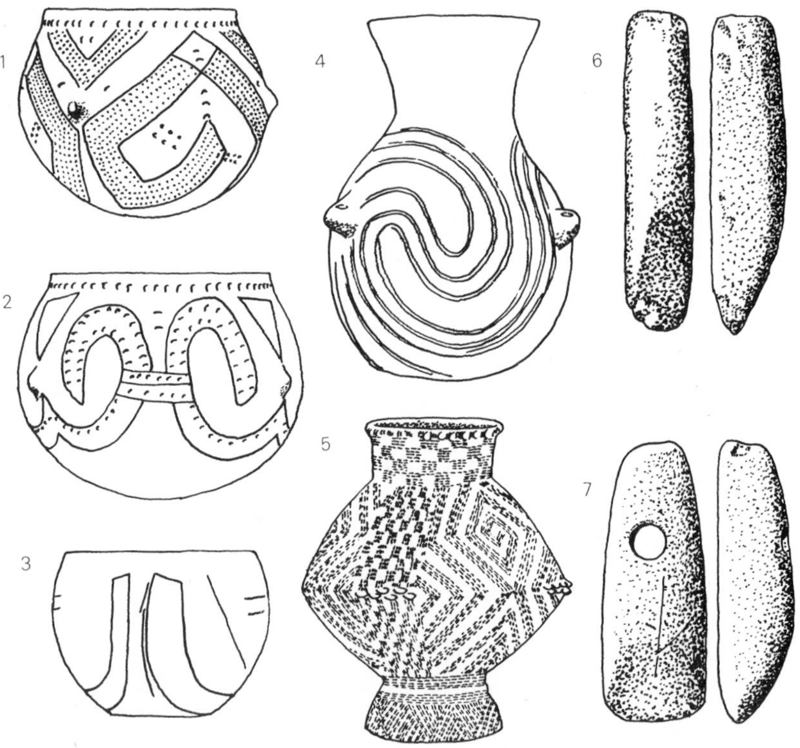

perate Europe where conditions did not favour sun-dried bricks settlements were no longer marked by mounds or tells. Houses were built on massive timber frames, commonly 20 to 30 metres and occasionally up to 50 metres in length. Apparently they were built on a tripartite plan, the family occupying the middle section with storage perhaps at one end and livestock at the other. As a rule the houses were oblong in plan but in Poland and occasionally elsewhere they might be trapeze-shaped having one end markedly wider than the other. Polished stone adzes of shoe-last form, blades and trapezi-

58 Danubian I settlements, Limburg, Holland: (*upper*) part of settlement plan, Elsloo; (*lower*) house-plan and reconstruction, Geleen.

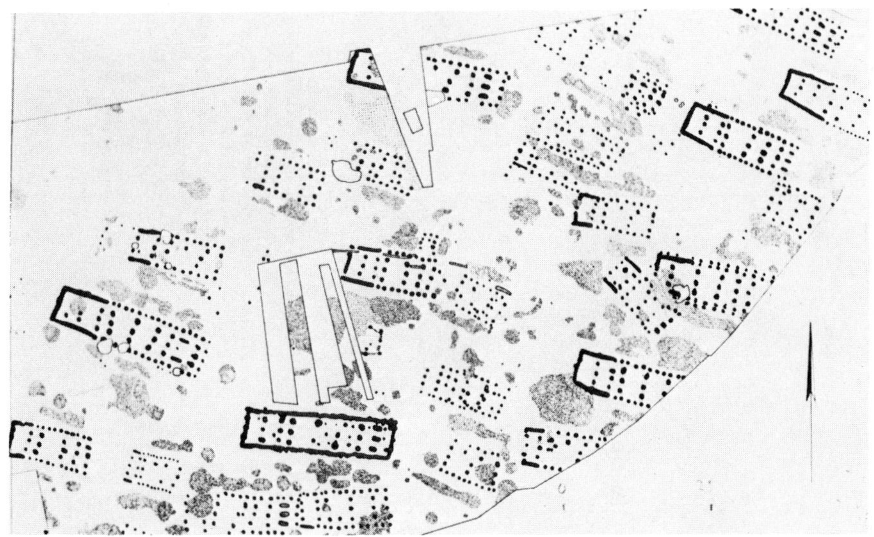

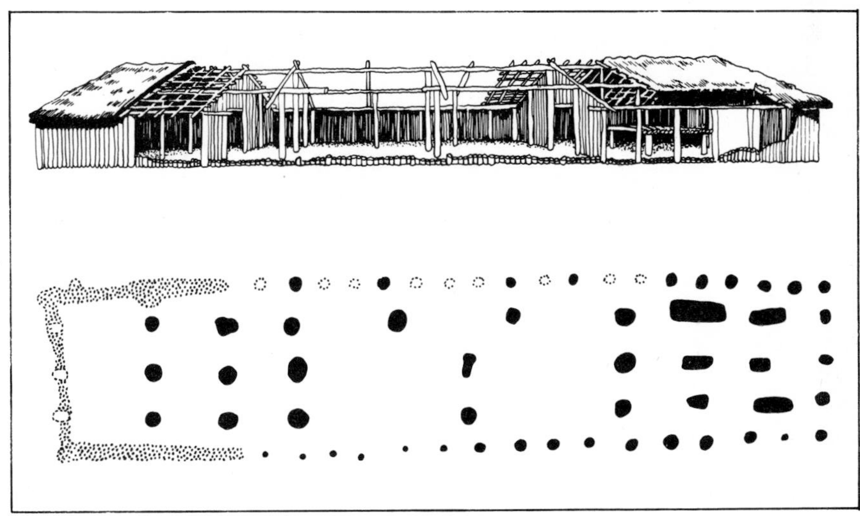

59 Ornaments of the Mediterranean mussel *Spondylus gaederopus*: (*upper*) shell and ornaments; (*lower*) map of Neolithic occurrences in Europe.

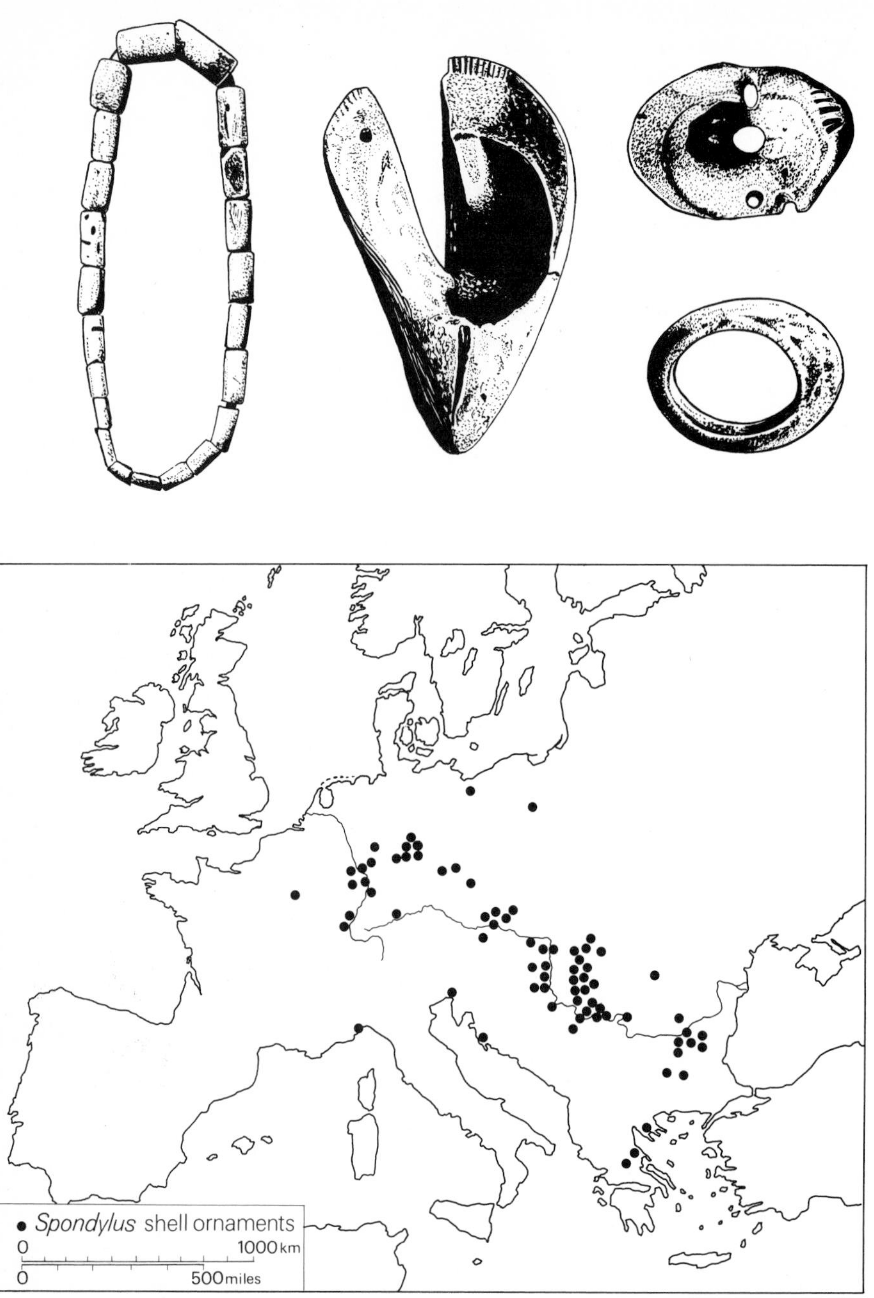

form arrowheads, the latter now having flat instead of steep side flaking, recall the lithic industries found in the south. The use of *Spondylus* shells as a material for making personal ornaments, documented as far west as the Rhineland and north France, shows that the Danube I people, like the Boians, shared in the same redistri-
59 bution systems for certain products as the south Balkans.

The next phase of settlement within the Danubian territory was marked by a change from long structures containing economic and living accommodation under one roof to smaller rectangular dwellings with a porch at one of the short ends, by the appearance of copper ornaments and by changes in pottery styles. Continuity with the older Danubian tradition is indicated by the use of the shoe-last adze, by the wearing of ornaments made from *Spondylus* shell and by spirals painted on the surface of pots after firing. Other elements which appear more sporadically hark back even further. These include anthropomorphic vases found with the repertoire of cylindrical jars and open bowls characteristic of the land east of the Tisza; or, again, female figurines and clay stamps which interestingly appear further north with Lengyel pottery in the forms of tall-footed bowls and biconical or pear-shaped jars. None of these last items is found with the Rössen pottery in territories to the north and west of the cortical area. Rössen pottery comprises hemispherical and globular vessels, sometimes standing on ringed feet, and most commonly ornamented by multichevron designs executed by notched furrows. The appearance of this pottery suggests the possibility of basketry prototypes and may even indicate contact with indigenous hunter-foragers. Certainly poorer soils seem to have been taken into occupation and there is evidence to suggest that hunting may have played a more important role in the food-quest. The evidence of defended settlements especially in the west argues for increased competition for land and there are signs that contact may have been made with alien groups.

Mediterranean. The first expansion of farming to the islands and coasts of the central and west Mediterranean is likewise marked by simple bowls and flasks often with round bases and with nothing more than lugs for handles. These were often plain, but they might be decorated by impressing the edges of cardium shells, a feature well known from the lowest levels at Mersin in Cilicia and Ras Shamra in Syria. The distribution of this ware in the Mediterranean is strongly coastal: it is found on the islands of Leukas and Corfu; on

the coast of Yugoslavia and the Adriatic coast of Italy, including the Tremiti islands; on Malta, Sicily, Elba and Sardinia; on the coast of Liguria; in the French provinces of Languedoc and Provence; and on the east and south-east coasts of Spain and the south coast of Portugal. The impressions, that might be made by toothed stamps and other objects as well as by cardium shells, were most commonly arranged as horizontal or vertical lines, zigzags or hanging arcs. Most of the settlement material has come from caves or rock-shelters and represents what appear to have been temporary occupations, though ones to which frequent returns were made. Excavations in caves like
244, 255 Arene Candide, Liguria, and Châteauneuf-les-Martigues, Provence, previously inhabited by Mesolithic man have shown that there was
60 very little change in the flint industries in the ceramic layers. This suggests that indigenous populations on the coast had been subject to acculturation or at most to some admixture of population rather than to displacement. Together with the art of potting, and the ability to make polished stone axes they must also have acquired not merely a knowledge of sheep maintenance, but actual stock.

60 Impressed and plain pottery with a blade and trapeze flint industry, Châteauneuf-les-Martigues, France.

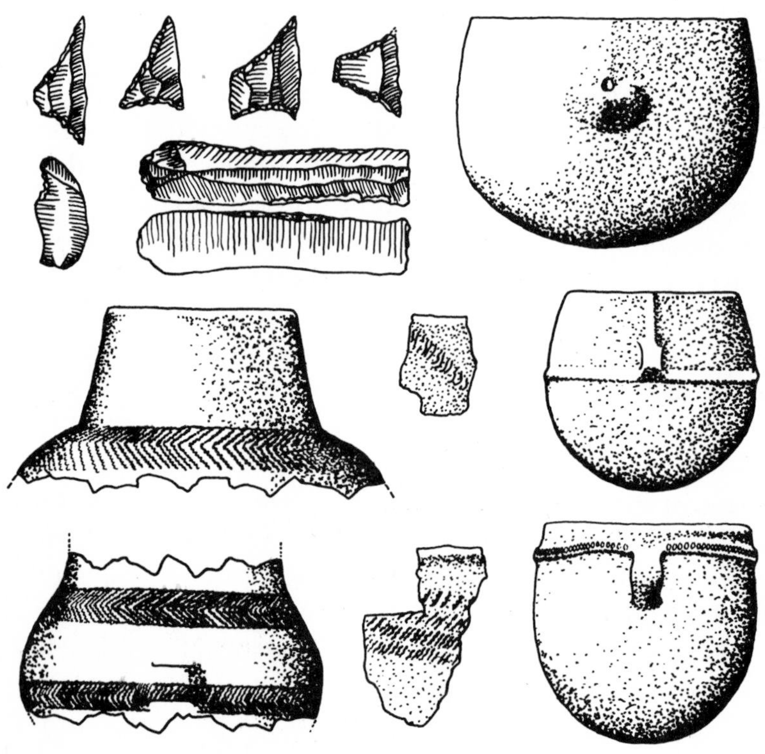

Knowledge of new territories was perhaps won by fishermen exploring the coastlines in quest of catches. In terms of radiocarbon dating impressed ware was already being made on the Adriatic coast of Italy early in the fifth millennium and by the middle it was certainly known on the south coast of France.

In the south of Italy cardial wares were succeeded by dark burnished and painted wares of Balkan inspiration. In the north on the other hand Danubian influences, shown for instance in ornaments of *Spondylus* shell, in clay stamps and in the use of the spiral motive in ceramic decoration, were complemented and finally replaced by influences emanating from the west.

Second expansion

West. It is reasonable to suppose that the peasant cultures that developed west of the Rhine during the fourth millennium B.C. and provided a platform for the later prehistory of Iberia, France, the Swiss foreland and the British Isles stemmed from the primary Mediterranean settlement. The new form of economy spread to the very margins of the Atlantic zone as far as western Ireland, the Hebrides and the Northern Isles of Scotland. Indeed the most intimate insight into the furnishing of a peasant household of this

61 Skara Brae, Orkney: interior of Neolithic house with slate furniture.

phase is provided by the stone-built houses preserved by the sand
61 dune that enveloped the site of Skara Brae on Orkney. Over most of western Europe the earliest peasants may be identified by pottery which, while exhibiting regional differences at sites like the Camp
239, 241, 257 de Chassey, France, or Windmill Hill in southern England, shared
265, 280 the same general character. In shape it was round-based, hemispherical, carinated or globular. As a rule it lacked handles other than lugs. The surface was often left undecorated, though in France and north Italy it might for instance have designs scratched on after firing and in Switzerland even be ornamented by cut-out designs of birch bark stuck to the surface by resin.

Subsistence in the western province was everywhere based to some degree on growing cereals among which varieties of wheat predominated over barley. This involved a major effort in clearing the forest on which Mesolithic man had made only comparatively small inroads. In calcareous regions lime-rich soils were preferred and there is evidence from south Britain that the light plough or ard had already come into use at this time. Livestock were another major resource. The most important animals were cattle and swine, each of which had long been at home in the Neothermal forest. Sheep and goat on the other hand, which had predominated in Crete and

62 Grimes Graves, Norfolk, England: view of gallery with flint seam and antler 'picks'.

Greece, were as a rule only of subsidiary importance in the early stage of farming in western Europe. The hunting of wild animals, which must have been necessary in any case to protect crops, added a useful source of food and raw materials. Generally this was only of minor importance. In the Alpine foreland on the other hand with its lakes and steep mountain slopes fishing, hunting and the gathering of wild plants made the most economic use of resources and in such a region may even have contributed more to the food quest than farming.

From limited evidence it looks as if British and French peasants at this time occupied small hamlets or clusters of houses. The dwellings themselves, basically of timber-frame construction, though in some terrains having stone wall-foundations and possibly turf walls, were gabled and rectangular in plan. Like more or less contemporary structures on Danubian II settlements east of the Rhine they were comparatively small and intended primarily for domestic use.

Although contemporary with people who had developed a copper metallurgical industry in the south Balkans and central Europe, the peasant communities between the Alps and the Atlantic relied primarily on flint and stone for their basic technology. The most important craft was fabricating flint or stone tools adapted to cutting, piercing or scraping a variety of other materials. Other activities included the shaping of wood and the utilization of bark and resin, basket- and net-making, the preparation and use of animal hides, weaving and potting. In a forested environment it is only to be expected that flint or stone axe-blades should have been of key importance since farming was only made possible by clearing trees. It follows that great care was taken to ensure the best materials for the blades of these crucial tools. In the case of flint, surface nodules, though adequate for certain purposes, were markedly inferior for axe blades to ones obtained from the parent chalk. These could sometimes be won from outcrops, but frequently they had to be mined. Traces of this activity in the cretaceous zones of Britain, France and Holland are only rivalled in sophistication by those associated with the Funnel-neck Beaker settlement of Poland, a country where flint-mining had already been practised since the Late Pleistocene. Many kinds of rock obtainable from surface outcrops were also used. The sites of axe factories associated both with flint-mines and stone outcrops can usually be recognized from the accumulations of waste that result from the initial process of roughing out the blades. The processes of grinding and polishing were evidently carried out either in the course of distribution or at the point

of use. It has long been possible to trace stone axes to their sources
and latterly the same has been possible for flint. Already it is plain
how complex were the redistribution net-works by which axe-blades
152: 247–50 found their way from source to user. For instance in the British Isles
stone blades made from material originally quarried in Ulster passed
to Scotland and to parts of England in the remote south and south-east.
Blades from sources in north Wales and the Lake District of England
had similarly wide distributions as did ones from unlocated quarries
in Cornwall. Again, before the flint-mines opened up at Grimes
62 Graves in Norfolk around the beginning of the second millennium
B.C. the people of East Anglia depended on flint axes imported from
Sussex where the mining had started a thousand years earlier.

63 Los Millares, Spain: reconstruction of corbelled passage-grave (*tholos*).

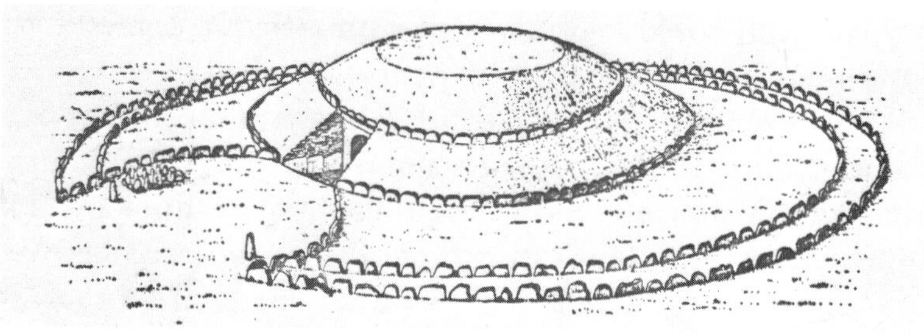

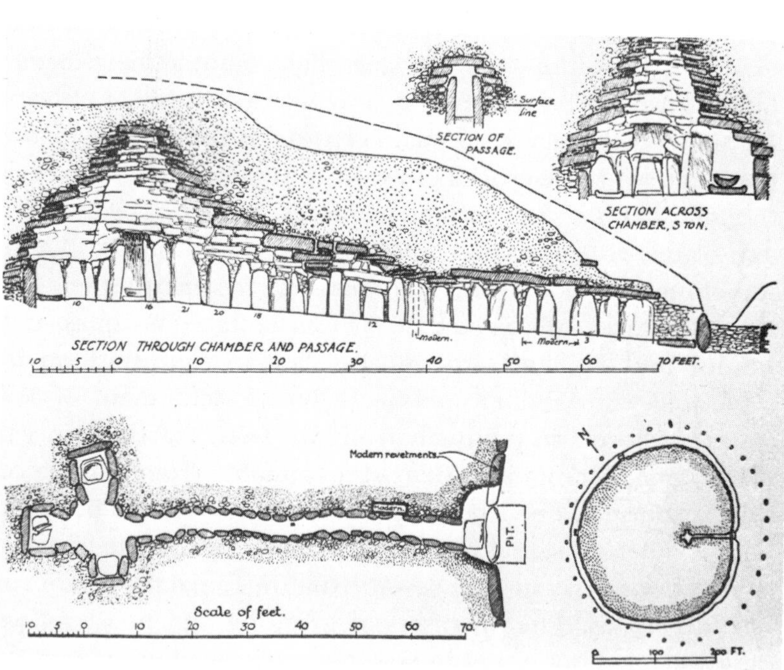

Quite another aspect of Neolithic settlement in western Europe was
the construction of collective tombs and sacred monuments on a vast
scale. The larger and more elaborate tombs fall into two classes, those
250 in which the chamber was approached by a distinct passage and those,
often termed gallery graves, in which there was a single chamber with
268 sometimes a short antechamber. Structurally passage-graves might
be cut out of the living rock, as in the cemetery at Palmella, Portugal,
63 or built of drystone walls and roofed by corbelling as at Los Millares,
Spain, or, as was generally the case along the Atlantic route from
Iberia and western France to the British Isles and the West Baltic,
walled and roofed by megalithic slabs. Alternatively two techniques
64 might be combined as at New Grange, where a megalithic passage
262 and chamber was roofed by oversailing slabs in a corbelling tech-
nique. Again there was scope for variation in the form of the chamber which might, for example, be round, polygonal, rectangular or cruciform. Despite such variations which were commonly favoured in particular regions, the occurrence of collective tombs in most cases of megalithic construction over so great an extent of the Atlantic seaboard has often been attributed exclusively to seaborne diffusion. On the other hand the notion that burial in collective tombs of monumental construction originated in the east Mediterranean has recently been disproved by radiocarbon dating. Passage-graves were apparently being built in Brittany early in the fourth millennium and both chambered and earthen long barrows in the British Isles in the second half of the same millennium, in both cases, that is, before Early Cycladic people were depositing female figurines in the rock-cut tombs sometimes claimed as prototypes.

Since western tomb-forms and grave-goods are not to be found
in the Aegean the problem is hardly to be solved by reversing the
direction of diffusion. A more likely explanation is that collective
burial was autocthonous to the Mediterranean basin and southern
Iberia. It is significant that the earliest pottery-using peoples of this
area, the makers of impressed ware, had been burying their dead
collectively in caves since the middle of the fifth millennium. Again
the distributions of impressed wares and of artificial collective tombs
coincide to a significant extent. The objection that this fails to take
65 account of the representations or symbols of female figures is hardly
one that stands up to scrutiny when it is remembered that there was
a strong Balkan element in the make-up of Mediterranean impressed
ware. The representation of women in more or less symbolic form
is deeply embedded in the earliest peasant traditions of Greece and

the Balkans in the form both of clay or stone figurines and of anthropomorphic and specifically female pots. Again, discussion of the spiral as a link between Mycenae, Hal Tarxien or New Grange sometimes overlooks the fact that this motive is common not merely to Early Neolithic traditions in Greece and the Balkans, but also appears on Middle Neolithic wares both in south Italy and on the Ligurian coast as at Arene Candide. It remains a fact that certain tombs found on the sea-board of Atlantic Europe embody notions which can only have spread by sea. The suggestion that this had anything to do at least initially with prospecting for metals is difficult to sustain when we remember how early collective tombs of megalithic construction were being built in north-west Europe. More likely the idea of building collective tombs spread northwards by routes opened up in the course of normal fishing activities. Species like hake and mackerel, which can be taken on simple hook and line tackle, regularly ascend from deep water to breed in southern zones before they do further north. Anyone depending on fishing for a living would therefore tend to move up the coast of Britanny to the Celtic
253 sea and ultimately round the west coast of Ireland to south-west Scotland.

The large number of megalithic tombs in south Scandinavia and adjacent parts of the North European Plain provides another puzzle. On the other hand more than four-fifths of these were small closed chambers (*dysse*) designed for single or at most for very few burials, a form generally accepted as of indigenous origin and already well established before collective burials in passage-graves began there during the northern middle Neolithic around 2600 B.C. The mere fact that the inhabitants of this region were already familiar with using megalithic blocks and slabs to construct burials probably made them more receptive to the notion of building passage graves when the basic notion had once been implanted. The degree of continuity displayed in the grave-goods of *dysse* and passage-graves shows that the latter can hardly have been introduced as part of a large-scale ethnic movement. Instead we may think in terms of stimuli brought perhaps accidentally by fishermen exploring the Channel route. This is quite consistent with the fact that the construction of passage-graves lasted for no more than a century or two in this region, even if the tombs were used for perhaps a millennium. In the parts of southern Europe where the tradition of collective burial was more deeply rooted, on the other hand, the construction of the tombs had a much longer life.

FOUNDATIONS OF EUROPEAN CIVILIZATION

65 Knowth (west), Ireland: anthropomorphic design pecked on stone slab.

Although less numerous than tombs, other kinds of sacred structure are in some respects of even greater interest. Outstanding
66 examples in the Mediterranean are the Hal Tarxien and earlier
256 'temples' on Malta, structures cut from solid rock or built of megalithic elements backed by stone-faced earthen walls. The fact that the earlier versions are reminiscent of rock-cut tombs and the later ones recall passage-graves in plan suggests the possibility that the cults practised in them symbolize the connection between life and death.

Even more impressive sacred monuments of megalithic construction are found in France and above all in the British Isles. Two main classes are represented, one elongated, the other more or less circular. The former range from small rows of upright stones like those of Dartmoor in south-west England to the sometimes much larger cursus monuments of southern Britain, enclosures formed by parallel banks and ditches, or the multiple stone alignments of Carnac in Brittany, extending over nearly four miles. There is an equally broad range of scale among circular structures in Britain. At one end are small circles of standing stones and at the other large and often complex monuments with stone or timber uprights set in areas defined by banks and ditches and sometimes approached by
67, 97 avenues. The function of monuments like Avebury and Stonehenge
240, 265, 285 in southern England has often been debated. Whatever role they played in religion it seems certain that they served as centres of social interaction, something documented by the concentration of stone axe-blades from factories in many different parts of the country.

66 Hal Tarxien, Malta: plan of megalithic temple.

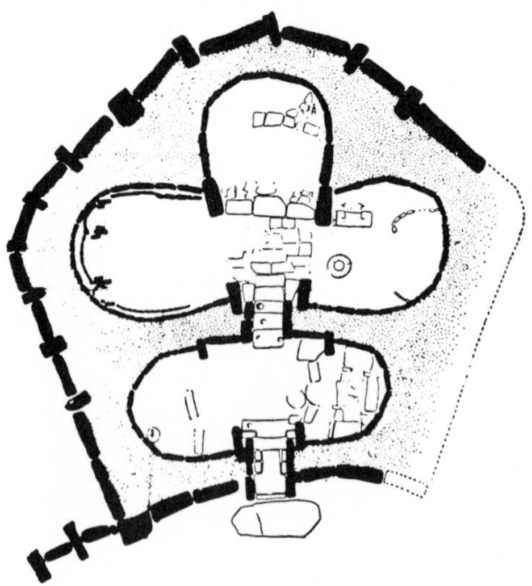

East. Expansion to the east was initially marked by a distinctive 161, 186 pottery style named after the Boian Lake at the head of the Dobrudja in Romania. The Boian pottery is found at the base of numerous tells in the region and shows that the peasants who occupied this new territory, while practising the same basic economy and living the same kind of life as those of relatives in the south Balkans, were nevertheless independent pioneers with a separate identity. They made large biconical storage vessels as well as smaller pots and some distinctive peg-footed cylindrical vessels which look as if they were inspired by wooden prototypes. Curvilinear designs including spirals were incised on the surface and angular ones excised to form patterns that might be emphasized by encrusting red or white pigment. Although evidently exploiting a separate social territory effectively enough to support permanent tell-settlement, the makers of Boian pottery shared in the re-distribution net-work which brought *Spondylus* shells from the Mediterranean to Thessaly and by way of the Danube basin over a substantial part of middle Europe. Copper was sometimes used for small ornaments but reliance was placed on stone

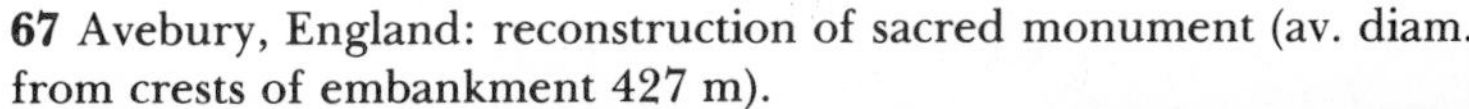

67 Avebury, England: reconstruction of sacred monument (av. diam. from crests of embankment 427 m).

tools including polished shoe-last adzes and bevelled adze blades.

During the next stage of settlement copper came into more general use and farming economy was extended from the Danube to the Dnepr. Cultural configurations also changed. Over much of Romania a Boian gave place to a Gumelnitsa pattern. In Bessarabia and new Ukrainian territories the Cucuteni–Tripolje culture derived some
167 elements from the Boian and others from the Danubian colonists who during the preceding period had advanced north of the Carpathians to reach the Dnestr and the Prut. On the other hand the forms of the pottery and above all its decoration featuring curvilinear and spiral designs rendered in white incrusted grooves or paint, often in several colours, gave it a unique character. The high and controlled firing of these wares was made possible by the great clay ovens

68 Tripolje settlement and house: (*upper*) Kolomysczina settlement; (*lower*) reconstruction of house at Vladimirovka.

represented in models, but also uncovered during excavations.
68 The houses themselves, built of timber plastered with mud and roofed by gabled thatch, were grouped in hamlets or small villages. These were sometimes defended by earthworks, but at Kolomysczina in the frontier zone near Kiev the houses were disposed radially to give some measure of security, rather as with the covered waggons on the trail to the far west of North America.

Beyond the Dnepr the steppes of south Russia extending to the Caspian, the Sea of Aral and beyond offered an independent corridor complementary to the Danube and the Mediterranean by which impulses were able to reach temperate Europe from western Asia. Again, the distinctive grass and steppe environment of the region was the setting for unique adaptations in the cultural field. One of the most striking contributions of South Russia was ultimately the domestication of the horse, but this animal first became important in the context of the chiefdoms which emerged during the final stages of prehistory. The speed of the horse, its spirit and grace of movement were to make it ideal both as symbol of rank and a fighting machine, at first harnessed to chariots and then as cavalry. An earlier contribution to transport was made by vehicles of homelier use, ox-drawn carts and waggons, originally formed by applying one or two pairs of wheels to vehicles previously dragged over the ground on runners. Although the earliest evidence may still be the representations in pictographs from Uruk dating from the closing centuries of the fourth millennium B.C., it is certain that South Russia played a key part in the transmission of such vehicles to the west.
69 The series of more or less complete vehicles from the pit-graves of
180 Transcaucasia and Caucasia dating from throughout the third millennium B.C. allows a close insight into vehicles that were equally useful to settled farmers and pastoral transhumants. The spread of such vehicles across south Russia to the west is defined by numerous finds of tripartite solid wooden wheels. During the course of the third millennium these reached the Danube basin and traversed the North European plain as far west as the Netherlands.

North. During the Initial and First Temperate phases in the spread of peasant economies in Europe, the inhabitants of the northern zone intermediate between east and west continued to support themselves by hunting, fishing and a variety of foraging activities including the occasional gathering of shellfish on the coasts. Already during the First Temperate phase to the south they had acquired or developed the art of potting. The large vessels, which accompanied pottery lamps at Ertebølle and comparable sites in Denmark and may well have been used for boiling shellfish, had the pointed bases so often found on the earliest pottery from Iberia to Japan and the New World and owed its form at least in many cases to basketry prototypes.

The Early Neolithic pottery of this region is often designated by
187, 220 the widespread funnel-neck beaker form extending from the Netherlands to the eastern frontiers of Poland. In its mature stage it comprised a variety of bowl- and bottle- or flask-like forms, commonly decorated by vertical motifs in incision or cord-impression. Tree-felling and wood-working tools as well as insignia of status were for the most part made of flint or stone. Copper, obtained from the south probably in the form of ready-made axe-blades and ornaments, was too expensive for common use. Amber continued to be favoured for personal adornment, as it had already been for some thousands of years, until it came to serve during the Bronze Age predominantly as an export commodity in exchange for bronzes or metal ingots.

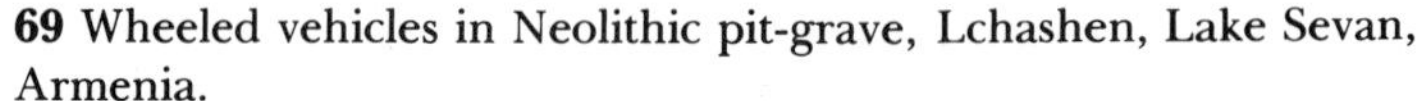

69 Wheeled vehicles in Neolithic pit-grave, Lchashen, Lake Sevan, Armenia.

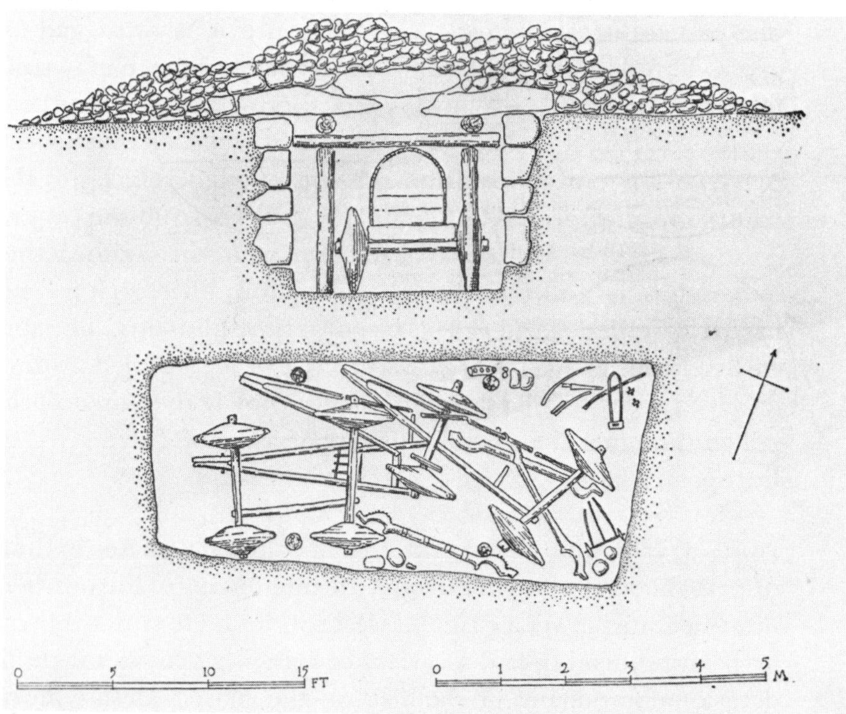

Whereas during the initial Ertebølle phase wild animals contributed almost the total supply of meat, by the Early Neolithic these had sunk to between 5 or 10 per cent of the total. Among domestic animals the proportions at the Polish site of Cmielow for instance revealed sheep and goat as constituting a mere tenth as against more than three-fifths of cattle. In Denmark on the other hand swine accounted for between a half and a third with sheep and cattle at rather over a quarter each.

The makers of funnel-neck beakers lived in short houses with gabled roofs. As a rule these were individual structures but there was a remarkable exception at Barkaer in Jutland where two parallel gabled terraces were each divided into sub-units. Burial was normally by single inhumation. As a rule these were in simple earth graves, but for the first time we encounter in this sector of Europe indications of monumental structures associated with the dead. These include the Kujavian graves of northern Poland, in which the burials were heaped over by long mounds defined by oblong or triangular settings of stone boulders. In Denmark and north Germany the dead were buried in closed megalithic chambers (*dysse*) under oblong or round mounds outlined by stone boulders.

The succeeding Middle Neolithic gave plenty of signs of continuity as well as displaying innovations in pottery and other equipment. In ceramic decoration, vertical motives gave way to mainly horizontally disposed chevron designs, new forms of battle-axe replaced the knobbed form and during the later stages thin-butted gave ground to thick-butted flint axes. In respect of burial single graves were now supplemented, though by no means replaced, by collective tombs of megalithic construction. Some of those in Denmark, south Sweden and north Germany resemble in plan the passage-graves disposed at intervals along the Atlantic sea-board to such a degree as to suggest inspiration from the west. On the other hand distinctive forms developed in the south Baltic area, more particularly tombs with elongated chambers, and at the same time anthropomorphic representations and constructional techniques like corbelling were absent, the latter probably for geological reasons.

The last substantial extension of Stone Age farming in northern Europe took place in the opening centuries of the second millennium
231 B.C. The most pervasive archaeological indicator of this Late Neolithic expansion is the perforated stone battle-axe. This class of artefact had already appeared in northern Europe in a knobbed polygonal form before the close of the local Early Neolithic as in a sense a

surrogate for the copper form on which it was ultimately modelled. For whatever reason stone battle-axes came strongly into fashion, presumably in their more finished forms as symbols of manhood, during the final stage of the Neolithic phase of settlement over a large part of north temperate Europe. Although everywhere associated with individual inhumation burial and in many areas with cord-impressed pottery, there was no uniform 'battle-axe culture' over the
70 territory as a whole. The axes themselves and their associated pottery took a number of local forms. Again, burials were sometimes flat, sometimes under mounds. Against the idea formerly held particularly strongly in northern Europe which equated battle-axes with groups adapted to pastoral activities, it is now widely accepted that the Late Neolithic of this region was one in which agriculture was intensified and extended. This was done in part by taking up poorer

70 Denmark: Early Neolithic 'C' artefacts: (1–5) pottery, including funnel-neck beakers and collared, eared and lugged flasks; (6) thin-butted flint axes; (7) copper flat axe; (8) knobbed stone battle-axe; (9–10) amber ornaments; (11) copper disc.

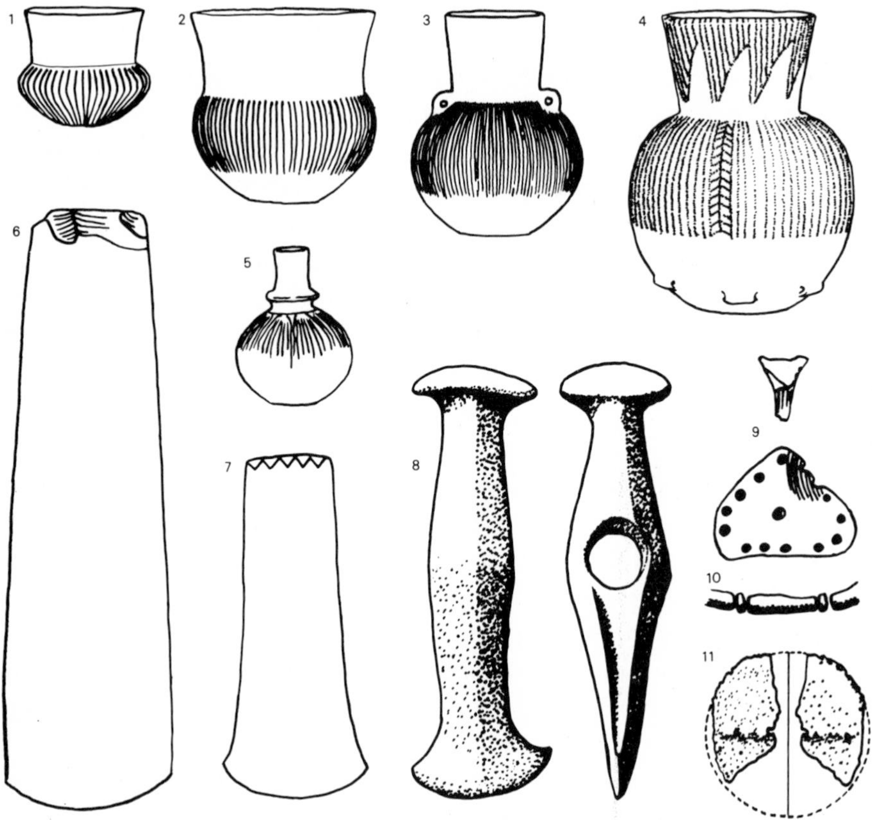

soils as in central Jutland, but still more by extending the geographical range of farming. Thus battle-axes of boat-axe form are to be found in Norway concentrated in the agriculturally richest parts of the country, namely the lands either side of the Oslo Fjord, Rogaland in the extreme south-west and the Tröndelag. In south Sweden, where in the local Middle Neolithic farming had been concentrated on restricted areas of lime-rich soils, boat-axes are now distributed much more widely over the country up to the margin of the deciduous forest in Uppland and small colonies were even sent at this time as far north as the coastal zone of Västerbotten. East of the Baltic Latvia and much of Esthonia were taken in as well as the extreme south-west of Finland. Even more extensive gains were
163 made in European Russia where farming was introduced for the first time to the southern taiga as far east as the Oka and Upper Volga basins, the focal area of the Fatyanovo style.

Farmers and hunter-fishers

Scandinavia and north Russia

The spread of peasant economy over the greater part of Europe during the later Stone Age was accomplished in part by the acculturation of the local Mesolithic populations but in large measure also through the expansion of population made possible by the successful prosecution of farming. The formation of better organized communities and the sheer weight of numbers stemming from a more secure basis of subsistence ensured the domination of the new economy. Although the peasants concentrated first on the richest and most tractable soils, they must at the same time have exploited, though in a much less intensive fashion, the wild resources of the surrounding territory, very much as happened down to modern times over much of Fennoscandia. A continuing process of acculturation may be presumed to have occurred along the margins of the new advancing economy. We have already seen how the occupants of caves in north Italy and the south of France acquired the arts of potting, cereal growing and herd maintenance during the fifth millennium while maintaining an ongoing tradition of flint-working. Early in the fourth millennium the hunter-fisher population of Denmark and adjacent parts of the North European Plain acquired the idea of potting and began to make the ware named after the midden site of Ertebølle in Jutland, large coil-built jars with pointed base, and oval lamps. About the same time the forest dwellers of European Russia acquired the art of making coil-built pots probably

from the Aral region. They made simple egg-shaped forms lacking
163, 167 handles which they decorated in horizontal bands by comb-
71 impressions and pits. Similar pit and comb ware continued to be made in various forms throughout the remainder of the Stone Age and often later over vast tracts of the Russian taiga, in Finland, the East Baltic states and beyond.

Although the peasant economy soon prevailed over the territories into which it was introduced, its advance was limited by climatic factors. In territories proximate to the ecological limit of prehistoric farming, defined more or less by the northern limit of the deciduous forest in Fennoscandia and by the frontier between the southern and middle taiga in European Russia, the situation was less clear cut. In south Sweden for example farming was dominant only during the third millennium on the most favourable soils, notably the lime-rich coastal moraine of Scania and the carboniferous limestone region of Västergötland. Elsewhere it was secondary to 'Mesolithic' activities such as seal-hunting, fishing and elk-hunting. As we have seen it was not until the Late Neolithic spread of battle-axes that the new economy extended its grip over south Sweden as a whole, advanced into south-west Finland and spread over much of the southern taiga in European Russia.

Beyond the northern frontier of the deciduous zone the great tracts of birch and coniferous forest and tundra, extending from Norway to the Urals, were only capable of supporting an economy based fundamentally on catching and foraging. Such an economy, enriched through sharing in the markets created by settled life further south, prevailed in essentials down to modern times. The emphasis laid on particular aspects of the food-quest varied according to local circumstances. On the Atlantic and Arctic coasts of
225: 109–75 Norway line-fishing for cod, ling and haddock was, as it still remains, of key importance during the winter months when they come closest to the coast. At this time of the year families congregated in settlements strung out along the shore and lived in houses built for warmth, semi-subterranean with low walls of earth faced with stone, tunnel-like entrances and roofs of sods supported on timber or whale-bone. During the summer groups broke up into smaller family units and moved into the interior to hunt and take salmon from the rivers. In Norrland and Finland the seasonal rhythm was different. There the winter was spent, at least by the active men, hunting elk and trapping birds and fur-bearing animals in the snow-covered interior. The most important source of food in the spring was seals,

principally the harp and ringed species. On the Swedish side of the Gulf of Bothnia this was followed by fishing for salmon and whitefish, first as they congregated in early summer off the mouths of the rivers and later as they passed upstream to spawn.

The ability to conduct line-fishing for cod and allied fish and at the same time to pursue the small toothed-whales depended on easily manoeuvred boats. To judge from many representations on the
72 Norwegian rock-engravings, these were skin-covered craft like the Eskimo *umiak* or the Irish curragh. Conversely with the primitive weapons available elk could most successfully be hunted by speeding

71 Finland: artefacts from the Arctic Stone Age.

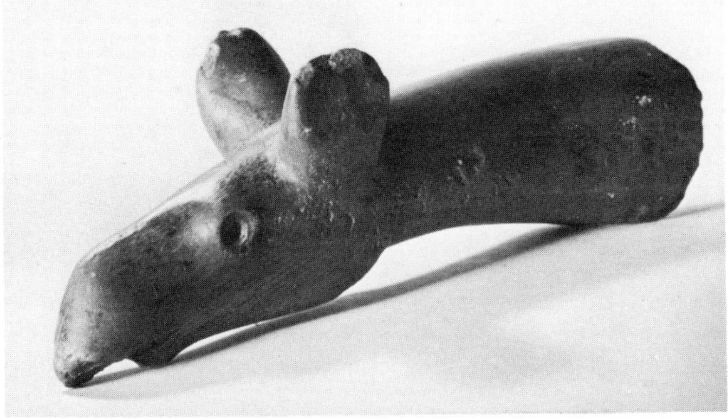

72 Rock-engraving, Zalavrouga, Russian Carelia, showing elk hunters mounted on skis and armed with bows.

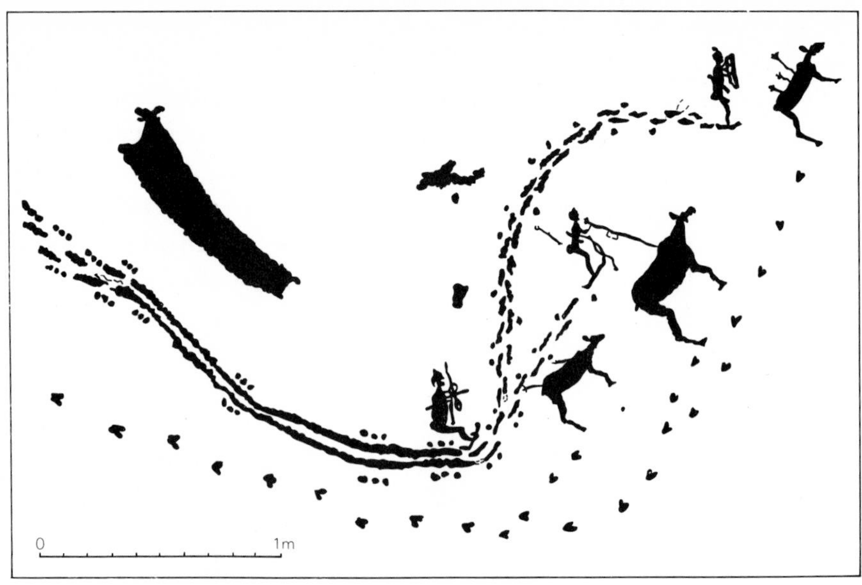

73 Snow-travelling gear from the Arctic Stone Age of Scandinavia: (*upper*) 'Arctic'-type ski with stick, Kalvträsk, Västerbotten, Sweden; (*lower*) runner (3.17 m long), Kuortane, Finland, and reconstruction of sledge.

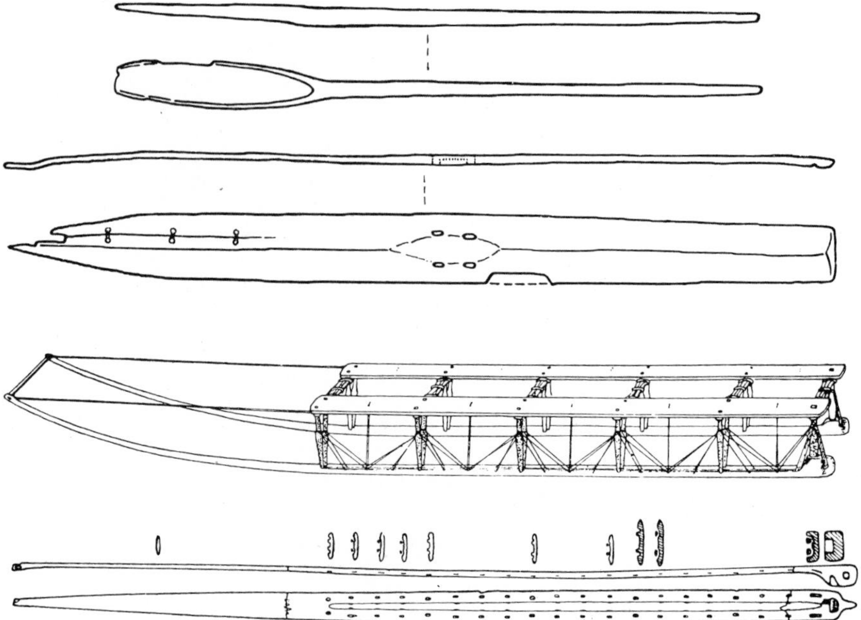

over the snow on skis. Similarly the carriage of elk meat and the pelts of furred animals during the period of snow cover was accomplished by the use of sledges drawn by dogs. Thanks to many finds from bogs
73 it is known that skis and ski sticks were available at this time as well
152: 293–301 as sledges. These were up to 3·5 metres long and had platforms supported on vertical struts set in grooves on the upper surface of the runners to which they were secured by sinews. The use of snow-travelling equipment makes it easy to understand how it was that sledge-runners and duck-headed wooden ladles of identical form should occur as far apart as Finland and the Gorbunovo bog in the mid-Ural region. Again the availability of snow and water transport facilitated the dispersal of scarce materials. South Scandi-
74 navian flint axes found their way to Norrland and across to the west coast of Norway which also received amber from east Prussia. Likewise axe-heads of green slate from factories at Olonets on the west shore of Lake Onega were distributed over much of Finland and the East Baltic states, a testimony to the web of obligations which knit together the populations of extensive social territories.

The scale of some of the cemeteries – that at Olen on Lake Onega contained over 150 individual graves even though partly destroyed – also points the same way. The wealth of grave goods and the fact

74 Hoard of adze blades of west Baltic flint from Bjürselet, Västerbotten, Sweden.

that the dead were apparently buried in their expensive skin garments fringed and embroidered with perforated animal teeth suggests an economy at least as effective in its own terms as that practised further south by farmers. Another sign of well-being is a vigorous body of art, concerned in the main with the celebration of animals sought for food, notably elk, reindeer, bears, seals, toothed whales, fish and water birds. Some of its manifestations, notably the engraving on hard rock-surfaces by pecking and grinding of large-
75 scale outlines of animals, implied a considerable input of labour. Rock engravings, concentrated in Østfold, west and north-west Norway and Swedish Norrland, are almost certainly over-represented in relation to the rock-paintings which are so much more perishable and only survive in a desultory way over a territory extending from Norway to Finland.

Another outlet for artistic expression was the shaping of small artefacts into animal forms. The special interest of these is that they appear to indicate the extent of distinct social territories. Thus, the trick of carving elk heads on the handles of slate knives defines a province centred on Swedish Norrland but extending to the north-west coast of Norway; perforated stone mace- or axe-heads in the form of bear or elk heads are concentrated in Finland and Karelia; and flints flaked into the profiles of a variety of animals occupy a territory centred on the Upper Volga basins with outliers on the Middle Volga and the White Sea.

75 Engraving of reindeer on steep rock surface by waterfall, Böla, North Trondelag, Norway.

4

Europe: from metallurgy to civilization

Early metallurgy

Before reviewing the adoption of metallurgy in particular parts of Europe it may be worth reflecting briefly on the context of this innovation in the attainment of civilization. The example of Middle America, where the Maya and cognate peoples developed what is commonly accepted as an independent civilization on the basis of a stone-using technology, reminds us that the practice of metallurgy was not a necessary hall-mark of this type of social development. Conversely, the change from a stone to a copper or even bronze technology was far from a guarantee of civilization. Thus in Europe civilization developed in a Bronze Age context only in the Aegean, whereas bronze technology spread to the limits of agricultural economy and even to a slight degree beyond. Over Europe as a whole literate societies first appeared among peoples equipped with an iron technology. Yet if bronze technology can hardly be reckoned a sufficient explanation for the rise of Minoan–Mycenaean civilization its requirements certainly played some part in its development.

The east Balkans

The first metallurgical industries to appear in Europe grew up by the beginning of the fourth millennium at a time when the peasant societies of the Aegean area were still restricted to a stone-based technology. They did so in a territory extending from the north shore of the Aegean to the Sava, Tisa and Prut rivers. Since this was adjacent to west Asia, where metallurgy had been established some time earlier, it has sometimes been assumed that its appearance in Europe can be adequately explained in terms of a simple process of diffusion from a more to a less advanced region. If today a fuller understanding of the ecology and dynamics of culture renders diffusion as an 'explanation' naive if not irrelevant, this is not to say that we can dismiss as coincidental the fact that the earliest centres of European metallurgy were those most accessible to contacts with western Asia. Contact has always been a major factor in stimulating innovation, and proximity in promoting contact. This does not alter the fact that the reasons why the inhabitants of the east Balkans adopted metallurgy are to be sought in local and regional circumstances, of which proximity to Asia is only one. The east Balkan people shared two advantages. One is that they had perfected their farming technique to the point at which they were able to settle permanently in the manner of the Asiatic tell-dwellers. Removal of the need to change settlements and clear new territories every few years for farming provided a platform for further advance, among other things in the field of technology. It was after all the occupants of tells who had first developed metallurgy in west Asia itself. The other great advantage enjoyed by the Neolithic peasants of the east Balkans was their occupation of a territory rich in both native copper and copper ores, not merely in the Transylvanian mountains but also in localities south of the Danube. In this respect they were more fortunate than the peasants of peninsular Greece, a country poorly endowed with copper resources.

Products of the copper industry included a number of forms,
76 notably flat axes, awls and pins with opposed spirals, that could have been made by hammering native copper, that is with no more knowledge of metallurgy than was possessed by the hunter-foragers
445, I: 261–4; responsible for the Old Copper culture which flourished about the
479: 75–6 same time in the Greak Lakes region of north America. On the other hand it has long been accepted that more complex forms, including perforated axe-hammers and axe-adzes, could hardly have been

76 Copper axes and axe-adzes, Hungary.

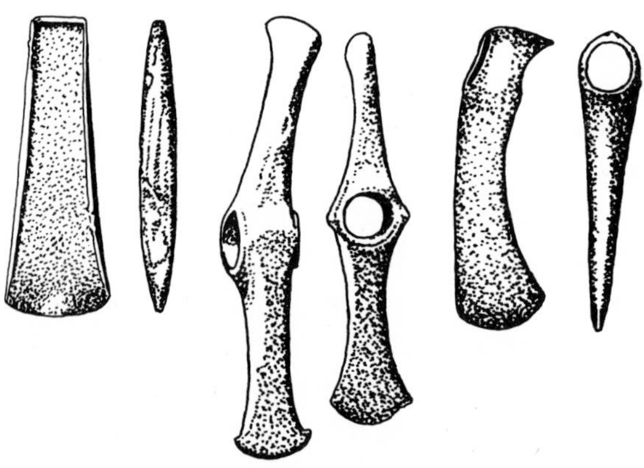

made in this primitive fashion. Recent research has shown beyond
181 question that these perforated forms had been cast in moulds before being subject to hammering and annealing. Moreover it has been pointed out that, although in some cases artefacts were made from copper so pure that it can only have been native, in others impurities were present to such an extent as to suggest that the metal had been smelted. The matter has recently been proved beyond doubt by the discovery at Rudna Glava in eastern Yugoslavia of mines dating from a period when Vinča pottery was still in use and which had evidently been sunk 20–25 metres deep to tap veins of chalcopyrites. What is implied therefore is a fully metallurgical industry based on an ability to mine and smelt copper ores as well as to utilize native copper, one moreover in which the principle of casting was known, including the use of cores for making the perforations. To judge from their pottery the people who carried on this industry were indigenous to the country: the Vinča C–D and Bodrogkeresztur wares made by them in Yugoslavia and Hungary appear to have stemmed from the preceding Vinča A–B ware; the Gumelnitsa pottery made by the chalcolithic inhabitants of Bulgaria and southern Romania was probably a development from Veselinovo ware; and the Cucuteni ware of north Romania evolved from the Neolithic Boian.

Much has lately been made of another attribute of the chalcolithic peoples of the east Balkans, notably the signs on Vinča C–D pottery and more dramatically on pottery roundels of uncertain age from Tartaria in Romania. The wealth of figurines has also been remarked. Yet before accepting these as pointers to civilization it is worth recalling that signs denoting some kind of notation stopping far short of writing as well as figurines were both current around a thousand generations earlier among the Upper Palaeolithic hunting bands of both east and west Europe. The most impressive fact, historically speaking, about the east Balkan peasants, apart from their early practice of metallurgy was their stagnation, something thrown into sharper relief with every backward extension of the date at which they began to work copper. By contrast the decisive advance towards the first civilization in Europe was made in Crete and peninsular Greece, territories comparatively deficient in copper resources and relatively late in adopting metallurgy.

Middle Europe

Before going on to consider the factors underlying the genesis of Minoan and ultimately of Mycenaean civilization it may first be convenient to review very briefly the early adoption of copper-working in some other parts of the continent where the metal occurred in nature. The occurrence of perforated copper axes of Hungarian type at the head of the Drava tributary of the Danube in Kärnten, Austria, is a pointer to east Alpine copper. The probability that this was being worked so early is suggested by the use of copper dagger-blades and flat axes among the otherwise 'Neolithic' makers of Mondsee pottery in the Salzburg region and adjacent part of Bavaria as also by the occasional presence of similar axes with Michelsberg pottery dating from the latter part of the Early Neolithic settlement of Switzerland.

Another and more important focus of early copper metallurgy in middle Europe was central Germany. The most easily diagnosed of the several sources of copper in this region is that from the Saalfeld district of Thuringia on account of the high silver content of its ores combined with the presence in lesser quantities of arsenic and antimony. Axes made from this ore entered into redistribution networks which carried them east to Silesia, south-west to the Rhineland and north over the plain of northern Europe extending during the final phase of the local Early Neolithic into Denmark and south Sweden. In this connection it seems likely that the flattening of the sides of flint axes in the north about this time may have been suggested by the form of the copper axes taken into use by the 'Neolithic' peasants.

Iberia

The Mediterranean formed an alternate, though subsidiary line of entry for metallurgy as for cereal growing. The earliest metallurgy on any scale in southern Iberia developed around 2400 B.C. in proximity to sources of copper in Almeria, Spain, and Algarve and Alemtejo, Portugal. It occurs in a basically indigenous context. The corbelled passage-graves and other forms of collective tombs carry forward a tradition already established in the same territories. The pottery from the tombs and defended sites like Los Millares and Vila Nova stems from plain wares of El Garcel type with close analogies in north-west Africa, and in this last connection it is worth remarking on the use of ivory for combs, dagger-pommels and small receptacles as well as ostrich shells for vessels. Again the flint industry, although enriched by new types, shows a continuing use of blades and of a form of triangular arrowhead derived from trapezes. It is further worth remarking the combination on the same pot of symbolic oculi and schematic representations of deer in a pre-Neolithic style. The metal objects themselves, including flat axes or adzes and chisels, daggers, curved knives and saws suggest that casting in moulds was practised and this is confirmed by direct evidence of metallurgical activity from actual settlements. A further indication of sophistication is that Iberian copper artefacts have sometimes been found to contain arsenic in proportions so high that it can only have been added intentionally as an alloy, a practice widely used in western Asia and the Cyclades, so that the development of bronze technology need no longer be thought of as conditioned by the availability of tin.

Greece and the Aegean

As already indicated peninsular Greece and the Aegean islands were comparatively late in developing a metallurgical industry of their own. There is no evidence that the rare metal objects found in 'Neolithic' contexts in this area were other than imports. The reason for this backwardness was not lack of example, since the Balkan province impinged on the north coast of the Aegean as the Troad did on the north-east. It was above all due to the relative scarcity of local copper resources whether native or in the form of ores. Conversely it was the poverty of the region in this respect, the need to remedy an environmental deficiency by the only means possible, that is by exchange, which more than any other single factor underlay its rise both socially and politically as well as economically to a level far beyond that of the better endowed Balkans.

The scarcity of metal objects from period I of what is con-
205 ventionally termed the Early Bronze Age in Greece, Crete and the Cyclades has often been contrasted with their relative abundance in the Troad, Lemnos and Lesbos. Troy I and II, Poliochni and Thermi the main centres in these territories each supported specialized smiths. These not merely smelted copper ores and cast them into flat axes, chisels and tanged daggers with marked midribs, but understood how to strengthen them by adding alloys. It is plain also that they had access to tin. Wherever they obtained their supplies – and there is no firm knowledge of the sources of the tin used in the Aegean world – it is certain that the metal was rare and only obtainable through an effective exchange net-work. The operation of such a net-work, which also brought other materials including gold, silver and lapis lazuli, as well as finished goods, combined with the marked advance in craft-specialization documented by fine jewellery, silver vessels and the introduction before the end of the period of

the potter's wheel, went hand in hand with a class differentiated from the various categories of artisan by status as well as social function. Treasures like those unearthed by Schliemann at Troy were symbolic of chieftains, predecessors, if remote ones, of Homer's Priam. The existence of leaders of this kind is further confirmed by the palatial scale of such a rectangular porched structure as that opposite the entrance to the city of Troy. The hierarchy of settlement witnessed by the existence of smaller centres and the trouble taken to defend the various capitals likewise confirms the existence of concentrations of wealth. Yet the scale of things in the Aegean world around the
81 middle of the third millennium was still modest. The first city of Troy covered a mere acre and a quarter and the second less than two acres. The limited scale and relative simplicity of the economies is also shown by the fact that they were able to function without writing or even seals.

During the second phase of the Early Bronze Age in this part of the world there is ample evidence for commercial activity between
77 the Troad, Greece, the Cyclades and Crete. As for the first three one
205, 206 might quote as one example the distribution of the two-handled *depas*
cup. Silver prototypes as well as pottery versions occur at Troy and pottery ones at other sites in western Anatolia as well as the north

77 Objects circulating within the Cycladic redistribution system in the Early Bronze Age: (*middle*) stone folded-arm figurine; (*above*) two-handled *depas* cups of silver and pottery; (*below*) sauceboats of gold and pottery.

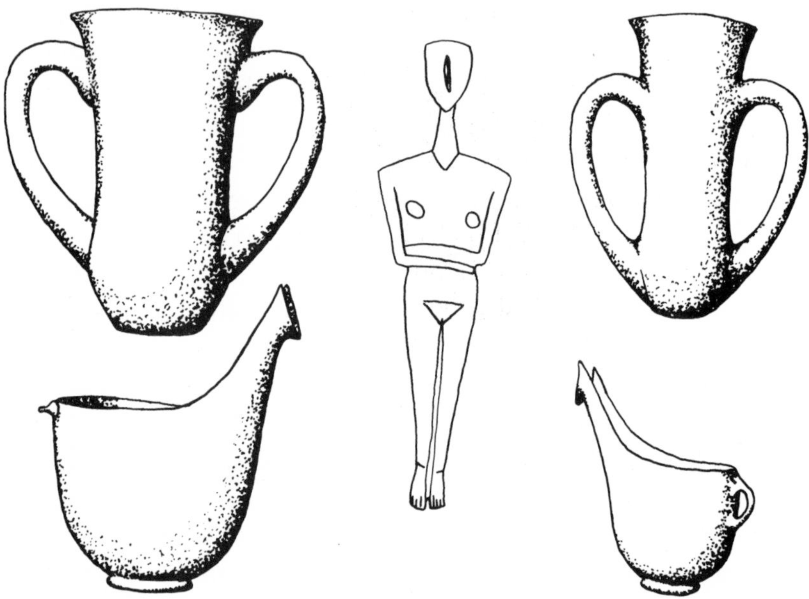

Cyclades and the Greek mainland. Another unusual ceramic vessel common to the three areas is the sauce-boat which also occurs in Early Helladic Greece in gold. A clear indication that exchanges were by now reciprocal is the appearance at Troy I of exotic coarse vessels, most probably containers of olive oil, one of which was stamped with a spiraliform seal of Early Helladic type. That Troadic forms reaching Greece were transmitted by way of the Cyclades is confirmed by the occurrence on the mainland of such a highly idiosyncratic Cycladic form as the ceramic fictiles of 'hour-glass' form. A clear sign that the islanders were maintaining close relations with Crete as well as Greece is the occurrence in both areas of stone figurines with folded arms, a type of Cycladic origin that was both imported and copied.

The rise of the Cyclades was due in the first place to their intermediate position between Greece, Crete and Anatolia. Another reason was the diversity of raw materials available on different islands – silver on Siphnos, copper on Paros and Siphnos, marble on Paros, emery on Naxos and obsidian on Melos – a diversity which involved the maximum degree of interaction between the islanders and their neighbours. Spectrographic analysis has shown indeed that Melian obsidian was being obtained – one can hardly say traded if

78 Representations of Bronze Age boats of the Aegean: (*left*) rowing galleys incised on Cycladic pottery 'frying-pans'; (*right*) sailing vessels engraved on Minoan seals.

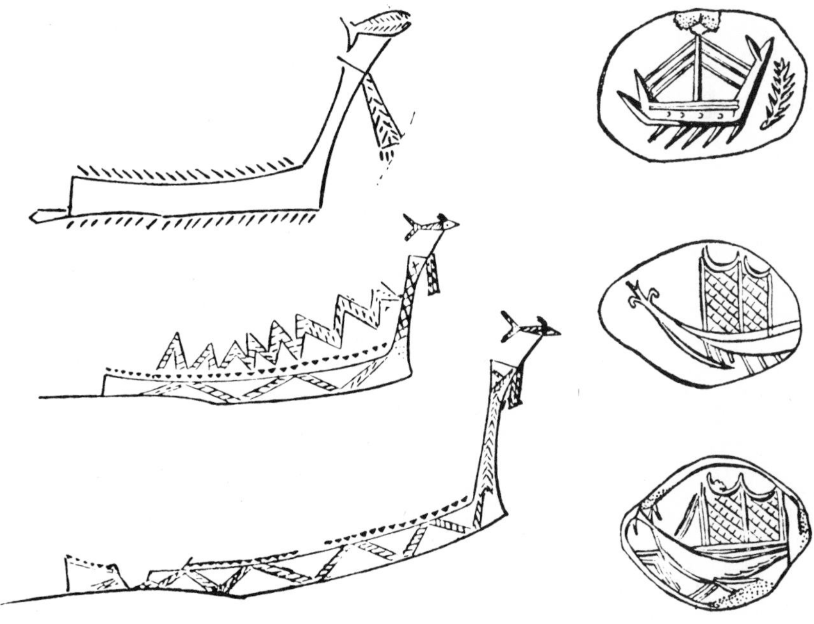

the island was uninhabited at the time – as early as the sixth millennium when it was being distributed to territories as far afield as Crete, Thessaly and west Macedonia. The Cyclades were thus known before most at least of them were inhabited. The fetching of obsidian from Melos is a reminder that as the colonization of Crete must already have made clear, navigation in the Aegean goes back at least to *c.* 6000 B.C. Of the craft themselves no direct evidence survives, but even in Early Neolithic times the vessels must have been large and stable enough to transport families and livestock as well as
78 mariners. From the Early Bronze Age there are two iconographic sources, incised designs on fired clay artefacts and models of lead and fired clay. These show long boats with upturned prow. Sails apparently did not come into use until the Middle Bronze Age in Crete. Previously oars were the only means of propulsion. This was a time of intense coming and going between Greece, the Troad and Crete with much of the traffic stopping to pick up or discharge cargo in the Cyclades, a time in which skills and ideas as well as materials and products were interchanged, leaving all manner of stimulus and profit in the hands of the middle-man. So long as they were at the heart of the web of redistribution in the Aegean the Cycladic islands enjoyed a period of prosperity and cultural achievement
195 all the more remarkable that many, Saliagos near Antiparos apart, remained uninhabited in Neolithic times. With so much wealth passing by it would be surprising if piracy, endemic in these parts down to recent times, had not already begun. The defences erected during the Early Bronze Age were probably, like their more recent successors, set up with sea plunderers in mind. By the same token when the Minoans established their hegemony during the Middle Bronze Age they did so in part through naval power. According to the legend of Minos, the king of Knossos was not only ruler of a hundred cities but lord of fleets that swept the seas.

If by the second phase of the Early Bronze Age the Cycladic islanders were riding a boom by controlling commercial net-works linking west Anatolia with peninsular Greece and Crete, it was the inhabitants of these latter territories who created the civilization which engulfed not merely the Aegean, but much of the east Mediterranean. Each controlled land areas sufficient to produce subsistence for relatively dense populations with enough to spare to feed craftsmen and other specialists and each inherited peasant populations fortified by an experience extending over three millennia.

Table 16. *Sequences in Greece and Crete*

B.C.	Egyptian synchronisms	Greek periods		Written records
		CLASSICAL		Literature, history
750				1st Olympiad 760
		GEOMETRIC		Alphabet
900				
		PROTOGEOMETRIC		None
1100				
	Bronze sword (cf. 4, Mouliana, Crete) from Nile Delta: with cartouche Seti II (d.c. 1200 B.C.)	HELLADIC LH IIIC MYCENAEAN CIVILIZATION	MINOAN	
1230				
	Mycenaean pots, Ahiram tomb, Byblos: Ramesses II (d.c. 1232 B.C.)	IIIB	LM III	
1300				Linear B script
	Mycenaean pots at Tell el-Amarna (*c.* 1370–1350 B.C.)	IIIA	PALATIAL MINOAN	
1400		II	II	
1500				Linear A script
		I (Shaft-graves)	I	
1580–50				
	MMII pots, Egypt: Middle Kingdom (XI–XII dyn.) scarab forms, Crete	MH III II I	MN III II I	Seal hieroglyphs
2000/1900				
		EH III II I	EM III II I	None
3000/2500				
		NEOLITHIC		
6000				

193, 204 The use of the terms Early, Middle and Late Minoan to denote the main divisions of the entire Cretan Bronze Age although consecrated by long use is in a way unfortunate. The social system which supported the fabric of Minoan civilization first began with the opening of the Middle Bronze Age between 2000–1900 B.C., a period marked in the archaeological record most plainly by the appearance of palatial architecture. Again, Minoan civilization in effect gave place to Mycenaean with the final destruction of Knossos marking the transition from Late Minoan II to III between 1400 and 1375 B.C. The
216 change from small and modest village communities like Myrtos to the palace-centred hierarchy of the Minoan civilization proper
198 was rightly categorized by R. W. Hutchinson, a former Curator of

79 Plan of Late Minoan township of Gournia, Crete.

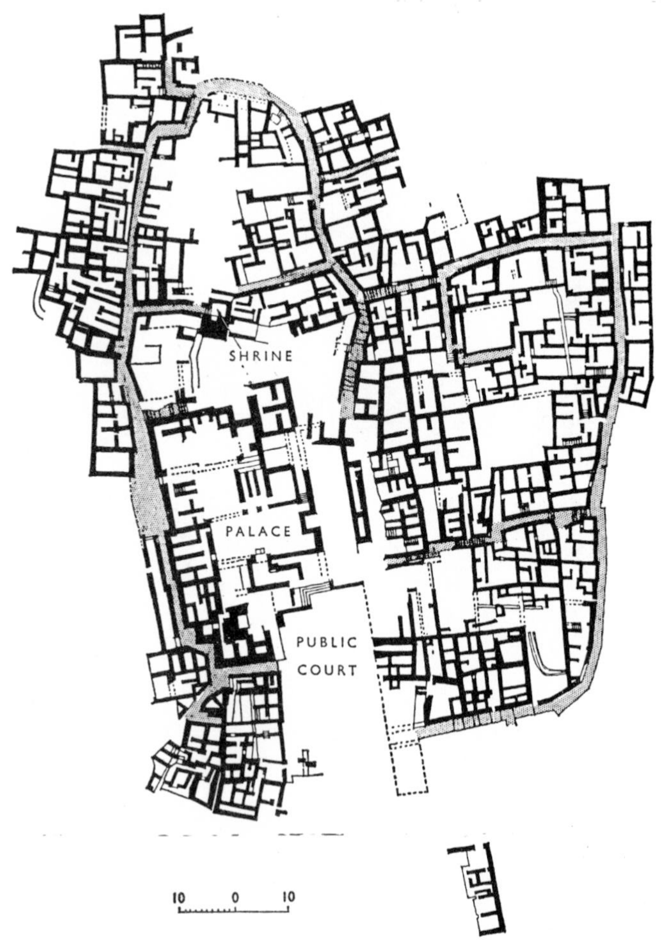

Knossos, as one of 'startling rapidity'. Several of the preconditions were already there during the Early Bronze Age. The domestication of the olive and the vine not merely increased the returns from land, but also multiplied the processes and skills required in production and processing as well as adding commodities of great importance for exchange. Again, the practice of metallurgy was of extreme moment in stimulating both the sub-division of economic functions and in some decisive areas the redistribution of raw materials. These developments along with the stimulus brought by commercial activities were alone enough to strain the old subsistence economy to the point at which it was easier to replace than reform. The new system arose above all to ensure an adequate distribution of products and services. The new classes and organizations which this called into play in turn gave a powerful thrust to the process of social differentiation and interaction.

79 Over and above small townships like Gournia with its streets, its craftsmen-potters, carpenters and metal-smiths, its olive presses and

80 Late Minoan Palace, Knossos, Crete.

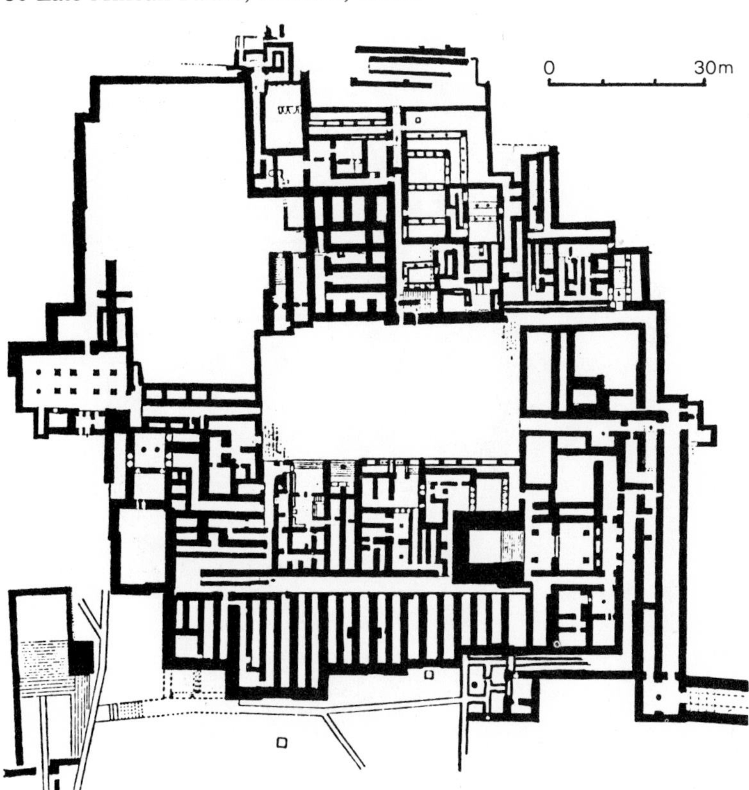

its shrines, Minoan Crete supported cities of which the most conspicuous and significant institutions were the large monumental
80 palaces. The Minoan palaces served as the economic, religious and socio-political centres of the most productive territories of the island. In the north Knossos tapped the extensive low lying area, on which the present capital, Heraklion, is sited, and further east Mallia drew upon its own separate tract. Phaistos on the south of the island concentrated and redistributed the produce of the rich Mesara plain. All of the palaces were provided with well laid out magazines for storage. The western one at Knossos held over 400 large storage jars
81 or *pithoi*, estimated to have had a cubic capacity of between 60,000 to 120,000 litres. Olive oil, which played a significant role in cooking, lighting and cleansing and was an important export product, was certainly one of the main materials concentrated in the palace magazines, but it is likely that wine and perhaps cereal grains were also assembled and stored at these centres. The task of assembling, accounting and disbursing this wealth called for a means of record,

81 Storage jar (1.43 m tall) from Minoan palace store, Knossos, Crete.

and the three kinds of writing known from Bronze Age Crete were apparently used solely for bureaucratic purposes and almost entirely in the context of palaces.

The earliest inscriptions dating from the beginning of the palatial period were brief, mainly on seals and clay sealings, and were written in hieroglyphic characters. The first linear script – Linear A – appeared on clay tablets dating from the close of the Middle Bronze Age and to judge from the fact that it used only a third of the hieroglyphs may be presumed to have been substantially a local development. The one thing we can be sure of about the language spoken by the people who used this script is that it was not Greek.
89, 191 As we now know, the people who devised Linear B on the other hand were Greek speakers. Yet they employed some two-thirds of the signs used in Linear A. These two facts have recently been elegantly reconciled by supposing that illiterate Greek speakers gained control of Knossos during the fifteenth century B.C. and, needing to maintain the palace records, were constrained to adapt the older script to accommodate their mother-tongue. As we learn from the Linear B texts, both from Crete and later from the Mycenaean mainland, they were concerned almost entirely with inventories of stores, produce, livestock and workers. Writing was not yet a vehicle for literature. It was solely part of the bureaucratic apparatus used in Minoan Crete and later in Mycenaean Greece for controlling the concentration, processing or storage, as the case might be, and distribution of produce and artefacts. That is why, when the intricate socio-economic system of the Aegean world disintegrated around 1200 B.C. under the impact of piracy and barbarian inroads, writing disappeared in this part of the world until the Greeks borrowed and adapted the Phoenician alphabet during the eighth century B.C.

One of the most noticeable features of the Cretan palaces and cities, by comparison for example with the situation on the Troad, the Cyclades or mainland Greece, is the absence of defensive works. This tells us two important things about the Minoan polity. It shows how effectively the island as a whole was shielded from piracy by the navy. Equally it points to peaceable conditions within Crete. Both point to a unified polity with a strong central leadership. Knossos was the only palace with a throne-room and unlike the others it was set about with the kind of villas for the rich and powerful one might expect to find at the centre of government. If this is so palaces like Mallia and Phaistos could be thought of as administrative centres for their respective territories, visited from time to time by the ruler.

The palaces also served in many other capacities. Among other things they were workshops at which were concentrated the specialist craftsmen required to make luxury goods for the court and foreign exchange. Prominent among the crafts practised at a site like Knossos would have been gem-cutting, ivory carving, faience manufacture, jewellery, silver-smithing, bronze-working, the making of stone vessels and the manufacture of fine painted pottery. In addition the construction, repair and replanning of the palaces themselves in-
82 volved the work of skilled masons and fresco painters. Several of the specialized crafts, more particularly those concerned with luxuries and insignia of rank, involved the use of metals and other materials either absent from or scarce in Crete itself. This is a reminder that the islanders drew upon a social territory embracing not merely the Aegean world but much of the east Mediterranean as well. This in turn went hand in hand with more effective sea-transport and in particular with the addition of sails, an innovation documented by Middle Minoan seal-engravings. Since the mariners of this time were unable to tack they had to take close account of prevailing winds. Reliance must almost certainly have been placed on the Etesian winds which blew fairly constantly and often strongly from the north during

82 Fresco painted on palace wall, Knossos, Crete.

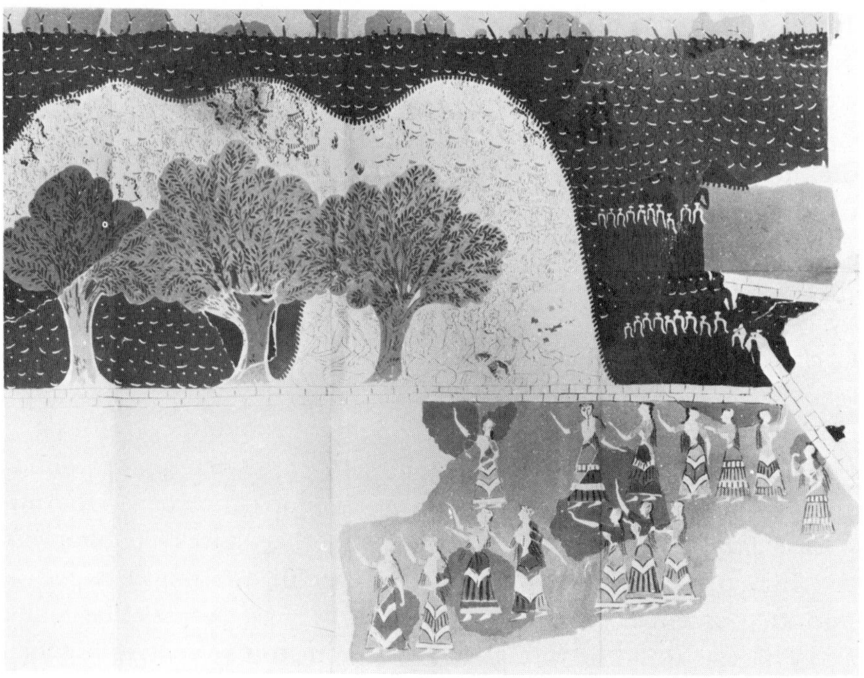

83 The Mycenaean world.

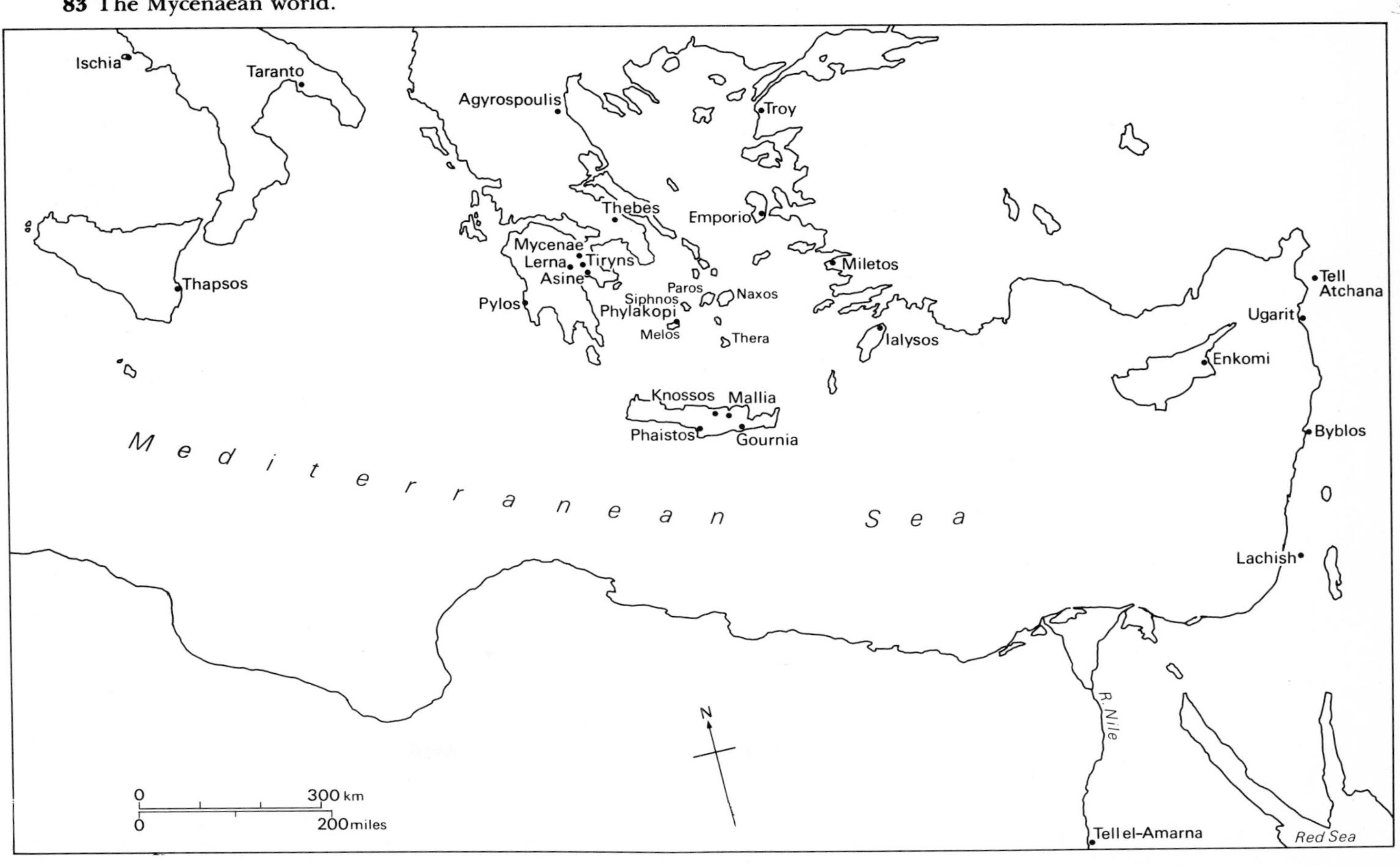

the summer months. Mariners could sail rapidly before these to Egypt and then catch them abeam to sail up the Levant coast and west again by Cyprus to the Cyclades and home. The cargoes carried in such craft belie the old idea that Minoan civilization was little more than an amalgam of Egyptian and west Asiatic elements. On balance the Minoans imported raw materials, though they certainly took a trickle of Egyptian exports, and exported their own distinctive manufactures, something easy to verify from Egyptian tomb paint-
84 ings and imports. Far from being a poor relation from a cultural
144, 146 point of view of Egypt or Syria, Minoan Crete was strikingly independent, an exporter whose products can immediately be distinguished in alien settings.

84 Mycenaean trade: man carrying ox-hide copper ingot and Minoan vase depicted on Egyptian tomb-painting at Thebes.

85 Minoan cult of the dead depicted on sarcophagus from Hagia Triada, Crete. Priests and priestess carrying offerings of animals and blood. Note the lyre and double axes mounted on pillars topped by birds.

The style of Minoan civilization was indeed unique. The fact that the Minoans were able as we have seen to focus resources from a wide range of territories through their command of the sea meant that they were able to live free of foreign pressure by virtue of their navy. They were spared the need for large armies expensive to maintain and too often associated with despotic rule. A spirit of liveliness and freedom blows through their art, whether this took the form of frescoes or was applied to pottery or metal-work. Depictions of flowers, sea-food or human beings have a spontaneity which proved immediately attractive when they first impinged on the modern consciousness. The decorative arts, as well as dancing and
85 the music of conch, lyre and double pipes played their part in religion as well as daily life. The religious aspect of Minoan life also differed radically in style from that of Egypt or Sumer. In place of large monumental temples the Minoans worshipped at small shrines either incorporated in domestic buildings or scattered over the
203 countryside in caves, on mountain tops or at the sources of springs. Even shrines designed for more public purposes like that facing the central court of the palace of Knossos comprised no more than two or three rooms screened from the worshippers. Among the furniture commonly found in Minoan shrines were snake goddesses, doves, sacral horns and double axes. Boxing and bull vaulting, though probably religious in origin, were also spectacles which like art, religion, ceremonial and games helped to maintain the cohesion of communities in which economic and social functions were increasingly specialized.

200 Another factor making for social cohesion was the care taken over the dead. In Crete, as in the Mediterranean as a whole, the central idea was collective burial over the generations in communal ossuaries. During the third millennium burials were inserted into natural caves or circular ossuaries built of drystone walling. The Middle Bronze Age saw the cutting of burial chambers with short passages in soft rock formations and the practice of cramming human skeletons into storage jars or clay coffins. During the Late Bronze Age collective tombs with ashlar-lined chambers might be constructed on even ground, but vaulted chambers of the same type as Mycenaean *tholoi* were also built into hill-sides and approached by passages.

Attention has of purpose been concentrated on Minoan civilization as a working system which retained its basic form over a period of around half a millennium. The palaces themselves more than once suffered damage if not destruction. During the latter part of Middle

Minoan II those at Mallia and Phaistos as well as at Knossos were severely shaken apparently by seismic disturbance, perhaps, as has been claimed, coinciding with earthquake disasters identified in the stratigraphy of the Levant around 1730 B.C. Another phase of seismic disturbance has been linked with the explosion of Mt Thera and the submergence of the Late Minoan I town of Santorin about 1500 B.C. under a thick blanket of ash and pumice. The intrusion of Greek speakers inferred for the fifteenth century left no structural trace at Knossos. Indeed according to the hypothesis followed in respect of Linear B they went to the length of inventing the new script in order to continue running the administration on its existing lines.

Mainland Greece

As we have already seen the latter half of the third millennium witnessed a quickening of the old peasant societies and the occupation for the first time of certain islands largely under the impact of the adoption of metallurgy and all that this implied in territories ill-supplied with metal. The concentration of wealth and power in

86 Royal shaft-graves enclosed in stone circle at west end of the citadel at Mycenae, Greece.

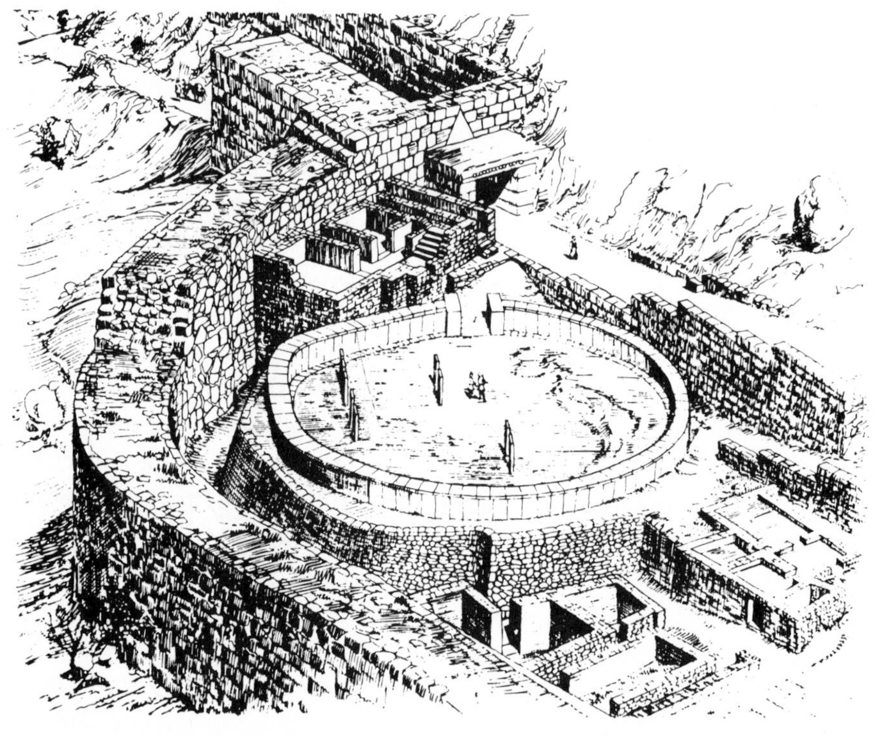

the hands of chieftains which went with increasing specialization and a greater intensity and range of social interaction found architectural expression, for example in the third phase of settlement at Lerna in the Argolid, in defended citadels containing halls of palatial size.

The continuation of this process cannot yet be documented in detail for the Middle Helladic phase, but it reached a recognizable
86 climax in the shaft-graves at Mycenae. Situated on an easily defended
199 spur commanding the route between the Gulfs of Argolis and Corinth and well supplied with fresh water it is hardly surprising that this site should have attracted an important settlement already by Middle Helladic times. Before the end of this period a leading and presumably by this time princely family or clan had acquired sufficient status for its burial area to be marked off from the generality of graves by a circular wall (Grave Circle B). This practice continued during the following period to which belonged the Grave Circle A excavated by Heinrich Schliemann, the discoverer of Mycenaean civilization. The wealth and status of the family or clan buried in this circle dating from the latter half of the sixteenth century B.C. is shown by the scale of the tombs, by the veneration they were accorded in later times and by the richness of their contents. Each of the six vaults of Grave Circle A consisted of shafts lined with dry-stone walling to bear a timber roof. They were large enough, up to 4·5×6·4 m, to hold from two to five bodies. Above ground they were marked by carved stone stelae. The veneration in which they were held is shown by the fact that, when several generations later the settlement on the hilltop was enclosed, the wall was bayed outward to enclose the grave circle which was itself defined by a new and imposing stone wall.

The contents of the vaults bear witness to the princely status of

87 Combat scene on gold seal from shaft-grave III, Mycenae. Note the thrust over the shield to the throat.

the dead, as well as to the by now highly differentiated society over
87 which they presided. The dominant impression is that of a ruling
clan characterized by wealth and warrior qualities whose splendour
is reflected in their armament, their drinking vessels and the embossed gold diadems and earrings of their women, not to mention
89 their death-masks of beaten gold. The men wore conical helmets
made of plates of boars' tusks, themselves symbolizing prowess in the
hunt. They carried daggers, swords and spearheads and sometimes
88 rode in light horse-drawn chariots with four-spoked wheels. As if to
emphasize the status of the warriors their weapons were enriched
by precious materials: swords might have ivory pommels and gold-
bound hilts embossed with running spirals, and dagger-blades be
embellished with scenes inlaid by gold, silver and niello. Drinking
vessels included gold and silver rhytons in the shape of bull, sheep
or stag heads. Further to emphasize the link between hard drinking,
princely status and fighting, a fragmentary silver rhyton depicts a
spirited attack on a citadel by helmeted warriors. More will be said
214 later of the specialized skills embodied in Mycenaean products.
Meanwhile it should be noted that even at this early stage the
craftsmen were using in bulk, materials, both for weapons and ornaments, that must have come from overseas. In addition they utilized
motives derived from the more sophisticated civilization of Egypt
either as a by-product of trade or possibly even as a result of mer-
cenary service. Even more pervasive were influences from Minoan
Crete visible for instance in the figure-of-eight shields depicted
on a dagger-blade, the gold Vaphio cup reproducing pottery vessels
of Middle Minoan origin and metal rhytons recalling the steatite

88 Hunting deer by bow and arrow from four-spoked chariot: scene on gold signet ring from shaft-grave IV, Mycenae.

89 Gold funeral mask from shaft-grave V at Mycenae. This was the mask attributed by Heinrich Schliemann to Agamemnon.

prototype from Knossos. Yet the most important thing about the men
89 who stare out of the death-masks is that they were mainlanders,
descendants of the Middle Helladic people and forebears of the late
Mycenaeans. Although still illiterate they already spoke Greek,
something which makes it easier to understand how the traditions
embodied in the Homeric writings survived to draw Schliemann to
Mycenae and Tiryns.

Archaeology has shown that with the fall of Knossos *c.* 1400–1375
B.C. the Mycenaeans assumed leadership in the Greek world. It is
important to be clear about the nature of this leadership. To speak
of a Mycenaean 'Empire' during the Late Bronze Age would be to
risk misunderstanding. Mycenaean society was certainly geared to
produce warriors and by means of ships the Greeks were able to bring
force to bear when and where it was needed. Indeed it was because
of this that they featured in the archives of more highly developed
societies bordering the Mediterranean, as the Ahhiyawa of the Hittites, or the Island Peoples or Peoples of the North of New Kingdom
Egypt. Yet their power was commercial and cultural rather than
military. At home the Mycenaeans found it necessary to eliminate
Thebes, but in general they were content to live as citizens of one
of several realms even within the narrow territory of Greece. Less
188 than eighty miles to the west the lords of Pylos ruled over Messenia
from a palace hardly inferior to that of Mycenae itself. Again, many
petty realms contributed to the Catalogue of Ships given in Book II
of the *Iliad* with Pylos contributing almost as many as Mycenae.

It is seldom possible to determine how far the degree of uniformity
in ceramic styles from southern Italy to the Levant was due to trade,
fashion or colonization. What is certain is that the fall of Knossos
removed a barrier to the expansion of Mycenaean influence which
even before this had led to settlement on Rhodes and the appearance
of trade goods at Miletos on the west coast of Anatolia. The expansion
of Mycenaean influence in the west during Late Helladic III times
is marked by the appearance of characteristic pottery on Sicily and
210 Ischia, by settlement at Taranto on the heel of Italy and possibly
even by the import of amber of ultimately Baltic origin and the
transmission to central and western Europe of faience beads. To the
east the evidence is more impressive. This is hardly surprising since
many of the most important raw materials needed for weapons and
display came from that direction, copper from Cyprus, ivory from
Syria and gold probably from Nubia. The wealth of Mycenaean products found at Akhenaten's city of Tell el-Amarna (1379–1362 B.C.)

is a neat converse to the earlier impact of Egyptian art on inlaid dagger-blades from shaft-graves at Mycenae. Exports of this kind may have helped to pay for Nubian gold. Finds at Askalon, Gaza and inland at Lachish, and others further north at Haifa and Ras Shamra (Ugarit) at the terminals of trade routes from the coasts of Palestine and Syria point to the source of ivory and probably also of other more perishable products including textiles which may have carried exotic art motives such as the opposed griffins appearing on Mycenaean ivories. The great increase of Mycenaean influence on Cyprus at this time may well reflect a growth in imports of copper from this source in the form of ingots of ox-hide form like those recovered from a ship wrecked off Cape Gelidonya, south Turkey. On their side the Cypriots grew in wealth sufficiently to trade with the Levant on their own account and compete successfully with mainland Greece.

Although the structure of Mycenaean society retained many features already documented in the shaft-graves, several aspects are
90 known more fully from this later period. The Linear B tablets from
189 Pylos, Mycenae and other Late Mycenaean sites confirm the fact of social stratification and go some way to defining social classes. At the head of each realm was a *wanax*, prince or king, who might be assisted by a leader (*lawagetas*). Next came the king's followers (*hequetai*) who held their lands on a quasi-feudal footing in return for renders in kind and service in war. Below them were workers, including artificers and land-workers. At the bottom were slaves. The political structure of Mycenaean Greece is reflected in the small size and close spacing of strongly defended citadels at sites like Tiryns,
91 Asine, Gla, Midea, Mycenae on the mainland, Phylakopi on the island
201, 208, 211 of Melos and Troy II on the Asiatic mainland. The walls of such citadels averaging around 4½ m, but sometimes as much as 6½ m thick, were filled with rubble but faced with Cyclopean stone blocks, so called because ascribed by the ancients to the Cyclopes, a race of one-eyed giants. The rulers' palaces took the form of rectangular structures entered by way of a shallow porch with post-holes either side of the entrance. Passing through an inner antechamber the

90 Linear B tablet from Pylos, Greece. Length 165 mm.

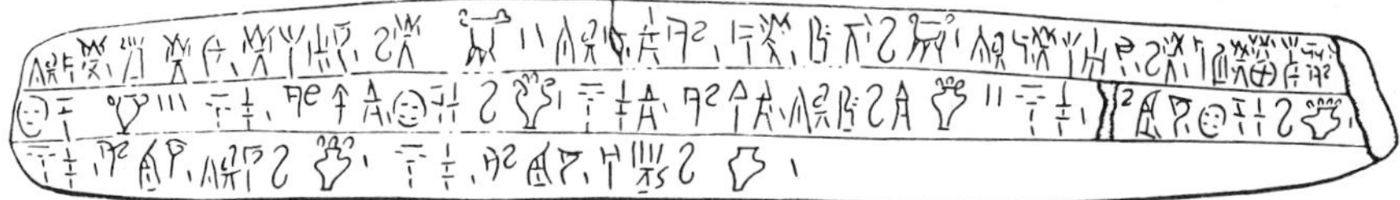

91 Bronze Age citadels in the Aegean area, each enclosing a megaron; (*left*) Tiryns; (*right*) Troy II.

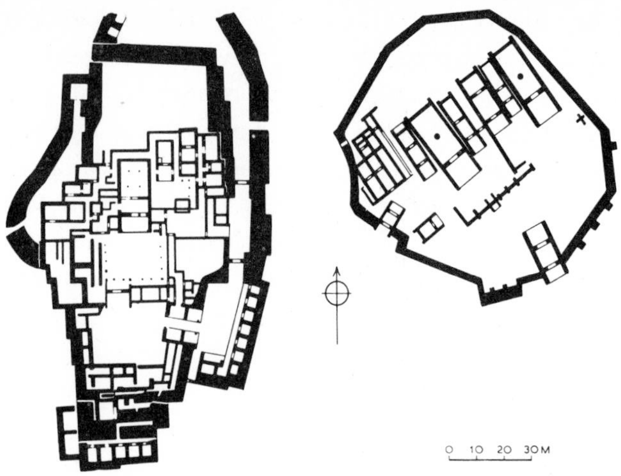

92 The Treasury of Atreus, Mycenae.

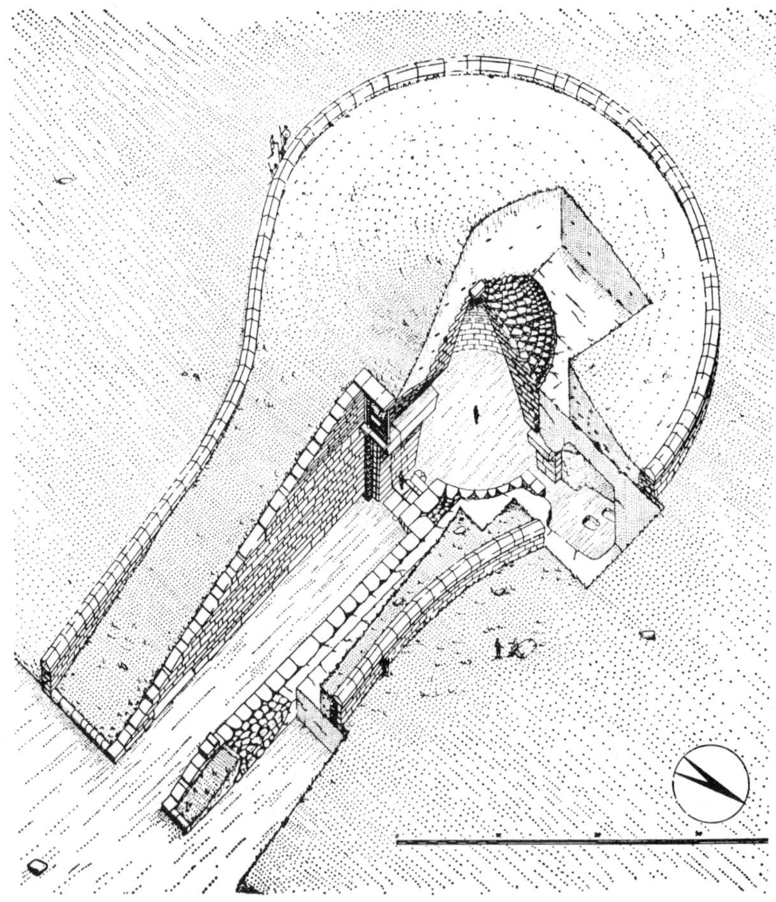

visitor reached a large hall or megaron with posts at each corner and a throne on one wall opposite a central hearth. Although the basic form of the megaron was Graeco-Anatolian, the finish, including the frescoes on plaster and the gypsum lining of entrances, were most probably derived, like so many other things, from Minoan Crete.

Tombs also reflect the nature of Mycenaean society. Whereas most citizens made do with rock-cut tombs, the ruling class built tombs with chambers resembling beehives in shape. The amount of work locked up in such structures suggests that, as with the pyramids of Egypt, the ruler commenced building his tomb during his life-time. The beehive tombs were remarkable for their size, finish and furnishing. All speak of majestic inequality. The chamber of the Treasury of
92 Atreus at Mycenae for example was nearly 15 m in height and diameter. It was approached by a grand entrance passage of sawn stone blocks and entered by a doorway nearly 5 m high capped by a lintel weighing a hundred tonnes and flanked by carved upright pillars. Only a few chamber tombs have survived intact. The beauty
93 and craftsmanship of their contents, as with tomb 10 at Dendra, testifies once more to the enhancement of civilization made possible by social hierarchy and marked inequality in the distribution of wealth.

93 Gold cup from chamber tomb 10 at Dendra, near Midea, Greece. Note the highly conventionalized 'sacral ivy' design and the double papyrus capital at the base of the handle.

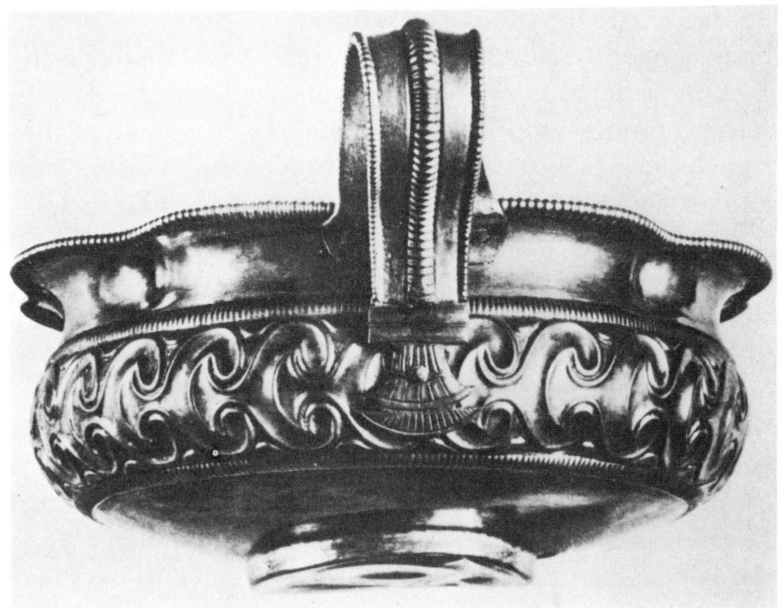

The earlier Bronze Age

The notion that bronze metallurgy first developed in central Europe under the influence of Mycenaean civilization can no longer be
181 sustained on chronological grounds. Even on straight radiocarbon dating the Únětice bronze industry of Czechoslovakia and adjacent parts of Germany was active by the nineteenth century B.C. and allowing for recalibration the true B.C. date must be earlier still. Despite the alternative of arsenic tin was of key importance. The northern part of the Únětice territory included highly important bodies of tin ores in the Fichtelgebirge and the Erzgebirge. The objection that these ores are particularly difficult to work and may have been beyond the capability of prehistoric man overlooks his ingenuity. As previously noted (p. 153) the mines recently found at Rudna Glava have shown that he was capable much earlier of obtaining copper from the difficult chalcopyrites ores. So it may have been with these tin ores. Alternatively it is possible that alluvial deposits, since exhausted, may once have been available. It is at least suggestive that a close correlation exists between early bronze industries and tin resources. The north Italian bronze industry is matched by the tin deposits of Tuscany, though admittedly it has not been proved that these were worked before the Etruscan period. The link between the bronze dagger industries of southern England and Brittany respectively and the alluvial tin of Cornwall and Morbihan can be accepted with more assurance. Whether the idea of adding tin to copper to make a tough alloy reached temperate Europe from outside is perhaps of less consequence than the fact that, once started, bronze industries could only be sustained by drawing tin from locally restricted sources or as was commonly done by adopting an alternative alloy such as arsenic. The more widely tin was adopted in adjacent territories like Hungary or south-west Germany the more vital the net-work of redistribution became. Archaeology shows that this extended far beyond the territories served by particular sources of tin. Close connections existed between Wessex and Brittany on one hand and north Germany and ultimately Únětician territory on the other. Even further afield the net-work extended to the Mycenaean world primarily in respect of exotic products, notably beads of amber and faience. Although a kind of amber occurs in the Mediterranean, physical tests have shown that much of that used by the Mycenaeans was of Baltic origin. This can only have reached the Adriatic by crossing Germany and passing through the territories of

the Únětice and probably also the south-west German tumulus culture. The presence in one of the earlier shaft-graves of amber spacer-plates perforated in the highly idiosyncratic fashion found on precisely similar objects from south-west German and Wessex barrows argues that some at least of the amber was imported in the form of beads. The passage of amber from Denmark to south and central Germany was almost certainly connected at the outset with the importation of finished metal tools and later of copper and tin to south Scandinavia, a territory lacking native sources of the key metals at least in a form in which they could be worked in antiquity. It is consistent with the idea that the bronze industries which sprang up first in central and western and later in northern Europe were to a significant degree independent, that Mycenaean influences are in the main confined to ornamental motives like the spiral and

94 Map showing spread of fashion of wearing segmented faience beads over Mediterranean and Temperate Europe. The metropolitan area in the Mycenaean period is enclosed by a broken line.

triskele designs found on antler and bone objects or on luxury prestige items like gold cups or bronze helmets. The commonest
283 novelties of east Mediterranean origin are beads made of faience, a composite product made of a cemented quartz core coated with a glass glaze mainly coloured blue by copper compounds. Although faience could be made locally wherever bronze smiths operated and the widespread segmented form of bead could easily be copied, it can hardly be doubted that the fashion and in many cases the beads
94 themselves stemmed from the east Mediterranean. The spread followed two main routes, by way of the Middle Danube and its tributaries to central Europe and by way of the Mediterranean to southern France, Brittany and the British Isles. Both routes converged ultimately on south Britain, and Wessex in particular, a territory which maintained close links at this time with Germany. The faience bead necklace from Odoorn in north Holland is in this respect significant because of its intermediate position. The fact that one of the segmented beads was made of tin only adds to its interest. Tin was evidently a potent magnet.

The bare existence of a European bronze technology, let alone the prosperity of the societies practising it, depended on the maintenance of redistribution net-works of some complexity, of which that relating to tin was only one. This and the degree of specialization inherent in bronze technology conduced to, though they did not of course demand, the emergence of a chiefly class. There are signs, though by no means conclusive ones, that this may have happened in parts

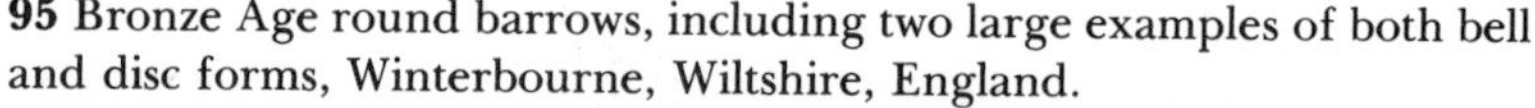

95 Bronze Age round barrows, including two large examples of both bell and disc forms, Winterbourne, Wiltshire, England.

96 Bronze castings of the best period of the Northern Early Bronze Age, comprising palstave, axe, spearhead, sword and neck ornament.

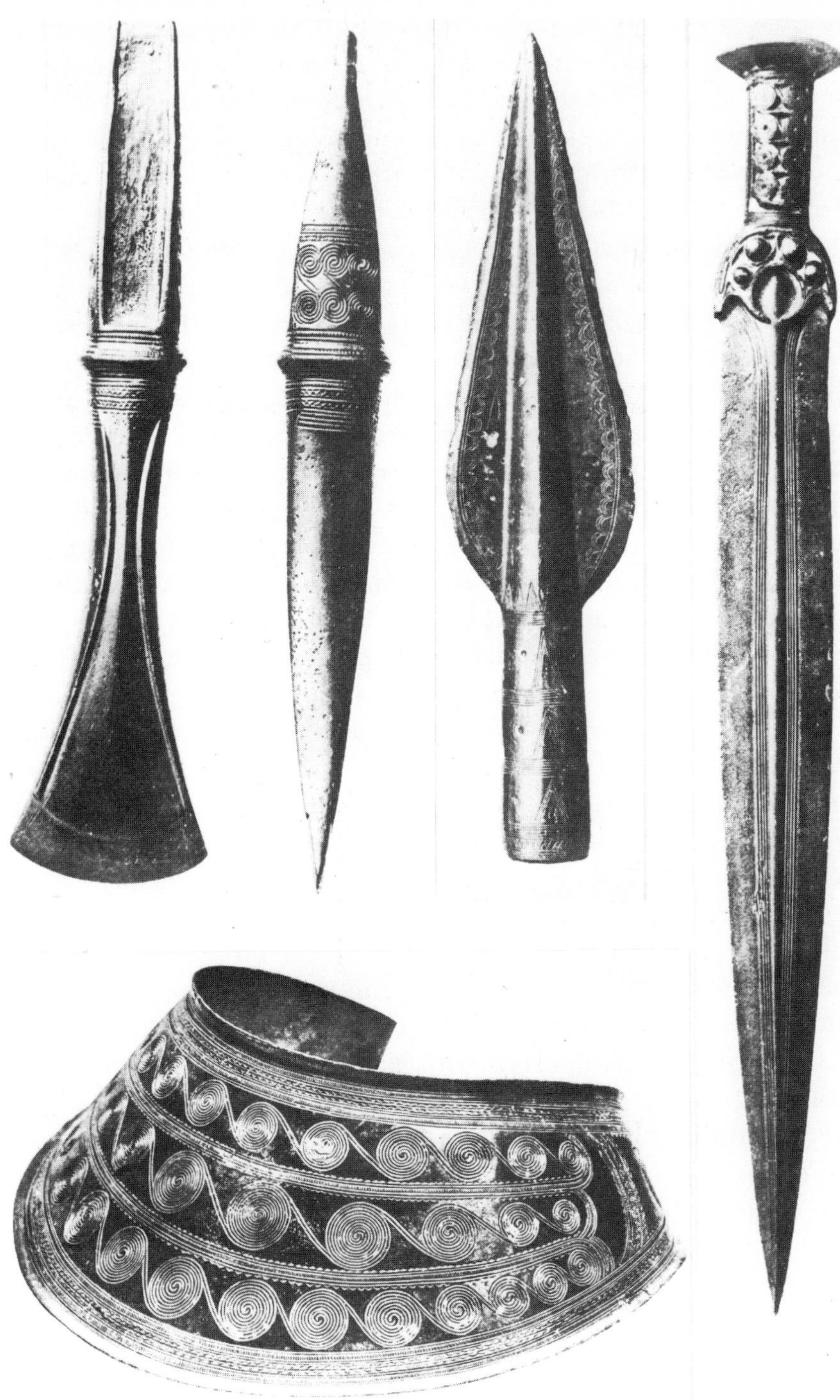

of Europe during the first half of the second millennium. The
95 construction of outstanding tombs – the round barrows of Wessex
are a case in point – and the provision of grave goods of a kind and
value outstripping the norm are two such indications. The emphasis
on daggers, a few with bronze hilts, others with ones of organic
materials sometimes studded by gold nails, points to a warrior status,
as do the bronze helmet from Beitsch or the occasional gold cups
like those from Rillaton or Fritzdorf. Wealth is indicated in outstanding burials such as the Únětician one of Leubingen with its
bronze daggers, halberd blade and axes and its gold arm-band, ring,
ear-rings and pins. Exotic objects or fashions, like the faience and
amber beads of the Wessex burials, are other symbols of superior
rank or social status which point in the same direction.

A point that can bear emphasis before leaving the Early Bronze
155: ch. 7 Age of temperate Europe is the sheer quality of some of its products.
The inhabitants of this territory may have been illiterate and their
polity had barely reached the level of incipient chiefdoms. Yet the
design and workmanship of their bronzes was hardly excelled by the
smiths of the Mycenaean world and so far as workaday objects were
concerned far transcended that of the products of Near Eastern, let
221: vol. II alone Egyptian, states of the period. This applies even to the products
of south Scandinavia, the latest territory to support an indigenous
bronze industry and one that depended wholly on imported raw
96 materials at this time. Even the bronze axes, let alone the daggers,
swords and personal ornaments of the earlier phases of the northern
Bronze Age are of quite outstanding excellence and quality.

A similar level of achievement can occasionally be matched in a
different sphere, for example in respect of the sarsen lintelled circle
and setting of trilithons, the altar stone and the bluestone circle which
240 constitute the third and early Bronze Age phase at Stonehenge.
Although puny by comparison with Sumerian temples and still more
with the great pyramids of Egypt – it comprised only *c.* 136 stones
by comparison with the 2·3 million incorporated in the Great Pyramid
of Cheops and a maximum height of only 7·3 m as against 146·6 m
– Stonehenge of course related to a community of quite another
demographic order. Yet in subtlety of design Stonehenge III, the
culmination of a thousand years or so of development, was in some
respects hardly inferior. Whatever dispute there may be on matters
of detail, the designers of Stonehenge must be credited with an
understanding of the movements of the sun and moon and a capacity
for prediction all the more remarkable that it rested on observations

unaided by the theorems of a later, more sophisticated age. From
a structural viewpoint one hardly knows which to admire more, the
skill in transporting and erecting stones up to 50 tonnes in weight
– the stones of the Great Pyramid averaged *c.* 2·5 tonnes – or the
nicety whereby the lintels of the sarsen circle describe a circle and
97 maintain so nearly a horizontal line on their crest.

The later Bronze Age

A commonly remarked feature of the later Bronze Age of temperate
Europe, corresponding broadly speaking to the Aegean dark age
between the fall of Mycenaean and the rise of Classical Greece, was
266 the widespread appearance of cremation cemeteries or urnfields.
These appeared first in Hungary, the Lausitz territory between the
Elbe and the Vistula, Lower Austria and the north Alpine area. In
due course they appeared south of the Alps in the Po Valley and
Latium where the Villanovan group emerged round about 1000 B.C.
261 on the basis of the earlier Appenine bronze-using population. The
prosperity of the Villanovans, displayed in such things as bronze
98 swords with antennae hilts, helmets, girdles, safety-pins and razors
resembling Danubian forms in style, rested to a significant extent on
the exploitation of Tuscan metal resources. In their practice of
urnfield burial they used pots decorated in Appenine style and
covered by cups or crested helmets, presumably those of the departed; or, alternatively, urns shaped like store-houses. The practice
of urnfield burial was apparently carried westwards by Celtic-speaking
peoples, crossing France and eventually reaching Catalonia during
the eighth century B.C. Perhaps it was the displacement of refugees

97 Stonehenge from the south-east showing the stone structures.

from the Loire that led to the rise of a distinctive school of bronze metallurgy on the Atlantic coast of Iberia, between which trading relations were apparently established with both Brittany and the British Isles. Close reciprocal relations were also established during the urnfield period between Britain, France and the Low Countries.

The other and more fundamentally significant feature of the Later Bronze Age is the evident cheapening of metal and the great range of artefacts for which this material was used. Associated with this were more advanced methods of mining. The best explored mines
99 are those of the Mühlbach–Bischofshofen area near Salzburg in
152: 189–92 the Austrian Alps, which tapped deep veins of copper pyrites. The miners had bronze-headed picks, but their main weapons were fire and water. Veins would first be attacked where they outcropped, but as soon as the miners had worked themselves into the hillside they were able to bring the fire to bear on the ceiling as well as on the rock immediately ahead. Very soon it would be necessary to build a wooden staging to carry the rock-waste and support the fires, and under this a passage would be left for the air currents needed to keep the fires burning and the atmosphere clear. By the time the workings had reached a practicable limit they might be as much as 160 metres in length and 30 metres in height at the entrance. Such a mine at the peak would probably have called for a labour force of some 180

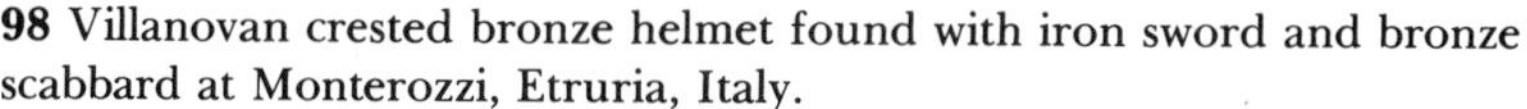

98 Villanovan crested bronze helmet found with iron sword and bronze scabbard at Monterozzi, Etruria, Italy.

men, a third of whom would have been employed on felling the wood needed for fuel and staging purposes.

Mining operations on such a scale greatly increased the supply of copper. Some of the metal was undoubtedly exported, to be incorporated for example in the products of the Nordic bronze-smiths in their splendid heyday; but the bulk was used by the Urnfield people themselves, either directly or for fabricating wares for export. Among the techniques first practised by Urnfield people in temperate Europe was the art of making buckets and cups from rivetted sheets of beaten bronze. Socketed axes, the idea of which may have originated in central Eurasia, were among the numerous forms to need core-casting. The cheapness of metal made it practicable to turn out an increased range of tools, and these included such things as chisels, gouges and saws, which in turn made possible notable advances in wood-working. The scale and number of the urnfields, the highly organized character of the extractive industries and the advanced standards of bronze-smithing suggest a dense population and a more productive basis of subsistence than that which sufficed for the earlier peasant communities of much of Europe.

99 Copper mining by fire-setting at Mühlbach-Bischofshofen, near Salzburg, Austria.

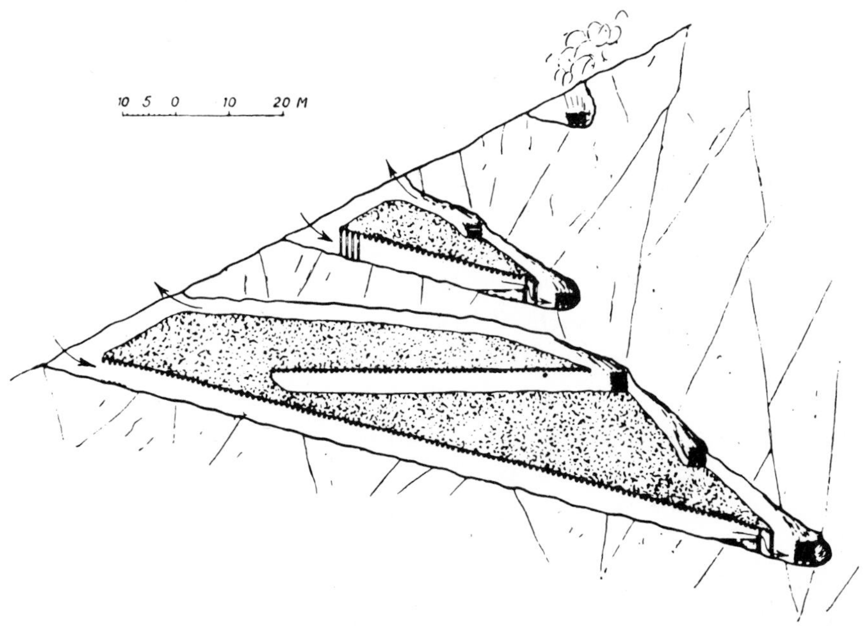

Breakdown and continuity

The signs of breakdown in the cultural and economic life of the Aegean area witnessed by archaeology are reflected in the historical records of neighbouring civilized powers and preserved in the oral tradition of the Greek people. Egyptian history tells of marauders from the sea and invaders from Palestine disturbing the peace of Ramesses III (*c.* 1198–1166 B.C.). Hittite records speak of enemies from without and rebellions within the empire. Indeed it was in the context of weakening Hittite power that the Mycenaeans were able to attack and sack the city of Troy (VII*a*) around 1200 B.C. in what proved to be the last phase of their own history. The time of troubles witnessed the breakdown of the stable political environment essential to the continued operation of the net-work of redistribution on which Mycenaean civilization rested. That is why the collapse when it came was so pervasive. The palatial economy could no longer function when the political framework in which it operated ceased to exist. Crafts like gem-cutting and masonry ceased abruptly. Nor should it occasion surprise that the system of accounting and record, including the Linear B script, should also have ended with the collapse of the system whose needs had called it into being. By the same token it is understandable that Bronze Age scripts should have survived on Cyprus which, because of its proximity to the Levant and its wealth in copper, remained within a viable net-work of redistribution and commerce.

Yet all was not lost. The age that followed the collapse of the brilliant but fragile Bronze Age Minoan–Mycenaean civilization was dark not only by contrast with what went before, but with what
190, 209 followed. The centuries during which Proto-geometric (*c.* 1100–900 B.C.) and Geometric (*c.* 900–750 B.C.) pottery was made were a time of gestation for the birth of a civilization which not only made possible the achievements of modern science, but also the very idea of history as we understand it today. Again, it would be wrong to underestimate the degree of continuity in Greece itself. If the Peloponnese witnessed the physical destruction of Mycenaean civilization, daily life in Attica, Boeotia and Ionia was less violently disturbed. The abrupt ending of literacy was of much less consequence than might appear, since as we have seen the script was little more than an adjunct of a particular economic system. The literature of the Mycenaean age as distinct from mere accounting was oral and for this reason able to survive the destruction of the material fabric.

If proof were needed one could point to the fact that when Homer composed the *Iliad* he was able to draw upon the resources of folk memory going back at least to the time of the Trojan war. The thread that drew Schliemann to Hissarlik and Mycenae had never been broken. Again, the mythology of classical Greece with its gods on Olympus subject to Zeus is basically Mycenaean in conception just as the temples themselves derived ultimately from the megaron prototype.

Iron technology

The most significant innovation from a technological point of view was the adoption of iron technology. The suggestion that on account of its greater ubiquity and cheapness it favoured a more democratic order is one of those pseudo-Marxist generalizations that does not bear examination. The decline of patriarchal kingship in most Greek states at the end of the Geometric period was followed in many cases by tyrannies on the Asiatic model. Looking ahead to the classical period Macedon under Philip II or Alexander was as firmly based on iron technology as ever had been the Athens of Pericles. The importance of iron is that its great abundance and cheapness allowed it to be used for tools in a great variety of trades and occupations. The idea that Greece owed iron-working to Dorian speaking invaders from the north can be disproved on chronological grounds alone. To the classical Greeks the traditional home of iron-working, in the

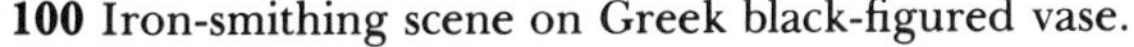

100 Iron-smithing scene on Greek black-figured vase.

sense of the extraction and forging of telluric iron as opposed to the utilization of rare pieces of sidereal iron from meteorites, was situated near the south shore of the Black Sea. Hittite records suggest that the process had already been developed by the fifteenth century B.C., but so long as the empire held together it seems that, on account of its military value, the process was a closely guarded secret. Its spread into neighbouring territories did not occur until the weakening of Hittite power around 1200 B.C. In the west iron working was adopted in Palestine during the eleven to twelfth centuries and by the tenth the metal was so cheap that it was used for such basic agricultural equipment as hoe-blades, ploughshares and sickles. The Greeks of
101 the Protogeometric period obtained iron daggers and swords and soon after the technique of iron-working from the Levant and west

101 Protogeometric cremation burial with iron sword, spear-heads, axe-heads, chisel, knife and horse-bits, Agora, Athens, Greece.

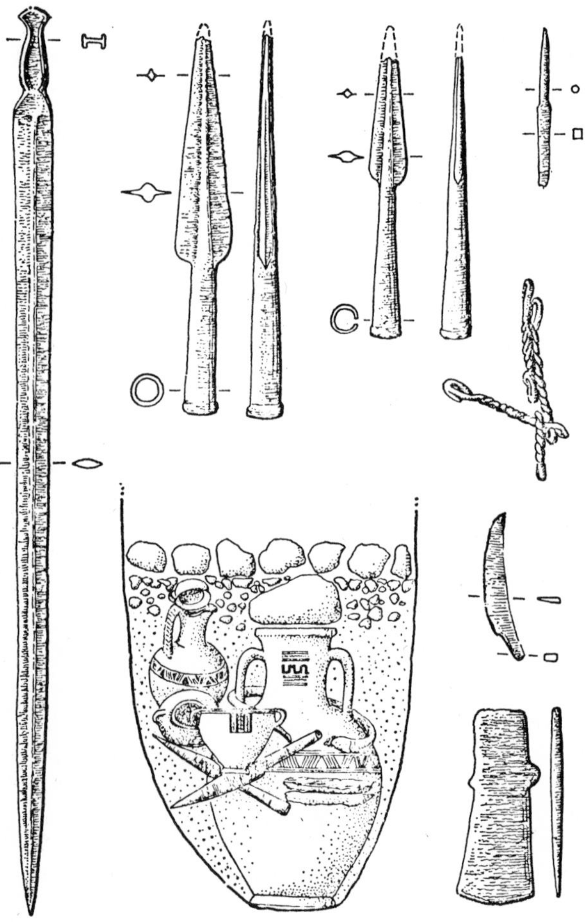

Anatolia. Central Europe on the other hand did not begin to acquire the new technology until the seventh century B.C. and then from a quite different quarter. Iron working had spread east from the Hittite world to Iran and also north-east across the Caucasus to the Koban where it was established by the eleventh or tenth century B.C. The suggestion that the craft spread to central Europe from this quarter by way of the Pontic zone is supported by abundant finds of horse-bits and harness furniture of Cimmerian style from the Middle Danube basin and from north of the Alps. During the early part of the first millennium iron-working was carried by Greek and Phoenician colonists to the islands and shores of the north and south Mediterranean.

Alphabet

If iron-working was important at a material level, it was the adoption and adaptation of the Phoenician alphabet around the beginning of the eighth century B.C. that made possible the fashioning of a vehicle for abstract thought and literature, which alongside the visual arts were the principal contributions of the Greeks to the heritage of mankind. The first alphabetic script in which each symbol stood for a particular sound was probably devised for a Semitic language somewhere in the Levant. Such a script was certainly in use among the Phoenicians by the eleventh century B.C. and prototypes are known from the earlier half of the millennium. In adopting the script from a territory with which they had enjoyed close trade relations since the Mycenaean age, the Greeks found it convenient to adapt it to suit their own language. Their most notable innovation was to introduce symbols for vowels as well as for consonants, a change which made it an altogether more flexible instrument. The power of the new alphabet was soon manifested in Homer's feat of reducing folk memories of the Mycenaean siege of Troy to the literary form of the *Iliad*.

Greek and Phoenician colonization

In spite of their possession of iron neither the Greeks nor the Phoenicians were able to support increases of population on their own narrow lands. The only outlet was colonization. In this they were rivals. The Phoenicians sailed due west. They secured control of the narrow passage between the east and west basins by planting colonies at Carthage (814 B.C.) and Urtica in north Tunisia, on Malta and at Motya in west Sicily. Beyond the strait of Gibraltar they founded settlements at Gades (Cadiz) and on the Atlantic coast of Morocco at Mogador. By planting colonies at Nora at the south end of Sardinia and on Ibiza they improved their grip on the west Mediterranean. Yet they failed to prevent the Greeks from gaining footholds at Massalia in Provence (*c.* 600 B.C.) and fifty years later at Emporion (Ampurias) on the coast of Catalonia. Meanwhile the Greeks had gained control of southern Italy from Calabria to Naples and of much of Sicily, territories reached centuries earlier by their Mycenaean forebears.

In the Black Sea the Greeks had a free hand. During the eighth century B.C. Ionian Greeks began to explore the north coast of Asia Minor and in due course trading posts were set up at Trebizond and Sinope, probably for shipping iron, copper and gold from Transcaucasia. Perhaps it was the adventures of these pioneers which nourished the legend of the Golden Fleece. During the next hundred years exploration extended to the west and north shores of the Euxine. The fish that abounded in the rivers of south Russia, the Bosporos and the Sea of Azov were traded either dried or preserved in jars. Salt could conveniently be prepared in the estuaries. Honey and wax were products of the region known to Herodotus. In addition to its value as a source of food and metals the Black Sea offered scope for settlement on its shores. Among the most prosperous colonies on the west coast were Apollonia and Mesembria and on the north Olbia at the mouth of the Bug and Tanais at the head of the Sea of Azov, both of which were in contact with the Scyths. Thus by around 600 B.C. the Greeks and Phoenicians between them had brought the Black Sea and the Mediterranean within the sphere of civilization. The impact of this on the native peoples of the interior, Thracians, Scyths and the like is manifest not merely in the Greek treasures buried in their tombs, but more interestingly in the stimulus given by exotic contacts to their native metal-workers and other craftsmen.

The barbarian world in the pre-Roman Iron Age

It is now the moment to take stock of what was going forward among the barbarian peoples of Europe beyond the limits of the Greek world. The Italian peninsula will be dealt with in a later section. We may here look first to the Celtic world in successive phases and then turn to the Scyths of south Russia.

Hallstatt

The Later Bronze Age Urnfield people had already begun to acquire iron as a precious or ornamental substance very much as the Mycenaeans had done during their final phase. The beginning of the
153: III.1 Hallstatt iron age proper dated from the seventh century B.C. when iron-working was introduced from the east. The most conspicuous feature of the period was the appearance of rich burials in timber chambers under burial mounds very much in the style of the Scyths and their relatives in the Altai. Apart from the insight they give into aspects of technology the main interest of these rich burials is the light they throw on social structure. As already suggested there are certain hints that something in the nature of chiefdoms had already begun to emerge in parts of temperate Europe at an earlier phase of the Iron Age just as they had done much earlier in Bronze Age Greece. The evidence for the Hallstatt phase is much more fully documented, more especially in the cortical area of Austria, Bavaria and Bohemia. The four-wheeled waggons recovered from certain tombs remind one vividly of the funeral carts described by Herodotus in connection with the burials of Scythic leaders. Grave goods and other finds reflect conspicuous consumption and display by members of a warrior class. Helmets, shields and greaves were made of bronze and sheet bronze was used to make several kinds of vessels. Even swords, though commonly with iron blades, might be made of bronze for display. Certain warriors at least rode horses, but there is no proof that they used them for true cavalry fighting; it could well be that they treated them, as the La Tène and other early charioteers did their vehicles, as means of transporting warriors to the most advantageous point for ground combat. In any case their ability to ride, which they doubtless owed to impulses from the steppe, enabled them to spread fairly rapidly over the old Urnfield territories in the west, down the Rhine to the Low Countries, into the Alpine area and across France to northern and central Iberia. In an opposite direction elements of Hallstatt culture appeared in several distinct Urnfield groups, among them the Lausitz culture, regarded by Polish prehistorians as the basis of the Slav people; the east Alpine, occupying much of the Middle Danube basin; and the Bosnian, extending over much of Yugoslavia south of the Sava and the Danube. The wealth of personal armament and protective armour leaves no doubt that the period was one of warlike activity. This is confirmed by the
252 construction of great hill-forts like the Heuneberg near the head-
102 waters of the Danube or the smaller but still impressive ones of

102 A British hill-fort: Herefordshire Beacon, Malvern, England.

remoter areas like Britain. The brick bastions of the defences of the Heuneberg are of special interest because they display a technique of fortification developed in the Greek world. Timber fortresses of the kind erected in marshes like Biskupin in Poland offer further evidence of violence. Yet how far the spread of Hallstatt types was due to mere fashion, how far to raids by warriors and how far to anything like folk-movements are problems which need to be considered on their merits in particular cases.

During the final phase of Hallstatt culture, defined by short swords
and beginning around 500 B.C., the centre of gravity seems to have
moved west, and it was then that Greek influence, stemming from
the colony at Massalia and passing up the Rhône and across to the
Upper Rhine and Danube, began to play directly, at least on the
upper classes of Celtic society. The most numerous imports from the
264 Greek world were concerned with wine-drinking, which seems to
have been taken up by Celtic chieftains almost as a symbol of status:
amphorae, still retaining traces of the pitch commonly added to wine
in the Mediterranean down to the present day, pottery wine-cups,
bronze mixing-bowls and flagons of Rhodian type combine to give
a convincing picture of a trade symbolizing an influence that was
to do far more than transform the drinking habits of the Celtic
aristocracy.

La Tène

During the last quarter of the fifth century a new art style, taking
its name from the famous votive find of La Tène at the eastern end
153: III. 1, 275–6 of Lake Neuchâtel in western Switzerland, came into being in the
territory between the Upper Danube and the Marne. Many elements
of La Tène art are most easily explained by the breakdown of
254, 263 Classical Greek motifs like the tendril and the palmette (an ornament
with narrow divisions somewhat resembling a palm-leaf), in the
hands of craftsmen schooled in the geometric Hallstatt style. Some
of the earliest vehicles of Greek art to reach the area in question
103 were bronze wine-flagons with beaked spouts, manufactured in the
Etruscan workshops of the Po Valley, but carrying Greek patterns
on the handle-attachments, which crossed the Alpine passes in the
course of trade; it was not until the conquest of the Po Valley by
Celtic-speaking people and the inauguration of Cisalpine Gaul
around the middle of the fourth century that contacts with Italo-Greek
art proceeded on a broader front. The fantastic treatment of animals
or parts of them was on the other hand almost certainly derived from

103 Bronze beaked wine flagon, probably made in Etruria, from Somme Bionne, Marne, France.

104 Bronze mirror from Holcombe, Uplyme, Devon, England, engraved in late provincial La Tène style.

the Scyths, immediate neighbours of the Hallstatt peoples in east central Europe. Celtic society was organized on an aristocratic basis and the finest products of La Tène art flashed in bronze or gold on the helmets, shields, spears, scabbards, harness-mounts, lynch-pins and terret-rings (driving rein rings) of warriors, their horses and
104 their chariots as well as on the heads, limbs, clothing and mirrors of their women; but some of the basic motifs were reflected in the work of humble potters and wood-carvers. From its original focal area La Tène art spread east into the Danube Valley, where was probably
105 made the silver vessel found in the bog of Gundestrup in Denmark, south into Cisalpine Gaul and west and north over France, the Low
243 Countries and the British Isles. Over the whole of this territory it continued to flourish until replaced by Roman provincial culture

105 Panel from the silver bowl found at Gundestrup, Denmark.

within the advancing frontiers of the Empire; and on the far north-west perimeter of Europe, in Ireland and the highland zone of Britain, it continued to survive until much later historical times.

During the prehistoric La Tène period the Celtic peoples of Gaul and Britain borrowed much from their more civilized contemporaries in the south. Thus, the revival of chariots was almost certainly due to contacts with the Etruscans. Again, during middle La Tène times the rotary lathe, used mainly for working wood and shale, reached south-west Germany from north Italy, where it had been introduced by the Etruscans, and from there spread widely over temperate Europe. The rotary quern, invented in the Graeco-Roman world for large-scale milling by means of donkeys and slaves, was introduced to barbarian Europe in the portable form used by legionary troops. The native coinage developed in Gaul stemmed from two main sources: the gold coinage was modelled on Macedonian staters; and the silver one on coins of Massalia and the Western Greek
106 colonies. The appearance of native coinage in Gaul, and in due
236 course in southern Britain, marked an important advance in political consciousness and organization and it is significant that the late La Tène period also witnessed the development in Gaul and south Germany of the considerable fortified townships or *oppida* described and in some cases stormed by Caesar.

The Scyths

An element in the make-up of Europe to which reference has already been made in connection with the early spread of wheeled vehicles to the west is the contribution of peoples adapted to life on the steppes. In addition to their positive role in contributing to the diversity of European culture these peoples also played a key part in

106 The earliest native British coinage and its Greek prototype.

the destruction of the Roman Empire. Reference has already been made to the role of the Cimmerians in the transmission of iron-working to central Europe. Attention may now be given to their successors on the Pontic steppe, the Scythic people who came into contact with the Greek cities on the north shore of the Euxine and
107 in the Caucasus absorbed important influences from Iranian art.

The Scyths were adapted to the steppe grasslands bounded on the north by the forest, on the south by the Euxine and east of the Volga
175, 176, 182 by the desert. They thus occupied a natural corridor linking the northern margins of China with the Altai, the southern Urals, Caucasia and the southern Ukraine, along which nomad horse-riders could move rapidly. Moreover, the fact that the nomads depended for their bare existence on the natural pastures of the steppe meant that pressure at any one point was liable to involve progressive displacements of population over vast territories.

To gain a living from the steppe called for a highly specialized knowledge of animal husbandry and a notable degree of cultural adaptation, notably in riding, clothing and habitations, so it is hardly surprising that well-defined nomad groups did not make their appearance until well into the first millennium B.C. One of the first indications dates from the end of the ninth century, when forerunners of the Huns began to harass peasant cultivators in the frontier lands of north China, and it may well have been the driving of these raiders to the west by the Chou emperor Suan that set in motion the widespread displacement of nomad groups which brought the Scyths

107 Scythic animal art of the 6/7th century B.C.: a gold shield-ornament depicting a lioness and displaying Iranian influence in the enamel inlay, from Kelermes, Kuban, Caucasia.

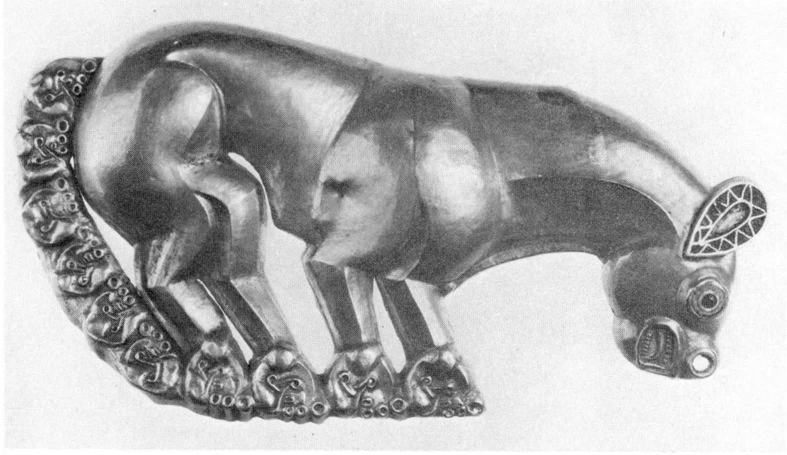

to south Russia, probably around 700 B.C. Although mainly concentrated in the south Ukraine and the Kuban, the Scyths penetrated
in some numbers into Hungary, where they formed immediate
neighbours of the central European Celts, with whom they appear
to have intermixed in Hungary and Transylvania. The Scyths were
pre-eminently nomads: by the fifth century B.C., it is true, some
groups in contact with settled peoples had adopted agriculture and
even occupied townships on the Dnepr and in the Crimea; but the
overwhelming proportion were at home on the open steppe. There
they subsisted to a large extent on mare's milk and cheese, helped
out by game and fish. Ever on the move from one pasture to
108 another, the men rode on ponies, on whose harness they lavished
the best materials and the most skilled craftsmanship, and the women
and children travelled in waggons under the shelter of felt roofs. It
is likely that when stationary they lived in felt tents which, to judge
183 from the frozen tombs of the Altai, where such things survived in
a wonderful state of preservation, had wool-pile rugs and brightly
worked wall-hangings. Leather, wool, felt and fur provided materials
for clothing, which in the case of men included soft boots, trousers
for riding, jackets pulled in tight round the waist to allow maximum
freedom in the use of the bow while in the saddle, and conical hats.
They wore plenty of jewellery, and bronze mirrors of Greek manufacture or copied from Greek models were common possessions.

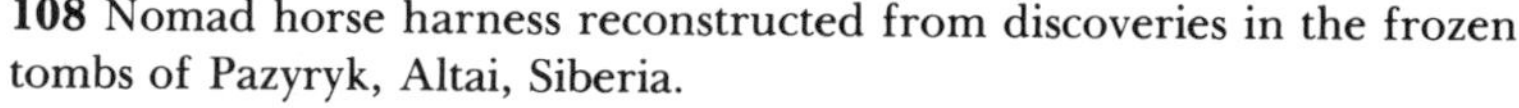

108 Nomad horse harness reconstructed from discoveries in the frozen tombs of Pazyryk, Altai, Siberia.

A notable feature of Scythic culture was the decorative art manifested in metal belt-plaques, harness-fittings, scabbards, dagger-hilts, drinking-vessels and jewellery and also in wood-carving, leather- and felt-work and even tattoo marks. Although much of the metal-work was executed by alien craftsmen and though the art derived elements from south-west Asia and Ionia, Scythic art was essentially barbaric in style and feeling. It was animated above all by a lively feeling for animals – stags, goats, lions and birds of prey prominent among them – such as one might expect to animate men who spent much of their life in the open and for whom hunting was a main interest. Yet there is a strong tendency towards stylization: the artist sometimes combined several aspects of a single animal into one representation, or he might use parts of one creature, such as the head and beak of a bird of prey, to enrich a representation of another quite different one; nor did he hesitate on occasion to contort and manipulate the beasts to conform to some decorative pattern. Among the tricks which the Scyths could have derived either from China or from south-west Asia, and which they probably transmitted in turn to Celtic art, was the rendering of projecting muscles on shoulders, haunches and other joints by means of curls.

As might be expected of a people to whom war, the chase and the management of animals were all-important, Scythic society was strongly masculine and authoritarian. This is brought out in the burials, which seem to have provided a main focus of religious sentiment and which incidentally have yielded by far the greater part of our information about the Scyths. The dead were buried under barrows in chambers roofed over with timber and provided with grave-goods. In the case of the leaders the tombs were sometimes of vast size and the grave-goods of outstanding wealth. The barrows of the royal Scyths in the Alexandropol region of south Russia, for example, might range from 9 to 21 metres in height and from 122 to 375 metres in circumference and the chamber might exceed 12 metres in depth below the old ground surface. The archaeological evidence strongly bears out the account left by Herodotus, who records that the body of the dead leader, having been embalmed, was laid on a waggon and for a period of forty days was drawn in procession round his territory. The great man would be accompanied to the grave, not merely by material possessions, such as clothing, jewellery, weapons, food, drink, drinking-vessels and containers, but also by his favourite horses, his wife and his chief servants, recalling the practices of the Han emperors of China or from much earlier times those of the Sumerian rulers, witnessed by the contents of the royal graves at Ur.

Antecedents and expansion of Roman civilization

Etruscans

Interesting in themselves the Etruscans have a double claim on our attention because of their close involvement in the beginnings of the Roman state. Rome itself was after all an Etruscan foundation and the Roman republic dates from the expulsion of the Tarquinian (Etruscan) dynasty in 510 B.C. The Etruscans have long remained mysterious. They spoke a non-Indo-European language and some of their art displays an exotic style. The fact that they borrowed the alphabet makes it the more tantalizing that their inscriptions, except for a word here or there, remain undeciphered. The notion given currency by Herodotus that they came with a ready-made culture from Lydia in western Asia Minor has now been generally abandoned, since their culture appears to be rooted in that of their
261 Villanovan predecessors. Their particular flavour comes rather from the play of Greek and probably also of Cypriote and Phoenician influences on an indigenous base. Their riches stemmed to a significant degree from their skill in working the copper, iron and tin so richly provided by the mountains of their homeland. The Etruscans gained control over most of Italy north of the Greek zone and west of the Apennines. Furthermore they appropriated Elba for its tin at an early stage and by *c.* 540 B.C. they had won Corsica following a sea battle in league with the Carthaginians against the Greeks. Before the end of the sixth century B.C. they had enlarged their occupation of the mainland down to the Campanian plain.

242 Whereas the Villanovans were essentially villagers, the Etruscans preferred, like the Greeks, to live in stone-built towns with public buildings: it was after all Etruscans who first enclosed the Seven Hills of Rome with a wall and converted a cluster of Villanovan villages into a city with forum and temple. The most impressive signs of their wealth are furnished by their tombs, great stone chambers domed or vaulted and heaped over with earthen mounds: the scenes painted on the inner walls, no less than the sculptured urns, the bronze figures, mirrors and vessels, the ivories, the imported Greek vases and the exquisite gold-smithery testify to a society that was not only affluent, but sophisticated and highly stratified. Politically the Etruscans were organized in self-governing cities, each with its dependent territory, a system which, as with the Greeks, was favourable to a high level of culture, but which was unable long to survive the pressure of larger and more coherent units. The overrunning of their territories in the Po basin by Celtic-speaking warriors between 450 and 350 B.C. began the process of disintegration which the Romans did so much to accelerate. By the middle of the third century B.C., indeed, Etruria had submitted to Rome, even if culturally the absorption was not complete until just before the beginning of the Christian era. Although the Roman republic ostensibly rose to power at the expense of the Etruscans they owed them not merely their capital city and its forum, but also some of their leading characteristics, notably their prowess with drains, their system of land survey by centuriation, their preoccupation with divination by the *haruspices* and, in the *fasces*, the very emblem of authority.

Expansion of Roman power

From a tiny rustic republic Rome step by step enlarged its territory until this engulfed the whole of the Mediterranean, Egypt and much of south-west Asia as well as most of the parts of temperate Europe occupied by Celtic-speaking people. Although the irruption of Celtic warriors had some time earlier seriously weakened the Etruscans, it

109 Europe, showing progressive expansion of literate civilization.

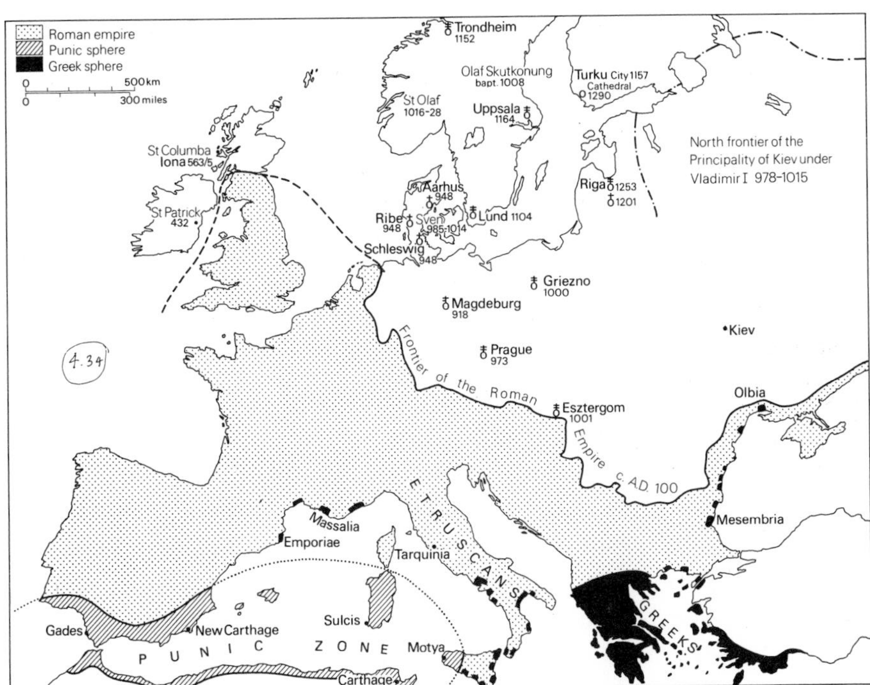

was not until they had won their victory at Segontium in 295 B.C. that the Romans finally emerged as the dominant power in middle Italy. In the second stage of their expansion they consolidated their hold on Italy as a whole: they began by bringing under control the Greek colonies of Magna Graecia, went on to evict the Carthaginians from Sicily in the course of the First Punic War (264–241 B.C.) and within the next twenty years had subdued the Po Valley. The third stage, during which they gained control of the Mediterranean, was initiated by the Second Punic War (218–201 B.C.), which not only brought them Spain, but also, as a result of the battle of Zama, Carthage itself and with it full control of the straits of Sicily; further than that, through the Carthaginian alliance with Macedon, Rome became involved in campaigns in the east Mediterranean which led indirectly to the conquest of Pergamum and so to Roman intervention in the affairs of Asia. The annexation of Syria and Crete in 62 B.C., and of Egypt in 30 B.C., virtually completed the encirclement of the Mediterranean, which became in effect a Roman lake. Meanwhile the fourth and final phase of expansion, during which the Romans incorporated within the empire most of the remaining territories of the Celtic La Tène peoples, had already been initiated with the conquest of the rest of Gaul by Caesar between 59 and 51 B.C. The subjugation of Britain, much of the southern part of which had since Caesar's incursion been subject to strong influences from Roman Gaul, was begun by Claudius between A.D. 43 and 47 and completed even beyond the Firth of Forth by Agricola (A.D. 78–84), appointed for the task by Vespasian. By the death of Trajan in A.D. 117 the Empire had reached the Rhine–Danube line, which it was destined to hold until the collapse of imperial authority in the west; and beyond this it had extended to the Low Countries, the enclave between the Middle Rhine and the Upper Danube, and the province of Dacia.

The Iron Age in northern Europe

The Earlier Iron Age

Meanwhile, beyond the most extended limits of the Empire the forces that were ultimately to disrupt it were gathering strength. The heirs
221: III, 1–273 of the Nordic Bronze Age had acquired a knowledge of iron-working from the south by 500 to 400 B.C. During the ensuing four centuries they drew their main inspiration from the Celtic La Tène peoples with whom they came into contact on their southern borders; but the opening centuries of the Christian era were marked predominantly by influences from the Roman world. Bronze accessories of

wine-drinking, manufactured in Italy, Gaul or the Rhineland, were
223 taken into use by prosperous farmers as far north as the Trondelag and new ideas were brought home by individuals returning from service in provinces of the Roman Empire. The free Germans were thus growing in wealth and knowledge at a time when the inhabitants of the Roman provinces were being thwarted by bureaucratic interference and fiscal exactions; moreover the provincials' power of war-like resistance was progressively lowered by the very peace secured within the frontiers by an army in which the barbarian element was ever on the increase. Beyond the frontiers the small possibility of internal growth allowed by subsistence farming and the barrier to northward colonization set by the adverse climate of Sub-atlantic times led inevitably to southern thrusts of population. The first of these identified in history was the drive of the Teutones and Cimbri from northern Jutland that began in 120 B.C. and was only checked by the destruction of the Teutones on the field of battle near Aix-en-Provence in 102 B.C. More widespread movements occurred during the second century A.D., when for example the Goths crossed the Baltic from their new homeland in south Sweden and drove north of the Carpathians down to the region of Olbia on the north-east shore of the Black Sea. Such movements as these increased the flow of new ideas back to the old homelands. It was from the Goths in their new territories that many exports from the Roman world, and art conventions from the steppes, reached the north. Another feature to spread north was the runic script, first adapted from the Latin in all probability by the Marcomanni of Bohemia, a script that was to reach Britain with the Anglo-Saxon invaders and remained the only form of writing throughout the Migration and early part of the Viking periods in northern Europe.

Although it has been argued that westward thrusts of Huns from the steppes, by engaging the eastern Germans delayed their assault on Italy, in the long run it was the complex system of folk-movements which they set in motion that brought down the Empire in the west.

The death of Theodosius I in A.D. 395 and the division of the Empire, the Latin west falling to Honorius and the Greek east to Arcadius, was the signal for wholesale invasions. The invasion of Italy and the sack of Rome by Alaric and his Visigoths in 410 was really decisive in that, bereft of an effective head, the provincial limbs proved unable to withstand the multiple and often lightning thrusts of the barbarians. No account of these can be offered here, but it is important to recognize a primary distinction between those of the eastern and western Germans. Whereas relatively small bands of the former, Visigoths, Ostrogoths, Burgundians, Lombards and Vandals, penetrated great distances and left little ethnic trace behind – the last-mentioned for example passed through Gaul and Spain and across North Africa to fall upon Rome from the Carthaginian shore – the latter laid the foundations of Anglo-Saxon Britain and Frankish Gaul in neighbouring territories.

The Later Iron Age

221: III, *Migration period.* The transition from the Early to the Late Iron Age
in northern Europe was marked by no sudden change in economic
277–444 or social life. It was rather the historical circumstances in which they
230, 235 lived that gave a special character to the peoples of the Migration
Period. The fall of the Roman Empire of the west deprived them of stability as well as of the employment and cultural stimulus that this had afforded. The new age was one above all of movement, of migration, trade and warfare, often inextricably interwoven.

A key part in these activities was played by the wooden ships which

110 Vendel-style art motifs from Sutton Hoo: (*upper*) man between animals executed in garnet and gold cloisonné on a purse cover; (*lower*) dancing warriors embossed on helmet plates.

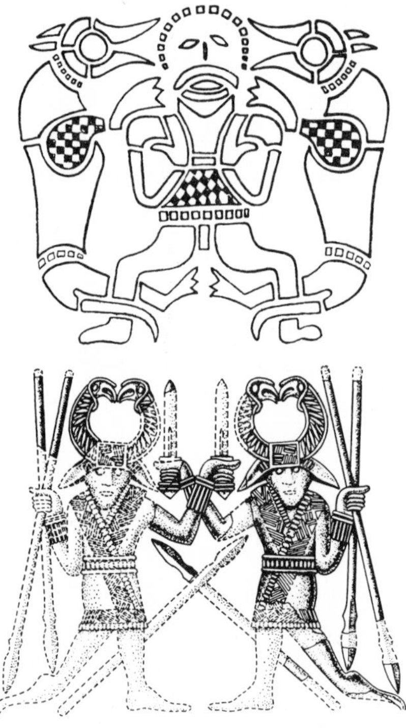

in the course of their development display a clear continuity from the prehistoric past. Although little is known in detail about the construction of the vessels depicted on the Bronze Age rock-engravings of Scandinavia, it is evident that they were long boats propelled by oars and that in some cases their upstanding prows were carved into the form of animal heads. The earliest vessel, as distinct from a mere dug-out, yet recovered from northern Europe is the
1: III, 31–41 ten-metre ship from Hjortspring, Denmark, dating from early in the
& 251–3 third century B.C. Like the long boats from Nydam (*c.* A.D. 400) and
245: ch. 4; Sutton Hoo (*c.* A.D. 600) this had a hull built up from side strakes
245: ch. 5* or planks having raised cleats on the inner face to which were attached the transverse ribs that lent rigidity to the whole. In the course of nearly a thousand years progress was deliberate rather than dramatic. The side strakes increased from two to five (Nydam) and nine (Sutton Hoo) in number and in the later vessels were joined by iron clench nails or rivets instead of being sewn together. Again, whereas previously the strakes were cut from single pieces of timber – and the Nydam boat was 22·8 m long – those of the 27 m Sutton Hoo vessel were made from shorter lengths scarfed and rivetted

111 Bronze dies for embossing helmet plates in early Vendel style (6th century A.D.), Torslunda, Öland Island, Sweden.

together, a technical advance which made it possible to build longer hulls from smaller trees. Another feature to undergo development was the keel. Whereas in the Hjortspring and Nydam boats these were broad flat planks, that of the Sutton Hoo vessel had a shallow projection on the under face.

Historical circumstances set a higher premium on leadership and concentrated executive power. Chieftains throve to petty kings, organizers of embryo states, leaders in war and monopolists of distant trade. The finest jewellery and personal equipment stemmed from concentrated wealth and served to symbolize and validate the authority of the rulers under whose patronage it was fabricated. The culture of pagan Anglo-Saxon England owed much to Teutonic settlers from between Frisia and Jutland, people who came first to serve but in due course to replace the Roman provincial government.
*245, 245** The grave goods from a royal grave like Sutton Hoo reflect distant contacts. The sword, shield and helmet, like the practice of ship
110 burial, point to the Vendel culture of Sweden. Some of the designs executed in cloisonné with garnet inlay or in embossed relief point in the same direction, as comparison with the designs on metal dies
111 from Torslunda, Öland, well shows. Representations of beaked birds of prey descending on ducks derive by way of Gothic art from south Russia. By contrast many elements come from the south. The gold coins from the purse were struck in Merovingian mints and the silver vessels were made in provinces of the Byzantine Empire.

274, 287 The prime significance of the Anglo-Saxons was the part they played in the history of England and so of the English-speaking world. It is essential to remember that the Anglo-Saxons were not only Teutonic, they increasingly became British. An indication of this can be seen in the Celtic spiral decoration found on the roundels or circular escutcheons attached to the base of the handles of bronze hanging-bowls from Saxon burials, including that of Sutton Hoo. An immediate result of the invasions had been a breakdown in both the urban civilization and the Christian tradition established in the Roman province. Continuity was re-established with the mission of St Augustine (A.D. 597) and the conversion within thirty years of rulers like Aethelbert of Kent and Edwin of Northumbria. With Christianity came literacy, coinage and monumental architecture, sculpture and painting. In Britain, as earlier in Merovingian Gaul, mediaeval civilization developed from an amalgam of Celtic, Teutonic and Mediterranean elements, both Classical and Christian.

The Vikings. The Scandinavian homelands remained untouched by
219, 224, 228 Christianity for some centuries after the conversion of the Anglo-Saxons. Although archaeologists recognize a conventional division between the Migration and Viking Periods at A.D. 800 there had in fact been no clear break since prehistoric times. Runes, the only form of writing during the opening phases of the Viking Period had come into use during the Roman Iron Age, and as recent excavations at Bergen have shown continued actively into the thirteenth century alongside the more sophisticated forms of writing that came in with Christianity. Viking art grew out of the abstract and sometimes convoluted animal forms of the Migration Period. Again, the Viking ships on which their power largely depended, though displaying a more developed keel with a greater degree of projection that made them stronger and more manoeuvrable under sail, marked a logical continuation of a tradition long established in the north. Many components of the trade net-work operated by the Vikings were also of long standing, not least the import of wine already established during the Roman Iron Age.

It was largely because of the relative poverty of their homelands that the Vikings were driven to look abroad for enrichment and expansion. To the west the British Isles, Atlantic and even to a slight extent the west Mediterranean held the attraction of richer lands offering opportunities for plunder, extortion and in some cases settlement. To the east on the other hand the Vikings played a more constructive role by opening up trade routes from the Baltic to the Black Sea and Byzantium on the one hand and the Caspian, Persia, the Islamic world and the Far East on the other. At a time when the Mediterranean was largely under Islamic control the Vikings offered an alternative route for interchange between such products of the north as furs, walrus ivory, ropes and honey and southern wares like spices, wine and silks. The Norsemen who controlled the main Dnepr and Volga routes and were known to the Slavs as Varangians and the Greeks as Russes had a profound effect on the character of the future Russian state through the close links they established with Byzantium.

The trade itself was apparently conducted by barter in which gold, but more particularly silver in the form of ingots and coins, mainly Arab, Anglo-Saxon and Frankish-German, served as media of exchange, weighed out on scales. To handle this trade the Vikings built trading posts and towns like Novgorod, Smolensk and Kiev in Russia or Helgö and later Birka in Sweden, Kaupanger in west Norway and

 Hedeby at the foot of Jutland, not to mention York in England and Dublin in Ireland.

The Vikings, apart from their impact on the west and their influence on Russia, contributed primarily to the building of the Scandinavian polities that entered the stage of history as a result of adopting Christianity. Again, if Romanesque had replaced Viking styles on monuments by the end of the twelfth century, the latter lived on for long in the popular arts. Beyond Scandinavia and adjacent lands the Norsemen extended the range of human settlement far to the west. The men who effectively occupied Iceland from Norway during the last decades of the ninth century A.D. did so in quest of independence as well as land. Before the end of the ninth century exiles from Iceland had made landfall on Greenland and established settlements on parts of the west coast that endured until the fifteenth century. According to the sagas the Norsemen ventured further afield to Vinland widely identified today with New England. They thus established contact with the Indians as well as the Eskimos and anticipated by about half a millennium the official discovery of the New World by west-European man.

Christianity and the end of European prehistory

The spread of Christianity

The prehistoric peoples beyond the old imperial frontiers were first
158 brought within the sphere of civilization by Christian missionaries. Although subject at times to severe persecution, Christianity spread widely throughout the Empire during the Antonine period (138–92) and between 313 and 325 it achieved a settled status through its recognition by Constantine and the clarification of its doctrines at the council of Nicaea. When the western Empire collapsed, much of its ecclesiastical organization survived even though in the areas most overrun by barbarians there was some relapse into paganism. Thus the continuity of civilized life in south-east Britain was so disrupted by the Anglo-Saxon invaders that Christianity had to be reintroduced from Rome when more settled conditions set in by the end of the sixth century. In the long run the Anglo-Saxons brought about an enlargement of the Christian world by displacing Christians from the most populous parts of the Roman province and driving them to the remoter parts of Britain and even across the sea to Ireland. As a result thriving centres of Celtic Christianity grew up in northern Britain and in the far west, separated from the remainder of Christendom by a welter of Germanic barbarians, and it was only during a lengthy

period after St Augustine's mission (597), in the aftermath of which the Synod of Whitby (663–4) was an outstanding episode, that the two were reunited. Even so the Celtic church continued as in a sense a separate force, making for example a distinctive contribution to the conversion of Bavaria and west Germany.

The bringing in of northern and eastern Germany had to wait on political progress. The defeat of the Huns at Troyes (451) and the conversion of the Frankish ruler Clovis to Christianity encouraged the emergence of a well-founded state under the Merovingian dynasty (486–751). Great advances were made under Charlemagne, who extended the Frankish frontiers to the Elbe and the Pyrenees and was crowned in the year 800 as emperor of the Romans at the hands of Pope Leo III. Yet the ninth century was to witness the temporary return of conditions reminiscent of those prevailing some four hundred years earlier, with Vikings taking the place of Germans and Magyars that of Huns: the former issued from Scandinavia to ravage the coasts of the Baltic, the North Sea, the Western Isles, the Irish Sea, the English Channel, the Bay of Biscay and even the west Mediterranean; and the latter, of remotely east Ural origin, were pushed by the advancing Petcheneg hordes from their immediate homeland in the Ukraine across the Carpathians into the Middle Danube basin, where their forays terrorized more settled peoples.

It was not until the middle of the tenth century, after half a millennium of unrest, that the German kings Henry the Fowler and Otto were able to establish more or less settled conditions in central Europe, the latter beating the Hungarians decisively at Lech and reviving the Holy Roman Empire at his crowning in 962. The extension of Christianity and indeed of literate civilization itself to the remaining parts of Europe was the work of missionary endeavour from Rome and Byzantium, the twin capitals of the Roman Empire. Henry and Otto had carried the frontier up to the Oder and the closing years of the first millennium were marked by a series of dramatic advances, among them St Adalbert's mission to Prussia (997), the adhesion of Hungary (1000), the conversion of Olaf Tryggvason, king of Norway (995–1000) and a former Viking, and
109 the establishment of Christianity in Sweden, whence in the twelfth century missionaries crossed to Finland. Meanwhile Byzantine missions had already before the end of the ninth century gone among the Bulgars, Croats and Serbs. In 988 Vladimir the prince of Kiev introduced Christianity to his dominions, which extended north to Novgorod over territory crossed by the old trade routes linking the

Swedish Vikings with Byzantium. Pressure of nomads from the eastern steppes led to Novgorod taking the lead from Kiev during the later twelfth century, but during the fourteenth and fifteenth centuries Moscow rose to prominence, and when at length the ancient capital of the East Roman Empire fell to the Turks it was to the metropolitan of Moscow that the headship of Orthodox Christianity passed and it was the principality of Moscow that formed the core of the future Russian Empire. It was the expansion of Muscovite power and Orthodox Christianity that brought the remaining areas of prehistoric Europe within range of literate tradition. By the death of Ivan III in 1505 the frontiers had reached the Arctic territories and the Urals and the prehistory of Europe was to all intents and purposes concluded.

A counterpart to the northward expansion of Christianity, which followed the achievement of more stable conditions towards the end of the first millennium, is to be seen in the staying and reversal of Islamic expansion in the south. Within twelve years of Mohammed's death in 632 his followers had overrun much of the Byzantine Empire, including Cyrenaica, Palestine, Syria and Iraq, and in addition Persia and Armenia; and by 700 they had added to their conquests the rest of North Africa, Afghanistan, West Turkestan and north-west India. At the peak of their power in the mid-tenth century the Moslems had come near to engulfing the entire Mediterranean, having occupied most of Spain, as well as Provence, Sicily and south Italy, and threatened Asia Minor and Byzantium itself. From this point of view the stability that made possible the Crusades came to Christian Europe only just in time: in the event not only was all Spain regained by the middle of the thirteenth century, but the fall of Byzantium was delayed sufficiently long for it to be in some respects an advantage to western Christendom.

The age of exploration: discovery of the world by Europe

By the middle of the thirteenth century Christendom was no longer on the defensive in the west and was indeed ready to reach out into other continents. Already by 1260 Venetian and soon after Genoese merchants had begun to establish trade relations with China from bases in the Crimea using the same route as that followed a thousand years previously for conveying silk to the Roman world; and during the earlier half of the fourteenth century envoys were reaching China by sea from the Persian Gulf. The conditions on which this eastern trade was based ceased to exist when the Mongol was replaced by the Chinese Ming dynasty (1368/70) and xenophobic influences regained the upper hand. The Europeans had to turn elsewhere for the spices and other eastern produce to which they had become accustomed. A new age of geographical discovery and as it turned out a new era in the history of mankind was inaugurated, in which the lead passed from the Mediterranean to the nations of the Atlantic sea-board. The Portuguese began by edging round the west coast of Africa and by 1498 had succeeded in reaching India by way of the Cape of Good Hope. Meanwhile, six years before Vasco da Gama's culminating exploit, Christopher Columbus, a Genoese holding the commission of Ferdinand and Isabella of Spain, made landfall on one of the Bahama islands and before returning planted a small colony of Spaniards on Haiti. Christendom had thus in the course of two or three centuries initiated a process that within the ensuing three or four was destined to bring the whole world within the purview of literate civilization and paradoxically made possible and necessary the concept of world prehistory.

5

The African achievement

In the total perspective of prehistory the contribution made by the African continent to the emergence of mankind and the enrichment of human life is by any standards impressive. The appearance of the earliest primates to make stone tools to standardized and recognizable patterns and the development of the earliest industries throughout the Lower Pleistocene would alone be enough to make the continent a focus of prehistoric research. Moreover the fact that it comprises much the larger part of hand-axe territory and occupies a central position between Europe and India suggests that Africa witnessed the evolution of the new mode in lithic technology.

The fundamental contribution of Africa during the long ages in the course of which human society first took shape is in no way impaired by the undoubted fact that the next great development occurred when man broke out of the frost-free zone in which the earlier primates up to and including *Homo erectus* had evolved. The colonization of much of Eurasia was facilitated by and at the same time encouraged the development of new modes in lithic technology. Although the key innovative centres now and in the future lay outside the African continent its later prehistory continued to follow its own indigenous course. Ancient Egypt for one thing gave birth to one of the major civilizations of mankind. Again the continent which received explorers, traders, missionaries and colonizers from Phoenicia, the Roman world, Islam and western Europe displayed aesthetic sensibilities of its own whether in music or the plastic arts which still enrich human experience.

The Stone Age

288–91 *Unspecialized cultures of the Lower and Middle Pleistocene*

During the Lower and Middle Pleistocene the development of human culture proceeded with extreme slowness: the Oldowayan lasted for a million or a million and a half years and the Acheulean for the best part of another million. With this went a notable degree of uniformity from the Mediterranean to the Cape of Good Hope. This in turn went hand in hand with the generalized nature of the lithic industries. It was this that made it possible for them to adapt to a wide range of environments as well as to last through immensely long periods despite the unfolding of climatic and other changes. An interesting point to emerge from the geographical distribution of industries in modes 1 and 2 is that they occur over extensive tracts of the Sahara, suggesting that at least during certain phases the climate rendered this area much more habitable than it is today. Another is that the only extensive territory into which the makers of these industries failed to penetrate was that of the present equatorial forest.

For the greater part of prehistory the only industrial tradition
91, 303 represented was the Oldowayan (mode 1), found in beds I and II
112 (lower) at Olduvai in the Great Rift Valley of East Africa, but also

112 Olduvai Gorge, East Africa.

far to the north at Ain Hanech, Tunisia. This elementary tradition
296 was enriched both in north Africa and in the upper levels of bed II at Olduvai by crudely made bifacial tools (mode 2) of Lower Acheulean character. In beds III and IV at Olduvai and over the continent as a whole the introduction of the soft hammer technique resulted in the production of thinner bifaces with the flatter flaking and more regular edges characteristic of the Upper Acheulean. At this level also cleavers having working edges formed by the intersection of two main flake scars were proportionately more numerous than before. Again, the small light-duty equipment was in some
298 instances more regularly made. Such an industry was found abun-
113 dantly in occupation layers at Kalambo Falls.

The fact that modified Oldowayan forms continued to be made alongside bifaces argues against the idea of the replacement of one culture by another and suggests rather that the new forms were called into being, possibly quite suddenly, to meet some new need. On the other hand there is no sign that the general way of life changed markedly during the Early and Middle Pleistocene. Traces of dwellings in the form of semi-circular or even in some cases of more or less circular patches of stones and concentrations of human activity were already observed in the upper part of bed I at Olduvai. Again the same kind of kill site, in which the skeletons of large mammals are found in close association with the stone artefacts presumably used to skin them and remove the meat, seems to occur throughout the period. A nearly complete skeleton of an extinct elephant (*Elephas reckii*) from bed I at Olduvai was associated with over a hundred stone artefacts. An elephant skeleton was found under similar circumstances at the Malawi site of Karonga of Middle Pleistocene age. Other Acheulean occurrences include a disarticulated *Deinotherium*

Table 17. *East African prehistory: the earlier phases (after G. Isaac)*

Industries	Localities	Potassium–argon ages (millions)	Hominid types
Upper Acheulian	Olorgesailie	B 1965 0·486	
		0·425	*Homo erectus*
	Olduvai IV (Wk)	*c.* 0·7	
Lower Acheulian	Kariandusi	B 695 0·928	
		B 1035 0·946	*Homo erectus*
		B 1061 1·1	
	Olduvai II (Upper)	*c.* 1·5	Transitional
Oldowayan	Olduvai II (Lower)		*Homo habilis*
	Olduvai I	*c.* 2·0	

from Isimilia and a hippopotamus from Olorgesailie. In each case
290:96 the associated tools were of the light-duty variety.

Specialized cultures of sub-Saharan Africa during the Late Pleistocene and Holocene

The prehistory of Mediterranean and sub-Saharan Africa diverged
310 for the first time with the appearance of men of modern type during the Upper Pleistocene. To balance the appearance of Neanderthal man (*Homo sapiens neanderthalensis*) in Morocco, Cyrenaica, Nubia and Ethiopia, fossils of a close cousin, Rhodesian man (*H. s. rhodesiensis*), have come from a number of sites between the tropics and
Table 18 the Cape, including the original finding place of Broken Hill, Zambia.

The First Intermediate Period of the sub-Saharan sequence was marked by the beginning of the process of specialization in the course of which lithic assemblages underwent progressive modifications in response to the varying nature of differing ecosystems. At a time when the Acheulian had already given place for some ten thousand years to the Levalloiso-Mousterian in Mediterranean Africa, we find it adapting to forest conditions in parts of central Africa and taking on the distinctive character defined as Sangoan. The Sangoan, named after the locality of Sango Bay, Lake Victoria, shows a marked emphasis on wood-working equipment, manifested most notably in

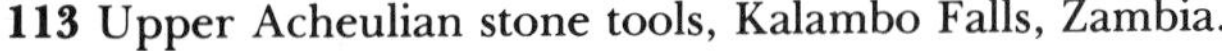

113 Upper Acheulian stone tools, Kalambo Falls, Zambia.

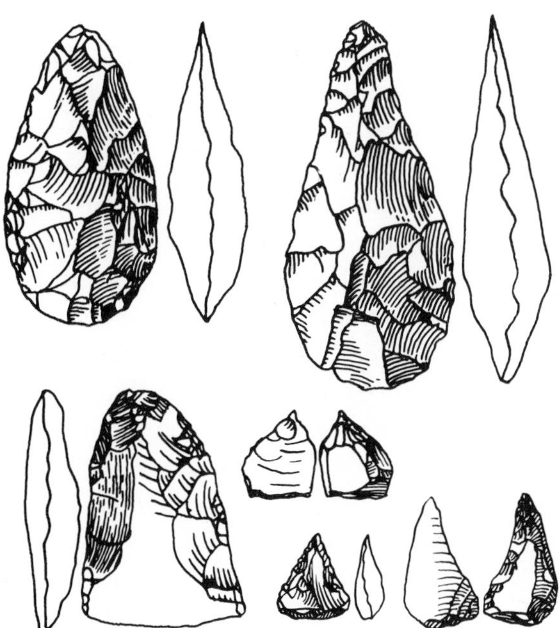

heavy bifaces and picks and in high-backed push-planes. Indeed it could well be that the people who used stone tools of Sangoan type depended for implements and weapons largely on wooden artefacts. Outside the forest, the grasslands and savannah supported people who continued the Acheulian tradition. This was now however marked, notably in the assemblages named after the township of Fauresmith in the Orange Free State, by a reduction in size and in increased refinement, both in bifaces and cleavers, and in the associated light equipment which now showed a more pronounced reliance on the prepared Levallois core technique.

A similar duality persisted during the Middle Stone Age which was also marked by a further overall reduction in the size of lithic
115 artefacts. In the equatorial forest Lupemban industries carried forward a basically Sangoan tradition, whereas the savannah territories extending from the Horn of Africa to the Cape carried assemblages characterized by blade-like flakes as well as squat ones struck from prepared cores and in addition bifacially flaked points, having the appearance of spearheads and named after Still Bay on the south coast of Cape Province. Towards the close of the Pleistocene the Second Intermediate phase witnessed a continuation of the process of reduction in size and a persistence of the distinction between forest
117 and savannah industries. With the former, one finds in the Tshitolian a continuation of some elements of the Lupemban together with new forms such as tranchets or miniaturized cleavers and thick narrow bifacially flaked points. The savannah on the other hand now carried assemblages of Magosian type (termed Howieson's Port in South Africa) which include lunates and other forms of steeply retouched blades intended for mounting in composite tools as well as miniature forms of flake tools struck from prepared cores of Levallois type.

Throughout the Holocene microliths, intended for insetting into composite artefacts including arrows, were a predominating element in the industries of almost the whole of sub-Saharan Africa. Other components included convex scrapers. As a rule these were small and of thumbnail form, though where, as in the Smithfield industries of the Orange Free State, a material like indurated shale was available, much larger ones might also be made. Other components, rarer, but to judge from the position in the twelve-thousand-year sequence established in the Nachikufan caves of Zambia, going far back in time, were edge-ground stone axes and bored stones perforated by sinking opposing hollows from either face. Similar, though as a rule heavier, bored stones (*! kwe*) were used quite recently by Bushmen to weight

Table 18. *The Stone Age sequence of different parts of Africa during the Upper Pleistocene and Holocene (the historical period is shown in black)*

	Periods	Sub-Saharan Africa				North Africa		
		Congo	South Africa	Zambia	Kenya	Maghreb	Cyrenaica	Nile
2000 A.D.	Later	Tshitolian	Wilton	Nachikufan	Kenya–Capsian	Capsian		Fayum–P.D.
10,000	Second Intermediate	Lupembo–Tshitolian	Magosian			Oranian		Qadan Gemaian
20,000 30,000	Middle	Upper Lupemban	Still Bay			Aterian	Dabban	Khormusan
40,000	First Intermediate	Lower Lupemban Sangoan	Fauresmith	Sangoan	Acheulo-Levallois	Levalloiso – Mousterian		
50,000 60,000	Earlier Stone Age	Upper Acheulian						

114 Main provinces of African Middle Stone Age.

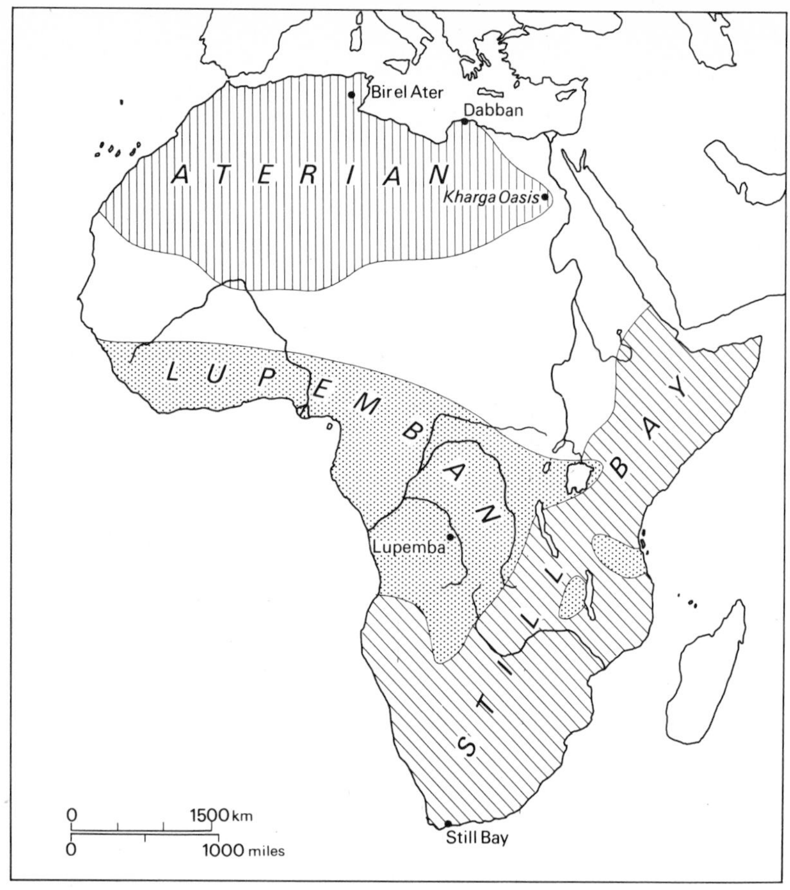

115 Lupemban stone tools from Kalina Point, Congo.

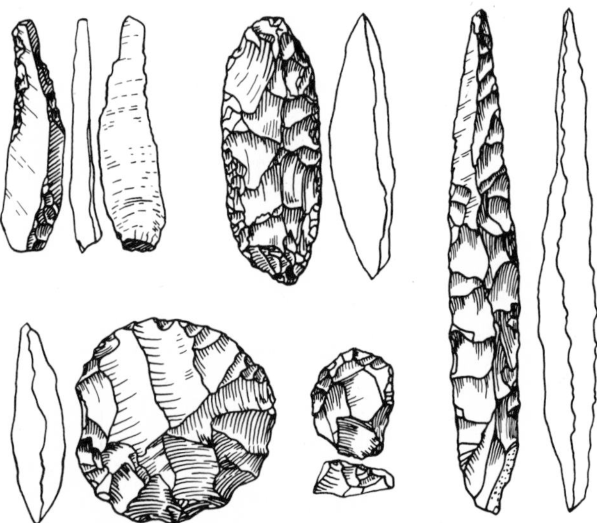

116 Main provinces of African Late Stone Age.

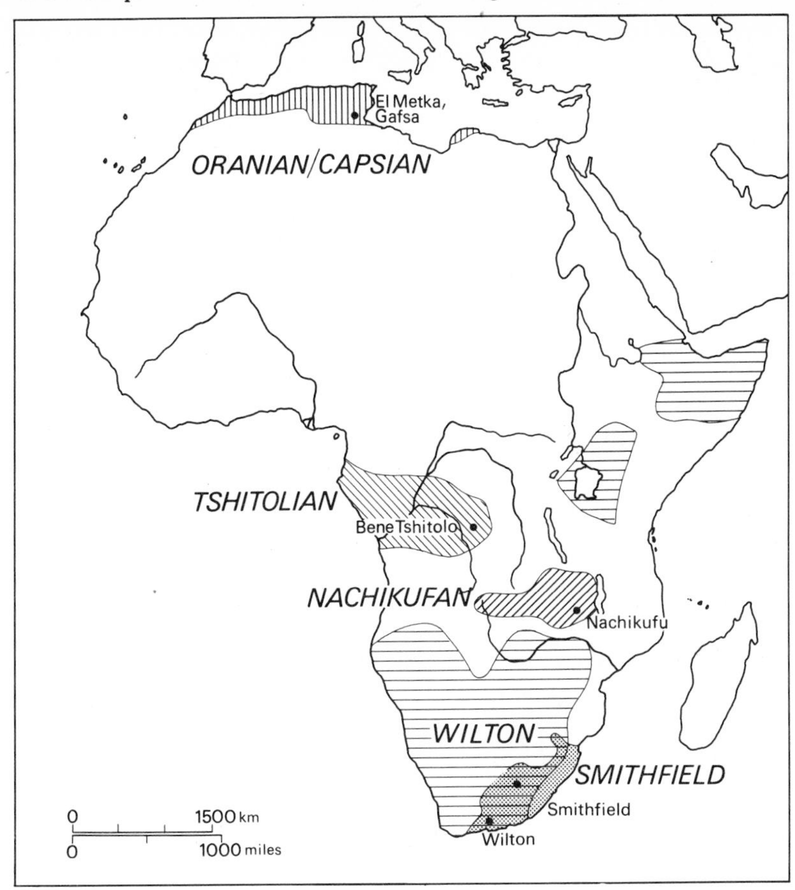

117 Tshitolian tools from Lower Congo and Angola.

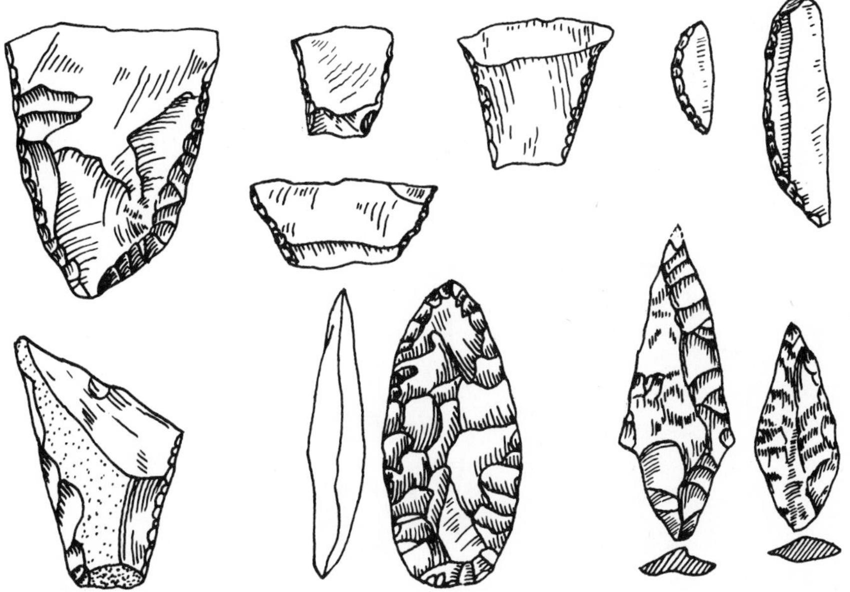

their digging-sticks. By around 5000 B.C. more or less standardized
Late Stone Age microlithic assemblages in mode 5, corresponding
118 approximately with those of level IIB in the Nachikufan sequence, but
usually termed Wilton after the rock-shelter of that name in Cape
Province, extended from the Horn to the Cape and, if we may judge
from the lower levels at Iwo Eleru, Nigeria, across the savannah tract
of West Africa. As we know from the occurrence of iron objects and
slag on Wilton sites in the Horn, Uganda and the Cape, the industry
was still being practised by hunter-foragers when iron-working was
spreading over sub-Saharan Africa. Indeed the use of glass as a raw
material shows that it lasted down to the European colonial period
in the Cape.

Indications of aesthetic feeling are found in the widespread occurrence of personal ornaments, including perforated shale pendants
and beads made from ostrich shell discs rubbed smooth on grooved
stones. More impressive is the distribution of rock engravings and
paintings. While it cannot be proved that these relate to the makers
305, 312 of Wilton industries there are two reasons for accepting this as a likely
hypothesis, namely the broad geographical correspondence and the
119 fact that Wilton assemblages have so often been found in rock-shelters
decorated in this way. Whatever the ultimate roots of this art may
be, a subject wide open to research, the consensus is that most at any

118 Nachikufan (*lower*) and Wilton (*upper*) tools from Zambia and South Africa.

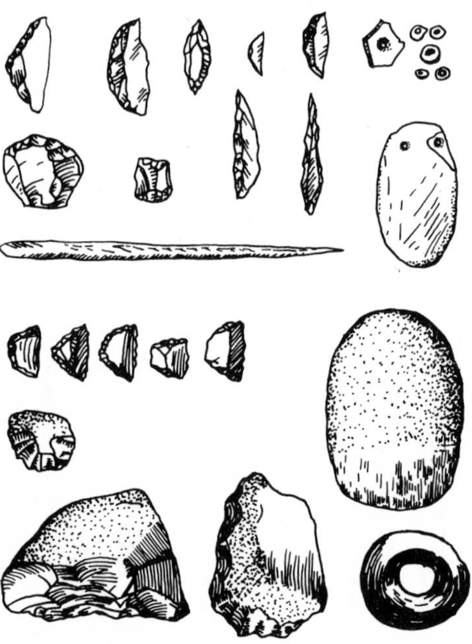

rate of the surviving rock-art of South Africa, even of the earlier group confined to naturalistic renderings of animals, goes back no further than two thousand years. The younger group, less well executed and featuring scenes of ritual and combat, in which people of varying racial stocks are distinguished, relates palpably to the recent Bushmen.

North Africa: Late Pleistocene and Early Holocene

306 The whole of northern Africa from the Maghreb to Cyrenaica and the Nile Valley and the greater part of the Sahara was occupied for much of the Late Pleistocene by hunter-foragers armed by a Levalloiso-Mousterian (mode 3) technology. Indeed, except in Cyrenaica, this tradition survived in modified form to between 15,000 and 12,000 B.C. There we find a well defined manifestation of mode 4 flint-working techniques in the Dabban industry, named after ed
307 Dabba, but most fully documented at the Haua Fteah, where it

119 Polychrome rock-painting of elands in cave in Cathkin area, Natal.

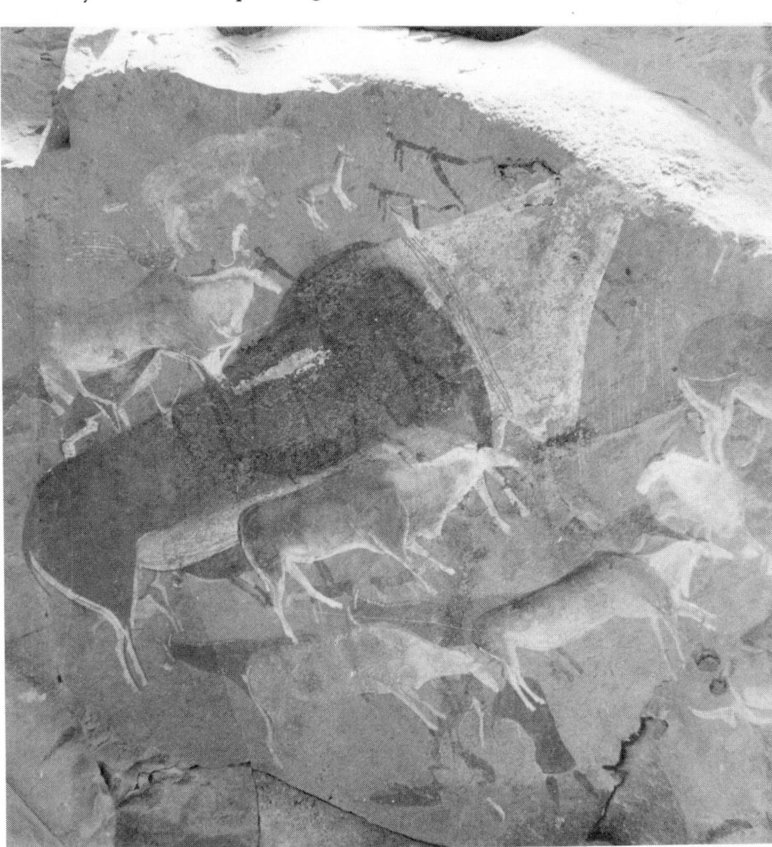

flourished between *c.* 38,000 and 12,000 B.C. The backed blades,
120 burins and end-scrapers conform to the pattern already met with in
the Upper Palaeolithic assemblages of Europe and parts of south-western Asia. The presence of chamfered blades closely resembling those of the Emiran assemblages at the base of Upper Palaeolithic sequences in the Levant suggests that the Dabban lithic technique may have intruded into Cyrenaica along the Mediterranean coast from the east.

The lithic technology which prevailed more or less contemporaneously over most of the rest of north Africa as far east as the Kharga
121 oasis and as far south as latitude 18° N was the Aterian, named after
297 Bir-el-Ater near Tebessa in Tunisia. In this a developed prepared
core technique yielded flake-blades as well as the broader facetted flakes usually found in Levalloiso-Mousterian assemblages. From these were made end-scrapers to set alongside the traditional side-scraper, as well as a variety of weapon heads. These included bifacially flaked leaf-shaped objects the symmetry and size of which suggest a use as spear or lance heads, as well as much smaller ones of leaf-shaped or tanged form which by analogy with later hafted specimens can be interpreted as arrowheads. Confirmation of the antiquity of the bow and arrow comes from the neighbouring territory of south-east Spain where similar objects occur at Parpalló stratified below Magdalenian levels and thus contemporary with some phase of the Aterian. This not only illustrates the close connection between Spain and north Africa but serves as a reminder that inventiveness was by no means lacking among those who maintained evolved Levalloiso-Mousterian traditions. Further east a different but parallel lithic industry, the Khormusan, was marked by denticulate flakes and burins for the most part conspicuously absent from the Aterian.

120 Dabban tools, Hagfed ed Dabba Cave, Cyrenaica.

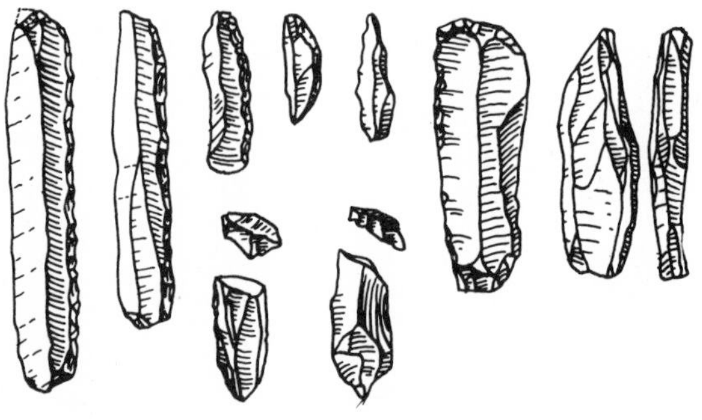

During the closing millennia of the Pleistocene a widespread and drastic change in technology occurred over north Africa. The Dabban and each of the Levalloiso-Mousterian derivative industries were replaced by assemblages in which the predominant form was the narrow backed bladelet. In both the Maghreb and Cyrenaica this appeared in the context of Oranian (or Ibero-Maurusian) assemb-
314 lages which made an apparently sudden appearance. In Nubia the new lithic technique is found intermixed with earlier ones in the Halfan assemblage, but the Ballanan and Qadan industries were almost, though in the latter case not quite, free from a Levalloiso-Mousterian component. A microlithic trend also appeared in contemporary but distinct lithic industries in neighbouring parts of south-west Asia. This suggests that the lithic components were responding to a technological change which transcended cultural divisions. As time went on the process became even more marked, as can be seen from the Capsian industries which followed the Oranian over much of north Africa and the Arkinian and Shamarkian ones which succeeded the Qadan in Nubia. It is reasonable to suppose that this change in lithic forms went with the increasingly widespread adoption of composite tools in which the microliths were set to provide sharp points, barbs and cutting edges.

An insight into subsistence has recently been won from exploration of seasonal encampments on the Middle Nile in Nubia. The hundred or so hearths which testify to many returns to the site of Tushka have yielded a useful assortment of animal bones. These show that aurochs (*Bos primigenius*), hartebeest (*Alcelaphus boselaphus*) and gazelle (*Gazella rufifrons*) were still available and other sites have yielded hippopotamus and an equid, probably a wild ass (*Equus asinus*). On the other hand the high proportion (4:19) of human skeletons from the cemetery at Tushka embedded with splintered flint projectile

121 Aterian tools from Kharga Oasis, Egypt.

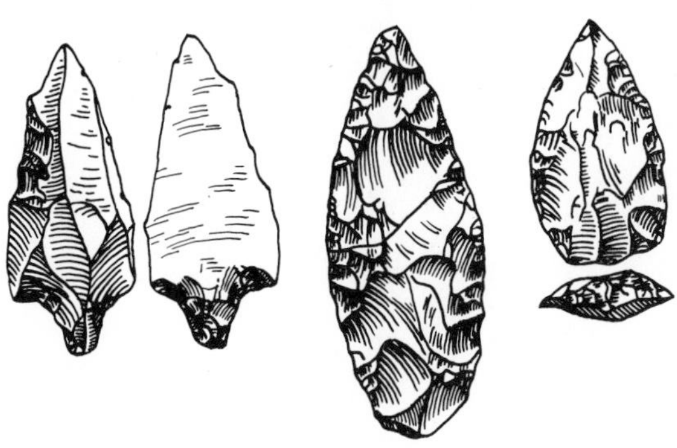

heads argues that the population was living under stress. It is not
surprising to find evidence for the exploitation of natural resources
on a broad front. Grinding stones and flints lustered at their edges
point to systematic use of plants at Tushka. Little attention seems
to have been paid to molluscs in Nubia, but these evidently had some
seasonal importance in the Maghreb at this time to judge from the
number and size of shell-middens. The Nile was an important source
of fish and it is evident that catfish played a significant part in diet.
122 The small overhanging rock-shelter below Wadi Halfa known as
Catfish Cave (site DI-21B) had clearly been used by fishermen when
situated on the very edge of the Nile at a time when it was presumably
approached by boat. The layer richest in fish-bones yielded a number
of barbed bone points of a kind that may well have been used to catch
them. Analogous points are known from lower down the Nile and
significantly in contiguous parts of south-west Asia, as well as higher
294 up the river in the neighbourhood of Khartoum and even as far south
as Lake Rudolph and the site of Ishango at the head of Lake Edward
where they again occur with remains of fish and hippopotamus as
well as antelope, buffalo and pig. Some, including those from Catfish
Cave, were evidently secured to spear shafts, but others were either
perforated or notched for securing to a line. Harpoon-heads of this
kind were doubtless used in some environments for hippopotami as
well as large fish. Closely similar objects are known from many sites
from the area of Lake Chad to Guinea. Their distribution defines
the route over the savannah and grassland along which pastoralism
and later iron-working may eventually have reached west Africa.

122 Barbed bone harpoon- and spear-heads: (1) Catfish Cave, Nubia; (2) Shaheinab; (3) Khartoum; (4) Ishango; (5, 6) Taferjit; (7) Araouan; (8) Kobadi.

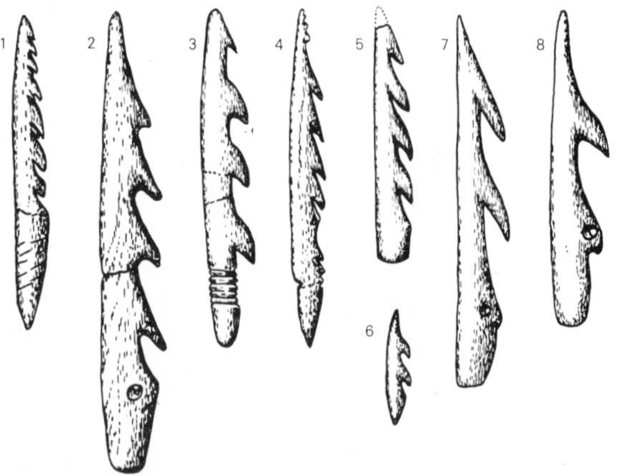

When considering the beginnings of farming in Africa it is natural to turn first to that part of the continent closest to south-west Asia where the animals and plants on which the early civilization of Egypt depended were apparently first domesticated. As we have seen in respect of Nubia the Nile Valley was already an important focus of human settlement during the closing stages of the Pleistocene at a time when epi-Levalloiso-Mousterian industrial traditions were being enriched by sophisticated blade and burin techniques (mode 4) of the kind developed more than twenty thousand years earlier in south-west Asia. The Nile dwellers can be assumed therefore to have been receptive to ideas reaching the Nile from Palestine and Jordan.

123 Artefacts from the Fayum Neolithic.

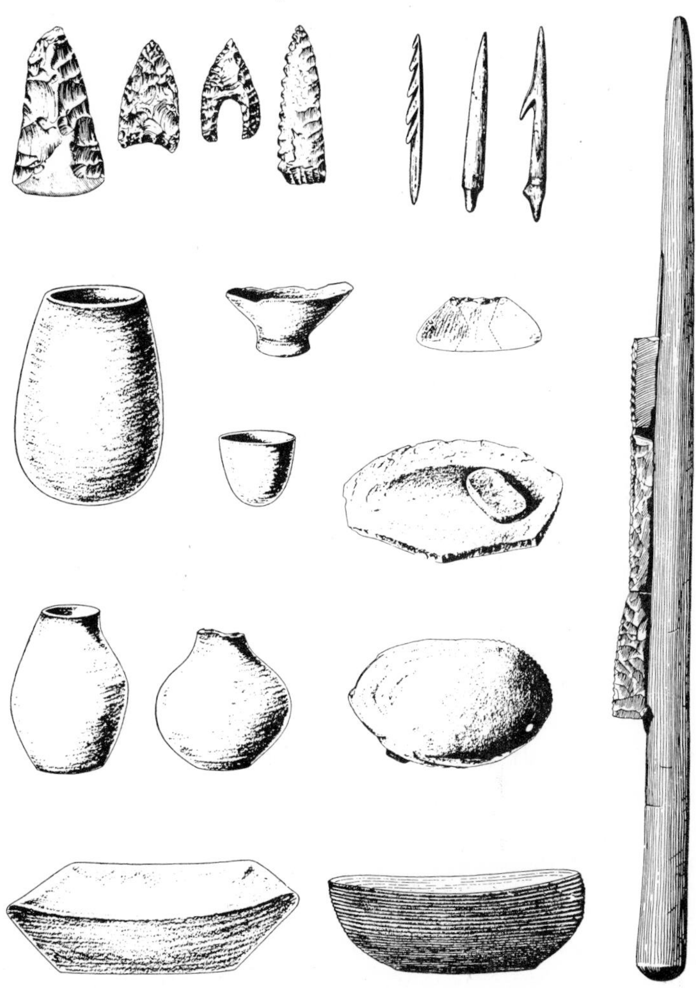

In particular they would have been well capable of adapting them to the favourable ecological conditions prevailing there. Not least among these were the annual inundations of the Nile and the deposits of silt brought down by them. Ironically it could well be that accumulations of such deposits have buried the earliest traces of farming in the Lower Nile Valley. We first encounter evidence for
123 these from the middle of the fifth millennium in the Fayum from which time the continuous archaeological record of ancient Egypt (p. 227) begins. Meanwhile the possibility has to be reckoned with in considering the position elsewhere in Africa that farming may have been established in the Nile Valley for longer than the archaeological record at present suggests.

In Mediterranean north Africa sheep/goat first appeared in the Haua sequence of Cyrenaica along with pottery at about the same time as in the Fayum. On the other hand there is evidence that both pottery-making and cattle-keeping were carried on in the Maghreb in earlier times. As in Cyrenaica these cultural elements were evidently taken over by the indigenous population. The lithic component is Capsian. The pottery conforms to west Mediterranean styles both as regards form, with round and pointed based bowls and perforated lug handles, and with respect to the impressed decoration. Indeed it is widely accepted that a common material-culture prevailed on either side of the Straits of Gibraltar at this time, a reminder of the situation prevailing during the Aterian. Similar impressed pottery from the western Fezzan has recently been dated by radiocarbon analysis as far back as *c.* 6000 B.C. Analysis of the animal bones from Uan Muhuggiag, Teshuinat, shows a marked shift in emphasis from ox (provisionally identified as *Bos brachyceros*) in the lower levels dating back to *c.* 4000 B.C. to a predominance of sheep in the upper ones. The Fezzan sites are also interesting from their association with the second or pastoral phase in the north African
124 rock-art in which bovines are strongly represented. The fact that this
313 carries forward a school of rock art that began with the delineation of large wild animals including *Bubalus antiquus*, which presumably dates from the Capsian or even Oranian lithic phase, only helps to confirm that the early cattle-keepers belonged to the indigenous population.

299, 308 Further south the Sahara offered a vast theatre for 'Neolithic' settlement at the height of Neothermal climate, coterminous with that of the Maghreb to the north and which to the east was linked by way of the Tibesti massif with the Upper Nile. Although certain

elements in the 'Saharan Neolithic', including probably stock-
keeping, may have come from the north, others, including Wavy
295 and Dotted Line pottery, resemble that made at Shaheinab near
Khartoum towards the end of the fourth millennium. Here, again,
though, we are dealing with a basically indigenous population which
appropriated cultural elements from its neighbours. The tanged
arrowheads which occur in such profusion stem beyond any doubt
from Aterian prototypes and like them are concentrated in the
western part of the territory. An abundance of arrowheads suggests
the importance of hunting. Rubbing-stones indicate that plant food

124 Rock-painting of cattle, Oua-n-Bender, Sahara.

 contributed to diet but there is no tangible evidence for cultivation.

There are some indications that the renewed desiccation which had already begun to affect parts of the Sahara by *c.* 2000 B.C. had the effect of displacing population south as well as north. This may provide one explanation for the new elements which appeared around this time in west Africa where, as we know from Iwo Eleru, Late Stone Age industries had been established since the close of the
311 Pleistocene. Excavation of a number of rock-shelters in Nigeria, including ones at Mejiro and Rop as well as Iwo Eleru itself, has shown that basic Late Stone Age assemblages including crescentic and trapezoidal microliths and thumb-nail scrapers, which in this part of Africa were usually made of quartz, persisted in the upper levels but were reinforced during the second millennium by a number of new elements, including pottery, polished stone axes and in some cases indications of husbandry. Although it is still too early to define differences between divergent groups at all closely, it must be evident that in so extensive a territory the inhabitants may be expected to have adapted their economies and therefore their artefacts to widely varying ecological circumstances. In the Kintampo group of the Lower Volta area of Ghana, the northern source of certain innovations is especially evident. For instance the pottery from Ntereso, a bush village with rectangular houses dating from the late second millennium B.C., was ornamented in some cases by coarse comb impressions, the hollow-based arrowheads were finished by shallow pressure flaking and a barbed bone point recalls those widely spread along the northern margins of the savannah from the former French Sudan to the upper Nile. The inhabitants evidently maintained livestock, including cattle, though engaging in hunting and fishing. In the case of the so-called Guinea Neolithic in which hoe blades flaked from rather soft stone were a feature, it looks as
293 if there was a greater emphasis on vegetable food and even as if some form of vegeculture may have been practised. Although the crops cultivated must at present rest on surmise, possibilities include sorghum, guinea rice (*Oryza glaberrima*), indigenous yams (*Dioscorea* sp.) and bullrush millet (*Pinnisetum*). Another question is whether and to what extent inroads were already being made on the forest during the Stone Age. Polished stone axe or adze blades which could have been used for clearing trees or breaking the ground have frequently been discovered in areas at present forested. The main uncertainty is the extent to which stone blades continued in use during the prehistoric Iron Age.

THE AFRICAN ACHIEVEMENT

No doubt it was in the wake of impulses from the upper Nile that pottery-making and cattle-keeping were adopted by the indigenous populations of parts of Eritrea and Ethiopia, perhaps as early as the
300: ch. X; 302 second millennium B.C. By the next millennium the Gumban A and B cultures of the Nakuru region show that they had penetrated the Rift Valley into Kenya. The obsidian industries on the Kenya sites are of Capsian type and confirm that the new traits had been adopted by the aboriginal population rather than introduced by any ethnic movement. The pottery was all hand-made and of elementary shapes. That from Elmenteita was of basket shape, with heavily impressed ornament on the outside and deep scoring on the inside.
304 The Hyrax Hill ware on the other hand comprised most notably tall ovoid vessels decorated by grooves, comb impressions and jabs. A widespread feature of the sites was the presence of stone bowls or mortars and pestles which occur as far south as Tanzania. These testify to the use of plant food on a considerable scale, but there is no clue as to its nature. Evidence for pastoral activities on the other hand is beginning to accumulate in the form of cattle bones from Kenyan sites of the first millennium B.C. In Zambia and territories further south cattle-keeping and potting appeared first in association with the spread of iron-working during the first millennium A.D.

Ancient Egyptian civilization

Early farmers in Lower Egypt

One of the earliest traces of farming settlement yet found in Lower Egypt – and the likely existence of earlier ones buried under the Nile
319 silt has already been indicated (p. 224) – is that of Merimde on the west side of the head of the delta, a huddle of flimsy huts of oval or horseshoe plan. The villagers made monochrome pottery by hand; shaped axeheads and maceheads from polished stone; flaked hollow-based arrowheads and knives or daggers from flint; and carved a variety of things from bone, including barbless fish-hooks of the same general class as those of the Natufian culture. They caught hippopotami and fish, but also planted cereals which they stored in large jars as well as in basket-bins or silos. One way in which they differed from the early farmers of the Fayum is that they buried their dead among their dwellings. According to radio-carbon analysis the culture already flourished in Lower Egypt during the first quarter of the fifth millennium; and if the pottery from the upper part of level VIII in the Haua Fteah in Cyrenaica belongs to the same tradition this date can be put back to the middle of the millennium.

 On the other hand the date from El Omari suggests that villagers may have preserved the same pattern of culture down to the Middle Predynastic period.

316 If the evidence for Neolithic settlement in the Fayum depression is fuller, this is due partly to the better conditions of preservation and partly to the care with which the environmental setting has been studied. Around the middle of the fifth millennium to which the Neolithic occupation can be assigned on the basis of radiocarbon analysis, that is at the peak of the Altithermal phase of climate, conditions were much more favourable than they are today. The level of the lake stood *c.* 55 metres higher and forest trees and swamps existed in what is now an arid environment. At this time the Fayum was no isolated oasis. It formed part of a territory linked to the Nile Valley as far south as the Sudan and extending thence in a westerly direction along the southern margin of the Sahara, a territory in

125 Upper and Lower Egypt.

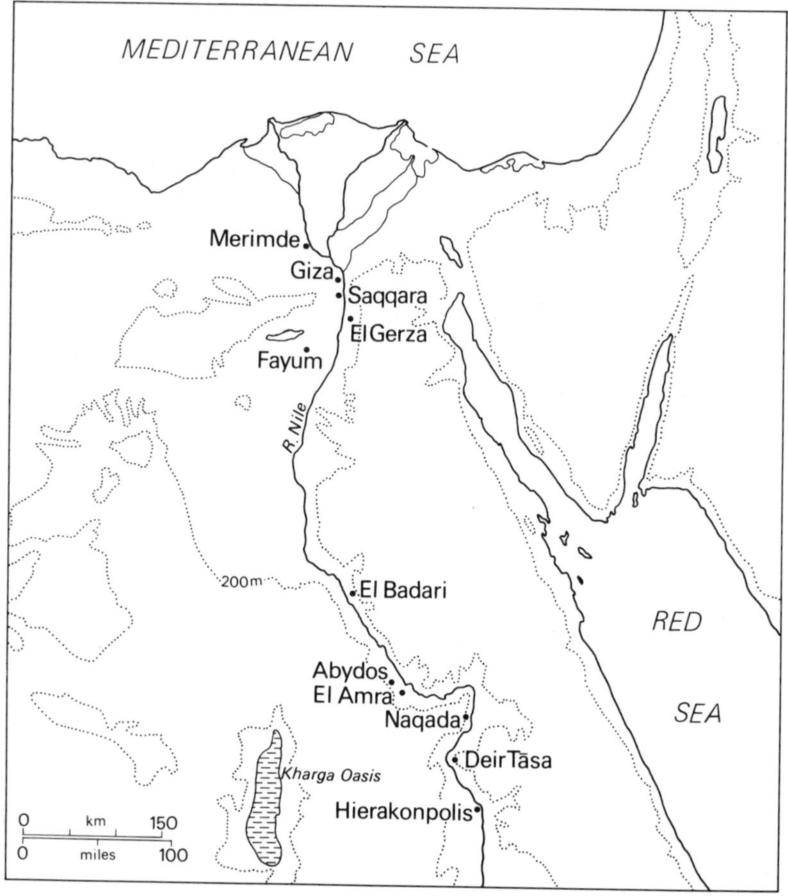

which fish, crocodiles and hippopotami were then able to flourish. That the Fayumis took advantage of this is shown by their equipment for hunting, including barbed bone harpoon-heads and flint arrow-heads of winged form; but the important thing is that they were farmers.

The Fayumi people kept sheep or goats, cattle and swine, and cultivated emmer and flax. The equipment used in harvesting, storing and grinding the grain, like the cereals themselves, were those developed long previously in western Asia. The silos lined with coiled basketry and containing carbonized cereals, yielded fine baskets, used in all probability for sowing, and wooden reaping-knives with flint blades set in slots, like the much older bone ones of the Natufians. Although fire-holes were noted in the mounds of midden material, no definite traces of dwellings were observed, from which it has been inferred that tents or similar structures were used. Numerous axe- and adze-blades made from polished flint or stone suggest that timber was nevertheless utilized on a considerable scale and it may prove that more substantial dwellings were in fact made. Traces of linen show that weaving was practised. Pots were made by

Table 19. *Some key radiocarbon dates for the Neothermal period in north Africa*

			B.C.
First Dynasty	Saqqara, tomb of vizier Hemaka	C 267 av.	2933 ± 200
Predynastic	El Omari, Egypt	C 643	3306 ± 230
	Naqada, Egypt		
	SD 36–46	C 811	3669 ± 280
	SD 34–8	C 810	3794 ± 300
Neolithic	Adrar Bous III, Niger	SA 100	3190 ± 300
	Shaheinab, Sudan	C 753	3110 ± 450
		C 754	3396 ± 380
	Dar-es-Soltan, Morocco	GrN 2805	4250 ± 82
	Haua Fteah, Cyrenaica:		
	Level VI, upper	NPL 41	2910 ± 97
	Level VI, lower	NPL 40	3850 ± 108
	Level VIII, upper	NPL 42	4420 ± 103
	Merimde, Egypt	U 6	4180 ± 110
	Fayum, Egypt	C 457	4145 ± 250
		C 550	4441 ± 180
Capsian	El Mekta, Algeria	L 134	6450 + 400
	Haua Fteah, Cyrenaica:		
	Level X, surface	GrN 3541	5050 + 110
	Level X, middle	GrN 3167	6450 + 150
Oranian	Haua Fteah, Cyrenaica:		
	Level XIV–XV	NPL 43	10,800 + 173
	Taforalit, Morocco	L 399E	10,120 + 400
			9950 ± 240

ANCIENT EGYPTIAN CIVILIZATION

hand in simple shapes, mainly undecorated flat-based bowls without handles, spouts or other features. Apart from shells, some of which were brought from the Red Sea and the Mediterranean, and beads of amazonite or microcline felspar of uncertain, but certainly exotic origin, the Fayumis made do with local materials and their economy was of simple subsistence type.

Badarian of Upper Egypt

Other communities of relatively simple farmers, depending on flint and stone for their basic technology, established themselves in Upper
315 Egypt, notably in the region near Badari, where they seem to have laid the basis of the Early Predynastic culture. Traces of the temporary settlement of such early farmers were found at Hammāmīya stratified below Early and Late Predynastic levels, but the bulk of our information comes from burials. The Badarian peasants cultivated emmer and barley which they harvested with reaping-knives set with bifacially flaked sickle-teeth and stored in clay silos; and they kept cattle and sheep or goats, though not apparently swine. In addition they hunted, using arrows tipped with heads of leaf- or hollow-based and winged form. As craftsmen they also wove, made baskets and turned out pottery by hand. This latter comprised bowls and open dishes, commonly black inside and near the rim, the lower part of the body being red or brown through oxidization; the finer ware was finished with a burnished rippled surface and patterns were sometimes made on the inner face of open vessels by means of burnished lines. Flint, stone and bone were freely used, but copper appeared only in the form of beads that had been hammered into shape, presumably from native metal. The dead were interred in a contracted attitude in oval trench graves clothed in linen with skin outer garments, as a rule with the head at the west end, facing south and so lying on their right side. The men were clean-shaven, but wore their hair long; and the women plaited theirs and wore ivory combs carved with animal heads. Finds of stone palettes, occasionally with red pigment or with malachite, suggest the use of cosmetics. Perforated shells were used for head-dresses, girdles and necklaces; and anklets, bracelets, rings and ear- or nose-plugs were also worn. A feature of Badarian practice of special significance for the future was their careful burial of domestic animals wrapped in textiles.

Among the graves with Badarian grave-goods were others with distinctive, though evidently closely related, furniture, which is commonly attributed to a separate culture named after the site of Deir

Tāsa. Although no radiocarbon or absolute dates are available for the Tasian it is generally held on not very impressive evidence to have preceded the Badarian. The absence of copper beads, on which some stress had been laid, could well be due to chance; and in any case the presence of absence of small trinkets of native copper has no real economic or technological significance. The distinctive beaker pots, slender, with round base and flaring rim, are decorated by incised patterns that suggest basketry prototypes.

Early Predynastic Egypt

The Early Predynastic or Amratian culture has been found at Naqada sandwiched between the Badarian, from which it apparently developed, and the overlying Late Predynastic. Radiocarbon dates suggest that it existed during the second quarter of the fourth millennium. Some marked changes are apparent. Whereas the villagers of Merimde and Badari camped on spurs overlooking the Nile and the Fayumis settled the margins of the Fayum lake, the Predynastic peoples seem to have been the first to exploit the possibilities of the naturally irrigated valley. The size of the Naqada settlement, an aggregation of mud and reed huts at least 92 metres across in either direction, and the number of the graves in the cemetery both suggest enlarged social units. Schematic representations of a variety of animals painted or scratched on pottery may have been intended as symbols of totems and it is significant that similar ones recur as emblems of nomes or territorial divisions during the historic period. It may well be therefore that the Amratian villages were occupied by totemic clans. The technology was still basically lithic, copper continuing to be used only in its native form and for such small objects as pins with rolled heads. On the other hand, flint was no longer obtained merely in the form of surface nodules; it was now mined and the roughing out and manufacture of tools was carried out on the site of the quarries. Bifacially flaked arrowheads continued to be made in numbers, including leaf and triangular as well as hollow-based forms. The finest pieces were fish-tail lanceheads and long dagger-blades, which had been ground into shape before being subjected to a final process of superbly controlled pressure flaking. This process, the object of which was no doubt to impart a surface finish, was also applied to polished flint axes and adzes. In general Amratian pottery was coarser than Badarian, probably because the Predynastic people were beginning to develop elegant stone vessels, cylindrical ones from alabaster and footed ones from basalt. Black-topped ware continued to be made, but a new departure was White Cross-lined ware in which patterns recalling basketry, together with others depicting animals, men and boats, were applied in dull white paint to a polished red surface. To judge from the clay figurines found in the graves, men appear to have gone unclothed apart from penis sheaths and sandals, though they wore plumes in their hair, and both sexes went in for a variety of ornaments, most of them elaborations of ones used by the Badarians, such as ivory combs carved with animal figures, glazed beads and a variety of bracelets. Stone palettes show that making up was still popular and indeed their more elaborate character – they might be shaped to animal profiles – suggests an even greater accent on cosmetics. In addition to personal ornaments the dead were accompanied by food and figurines, which might be carved from ivory, as well as being modelled more roughly in clay, in graves that were still simple holes in the ground.

Late Predynastic Egypt

The Late Predynastic culture, represented by Naqada II, extended further north into the northern part of Middle or the southern part of Lower Egypt and indeed takes its name from Gerza near the entrance to the Fayum depression. In the extreme south, however, it never displaced the Amratian in Nubia, nor at the opposite extreme did it penetrate northern Lower Egypt with the Delta, which was occupied by a quite different culture, represented by the settlement of Maadi near Cairo and by the cemetery of Heliopolis on the margin of the Delta. The Gerzean culture probably arose in Middle Egypt on an Amratian basis enriched by the permeation of cultural elements of Asiatic origin. Thus, whereas Black-topped pottery continued to be made for a while, White Cross-lined ware gave place to Decorated ware, painted in Asiatic fashion with dark red paint on a pale buff ground, to represent the natural markings of the stone vessels on which the forms were based. Stone vessels themselves continued to be made and the use of hard porphyry marks a further advance in an exacting craft.

A highly significant innovation was the introduction of metallurgy, which had appeared in western Asia a thousand years or so previously: in addition to the small objects which the Badarians and their immediate successors had made from native copper, the Gerzeans were now able to cast flat axes, ribbed daggers and flat knives. The ability to raise temperatures enough for casting copper also made

126 Predynastic sequences for Upper Egypt.

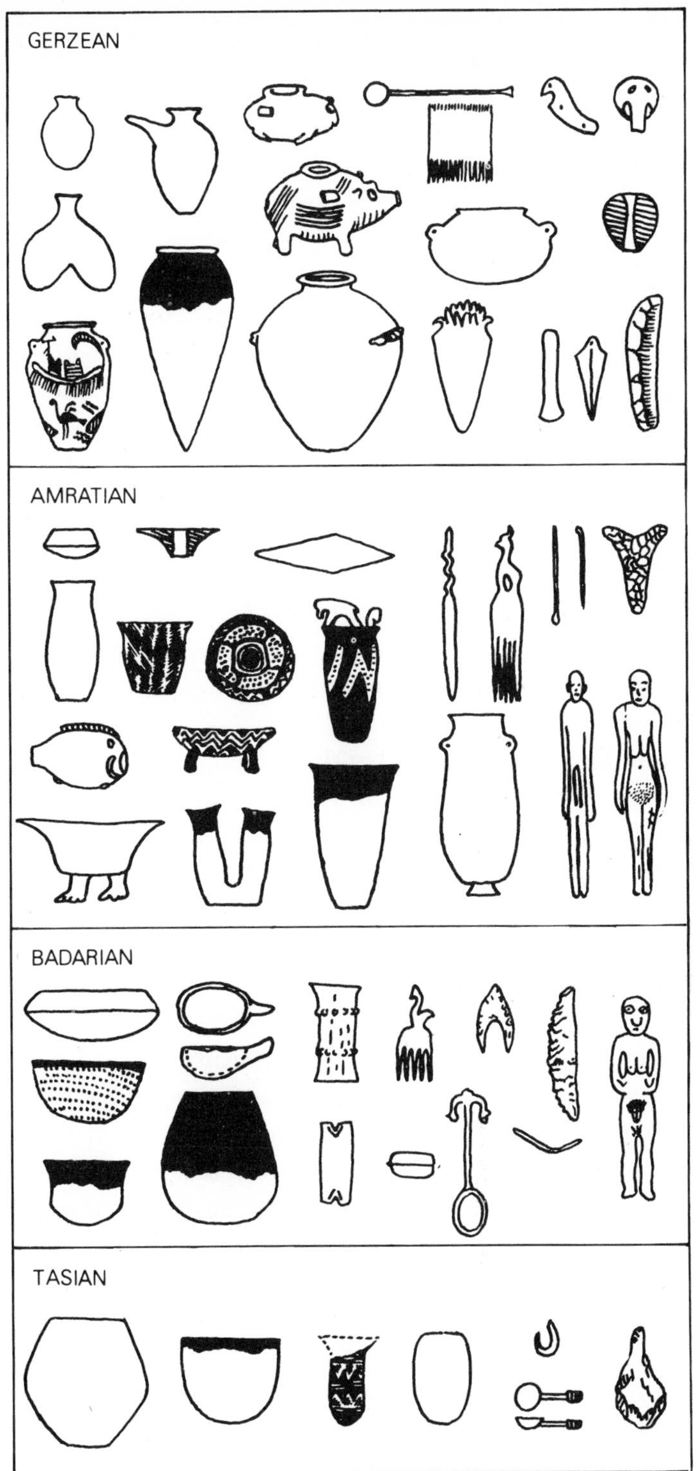

 it possible to manufacture faience, a substance consisting of an artifical core of finely powdered quartz grains cemented by fusion and coated with a glass glaze. Important raw materials were obtained from a distance: copper came from the eastern desert or from Sinai, but lead and silver were imported from Asia, and lapis lazuli from an ultimate source in northern Afghanistan, presumably by way of Mesopotamia. In this latter connection it is significant that a local copy of a Mesopotamian cylinder seal of Protoliterate type was found in one of the Gerzean graves at Naqada. Boats made of bundles of reeds, but of substantial size and provided with cabins, served for the transport of materials like mined flint or stone vessels on the Nile. These native boats were propelled by oars, but foreign-looking ones with upturned prow and stern painted on Gerzean pots were fitted with a sail. For overland portages asses were used, and it should be noted that wheeled vehicles, though long known in Mesopotamia, were not introduced in Egypt until the New Kingdom, which began *c.* 1570 B.C.

Gerzean society was firmly based on farming, and hunting had markedly declined as an economic activity. The villagers lived in more substantial houses, rectangular in plan and fitted with a wood-framed doorway in the side. Graves were no longer orientated regularly and it is noteworthy that they began to show a greater range of wealth in terms of burial offerings, some being provided with ledges, others with compartments separated off by wattle partitions, to contain extra offerings; the most one can say is that during Gerzean times there were signs of a growth in wealth accompanied by a more integrated social structure.

Unification of Upper and Lower Egypt

The ancient Egyptians attributed the unification of their country to a single individual, Menes, whom they supposed to have welded the twenty-two nomes of Upper and the twenty nomes of Lower Egypt into a single realm and to have initiated in his own person the First Dynasty of pharaohs. In reality the process must almost certainly have been a gradual one, lasting for at least two or three generations. The unification is unlikely, for one thing, to have been accomplished without a good deal of fighting, and we have evidence for this on a number of well-known archaeological objects. For instance scenes of royal conquest are carved in low relief on either face of a great
322 stone palette just over half a metre in length from the old royal
127 capital of Hierakonpolis in Upper Egypt: one depicts King Nar-mer,

127 Palette of Narmer, Hierakonpolis, Upper Egypt.

the crown of Upper Egypt on his head, despatching an enemy with a stone-headed mace and surrounded with captives and enemy dead; and the other shows the same ruler, this time with the crown of Lower Egypt, confronting four chiefs of nomes and surmounting a heap of decapitated enemies. It is interesting to note that two animals are depicted on this latter face with their necks intertwined, a convention also found on a dagger handle from Gebel el-Tarif, but only at home in Mesopotamia. Another knife-handle, this time of ivory from Gebel el-Arak, has been carved to show on one face combats between men and boats with standards and upturned ends and on the other a man dompting two lions. This last is especially interesting because the man is wearing a hat and skirt of Sumerian type and because the whole scene recalls the Sumerian epic of Gilgamesh.

The occurrence of elements of Mesopotamian origin among the representations on these key objects raises the question how far the unification of Egypt was brought about by foreign influence or even by alien intruders. There can be no doubt of the existence precisely
318 at the period of transition from the Predynastic to the Protodynastic or Archaic period of Egyptian history of innovations that stemmed from Mesopotamian sources of Proto-literate (Jamdet Naṣr) age. In addition to the cylinder seals and the art motifs already mentioned, one could cite brick architecture, which after a long history in Mesopotamia appeared suddenly in Egypt during the First Dynasty in the construction of tombs and which exhibited a series of detailed agreements, such as the size of bricks, the use of three rows of stretchers alternating with one of headers and the decorative use of buttresses and recesses. Another innovation to appear about the same time was writing, with ideograms, phonetic signs and determinatives, even though at first mainly as an element in monumental art rather than for the practical purposes for which it had been devised in Mesopotamia.

Dynastic Period

Yet it has to be emphasized that, important though Asiatic impulses undoubtedly were at this decisive juncture, the civilization that emerged in the Dynastic period was essentially Egyptian, the culmination of a thousand years or so of prehistory in the Nile Valley,
74 distinct from and in some respects in marked contrast to that of Mesopotamia. The continuity of Egyptian civilization from its prehistoric beginnings down to the Hellenistic Age and even to the spread of Islam owes much to geography. Whereas the inhabitants

of Sumer had to contend with rich and warlike mountain dwellers both in the east and north, as well as with occasional incursions from the western desert, the ancient Egyptians were comparatively insulated in the Nile Valley. They were not so remote as to be cut off from the stimulus of Asiatic civilization, deriving from that quarter first the arts of agriculture and then metallurgy and the techniques of incipient civilization, but they were far enough off to escape invasion, save at periods of exceptional weakness; and even when this did occur their civilization was too deeply rooted to be much affected by temporary political domination. Meanwhile the economic wealth conferred by the Nile floods and the cultural advantages derived from proximity to Asia ensured that the Egyptians were at all times so superior that they had nothing to fear from their neighbours in the deserts on either side or in tropical Nubia.

The main political danger was rivalry between Upper and Lower Egypt arising from the narrowness and great length of the alluvial zone of the Nile. It was because of this that the conquerors from the south found it worth while to set up an important centre at Memphis to match their old capital at Hierakonpolis and that down to the end of the New Kingdom the pharaohs wore the two crowns. The River Nile provided a physical means for uniting the country, but it was the supremacy of the pharaoh that guaranteed that unity. As a divine ruler he symbolized the whole community and it was his unchallenged sovereignty that engendered confidence and stability. The whole administration was carried on by authority delegated from the pharaoh, whether through governors of nomes or through officials of the central government, one of whose main concerns was to channel a sizeable proportion of the social surplus into the hands of the ruler. The importance of leading officials even during the Archaic phase of the Dynastic period is witnessed by the scale and richness of their tombs recently explored at Saqqara. On the other hand the supremacy of the pharaoh is well displayed on one of the great ceremonial stone maces from Hierakonpolis, showing Nar-mer raised up nine steps on his throne, confronted by captives and attended by a priest, a sandal-bearer and fan-bearers. Another shows the 'Scorpion' ruler presiding at the opening of a canal, a symbolic act emphasizing how the people of Egypt depended for their very sustenance on the mediation of the pharaoh. From the beginning crops must have benefited from the natural irrigation brought about by the Nile flood, but for any great extension of the fertile zone it was necessary to cut channels and lift the Nile water into them by

some such device as the *schaduf*. The increase in population that seems from all appearances to have marked the Predynastic period suggests that some such works must have been initiated before the end of the prehistoric period. On the other hand the institution of a highly centralized government, while in itself expensive to maintain, made it possible to undertake public works on a scale not
128 hitherto possible.

In addition to centralizing sovereignty and administration, the pharaohs were careful to promote an official religion. This was centred on the solar cult whose priests evolved a cosmogony, accounting for the genesis of nine main deities, at their headquarters in Heliopolis (the ancient Egyptian On), a little north of Memphis. Of the progeny of Ra-Atum, the sun-god, the most influential was Osiris, lord of the regions of the dead, whose cult was a direct counterpart. Preoccupation with death, or rather with the continuance of life after physical death, played an immensely important part in the life of ancient Egypt. The basic belief was that the spirit could survive only if the body was adequately preserved and provided with what was needed for its well-being in the after life. As the Egyptians grew richer and their social structure became more elab-

128 Part of scene in tomb of Egyptian nobleman of XIIth dynasty showing a colossus mounted on a wooden sledge hauled by a work party totalling 172 disciplined men.

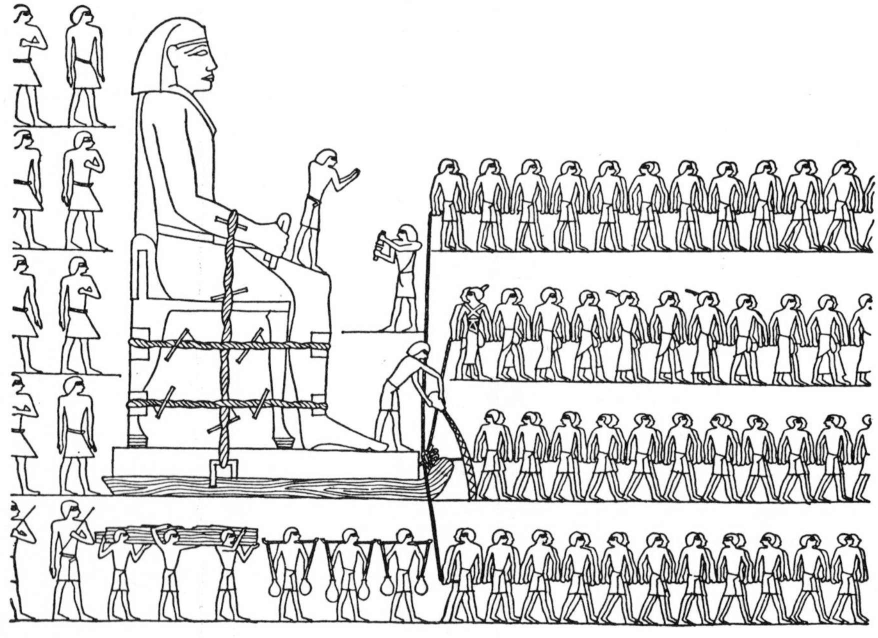

orate the tombs of the more important members of the community took on a monumental form and were furnished richly to accord with
321 the position in life of the dead. By the First Dynasty substantial structures of sun-baked bricks, known as Mastabas, began to be erected over the graves of prominent people, and by the Third Dynasty stone was employed for royal tombs. The first or Stepped
129 Pyramid, erected by Zoser at this time, was built over a Mastaba, already twice enlarged, and set in the midst of a large rectangular enclosure. The burial itself was concealed in a maze of passages and
317 rooms at the foot of a deep shaft beneath. The Old Kingdom was symbolized above all by the regular pyramids which began to be made in the Fourth Dynasty and reached an early climax in the Great
130 Pyramid built at Giza for Cheops and his queen. The dimensions of this structure – approximately 231 metres square at the base, which covered over 5·3 hectares, and rising, when complete, to a height of 147 metres – are impressive in themselves, but the great cause for wonder is the sheer labour involved in the preparation and transport

129 Stepped Pyramid of Zoser in its enclosure, Saqqara, Egypt: IIIrd Dynasty.

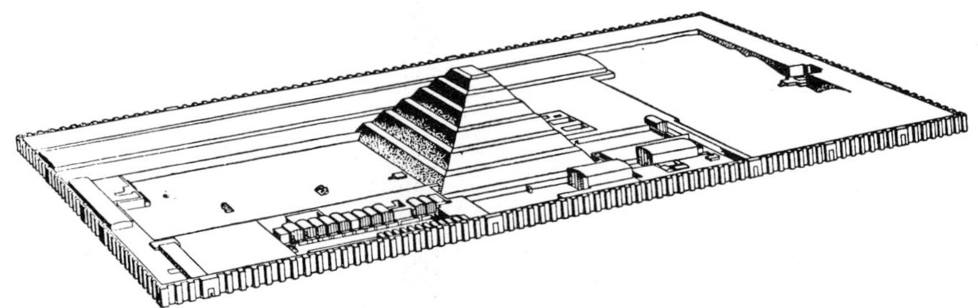

130 Great Pyramid of Cheops near Giza, Egypt: IVth Dynasty. Note passages and chambers seen in section.

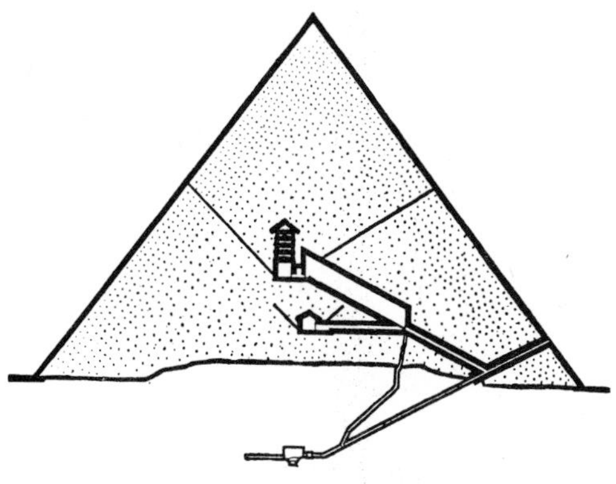

of the stone. Approximately 2,300,000 blocks, weighing on the average some 2½ tonnes, were used and the mere transport of these by manpower would have involved the labour of perhaps 100,000 levies for a three months' spell in each of twenty years, the time it took to complete the work, according to the story recorded by Herodotus; and in addition to this a permanent force of masons and labourers would have been needed on the site, perhaps as many as 4,000 in all. When it is recalled that upwards of twenty pyramids, none so large, but all substantial, were erected during the Old Kingdom alone, the overwhelming force of the idea behind them, the conservation of the bodies of the pharaoh and his consort and their provision for life after physical death, and the almost incredible concentration of the forces of an essentially poor society on the needs of one man will be even more apparent. Another expression of authority is to be seen in monumental sculptures of Pharaohs carved
131 in hard stone. The divine status of the ruler might be emphasized by his association in the monument itself with mythological figures.

By contrast, no trace of the houses or even of the palaces of these divine rulers survives. For the purposes of transient life even the greatest were content to live in flimsy structures, while lavishing their power and substance on the construction and provisioning of their own tombs. In this respect the difference between Egypt and Sumer is marked, even when we remember the riches of the Royal Tombs of Ur. Although in abstract terms civilization had progressed by way of the same broad stages of development, the actual expression or form of the two civilizations was markedly distinct. Nourished by the Nile and sheltered by protective deserts and their own superior technology, the ancient Egyptians were able to maintain their way of life with remarkably little change over something like three thousand years of recorded history. The breakdown of central authority that marked the end of the Old Kingdom would in an Asiatic state almost certainly have led to alien domination, but in Egypt it was the local nomarchs who profited and when the royal power was re-established with the Middle Kingdom (*c.* 2132–1777 B.C.) the construction of pyramids was begun again as though no interruption had been. During the second intermediate period, it is true, Egypt fell under the yoke of foreign rulers, the Hyksos or

131 IVth Dynasty ruler Mycerinus between cow-goddess Hathor and goddess of the jackal-nome.

Shepherd kings, but it is significant that their eviction (1573/70 B.C.) inaugurated, in the New Kingdom, the greatest phase in the history of the land, during which Egyptian armies warred against the leading powers of western Asia and campaigned as far east as the Euphrates. Even during the period of decline that followed the close of the Twentieth Dynasty (*c.* 1090 B.C.) and witnessed conquests by Assyrians, Persians and Greeks the fundamentals of Egyptian civilization survived: indeed, under the earlier Ptolemies, whose rule began with the death of Alexander in 323 B.C., the Egyptian state experienced something of an imperial revival; and independence was only ended with its conversion into a province of the Roman Empire on the death of Cleopatra in 30 B.C.

Ancient Egypt owed its history to the twin facts of being near enough to share in the basic advances made in the creative zone of south-west Asia, while at the same time being remote and self-sufficient enough to mature and conserve its own distinctive civilization over what in terms of other and later traditions must be accounted an immensely long period. For the rest of Africa the consequences were less happy. The ancient Egyptians, secure in their homeland, made no conscious effort to extend their civilization or even their sphere of influence over other peoples: they defended their frontiers and during the New Kingdom extended these far into south-west Asia; but in their African homeland they contented themselves with holding their neighbours at arms' length. This is not to say that the ancient Egyptians refrained from all contact with other African peoples: apart from anything else they were compelled from time to time to campaign in Nubia, they employed Libyan mercenaries and they even sent trading expeditions to the land of Punt, activities which between them must have resulted in some limited amount of cultural interchange. The fact remains that pharaonic Egypt, in itself technologically sheltered and conservative, served even more as a buffer than as a mediator of higher culture.

The opening up of sub-Saharan Africa

329 *The spread of iron-working*

Few things illustrate more plainly the peripheral nature of sub-Saharan Africa during the later stages of prehistory than the spread of iron-working from western Asia. Iron-working was first established on African soil with the implantation of the Phoenician colony of Carthage traditionally founded in 814 B.C. The ancient Egyptians had utilized meteoric iron on a miniature scale since Predynastic times and the pharaohs had received presents of weapons of forged iron in the course of diplomatic exchanges with the Hittite kings in the early days of the New Empire, but iron working as such was not established in Egypt until the country had been conquered by Asshurbanipal in 662 B.C. and incorporated as a province of the Assyrian Empire. From Egypt it spread south to the Sudan where it appeared as a component of the basically derivative technology of the Kushite kingdom. The quantity and extent of the slag together with the number of open hearths and, at a certain stage, of shaft furnaces bears witness to the importance of iron-working at Meroe during the latter half of the first millennium B.C.

132 Iron Age Africa (see fig. 125 for inset detail).

Primitive iron technology spread fairly rapidly over the savannah
of sub-Saharan Africa. It appeared to the north of the equatorial
forest on the Jos plateau of Nigeria, to judge from the date of the
iron-smelting site of Taruga, as early as the late fourth century B.C.
327 The context in which it was found, that of the Nok culture, shows
clearly enough that the new technology was being practised by
133 Negroes. The terracotta representations of Negro mens' heads, not
only emphasize this, but also provide a convincing prototype for later
330 Yoruba art including the terracotta and bronze heads of Ife. East
of the Congo iron-working was being practised by the inhabitants

133 Terracotta head from Nok, Nigeria.

of Kenya, Ruanda, Uganda and Tanzania, identified in the arch-
134 aeological record by bowls and globular pottery vessels with dimple
309, 325 bases, as early as the first century A.D. About the same time it extended as far south as the Zambesi where it was associated with analogous pottery. Beyond the Zambesi iron-working was practised by the first inhabitants of Zimbabwe whose settlement, dating from before A.D. 300, was found stratified under the stone necropolis. By the fifth century it had spread beyond the Limpopo, where it was carried on by stock-keeping farmers at the site of Broederstroom.

The prehistoric iron-using communities of sub-Saharan Africa evidently lived in open village settlements comprising from twenty to thirty biological families. The shallowness of their deposits and the wide extent of hut remains – anything from ten to forty acres – suggest that the villages were rebuilt on adjacent sites. It is relevant that at the present day the Nyakusa and Ngonda peoples do so each generation. This made it possible to cultivate the sites of old dwellings and to benefit from the organic refuse stored up in the soil. The huts were characteristically round. They might be built, as they apparently were at sites near the Kalambo Falls, of poles daubed with clay and roofed by conical thatching. In Zambia and further south iron-working spread in the context of the initial agriculture and stock-raising to appear in successive regions. The occurrence of numerous large grindstones at Kalambo argues for the importance of plant foods, which in the absence of actual traces may plausibly be assumed to have included finger-millet and perhaps sorghum, cow peas and ground-beans. Animal remains were similarly absent. Domestic cattle as well as sheep and goats were kept at Broederstroom, but it is uncertain when the former first appeared in sub-Saharan Africa. Among the artefacts fabricated from iron were axe- and adze-heads, as well as arrowheads and rings.

In the long run iron technology wrought one of its main effects on African history by making easier the clearance of equatorial forest

134 Dimple-based bowls from Yala Alego, Kavirondo, Kenya.

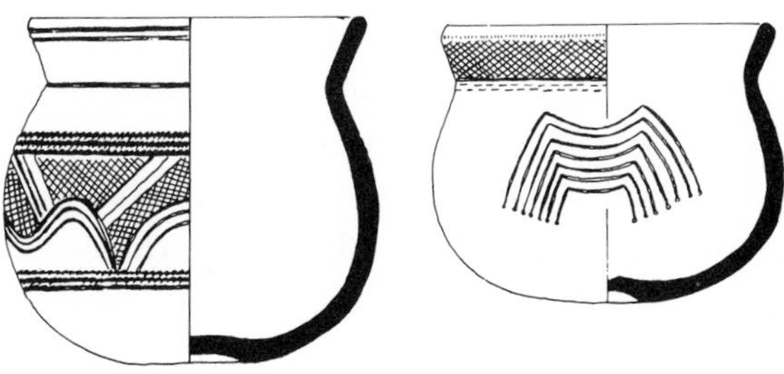

and the creation of yam gardens and banana plantations. The yams grown in Africa in recent times were partly (e.g. *Dioscorea cayenensis* and *rotundata*) native, but partly (e.g. *D. alata, esculenta* and *bulbifera*) they originated like the banana in south-east Asia. When and how these last reached Africa and whether their arrival succeeded or stimulated the domestication of indigenous species is still unknown. Ethnology suggests that the south-east Asian species may have been carried as food by sailors: the outrigger boats of the East African coast, like the widely distributed xylophones, could both have come from this direction; and Malaya–Polynesian affinities have been claimed for the Malagache language of Madagascar.

292 *The impact of more advanced economies*

The process by which iron-working spread over most of sub-Saharan Africa was complemented by the impact of more advanced economies based on north Africa and outside. When this began is obscure. There are no solid grounds for thinking that the ancient Egyptians drew significantly on the resources of sub-Saharan Africa. The same applies to the Meroitic kingdom and again to the kingdom of Axum which arose in north Ethiopia near the beginning of the first millennium A.D. and adopted Christianity during the fourth century. The first undoubted indications that the mineral resources of sub-
326 Saharan Africa were being tapped for export comes from the Transvaal where copper mining began in the fifth century in radiocarbon terms. Since the aboriginal population was not then exploiting the metal the inference is that mining was carried on by intruders for
135 use elsewhere. More conclusive evidence comes from Zimbabwe in
328 the neighbourhood of the Mashonaland goldfields. By contrast with the earliest settlement relating to subsistence farmers the second phase (*c.* 600–11th century A.D.) was marked by two complementary features: the people were not only wearing gold ornaments for the first time, but also and significantly cylindrical glass beads of kinds known from Arabian, Persian and Indian sources. The presence of opaque oblate beads of undoubted Arabic origin in the third occupation strengths the idea that Arab traders were by this time actively exploiting African resources. Indeed we already know that from the ninth and tenth centuries onward the Arabs maintained trading townships along the eastern coast of Africa from Mogadishu and Brava on the Somali coast to Kilwa and Sofala in the south. About the same time as this was going forward on the east coast the Arabs of Mediterranean Africa were tapping the gold of the Upper Niger

and Ashanti, as well no doubt as ivory and slaves, by means of
caravan routes across the Sahara for which camels were by then
available. In return the Nigerians obtained not merely salt and
copper but the technique of *cire perdue* casting which made possible
136 the bronze heads of Ife. It was on the control of such trade that the
Moslem rulers of the states that grew up in the savannah zone
between the desert and the forested coastal zone of west Africa based
their power.

When in due course the Portuguese broke the Arab monopoly they
built forts of their own on the east coast and it is hardly surprising
323 to find that in the fourth phase at Zimbabwe imports derived from
the Portuguese connection, notably glass beads from India and
Indonesia and Ming porcelain from China. Meanwhile in finding
their way to India the Portuguese perforce explored the coast of west
Africa. Between 1433, when Henry the Navigator began to open up
the coast of west Africa and 1488, when Dias first rounded the Cape,
successive expeditions had identified the main gold-bearing rivers.
The castles they built on the Gold Coast were forerunners of the
many defended posts established by the north European nations who
followed them in the quest for gold and in due course for slaves.

It is ironic that the heaviest price for the untold misery of the slave

135 The citadel of Zimbabwe.

trade has in the long run been paid by the western world, even though it had been carried on for long centuries before Europeans had first appeared on the scene. The ultimate result of European trade and exploration has been to draw the country within range of modern science and technology, to bring its economy within the world market and to stimulate the growth of modern political institutions including the sovereign independent state. In the course of doing so it has inevitably damaged the integrity of indigenous cultures and institutions. Yet, partly owing to the fact that direct European influence was for long confined to the coast, but in large measure due to the vitality of the cultures surviving from prehistory, the peoples of
331 sub-Saharan Africa have preserved their heritage of music, sculpture and socio-political styles more fully than for instance the populations of some highly industrialized states in the west have managed to
137 retain their own folk cultures. The bronze plaques of Benin combine
324 Negroid and Portuguese elements in an art already ancient in west Africa. In modern times artists in many lands have sought inspiration in the products of miscalled 'Primitive Art' to aid them in breaking through the constrictions of their own academic traditions. Africa has not been the only source, but it is one which in respect of west African sculpture in particular has been made explicit in the collections formed by creative artists in the west.

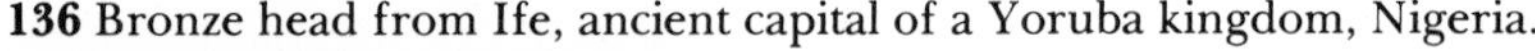

136 Bronze head from Ife, ancient capital of a Yoruba kingdom, Nigeria.

137 Bronze panel from Benin, showing Nigerian wearing helmet of European character.

6

The Indian sub-continent

It is still an open question when the Indian sub-continent first began to be occupied by man, but it is already evident that continuous human occupation goes back at least to the latter half of the Middle Pleistocene, perhaps a quarter of a million years ago. The upper limit of Indian prehistory as defined by written records varies slightly in different territories. The north-western provinces featured first in the histories of the ancient world as a result of invasions beginning with that of the Persian king Cyrus (*c.* 530 B.C.). By the time of Herodotus this region, under the name Gandhara, was one of the richest satrapies of the Achaemenid Empire. Alexander of Macedon's incursion (*c.* 327–325 B.C.) made an even sharper imprint on history since some of the most vivid accounts were written by eye-witnesses, notably by his admiral Nearchus. For the greater part of the sub-continent indigenous historical records began with the rock-cut inscriptions of the Mauryan emperor Ashoka (*c.* 272–232 B.C.). Since these extend from the north-west as far south as Mysore they form a convenient watershed between the prehistoric and historic periods for the greater part of the sub-continent. Even so tribal societies continued to shelter in jungle areas down to the time they were brought within the range of history by western ethnographers.

Early prehistory

The earliest traces of human occupation at present known from the sub-continent are those from the Potwar district of the Punjab and
363 more particularly from sites along the Sohan river between
Rawalpindi and the Indus confluence. The only hint of earlier occupation is offered by a handful of worn flakes from deposits of the second glaciation. On present evidence it must be accepted that India, though occupied in historical terms for an immensely long

138 Microlithic industries in India.

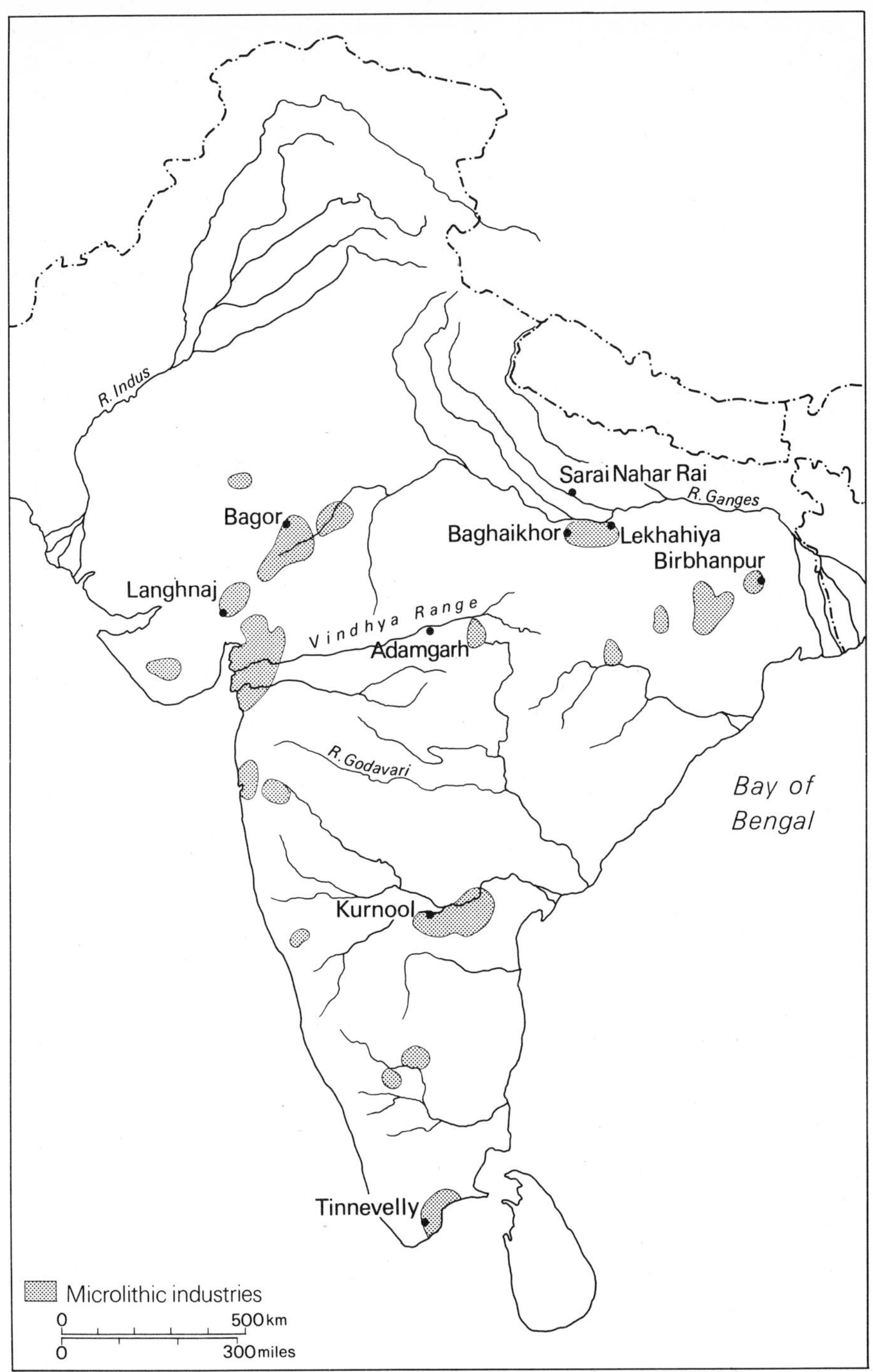

time, was in fact settled comparatively late with respect to Africa. Again, whether or not the original colonization which must have come from the west was reinforced by further migrations or movements of ideas, the lithic technology of the sub-continent passed through the same broad evolutionary stages as Africa and south-west Asia. On the other hand the later developments of the Indian Older Stone Age were by comparison restrained in their expression.

Lithic technology

The early Potwar industries combine two basic modes of working. Clumsy scraper and chopper-like tools and their attendant flakes were accompanied by traces of bifacial flaking. Thus the Middle Pleistocene industries of India resembled those which existed at a relatively advanced stage of the Olduvai sequence in east Africa. The same duality persisted in the lithic assemblages dating from the third interglacial: over a territory extending from the Gujarat to the Punjab and Orissa and down to Madras rougher forms were reinforced by more refined forms of cleaver and hand-axe comparable with those of Upper Stellenbosch assemblages in south Africa and Upper Acheulian ones in Europe; and the flake and core component came to display, admittedly sparingly, a technique of producing flakes from prepared cores comparable with the Levalloisian in Africa and Europe.

Overlying this Acheulo-Levalloisian level at Nevasa on the Pravara river assemblages have been found which show a predominance of flakes and an overall reduction in size. Similar Middle Palaeolithic assemblages occur over great tracts of the sub-continent from the Punjab to Madras. Bifacial tools continued to be made, but the emphasis was now firmly on flake tools. Some of these had been struck from tortoise cores, but the Levallois technique, though present, was not prominent. Again, the points and sidescrapers shaped by careful secondary retouch applied to the edges of flakes, not to mention the thin bifacially flaked points found with some mode 3 assemblages elsewhere, are conspicuously absent.

The industries which follow are even poorer in secondary features. This is one reason why they have only lately been recognized. Another is that little is known about final Pleistocene and early Neothermal stratigraphy in India and that in any case so many of the reported finds come from the surface. Some of the few chronological clues come from Rajasthan where dunes accumulated during arid phases coinciding with extensions of the Great Indian Sand Desert or Thar. Observations at sites like Pavagadh Hill and Visadi suggest, though they hardly prove as yet, that an unspecialized blade and burin industry in mode 4 relates to an arid phase dating from the final phase of the Pleistocene. A similar industry, this time enriched by backed blades and a greater variety of burins, has been recovered from the surface at Renigunta in the Chittor district west of Madras. Renewed excavations at caves in the Kurnool district of Andhra Pradesh has produced a similar flint industry together with unspecialized bone artefacts. These are in the main crudely made by breaks and edge-flaking, but there are signs that burins had been used in some cases to isolate the blanks. Further evidence for the existence of blade and burin industries intermediate in age between flake and microlithic assemblages in modes 3 and 5 has recently been recovered from the Belan river gravels near Allahabad and from the Bhimbetka rock-shelter, Madhya Pradesh.

2;347 *Mesolithic settlement*

As in so many other parts of the Old World the opening phases of the Neothermal period were marked over much of the Indian sub-continent by the adoption of a lithic technology associated with the use of composite artefacts and featuring points, barbs and blades for arrows, spearheads and cutting tools. Since industries of this kind
139 from Adamgarh and Bagor have been dated to the late sixth and fifth millennia respectively in terms of radiocarbon, that is earlier than the chalcolithic intrusions in the north-west, they can reasonably

139 Microlithic implements from Bagor.

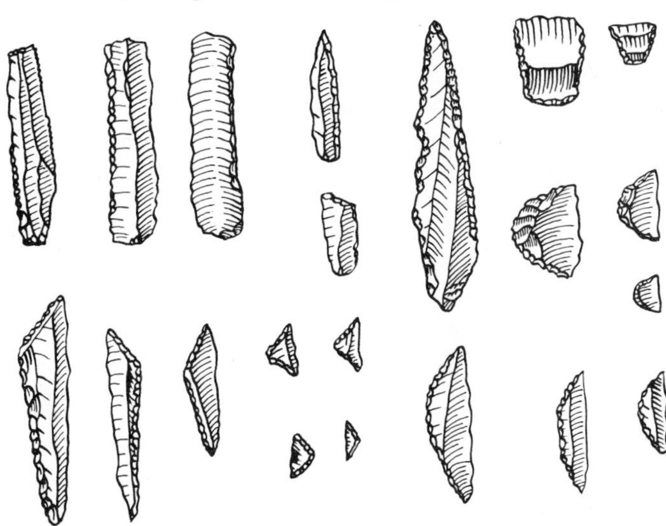

be identified with the indigenous population. Although the present pattern of finds reflects to some extent gaps in research, it is evident that microlithic industries are widely distributed over the modern state of India apart from the Ganges basin. Many kinds of environment were exploited. Sparsely wooded rocky territories were favoured as well as sandy areas like those of North Gujarat and the Tinnevelly district of the extreme south. On the other hand many sites occur in the sandstone Vindhya and Kaimar ranges which still carry heavy tree cover in places. River banks and in the Bombay district sea coasts also attracted settlement. Individual sites were as a rule small and concentrated. Fire-places accompanied occasionally by traces of stone paving are as a rule the only structures relating to settlement, suggesting that dwellings were lightly constructed from organic materials. Comparison of the stone artefacts from Sarai Nahar Rai on the margin of a fossil loop of the Ganga and from sites on the Vindhya hills some 160 km distant argues for seasonal movement within extensive annual territories. The probability is that the traces found at a site like Sarai Nahar Rai relate to a number of seasonal visits on the part of a group even smaller than the total area of 1,800 sq. metres would suggest. On the other hand this and other comparable sites were evidently occupied long enough to involve the need for burial. At every open site where they are found graves occur within the restricted area of settlement and burials also occur in occupied caves as at Baghạikhor and Lekhahiya near Mirzapur. Two main forms of inhumation occur. Whereas at Langhnaj the bodies had been buried in a tightly flexed attitude with the heads facing west, at Bagor and Sarai Nahar Rai the heads faced east and the bodies were extended with one forearm placed diagonally across the abdomen. The Sarai Nahar Rai cemetery yielded information of exceptional interest on the socio-economic life of these people. A double burial, in which two men were placed on the right and two women on the left of the grave, reflects the distinct status of the two sexes founded probably on an economic division of labour as well as upon complementary biological functions. The fact that ten out of the eleven individuals died between the ages of sixteen and thirty suggests that children and infants were buried elsewhere or otherwise disposed of and the presence of only one adult over thirty years of age underlines the brevity of human life at that time. Another fact of extreme interest is that in three instances microliths were found in a position to suggest that individuals may have been shot; the one case in which a microlith was actually embedded in a rib can hardly admit of any other explanation. How this phenomen, observed also in Africa and Europe, is to be interpreted is another question. Does it imply competition for scarce resources or could it not reflect the danger inherent in the hunting method represented by some Iberian rock-paintings in which during the closing stages of the hunt the archers formed a circle and shot their arrows at close range?

At a number of caves and rock-shelters yielding microlithic industries, and notably at Adamgarh, Lekhahiya and Mirzapur, rock-paintings have been observed. As is usually the case no connection can be proved between the makers of the lithic assemblages and the art. Certain scenes, notably those depicting elephants and warriors mounted on horses must belong to the historic period. On the other hand hunting scenes such as those which at Mirzapur underlie these historical paintings may well date from the local prehistoric period and could even have been executed by the people responsible for the microlithic industries.

Something, though as yet nothing definitive, can be learned about the basis of subsistence of these people. To judge only from the data available from archaeological sites it would seem that diet was focused on meat. Remains of fish, tortoise, turtle and monitor lizard suggest that the food-quest was wide-ranging, but the main bulk of animal protein from sites like Adamgarh, Bagor, Langhnaj and Sarai Nahar Rai comes from herbivorous mammals. Whether the indigenous population had domesticated animals like cattle and swine before these were introduced together with sheep and goat from the Iranian plateau by relatively sophisticated farmers can hardly be answered until we have adequately diagnosed and accurately dated faunal assemblages from deposits secure against later intrusion. Meanwhile it is significant that the microlith-makers who camped on the dunes at Langhnaj ate cattle and swine (*Sus scrofa cristatus*) as well as hog deer (*Axis porchinus*), swamp deer (*Cervus duvauceli*), spotted deer (*Axis axis*), black buck (*Antelope cervicapra*) and nilgai (*Boselaphus tragocamelus*), but not sheep or goat the two animals which must necessarily have been introduced. Again, where these do occur as at Bagor and Adamgarh there is evidence for later occupation. On the other hand studies on the plant remains from
364 natural deposits in the beds of former salt-lakes in Rajasthan in north-west India dating from between 7500 and 3000 B.C. have yielded evidence that point to the likelihood of cereal cultivation. This comprises evidence for extensive scrub burning combined with

Cerealia pollen. Although cultivated cereals have yet to be recovered from archaeological sites of this period, it is suggestive that high values for *Cerealia* have been noted from pre-Harappan levels at the major site of Kalibangan.

Later prehistory

As a peninsula cut off from central Asia by the Himalayas the Indian sub-continent must have received its main accessions of population and ideas during prehistoric times as it did during the historic period from the north-west. Through the Hindu-Kush there was entry by way of the Khyber–Peshawar route and further south there was access from the Iranian plateau by way of Kandahar and Quetta. It was from Iran that the uplands of Baluchistan and the lowlands of Sind were first colonized by farmers just as during proto-historic and historic times it was from the north-west that there came Aryan speaking barbarians, Persians, Greeks and the rest. The view that the history of India was for long the product of 'diminishing ripples of alien influence radiating from an entry in the north-west', while not fully sustainable, does help one to understand another feature of Indian archaeology, namely that the further south one looks at any moment of time the more backward in stadial terms the culture. Yet this picture needs serious qualification. For one thing the north-east route from Thailand and Burma by way of Assam, though subsidiary, certainly played some part in the enrichment of India. For another it is of the essence of peninsulas to be accessible by sea. Already during the third millennium the Indus Valley was linked by sea with Sumer. In later times trading contacts between the Middle East and ultimately the Roman world on the one side and the Far East by way of south-east Asia on the other helped to redress the balance by enriching and stimulating the far south of the sub-continent. Lastly and most importantly it would be entirely wrong to view the sub-continent as culturally inert, a mere recipient of influences from without. The population of India had been in continuous occupation for a period of almost unimaginable length in historical terms before the first pot or copper artefact appeared there. It is hardly to be wondered at that the settled cultures that developed were distinctively Indian in style and character.

Chalcolithic farmers of Baluchistan and Sind

To judge from radiocarbon dating of the first settlement at Kile Ghul Mohammad farmers with a comparatively sophisticated technology

had already colonized northern Baluchistan by way of Seistan and
366: 9–17 the Helmand River as early as the middle of the fourth millennium
B.C. These people were already turning their pots on the wheel and making copper artefacts. Within a few hundred years they had colonized an extensive territory including Sind and the lower Indus Valley. The designs painted on their pots define a number of distinct social territories. The Zhob potters of northern Baluchistan and the makers of Togau ware extending over the southern part of the country applied friezes of humped oxen with stylized elongated legs in a manner that compares tellingly with that seen on painted vessels from the mounds of Hissar and Sialk two thousand kilometres or so to the west on the inner flanks of the Elburz and Zagros mountains of Iran. Oxen were conspicuously absent on the other hand from the repertoire of the Nal and Amri potters, the former of whom kept
342 to the higher ground, the latter to the foot-hills and the lower Indus
plain. The Nal potters distinguished themselves by using polychrome paints as well as by making some use of animal designs alongside the geometric patterns which predominate in both groups. The makers of black-painted Kulli pottery, direct successors of the Nal potters,
140 were fond of depicting bulls, though in this case tethered to trees
in precisely the same style as those found on painted vessels from Susa and Early Dynastic Sumer. This stylistic borrowing is matched by the westward distribution of Kulli ware, both on the high ground forming the hinterland of the Makran coast and even more strikingly on the island of Abu Dhabi off the Trucial coast on the south shore of the Persian Gulf. This suggests that the people who made this pottery may well have played a key role in linking the great riverine civilizations of Mesopotamia and the Indus Valley.

345–6, 352, *Harappan florescence*

357, 366 If the peasant societies of Baluchistan and Sind are best regarded
as regional manifestations of a way of life common to large parts of

140 Painting of humped back cattle on Kulli ware.

the Iranian plateau and beyond, the Harappan civilization of the Indus basin must surely be accounted an independent and original florescence even if it issues from the same stem. There are two cogent reasons for saying this. First is the fact that the form and style of Harappan civilization and its material products are manifestly recognizable when seen in alien contexts. Then again, excavation and the application of radiocarbon analysis have made it plain that cultural antecedents exist for this civilization in the Indus basin itself, even if details of the pedigree have yet to be recovered. Harappan civilization was not an outpost of Sumerian but an independent entity.

Before touching further on its antecedents it will be convenient to indicate the age of this civilization as precisely as possible. One way of doing so is to note the chronological contexts in which

Table 20. *Some key radiocarbon dates for early village and urban settlement in the Indian sub-continent*

			B.C.
Pre-Harappan			
Damb Sadaat, Baluchistan	Amri ware	L 180B	2400 ± 350
Kot Diji, Sind	Layer 14	P 196	2471 ± 141
Kile Ghul Mahammad, Baluchistan	Preceramic	L 180A	3500 ± 500
Harappan			
Mohenjo-daro, Sind	Final Harappan	TF 75	1650 ± 110
Lothal, Gujarat	Layer 10	TF 136	1965 ± 130
Ahar, Rajasthan	Range at 11·3 m	(V 56)	1765 ± 95
		(V 57)	2025 ± 95
Kalibangan, Rajasthan	Range	TF 150	1790 ± 100
		TF 139, 145, 147, 151, 163	
		TF 160	2110 ± 100
Kot Diji, Sind	Layer 4*a*	P 195	1975 ± 134
	Layer 5	P 179	2211 ± 151
Peninsular chalcolithic			
Nevasa, Bombay	Topmost chalcolithic	P 181	1250 ± 122
Navdatoli, Madhya Pradesh	Trench 1,		
	Layer 2	P 205	1344 ± 125
	Layer 3	P 204	1499 ± 127
	Layer 6	P 202	1553 ± 128
'*Neolithic*'			
Bainapalli, Madras	At 1·8 m	TF 349	1390 ± 100
Tekkalakota, Mysore	Range	TF 239	1445 ± 105
		TF 266	1675 ± 100
Burzahom, Kashmir	At 2·9 m	TF 129	1720 ± 90
		TF 128	2255 ± 115
Utnūr, Andhra Pradesh	Phase II A	TF 167	1940 ± 110
	Phase I B	BM 54	2170 ± 150

141 Chalcolithic India.

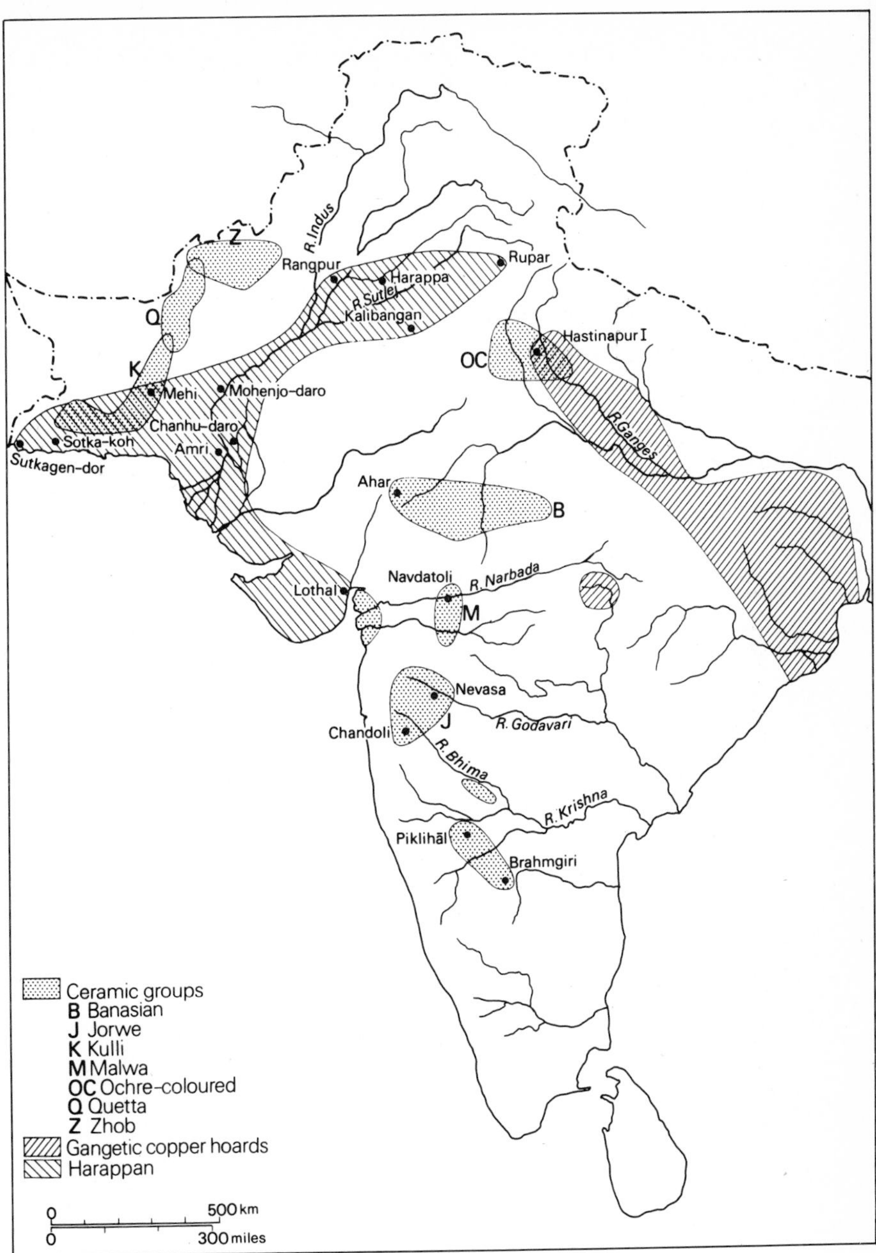

recognizably Harappan seals occur in Mesopotamia. The great majority fall within the Sargonid and Isin-Larsa periods, that is between *c.* 2350 and 1770 B.C., and having regard to the long life of such objects this is not contradicted by the few examples known from Kassite contexts. Again, the few references in Mesopotamian literature that can plausibly be related to such contacts date from the IIIrd dynasty of Ur and the ensuing Larsa dynasty. These historical dates are interestingly confirmed by the conventional radiocarbon dates ranging from *c.* 2300 to 1750 B.C.

Turning now to immediate antecedents it is reasonable to consider first and foremost material recovered from levels underlying Harappan layers at three widely separated sites in the Indus basin, namely Amri, Kalibangan and Kot Diji. This includes pottery, stone tools and, in the first two, copper objects. The most diagnostic of these, the pottery, although resembling in certain technical respects Harappan ware, for instance in the common use of the wheel and of painted designs, differs in shape and also in being pink or creamish in colour rather than red. On the other hand it compares in some instances closely with certain of the Baluchistan wares already mentioned. Again the mud-brick structures, including at Kalibangan bread ovens, remind one of west Asiatic usage but at the same time point forward to the Harappan. On the other hand, although radiocarbon analysis confirms the priority of Amri and Kot Diji wares, it also shows that they persisted into the Harappan period. From this it has been argued with some force that the Amri culture, for instance, can hardly have given rise directly to that of Harappa or Mohenjo-daro. The most likely place to find direct antecedents is underneath the metropolitan cities themselves. The depth of alluvial deposit would make this a formidable task. Already Harappan material has been found nearly 12 metres below the flood plain level.

Something can be learned about the physical character of the Harappans from their skeletal remains. It is evident that they were of mixed stock. Significant elements in the population, including tall, long-headed people of Mediterranean and northern types and broad-headed Alpine types, could well have entered the Indus basin by way of Baluchistan. On the other hand low-headed people with retreating foreheads, pronounced supraorbital ridges and relatively broad noses with depressed roots appear to be related to a Veddoid-Australoid stock of indigenous character. The presumption is that these people correspond to the dark-skinned, flat-featured *Dasas* whose defeats by Aryan-speakers are a recurring theme of the *Rigveda*.

By comparison with the tribal territories defined by the various ceramic styles in Baluchistan and Sind the zone comprehended by the Harappan civilization was of another order of magnitude, around 1,300,000 sq. km as opposed to an average of perhaps 130,000 sq. km. Indeed in sheer extent – Lothal and Rupar are some 1,700 km apart as the crow flies – the Harappan realm was substantially larger than that of either ancient Egypt or Sumer. Within this broad territory there was a high degree of conformity whether as regards material culture, the decorative arts, architecture, weights and measures or script. Again, the regularity with which the two great centres of Harappa and Mohenjo-daro, themselves some 600 km apart, were planned has long excited comment. Yet no traces have been found of any ruling authority comparable with the pharaohs or even the dynasties of Sumer. One of the key problems posed by the material manifestations of Harappan society, is what gave it coherence and cohesion over so wide a territory.

Turning first to the economic basis on which the archaeological evidence bears most fully and directly, the dominating feature is the emergence of true urban centres whose population, pursuing a variety of specialized vocations, depended for their food on the surrounding countryside. The peasants who produced at any rate most of it continued to live, like their forebears, in village communities. Subsistence was based primarily on cultivating cereals well adapted to the comparatively dry climate of the Indus basin. Of these club wheat (*Triticum compactum*) and barley (*Hordeum vulgare*), originally domesticated in south-west Asia, had presumably been introduced to Baluchistan and Sind from the Iranian plateau. From the same quarter no doubt came sheep and goat and in all probability the humped cattle depicted on some of the Baluchistan wares and on pottery as far afield as northern Iran and Mesopotamia. On the other hand short or Indian dwarf wheat (*T. sphaerococcum*) was apparently a genetic mutation that arose in this part of the Indian sub-continent. Traces of rice husks at Lothal and Rangpur point to a spread from the Ganges basin. The cotton textiles from Mohenjo-daro argue for the cultivation of *Gossyprium arboreum*. Although cotton textiles were apparently unknown in Babylonia at the time of Herodotus and in Egypt down to Meroitic times, it has been argued on cytogenetic grounds that the progenitors of the cottons cultivated in the Indus valley are likely to have been introduced from southern

142 Pottery from Mohenjo-daro.

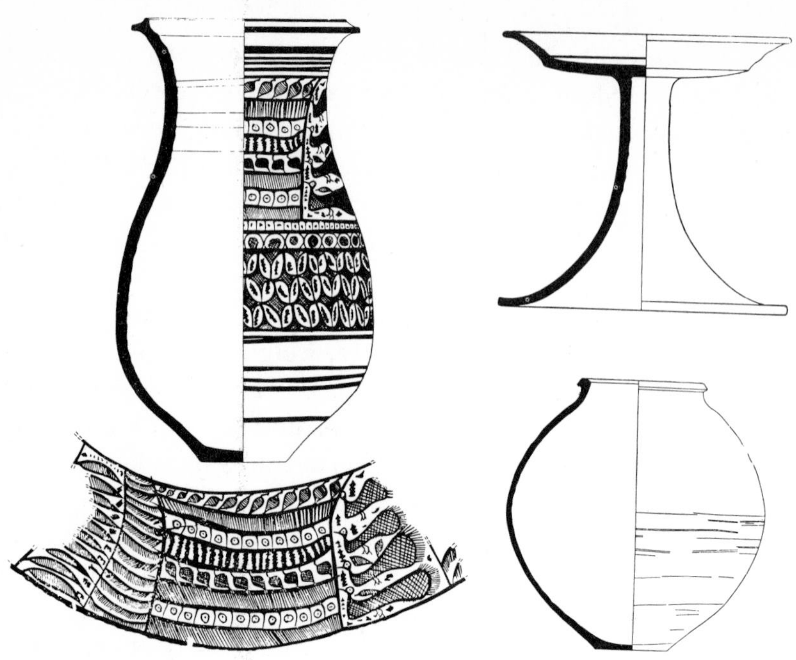

143 Copper and bronze vessels from Mohenjo-daro.

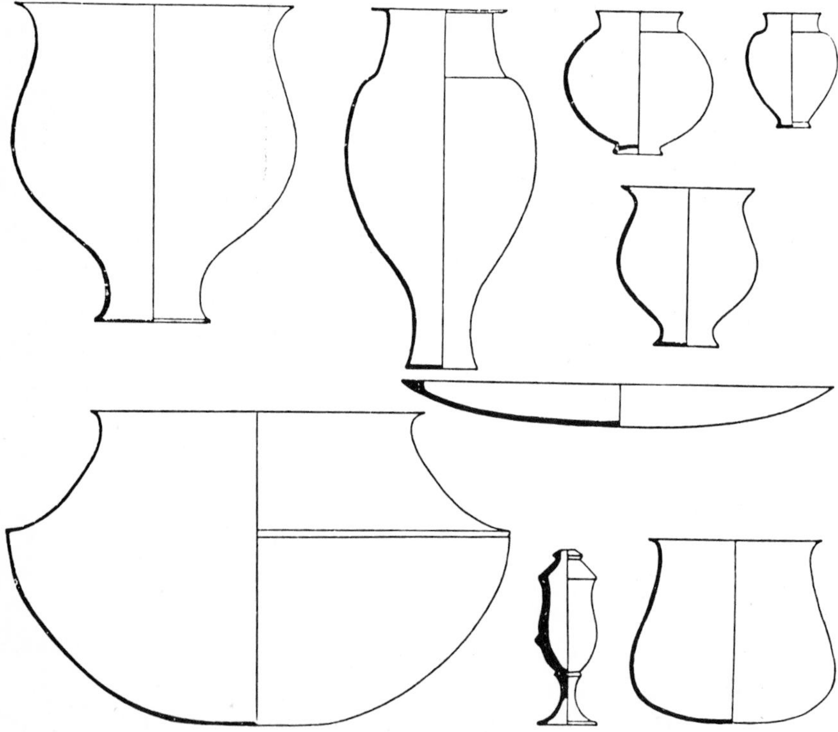

Arabia or north-east Africa. As to methods of cultivation it is of interest that the pattern of cultivation visible in the ground surface under the Kalibangan settlement mound compares closely with that still in use. This implies the presence of the traction plough, drawn presumably by humped oxen, and signs of cross cultivation may point to a regime of spring-sown wheat and barley and autumn-sown cotton. Although no evidence has been found for extensive or large-scale irrigation, some use of the Indus water for cultivation may be assumed, and there is ample evidence for flood control in massive brick platforms and in intricate drainage systems in the main cities.

The natural waterways of the Indus Valley system provided a ready means of transporting food to provision the urban populations by concentrating resources from surrounding regions. The craftsmen occupying the residential areas of the city were highly specialized and their products, standardized and displaying a high grade of finish, exhibit the effect of a finer subdivision of labour than prevailed in
142 the earlier village communities. The potters turned out their red vessels painted in dark paint in a variety of designs, the metal-smiths made a number of objects including flat axes, spearheads, arrow-heads, pick-axes, chisels, knives and daggers as well as a variety of
143 footed, carinated, open and constricted-neck vessels from hammered sheets. Then there were artificers making objects of personal adorn-
144 ment like beads, who at Chanhu-daro were found to occupy a distinct quarter. Ornaments were made from several different substances, some artificial like faience or pottery, others made from a range of natural materials including gold, silver, copper, steatite, shell, agate and carnelian, materials which often needed drilling by chert drills or tubular bronze ones. Others made objects for leisure
145 activities such as gamesmen, or the steatite seals used to denote ownership. Then, again, there were sensitive craftsmen capable of
146, 147 carving human figures in steatite, alabaster or limestone, modelling

144 Beads from Mohenjo-daro: (1–3, 8–10) faience; (4–6) steatite; (7) shell; (11) etched carnelian; (12) banded agate.

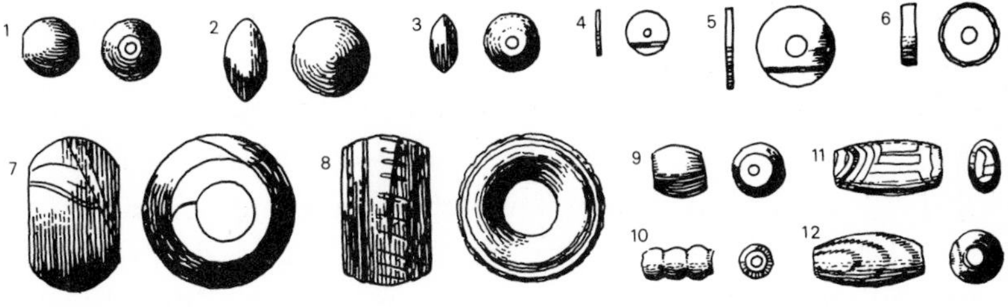

them in clay or casting them in metal for a sophisticated clientele. Many of the raw materials, and more particularly those used for personal ornaments, were derived either, like gold, from distant parts of the sub-continent, probably from Mysore, or from further afield: silver could have come from south India, Afghanistan or Iran, turquoise from Iran, Kashmir or Tibet, lapis lazuli from north-east Afghanistan and jade from inner Asia. There is nothing novel about the movement of valuable materials of small bulk over great distances through the ordinary mechanisms of social interaction. This had been happening with respect to obsidian since Late-glacial times in South-west Asia. Of greater interest as reflecting another level of social development is the evidence for a more organized form of overseas commerce. Although far from explicit, inscriptions dating from the time of Sargon of Akkad and the IIIrd dynasty of Ur down to the fall of the Larsa dynasty give many clues to the existence of sea-borne trade between the Indus Valley and Sumer. Tablets from Ur dating from the Dynasty of Larsa (*c.* 1950 B.C.) refer to sailors. There are hints that this trade was not direct but conducted through an entrepôt on the Persian Gulf, Dilmun or Telmun, which some have identified with Bahrain. Support for this comes from the Danish excavations at Bahrain and it is suggestive that Al'Ubaid pottery has recently been found at Qatar. The existence of Harappan outposts on the Makran coast at Sutkagen-dor and Sotka-koh, the former with a citadel, points in the same direction. So does the occurrence of Harappan seals at Lothal, Tell Asmar and other Sumerian sites and the complementary occurrence of a Persian Gulf seal, similar to ones from Bahrain. This occurrence at Lothal is of particular significance both because of its geographical situation and because of the occurrence at that site of a large oblong structure (216·4×36·5 m) sometimes interpreted as a dock. No signs even of an iconographic kind either of the sea-going boats that must have been used for the Gulf trade or of the Indus boats have yet been found.

A significant indication of the uniformity established over the whole extent of Harappan territory was the existence of a more or less standard system of weights and measures. The main linear units appear to have been feet (330–335 mm) and cubits (515–528 mm): the granaries of Harappa itself were 10 cubits wide and 30 long. The lower levels of weights were divisions or multiples of the traditional and still prevailing Indian unit of sixteen (e.g. 16 annas = 1 rupee). On the other hand, although Indian units differed from those prevailing in Sumer, it is significant that the bun-shaped type of

145 Stamp seals from Mohenjo-daro engraved with animals, mythological scenes and script.

copper ingot found at both Harappa and Mohenjo-daro was also favoured in Sumer.

Great emphasis has rightly been laid on literacy as an index of social advancement, but care has not always been taken to distinguish between a situation in which at least the members of an upper class are accustomed to communicate and maintain records in writing and one in which signs or scripts are used as a device for highly restricted and technical purposes. The mere use of signs, as we know from the advanced hunting cultures of Late-glacial Europe, is not sufficient to qualify people as civilized. Similarly, if the Harappan people are so termed this would be on account of the scale and nature of their society rather than because something like two thousand inscribed objects have so far been recovered by archaeology. The great majority of these occur engraved on steatite seals. These were of the stamp variety like those of Iran and so differed markedly from the cylinder seals characteristic of Sumer. Other inscriptions occur on pottery, either moulded on the base or scratched in the surface, on metal objects and on ivory or terracotta rods, possibly amulets. While not excluding other symbolic purposes, the prime function of

146 Figurines of bronze and stone from Mohenjo-daro.

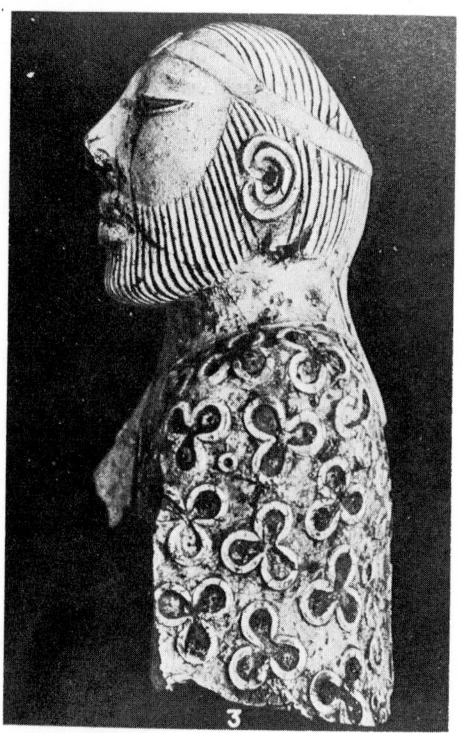

inscriptions in this context was to identify the goods of individuals, notably bales or containers used in commerce. It is perhaps not surprising that the inscriptions were brief, ranging from one to twenty symbols and averaging around five. By the same token they present formidable difficulties to anyone seeking to discover the language in which they were written. Although not widely accepted it is worth mentioning the conclusion of a Finnish team of investigators that it was Proto-Dravidian, a language of which enclaves exist in Baluchistan, cut off from the main areas of Dravidian speech, but which is found today mainly in South and central India.

The layout of the settlements throws a significant light on the
nature of Harappan society. At the two major sites, but also for
366: 22 example at Kalibangan, the cities were divided into two, a tightly
packed residential area with artisans' quarters laid out on a grid
148 system, which at Mohenjo-daro was about 1·5 km across, and well
provided with drains and fresh water supplies, and a powerfully
149 defended citadel containing public buildings and installations. The
buildings were made of kiln-fired bricks built with alternate courses

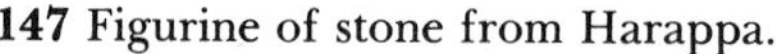

147 Figurine of stone from Harappa.

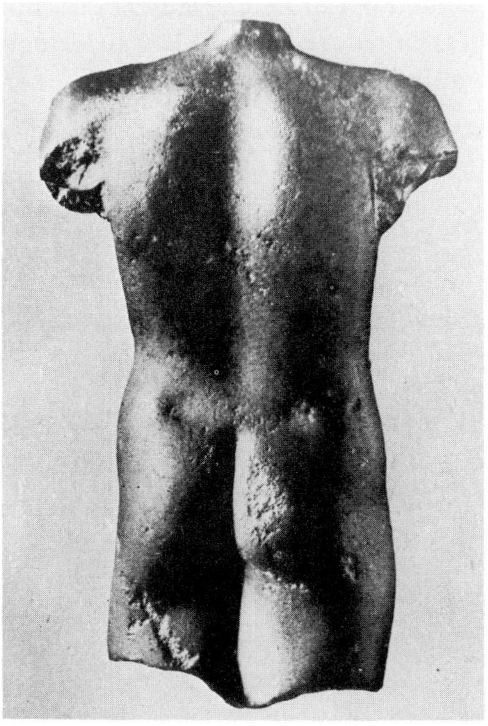

of headers and stretchers and had stairways to upper floors. Among the most important public buildings were large granaries built of timber but resting on massive brick podiums. These were designed to house the grain needed to feed the citizens and act as an insurance against hard times. They symbolize in monumental fashion the redistributive aspect of Harappan society, an aspect which went hand in hand with the high degree of specialization that was an essential part of the process of urbanization.

The existence of citadels over against the more extensive living areas of the population at large confirms the impression of authority given by the regularity of the street plan and the extent and excellence of the drainage systems, no less than by the geographical extent of cultural conformity in the Indus basin. The scale and complexity of Harappan society meant that it can hardly have operated on the basis of mere kinship adequate for the villages that immediately preceded and continued to sustain it. Yet neither symbols of dynastic rule, royal tombs or temples in any way comparable with those so well represented in Sumer have so far been recognized despite the extent of excavation and the wealth of objects recovered. It may be significant that the only large structures other than granaries and the defences themselves are buildings of a collegiate character provided with bathing tanks. If Harappan society was not held together by force, if it had not yet acquired the sanctions of a state, the conclusion

148 Residential quarters at Mohenjo-daro.

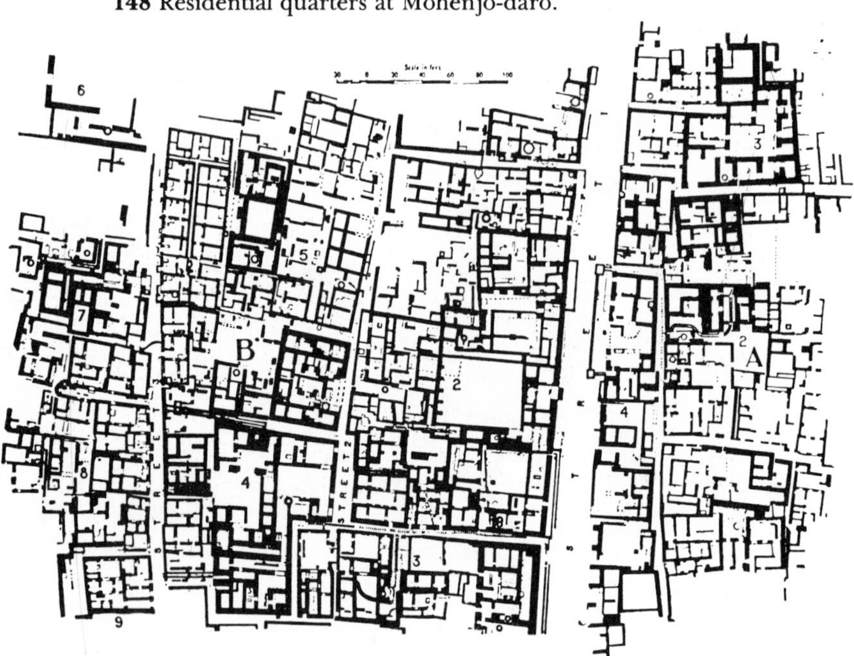

149 Citadel and public buildings at Mohenjo-daro.

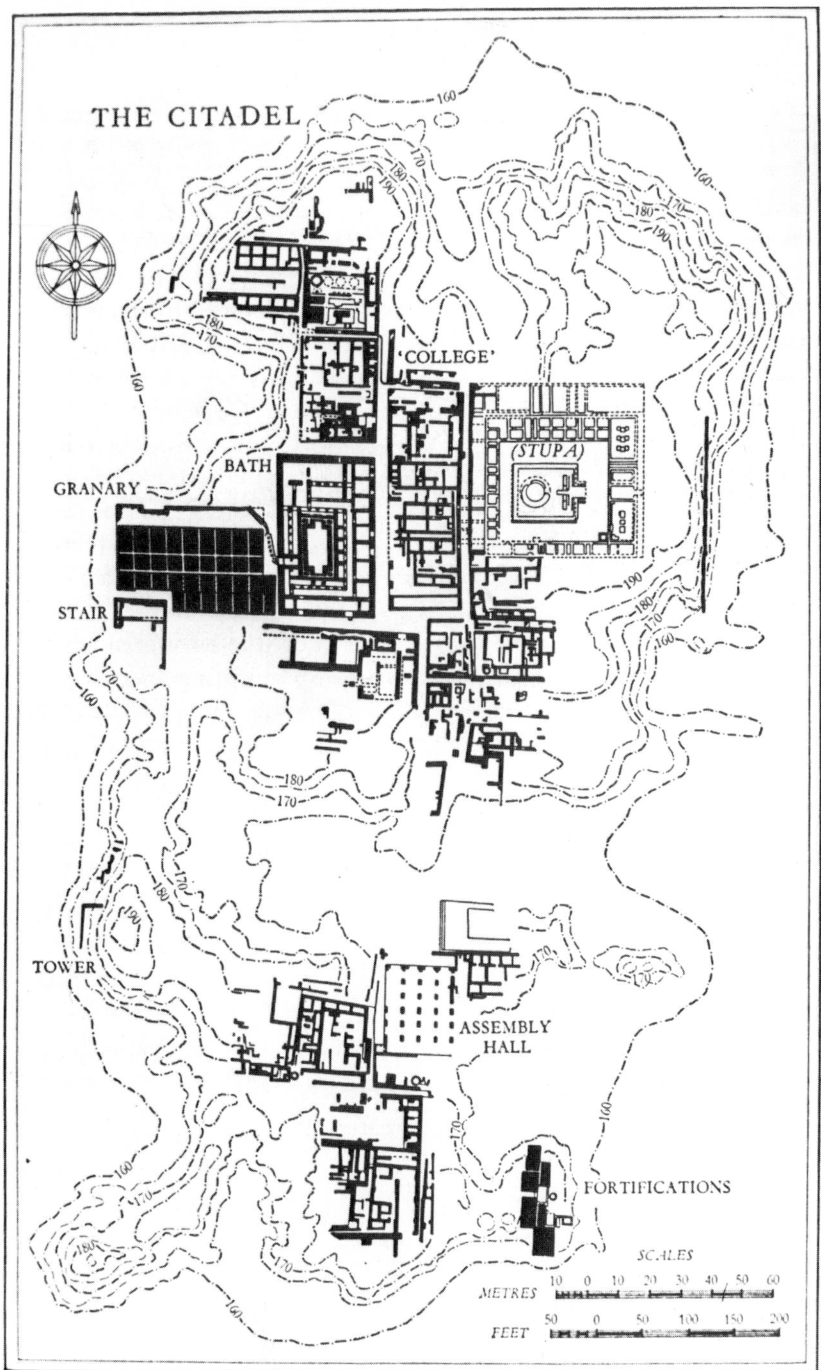

can only be that cohesion was given in part by its social structure and in part by the ideology which validated this structure in the minds of individuals and social groups.

The most likely explanation is one that emerges if we regard the Harappan phenomenon less as something to be classified in western stadial terms as a 'civilization' and more as marking a formative phase in the development of the Indian civilization known from history. Many 'Indian' traits indeed have long been recognized in the material excavated from Harappan sites. At the level of basic sub-
365: 30 sistence the methods of cultivation under Kalibangan, the prevalence of humped cattle and the growth of cotton for textiles, have already been noted and to these may be added the toy wheels and chassis
150 of baked clay which reproduce precisely the carts still in use today and incidentally confirm the use of animal traction. In the sphere of ideology one can only mention a few suggestive, if at the moment slender, clues, such as the prevalence of the swastika symbol, the depiction on a seal of a figure resembling Siva squatting on a low stool or, again, the bathing tanks already mentioned. Excavation and radiocarbon dating between them have recently strengthened the likelihood of historical continuity by bringing to light the chalcolithic societies of Malwa and the Deccan (see pp. 272ff.). The possibility that the script was written by speakers of a Proto-Davidian language has already been canvassed; if validated it would be another compelling argument for continuity. If one adopts an 'Indian' hypothesis one might think in terms of a prototype of what was later to develop into a caste system, a system which, because it was hereditary, was both self-sufficient and self-perpetuating.

Many theories have been advanced to account for the rather sudden end of the efflorescence of Indian civilization in the Indus basin. Some of these are physical. For instance it has recently been claimed that a dry period of some intensity set in around 1800 B.C. in Rajasthan. Again, it has been suggested that a tectonic uplift may have occurred in the region of Sehwan below Mohenjo-daro. By forming a barrier sufficient to retain the silts brought down by the current of melt-waters, while at the same time allowing most of the water to escape by seepage or evaporation, this could not only have created the highly fertile conditions which made possible the process of urbanization in the Indus basin, but may also explain the accu-
355 mulation of between eleven and twelve metres of flood-deposit during the life of Mohenjo-daro. Conversely the breaching of such a barrier would have exerted an extremely adverse effect on the

prosperity of the region as a whole. The onset of drier climate
364 may also have been a critical factor. Again, it is possible that intensification of settlement and the burning of the large number of bricks needed to keep abreast of flood-waters might itself have resulted in deforestation, so encouraging erosion and increasing the flow of silt. Alternatively the system of cultivation practised by Harappans may itself have contributed to its own run-down. Ecological and environmental factors of this kind may well have served to weaken the system or at least to create conditions which undermined its resistance to external forces. Indeed the impact of Aryan-speaking invaders has even been invoked as in itself a full and sufficient cause of the end of the Harappan cities. The most obvious check on this last hypothesis is its chronological feasibility. The *Rigveda* certainly refers to assaults on defended strongholds. The question is how far these can be identified with the Indus cities. We know from radiocarbon analysis that the metropolitan sites came to an end in all probability as early as *c.* 2000 B.C. and even secondary sites in the Indus basin by *c.* 1750 B.C. When the Aryan speakers first reached India is still unknown. Internal evidence suggests that the society mirrored in the earlier parts of the *Rigveda* was accustomed to copper and bronze, but ignorant of iron, something that would put the earlier waves of immigration back before *c.* 800 B.C. How far back is still unknown, but the occurrence of the names of gods familiar from the Indian pantheon in the treaty between Hittite and Mitannian rulers dating from *c.* 1380 B.C. suggests that the mythology of the Aryan speakers reflected in the *Rigveda* had taken shape around

150 Harappan clay model wheels and chassis compared with a modern cart of the region.

the middle of the second millennium B.C. Another test is topographical. The two basic features of the landscape encountered by the early Aryan-speakers in India included great rivers and snow-capped mountains. This points to the Sutlej and upper Ganges basins as the focus of Aryan-speaking invaders rather than the Indus.

Early farmers and villagers of the Deccan

If the breakdown of the urban centres of the Indus basin is no longer
361 viewed in a tragic light, this is due very largely to a fuller appreciation
of the essential continuity of Indian history. The presence of so many
'Indian' traits in the evidence recovered from the Indus Valley
settlements has already been remarked. What also needs to be emphasized is the degree of historical continuity documented by recent
excavation and radiocarbon dating. It is already apparent that copper-
using communities were flourishing on the upper Banas and Berach
354, 360 rivers of south Rajasthan between *c.* 2000 and 1600 B.C., that is
throughout the latter half of the Harappan. Excavations at such sites
as Ahar and Gillund have revealed settlements of rectangular houses
with mud walls on stone foundations. Although practising metal-
151 lurgy, and in most cases the same lithic technique as the Harappans,
making their pottery on the wheel and living on one site sufficiently
long to leave settlement mounds, these people were distinct in culture – Banasian ware was basically monochrome – as well as being
inferior in wealth to the Harappans. The decline in wealth applies
with even more force to the copper-working groups of Malwa and
the Deccan, which in conformity to the ripple image were progressively poorer and younger the further south one looks. Although
all of them made or at least used simple copper tools like flat axes,
none made metal vessels, engraved seals, had even an elementary
script or lived in cities. This was not because they were degenerate,
so much as because in the prevailing state of technology the relatively
confined alluvial strips available to them were incapable of supporting anything as elaborate as the extensive alluvial plains of the
Indus. The communities which flourished in the Narmada valley
between *c.* 1700 and 1400 B.C. were no more than villages of small
round or rectangular huts built of wooden posts with walls of split
bamboo and clay plastered with cattle dung. Nevertheless the
351 villagers of Navdatoli made bronze axes with *c.* 3% tin as well as
152 faience beads and decorated their red Malwa-style pots with animal,
anthropomorphic and geometric designs in black paint. At sites like
350 Nevasa and Chandoli near the headwaters of the upper Godavari

151 Chalcolithic blade and microlith industry from Maheshwar on the Narbada.

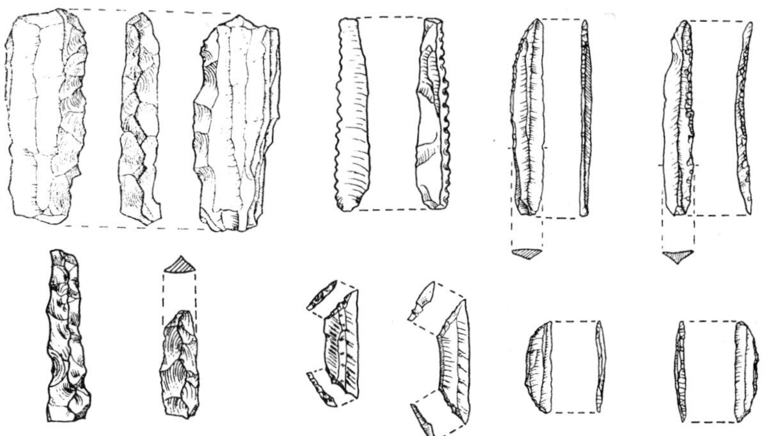

152 Malwa style pottery from Navdatoli on the Narbada.

and Upper Bhima rivers marked by Jorwe ware with designs in black
153 paint on burnished matt surfaces (*c.* 1400–1100 B.C.), copper axes
continued in use, but polished stone axes were now common. Further
339 south still, for instance at Piklihāl in the upper Krishna basin and
Brahmagiri, the cultural assemblages are basically Neolithic with
only the odd object of copper.

In southern India farming communities with a 'Neolithic' technology had already been established as early as the latter half of the
third millennium B.C. according to the radiocarbon dates for Kodekal
340 and Utnūr. To judge from their material equipment these 'Neolithic'
communities were but the impoverished representatives of a population which in Baluchistan and Sind still retained the 'chalcolithic' character of their Iranian forebears. The people lived in light wooden houses mainly round but occasionally oblong in plan. They used edge-ground stone axes often with pointed butt of a kind that would have served to clear the ground and provide timber for building. They made blades and microliths from chert and chalcedony using the same technique as is known from the Harappan and simpler chalcolithic centres. Their pottery, mainly in grey monochrome, although hand-made, included alongside convex and carinated bowls and tall jars with concave neck such sophisticated forms as spouted bowls and flasks. Although saddle-querns suggest that they grew crops, their main source of wealth was apparently cattle which they evidently kept in timber enclosures to protect them at night from predators. It may well have been fires maintained for the

153 Jorwe style pottery from Nevasa on the Godavari.

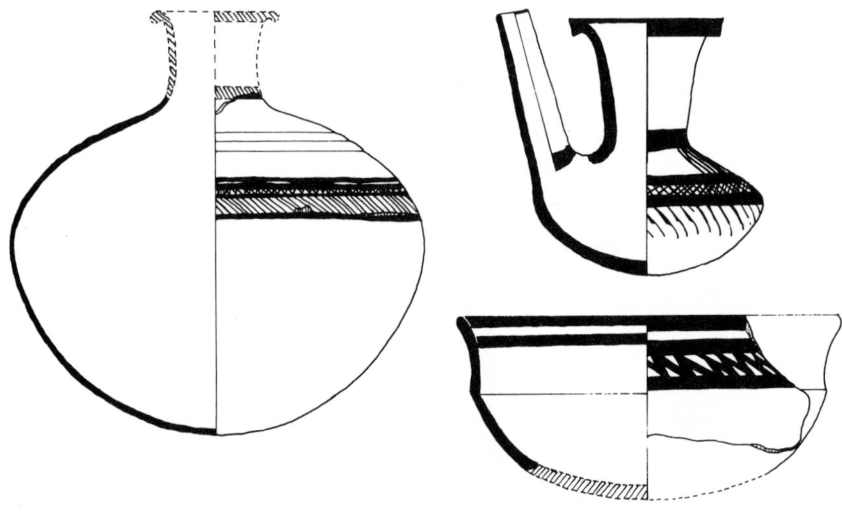

same purpose that from time to time set light to the great heaps of
341 dung at the sites of their cattle kraals, causing the formation of the characteristic ash-mounds that first drew archaeologists' attention to them. The evident neglect of dung as a source of manure suggests that agriculture was poorly developed, though the presence of worn saddle-querns certainly argues for cereal crops of some kind, and remains of finger-millet (*Eleusine coracana*) have been found at Hallur and Paiyampalli. It is consistent with their remoteness in the cul-de-sac of south India far from the main areas of change that there is no good evidence for culture development for over a thousand years, apart that is from the reception at later settlements of an occasional copper axe from the 'chalcolithic' zone further north. The importance of cattle, which were of the humped variety found over the whole of Iran and the Indian peninsula in early times, is reflected
154 in the rock paintings at Piklihāl and other sites in the Raichūr district for which the neolithic tribes were almost surely responsible.

Protohistory

The Aryan speakers

From an archaeological point of view the period between the end of city life (*c.* 1750 B.C.) in the Indus basin and the beginning of iron-working (*c.* 800 B.C.) is the most obscure in the later prehistory of the sub-continent. As far as the Indus basin and Sind are concerned there is no sign of any major shift in population. The collapse of urbanization entailed no marked cultural break. Both the Jhukar ware which overlay Harappan levels at Amri (III) and Chanhu-daro (II) and Jhangar ware which succeeded it at Chanhu-daro (III) carry forward established ceramic traditions with at most influences from south Baluchistan. In Baluchistan itself the pottery from the cemetery sunk into an abandoned Kulli mound at Shahi-tump is again a local development. The only clear traces of exotic impulses appear in the context of metal-work, notably in the stamp-seals and shaft-

154 Pecked and painted respresentations of humped back cattle on rocks near Piklihāl Neolithic settlement.

hole axe from Shahi-tump, an animal-headed pin from the H cemetery at Harappa, post-dating the city, and number of objects from Chanhu-daro II including a faience version of the metal stamp-seals from Shahi-tump. At most these reflect the restlessness which affected not merely Iran but much of the ancient world. For archaeological traces of the intrusion or more likely intrusions of Aryan-speakers it is more profitable to turn to the north-west and more particularly to the region of the Sutlej and the Upper Ganga not too far from the snow-capped mountains that impressed so many of the intruders in their new homeland.

A key source of information about the culture of the Aryan speakers as they entered the country is to be found in the *Rigveda* itself. Although first committed to writing at the instance of European scholars of Sanskrit as recently as the late eighteenth and early nineteenth centuries, this collection of more than a thousand hymns, prayers and spells can be accepted within limits as a valid source of information about the remote period when they were first composed. This is because they were transmitted in the form of chants memorized by priests for whom the exact repetition of sacred texts was a matter of vital significance. The picture they give is of people who by comparison with the citizens of Harappa were rustic barbarians. The Aryan-speakers cultivated cereals by ox-drawn ploughs, but animal husbandry played a leading role in their economy. They kept sheep and goats, but cattle were their main source of wealth and horses were important for harnessing to chariots. Those vehicles had light spoked wheels and were valued for transporting archers in warfare and also for racing. The people occupied farmsteads that might be grouped at most in villages. Their houses were constructed of timber and other organic materials. Great importance was attached to the hearth as a focus of social life, feasting and drinking played a prominent role. In this, as in many other respects, the heroic society reflected in the *Rigveda* compares with those familiar from Mycenaean Greece and the Celtic west.

A point of crucial importance in any attempt to establish the archaeological context of the arrival of Aryan-speakers are clues to their technology in the *Rigveda*. The problem here is that whereas early components refer only to copper-bronze, other presumably later ones imply an iron technology. Do these relate to two phases of entry, or do the references to copper refer to a phase prior to the actual descent? Finds in the Gandhara region, comprising Rawalpindi, Peshawar and the Khyber pass through which any movements from beyond the Hindu-Kush must have passed, are consistent with the former hypothesis. Burials from periods I–II of the Gandhara grave culture display a copper, and those from period III, an iron technology. Radiocarbon analysis suggests that period I dates from the fourteenth and fifteenth and period III from the ninth century B.C. The physical characteristics of the population represented by the burials is consistent with people entering from the north. The monochrome grey ware accompanying each phase of burials is suggestive because it superseded pre-existing wares also over extensive areas of northern Iran and Turkmenia. The pottery is of fundamental interest in the Indian context quite apart from whether or not it can be accepted as an archaeological indicator of an initial ware of Aryan speakers, since it provides an obvious point of departure for the Painted Grey Ware which developed in the upper Ganga basin in association with an iron technology and horses and marks the first large-scale exploitation of this region by settled populations. Whatever else may be learned about the initial penetration there are good grounds for thinking that the people who made Black Painted Ware and effectively initiated the Iron Age in India spoke an Aryan tongue. Before turning to this something needs to be said of the Gangetic plain and the adjacent zones of Bihar and Orissa.

The Gangetic plain

Although it was destined to form a base for successive empires during historic times, the Gangetic plain was intensively settled relatively late by comparison with the Indus basin. One reason for this is to be sought in the different opportunities provided by the two territories. Whereas the Indus basin offered relatively easy conditions for cultivation, the hard calcareous soils of the Gangetic plain were not easily tackled until iron equipment was available.

Again, there were significant disparities in both climate and vegetation. Whereas the Indus flowed through a territory of low rainfall well adapted to the cereals domesticated in south-west Asia, much of the Gangetic plain and the whole of the north-eastern provinces of the sub-continent were subject to high rainfall and under natural conditions carried tropical forest. It is not surprising that Harappan settlers, adapted to quite different conditions, penetrated no further than the upper Gangetic region, where for example late Harappan material is found in the bottom level at Alamgirpur between the Yamuna and Ganga rivers. Conversely the territory marked an

obvious extension from an ecological point of view of south-east Asia.
It is hardly surprising to find the distribution of shouldered stone
356 celts of a type distributed over a territory as far east as south China
confined to the zone of 100 cm or more of tropical rainfall in Bihar,
Orissa and the lower and middle Gangetic plain, and the same with
copper versions of the same form. At Daojali Hading in the north
Cachar hills of Assam shouldered stone celts of this kind were found
with coil-built pottery finished by wooden beaters wrapped with cord
or roughened by surface engraving to prevent them sticking to the
20: 146 wet clay. Within this territory rice (*Oryza sativa*) was the most
important food crop and it is widely accepted that the monsoon
rainfall zone of the Gangetic plain and the north-east of the Indian
sub-continent formed part of the territory within which this crop was
originally domesticated. Rice was certainly grown before iron had
come into use in west Bengal as shown by finds from Mahisadal and
Pandu Rajar Dhibi on the west margin of the Ganga delta. By early
in the second millennium it had already spread down the Narmada
valley to the late Harappan sites of Lothal and Rangpur IIA. Its use
is referred to in later parts of the *Rigveda* and its occurs significantly
with Painted Grey Ware at Hastinapur II and Noh.

It is still an open question whether the people who made the
155 ochre-coloured pottery found in the bottom layer I at Hastinapur
344 and at many sites between the Upper Yamuna and the upper Ganga
were Aryan speakers. The pottery itself could well have been a
regional development in much the same way as the Jhukar ware of

155 Ochre-coloured pottery from Hastinapur I.

the lower Indus. Its main interest is that it marks the first substantial evidence for settled life in this region. Some of the most plentiful
65: 38–41 archaeological finds of prehistoric antiquity found in the region are
156 hoards of copper artefacts. As a rule these occur apart from dwelling sites, but in a few cases in the northern part of the Gangetic plain they have been found in apparent association with ochre-coloured pottery. On the other hand the majority of these hoards occur as strays in the middle and lower Gangetic plain and adjacent areas of Bihar, Orissa and west Bengal, a territory for which information about settlement prior to the Iron Age is still slight.

Spread of iron-working

Iron-working was first adopted around 800 B.C. in the territory traditionally associated with Aryan-speakers between the Sutlej and the middle Ganges and the Painted Grey Ware with which it was often found could well have been developed from the monochrome grey ware encountered in the Gandhara graves. The Painted Grey Ware, which for the first time serves to define Aryan-speaking people with some certainty in the archaeological record, was shaped on a turntable or spun wheel to form shallow dishes, bowls and necked
158 jars of elementary shapes, lacking spouts or handles. Before being fired under carefully controlled conditions the pots might sometimes

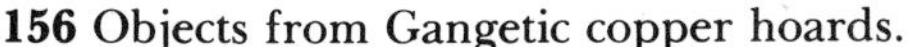

156 Objects from Gangetic copper hoards.

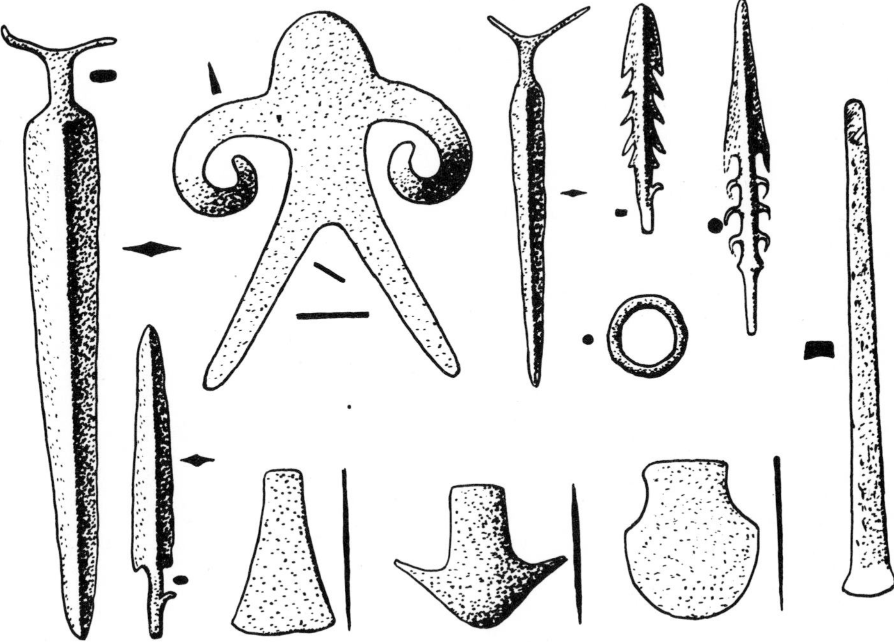

157 India in the third century B.C.

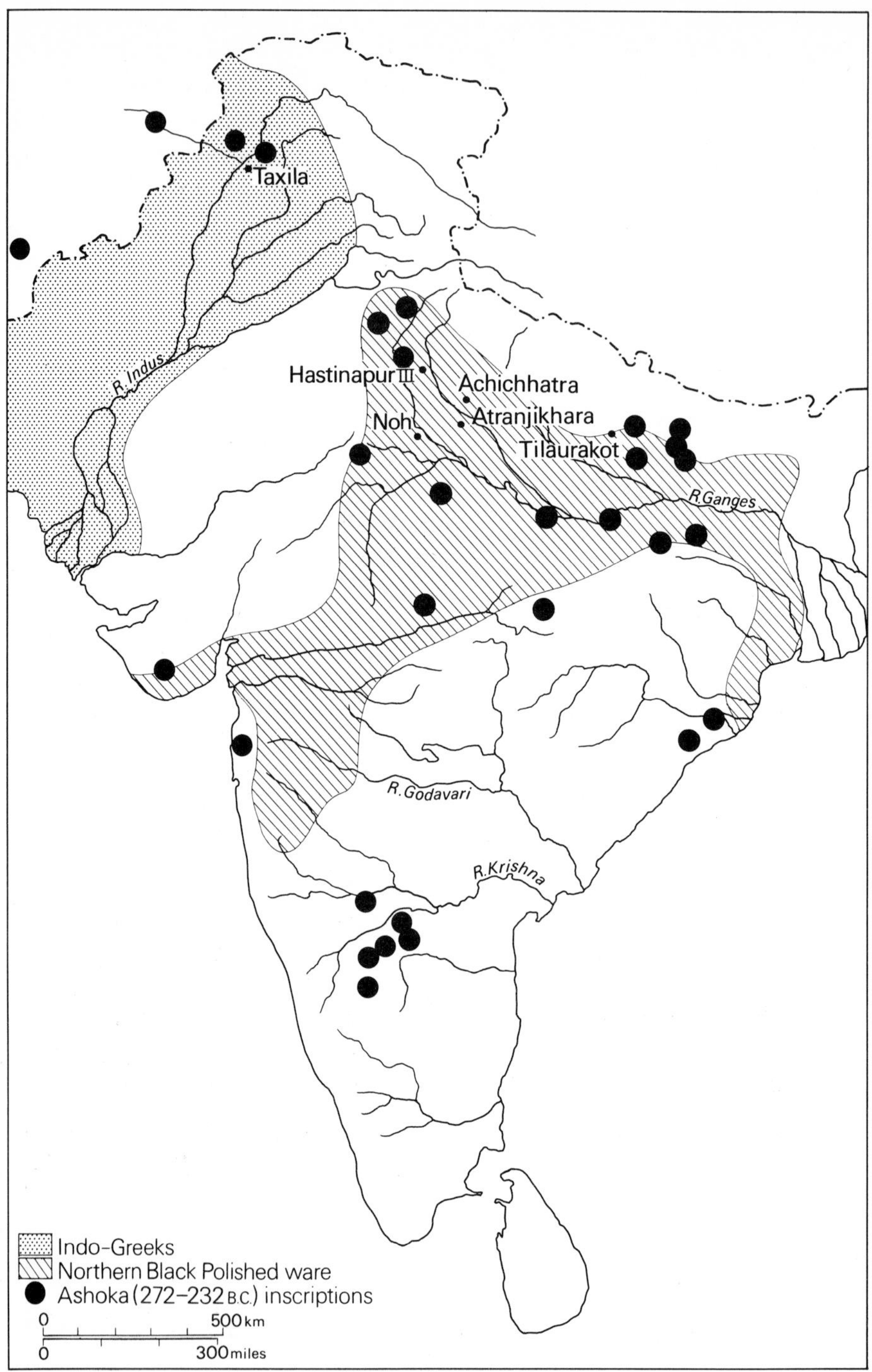

be decorated in black paint with simple, standardized patterns such as zones of parallel lines, commonly bent, circles enclosing dots and recurring spirals. Pottery of this kind which appeared at Hastinapur in level II, overlying ochre-coloured ware, was current between *c.* 800 and 500 B.C. in terms of radiocarbon. The people who used it lived in timber-framed mud-walled houses and their material equipment, though now including iron and glass, was in some ways inferior to that of the city-dwellers of the Indus basin who lived some fifteen hundred years earlier. Yet it was at this very time that the clearance and exploitation of the upper and middle zones of the Gangetic plain, the heartland of later empires, effectively began.

The process of deforestation and the breaking up of the hard calcareous soils was sharply accelerated when iron-working technology expanded down the lower Gangetic plain during the sixth and fifth centuries B.C. to reach the rich iron deposits of Bihar. This decisive phase is well defined in the archaeological record by the appearance of a distinctive new pottery, Northern Black Polished Ware. Although at Hastinapur and elsewhere it replaced Painted Grey Ware the change was evidently a matter of fashion rather than one involving movements of population. The new pottery retained the hard grey core and many of the basic shapes of the old. The essential change was in surface treatment, the replacement of painted designs by a surface slip. This was applied after the pottery had been given an initial firing at a comparatively low temperature. After application of the slip the pottery was fired at high temperatures under sealed conditions. This caused it to acquire the characteristic colours, mainly coal-black, but also fairly often from brown-black to steel-blue, and the noteworthy burnished or polished surface. The distribution of this ware defined an expansion of iron technology from the upper and middle Gangetic plain to its lower portion and adjacent Bihar, and, in addition, to central India as far south as the headwaters of the Godavari and Krishna rivers.

158 Painted grey ware from Hastinapur II.

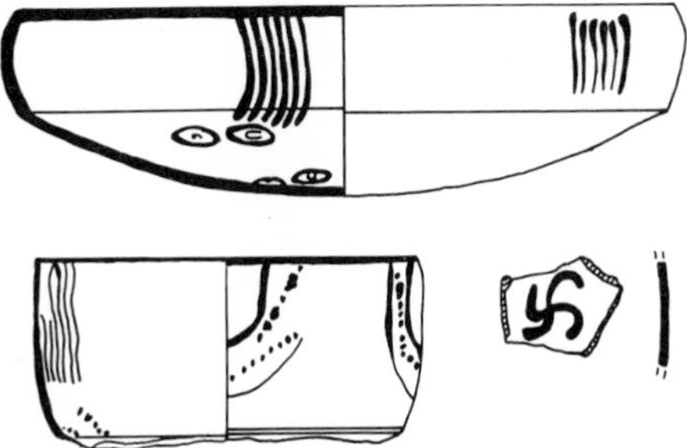

The territory over which Northern Black Polished Ware was current formed the core or heartland of successive empires from the Mauryan to the British. It is symbolic therefore that the pottery should recently have been found in a mound buried under the sixteenth-century site of Purana Qila one of the many ancient capitals at Delhi. Significantly the deposits containing this pottery incorporated such indicators of urban life as baked-brick drains and terracotta well-linings. The economic basis for urbanization and so for the emergence of political structures culminating in empires was already laid.

In the meantime north-west India had suffered two more intrusions. In *c.* 516 B.C. Darius incorporated the Gandhara region where Aryan speakers had first established a foot-hold, together with Baluchistan and much of the lower Indus, as satrapies of the Persian empire. Paradoxically the temporary incorporation of a small part of the sub-continent within an empire which then extended as far north as Aral and Caucasus and west to Egypt and Thrace made less impact than the overthrow of that empire by Alexander the Great nearly two centuries later and his invasion of the Indian provinces. Entering by the traditional route of the Kabul river and the Khyber pass Alexander had no difficulty in replacing Greek for Persian rule in the territories conquered by Darius. For India his conquest was mainly significant for the stimulus it gave to the growth of a distinctive Indo-Greek culture in the north-west and for the political development of the upper and middle Gangetic plain.

The Mauryan empire

Alexander's death at Babylon in 323 B.C. gave the signal for something of a national rising. One outcome was the establishment by Chandragupta Maurya of a dynasty that marks the effective beginning of Indian history. The main achievement of the Mauryan kings was to link together for the first time the peoples of the Indus and Gangetic plains and create by means of the elaborate bureaucracy admired by Megasthenes the administrative machinery needed for a large scale polity. As testified by rock-cut inscriptions extending from Gandhara on the North West Frontier to Orissa and Mysore, the Mauryan empire attained its maximum extent under Chandragupta's grandson Ashoka (272–232 B.C.).

Beyond his southern frontier Ashoka contented himself with establishing friendly relations with the small kingdoms that were then in process of emerging from tribal chieftainships. It was probably as a result of these contacts that the Tamil-speakers of the extreme south began to adopt the Brahmic script and thus attain literacy. More significant in historical terms were the close connections maintained with Persia and the missions exchanged as far west as Syria, Egypt, Macedonia and Epirus. Material embodiments of the Iranian enrichment of Indian culture may be cited in the very concept of rock-cut inscriptions based on those of Darius or, again, in the capitals of Ashokan pillars modelled on those of Persepolis and which interestingly enough were among the first symbols used on its postage stamps by the modern Indian state. Cultural enrichment from the Iranian plateau was of course no new thing in Indian history.

Trade and commerce

The Mauryan empire, like all those which succeeded it after longer or shorter intervals, disintegrated fairly rapidly and even reverted in some areas to something like chaos. Yet the period *c.* 200 B.C. to A.D. 300 witnessed a significant phase of mercantile development in the course of which India was linked with lands far to the east and west. Internally the Mauryan Empire opened up and rendered secure the links by which commodities and manufactures circulated extensively within the sub-continent. Merchants, money-changers and the like formed thenceforth an increasingly important element in Indian urban society. One conspicuous way in which they helped to shape Indian history was to form a nexus of wealth relatively independent of the ups and downs of political life. Another was to consolidate and amplify external relations initiated in the political sphere.

Other factors operated to further this latter process. The Bactrian Greeks took advantage of Ashoka's death to re-establish Greek control of the north-western territories previously under Achaemenid rule and subsequently conquered by Alexander and Chandragupta. As a result a genuinely Indo-Greek culture developed in Afghanistan and the north-west provinces of India. In the archaeological record this is manifest in the coins issued by the Indo-Greek kings, inscribed in Greek and later also in Brahmi, and even more impressively in Gandharan sculpture. Although derived from the Graeco-Roman style current in Alexandria, Gandharan art was most potently applied to the service of Buddhist iconography. Sculptures in stone, stucco and terracotta reproduced Buddha and his saints and not least the mother of Buddha who no doubt served the populace as a species of mother goddess. Buddhism met an essential need of the Greeks, who found themselves barred from Indian society by the institution of caste deeply embedded in Hinduism. It was largely because Buddhism provided a way into social life that it was so eagerly embraced. The rich and powerful of Indo-Greek society competed to build up Buddhism in the north-west by endowing monasteries and supporting missionary enterprise in Inner Asia. This in turn played an important part in developing trade with China.

The Indo-Greeks indeed opened up Indian commerce to the outer world from two complementary directions. Buddhist missionaries from Gandhara ultimately reached China by way of Inner Asia and in this way helped to pioneer the Inner Asian route along which Chinese products, notably silk, reached the west. Their own contacts with the Hellenistic west made them natural middlemen between China and the Roman world and the conflict between Rome and Parthia meant that the silk trade from China was deflected from the direct route to north-west India. From Taxila the commerce was able to flow down the Indus to Broach. From there the silk was shipped direct to Babylonia, as more than two thousand years earlier had been the cotton of Mohenjo-daro and Harappa. A reference in the *Periplus* to silk among the commodities traded to the east coast of south India suggests that some of its must have passed down the Ganges to the Bay of Bengal. It is also possible that some crossed the Indian ocean direct to Aden and passed up the Red Sea to Suez *en route* for the great entrepôt of Alexandria. Direct contact had been established between Broach and Rome as early as the reign of Augustus to whom a special mission brought specimens of the Indian fauna, including tigers, pheasants and snakes.

If the Roman appetite for silk was satisfied by a combination of overland, riverine and maritime routes, that of spices could be met by long sea voyages interrupted only by brief portages. Direct evidence for Roman commerce in the form of coins, objects of Roman manufacture and even traces of settlement are mainly concentrated in the south of India beyond the limits of the Mauryan realm. This was doubtless linked with the fact that the Romans were as keen on spices as on silk. Malabar was itself an important source and Coromandel faced yet more important sources, those of south-east Asia. In addition the Coromandel ports were open to traffic from the Gangetic ports across the Bay of Bengal. The distribution of Roman coins strongly suggests that the two coasts were linked overland through the Coimbatore gap. This makes it the more significant that archaeology should have disclosed a major centre of Roman settlement and commerce at the eastern end of this route at Arikamedu or Negapatam, most probably to be identified with the Padouke of the *Periplus*. Excavation has shown that the site was not merely a port, but a settlement at which glass and pottery of Italian manufacture were used. In addition to spices and silk, the merchants of Arikamedu handled pearls, precious stones and muslins of local manufacture. The Syrian church which still flourishes on the Malabar coast is a direct descendant of the Christianity introduced as a concomitant of this first-century commerce.

Caste

The network of commerce and the rise of a mercantile class in the cities of India may be one reason why Indian civilization was to show itself so relatively immune to the rise and fall of successive civilizations based on the Gangetic plain. Another was the caste system which provided an all-pervading and self-perpetuating social structure. The degree of craft specialization in the Harrapan cities has already been emphasized and a hint has been offered that social hierarchy may have been a major factor in the cohesion and stability of the society represented. The economy of the originally strongly pastoral but progressively more agricultural Aryan speakers at the time of their early settlement hardly called for the sub-division of labour on anything like the same scale. On the other hand the Vedic hymns indicate a pronounced differentiation of broad social classes. Among those distinguished were rulers, aristocrats and warriors (*Ksatriyas*), priests and philosophers (*Brahmans*), artisans (*Vaisyas*) and cultivators (*Shudras*). More fundamental still was the distinction between the Aryan-speaking intruders and the indigenous populations in whose lands they settled. The latter, the *Dasas*, were distinguished by their racial characteristics and above all by their squat noses and the darker colour of their skins, a distinction which still forms a ready guide to status in the system of caste, the very word for which in Sanskrit, *varna*, signifies colour.

Religion

Another factor making for stability and continuity was religion. The earliest real insight into Indian religion is that to be won from the Vedic writings. Like other Indo-Europeans the Aryan speaking intruders into India personified natural forces in a variety of gods and goddesses. Indra, god of strength, thunder, rain and battle, and Agni, god of fire and the domestic hearth, were only two members of a pantheon that also included personifications of the sun, death, the intoxicating juice *soma* and many others. In Aryan religion the aid of such deities could only be effectively enlisted by means of the rituals of sacrifice. The priests owed much of their power to the fact that they alone were equipped to preside over these. The metaphysics of the early brahmans centred to a significant degree on the fate of the soul after death. Orthodox doctrine enshrined the idea that fate in the after life depended on conduct in the present and combined this with the notion of the transmigration of souls. From this followed the doctrine of *Karma* according to which the nature of rebirth itself, whether higher or lower, depended on personal merit. Such a combination of ideas provided a useful endorsement of the caste system, since every individual was placed according to his deserts in a previous life. Again, it held out the hope to every man of being able to improve his status by leading a meritorious life. In this manner *Dharma*, the natural law of society, was maintained.

The Hinduism encountered by the Arabs as they introduced Islam to present day Pakistan in the eighth century A.D. was the outcome of a long history. In the course of this the Aryan religion reflected in the Vedic literature had been modified from two directions. On the one hand the brahminical priesthood had to accommodate to the popular religion of the aboriginal population as the Aryan speakers spread more widely over the Gangetic plain, central and southern India. It is from this source that the cults of popular Hinduism centering on Brahma the creator, Vishnu the preserver and Siva the destroyer must surely stem. Their antiquity and indigenous nature is neatly confirmed by the well known engraving of what may
145, *upper* well be Siva on a Harappan seal. On the other hand the metaphysics cultivated by the brahmans was strongly influenced by the heresies which multiplied in the context of growing urbanization and reached a climax around the middle of the millennium.

Of these, two in particular, Jainism and Buddhism, continue to exert their influence as independent religions in the modern world. Each stemmed from the renunciation of family and the adoption of an ascetic life by outstanding individuals. The sermon preached in the Deer Park at Sarnath near Benares by Gautama Buddha (*c.* 566–*c.* 480 B.C.) identified salvation with the attainment of freedom from the cycle of rebirth and emphasized that *Nirvana* or extinction could only be achieved by following principles conducive to a moderate, well-balanced life. The Jainist doctrine taught by the conqueror (*Jina*) Mahavira, who entered on his ministry *c.* 510 B.C., again stressed the supreme value of purification through moderation and the avoidance of physical violence. By rejecting animal sacrifice and the caste system both made a strong appeal to the poor as well as, more particularly in the case of Jainism, to the mercantile class emerging in the cities. Yet both made their chief impact on the peoples of India as a whole through their impact on Hinduism. Jainism never catered directly for more than minorities, more particularly the merchants operating in the cities of the Gangetic basin, the north-west and Mysore and later on the west coast where alone it still has a substantial body of adherents. Buddhism on the other hand was a proselytizing faith aiming at mass conversion. The zeal displayed by Ashoka in his widespread inscriptions is only one illustration. Of more lasting significance was the introduction of monastic orders. Individual monks spread the religion by wandering from place to place depending on the alms of the people among whom they moved. Monasteries consolidated this missionary work by providing permanent institutions for education and learning. As a result a faith born in northern India was carried south to Ceylon as well as far and wide over East Asia. On the other hand whereas, as explained earlier, it flourished in Indo-Greek India until it was overwhelmed in what is now the core of Pakistan by Islam, in India proper it failed to replace though it did influence the more deeply rooted Hinduism. Its main impact on Brahminical teaching reflected in the Upanishads lay in the direction of monotheistic thought and the concept of universal soul.

7

East Asia

Few useful generalizations can be made of a territory ranging over 80° of latitude, extending from the tropics to far north of the arctic circle and comprising lands as different as China, east Siberia and Japan, the mainland of south-east Asia, the Indonesian islands and the Philippines. Separate consideration will therefore be given to each region. If these receive differing emphasis, this is because they vary so greatly in the importance of the contributions they have made to the subject of this book, the understanding of the history of mankind.

China

Early Stone Age

East Asia was accessible to human settlement from both north and south of the Tibetan plateau. The more southerly route was certainly used by the Middle Pleistocene and possibly earlier, whereas the northerly does not appear to have been followed until the Late Pleistocene. Assuming that the earliest migration is likely to have proceeded over dry land with no more than narrow traverses of water, movement is most likely to have occurred at times of low ocean level corresponding with periods of glaciation in alpine and temperate latitudes. Even at such times the Bay of Bengal was only slightly less indented than it is today. If we accept his African genesis, early man must have expanded eastward from north India through a comparatively narrow funnel between the Bay and the extended glaciation of the Himalayas. From Assam it seems logical to imagine that he would have expanded fanwise downstream to Burma, Thailand and Vietnam and so north-eastwards (by the Burma trail) to south China and south-eastwards by the Sunda shelf to Sumatra, Java, Borneo and Palawan.

EAST ASIA

Stone industries made in mode 1 and featuring heavy chopping
367 equipment, hand-adzes and flakes occur in most of these countries,
but their precise character was influenced to some degree by the
varying raw materials from which they were fashioned. Although
dating evidence is sometimes lacking and never precise, it is evident
that they were established by the Middle Pleistocene and in some
cases possibly even earlier. The clear association of such an industry
54: 235; with plentiful remains of *Homo erectus* at Choukoutien remains at the
376: ch. 2 moment unique, but it is suggestive that industries of Patjitanian type
have already been recovered from the Upper Trinil beds in Java
immediately overlying the Lower Trinil deposits from which the
377: 3–6 original find of *Homo erectus* was made. Meanwhile new discoveries
have shown that the finds at Choukoutien in Hopei are far from being

159 East Asia at a period of minimum sea-level.

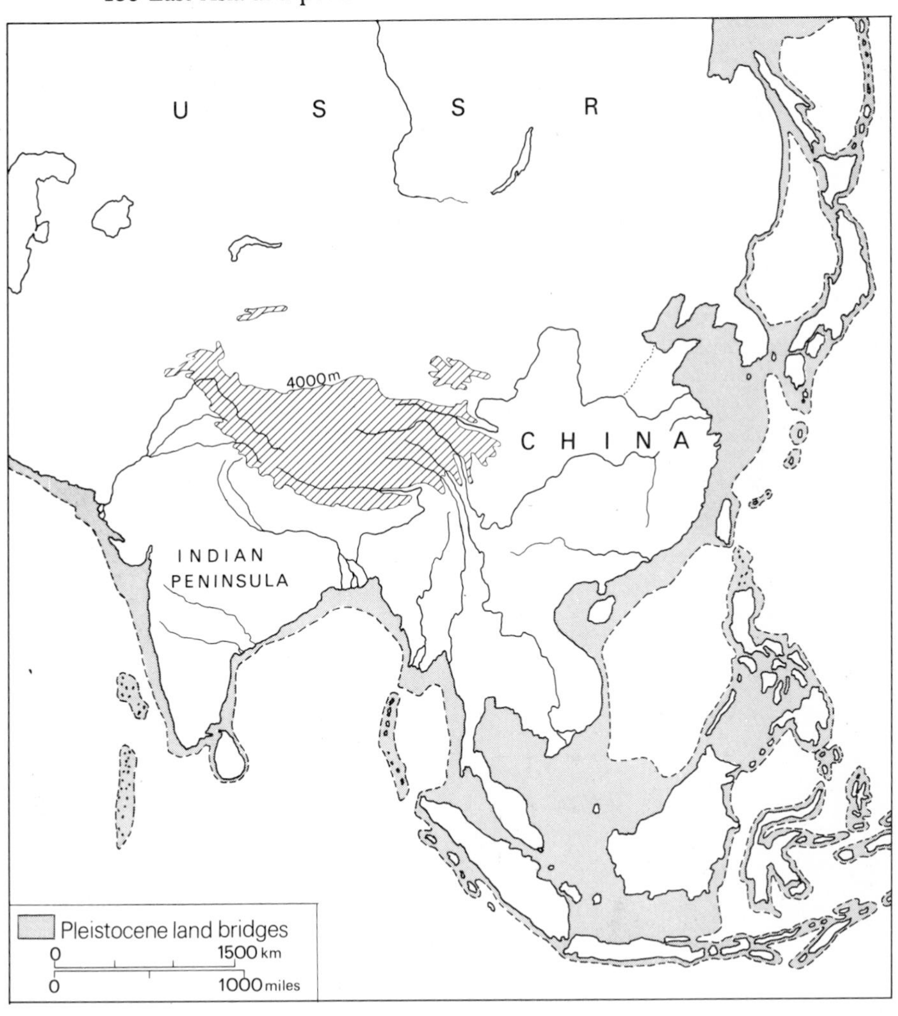

CHINA

the only ones in China. In fact the gap between Peking and the Burma road is already beginning to fill, as one can see from the *Homo erectus* mandible and skull from Lantien and neighbourhood and similar remains from Yunnan, as well as from the early stone industries found at Ko-ho and in the Lantien area.

Information about the history of human settlement in China
373: ch. 2 during the ensuing phases of the Pleistocene is still deficient, but there are signs that it was continuous. The stone industries dating from the latter part of the Middle or the early part of the Upper
391 Pleistocene from locality 15 at Choukoutien and from the lowest terrace of the Fen river at Ting-ts'un in southern Shensi carry forward earlier traditions, though displaying certain changes. Among these may be noted a greater regularity of workmanship on stone flakes, slight traces of bifacial flaking recalling that of the Patjitanian industry of Java and the appearance of keeled pointed forms made from thick flakes. Again it is worthy of note that the three teeth from
160 Ting-ts'un relating to a primitive (cf. Neanderthaloid) form of *Homo sapiens* display the shovel form of upper incisor noted in the case of the *Homo erectus* material from Choukoutien.

This same feature, which characterizes the existing Mongolian stock, is found in the human skeletal remains of *Homo sapiens sapiens* type from Late Pleistocene deposits over the whole of China from the upper cave at Choukoutien in the north to Tzu-yang, Szechwan, in the west and Liu-chiang and Lai-pin, Kwangsi, in the south. The archaeological material from this period, while again showing continuity, is notable above all for clear evidence of influences reaching China for the first time from north of the Tibetan plateau. This was visible in the stone tools from the Hsiao-nan-hai cave near

160 Shovel-shaped upper incisors of ancient and modern man from China: (1–2) from Choukoutien (*Homo erectus*); (3–4) from Ting-ts'-un (*H. sapiens* cf. *Neanderthalensis*); (5–6) modern Chinese.

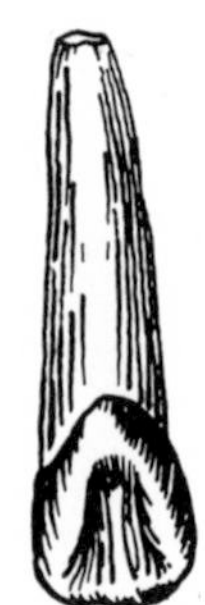

Anyang in Honan and from a number of sites in Ordos, Inner Mongolia, notably Shui-tung-kou and Sjara-osso-gol. These industries include a blade component notably burins, end-scrapers and pieces with steep retouch. The material from the Upper Cave at Choukoutien helps to complete the picture by providing artefacts of
161 antler and bone. Among these were eyed needles, implying most probably skin clothing, and a wealth of personal ornaments including beads made from the perforated teeth of red deer and badger, from sections of tubular bird bone and interestingly from fish vertebrae, all features which find ready parallels in assemblages dating from the final stages of the Upper Pleistocene over extensive tracts of Eurasia. The impact of north Asiatic culture was, as will be shown (p. 323), even more pronounced in the case of Japan. For China it was chiefly significant in that it set the pattern of its later history. Essentially this was one of indigenous development continuing from early in the Middle Pleistocene and enlivened towards the end of the Pleistocene and increasingly during recent millennia by the stimulating effect of contacts with the north and west.

Context of Chinese civilization

The notion universally held among the Chinese down to modern
368; 373: ch. 1; times that their country was the centre of the world and that other
388: ch. 4 peoples were by comparison barbarians, corresponded with reality, at least as far as east Asia is concerned, much more closely than did comparable notions prevalent among many other peoples. China was

161 Artefacts from Late Pleistocene deposits in the Upper Cave at Choukoutien.

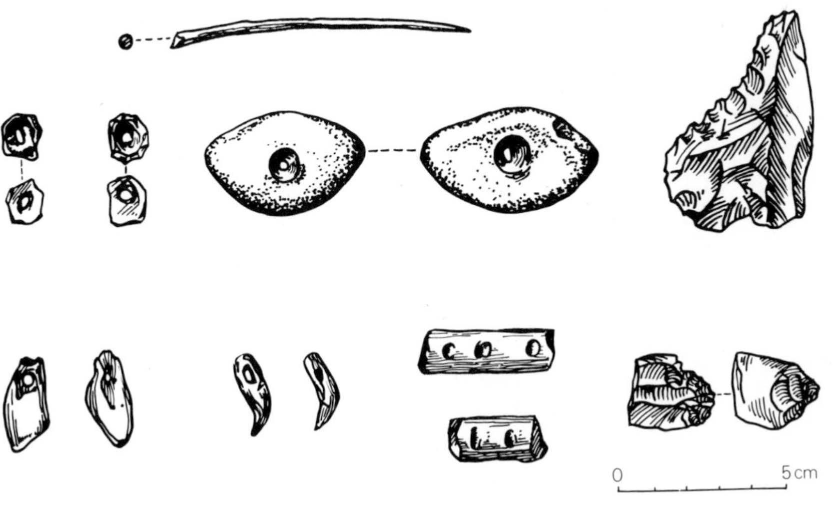

shut off in part at least by the Tibetan plateau and to the east surrounded by the sea which down to recent times served more to isolate than to connect it with territories overseas. Although China was originally populated from the south and despite some important contributions such as rice-cultivation, the population of this region remained too barbarous to threaten the fabric of Chinese civilization. The basis of this civilization was laid in the eastern part of the temperate provinces of north China mainly in the basins of the Hwang-ho or Yellow River and the Yangtze. It was not until the Han period that Chinese civilization incorporated the tropical zone of south China. Until the intrusion of advanced civilizations by sea during recent times the main stimuli applied to the essentially autochthonous civilization of China came from north of the Tibetan plateau. The more southerly route skirted the plateau traversing Mongolia and Sinkiang on the way to Turkestan with a side branch to the Indus valley, but its use cannot be certainly documented until Indian Buddhist missionaries followed it to reach China and opened the way for the silk trade of the Han period. There is strong evidence that the northerly route linking north China with Manchuria and so by way of the upper Amur river and its tributaries to Baikal and Minusinsk had begun to operate during the Shang dynasty.

The Chinese thought of their history in mythological and dynastic terms. Yet it is significant that they identified the same requisites for the formation of their civilization as modern archaeologists, namely the establishment of an economy based on farming and the subsequent formation of states. The basic achievement of settled life was identified with the activities of two mythological characters. Shen Nung is said to have invented agriculture, pottery-making, textiles and markets and Yu to have harnessed rivers ensuring the population against the menace of floods, traditional destroyer of life in the low-lying basins in which the population is chiefly concentrated. It was only after these accomplishments that the Yellow Emperor was able to found cities and develop the notion of a polity transcending kinship and ensuring the integrity and prosperity of more or less extensive territories through the ultimate sanction of force.

373: 78–80 According to legend Shen Nung taught the Chinese people to cultivate the land when they had become too numerous to continue subsisting on the meat of animals and birds. Regrettably little is known of the history of human settlement in China during the first four millennia of Neothermal time. The excavation of caves from

390, 374 Szechwan to Kwangsi and Formosa shows that the inhabitants of the southern provinces continued to make their stone tools from pebbles according to a mode already established during the Middle Pleistocene. They certainly hunted wild animals and may well have established mutually profitable symbiotic relations with certain of them. The concentration of population on rivers and in coastal territories argues that fish were already significant in diet. There is no definite evidence for their plant food, but it may be relevant, more particularly in relation to north China, that Shen Nung was credited with knowing the taste of a hundred grasses. If the earliest peasant societies in north China were essentially the product of indigenous development, it becomes more than ever important to learn more about their immediate antecedents.

373: ch. 3 *Yang-shao peasants*

There is no mystery why Chinese farming or for that matter the Chinese state should first have developed along the middle course
368 of the Yellow River. The river was yellow because it was eroding loess, a wind-blown deposit that mantled much of north-west China. This soil was ideal for farming even under primitive conditions: it was extremely fertile and it was easy to work. Another reason why north China was to prove so much more progressive than the south is that since Late Pleistocene times it had been exposed to influences from the west and north. Indeed, when traces of peasant economy were first brought to light at Yang-shao-ts'un, Honan and at sites in Shensi and Shansi, archaeologists were prone to assume that it was the outcome of diffusion from western Asia. Domestication, the use of polished stone axes and the manufacture of pottery were all accomplishments thought to have been acquired along the route followed much later by the silk trade. Much play was made in particular with the fact that the Yang-shao potters applied painted decoration to their vessels before firing, a method perfected long before in south-west Asia. Fuller knowledge has since made it plain that anything in the nature of transference is out of the question. Whatever stimulus the inhabitants of north China may have experienced from the west, it is abundantly clear that they developed primarily along autochthonous lines. As they multiplied the Yang-shao peasants of the nuclear or Chung-yüan area evidently sought additional land on
372 the loess of Kansu and even as far west as Chinghai. Radiocarbon analysis has confirmed the conclusion originally based on stylistic grounds that the painted pottery of Ma-chia-yao and other sites in

Kansu is younger than the early Yang-shao of the nuclear area. The fact that the Yang-shao peasants spread west rather than east is only another indication that, whatever stimulus may have been received from the west, the early peasant culture of the nuclear area was essentially an autochthonous growth.

For crops the Yang-shao farmers depended mainly on millets, fox-tail (*Setaria italica* var. *germanica*) and brown corn (*Panicum miliaceum*). Too little is known yet of the early history of the millets to speculate fruitfully about the source of the staple crop of the earliest peasant societies of north China. There is no record so far for millet in Mesopotamia earlier than Jamdet Naṣr (*c.* 3000 B.C.), but it was certainly being cultivated in central Europe by the fifth millennium. The relevant point so far as China is concerned is that millet was a crop capable of withstanding long periods of drought.

162 Map of China with Yang-shao, Lungshanoid and Shang territories.

It was thus particularly well adapted to the climate and loess soils along the middle and upper course of the Hwang-ho, a territory in which it still features as an important crop. In respect of livestock attention was concentrated on pigs and dogs, each of which could have been local domesticates. Farming produce was supplemented by hunting and foraging. Wild plants and their seeds were harvested and wild cattle, deer and horse, among other animals were hunted. A feature of Chinese culture already marked at this time was the
163 importance accorded to fish both as a source of animal protein and as a motive for ceramic decoration.

By far the most numerous artefacts made by the Yang-shao peasants to survive in the archaeological record are the pots they made for storing, cooking and serving food as well as for drinking. The commonest forms were open dishes, bowls, tall jars and globular vessels with necks. They were made entirely by hand except perhaps that the rims have been finished while the pots stood on turn-tables. The methods used for building were coiling and moulding. For firing the pots were placed on ledges in the upper part of kilns heated by fires placed at the open ends of short passages to ensure a draught. Before this process, which brought them to a red colour, some of the vessels intended for personal use or for funerary ritual were decorated by designs painted in a black or purplish brown slip pigment by means of a brush. Here, again, we see the beginning of a long tradition, not merely of ceramic decoration, but also of calligraphy and pictorial art. The stylized designs include human and animal as well as geometric forms and gave ample scope for diversity of taste and fashion, a medium through which social groups were able to express their identity and solidarity. Some of the richest
164 decoration is that displayed on vessels from the cemeteries and settlements of Kansu.

Indications that the pots were stood and perhaps even turned on

163 Fish designs painted on Yang-shao pots from Pan-p'o-ts'un, Siam.

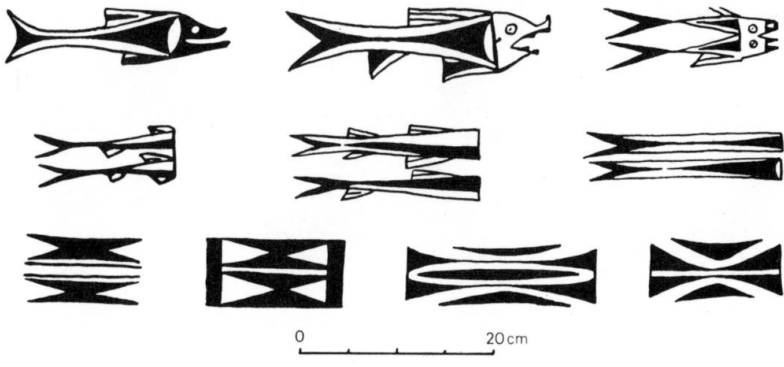

mats and baskets before firing is given by impressions on their bases. These clearly demonstrate the skill of the Yang-shao peasants in different varieties of plait-work. The large numbers of spindle-whorls suggest that weaving was also an important craft at this time. Although too much significance ought not perhaps to be attached to the find of a single half-cut cocoon of the silk worm (*Bombyx mori*) from the site of Hsi-yin-ts'un in Shanshi, it may hint that the silk industry amply documented for the Shang period had already begun during the stone age.

Among the other main crafts practised were carpentry and the
165 working of stone, antler and bone. Heavy stone axes must have been important for tree-felling and clearance. Lighter adze blades would have served for dressing house-timbers and probably for making the wooden appliances and equipment needed in farming. Bone served for making tools used in potting and leather-work, as well as for fish-hooks and a variety of tanged arrowheads. A feature of Yang-shao technology widely shared among the early peoples of northern Eurasia and north America was the use of polished stone for projectile heads and knives. Rectangular knives of iron closely resembling the stone ones from Yang-shao sites, perforated near the back to secure straps and backing of leather and cloth to secure the thumb and provide a hand grip, have been used down to recent times in China for harvesting kaoling (*Andropogon sorghum*). This type of reaping equipment differs markedly from that employed by the early barley and wheat farmers of western Asia. It is noteworthy that bone knife-handles slotted to receive flint blades found in Yang-shao contexts are few and relatively late.

Important information about the economy and social life of the Yang-shao peasants is given by their settlements. Sites were clus-

164 Painted pottery of the Ma-chia-yao phase from Kansu.

tered in favoured locations. There is no indication that any particular one was inhabited for any great length of time, though some were occupied on more than one occasion. The most reasonable hypothesis is that the Yang-shao farmers practised a form of shifting agriculture which may well have been associated with a slash and burn regime. This was capable of yielding good crops without the need for elaborate cultivation, but it involved the clearance of new patches of forest every few years. The peasants lived in villages – forty-six
166 houses were excavated at the Pan-p'o-ts'un settlement – rather than
370: fig. 8, 9 on scattered farmsteads. The archaeological evidence bears out the legend that in the days of Shen Nung the people did not think of harming one another. The settlements were defined by ditches, but displayed no elaborate defensive works. Similarly the architecture agrees with the smaller artefacts in reflecting a society lacking any marked hierarchy. On the other hand there is some suggestion, notably in the plan of Pao-chi in central Shensi, in which the dwellings were arranged in two rows either side of an open space, that Yang-shao society was of segmented structure. Individual houses, which were often semi-subterranean, might be round or oblong in plan. In each
167 case the pitched roof, probably thatched, was carried on stout vertical posts, the main structural members of the buildings. When walls were needed these were made of wattle and daub and served no other purpose than to screen the interior. The floors were either of stamped earth or were plastered. Each housing unit had its own hearth. The pottery kilns tended to be grouped in one quarter possibly on account of the fumes. The pigs were liable to be penned in the middle

165 Polished stone objects used by Stone Age peasants in North China.

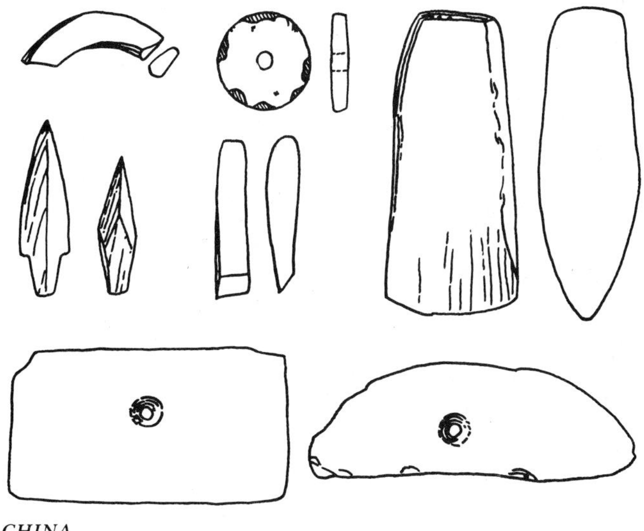

166 Yang-shao village of Pan-p'o-ts'un in course of excavation.

167 Oblong and round houses at the Yang-shao village of Pan-p'o-ts'un, Shensi.

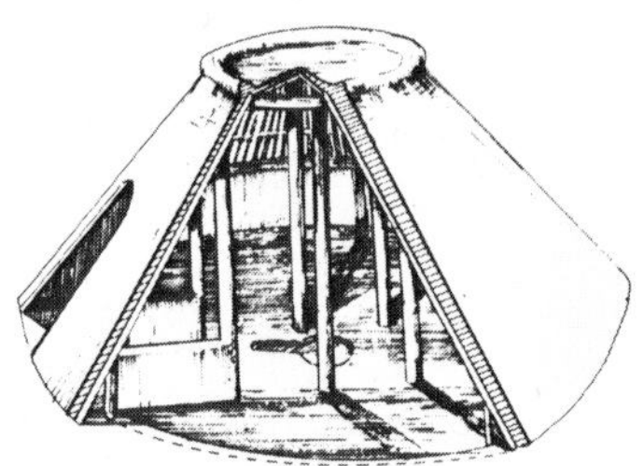

of the village, a sensible enough arrangement if they were largely fed on waste. Adult members of society were buried in cemeteries outside the villages in contracted or extended positions accompanied by food and pottery.

373: ch. 4 *Lungshanoid and Lungshan peasants*

The first indication of a more complex situation came with the discovery at Lung-shan-chen in Shantung of a peasant culture having many traits in common with Yang-shao, but distinguished by a
168 markedly different kind of pottery. Classical Lungshan ware was wheel-turned, thin-walled, had a plain black burnished surface and included a series of novel forms. These included cooking vessels with solid feet (*ting*), cauldrons with hollow feet (*li*), sometimes with necks, spouts and handles (*kuei*), stemmed cups and handled mugs. The fact that this kind of pottery was concentrated in the provinces of Shantung and Hupei, adjacent to that occupied by the hand-made painted Yang-shao wares, suggested the existence of two related associations of peasant communities, one on the primary loess of the middle Hwang-ho, the other on the redeposited loess of the lower Hwang-ho and the Shantung peninsula. When ceramic wares began to be recognized which conformed to neither model, the tendency at first was to explain them as if they were hybrids rather than products of self-standing groups. At least five such 'Lungshanoid' wares have already been recognized, two in the Hwang-ho basin, two in that of the Yangtze and one in the south-east China coastal zone, namely

(a) Miao-ti-kou found overlying Yang-shao ware in the Chung-yuan nuclear region,

168 Forms of classical Lungshan ware.

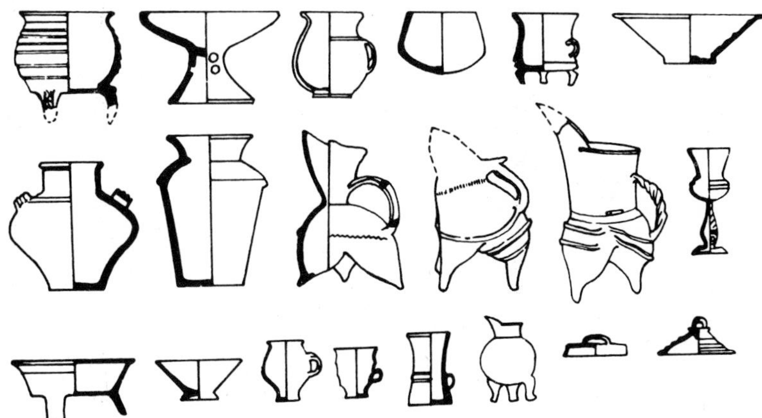

(b) Ta-wen k'ou found underlying classical Lungshan ware in Shantung,
(c) Ch'ü-chia-ling in the Hanshui and middle Yangtze basins,
(d) Ch'ing-lien-kang in the lower Yangtze basin,
(e) Feng-pi-t'ou on Formosa and in the coastal zones of Fukien and Kwangtung.

371 The first radiocarbon dates to become available, although far from sufficient, are beginning to provide a framework or at least to suggest the main lines of development in time. It is already apparent that the Chung-yuan area was in fact the earliest focus not merely of the Yang-shao but of Chinese peasant culture in general. Good evidence for the antiquity of Yang-shao ware in its nuclear region comes from the well excavated site of Pan-p'o in Shensi which was evidently occupied at intervals during the first half of the fourth millennium. On the other hand the western expansion to Kansu evidently did not take place until the middle of the third millennium and Ch'i-chia ware was still being made into the middle of the second. The appearance of Lungshanoid wares was also relatively late. In the nuclear area Miao-ti-kou ware was dated to late in the third millennium at the name site where it appeared on a long abandoned Yang-shao settlement. The only date for Ch'ü-chia-ling ware, that from Ching-

Table 21. *Radiocarbon dates for Chinese neolithic wares (after Barnard)*

Lungshanoid		
Miao-ti-kou ware		
Miao-ti-kou per.II	ZK III:	2174 ± 95*
Ch'u-chia-ling ware		
Ching-shan Hsien	ZK 81:	2162 ± 95*
Ch'ing-lien-kang ware		
Ch'ien-shan-yang	ZK 49:	2628 ± 100*
Yang-shao		
Ch'i-chia ware		
Ch'i-chia, Kansu	ZK 15:	1620 ± 95
	ZK 23:	2085 ± 95*
Ma-chia-yao ware		
Ma-chia-yao, Kansu	ZK 21:	2070 ± 100
	ZK 108:	2458 ± 100
Classical Yang-shao		
Miao-ti-kou per.I	ZK 110:	3109 ± 100*
Pan-p'o		
Site 3	ZK 127:	3490 ± 105
Site 1	ZK 122:	3735 ± 105
Site 1	ZK 121:	3798 ± 105
n.d.	ZK 38:	3953 ± 110

* Corrected from 5700 to 5568 half-life.

shan Hsien, was closely similar in age. On the other hand the single determination for Ch'ing-lien-kang ware, that obtained from rice husks from the site of Ch'ien-shan-yang, dated from late in the first half of the third millennium. No determinations are yet available for the classical Lungshan ware of Shantung which on the other hand was found overlying the local Ta-wen-k'ou version of Lungshanoid pottery.

In the course of over two thousand years it is hardly surprising that the peasant way of life should have expanded over such extensive parts of China. It was of the very nature of an extensive system of agriculture to spread at least to the limits of the soil and climate in which it came to birth. In this respect neither the primary loess of Kansu nor the redeposited loess of the lower Hwang-ho and the Shantung peninsula presented obstacles to the spread of an economic system first developed on the loess of Honan and Shensi. Expansion to the Yangtze basin and the coastal zone of south-east China involved adaptation to higher rainfall and temperature and different soils. The fact that this was accomplished so readily was almost certainly due to experience accumulated by the aboriginal inhabitants. It is significant that rice, a crop almost certainly first harvested and probably domesticated in south-east Asia, was adopted by both the Lungshanoid groups in the Yangtze basin and by the Feng-pi-t'ou people of the south-east. In respect of livestock the economy of the later Neolithic farmers of China was enriched from two directions. The makers of K'o-hsing-chuang ware, the Shensi equivalent of the classic Lungshan, kept sheep, horses, cattle and water buffalo as well as the perennial dogs and swine, the first presumably derived from the west, the last from the south and ultimately from south-east Asia.

The evidence for rice cultivation and a wider range of livestock argues for a more productive basis of subsistence. Again, the fact that the Lungshan peasants were apparently already building earthen walls round their settlements argues for greater permanence. The probability is therefore that they practised a more settled form of agriculture than their predecessors. As on the loess of central Europe the duration of an extensive system based on the clearance of successive zones was limited by the capacity of the forest to rejuvenate. Once the loess of the Hwang-ho basin was fully colonized on an extensive basis the normal build-up of population would have led to a speeding up of the cycle of clearance until the point was passed at which the forest could replace itself sufficiently fast to allow swidden agriculture to continue. When this stage was reached the development of a more effective system of farming permitting more permanent settlement was the only alternative to a reduction in the growth of population. In such a process there was a close interaction between the nature of subsistence and settlement. If greater productivity permitted a more established form of settlement, fixity of settlement prompted the return of accumulated organic refuse to the soil and higher returns from fields in the immediate area of habitation. Again, greater permanence facilitated advances in technology which in turn helped to increase the returns from agricultural labour. Such a process once begun was likely in a territory combining a fertile soil with a stimulating climate to be self-perpetuating. It should be no surprise that at one site after another archaeologists have recovered evidence for more developed economies and social systems from deposits overlying ones containing Lungshan pottery.

Shang dynasty (1523–1027 B.C.)

3: ch. 6; 382, The earliest dynasty recorded in the Chinese annals to be identified
'3, 397: ch. 2 by archaeology is that of the Shang. The truth of this identification is proved by the degree to which the king-lists preserved in the histories have been confirmed by study of the inscribed oracle bones excavated from the final capital of the dynasty at Anyang. The accuracy and span of the Chinese historical tradition stems ultimately from the reverence for ancestors that formed an integral part of Shang civilization, yet the earliest history of China only assumed its traditional form in the time of Confucius (d. 479 B.C.) whose teachings did so much to confirm the Chinese people in their respect for history. Modern critical scholarship working on such early sources as the bamboo strips recovered from the time of the eastern Chou dynasty and the oracle bones of Anyang has sometimes been able to correct the Confucian canon in respect of the earliest phases of Chinese history. This applies notably to the chronology of the Shang dynasty. Whereas the beginning of the dynasty was traditionally set at 1765 and its replacement by the western Chou at 1122 B.C., the dates most commonly accepted today are 1523–1027 B.C. According to the traditional history the capital was moved several times during this period, and archaeology has revealed at least three focal areas equivalent in all probability to successive capitals. Around 1300 B.C. on the short chronology here favoured the Shang ruler moved his headquarters from Cheng-Chou to Anyang some 160 km to the north. To judge from excavations at Ehr-li-t'ou a yet earlier capital was located in the Lo-yang-yen-shih area further west.

The fact that Anyang happened to have been excavated first meant that the material manifestations of Shang civilization burst on the
375, 379 consciousness of western archaeologists in their fully mature form. At a time when it was customary to account for the appearance of bronze technology in the old world in terms of diffusion from a limited zone of south-west Asia these new finds from China were disconcertingly distinct in form and style. As knowledge increased it soon became evident that the Shang bronze age was so largely an indigenous development that the question of a possible stimulus from the west has lost much of its relevance. This is supported by the fact that it grew up in the nuclear area of Chinese peasant culture in northern Honan and that the excavation of key sites has frequently revealed a more or less continuous sequence of occupations in some cases going back to Yang-shao times.

If geographical and stratigraphical indications agree in pointing to the gradual emergence of Shang civilization from indigenous and specifically Lungshan roots, the same conclusion is suggested by the maintenance of basically the same form of subsistence economy. Cultivation continued to be carried on primarily by digging-sticks and hoes, though symbols on the oracle bones have been construed as indicating the use of traction ploughs, and there is still no evidence

169 Shang territory with key sites.

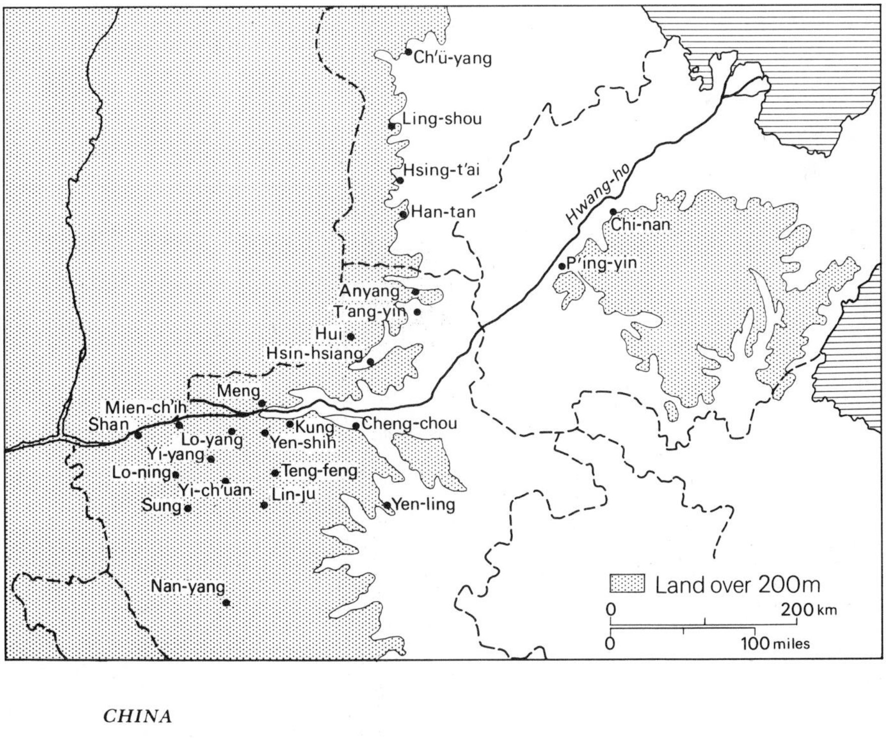

for irrigation on more than a very local basis. Millet continued to predominate over rice and wheat as food crops, and hemp and silk-worms were now raised on an ampler basis to provide fibres for textile industries. Among other evidence to show continuity may be cited the use of nephrite, pottery, certain of the forms of bronze ritual vessels and the practice of scapulomancy.

Yet continuity has to be viewed in the light of a major historical evolution. What emerged in the nuclear region of the Hwang-ho loess around the middle of the second millennium B.C. was nothing less than a different form of society. In place of basically egalitarian communities living peaceably together and practising subsistence economies with only a rudimentary degree of craft or social specialization, Shang China showed the beginnings of an organized polity. Yet it would be easy to overdraw the analogy between the Shang dynasty and that of the later historical period. Quite apart from the restricted territory involved, the emperor's position was still tenuous. The royal clan over which he presided was only one of a confederacy of clans each of which had its own petty chieftain and maintained its own ancestral cult. His position was more that of first among equals than of absolute ruler. He owed his status primarily to the fact that the royal clan was able to claim divine descent and that it fell to him as its leader to mediate between heaven and the people.

Shang society was hierarchical, warlike and one in which labour was more finely sub-divided and social roles more specialized than

170 Design of Shang house at Anyang. Length *c.* 24 m.

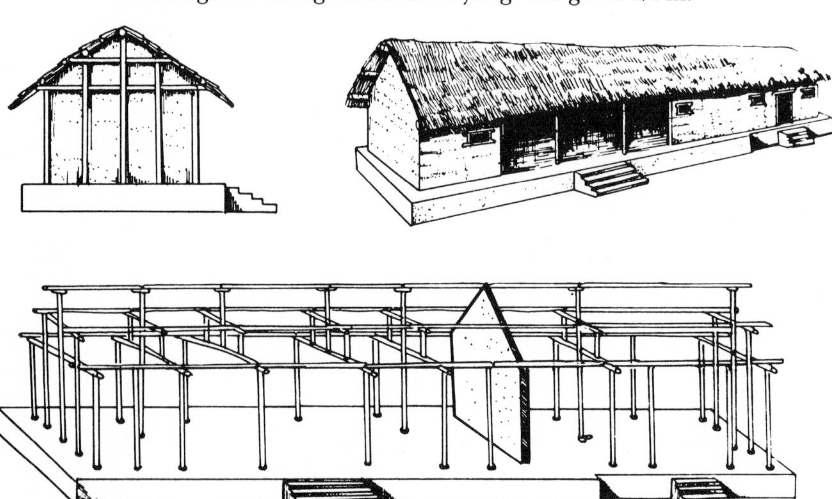

in earlier times. It was also for certain limited purposes literate. One of its most conspicuous manifestations was the large capital city, the focus of political authority and the home of many kinds of specialist craftsmen. Excavation of the earlier capital at Cheng-chou shows that even this was nearly three and a half hectares in extent. In several respects it resembled the much more recent imperial city of Peking. Thus it was rectangular in plan, measuring 2,000×1,725 metres, was orientated to face the four cardinal points, had a regular street-plan and was defended by a powerful earth wall, in this case of rammed earth some 19–20 metres across the base. Palaces and other public buildings were likewise concentrated in a palatial quarter and built mainly of wood on rectangular podia or platforms of rammed earth.
170 The roofs were gabled and were carried on vertical posts set in some cases on stone or bronze bases. The houses of the common citizens, though smaller, were also rectangular gabled structures. They now had plain earth floors which might, as in earlier times, be sunk below ground surface. The concentration of population in a city as large as Cheng-chou implies the existence of a redistributive mechanism. The various crafts – potting, metal-smithing, jade-working and the like – occupied their own quarters as they did down to recent times in European cities. Many of their products were absorbed by the court and the citizens, but others, particularly the more modest ones, were traded to the peasants of the attendant territory in exchange

171 Plan of cruciform pitgrave, Hsi-pei-kang, Anyang.

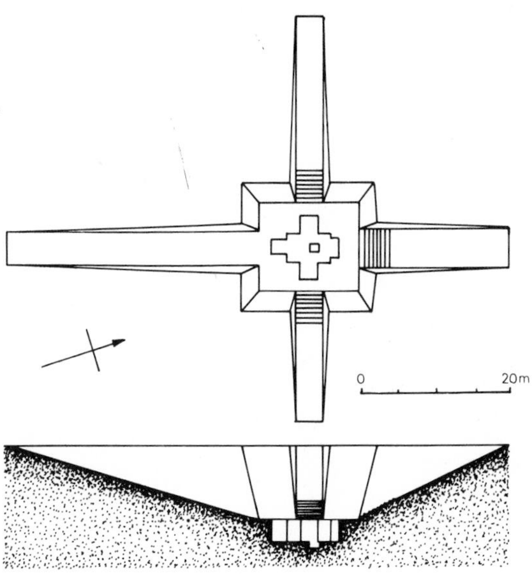

for food. The capital was thus a centre of production and a market as well as a political capital. It was rich as well as the centre of authority. Not surprisingly it was well defended, more especially when it is remembered that the royal clan was only one of many.

Even more dramatic evidence for social hierarchy in later Shang society is afforded by the cemetery at Hsi-pei-kang, Anyang, where eleven royal graves contrasted by size, character and content with
171 over 1,200 private ones. The royal dead were buried in deep pits up to fourteen by nineteen metres in plan sunk ten metres or so below the surface and approached by a cruciform arrangement of ramps. The burial pits were provided with a double lining of jointed timbers, the inner one forming a coffin and the outer a receptacle for grave-goods. In an exceptionally well-preserved tomb at Wu-kuan-ts'un the chamber could be seen to have been covered by a painted and inlaid wooden canopy. Apart from their size and elab-

172 Shang chariot burial with skeletons of horses and groom, Ta Ssu K'ung, Anyang.

orate structure the Shang tombs impress by the wealth of their grave goods, including weapons, ornaments and chariots, but even more
172 by the evidence that animals and servants were despatched to accompany their master. In the case of the Wu-kuan-ts'un tomb sixteen horses had been buried in the shaft and others, as well as dogs, in the ramps. Numerous human victims were found in the burial pit and ramps and no less than thirty-four human skulls were set in rows in the upper layer of the shaft infill. The idea of burial in timber-lined shafts as a rule under mounds was of widespread occurrence in Eurasia during the prehistoric period and reached a climax
183 in the nomad burials of Pazyryk in the Altai. The custom of burying vehicles, steeds and attendants with the great man reminds one
127 vividly of the royal graves at Ur. Quite apart from any consideration for the comfort of the departed in a future life, ceremonial burials of this kind served the vital role of reinforcing hierarchy. The same

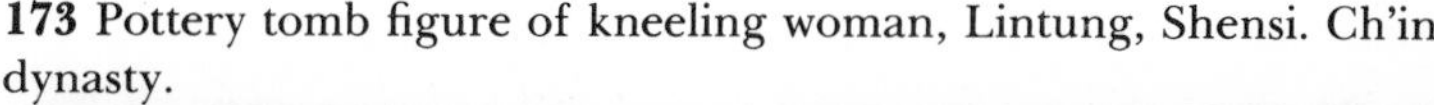
173 Pottery tomb figure of kneeling woman, Lintung, Shensi. Ch'in dynasty.

basic idea informed the burial practices of later dynasties even when horses and men and women were replaced by pottery models, which in Ch'in times might be of life size, but were later reduced in scale
173 sometimes to mere figurines. By the Tang dynasty the display of funerary models was so palpably directed at advertizing the status of the deceased and relatives that it was the subject of imperial edicts designed – often vainly – to ensure that the size and number of models was appropriate to the official status of the deceased.

Weapons and, during the Anyang phase, chariots played a key role in hunting and warfare as well as serving to maintain the prestige and define the status of the elite. Although the Shang chariots must
180 be viewed in the context of Eurasia as a whole, extending as far west

174 Reconstruction of chariot from fifth-/fourth-century tomb at Liu-li-ko, Honan.

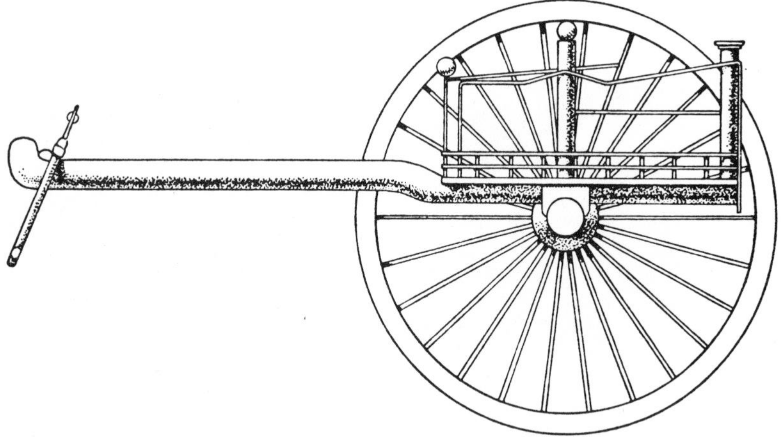

175 Shang bows (script signs) and arrows (bronze).

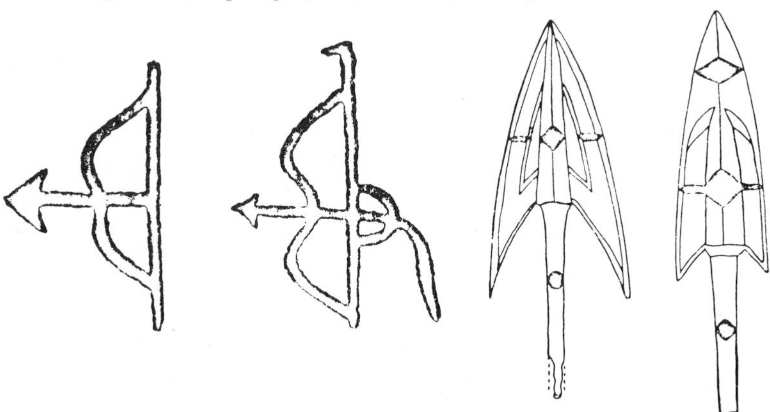

as south Scandinavia, Germany and Greece and including parts of
south-west Asia, they were distinguished like so many cosmopolitan
features of Chinese technology by a number of distinctive and
original features. Instead of being set near the rear end of the
driver's platform the axle was placed directly under it. Again, the
harness was attached to the yoke by means of mounts of inverted
V form peculiar to China. The Chinese chariots, which were normally
397: 63–5 drawn by pairs of horses, were lightly built of wood with wheels of
particularly fine construction, having numerous tapered spokes, up
174 to eighteen during the later Shang and as many as twenty-six at the
time of the Warring States in the latter half of the eastern Chou
dynasty. Bronze was used as mounts for harness, hubs and yokes,
as well as for axle caps and the cheek pieces of horse bridles, to impart
a gleam to the equipages and symbolize the superior rank of leading
men. In China as elsewhere in the ancient world the chariot was
designed basically as a moving platform to transport leading warriors
397: 118–23 to decisive positions in the field. The bow and arrow played an
175 important role in war and chase. Arrowheads might be made of bone
or bronze. Bows, to judge from the symbol used to denote them, were
of reflex form and compound construction, made, if one can go by
an example from the third century B.C., of strips of bamboo and
animal sinew. The spear was used, though whether for hurling or
176 serving as a pike is unknown. For close fighting the halberd or *ko*
with bronze blade was the main weapon and remained so for a
thousand years during which it underwent developments unique to
China. For body armour the Shang warrior may well have worn
bamboo or quilted breast guards. Bronze helmets were certainly
made, but their rarity makes it likely that these were confined to
leaders.

The crafts most abundantly represented in the archaeological

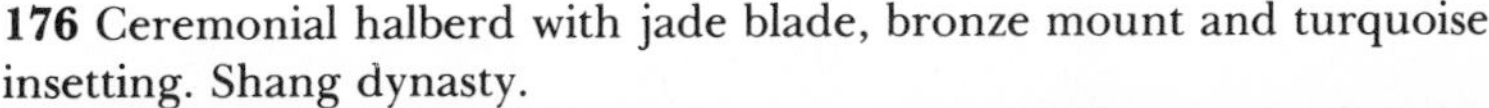

176 Ceremonial halberd with jade blade, bronze mount and turquoise insetting. Shang dynasty.

material and probably of leading importance during the Shang
period were potting and bronze metallurgy. Although serving dif-
397: ch. 3 ferent purposes these were from a technological point of view closely
interlocked. The Shang potters knew how to produce high temperatures under controlled conditions. In the construction of their kilns
the firing chamber was separated from the heat-flue and furnace and
provided with holes in the floor in order to admit the heat directly
to the pots. The reducing atmosphere, in which, following Lungshan
practice, the Shang potters produced their grey-walled vessels, was
one well adapted to removing oxygen from metallic ores. In addition
to producing the pottery required for cooking and daily use the
Shang potters made two luxury wares, one featuring tall lugged jars
177 made from white kaolin, the other bowls and vases having for the
397: 70 first time a felspathic glaze. Although lead fluxed glaze did not
appear in China until the third century B.C. and the first true

177 Lugged water-jar of kaolin from Anyang.

porcelain was not invented until the Tang dynasty, the Shang potters had already made key advances towards the world-wide supremacy of Chinese ceramics.

The absence, at any rate so far, of a distinct chalcolithic phase in north China and the appearance of such forms as socketed axes and spearheads suggest that the initial stimulus to bronze metallurgy
378 reached China from the west most probably by way of the Baikal region. On the other hand, it is certain that during the later Shang
178 period the bronze workers of Anyang produced castings, more particularly for ritual vessels required for the cult of ancestor worship, of an outstanding level of excellence using highly original methods. Techniques like sheet-metal work and rivetting used in the west for manufacturing metal vessels were conspicuously absent. The
179 ritual vessels of Anyang, which might weigh up to 900 kg and stand as high as 1·33 m, were apparently made by direct casting in multiple

178 Ritual bronze wine vessel (*tsun*) with animal mask design. Western Chou dynasty.

clay moulds. The elaborate symbolic ornamentation, often in deep relief, was modelled on the inner face of the moulds, which in themselves were outstanding examples of ceramic skill. Sources of copper and tin exist within comparatively easy reach and it is interesting to note that bronze halberd blades have been found to contain between 13% and 20% of tin alloy.

Jade in the form of nephrite continued in favour and the discovery of regular workshops shows that it was imported as a raw material,
392, 397: 59–60 most probably from the Vostochny Sayan mountains in Baikalia. A substance so hard to work represented a heavy investment in human labour and the fact that finds were concentrated in royal tombs only emphasizes the role of jade artefacts in reinforcing status. At the same time it may well have acquired the magical or therapeutic qualities with which it was certainly invested in later times. Nephrite continued to be used for *pi* rings, either cut from a single piece or made up from three segments. Other objects made from this precious and intractable material included dress ornaments, amulets in the form of animal profiles, animal sculptures up to 27 cm long and the blades of ceremonial knives and halberds. The fact that the mounts of halberds with jade blades were sometimes set with
176 turquoise is significant, since both materials are available in Baikalia.

Another craft to call for comment is that of silk weaving, one of China's signal contributions to the luxury of civilized living. Silk textiles were common enough during the Shang period to use for wrapping bronze halberd blades and the only direct evidence for silk

179 Bronze tripod wine goblets (*chueh*) showing pottery moulds in position. Shang dynasty.

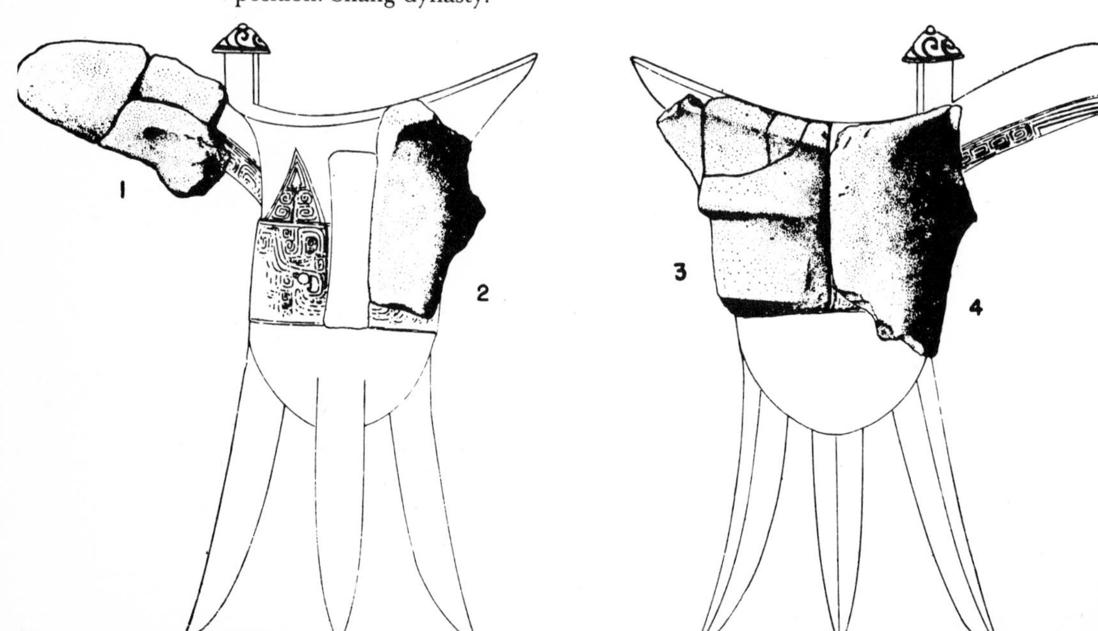

at this time is in fact provided by impressions preserved by surface decay of bronze objects.

The later Shang period was notable for its art. The discovery in a tomb at Hou-chia-chuang, Anyang, of a musical stone and of traces of a drum and the frame on which they were both hung is a reminder of the part played by music presumably in court ceremonial and in the performance of ancestral rites. Graphic art took the form of sculptures in jade, limestone and marble. These included
180 representations of kneeling and squatting human figures, animals, including buffalo, elephant, frogs and turtles, and in addition mon-

180 Tiger-headed monster of marble, tomb 1001, Hsi-pei-kang. Shang dynasty.

sters with eagle or tiger heads. Much more numerous are decorative
181 elements applied to ritual objects, chariot fittings, knife-handles and the like. Although a variety of spiral and other abstract designs were used, animal and to a less extent human figurations were an important element in the repertoire. The emphasis on animal representations reflects the intense preoccupation of Shang rulers with hunting wild animals and keeping them in captivity. Stylized animal masks recall later occurrences in Maori and Kwakiutl art and the motive of opposing pairs of tigers or other animals with a human face or the symbol for a ruler placed between the heads, reminds one of much earlier Sumerian and Pre-dynastic Egyptian art. Yet it is well to remember that the desire to avert evil is as universal as man himself.

Another highly significant feature of Shang civilization was the

181 Bone knife handle with animal head masks, Hsiao-t'un. Shang dynasty.

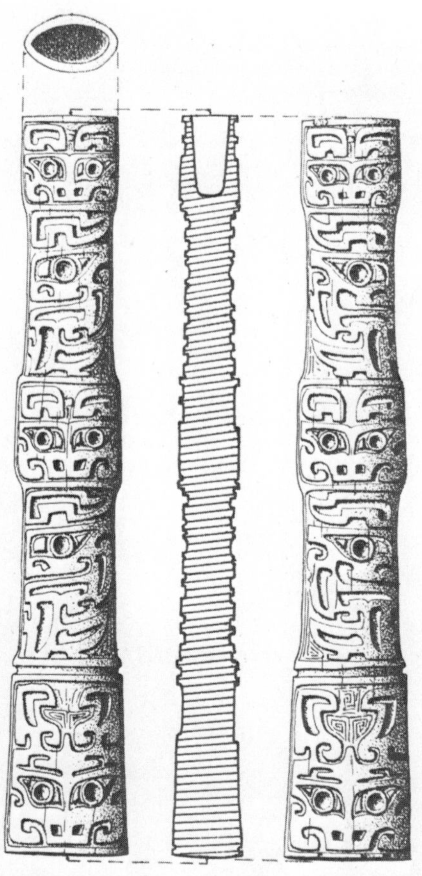

script. Whereas oral communication sufficed for prehistoric peasant societies in China as elsewhere, the scale and complexity of Shang civilization called for literacy at least among the official class. We owe the earliest body of Chinese writing to the fact that the Shang ruler and his advisers sought guidance from oracles on such topics as the weather, the time of hunting and warlike expeditions, the health and movements of the ruler and the appropriate sacrifices to the
182 ancestors. The basic technique invented by the Lungshan peasants was to apply heat to pits sunk in one face of a scapula and observe the positions of the cracks on the opposite one. The innovation made by the Shang was to paint or more often incise questions on the surface and observe the way the cracks behaved in relation to these. Towards the middle of the Shang dynasty the use of the carapaces of tortoises (*Testudo anyangensis*), as an alternative to scapulae, came

182 Oracle bone inscription.

into fashion, a sign that supplies from south of the Yangtze were already being drawn upon. It is possible for modern scholars to interpret these oracle inscriptions because, despite the reform of the script during the second century B.C., around a third of the symbols closely resemble those still in use. Apart from insights into the preoccupations of the Shang rulers, the inscriptions provide striking testimony to the historical reality of the dynasty. Of the thirty names of rulers listed in the bamboo records of *c.* 100 B.C., no less than twenty-three have already been identified in the oracular inscriptions.

373: ch. 7

Chou period (1027–221 B.C.)

Whereas the territory of the Shang polity was narrowly confined to northern Honan and immediately adjacent areas its impact was felt by peasant communities as far afield as the Liaotung peninsula and the maritime zone of south China. In certain cases it stimulated social changes which were of more than local significance. This was notably the case in respect of the Wei valley where a hierarchic civilization known to history as the Chou developed to the point at which it was strong enough to extend east and replace the Shang. As might be expected the Chou civilization which dominated north China for eight centuries shared many of the characteristics of its mentor. It was not merely that it had developed in its homeland under Shang influence, but as so often happened in later Chinese history the intruders were to a large extent absorbed by the already ancient culture of the heartland of north China. Cities continued to play a key role and increased in numbers as the territory expanded. Despite differences in form and style the bronze vessels, chariots, ornaments and weapons of the Chou period carried forward the basic modes established during the preceding era.

The new era was chiefly notable for the establishment of political dominance over an area extending from Manchuria to south of the Yangtze basin and at the same time for technological developments that helped to give further shape to the form of Chinese civilization as this appeared in the fuller light of history. Iron was now brought into use, something which profoundly influenced the productivity of farming and therefore of the economy as a whole. During the opening centuries of the new era bronze continued to be the only metal available for tools and weapons. Iron was not taken into use until around the middle of the first millennium B.C. Technical considerations suggest that the innovation was made by the Chinese themselves. Whereas in the west iron-working was carried on exclusively by forging until the adoption of casting as late as the fourteenth century, in China the sequence was reversed. Iron-working began by casting and was only supplemented by forging during the third century A.D.

Lacquer work based on the use of the natural sap of the lac tree was first invented during the Shang period when it was applied to tomb painting, but it was during Chou times that it first came into wider use and notably improved the amenity of daily life. Applied to a base of wood and sometimes textile it was capable of producing a wide range of articles that combined strength and resistance to water with lightness and a surface both pleasing in itself and affording an ideal base for painting. Among other things lacquer was particularly well adapted to containers and the surface covering of sword-sheaths and a wide range of furniture. It is in large measure due to scenes painted on lacquer, but now increasingly also on silk, that we owe our knowledge of early Chinese painting. Another field for brushwork which now becomes prominent was the bamboo writing-slip, a reminder that calligraphy and painting went and still go together in Chinese art. Between them representations, documentary sources and not least material products from tombs combine to present an insight into the standards of refinement and taste which already prevailed in the higher levels of Chou society.

The nature of the polity inherited from the Shang dynasty combined with the large extension in territory meant that, as happened so often in later times, China reverted during the Eastern Chou period to a situation in which extensive fiefs had become largely independent of any central authority. It was precisely during this time that scholars and philosophers first achieved power and influence. They did so at the courts of quasi-independent dukes and their teachings were reinforced and perpetuated institutionally through the founding of academies. In this way the foundation was laid for the education of the official bureaucracy which from the Han period onwards was to ensure the stability of the Chinese empire even during the many periods of trouble that intervened between effective periods of dynastic rule. The teaching of men like Confucius and Mencius in itself reinforced the stability inherent in the long-established veneration of ancestors. The new teaching emphasized the virtues of harmony, tolerance and mutual respect between members of families, master and servant, ruler and people and in this way provided a social cement capable of withstanding powerful stresses.

One outcome of the increases in wealth and amenity evident during the Chou period was that China became increasingly attractive as a focus of pillage both to the nomadic peoples of desert and steppe and to rival contenders, not to mention the under-privileged, within the frontiers. One response was yet another Chinese invention, the cross-bow operated by a bronze trigger-mechanism which first appeared during the fourth century B.C. Another was that a beginning was made with the construction of passive defences in the north.

Ch'in dynasty (221–210 B.C.)

The reign of the house of Ch'in, which emerged victorious from the confused world of the Warring States, was brief. It was nevertheless of great moment in the history of the Chinese state quite apart from giving a name to the Chinese people. When Cheng assumed the title of emperor one of his first acts was to reduce the fiefs and principalities to the status of imperial provinces. Another was to impose conscription and employ the army as an engine of state. The territory of the empire was extended west to Szechwan and south to the Canton delta and Annam. Military success was aided by the deployment of cavalry, and the development of canals and roads assisted control by the central government. The great degree of central control made it easier to ensure a more adequate defence of the northern frontier and it was at this time that earlier defences were replaced by a continuous wall over some 2,250 kilometres. In the form in which it was reinforced during the early Ming dynasty this still survives as a symbol of national integrity.

The Han dynasty (202 B.C. *to* A.D. 200) *and the west*

The founder of the Han dynasty, Liu Pang, a minor official of peasant origin who seized power during a period of disorder and reigned as emperor Kao-tsu, further consolidated the basic achievements of the Ch'in. The Chinese state, now centred on the Yangtze basin, assumed the form in which it was to endure for some two thousand years. The official examination system was established and the ideological basis of the state firmly fixed. Many early texts prescribed during the brief period of the Ch'in were rescued and Confucianism elevated into something like a state religion. At a technical level these developments were powerfully affected by the invention of paper in *c.* A.D. 105. One of the early uses of lamp-black ink invented *c.* 400 A.D. was to make paper rubbings of Confucian texts carved on stone. This in turn suggested by the seventh century the employment of wooden blocks with inscriptions carved on one face for printing on paper sheets.

The appearance of the Chinese empire in its modern extent endowed with many of the institutions which lasted down to recent times coincided with the establishment of contacts with the civilizations of India, western Asia and the Mediterranean. As so often happened in history the catalyst was not economics but religion. The overland route could well have been opened up by Buddhist missionaries from north-west India at the time of the Han dynasty. Traces of Buddhist monasteries have been found along the Inner Asian route skirting the north of the Tibetan plateau. It is possibly in the wake of the missionaries that nephrite from the sources between Yarkand and Khotan, known to have been that mainly drawn upon during later times, first reached China. From the opposite direction silk textiles flowed towards the rich markets of Syria, Egypt and Rome. Not for the last time religion opened the way to commerce. The direct overland route by way of Iran and Syria was subject to interruption from Parthian enmity to Rome. This only enhanced the value of the sea routes to Alexandria from the mouths of the Indus, the Narmada and possibly the Ganges. There is no evidence that

183 Commercial links between China, India and the West.

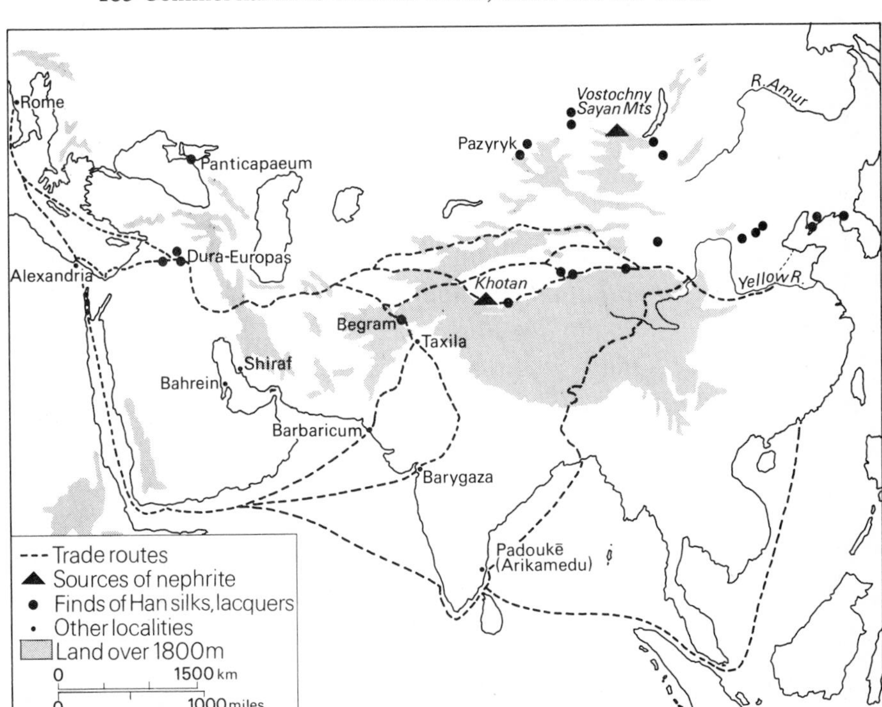

trade flowed direct from the China coast before the Tang period and even then, as we are reminded by a Kufic inscription under the glaze of a pot found at Shiraf on the Persian coast but made in China, the initiative came from the west as it had done in the case of the Inner Asian route and was to do a thousand years later by sea. The very self-sufficiency of Chinese civilization testified by the archaeology of six millennia, while it helped to maintain the continuity we admire; at the same time deprived it of the ability to adapt to foreign contacts when these broke upon the country in the wake of the industrial revolution. The ambivalence of the present regime to the glories of China's traditional culture is easy to understand. Yet if history is anything to go by the millennial civilization will surely reassert itself when a new balance has been achieved between immediate needs and long-term values.

Japan

Two of the main questions posed by Japanese civilization is why it was so late in developing and why, more especially since it went to school so to say in Tang China, it differed so greatly from that of the mainland. It follows from the line adopted in this book that in seeking to account for the distinctive character of any particular civilization one should turn to the antecedent, prehistoric phases in its cultural evolution and at the same time take account of the ecological setting in which these unfolded. In the case of the Japanese the first point to make is that for thousands of years they have been insular. Moreover, although three of the four main islands of Japan are at the same latitude as north China, their main axis is inclined towards Siberia. Whereas the northern part of Sakhalin approaches within ten miles or so of the lower Amur region and Hokkaido is linked by the Kurile island chain to Kamchatka, the island of Kyushu is separated by some 190 kilometres from Korea, the immediate source of most of Japan's borrowings from China during proto-historic times. Yet if the Japanese were cut off from China their insularity gave them a secure base as well as encouraging use of the sea. This made them both receptive and adaptable when the time came for selective assimilation. Insularity was also important for economic reasons. The seas round the Japanese islands compensated to a degree for their own limitations. Japan is mountainous. Five sixths of the land area contributes only marginally to subsistence and part even of the cultivable area could be exploited effectively down to recent times only by means of an extensive slash and burn regime.

The limited extent of good cultivable land meant that it had to be given almost entirely to the growth of crops for direct human consumption. Meadows for feeding livestock, still more fodder crops, were far too inefficient to be readily afforded. Animal protein had to be obtained either from hunting or from fish and molluscs, both from inland waters and from the surrounding or even in some cases comparatively remote seas. Another feature is that cultivable land was not merely limited in total extent, but fragmented. Even the most compact areas like those on which Kyoto and Tokyo developed were of minuscule area by comparison with the loess plains of north China. Many were even smaller and separated from one another by relatively unproductive mountains. Geographically Japan was designed for petty states rather than a united realm. This is why the Japanese had to propagate and emphasize the divinity of the rulers of the leading clan. Nominally both the Japanese and the Chinese had emperors, but their roles in history differed as much as the territories and the societies over which, in whatever manner, they presided.

Early Stone Age

When sea-levels were lowered at the time of major glaciations the Japanese and associated islands would have been much more accessible to and at times certainly formed part of the Asiatic mainland as is proved by remains of glacial animal species. So far there is no certain evidence that the country was occupied by man during the Middle Pleistocene. The earliest certain traces date indeed from the latter part of the Late Pleistocene and even so are unfortunately limited to the lithic aspects of material equipment. The possibility of learning more about the economy or even the technology of the Early Stone Age inhabitants of Japan depends on the discovery of sites with the necessary organic data. At present one can only say that over much of Eurasia comparable stone industries are associated with economies based to a notable extent on hunting. Detailed plotting of stone implements, waste and traces of fire on recently investigated
412 sites like Sunagawa points to settlement in small groups of light shelters each hardly more than two or three metres across.

400, 403 So far it is scarcely possible to do more than detect a broad sequence in time and define a limited number of regional variations. A tempting clue to the sequence on Honshu is provided by the
411 sequence of black bands in the Kanto loams of the Tokyo area, but these have to be used critically. Not all researchers have allowed for the fact that individual bands consolidate or remain separate

according to local circumstances, a fact which invalidates hasty attempts to produce a uniform sequence. Direct archaeological stratigraphy arising from the occupation and reoccupation of particular sites over a period of time – Heidaizaka, Nogawa and Tsukimino are cases in point – has proved helpful. Even more valuable results are being obtained from the application of geophysical dating methods, including radiocarbon analysis and measurement of surface hydration in respect of obsidian tools. One of the beauties of these techniques is that they can be applied to natural sequences like the black bands in the Kanto loam as well as to archaeological stratigraphy. The lithic industries, which occur in the Tachikawa loam formed between *c.* 30,000 and 10,000 years ago, belong to a mode 4 tradition with blades, burins and end-scrapers. From time to time assemblages were enriched by secondary traits. The first of these
184 were portions of blade shaped by a steep retouch but retaining untouched one sharp flake edge, which might be transverse but was more often oblique to the main axis. None of these have been found mounted on their hafts on Japanese sites, but examples with transverse edge are known from northern Europe hafted as the heads of cutting arrows. Around 13,000 B.C. the Japanese industries
185 were enriched by a bifacial technique applied to symmetrical forms of sizes suited both for arrow- and spearheads, but also to asymmetric pieces that may have served as knives. Another technique to appear

184 Backed blades with sharp oblique or transverse edge.

in this context was designed to produce small regular bladelets of
a kind found hafted in slotted bone knife-handles or projectile heads
over extensive tracts of northern Eurasia and north America.
Although none have yet been found in their mounts in Japanese
sites it is likely that they served to provide sharp cutting edges.
Bladelets of this kind were struck from very carefully prepared cores.
406, 410 According to the Yubetsu technique best exemplified on Hokkaido,
cores of this kind were made on portions of large bifacially flaked
points prepared by removing ski-shaped slices. It is relevant to the
northern connections of Hokkaido in the closing phase of the Late-
glacial period that close analogues to this technique are known from
413: fig. 1, 25 Kamchatka, Manchuria and arctic North America. It was in this
context that the first, pre-Jōmon pottery appeared in Japan.

185 Bifacial points, microblades and Yubetsu core.

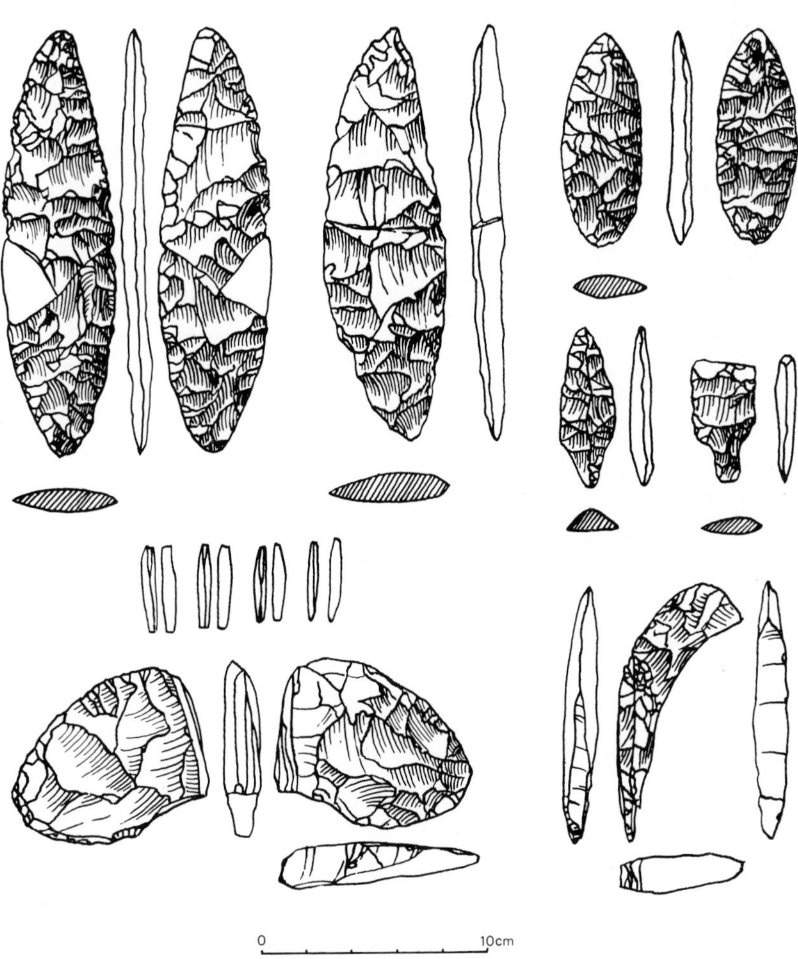

When cord-marked (*jōmon*) pottery was first systematically excavated from the Ōmori shell-mounds near Tokyo, this was thought to mark the earliest phase of human settlement in Japan. As we now know Japan was inhabited well back into the Late Pleistocene before pottery had come into use. Again it has since appeared that the Ōmori pottery was relatively late in the Jōmon sequence (phase 4). Leaving on one side the many regional variants which correspond to the fragmentation of productive territory arising from the mountainous character of the country, Jōmon pottery has been divided on stratigraphical and typological grounds into five main temporal divisions. These have since been confirmed by radiocarbon dating, a technique which has also made it possible to recognize the existence of a pre-Jōmon phase in the ceramic history of Japan.

Table 22 If the high radiocarbon dates assigned by two laboratories in Japan
405:285 and five in the United States are accepted – and their number and consistency leave us with no real alternative – the appearance of pottery in Japan can hardly be accounted for in terms of immigration or cultural borrowing from the mainland of east Asia. In seeking an indigenous explanation it is logical to turn to subsistence economy. Before doing so it is important to dispel one important source of misunderstanding. This arose from the circumstance that Jōmon pottery was first located by modern archaeologists in shell-mounds, which, because they were easy to recognize, bulked as unduly in the archaeological record of Japan as of northern Europe. At a time when prehistorians were too preoccupied with the chronological

186 Radiocarbon dating of pre-Jōmon and Jōmon pottery.

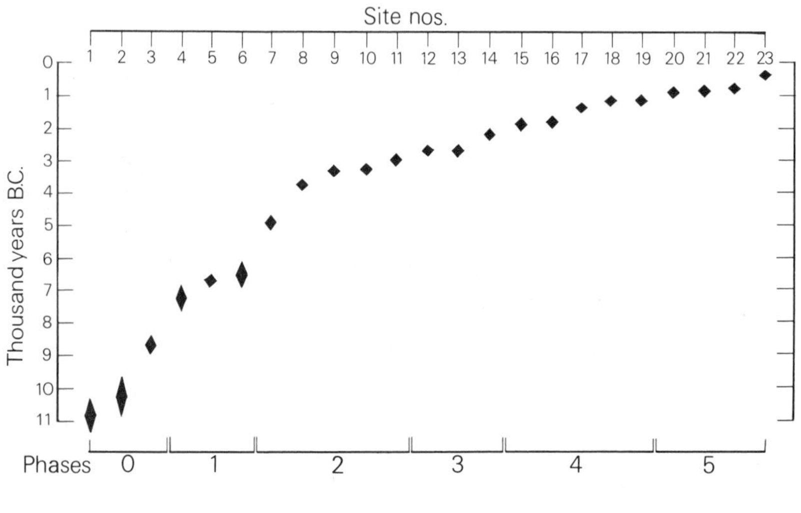

ordering of primary data to give much critical thought to its meaning, it was easy to assume that eating shell-fish was a way of life at a particular period of time rather than providing only one component of diet. The earliest Jōmon pottery is widely distributed in Japan including the mountainous interior. This is not to deny that coastal activities were unimportant at a time when Jōmon pottery was in use. Indeed the indications are that they contributed to subsistence on an increasing scale. This trend may have been in part due to the increasing warmth of the Neothermal seas. On the other hand it may reflect wholly or in part demographic factors. By and large, marine resources complement terrestrial ones. While the sea-shore may always have been exploited as a foraging zone, it may be supposed the main food resources exploited by the earliest inhabitants would have been the animals and plants existing on dry land. As population grew and spread over the habitable area, the point would be reached when resources were no longer adequate in poor seasons. The only

Table 22. *Radiocarbon dates for Stone Age ceramic phases of Japan*

Jōmon phases		Localities	Lab. Ref.	Age C-14 B.C.
(5) Latest	23	*Arami, Chiba	N 166·2	340 ± 120
	22	Nishippara, Toshigi	N 53	750 ± 170
	21	Yahatazaki, Aomori	N 110	870 ± 130
	20	Shimpukuji, Saitama	N 117·2	990 ± 130
(4) Late	19	Takayagawa, Chiba	N 37	1120 ± 120
	18	*Ishigami, Saitama	N 94	1140 ± 120
	17	*Sobata, Kumamoto	N 269	1350 ± 125
	16	Ōyu, Akita	N 114	1730 ± 130
	15	*Harinouchi, Ichikawa	N 59	1830 ± 150
(3) Middle	14	*Todoroki, Kunnamoto	N 317	2130 ± 180
	13	Osawa, Mitaka, Tokyo	UCLA 279	2620 ± 150
	12	Omiyama, Nagano	SI 93	2630 ± 60
(2) Early	11	Ishigami, Aomori	N 242	2920 ± 130
	10	*Sobata, Kumamoto	N 268	3240 ± 130
	9	*Kamo, Chiba	N 386	3340 ± 140
	8	*Ta, Ibaragi	N 191·1	3690 ± 130
	7	†Ōmagari, Hokkaido	GX 281	4845 ± 150
(1) Earliest	6	*Kijima, Okayama	M 237	6450 ± 350
	5	†Tochihara, Nagano	Gak 1056	6650 ± 180
	4	Natsushima, Kanagawa	M 770	7290 ± 500
(0) Pre-	3	Saishikada, Gumma	Gak 311	8700 ± 250
	2	†Kamikuroiwa, Ehime	I 943/4	8135 ± 220 10215 ± 600
	1	†Fukui, Nagasaki	Gak 949/50	10450 ± 350 10750 ± 500

* Midden. † Cave, or rock-shelter.

practicable alternatives short of a limitation of population were either to exploit terrestrial resources more effectively or to intensify the utilization of coastal and marine foods or to do both simultaneously. Either course would imply a more sedentary mode of life. This in itself was consistent with the manufacture of pottery for which the need to boil plant food and molluscs alike would have provided positive incentives.

The oldest pottery from Japan and possibly in the world comes from cave sites widely distributed in central Honshu, Shikoku and Kyushu. This comprises rather sparse remains of small, apparently round-based pots built by squeezing together slabs of worked clay. The earliest of these were ornamented solely by a linear relief-technique suggested perhaps by the technique of building the pots, but ornamentation by finger-nail impression was also used before the first appearance of cord-impression.

187 Earliest Jōmon sites in Japan.

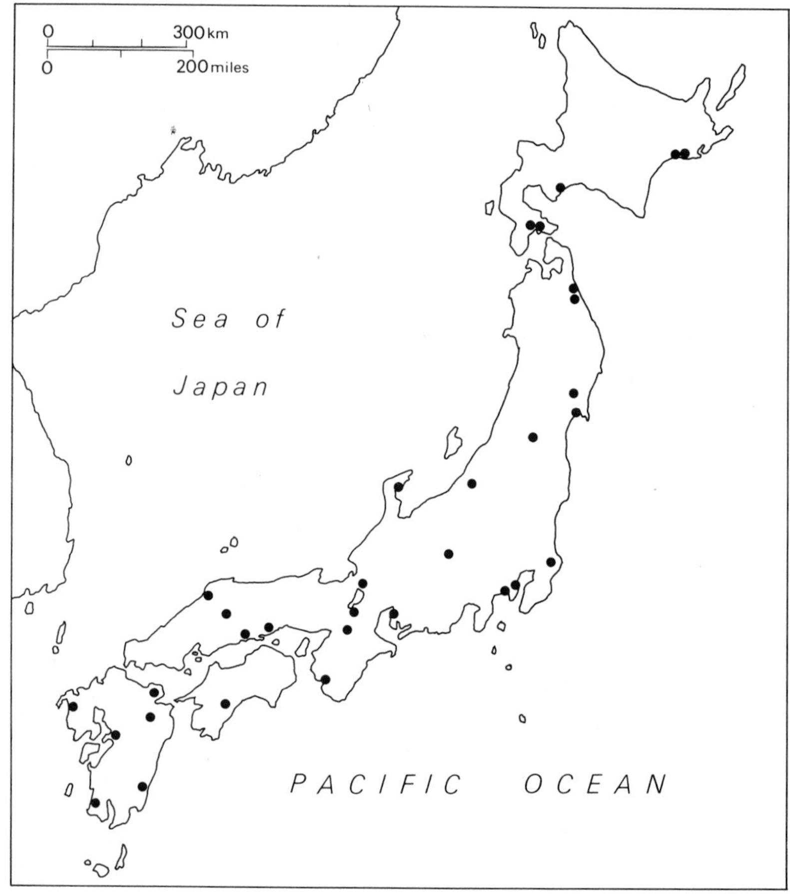

188 (a) Conical based Earliest Jōmon pot of Entō Lower type.

(b) Flat based Middle Jōmon pot of Tado I type.

(c) Middle Jōmon pot of Umataka type with luxuriantly ornamented rim.

Jōmon pottery proper, although exhibiting a variety of local and temporal styles in the course of seven millennia, was nevertheless marked by persistent features. All of it was made by hand by pressing together clay coils and fired in the open. Imprints on the bases of pots made in periods 4–5 suggested that they were stood on mats during the process of building. Cooking vessels were the only kind of pot during the earliest stages, but in periods 3–5 vessels were also made to meet a variety of needs, notably 'tea-pot' forms, plates, cups
188 and bowls. The commonest shape to begin with was conical with a pointed base resembling a basketry prototype, but pots with flat bases became dominant in period 2 and remained so to the end, though accompanied by ones with ringed (per. 2) and footed (per. 3–5) bases. The rims of most pots were smooth, but wavy or peaked profiles were a continuing feature of Jōmon pottery and handles featuring snake motifs (per. 3) and human heads (per. 3–5) appeared in the later stages. Cord-impression, the diagnostic feature of Jōmon pottery, which took a variety of forms, persisted throughout as did groove decoration. Shell imprints occurred in per. 1–2 and red paint and lacquer coating in per. 3–5.

Whereas pre-Jōmon pottery is most commonly found in caves and rock-shelters in the interior, Jōmon pottery itself comes mainly from
402 riverine and coastal shell-mounds and from open settlements in the interior. Clusters of up to fifteen dwellings suggest cohesive groups, though whether all were occupied at once can hardly be proved. The dwellings themselves were humble enough. Round, oblong or wedge-shaped, their floors were sunk into the sub-soil to allow head-room
189 without an elaborate superstructure. The gabled roofs supported on timber uprights and cross pieces were made of materials like bark

189 Jōmon and Yayoi hut plans.

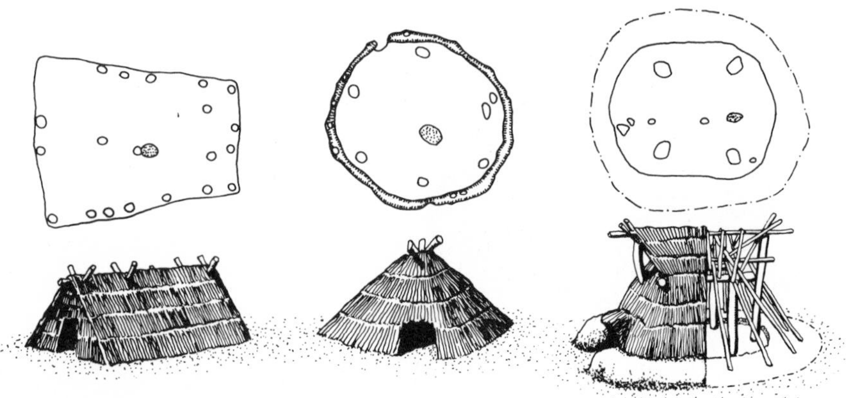

or foliage and rested on the ground. There is no indication of elaborate carpentry and the primitive edge-ground axes sufficed until the closing phases when they were supplemented by polished blades with oval or flattened section.

Subsistence even at sites marked by mounds of the discarded shells of oysters, mussels and other edible shell-fish, was based on a wide range of resources. Deer and wild pig were the main sources of meat though dogs, which were apparently kept throughout, were also probably eaten as well as smaller game. The bow continued in use from the pre-ceramic period and arrows were tipped with bone heads or bifacially flaked stone ones of hollow-based and, during later phases, barbed and tanged form. Harpoons with antler or bone heads may have served for hunting land mammals, but also for catching large marine fish such as tunny, shark and sting-ray whose remains appear in the middens. One of the most significant facts about Japan from this point of view is that deep Pacific waters approach the east coast so closely. Analysis of the fish remains from Jōmon middens suggests that certain species were caught on relatively distant fishing-grounds implying seasonal absences of the active men, while nuclear families remained at their home bases with secure sources of food. The Sea of Japan off the west coast also had its attractions for fishermen as did inshore fisheries round the entire coast. Fish-hooks and indications of nets are further reminders of the importance of fish in diet. It is likely that the cooking pots which abound in the middens were mainly used for boiling fish and molluscs, but in the interior at least they may well have served to a significant extent for cooking plant food. Here the evidence is still defective, but recent studies are emphasizing the importance of this resource. It seems likely that walnuts, chestnuts, horse-chestnuts, acorns and lily bulbs for example were not merely foraged, but discarded or even planted close to dwellings where they would have flourished on concentrations of organic refuse and provided annual crops in immediate proximity to home bases. Indeed there is evidence that crops were being cultivated on however small a scale before the end of the Jōmon phase. Charred plant remains from the floor of a house at Uenohara, Kumamoto, dated to *c.* 1400 B.C. in terms of radiocarbon, included a few grains of barley and rice as well as remains of wild species such as knotgrass, wild red bean, acorns and bamboo stems. Already during period 4 in the currency of Jōmon pottery the foundations were being laid for the economic basis of the Yayoi phase.

Before turning to this a word may be said of the way in which

Jōmon man satisfied his psychic needs. The dead were buried very simply in contracted or extended positions occasionally protected by stones. The only monumental structures associated with him were built in periods 4–5 and concentrated in northern Honshu and Hokkaido. These comprised plain stone circles with uprights up to a metre high and sun-dial formations with an upright monolith surrounded by a radial arrangement of recumbent stones enclosed in a kerb. Plastic representations of an anthropomorphic kind sometimes appear on pottery in addition to the heads already noted on rim handles. In period 3 schematic free-standing figurines appeared and in periods 4–5 ones of a more naturalistic appearance including
190 some of undoubted female character. Among personal ornaments it is interesting to note the popularity of perforated animal teeth and claws, prototypes of the imperial curved jewel (*magatama*), but traces of hierarchy or even of social differentiation are conspicuously absent from the Jōmon phase.

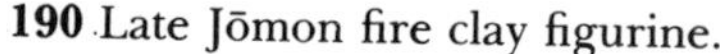

190 Late Jōmon fire clay figurine.

404: *ch. 3* The contact with Korea already indicated by the appearance of barley and rice during the later Jōmon phase was greatly intensified during the third century B.C. in northern Kyushu. The establishment and general acceptance of rice as the principal basis of subsistence inaugurated the new Yayoi phase of settlement. By around 200 B.C. the new economy had been adopted in Shikoku and western Honshu and by A.D. 100 it had spread to the Kanto plain and central Tohuku. By middle Yayoi times the whole of the western half of Japan had adopted a basically agrarian economy but it is important to note that rice cultivation was not established on Hokkaido during the prehistoric period owing no doubt to the colder climate. Rice cultivation is documented by botanical data, and also by many cultural indications. These include traces of paddy fields and irrigation channels, crescentic or rectangular reaping-knives like those used two or three thousand years earlier by the peasants of north China, and a wealth of wooden implements for cultivation, including spades, hoes and rakes, as well as pestles and mortars of the kind used for pounding rice. Hunting and fishing were actively pursued as sources of protein, all the more so that animal husbandry at no time played a significant role in Japanese economy. The more sedentary basis of subsistence is reflected in the settlements. Dwelling houses, normally rectangular or sub-rectangular in plan, might be as large as seven by eight metres, but though embodying stouter timbers, they were still of primitive construction. The much greater volume of crops is reflected in specialized granaries raised on stilts and approached by ladders made of notched logs. More secure supplies of food allowed a marked increase in the sub-division of labour and a parallel advance in technology. The general introduction of the potter's wheel by the middle Yayoi phase went with the manufacture of pottery by craftsmen and resulted in a more standardized product. Weaving, which was certainly practised at this time, may well have remained a domestic craft. On the other hand metallurgical industry reached a level in respect of bronze-work in particular that must surely indicate specialist smiths. Iron was only used sparingly and much equipment continued to be made of flaked or polished stone, including many axes and adzes, reaping-knives and arrowheads. Bronze served in the main to define status, in the first instance no doubt that of immigrants, but also for ritual objects.

The existence of close contacts with the mainland during the Han dynasty is reflected both in Chinese records of the time and in the

191 Yayoi bronze weapons.

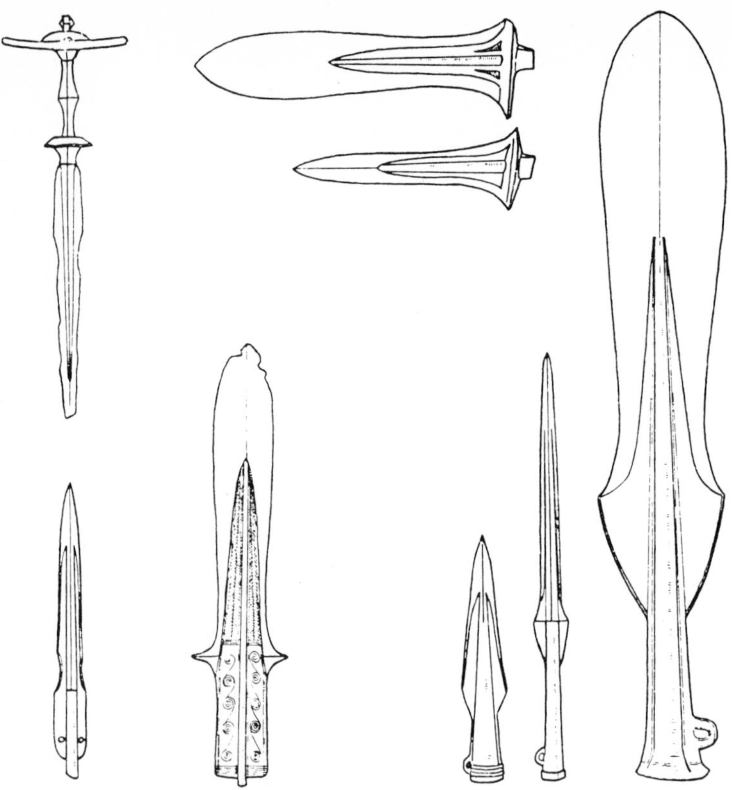

192 Yayoi bronze bell.

archaeological data, notably in respect of bronze weapons and mirrors, sporadic coins and personal ornaments such as glass beads and bracelets. Yet the Yayoi culture was far from being a ready-made import. Rice had been grown on however small a scale for a thousand years before it was adopted as the staple food of western Japan. Again, although bronze weapons were based on Chinese prototypes and included a number of imports, those made by Yayoi smiths
191 showed a marked tendency to diverge. Indeed the blades of some Yayoi halberds and spears were so expanded that they can only have served to symbolize status. On the other hand, as burials show, the trend towards a hierarchic ordering of society was still restricted. Although Yayoi burials were slightly more elaborate than Jōmon ones, none was on the monumental scale indicative of widely separated ranks. The dead were placed in small stone cists or buried in two or three pottery jars. The nearest approach to monumentality came when jar burials were protected by heavy capstones resting on a number of small shallow ones, but it is noteworthy that Chinese objects were concentrated in certain burials. The most outstanding
192 things made during the Yayoi period were bronze bells which might be over a metre tall and were notable feats of casting by indigenous smiths. The fact that they have nearly all been found in isolation and that the subjects depicted in relief on their surfaces concern the food quest argues that they may have played a key part in rituals designed to ensure plenty.

Protohistory and the Nara–Heian period (710–1185)

404: ch. 4 During the fourth century A.D. Japan entered on the Protohistoric phase which lasted down to the establishment of the imperial court at Nara in 710. The main information is derived from the burials
401 of leading men. Their tombs were often of monumental scale and

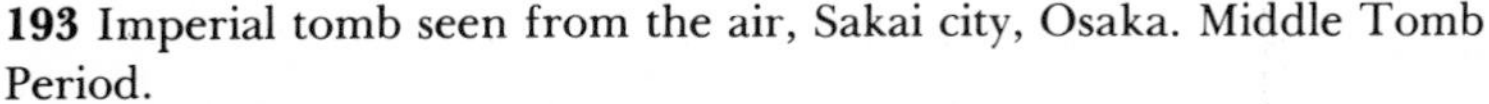

193 Imperial tomb seen from the air, Sakai city, Osaka. Middle Tomb Period.

might occupy areas, including surrounding moats, of as much as 32·4
193 hectares. The mere construction of such monuments testifies not merely to increasing population and wealth, but above all to a hierarchic ordering of society, in which the most important role was played by warrior clan leaders and their henchmen. The dead men were provided with body armour, helmets and a variety of weapons, including swords, daggers, spears, bows, arrows and quivers. The
194 tombs also included clay *haniwa* models of heavily armed warriors, veritable prototypes of the *samurai* known to history. Other tomb models show a marked differentiation in architectural forms as between town and country, palace and shrine. Already at a time coinciding more or less with that of the barbarian migrations into the European territories of the Roman Empire, the main social institutions of historical Japan had taken shape. As if to emphasize the fact of historical continuity, wooden Shinto shrines have continued to be rebuilt on the same site and according to the same design as those of the Protohistoric period. Again, although Shintoism may itself have been institutionalized first in reaction to the introduction of Buddhism, its basic belief in the value of thank-offerings and sacrifices to natural spirits inhabiting such places as groves, mountain tops, sources of water or stones of unusual size surely stems from the prehistoric past.

408 During the early historic period the Japanese distinguished themselves from the Chinese above all by their contrasted attitude to foreign cultures. Whereas the Chinese had developed over a long period of time a civilization so superior to the attainments of the peoples with whom they came into contact that they acquired the habit of ignoring or rejecting what was non-Chinese, the Japanese were more empirical in their attitude. The islanders when they first came into contact with China saw the advantage of borrowing and adapting elements of a civilization so evidently more powerful and effective than their own. Already in the course of the sixth century they had begun to read Chinese and to modify the script to suit the needs of their own language. They studied Buddhist and Confucian texts, imitated the conventions of Chinese art, adopted Chinese processes and introduced an official bureaucracy on Chinese lines. The sophisticated arts, crafts and manners of the imperial court established to begin with (710/794) at Nara and later Heian (Kyoto) were modelled on those of Tang China, but nevertheless found expression in a distinctively Japanese idiom or style.

The period of rapid, almost precipitate acculturation was followed

194 Fired clay *haniwa* model of armoured warrior. Late Tomb Period.

by a prolonged one during which the native culture of Japan reasserted itself ever more strongly. A clear sign of the onset of a new phase was the court's refusal towards the end of the ninth century to sanction the despatch of another mission to China, where the Tang dynasty was in any case in marked decline. Already during the tenth century a vernacular literature began to develop alongside that modelled on Chinese taste. In the field of government the bureaucratic institutions imported from China gave place to aristocratic rule by leading families. The emperor whose deification served as a counterpoise to the centrifugal forces inherent in Japanese society remained as nominal ruler, but he and his court were gradually enveloped in the silken cocoon which nevertheless preserved them for a thousand years. Effective power came to be concentrated in the hands of the dominant one of the rival leading families whose head emerged as commander-in-chief and overlord of the clan leaders with the official title of Seii-Tai-Shogun.

The attitude of the Shoguns and their feudatories to the western contacts that began fortuitously in 1542 with the grounding of a Chinese junk carrying Portuguese on an island south of Kyushu differed profoundly from that adopted many centuries earlier to Chinese civilization. Whereas in the latter case it was the Japanese themselves who took the initiative, the westerners who reached Japan from western Europe by way of south-east Asia in increasing numbers and variety were intruders. The Japanese of the feudal age, who for centuries had been indulging in their indigenous culture, were in no mood for another dose of acculturation. They were happy enough to acquire fire-arms, but, despite their brief tolerance of St Francis Xavier on Kyushu, they were totally disinclined to allow their societies to be transformed by Christianity or by western ideas in general. Their reaction soon reverted to that adopted by the Chinese through much of their history. When after nearly three centuries western power could no longer be resisted, it was fortunate for the Japanese that they had the divine emperor in reserve. The Meiji restoration of 1868 which brought the emperor and his court from the religious seclusion of Kyoto to the seat of temporal power at Tokyo initiated a period during which western technology was absorbed as rapidly as Chinese civilization had been a thousand years before. On the other hand, ironically, western political and social objectives were only accepted after the destruction of Hiroshima had terminated another, perhaps final, outburst of the warrior mentality already objectified in the *haniwa* figures of the Protohistoric era.

South-east Asia

The archaeology of south-east Asia is in some respects paradoxical and more than that of most regions calls for more rigorous research. Although polities based on hierarchically organized societies, writing and advanced religions only developed there under exotic and primarily Indian inspiration, the civilizations which ultimately emerged wore their own distinctive masks. Again, despite being late in attaining to civilization themselves, these territories almost certainly contributed in a significant manner to the subsistence economies of ones which had attained this state much earlier. Ethnobotanists have for some time held that the south-east Asian zone of the tropics is likely to have given rise to a number of major food crops including not merely roots and fruits, but outstandingly rice. Adequate testing of this is a primary requirement on which so far only a beginning has been made. Definitive results can be reached only when an adequate number of sites occupied over a period of time and having well-defined series of relatively undisturbed deposits have been consistently dated and their organic as well as their artefactual content exhaustively assessed. An essential dilemma is that the earlier cultivation and metallurgy are shown to have appeared in Indo-China the more difficult it becomes to account for the tardiness of civilization in this region and for the fact that it only emerged as an outcome of external stimulus, substantially as an Indo-Chinese amalgam.

Early Stone Age

There is an element of paradox in the role of south-east Asia even during the earliest phases of human settlement in the region. If the hypothesis (see p. 288) that *Homo erectus* first reached the Far East from India and ultimately from Africa by way of the Burma road is accepted, it follows that Indo-China together with Indonesia was something of a cul-de-sac. On an east–west axis it may have been. On the other hand at periods of low sea-level, when the Indonesian islands and the Philippine island of Palawan were joined by the Sunda shelf to Malaysia and Indo-China, the region formed something of a bridge to Australia, a continent once tellingly described as a peninsula of Asia. From the point of view of Australian prehistory the task of establishing a detailed sequence in Indonesia during the Late Pleistocene is a prime objective of research. At the present juncture only the barest comments are in order. The oldest industry
432: 248–51 as yet identified from Java, the Patjitanian of late Middle or early

Upper Pleistocene age, combined flake tools with a heavy element
of massive plano-convex choppers and hand-adzes flaked mainly on
their convex face. Later Upper Pleistocene deposits from the same
island yielded industries of a pronouncedly flake aspect, notably at
429 Sangiran and at Ngandong in the Solo Valley, a locality also
425 associated with remains of a Neanderthaloid type of man. Comparable flake industries from the Niah cave, Borneo, have been
dated to *c.* 38,000 B.C. and in the Tabon cave on Palawan to a
419 period ranging from *c.* 30,000 to 7,000 B.C. In the Tabon cave the
flakes showed a tendency to get progressively smaller at successively
younger levels.

195 South East Asia during period of low sea-level with key Early Stone Age sites.

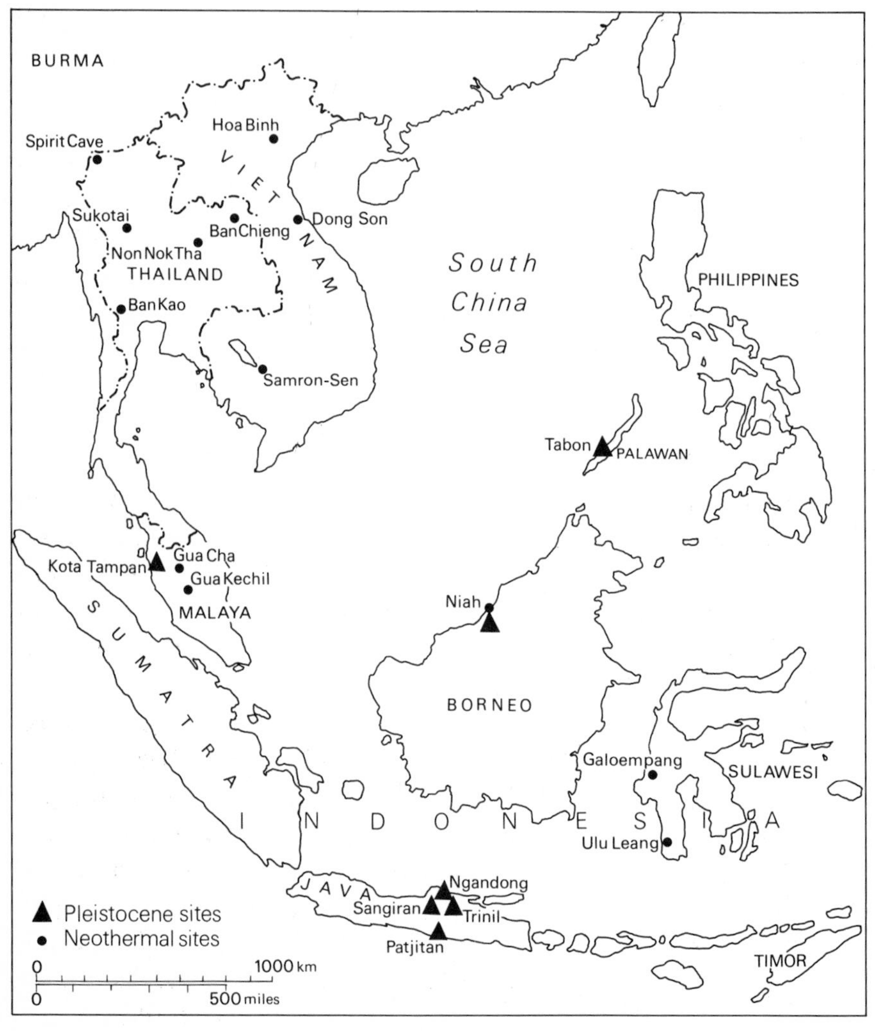

Hoabinhian phase

The best defined adjustments to the onset of Neothermal conditions over much of Indo-China, Malaysia and north-east Sumatra are displayed by lithic assemblages which take their name from the site
418, 422, of Hoa Binh west of Hanoi. The Hoabinhian, although continuing
428, 430 in a developed and stylized form the primitive mode 1 tradition in stone-working established in the region since the Middle Pleistocene, was highly successful. It served the needs of its makers for several thousand years without itself undergoing significant change, a fact which in itself makes one doubt how far the economy it served could at the same time have been undergoing a process of significant
196 intensification. Technically the industry rested on the shaping of pebbles and large flakes by percussion as a rule from one, but occasionally from two faces so as to produce a tool of highly generalized utility. This percussion technique was complemented by edge-grinding applied to edges of heavy tools, but also on a limited scale to scraping equipment and, in the case of Spirit Cave, to thin stone knives resembling harvesting equipment. The rarity, if not absence, of bone equipment argues that materials like wood and bamboo were used to make the variety of gear required for a wide-ranging hunting and foraging economy. Signs of wear on small stone tools from Spirit Cave are consistent with the shaping of wood. In the interior, industries of Hoabinhian type are characteristically sited on upland karst formations and commonly occur in caves or rock-shelters, situated close to streams. Another favoured location was on the sea coast where settlements are normally marked by shell-mounds. This by no means reflects a cultural dichotomy. It

196 Hoabhinian stone tools.

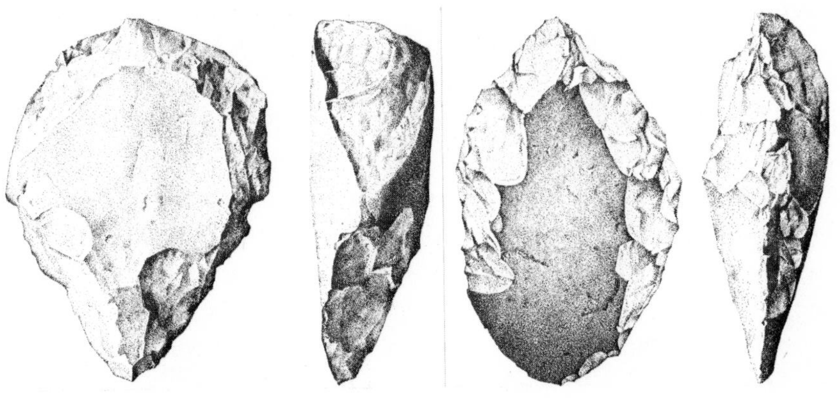

merely shows that the Hoabinhian people exploited the resources within range of their home bases. This is amply reflected in the organic contents of their settlements, even despite the fact that these have only rarely been adequately analysed. The shell-mounds show that though the coast dwellers made the most of molluscs, a resource of special value as a standby against lean periods, they also caught sea-fish and at the same time hunted land mammals in the hinterland. As it happens the only adequate analysis of food refuse from a
423 Hoabinhian site is that from Spirit Cave in northern Thailand, a site which appears to have been occupied intensively during two periods between 10,000 and 7,500 years ago. Consideration of the biological data suggests that during each of these the cave served as a home base substantially the year round. The organic refuse can thus be taken to give a useful indication of the dietary resources exploited at this time. Among land mammals deer, pig and bovines were important sources of animal protein as they were in the case of the coastal midden sites, but rhinoceros and large carnivores were also hunted. It is also of particular interest in view of indications about early hominid behaviour obtained from Early and Middle Pleistocene deposits at Olduvai in East Africa that the Spirit Cave people ate fellow primates including gibbons, langurs and macaques. Proximity to a stream gave not only water but additional access to animal protein in respect of fish, crustacea and shell-fish. An aspect of the food quest on which Spirit Cave has thrown a unique light is the importance of plants in diet. These included a variety of nuts, including almonds and betels, gourds, pepper, water-chestnut, peas and beans. The water-chesnut, still a significant plant food in China as well as south-east Asia, is a good instance of a plant which once discarded in warm water continues to replace itself without human intervention. The same must have applied to other plants which, foraged from the wild, flourished on refuse-enriched soils close to home bases. In a tropical environment the utilization of plant resources must have played a key role, more especially in the interior, in promoting a sedentary mode of life, but it does not follow that such conditions were necessarily conducive to progress. The very perfection of the relations established between the Hoabinhians and their environment might arguably have made for stability. On the other hand there are signs that they may well have embarked on some form of cultivation. The large size of a bean (*Phaseolus* or *Glycine*) from Spirit Cave could well testify to nothing more than the extra wealth in plant nutrients of soils immediately associated with human

settlement. It is however clear that rice entered significantly into the diet of the inhabitants of the open site of Non Nok Tha since grains
417 as well as husks in pottery have been recovered from low levels. Unfortunately two discrepant chronological horizons have been suggested for these levels, an earlier going far back into the third millennium and a later to the first millennium B.C. More information about the extent to which this rice had been modified genetically as a result of cultivation is awaited from plant geneticists.

It is significant that pottery, an attribute that commonly goes with a sedentary mode of life, appeared in Hoabinhian contexts over a wide-ranging territory. At Spirit Cave it appeared as early as the sixth millennium, at caves in Cambodia (Laang Spean) and Burma (Padah-lin) by the fifth and in Malaysia (Gua Kechil) already well before the opening centuries of the third. In every case the pots were of simple forms ornamented by impressed cords. The early occurrence of
197 cord-impressed pottery of elementary forms in south-east Asia falls easily into place in view of the high antiquity of Jōmon pottery and the early presence of similar pottery in Formosa. The people who made this ware were habituated to the use of cord both from their familiarity with fibre-producing vegetation and because they were used to making nets and lines and probably also to caulking boats in connection with fishing. Again, the use of pottery over this whole region evidently went with a trend towards settled life based on fishing, shell-fish gathering and a more intensive use of plant foods. How far this included the purposive concentration of selected plant species close to the home base and how far, if at all, the soil was cultivated are questions yet to be answered.

197 Cord impressed pot.

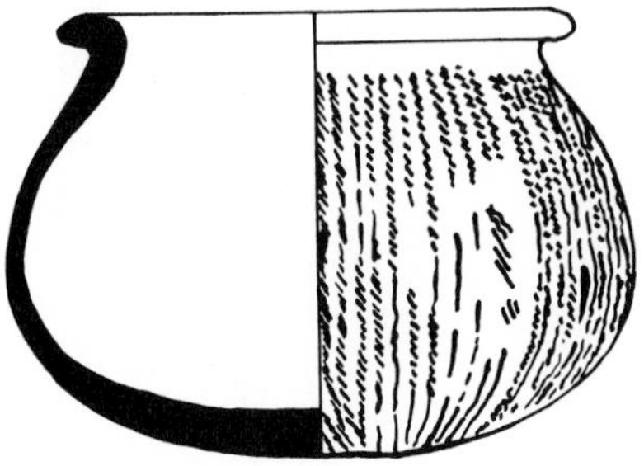

The lithic industries dating from the Neothermal period in Indonesia and the Philippines differ profoundly from those of the Hoabinhian zone. Instead of heavy tools of relatively coarse-grained materials we find light assemblages, frequently as in those from Bandoeng, Java, and from the Djambi district of central Sumatra, made from obsidian. Industries of this kind were first recognized in the Celebes where they were termed Toalian on the questionable assumption that they were made by the remote ancestors of the existing To'ala aborigines. They include scraping and perforating equipment and a variety of points including crescentic and triangular microliths and hollow-based points named after the Moros locality. Since the makers of Toalian industries occasionally used caves there is already some evidence for their cultural and economic context. As a rule they occur with pottery which has been dated well back in the second millennium by radiocarbon. Already, though, in the Celebes cave of
431 Ulu Leang, a Toalian assemblage has been found stratified below a level with pottery and dated by radiocarbon to the mid-fourth millennium. Much more detailed stratigraphic work needs to be done before one can decide whether the Toalian stemmed from indigenous sources or spread from south India and Ceylon or conceivably from Korea or Japan. An industry marked by tanged points and flake axes which appears at the moment to be a manifestation local to Timor occurs in the same context as pottery, dogs and swine-keeping.

198 Polished stone adze blades; shouldered (*left*) and beaked (*right*).

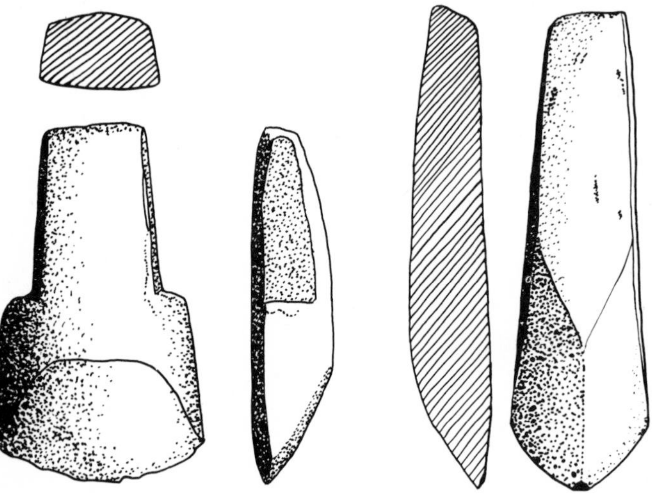

Richer and more diverse configurations of culture marked by completely polished stone axe- and adze-blades and more sophisticated pottery serving a wide range of distinct functions have frequently been found overlying Hoabinhian levels on the mainland of south-east Asia. Beyond this elements spread over the islands of Indonesia and the Philippines both from Indo-China and from the Chinese mainland. Four-sided axe- and adze-blades are among the prolific features common to this widespread territory. A well defined form
198 shouldered to facilitate hafting occurs on the mainland from China to the north-east of the Indian peninsula and also in Borneo, the Celebes and Philippines. Polished stone arm-rings, shell beads and barbed bone fish-hooks and harpoon-heads are other features liable to appear over this extensive territory. Common antecedents and the practice of similar economies may help to explain such widespread

199 Tripod and high-footed pots from Ban Kao, Thailand.

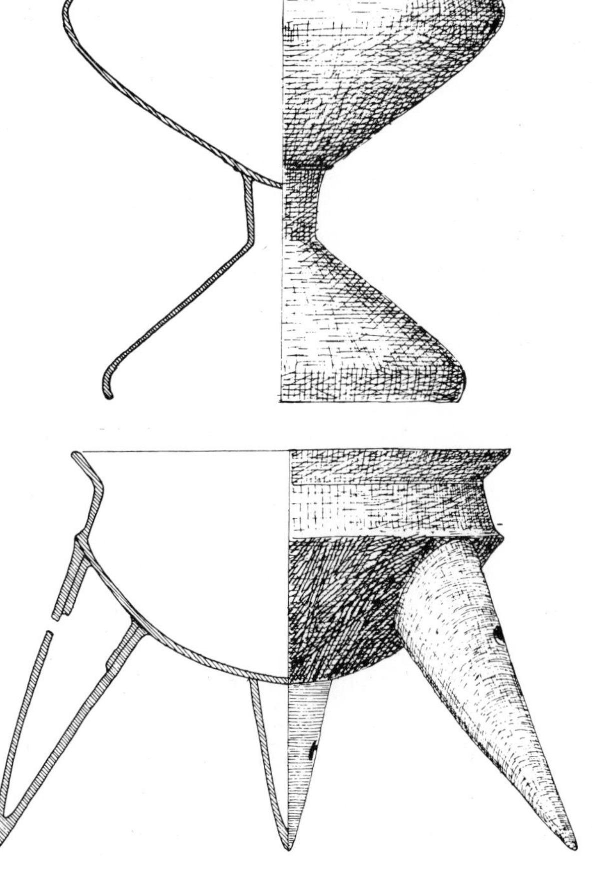

similarities, but the use of boats for sea-fishing in and around the South China Sea provided a mechanism for the movement of ideas. There are also hints of an overland spread from the upper Yangtze across Yunnan and down southward-running valleys into Thailand.
437 The burials from Ban Kao in the Kwae Noi valley of the west central part of that country were mongoloid in race and approximate closely to the existing Thai population. The pots buried with them exhibit a number of features in common with Lungshanoid wares in the Yangtze basin. These include fine black and red wares with burnished
199 surfaces, high-footed bowls and jars and vessels with hollow tripod
435 legs. Pottery recovered with burials from the later phase at Gua Cha, Kelantan, Malaysia, shows the same general character, but tripod feet reached only the northern part of Malaya and the ringed feet at Gua Cha were markedly shallower. The form of burial was closely similar. Corpses were laid on their backs and pots were placed at head and foot and sometimes over the lower limbs in marked contrast to the contracted burials from the Hoabinhian levels at Gua Cha. Features of the Gua Cha stone equipment absent from the Thai site include
198 a Malaysian type of beaked adze-blade and stone bark cloth beaters of a kind known from Tongkin. Pottery from different parts of Indo-China displays a wide range of variation. In much of Vietnam the surface is ornamented by cord-wrapped paddles, but the pottery from Ben-Do in the Bien Hoa district near Hanoi sometimes displays red paint in addition and that from Samron-Sen north of Phnom Penh, Cambodia, is richly ornamented with spirals and meanders among other geometric patterns. Patterns similar to those on Samron-Sen ware occur on pottery from Galoempang in Celebes together with shouldered stone adze-blades.

Metallurgy

There are indications which too often lack precision, for example at Samron-Sen, that copper and bronze were known to at least some of the communities which made do with polished stone axe- and adze-blades. The question of the genesis of metallurgy is second only to the beginnings of rice cultivation as a theme for prehistoric research in south-east Asia.

Bronze metallurgy has generally been regarded as a comparatively recent introduction to south-east Asia under Chinese influence. A late date was suggested by the absence of primitive forms and the
202 presence of iron alongside socketed axes and other bronze forms recovered from the cemetery of Dong Son, the type site in Tongkin.

Exotic inspiration was inferred from the bronze forms and from
201 elements in the decoration of kettledrums apparently derived immediately from Chou China. The application of geophysical dating methods to cave deposits in the interior of Thailand on the other hand has opened up the possibility that bronze-working may have begun much earlier, indeed at dates so remote as to place Indo-China in the very van of progress. It is well to reflect on the implications of recent claims. If metallurgy was flourishing in Thailand by the middle of the fifth millennium, one may ask how it was that the Thai smiths should have marked time for four thousand years and why having gained so great a start technologically on China and India the peoples of south-east Asia should have fallen so far behind these territories in the race to literate civilization. These would be interesting questions for research, but before embarking on them a rigorous substantiation of such claims is called for. The published evidence is unimpressive. The radiocarbon dates for layers containing metal objects at the settlement mound at Non Nok Tha is as anomalous as one might expect of a sequence which to judge by the

200 Painted pot from Ban Chieng, Thailand.

published section of the 1968 excavations was so heavily disturbed by burials, rootholes, termites and washouts.

200 The discovery of pottery with red painted spiral designs on the
Korat plateau has recently directed further attention to northern
424 Thailand. The excavators of Ban Chieng claim that the new ware
did not appear until phase V (*c.* 1000–500 B.C.) of the prehistorical burial sequence, that bronzes occurred in phases I–III (*c.* 3600–2000 B.C.) with burnished, incised and cord-imprinted wares and that iron came in with painting already in phase IV (1600–1200 B.C.). If this chronology were to be substantiated it would establish the region beyond doubt as a major focus of technological innovation.

421, 427 Whether or not the Dong Son bronze industry proves to have such
deep roots considerable interest centres on its largest product,
201 namely the metal kettledrum. Objects of this kind, still used by the
Karen tribesmen of Burma and north Thailand, were plainly of ceremonial use intended both to summon the population and to intensify participation. Representations of dancing figures remind us of one reason for the use of kettledrums. Models of frogs attached to rims point to rainmaking ceremonies, and the placing of miniature drums in graves suggests that they played a part in mortuary ceremonies. Their importance is witnessed not only by the size and ornamentation but also by the wide area over which they were disseminated in Indonesia as far as islands to the east of Celebes and

201 Dong Son bronze kettledrum.

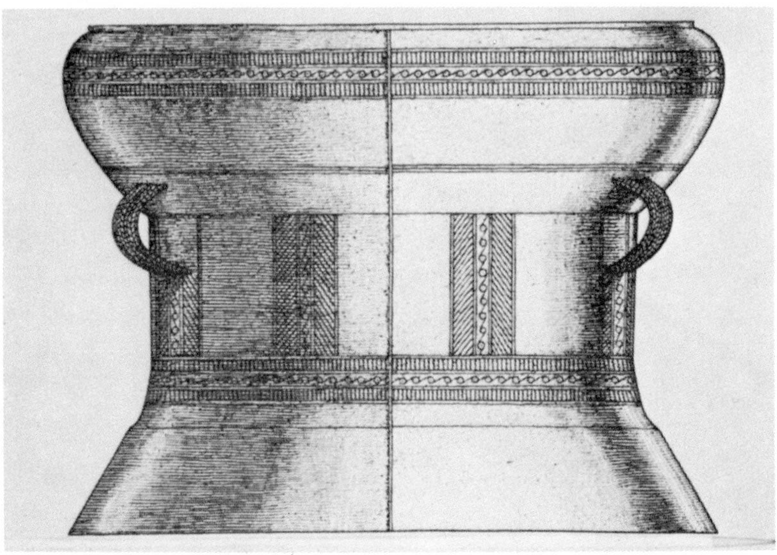

Timor. Their manufacture was in full swing when Tongkin was incorporated into the Han empire and barbarians continued to offer them as tribute to the emperor at least down to the Tang dynasty.

The handled axes with expanded and ornamented blades that formed part of the Dong Son complex presumably served as symbols
202 of status rather than as weapons or tools. Even the socketed bronze axes can hardly have played more than a subsidiary role in daily life. Similarly, although iron was known, it was not taken widely into use until Indian merchant enterprise had spread as far as Java, Bali and Borneo early in the Christian era. Until this happened polished stone axes and adzes played the key role in dressing timber and shaping the boats that linked together the islands and the mainland.

Indo-Chinese civilization

The civilizations which arose in the great river basins of Thailand
424, 433 and Indo-China did so primarily under Indian but also to some degree Chinese influence. These were brought to bear in rather different ways.

The territory most open to influence from China proper was that of the Red River basin and the coasts of the Bay of Tongkin and the South China Sea. During the historic period this began with the expansion of the Yueh people from south China during the third century B.C. under the brief Ch'in Empire. Even when northern Vietnam was taken over by the Han Empire administrative control

202 Dong Son bronze axe, Indonesia.

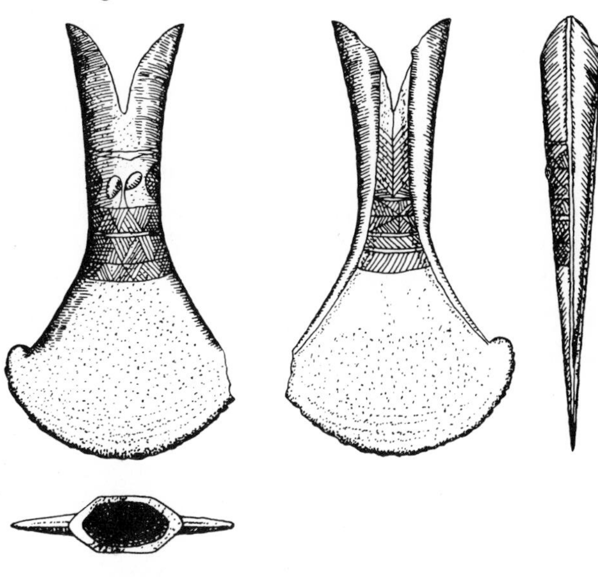

sat lightly on the local powers. Admiration and emulation between them were as ever more potent agents of cultural change than force. Despite the manifest superiority of Chinese culture something of the native genius survived. The porcellaneous wares of different parts of Indo-China, though made by Chinese techniques and often by Chinese potters, are still in many cases recognizable as distinctively Annamese, Khmer or Sawankhalok (Thai). By contrast in the case of the Philippines the cultural gap was too great for fruitful interaction. Vast numbers of porcellaneous vessels of Chinese, Sawankhalok or Annamese manufacture were imported in exchange for Philippine commodities like wax, beads, tortoise-shell, cotton or coconut-pith. Not one was made in a Philippine kiln.

The influence of Indian civilization stimulated far more positive results both on mainland south-east Asia and in parts of Indonesia. Perhaps this was because it was mediated by merchants to tribal societies which had attained a level of culture sufficient for fruitful interactions. By making the south-east Asians aware of new ideas and providing them with new social mechanisms including writing, the Indian traders stimulated the growth of kingdoms among hitherto tribal peoples. The earliest of these, known to Chinese annals as the Kingdom of Fou Nan, grew up west of the delta of the Mekong river in Cambodia as early as the mid-third century A.D. The importance of its situation on the trade routes between India, the West and China is illustrated by the occurrence on Fou Nan sites of Han bronzes, Roman coins and objects of Sassanian and Ptolemaic manufacture. By the sixth century the focus of political power had shifted to Chen La in the midst of the Mekong basin with its broad expanse of wet rice lands. The moated cities, the temples and the monumental sculptures of Buddha, Vishnu and Siva that adorned these were all palpably Indian in inspiration. About the same time as the Fou Nan Kingdom was emerging Indian trading posts were being established in Java and once again we find principalities emerging with monumental trappings in the Indian mould. The Indianized art of Java in turn contributed to the distinctive Khmer art, which arose in Cambodia on the basis of that practised at Fou Nan and Chen La, and reached a climax in the vast and intricate complex of Angkor late in the ninth century.

The story in Thailand was more complex, but once again Indian seaborne influence predominated. Minor kingdoms arose in peninsular Thailand but the main developments occurred in the Menam basin which though not so extensive as that of the Mekong was still capable of supporting powerful polities on a basis of wet rice cultivation. Already in the fifth and sixth centuries, as the monumental structures of Lopburi embellished by sculptures in the Indian Gupta style so vividly illustrate, the Mon who spoke a language akin to that of the Khmer had developed states based on kingship and the practice of Buddhism. The extension of the Mon over northern Thailand was followed by powerful intrusions from neighbouring territories. Between the tenth and twelfth centuries the Khmer had extended their empire from Cambodia as far as the centre of the country and occupied all but the extreme north of Mon territory. In the thirteenth century this northern region was infiltrated by the ancestors of the modern Thai from their homeland in south China following the pattern of Lungshanoid expansion some three thousand years earlier. Having assimilated the Mon, though at the cost of founding a northern capital at Chieng Mai, the Thai proceeded to overthrow the Khmer in the south and found the kingdom of Sukhodaya in the midst of the basin. The earliest historical document of the founder of modern Thailand, the obelisk set up at Sukhodaya *c.* A.D. 1292, aptly summarizes its own pedigree. The script was based on a cursive form of Khmer which was itself of Pāli, that is of Indian, origin. On the other hand the modern Thai speech is a combination of Indian and Chinese elements, a reminder, embodied materially in the porcellaneous ceramics of Sukhodaya and Sawankhalok, that China contributed something to the amalgam, though as in Cambodia to a degree quite subsidiary to that of India.

8

North and Middle America

When Christopher Columbus returned from his rediscovery of the New World in 1493 he brought home not merely gold, plants and wild animals but six inhabitants of the West Indies. These showed every sign of being men, but it took more voyages and twenty years before it could be pronounced officially that the Amerinds were in truth fellow descendants of Adam and Eve. This provided both a licence and a stimulus to the conquistadors. Cortes' conquest of the Aztec capital of Tenochtitlan on the site of the present Mexico City in 1519 and Pizarro's overthrow of the Incas of Peru in 1532 between them spelt the beginning of European domination of indigenous American civilization, a domination extended in ensuing centuries over the whole extent of both continents.

The riches of the Aztecs and Incas were at first esteemed by their captors in terms of bullion and their monuments as something to be out-matched by the Spanish state and the Catholic Church. When the time was ripe to view these things in their own right as products of human art some European scholars found themselves unable to accept them as the unaided work of the Amerindian peoples. Indeed
446:25 the impetus behind Lord Kingsborough's massive nine volume *Antiquities of Mexico* (1831–48), a work lavish enough to undermine the finances of its author, was his conviction that the American Indians were descendants of the Lost Tribes of Israel.

For some time prehistorians have taken as a working hypothesis that the most advanced societies encountered by the conquistadors in the New World were in essence the outcome of indigenous development. Whereas hunter-fishers had only to cross from the Old World to the New by dry land, by ice or at most by traversing a narrow strait, the temperate zones which supported farming economies were separated by thousands of kilometres of what, from a farming point

of view, were desolate wastes. Contact between Old World farming cultures and the inhabitants of parts of the New World in which farming was practicable would only have been possible across the Pacific ocean. The voyages of the Polynesians, not to mention the Kon-tiki, warn against discarding this possibility out of hand. But the fact is that the question of Old World influence has lost most of its bite since research has gone so far in demonstrating how the indigenous inhabitants of different parts of the New World have
441, 445 unlocked the varying potentialities of the several environments open to them. It is not merely that they domesticated animals and plants quite different from those of the Old World or that conversely they lacked elements of technology common to many Old World
439, 440, 442 communities. More positively they developed civilizations unique in form and style, civilizations which differed profoundly from those known in any other part of the world. This is all the more remarkable when it is realized for how comparatively short a time America has been occupied by man.

The New World was first occupied so far as is known at an advanced stage of the Upper Pleistocene. The Paleo-Indians arrived in small bands equipped with a meagre technology. Yet by the close of the Pleistocene they had transversed both continents, reaching central Chile by the mid-tenth and the strait of Magellan by the mid-ninth millennium. The spread of the colonists was matched by their skill in adapting to a wide range of environments. Over extensive tracts, including those uncovered by the melting and contraction of the North America ice-sheets since the original colonization, men continued to perform catching and gathering activities. In the Arctic zone extending from Bering Strait to Labrador and Greenland highly effective systems were evolved based primarily on the catching of sea-fish and mammals. Since they provided not merely the most efficient but in the final resort the only way of surviving in this environment it is hardly surprising that they should have endured. The fact that in modern times the world market has provided the Arctic fishers and hunters with technical and social aids, including more efficient gear, expert assistance, education and medicine, does not alter the reality that over this extensive territory life still depends on catching.

More extended possibilities were open to the inhabitants of the temperate and above all the tropical zones of America as the several ecosystems took shape in the course of Neothermal times. During the Archaic phase of settlement subsistence became more broadly based. Hunting persisted and locally, as in the Plains area, even predominated, but where circumstances were favourable, as in the rivers of the north-west of North America, fishing might play a key role. On the other hand the most striking fact of the new age was the increasing contribution made by plants to subsistence. The Amerinds seldom established relations with animals close enough to give rise to the kind of genetic mutations which make it possible to infer domestication from skeletal remains. Dogs were introduced at an early stage but the only significant native animals to be domesticated in the full sense of that term, if we except the turkey, were the Andean llamas and alpacas. The sources of ampler, more concentrated and more secure supplies of food were vegetative. It was by manipulating plants and modifying the conditions under which they grew that the societies which so much astonished the conquistadors developed. The stages by which this was effected will feature prominently in this account. Attention will also be given to the far more extensive territories of more modest achievement in which social development was arrested at petty chieftainship, village communities or hunter-forager bands. From a cultural point of view each of the two Americas was like a pyramid, albeit a pyramid of highly asymmetrical form.

Late Pleistocene settlement

Amerinds

It has been recognized since the middle of the seventeenth century that the New World must have been populated by way of Bering Strait. The physical relationship between the Amerinds and the Mongoloid peoples of eastern Asia is sufficiently evident. Both share to varying degrees such basic traits as yellowish to reddish-brown skins, brown eyes, straight black hair, broad skulls and high cheek bones. On the other hand the original immigration from north-east Siberia must have occurred before Mongoloids had spread so far north on the Asiatic side, since the earliest human skulls from the New World, whether from Minnesota, Arizona, east Brazil or the strait of Magellan, are predominantly long-headed. It follows that the Mongoloid strain in the composition of the Amerinds must relate to later phases of immigration. Physical anthropologists have explained the range of variability observable among the aboriginal inhabitants of the New World in different ways. Some account for the main groups by supposing separate invasions or phases of immigration. Others prefer to explain regional differences in terms of adaptation to varying ecological circumstances. If there is truth in both the predominant factor is surely ecological. The fact that both the Eskimo of the Arctic and to a lesser degree the Indians of the west Sub-arctic zone stand closest to their Asiatic relatives in respect both of race and of material equipment suggests ethnic movements of relatively late date. Yet even here it is worth emphasizing that the environments to which they were adjusted were of specialized kinds. Again, the Plains Indians and the Appalachians correspond respectively with the prairies and forest zones of north America and the Amazonians with the extent of that great river basin.

More interesting in some respects is the Sonora group occupying the Pueblo territory of the North American south-west, Middle America and Andean South America, since here the unifying environmental factor is economic rather than geographic namely the cultivation of maize. On the face of it the genetic mutations selected for survival might be expected to be those best adapted to prevailing conditions whether economic or physical.

The crossing from Asia to North America is most likely to have occurred during a period of glaciation. A lowering of sea-level of only 35 metres would have been enough to convert what is now a strait 80 kilometres wide with a current strong enough to disturb even
451 the winter ice, into a broad land bridge. The plain of Beringia so formed united the ice-free parts of Siberia, Alaska and the Yukon and carried herds of herbivorous animals of species known to have been predated by man. Localities on the Old Crow River, Yukon, have yielded tools flaked in a lithic technique from portions of mammoth limb bones and the metacarpals and metatarsals of horse as well as artefacts shaped from caribou antler. These include tines converted into wedges and a remarkable tool made from a longitudinal section of an antler beam, itself dated by radiocarbon to *c.* 25,000 B.C., finely toothed at one end in the style found on fleshing tools made by North American Indians. Evidence from either side of Bering Strait suggests that the plain was already inhabited between 5,000 and 8,000 years earlier. The stone artefacts so far recovered from the Yukon deposits, including bifacially flaked chert and obsidian pieces, unfortunately derive from redeposited gravels. A fuller picture must await the recovery of traces of human settlement in undisturbed beds.

Access to territories further south was blocked during glacial phases by the united Cordilleran and Laurentide ice-sheets. A pass-
452 age east of the Rockies could only have been effected either during

an interglacial or during the interstadial of *c.* 28/27,000 to 21,000 B.C. or, again, since the ice began its final retreat around *c.* 11,000 B.C. Many claims have been made in support of the earlier alternatives. In the last analysis these rely on four main categories of data. Of these traces of burning dated by radiocarbon can be summarily dismissed unless accompanied by contemporary artefacts, since fires and consequently charcoal can easily be produced by agencies other than man. Assemblages of stone artefacts of apparently primitive form are another source of error. This can arise embarrassingly from a failure to distinguish between flaking certainly made by man and that which could equally well have been made by natural forces. Conversely there is the danger, long ago exemplified by the finds from the Trenton gravels, of drawing false conclusions from typological crudity. Another source of error, that of recovering undoubted artefacts by superficial collecting from contexts only apparently early, is well illustrated by reference to Tule springs, Nevada. It needed full-scale excavations to establish that the artefacts, so far from being associated with remains of fossil animals up to 28,000 years old, in fact came from erosion channels and could not date from before *c.* 11,000 B.C. A fourth category, human bones dated by the racemization method, can only be assessed when the method itself has been validated. In the meantime dates of between 30,000 and 65,000 years have been claimed by applying this method to human bones from La Jolla, a suburb of San Diego, California.

203 Radiocarbon ages of Paleo-Indian projectile points, North America.

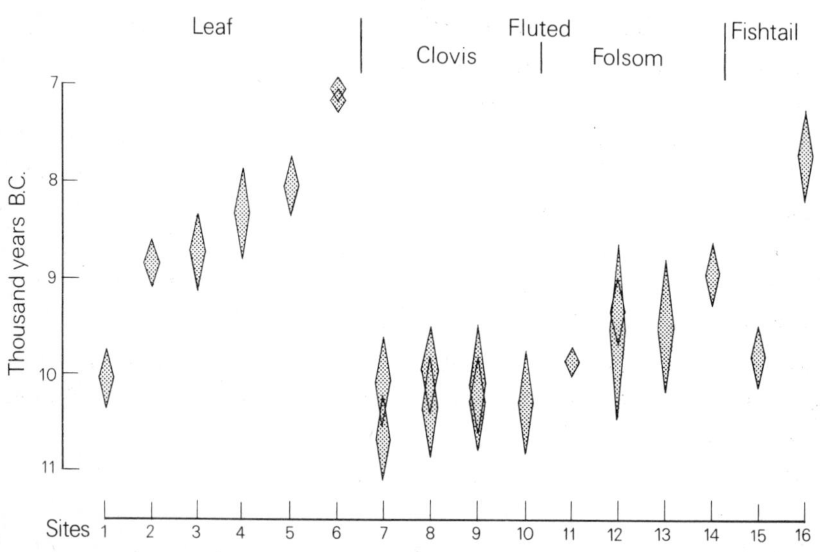

Table 23. *Radiocarbon dates for early man in the New World*

		B.C.
NORTH AMERICA		
Desert culture		
Fort Rock Cave, Oregon	C 428	7103 ± 350
Danger Cave, Utah	Tx 85	8650 ± 200
Gypsum Cave, Nevada	C 221	8505 ± 340
Leonard Shelter, Nevada	C 599	9249 ± 570
Ventana Cave, Arizona	A 203	9340 ± 500
Cordilleran culture		
Fraser Canyon, British Columbia	S 113	7050 ± 150
Five Miles Rapids, Dulles Reservoir, Oregon	Y 340	7835 ± 200
Folsom culture		
Lubbock, Texas	C 558	7933 ± 350
Brewster, Wyoming	I 472	8425 ± 700
Bonfire Shelter, Texas	Tx 153	8280 ± 160
Lindenmeier, Colorado	I 141	8900 ± 550
Blackwater Draw no. 1, near Clovis, New Mexico	A 379–80	8300 ± 320
	A 386	8500 ± 900
Hell Gap, Wyoming	I 167	8900 ± 500
Clovis culture		
Blackwater Draw no. 1, near Clovis, New Mexico	A 490	9090 ± 500
	A 481	9220 ± 360
	A 491	9680 ± 400
Dent, Colorado	I 622	9250 ± 500
Lehner, Arizona	A 40b	8950 ± 450
	A 375	8990 ± 100
	K 554	9220 ± 140
	A 42	9290 ± 190
	M 811	9340 ± 500
Domebo, Oklahoma	SM 695	9095 ± 647
	SI 172	9270 ± 500
MEXICO		
Lerma culture		
Diablo Cave, Tamaulipas	M 499	7320 ± 500
San Bartolo, Atepehuacan	M 776	7720 ± 400
Santa Isabel Iztapan (Upper Becerra beds)	C 205	9053 ± 300
SOUTH AMERICA		
Various		
Intihausi Cave, Argentina	Y 228	6020 ± 100
	P 345	6110 ± 100
Palli Aike Cave, Chile	C 485	6689 ± 450
Lagoa Santa (levels VI–VII), Brazil	P 54	7770 ± 128
Cerro dos Chivateros, Peru	UCLA 683	8480 ± 160
Fell's Cave, Chile	W 915	8770 ± 300

The earliest phase of human settlement adequately documented by archaeology dates from the final stage of the Pleistocene. The
454 evidence comprises first and foremost bifacially flaked projectile points of stone, frequently found in conjunction with the bones and sometimes with the skeletons of extinct animals. On many occasions
203 these occurrences have been dated by radiocarbon to between eight and ten thousand B.C. The bifacial percussion technique by which the earlier of these were shaped was developed in the Old World long before on any reckoning man had appeared in the New. In the form of hand-axes in mode 2 of lithic technology it goes back to the Middle Pleistocene. Leaf-shaped points of a form and size that would have fitted them as spearheads appeared already in mode 3 contexts of early Upper Pleistocene date and during the latter part of this period they were featured by many different industries in mode 4 from western Europe to Siberia and Japan. It would be perverse not to accept that their appearance in the New World was due to transmission by way of the Bering land bridge. This is all the more so when account is taken of other elements in Paleo-Indian technology, notably the much neglected punch-struck blades and burins
450 from the grey sand layer (bed 2) at the key site of Clovis, New Mexico. Another conspicuous occurrence of blade tools of high quality accompanied the mammoth skeletons at Santa Isabel Iztapan,
204 Mexico. In respect of burins, which Old World archaeologists sometimes refer to as gravers, it is important to stress that these tools were typologically and technologically quite different from New World 'gravers'. Whereas the burin is a chisel-like object having a working edge shaped by the punching out of one or frequently more flakes or spalls into the main axis of the tool, the American graver is a finely spurred tool, the points of which have been shaped by edge-flaking. These finely spurred 'gravers', which together with convex scrapers and spokeshaves were a recurrent feature of fluted-point sites, evidently served a continuing need in North America since they appeared in Anasazi sites in the south-west down to the first millennium A.D. The wooden handles on which the Anasazi mounted them suggest that they were intended for some purpose which involved precisely applied pressure. Another component which Paleo-Indian technology shared with the Old World was the use of antler, bone and ivory for weapon heads. Points from the Sandia Cave, bevelled ones from the Clovis Blackwater site, both in New Mexico, and barbed points from sites in the Colombia basin west of the Rockies give

some indication of what has for the most part been lost. The marginal fringes of incised lines on bone roundels from the Folsom site of Lindenmeier suggest that the Paleo-Indians shared with the Late-glacial hunters of Eurasia a proclivity for ornamenting bone artefacts.

The bifacial stone point in its many guises remains the most conspicuous artefact left by the Paleo-Indians. Analogues argue that it served to arm hunting weapons. This is confirmed by their repeated occurrence with the skeletons of herbivorous animals, on more than one occasion lodged in their rib cages. Their weight and the fact that there is no evidence for the use of the bow until millennia later in the New World argues that they served as spear- or dart-heads. It is likely that the necessary momentum was acquired by propulsion from a sling or a rigid spear thrower comparable with the recent Amerindian atlatl: rigid spear throwers made of reindeer antler were being made in western Europe already during the Late-glacial period and in the North American south-west wooden atlatls have survived on desiccated Anasazi sites dating mainly from the first millennium A.D. This does not mean that all bifacially flaked points were mounted as projectile heads. Some of the heavier ones may have been mounted on hand-held lances and asymmetric forms are likely to have served such functions as knives or flensing tools or alternatively as side armatures for weapons.

Although the bifacial point was introduced to the New World from

204 Basket-maker 'spurred graver' (1–2), and Paleo-Indian burins (3, 5, 6); burin spalls (4) and blades (7, 8).

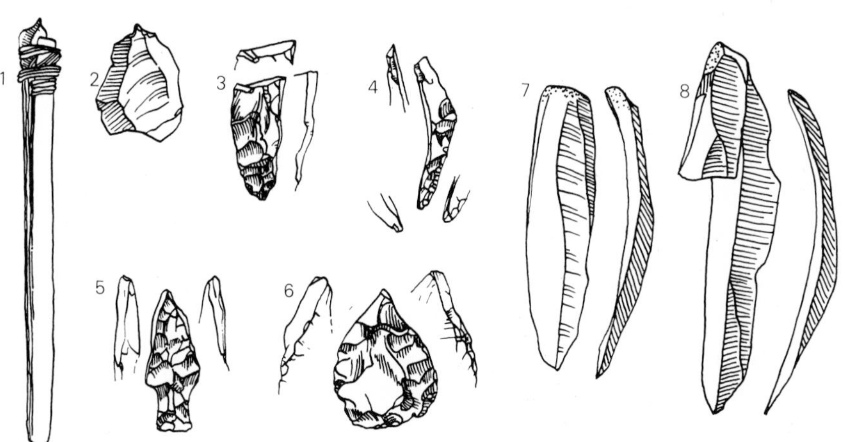

Asia, the overriding characteristic of the majority of examples found
205 in the New World is their indigenous character. The proliferation of varieties of bifacial point is a first portent of the inventiveness and diversity displayed by the Amerindians throughout their history in response to the variety of environments which they explored, appropriated and exploited. The exceptionally wide geographical distribution of the prototypical leaf-shaped point shows it to have been an early arrival even though as yet none has been found in contexts quite as old as the first occurrence of the indigenous Clovis
448 point. The form appears as Cascade points in the Old Cordilleran tradition of the north-west, as Kluane points in the Yukon, as Lerma points in Mexico, as El Jobo points in Venezuela and as Ayampitin points in the Argentine. A shouldered version occurred in the Sandia cave, New Mexico, and specimens with truncated base accompanied a Lerma point at Santa Isabel Iztapan.

The innovations made by the Paleo-Indians were designed to make the head more secure on its shaft. An original way of achieving this was to remove flakes from the base on either face in such a way as to produce well-defined grooves or fluting. Fluted points, though first noted in the Plains area, were soon recognized over a much more extensive territory. Their makers evidently occupied in addition the
456 whole of the East Woodland zone as far as Florida and New England
455 and north to Alberta and Saskatchewan, the Great Lakes and New-
453 foundland. Radiocarbon dating confirms the sequence of Blackwater Draw in showing that the Clovis variety preceded the developed Folsom type marked by its mitre-like form, by fluting extending almost to the tip and as a rule by pressure flaking. Again it can hardly

205 Paleo-Indian bifacial points, North America: Sandia, Clovis and Folsom (*two right*).

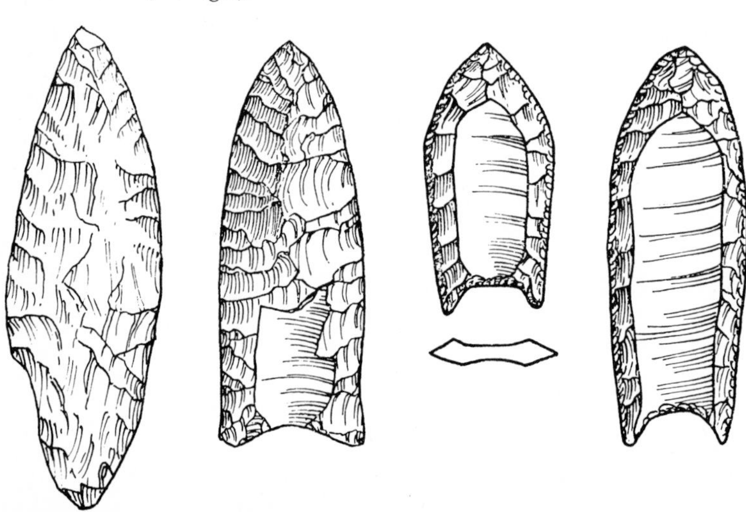

206 Key Paleo-Indian sites, North America.

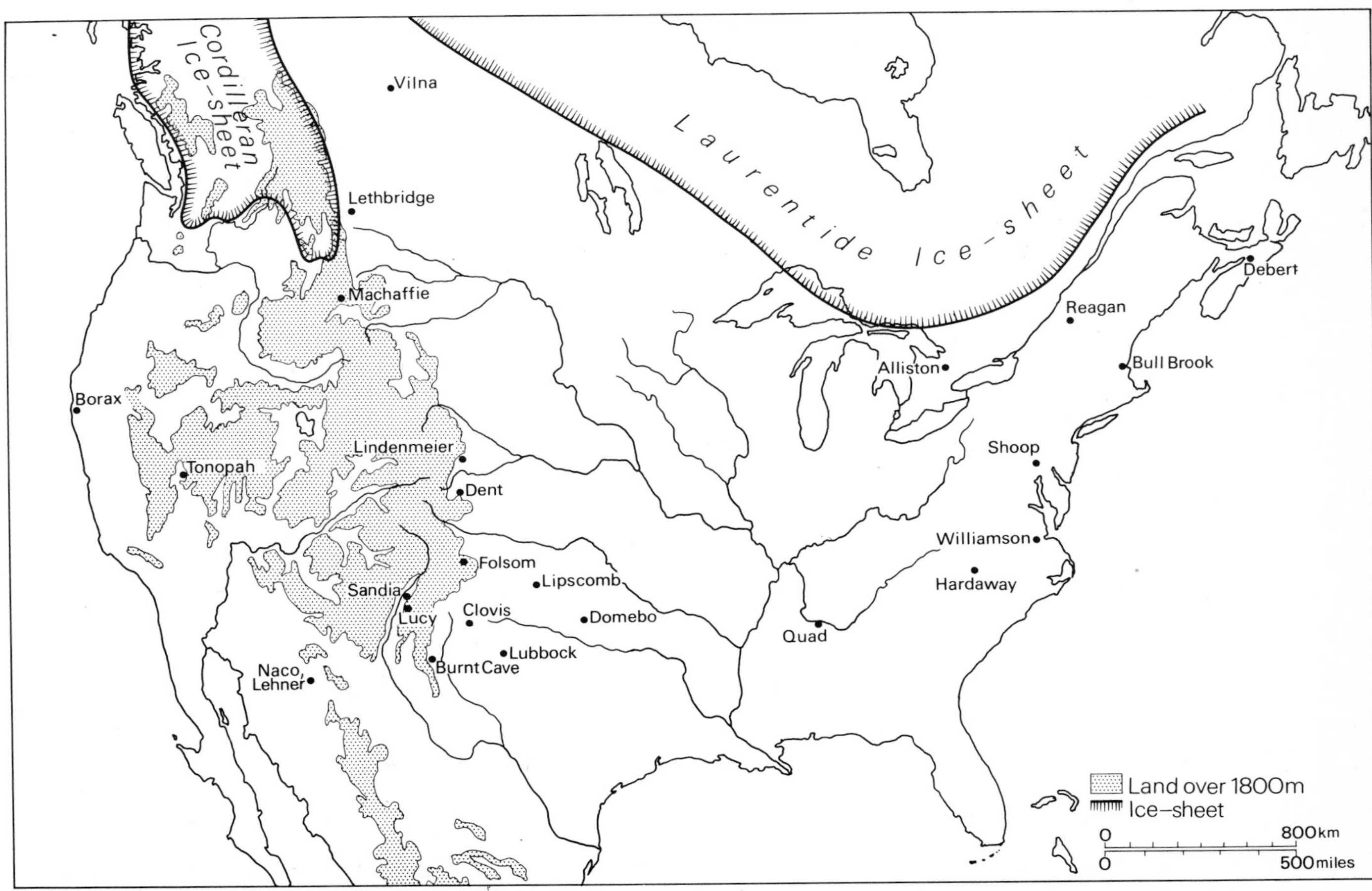

be accidental that whereas Clovis points have frequently been found with mammoths, Folsom points commonly went with bison. Clovis points have also been found with remains of Giant Sloth in Texas and there are indications that this animal was eaten in Gypsum Cave, Nevada, in Ventana Cave, Arizona and frequently in South America.

Since mammoths, which occurred from Alaska down to eastern Brazil, were the richest prize it is to be assumed that the Paleo-Indians would have concentrated on them first. The animals associated with Clovis points – at least a dozen at the Dent site, Colorado – belonged to the Columbian species (*Mammathus* (*parelephas*) *columbi*) in contrast to the imperial mammoth (*M. archidiskodon imperator*) skeletons from Santa Isabel Iztapan. How far the decline and ultimate extinction of mammoths in the New World was due to the depredations of hunters and how far to the change in climate and vegetation that marked the onset of Neothermal conditions is still unclear. What is certain is that by the ninth millennium the north American Paleo-
207 Indians were concentrating on bison over the whole territory from the Rockies to the Alleghenies and from Great Slave Lake to the Mexican Gulf. Where enough of the skulls remained the bison of Late-glacial and Anathermal age (*Bison antiquus figginsi* cf. *Bison*

207 Skeleton of extinct bison, Folsom, New Mexico.

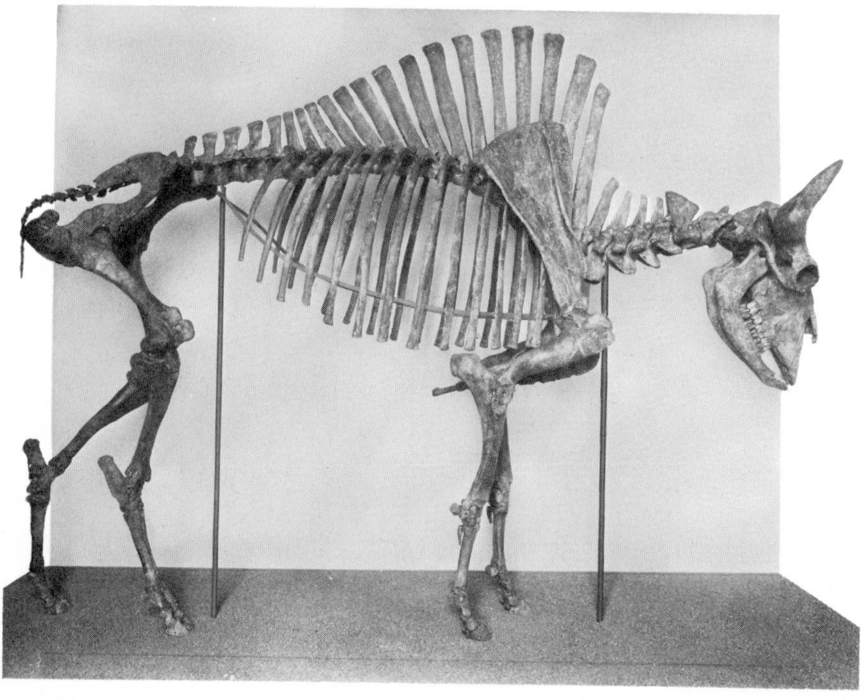

occidentalis) were seen to be distinguished from extant forms by the breadth of their horns. The gregarious character of bison and the
449 fact that they were subject to seasonal migration made them peculiarly vulnerable to hunters equipped with a knowledge of their movements and armed with spears or darts, even when operating in quite small bands. It was only necessary to intercept them in a critical situation, as when crossing the narrow gully or creek in Itaska park, Minnesota, at the south end of Lake Huron, to find an ample target. The task was further eased when, as at Itaska, the hunters concentrated on herds of cows and immature animals at the time of the autumn movement. In this respect the bison hunters conformed to the same pattern as the mammoth hunters of Dent, Colorado. To judge from the heaps of articulated bones found separately or adjacent to encampments, amounting in the case of the Horner site near Cody, Wyoming, to around 180 bison, the animals were skinned and the flesh removed, probably for drying, at the actual kill sites. The rarity of tail bones, observed for instance at the Folsom name site, may be due to their removal with the hide. The absence of the tops of the skulls at the prolific Horner site, one reason why special identification has frequently been impossible, may well have been due to the removal of frontlets and their attached horns for use as masks, either as a device for hunting or in connection with ritual activities concerned with ensuring success. The artefacts found at bison kill sites, notably knives, curved scrapers, spokeshaves and spurred tools (gravers), could all have served in butchery and the processing of hides.

Middle American sequence

The emergence of human societies at widely varying levels of attainment has taken place during the ten thousand years since the end of the Ice Age and predominantly during a quarter of this span. In North America the change from Late Pleistocene to Neothermal conditions implied changes in the options open to man of a profound and comparatively sudden nature. The contraction of ice-sheets uncovered extensive new habitats for human settlement in the present Sub-artic zone. Further south in the present temperate zone changes in the biosphere modified profoundly the potentials for man in relation to both subsistence and technology. The significant fact remains that the tropical zone of Middle America, in which the most significant economic and social advances were made, was that least affected by environmental change. Since in this work we are concerned above all with human achievement it will be logical to begin with the tropical zone and move outwards to those where development was increasingly more restricted.

In the highlands of Middle America the transition to Neothermal times was marked by the extinction of the big game animals symbolized by the imperial mammoth on which the Late Pleistocene economy was to a significant degree based. Henceforward subsistence rested mainly on the harvesting of plants. Developments in man/plant relations, which both made possible and reflect the impact of more advanced states of society, are best displayed in the sequence of organic food refuse from stratigraphic sequences in the valleys
208 of Central Mexico and Oaxaca.

During pre-conquest times the populations of the Mexican highlands depended substantially on plant foods. By comparison meat contributed to a relatively minor, though locally by no means negligible extent. During the Archaic phase in the occupation of the Oaxaca valley, a territory ultimately of high significance as the home
462 successively of the Miztec and Zapotec civilizations, white-tailed deer (*Odocoileus virginianus*) and rabbits (*Sivilagus cuniculus* and *S. floridanus*) made useful contributions. The fact remains that subsistence in the Oaxaca valley was won substantially from the systematic foraging of

- maguey (*Agave* sp.),
- succulent cacti, including organ cactus (*Lemaireocereus* spp.) and prickly pear (*Opuntia* spp.),
- tree legumes, including mequite (*Prosopis* spp.) and guaje (*Leucaena*, *Mimosa* and *Acacia*),
- acorns and pinon nuts.

There are signs that the process of domestication had already begun in early Neothermal times. Some species displayed a range of diversity and a concentration unusual in wild forms and others a degree of genetic divergence from wild prototypes difficult to explain except
465 in terms of domestication. The inhabitants of the Canon del Infiernillo near Tamaulipas were apparently cultivating pepper (*Capsicum annum*), bottle-gourd (*Lagenaria siceraria*) and pumpkin (*Cocurbita pepo*). At the same time the common bean (*Phaseolus vulgaris*) and
466 pumpkin were being grown in the Oaxaca area. In the Tehuacan Valley squash (*Cocurbita mixta*) were already being cultivated during the El Riego phase and by Coxcatlan times avocado pear (*Persea americana*) and pepper were domesticated in this region, as well almost certainly as maize.

208 Changes in the sources of subsistence in the Tehuacan Valley, Mexico, between 8000 B.C. and A.D. 1500.

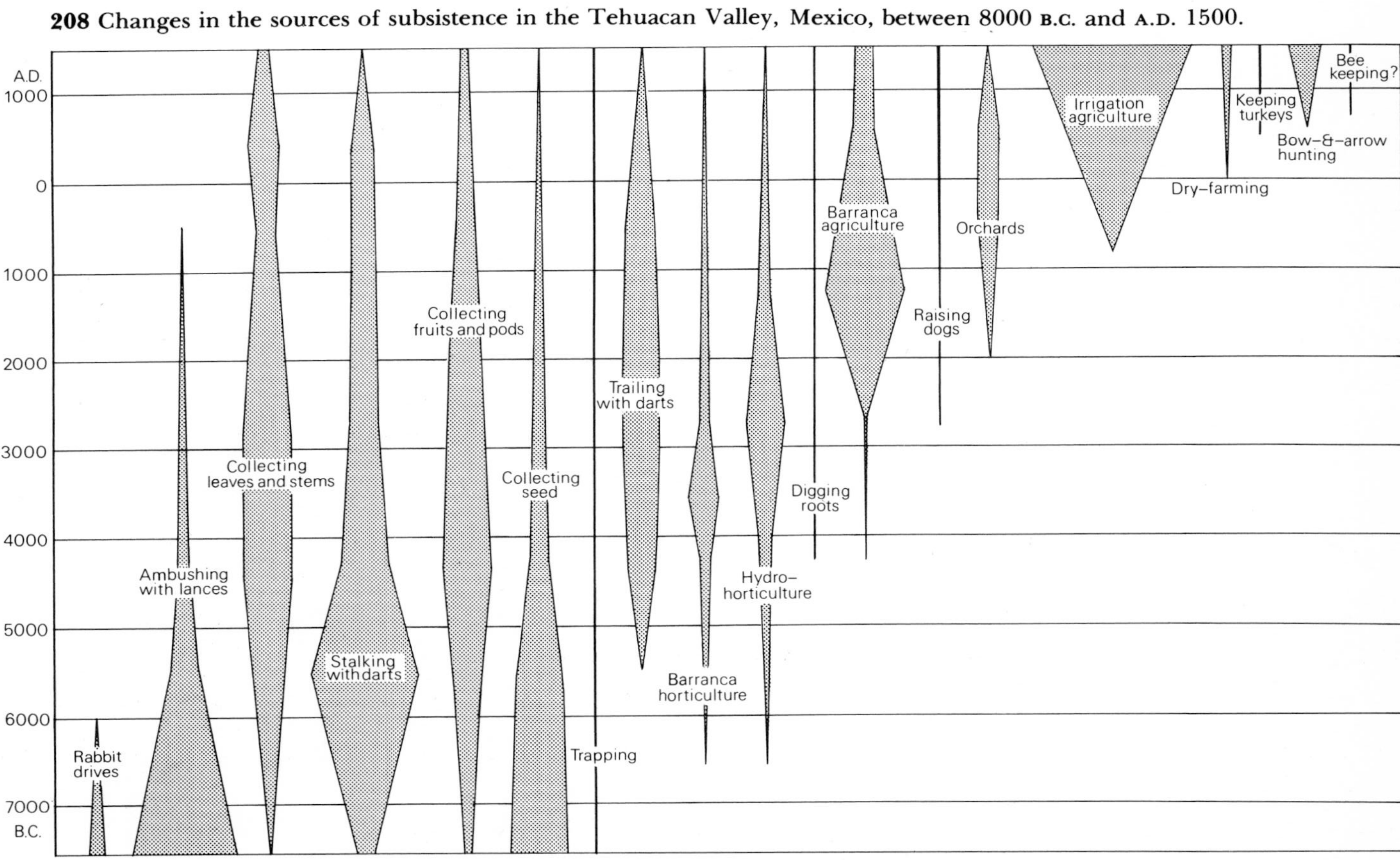

Table 24. *Chronological table for four zones of Middle America*

	C. MEXICO				
	Tehuacan	Mexico Valley	OAXACA	TABASCO	GUATEMALA LOWLANDS
1500 A.D. POSTCLASSIC		*Aztecs* Tenoch-titlan *Chichimecs*	*Miztecs* Monte Alban V : Mitla Monte Alban IV		*Maya*
900					
700 CLASSIC	Venta Salada	Teoti-huacan IV III	Monte Alban III	Tres Zapotes (upper)	Tikal 4 Tikal 3
300					
LATE O– FORMATIVE	Palo Blanco	II I	Monte Alban II	Tres Zapotes (middle)	Tikal 2
300					
MIDDLE FORMA-TIVE	Santa Maria	Zacatenco (middle)	Monte Alban I Guadalupe	Tres Zapotes (lower) La Venta I–IV	Tikal 1
1000					
1200 EARLY 1500 FORM-ATIVE	Ajalpan Puron	Zacatenco (early	San Jose		
2000					
3500 ARCHAIC 5000	Abejas Coxcatlan El Riego	Chalco	Guila Naquitz		
8000 B.C.					
PALEO-INDIAN		Santa Isabel Iztapan			

Appreciation that many other plants were cultivated and tended should not obscure the overriding importance of maize in Middle America, where it came to occupy a place even more central than that of wheat and barley in parts of the Old World. The Yucatec peasants occupying the Maya lowlands in modern times derive three quarters of their energy intake from maize and the proportion must have been even higher before they had access to the new food resources, notably pork, beef, bananas and plantains, introduced by the Spaniards. The rich mythology surrounding the origins of maize and the belief that the gods made men from this material show how sharply the Maya appreciated their dependence. The status of the Coxcatlan corn cobs has only lately been revised. Until recently they were thought to represent a hypothetical wild species, all living traces of which were expunged by domesticated forms. The more recent interpretation is to deny the existence of this hypothetical wild form and to derive maize (*Zea mays*) as a domesticate direct from teosinte (*Zea mexicana*). According to current theory maize arose through a process of unwitting human selection operating on mutations producing softer glumes which aided threshing, and a tougher, less brittle rachis making it practical to harvest the crop at one time. If this view is correct it means that maize was domesticated at the same time as the other species. On the other hand it looks as though the contribution of the various domesticates taken together played only a minor role by comparison with harvested wild plants in the diet of Archaic man in Middle America.

Early Formative communities

The transition from the Archaic to the Formative stages in the evolution of Middle American society followed rapidly on a shift from wild to domesticated plants as the principal scource of food and the simultaneous rise of maize as the predominant component. That this occurred during the final phase of the Formative is suggested by a veritable jump in the average length of maize cob and the concomitant increase in the average number of spikelets. The revolutionary nature of this change is well brought out by comparing the
209 subsequent development of maize in the Tehuacan Valley. Against a doubling in length and number in the final Formative, the maize grown under irrigation for the service of urban communities during the Classic period only increased by around a quarter in length of cob and a half in number of spikelets during the whole ensuing period. Whatever the explanation – and in the absence of irrigation

works at this stage there seems no need to look beyond the kind of genetic mutations that arise from cultivation – the huge increase in the productivity of maize measured in terms of increased output for the same input gave this crop an overwhelming selective advantage over others. At the same time by eliminating the need for extensive foraging it made it not merely possible but advantageous and even necessary to adopt a sedentary way of life. This had a number of implications in the socio-cultural sphere. Pottery began to supplement baskets as containers in the Puron phase and, by the Ajalpan, cotton, introduced probably from the south where it had been earlier cultivated on the coast of Peru, began to be used for thread in the Tehuacan Valley. In terms of society effective food production and the adoption of fixed settlement led to a change from exogamous bands which for much of the year lived as micro-bands to communities organized on a clan basis.

Ceremonial centres and their realms

Societies of the kind which first appeared in the New World during the Early Formative continued to flourish over much of the temp-

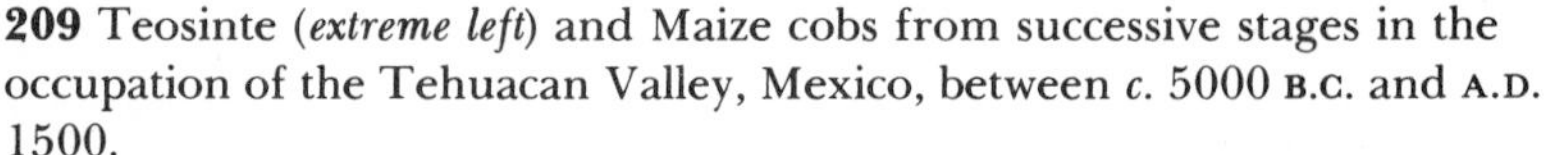

209 Teosinte (*extreme left*) and Maize cobs from successive stages in the occupation of the Tehuacan Valley, Mexico, between *c.* 5000 B.C. and A.D. 1500.

erate zones of North and South America, while hierarchically structured ones were developing in certain parts of the tropical zone, just as ones even more elementary depending for subsistence on hunting, fishing and foraging persisted and indeed still persist in the Arctic and Sub-artic zones. On the other hand it was the replacement of horizontally by vertically structured societies both in Middle America and the Andean zone that made possible and indeed determined the forms of the major civilizations of Pre-Columban America. On the face of it the territories one might suppose to have been best suited to this change were ones of ecological diversity in which the most favoured localities were able to take the lead and assume control of the redistribution of resources needed by less privileged ones. The centres from which this was organized came to dominate dependent territories in the very process of serving their needs. Concurrently they were the seat of specialized services, not least those connected with the observance of worship and the discharge of the ceremonial activities which sustained confidence and animated the flow of goods and services. Archaeologically they were marked by architectural manifestations, by monumental art and by evidence both of specialized crafts and of the redistributive process by which the leading hierarchs acquired their distinctive insignia. Conditions of this kind certainly prevailed in the highlands of Middle America where water, a commodity much more readily available in this zone at some localities than at others, was a major factor in the attainment of high population densities and prosperity.

On the other hand it looks, on admittedly incomplete evidence, as though ceremonial centres were first constructed, maintained and serviced in the more or less uniform tropical rain-forest rather than in the highlands. Why was this? For one thing the tropical rain-forest was disadvantaged in respect of food. Animal protein was not so scarce as is sometimes implied, since deer, peccary, iguana, tapir and turtle among others were available as well as fish and shell-fish in some localities. On the other hand the absence of domestic herds was a severe limitation. Again, while it is true that crops like beans and maize were available, their cultivation had to be carried on by the milpa system, a local variety of the swidden or slash and burn regime universally linked with shifting cultivation and a relatively dispersed population. Furthermore, the region was notoriously lacking in some of the materials most important for technology and the designation of social status. Obsidian, salt and the igneous rocks which made the best metates or corn-grinding stones had to be obtained from a distance and the main sources of jadeite were pebbles from the Motagua river and other localities in southern Guatemala. The limitation on food supply, mitigated though it may have been by a more intelligent cycling of clearance and regeneration and by the produce of garden plots, prevented large concentrations of population and so by definition the growth of urban communities, not merely during the Formative but throughout the Classic and Postclassic periods. On the other hand the scarcity of raw materials could only be resolved by means of an adequate mechanism for redistribution. Paradoxically therefore the tropical rain forest could only be settled effectively by people already at a certain socio-economic level. In this respect the Middle American rain forest presented certain analogies to the alluvial plains of Sumer. South Mesopotamia could only be exploited by people already familiar with farming and well equipped in techniques of social cooperation, experiences long since acquired within the rainfall zone which permitted dry cereal farming in Assyria and the Zagros. Similarly, the rain forest of the Gulf zone of Vera Cruz and Tabasco and on the other hand of northern Guatemala and Yucatan could only be tamed by people equipped with a knowledge of farming and socially experienced enough to organize and maintain redistributive networks capable of overcoming local deficiencies.

The analogy between Middle America and Mesopotamia has only to be stated for its limitations to appear. Although lack of rain

210 Middle America with key sites.

inhibited or at least rendered precarious the practice of dry cereal farming in Sumer, the alluvial soils and the sun between them were capable of yielding rich crops in return for the irrigation works in which relatively advanced societies were able to invest resources. In such a situation it was possible for nucleated cities to develop. In Middle America on the other hand the constraints on food supplies already noted were never mitigated sufficiently to allow the concentrations of population reflected in true urbanization. Yet it is important to realise that although not even the largest Maya ceremonial centres were associated with nucleated cities they were nevertheless the foci of organized realms, comprising populations of the order of up to fifty thousand people. The mere scale of the platforms and buildings implies substantial numbers of workers, and their elaboration and that of the minor artefacts associated with them argues for a relatively advanced sub-division of labour. Although it was only at times of outstanding significance in the sacred calender that people would have converged on the main centres, these were nevertheless of high symbolic value and may even have played a direct role in administration and economic life, notably in the process of redistribution.

Lowland

Olmec. According to radiocarbon dating, architecturally defined ceremonial centres first appeared in Middle America in Vera Cruz and Tabasco. Although the most complete sequence, extending from the Middle Formative to the Classic, has been found at Tres Zapotes, the
461 initial stage is best displayed at La Venta. The remoteness of this site set on an island surrounded by marsh emphasizes its sanctity. The fact that the island was only 5 sq. km in extent suggests that it was serviced by comparatively few hierarchs and their retainers on behalf of peasants scattered in small dwelling groups over an extensive dependent territory. On the other hand the scale of the
211 works – the La Venta pyramid measured 128×73 metres in plan and 31 metres feet in height – and the fact that they were maintained over four centuries argue that labour must have been contributed by this dependent population. The case is even clearer when it is observed that large quantities of lithic materials used in the structure must have been transported considerable distances by men without the assistance of animal traction or wheeled vehicles. The carved stelae, colossal heads and the columns enclosing the more northerly of the two courts attached to the pyramid were made from basalt that can

211 Key to lay-out of major structures at Olmec ceremonial centre of La Venta (site 4), Tabasco, Mexico.

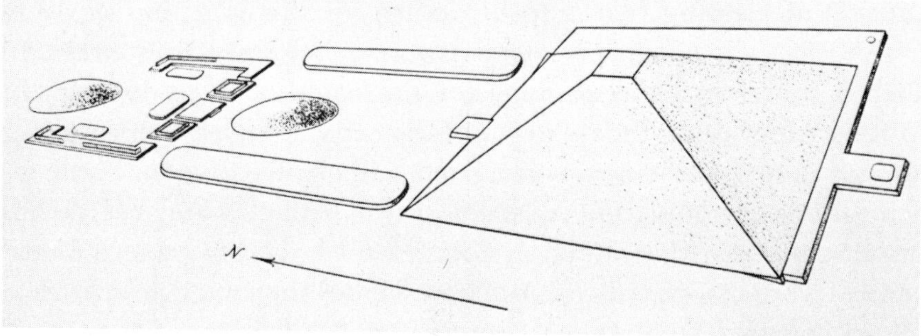

212 Jadeite adze with feline head in Olmec style, Vera Cruz, Mexico.

only have been won from volcanic beds 100 kilometres or more to the west or 240 to the south. Again, the many tons of serpentine blocks used for jaguar-mask pavements and deposited as offerings in several of the platforms must have come from outcrops of metamorphic rocks nowhere nearer than 100 kilometres away. The jade-
212 ite used for finely polished axes, figurines and personal ornaments and the ilmenite and magnetite from which were shaped the concave mirrors probably used for lighting fires were almost certainly collected in pebble form from the beds of rivers issuing from metamorphic rock formations. The existence of craftsmen highly skilled in working substances as hard as jadeite and ilmenite, no less than the conduct of the ceremonial activities themselves also argue for a fairly advanced sub-division of labour. Although much remains to be learned about its precise nature, the existence of a hierarchic social structure like that represented visually on painted vessels from
213 the Maya site of Tikal is the hypothesis which best fits the facts. It is even possible that the colossal stone heads so characteristic of the Olmec culture and some of the relief carvings may even depict or symbolize individual hierarchs.

458 A feature of Olmec iconography, as this is represented in stonework and pottery at La Venta, Tres Zapotes and other centres in the tropical Gulf zone, is a peculiar rendering of the face. The mouth is depicted like that of a baby incongrously combining elements suggestive of a snarling jaguar. This, in conjunction with the jaguar pavement at La Venta, argues that the jaguar, the most formidable beast of the tropical rain-forest, was the object of a pervasive cult. The appearance of Olmec features in central Mexico and at Monte

213 Maya hierarch giving orders. Scene painted on cylindrical pots from burial 116, Tikal, Guatemala.

Alban I in the Oaxaca region has sometimes been interpreted as evidence of expansion from the Gulf area to the highlands. Perhaps it is unnecessary to read more into this than evidence for intercourse between the hierarchs of neighbouring territories, something after all consistent with their role as controllers of redistributive networks. Whatever part Olmec influence may have played excavations at Monte Alban show clearly enough that an impressive ceremonial centre had begun to develop there during the latter part of the Middle Formative period. The large flat-topped mounds of Monte Alban I situated on a spur overlooking the fertile plain of Oaxaca in the highlands of southern Mexico were accompanied by the hieroglyphs, numerals and evidence of calendrical lore characteristic of early civilization in Middle America.

459, 463, 469, 470 *Maya.* The tropical rain-forest of lowland Guatemala and Yucatan, homeland of the Maya at the time of the discovery, was already occupied during the Middle Formative. By the Late Formative simple tribal societies were beginning to give place to ones with hierarchic structures. Monuments dating from the Classic Maya phase betray clear evidence of a grading of sites. House groups of four or five dwellings combined to form hamlets and four or five of these supported unpretentious ceremonial centres. On the average every ten such were subservient to a major centre at which stelae and glyphs were concentrated. At no point in this progression is it possible to detect nucleated urban settlements or towns.

The monumental expression of Maya culture reached a climax
214, 215 between *c.* A.D. 300 and 900. In their general lay-out and in the pyramidial form of their largest structures ceremonial centres like Tikal, Uaxactun or Lubaantun conform to the pattern found over
460, 464 much of Middle America on the highlands as well as in the lowlands. Although the core of the pyramids, which might be over 60 metres high, was made of earth or rock rubble, the mounds were faced at major sites with dressed stone masonry blocks set in mortar. The temple structures set on top of these and approached by flights of external stairs were primitive in the sense that in relation to their bulk their interiors were small and dark; the only method of vaulting known to the architects was that of corbelling by oversailing courses, a technique employed by some of the megalith builders of the Old World. Yet the loftiness achieved by placing them on acutely stepped pyramids, together with their carved and stucco-sculptured ornamentation and elaborate roof-crests, must have given them an over-

214 Oblique air view of part of Maya ceremonial centre at Tikal, Guatemala. Temples I and II on stepped pyramids with acropolis on left.

215 Sectional diagram showing four phases in the construction of the ceremonial centre at Tikal, Guatemala.

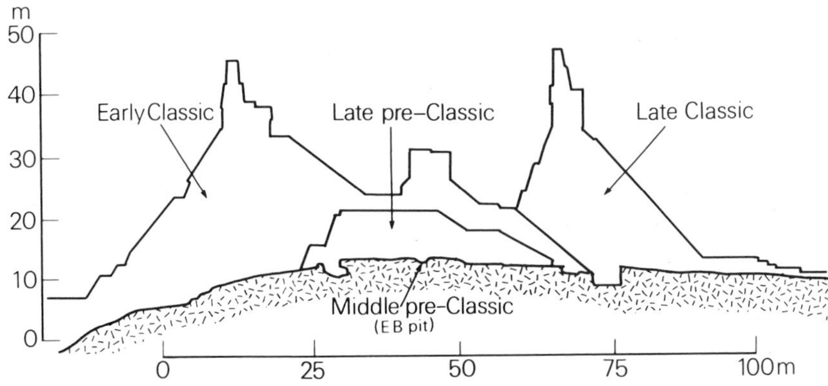

powering impressiveness to a population accustomed to living in small villages of humble dwellings in forest clearings. To modern observers the most striking thing about them is that they were built by people based on a lithic technology.

Impressive as were their architectural and sculptural monuments, the outstanding achievements of the Maya lay in the conceptual field. They were obsessed above all with a sense of the overriding need to ensure the continuance of time. To this end they deemed it of vital importance to schedule their ceremonials correctly. This in turn involved elaborate time-counts and the precise measurement of
467, 468 celestial events. The astronomical and mathematical achievements reflected in the glyphs and in the planning of their ceremonial centres provide striking illustrations of the conceptual capabilities of a Stone Age community. The Maya maintained two distinct counts. For religious purposes they used a sacred year (*tzolkin*) made up of thirteen twenty-day units. Since each day had its name and hieroglyph and since days were also numbered in series of thirteen it was possible to record the precise day of the religious year on monuments. Moreover by combining religious with secular years (*haab*) of 365 days, they arrived at the concept of the calendar-round of 18,980 days, in the course of which precisely 73 sacred and 52 secular years would pass. If for no other reason than that it came to be believed that the world was likely to end at the conclusion of a calendar-round, the event was looked forward to with some dread and when safely passed was followed by rejoicing. The Maya were well aware that the solar year was in fact rather longer than 365 days and developed a method of correcting the discrepancy between solar and calendrical years by calculating with surprising accuracy the length of the solar year: the Maya value of 365·2420 days was in fact closer to the modern astronomical value (365·2422) than was the corrected Gregorian calendar (365·2425). They also derived an accurate lunar calendar, and calculated the intervals between eclipses of sun and moon. Venus also claimed attention. Their calculation for the synodical revolution of this planet was remarkably accurate (584 as compared with the scientifically observed 583·92 days) and they were fully aware that in approximate terms 5 Venus years = 8 solar years. The priests owed much of their power to their control of the calendar and their ability to predict astronomical events that might otherwise have caused some consternation. One of their most important means of taking observations was to use the lines of sight to distant points on the
216 horizon obtained from the tops of their temples. For this reason their

ceremonial centres were laid out with astronomy in mind. The temple at Uaxactun was so planned that an observer standing on the steps of the opposite pyramid would see the sun rise at the equinoxes exactly over the centre of the middle temple and at solstices over the north corner of the front of the northern temple and the south corner of the front of the southern. In calculating periods of time culminating in Aluntuns of 23,040 millions of days by which they sought to assuage their anxieties about the continuity of time, the priests employed the concept zero and used a vigesimal system of numeration. Of no less importance for the control of the calendar
217 and the regulation of religious observance was the system of hieroglyphs devised for this specific purpose.

If the Classic Maya civilization, like the Olmec culture some twelve or thirteen centuries earlier, was subject to an abrupt decline, the explanation lies in its highly artificial character and its extremely narrow social base. It existed despite the natural disadvantages of the tropical rain-forest thanks only to a delicate socio-cultural mechanism. The architecture, the iconography, the inscriptions and

216 Astronomical lay-out of temple structures at Maya site of Uaxactun, Guatemala.

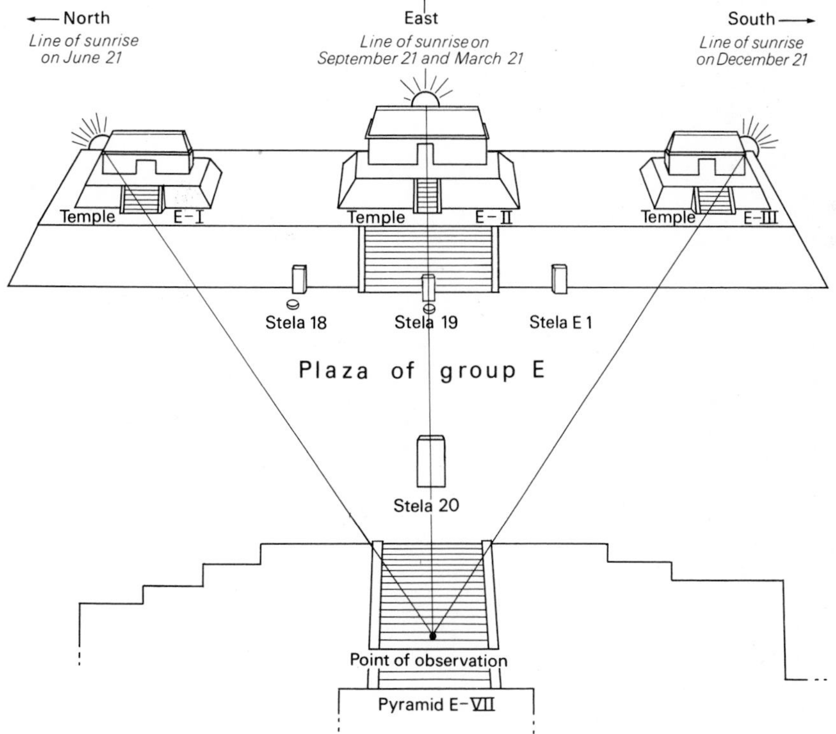

217 Maya stela with glyphs, Quirigua, Guatemala. The figure is that of the archaeologist Sylvanus Morley.

the elaborate calendrical systems related to an elite hierarchy based at a relatively few ceremonial centres. When for any reason these ceased to function – and the impact of barbarians could well have been the efficient cause in both instances – this did not mean the end of Maya people as such. Deprived of their elite they merely relapsed to a level at which they had nothing of note to leave for posterity. It is further possible that the swidden system (*milpa*) was pressed to the point beyond which the forest was unable to regenerate. When the Spaniards came they found the Maya concentrated in the northern third of Yucatan and in the coastal zones. The heartland of the Classic Maya only retained a much reduced population.

Highland

Classic: Teotihuacan and the first Middle American cities. Although central Mexico along with the Oaxaca Valley shared in the early phases of domestication, it was not until the final stage of the
457 Formative period that it rose to the dominant position it has ever since maintained. The classic phase in this area was presaged by the growth during the Late Formative of a settlement at Ostoyahualco on the northern edge of the eponymous site of Teotihuacan. The wide range of environments in the central Mexican highlands and in particular the varying accessibility to water made the territory highly conducive to a hierarchic ordering of settlements. It is symptomatic that the site of Teotihuacan was placed immediately above a concentration of some eighty springs.

After expanding over its valley during its second phase the classic Teotihuacan III attained the status of a city. The cortical area extended over 19 or 20 square kilometres and probably held a population of from 40,000 to 50,000 people. The only Middle American city to attain a comparable size during Pre-Columban times was the Aztec capital of Tenochtitlan on the present site of Mexico City. Teotihuacan III was not merely large, it was well planned and contained structures of monumental character. The ceremonial area was traversed by a grand avenue over three kilometres long, running more or less directly south from the Moon pyramid. Close to the crossing of the east–west axis stood a high palatial structure some 400 metres square with in the midst a temple adorned with symbols of the rain god and representations of feathered serpent heads,
218 probably identified with the historically known deity Quetzalcoatl, bringer of civilization. Between this and the Moon pyramid was the largest of the three, the pyramid of the Sun. In each case the

pyramids were built of earth, rubble and clay encased by stone blocks. The pyramids were stepped, devoid of decoration and carried shrines on their tops approached by flights of external steps. To illustrate their scale it may be mentioned that the pyramid of the Sun covered approximately four hectares, measured *c.* 210 metres square and stood 64 metres high. The main avenue was flanked by courtyard
219 houses which from their size and the religious nature of their interior wall-paintings can probably be interpreted as residences of the elite responsible for servicing the temples and governing not merely the city and its surrounding suburbs, but also the entire dependent
220 realm. The art styles and artefacts current at Teotihuacan III set

218 Temple of Quetzalcoatl showing reptile heads and masks of the rain-god.

219 Isometric view of courtyard house in Classic city of Teotihuacan, Mexico.

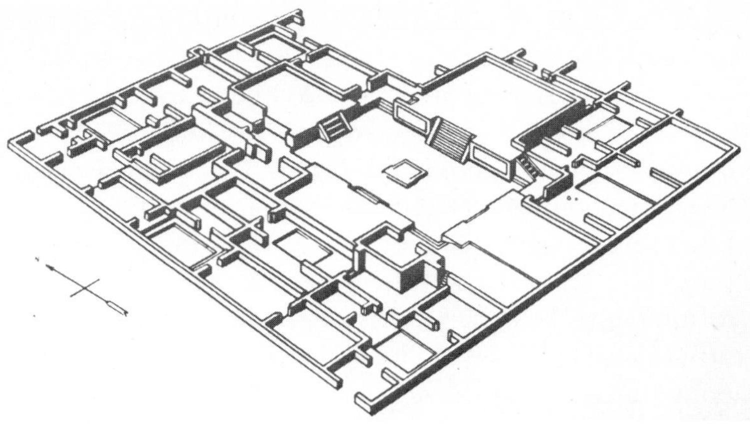

220 Serpentine mask of Classic period, Teotihuacan, Mexico.

fashions that were widely followed over the southern highlands, not merely at Monte Alban III in the Oaxaca Valley, but as far afield as Kaminaljuyu in the Guatemalan Basin during its Esperanza phase. Once again the explanation could well lie in intercourse between hierarchs rather than in invasion and conquest. At a conceptual level there is evidence for a restricted use of writing and it is significant that the hieroglyphs were notably central Mexican in character. The hierarchs maintained calendars based on units of 260 (52×5) days, but there are no signs that they emulated the long counts of the Maya system.

Around A.D. 600 there is evidence for the sudden collapse of Teotihuacan III. As in the case of other elaborate hierarchic civilizations the manifestations which proclaimed its existence in the archaeological record, although fabricated by the multitude, were imagined and commissioned by comparatively few concentrated at the apex of social structures which only functioned by virtue of an intricate socio-political mechanism. When for any reason this was dislocated the superstructure of civilization itself collapsed. In the case of Teotihuacan III signs of destruction by fire are consistent with barbarian intrusions. Although such may well have been the immediate cause of decline, it was the narrow basis and artificial nature of this as of other ancient civilizations that prevented an immediate recovery. Life continued at Teotihuacan IV as at Monte Alban IV but at a low ebb. Villages clustered on the former sites of the city of Teotihuacan.

Postclassic: Toltec and Aztec. During the Postclassic period the leading role in Middle America was taken by the inhabitants of central Mexico. Here the abandonment or destruction of many ceremonial centres had been brought about by the incursion of Chicimecs, or northern barbarian tribes driven or attracted south by crop failure, population pressure or the prospect of easy loot. As so often happened in other parts of the world, the barbarians having triumphed were themselves absorbed by the traditional culture. The first group to reach prominence were the Toltecs, who built their most important ceremonial centres at Tula in the tenth century A.D. and ultimately grew to be a powerful force in Middle America as a whole. Yet by *c.* A.D. 1160 the incursion of another wave of semi-civilized tribes from the north overwhelmed Tula and initiated another period of turmoil.

471 The Aztecs emerged as victors and by the end of the first quarter

of the fifteenth century had made themselves undisputed masters of central Mexico. The growth of their power and authority was
221 symbolized by the great city of Tenochtitlan, on an island in Lake Texcoco to whose shores it was linked by numerous causeways. It seems likely that at the time of the Spanish conquest the city numbered two or three hundred thousand inhabitants. The ease of transport over the lake helped to make it possible to concentrate the food needed for such a large population. Another factor was the productivity of chinampa beds, made up artificially from water vegetation and muck from the lake bed. In addition to its key role as a market and centre of government and religious ceremonial, the city was a centre for specialized craft activities. Besides such basic manufactures as pottery and now metal-working, the artificers of Tenochtitlan made luxuries for the upper classes including featherwork and jewellery. From this base the Aztecs entered on a career of warfare and imperialism. Under the reign of Ahuitzotlo (1486–1502) their empire extended to the shores of the Pacific and the Gulf of Mexico and from the valley of Mexico in the north to Guatemala in the south. As a people who emerged and attained success by defeating, incorporating and dominating their neighbours, the Aztecs were so to say self-selected for fierceness and cruelty. Their social structure was strongly hierarchical and was crowned by a

221 Reconstruction of main square of Tenochtitlan, now under Mexico City, with large temple on left.

semi-divine king. They worshipped a god Huitzilopochtli whose inordinate desire for human sacrifice could most conveniently be met by prisoners taken in war. They were a scourge to their weaker neighbours, Huaxtecs, Mixtecs, Zapotecs and the like. Ironically the authoritarian structure of their society contributed to their undoing when challenged by the Spaniards. Excessive veneration for their ruler Montezuma II made them incredulous of his seizure by Hernando Cortes and hatred of their Aztec overlords prevented the subject peoples of Mexico from rallying against the invader. Yet this merely accelerated an outcome that was in any case determined by an overwhelming superiority in armament. The Aztecs had no reply to steel armour and weapons, gun-powder and cavalry. Their state and empire was brought abruptly to an end between 1519 and 1521.

9

North America

Temperate zone

Hunter-foragers

The Indian population of Temperate North America had to adapt to a wide range of ecological conditions. In certain areas, notably the Plains, California and the north-west, economies resting on varying combinations of hunting, fishing and foraging continued to prevail down to historic times. It was only over the extensive zone of eastern North America where forest conditions prevailed during the Neothermal period and in highly restricted parts of the desert zone of the south-west that farming began to be practised and then only during the last two or three out of the twelve millennia of Neothermal time.

Plains. The Plains region continued to provide ideal grazing grounds for bison. These animals grazed the Plains in huge numbers – there are thought to have been from forty to sixty million of them at the time of the first European settlement. Finds like the Powers-Yonkee kill-site in Montana dating from the third millennium reflect the ease with which these animals could be stampeded and killed under confined conditions. Down to the moment when the balance between predator and prey was finally upset by the introduction of horses during the Colonial period the bison herds continued to provide the Plains Indians with almost everything they needed in respect of food and raw materials. Looked at another way this meant that they were trapped in a system of which the bison was the prime component. It is symptomatic that the key archaeological fossils of these Indians were the stone heads of their projectiles.

California. The food resources of California and more especially of the coastal zone and the lower reaches of rivers were much richer than those of the Great Basin in recent and by inference in prehistoric times. The recent Pomo tribe occupying the northern part of the central coast zone possessed a food-base proof against serious failure because based on different resources, each normally prolific. Harvests of acorns and grass seeds, supplemented by fish, waterfowl, deer and elk, allowed them to live in tribelets of around five hundred people divided into from three to four to as many as fifteen to thirty hamlets. Further south the Chumash were so successful at sea fishing, for which they made canoes of sewn planks, that they could concentrate as many as a thousand men at a time. Artefact assemblages from successive phases of the Neothermal share many characteristics with the eastern Archaic. These include bifacially flaked stone points, stone milling equipment, bone artefacts including awls and the barbed points of composite fish-hooks, baskets, stone vessels and ornaments made from abalone shell.

222 Plano points: (1) Midland, (2) Plainview, (3) Meserve, (4) Milnesand, (5) Scottsbluff, (6) Eden, (7) Angostura, (8, 9) Agate Basin, (10) Browns Valley.

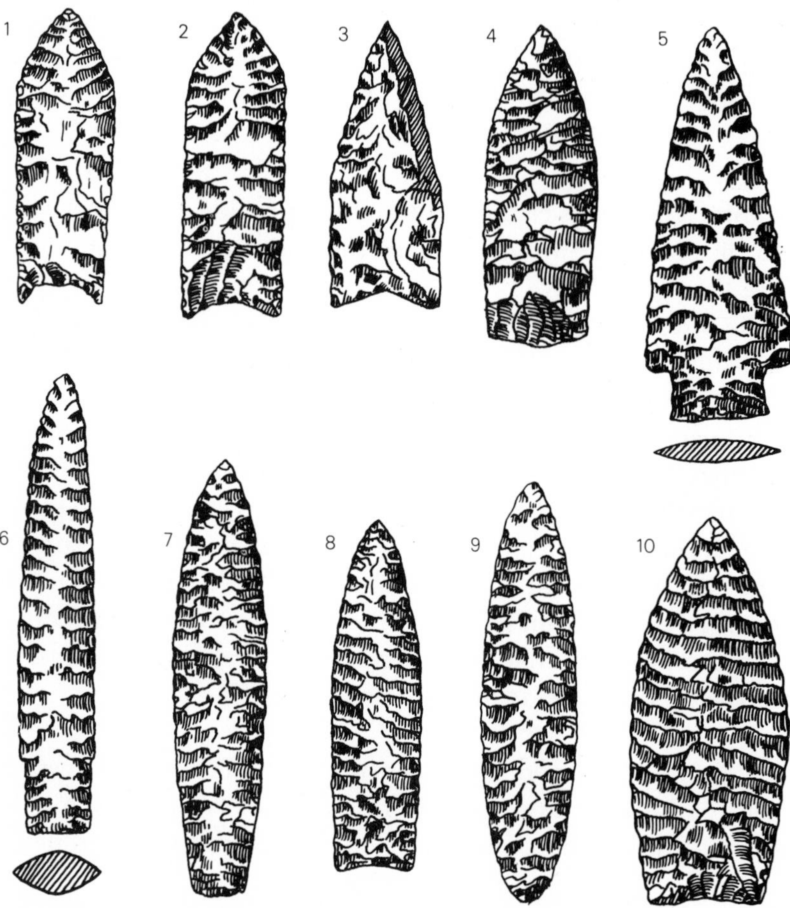

North-west. The abundance of marine resources, including seals, sea lions and sea otters as well as fish and sea-birds, and not least the salmon which ran up the Columbia and Fraser rivers from the Pacific
472 ocean, served greatly to enrich the economy of the Indians who inhabited the North-west coasts at the time of Captain Cook's visit of 1778. Archaeological investigations at Five Mile Rapids near the Dalles on Columbia river show that it was a key salmon-catching station as early as the eighth millennium B.C. Over 125,000 salmon vertebrae were recovered in the opening season of excavation and a like number in the next. At the present time the river is visited by five species of salmon was well as by the related steelhead trout. The main run lasts from May to early July. At this time of the year the Wishram Indians were accustomed to net the fish as they swam upstream. Spears might be used during the fall, but never at the same stations. This makes it interesting that the Dalles site yielded only one barbed bone leister prong. The salmon were presumably taken by nets. Bones of inland and marine birds and mammals show that salmon, though the most important, was by no means the only source of animal protein exploited at the time. Traces of successive
447: fig. 5 occupations on the Lower Fraser river unfortunately lack organic remains but their situation argues that salmon once again played a leading role. The predominant importance of salmon and allied fish is that they are abundant and dependable in nature, easy to catch at the correct locations and capable of being stored for lengthy periods. The Wishram Indians after splitting and drying salmon in the sun made a practice of pounding them into meal and packing them tightly in baskets lined and covered with dried fish-skins. In this condition they were reputed to keep sound and sweet for two or three years or more.

One should be careful not to project into the remote past the elaborate social arrangements of the recent Indians. In the course of prehistory the regions received fresh impulses overland from the north-west. Instances readily identified by archaeology include the micro-blade technique (p. 412) as well as toggle harpoon-heads. The region was also on the eastern rim of the North Pacific cultural pool. The several art styles of the north-west, Nootka, Kwakiutl, Haida and Tlingit, were original expressions of indigenous groups, but may nevertheless register influences from afar. The existence of plentiful and secure sources of food made it possible for the recent north-west coast Indians to live in settlements of up to thirty houses built of massive timber frames and planks and up to 159 metres long and

18 broad, a single one of which might accommodate up to a hundred
223 people. Again, ceremonial feasting and the ostentatious destruction of wealth was possible out of the superfluity. From a culture-historical viewpoint the Pacific coast Indians may have lived in a cul-de-sac. Their way of life was so satisfying that there was no place for them to go. If their culture survives today only in the memory of the very old, in the monographs of ethnologists or in museums, that is part of the price they have had to pay for ten millennia of equable well-being. While it lasted they were better off by far than most communities based on farming.

Eastern Archaic. From the Mississippi basin to the Atlantic coast the onset of Neothermal climate was accompanied by the spread of forest cover and a changed fauna. Whether or not it provided richer food resources, it certainly offered new options. Big game hunting of herd animals gave place to the exploitation of a wider range of resources in a variety of habitats. As a result marked differences of emphasis appeared in the food-quest and so in the overall pattern of culture, even if this did not become pronounced until the Neothermal transformation had attained its climax.

The Early Archaic phase of settlement was one of transition during which populations accustomed to herd hunting in a relatively open landscape were adapting to a more forested environment, rather as was the case with the Mesolithic populations of temperate Europe at about the same time. This can best be documented where the organic data have survived as in Russell Cave, Alabama or the

223 Interior of house, Nootka Sound, British Columbia, 1778.

shell-mounds of Tennessee. Comparison of material from successive
474 deposits in the Russell Cave shows that there was no substantial change in the pattern of subsistence from the Early Archaic up to the Colonial period. Apart from the extinct peccary (*Mylohyus* cf. *M. nasutus*), represented by a single individual from the basal layer, all the animals from the cave are still to be found living in the region. The fact that remains of twenty-two mammals, nineteen amphibians and reptiles, thirteen birds, seventeen fish and fourteen molluscs have been recovered from the cave argues for a wide-ranging food-quest. Yet throughout this time the main emphasis rested on a comparatively few species. The main source of meat was the whitetail deer (*Odocoileus virginianus*) with grey squirrel, turkey and box turtle making significant contributions. Fish was notably scarce throughout the Archaic levels at this site, but freshwater mussels and snails from the Tennessee river featured strongly from the Middle Archaic onwards. The most prominent component of material equipment continued to be bifacially flaked stone projectile-points, among which Paleo-Indian forms gave place rapidly to tanged and side-notched shapes.

The Middle Archaic was marked by several innovations. Among the most notable was the appearance of the dog, whose domestic status was sometimes emphasized by burial with human beings. Others included a variety of equipment made from antler and bone, including barbed points and barbless fish-hooks. Even more prominent because more often preserved were objects made from
224 polished stone. This included atlatl weights, adze-blades with straight and hollow blades, grooved axeheads and knife-blades and projectile-heads made of ground slate. The fact that many of these were common to the circumpolar zone of Eurasia prompts one to ask whether they were derived from that quarter. Yet the wide geographical gap between Eurasia and eastern North America is a formidable obstacle. The technique of polishing could readily have been applied from bone to stone in disconnected territories. Again the device of hollow-grinding the edges of polished stone adzes could readily have been suggested independently by the medullary cavity of split long bones adapted to tool-making. A good illustration of the way in which hunter-gatherers responded to local opportunities is afforded by the effective exploitation of native copper by the Middle Archaic population in the western zone of the Great Lakes. The metal came from outcrops on the south of Lake Superior and from detached fragments carried by the ice over much of Wisconsin and

Minnesota. No knowledge of metallurgy was implied any more than it was among the recent Indians of Alaska and the Coppermine River district of Canada. According to the late-eighteenth-century traveller Samuel Hearne these Indians were able to 'beat the piece of copper into any shape they wished' with the aid of fire and a couple of stones.
225 From such native copper the Archaic Indians beat out awls, tanged knives and projectile-heads and broad spud-blades both with wrapped over sockets. The products of this Old Copper industry were distributed by a mechanism akin to trade over much of the Laurentian area, New England and New York and even as far as the shell-mounds of the middle South. Copper was not the only material to be distributed by social mechanisms far beyond its zone of primary occurrence in nature. For instance bowls of Appalachian steatite were traded as far as Florida and the lower Mississippi and objects of

224 Some lithic components of Great Lakes Archaic.

shell were also widely diffused from their sources in the extreme south-east.

A feature of the Late Archaic was the appearance of the earliest pottery in North as opposed to Middle America, namely the fibre-tempered ware (see p. 403) which began to be made about 2000 B.C. in the coastal zone from Florida to Virginia and apparently spread inland to Tennessee and Kentucky in the course of the millennium. More importantly the period witnessed a northward expansion of
485 the Archaic way of life over much of the Canadian Shield from Great Slave Lake to Labrador, and the emergence on the coasts of New England, the Lower St Lawrence zone, Nova Scotia and Labrador of a distinctive Maritime province. This last was a facies of the Laurentian province of the Archaic with which it shared much basic equipment including polished straight and hollow-edged stone adze-blades, polished stone plummets, ground slate points and knives and barbed bone points. It was differentiated by the absence of common Laurentian forms like bifacially flaked stone points and copper artefacts and the presence of some absent from the Laurentian
226 including bayonet-forms of antler and ground stone point and harpoon-heads of stemmed and toggle form. The maritime orientation is amply documented by the food-refuse from maritime sites. Ringed, harp, grey and harbour seals and walrus testify to marine hunting. Salt-water fish were caught and sea-birds, including the great auk, were taken. This does not mean that the resources of the

225 'Old Copper' artefacts, Great Lakes Archaic.

interior were neglected. Salmon were caught as they moved upstream from the Atlantic and in the interior caribou were hunted. It was nevertheless the addition of rich marine resources that helped to give a special character to the Northern Maritime Archaic. The excavation
480 of well-preserved cemeteries of which Port au Choix, Newfoundland, is a recent and conspicuous example, throws light on quite another aspect of the culture. A point to note is the elaborate ceremonial nature of the burials. These were sprinkled with red ochre, covered by layers of limestone boulders and accompanied by up to a hundred grave goods each. Fine eyed needles which might occur in caribou

226 Objects from Port aux Choix cemetery, Newfoundland, North Maritime Archaic.

bone cases, point to the use of skin clothing, and harpoon- and lance-heads of antler, bone and stone remind us that many of the people buried were hunters. Particular interest attaches to hunting amulets like those still used by the Netselik Eskimos. These included the teeth, feet and claws of marten, otter, seal, caribou and fox and the beaks of ducks, loons, gulls and great auk. Stone figurines of birds and killer whales and the carving of animal heads on such things as bone combs also recall Eurasian practice.

476 *Desert adaptation.* Very different conditions applied to the Great Basin between the Sierra Nevada and the Rockies as well as in some degree to the south-west and the Interior Plateau on the north. Contrary to earlier opinions it seems likely that climatic and biotic conditions have been relatively stable in this part of the world for the last ten thousand years or so. Aside from local variations the prevailing vegetation was a steppe type featuring sagebush, juniper, spruce and pinon pine. Survival in such an environment depended on a detailed knowledge of sparse resources, on knowledge of how to exploit them most advantageously, and on mobility. Although bison, antelope or mountain sheep provided the larger part of their animal protein the Desert people supplemented the meat obtained from these herbivorous animals with flesh from carnivores like desert fox, bobcat, coyote and skunk and rodents such as desert wood-rat, bushy-tail rat, gopher or kangaroo rat. For their catching activities they used nets, snares and traps as well as darts propelled by atlatls and tipped with bifacially flaked stone heads, including side- and base-notched points of the type encountered in the eastern Archaic. Plants, notably nuts, seeds and rhizomes, were laid under heavy contribution. Exception-
477 ally arid conditions in certain caves – notably Danger Cave, Utah; Roaring Springs and Fort Rock Caves, Oregon; Leonard Shelter near Lovelock and Gypsum Cave, Nevada; and Ventana Cave, Arizona – have led to the survival of a broad range of organic materials. These include baskets, at first twined but later supplemented by coiled, nets, cordage and matting, digging-sticks, fire-drills, darts and
227 atlatls, all readily portable. The adjustment to a severe environment was so tight that there was little scope for change in terms of the indigenous culture. It is significant that new developments like those in the south-west (p. 394) only occurred under the impact of more advanced centres to the south. Conversely it is hardly surprising that groups like the Paiute Indians should have continued down to modern times to live for most of the year in family groups and

227 Plaited work, Desert Culture.

depend largely on harvesting nuts of the pinon pine supplemented by hunting. Much even of their equipment agrees closely with that from the prehistoric caves, including atlatls, artefacts of shredded fibre, fur blankets, moccasins and stone pipes.

Farmers

Farming and the kind of settled village community that sometimes went with this appeared in two distinct parts of the United States
475 during the pre-Columban period, namely the south-west with a focus on Arizona and New Mexico and the extensive region east of the western margin of the Mississippi basin. These were not merely separated from one another by a territorial gap in which agriculture was apparently not practised during prehistoric times. Their economies, like their ecologies, differed in some notable respects, but above all in the relative importance of maize in diet and the varying degrees of intensity with which it was cultivated. The emphasis on maize was much more pronounced in the south-west than in the east. There it was grown wherever cultivation was practicable. The prehistoric inhabitants of Arizona and New Mexico and contiguous areas pressed maize cultivation to its geographical limits if we may judge from the fact that no significant extension has been made since. The fact remains that the overwhelming proportion of this area consists of desert and mountain too arid for cultivation. It has been estimated that hardly more than 300 or 500 were cultivated out of between 500,000 and 800,000 square kilometres. This explains why the overall density of population remained low while at the same time it was possible for quite large aggregations to inhabit the small areas enjoying a supply of summer rainfall adequate for maize cultivation. In the east the situation was quite different. Whereas almost the whole territory up to the Great Lakes had sufficient sun and the hundred or more frost-free days in the year required by maize, only about one per cent of potentially arable land was in fact cultivated at one time during the pre-Columban period.

In both cases this implied a relatively low level of population. It has been calculated that the million or so inhabitants of pre-Columban
443 North America were distributed broadly as in Table 25.

The relatively high density for the Pacific coast emphasizes the great importance of coastal resources. Although eclipsed by the Pacific coast, it is noticeable that the farming areas were five times more thickly inhabited than those depending solely on catching and foraging. But this generalized picture obscures the important differences between the south-western and eastern zones of farming. Despite the small proportion of its territory given over to farming, the former supported *c.* 33·3 per hundred square kilometres by comparison with only 9·1 in the much more extensive east. This reflects a fundamental contrast not merely in the economic but also in the socio-cultural dimension. Whereas the easterners remained essentially catchers and foragers who complemented their diet by the produce of cultivation, the south-westerners or at least those of them with access to cultivable land were essentially maize-growers who also foraged and hunted and maintained contact with groups which lived off the sagebush and juniper vegetation of the semi-desert and its wild animals. The fact is that despite the poverty of much of their terrain the population density of the south-west was nearly half as much again as that of the Pacific coast and nearly four times that of the east. Both were able to support structures which marked them off from their Archaic predecessors and from the hunting bands of the far north, but whereas to some of the south-westerners maize farming was a way of life, among many of the easterners it served merely to provide the extra surplus needed to support a life of war-like exploit.

75: 112–225; 478 *South-west.* Although during the initial stages when agriculture was being introduced to supplement and in some localities in large measure to replace the foraging economies of the old desert tradition the same broad pattern prevailed with only minor exceptions over the south-west, development proceeded on increasingly divergent lines as finer adaptations were made to the varying ecologies of each
228 of four main zones. The largest of these, commonly termed Anasazi, the Navaho word for 'Old Peoples', occupied the high plateau of northern Arizona and New Mexico with contiguous parts of Utah and Colorado. Below this and occupying the southern parts of Arizona and New Mexico the Mogollon territory comprises dry grasslands in the valleys and coniferous forests on higher ground.

Table 25. *Population densities in pre-Columbian North American (after Kroeber)*

	Area (%)	Population (%)	Density per 10 sq.km
Farming zone	20	40	10
Pacific coast	6	30	25
Remainder	74	30	2

The south-west corner is shared by the intensely hot territories of Hohokam and Patayan, neither of which played a prominent role in prehistory. Systematic application of tree-ring chronology to the often well-preserved timbers used in construction, has made it possible to subdivide the settlement history of the South-west with Table 26 some precision, more particularly in the case of the Anasazi and Mogollon sub-areas.

Although it is commonly accepted that the Anasazi, Mogollon and other patterns of settled life in the south-west derived from an amalgam of exotic and indigenous elements, it is neither practicable nor would it be particularly meaningful to define these in detail, since as we have seen settled life in Mexico had developed from much the same basis. The process of cultural borrowing from the south is one that still operated in the mid-nineteenth century when the Pueblo Indians acquired the art of silver-working, which they still employ for mounting turquoise, from Mexico. According to pollen-analysis the cultivation of maize had already spread as far north as Colorado by around 1000 B.C. Yet, as in the valleys of Tehuacan and Oaxaca, the mere fact of domestication was not in itself important. What mattered from a social point of view was the adoption of a sedentary mode of life, something which itself was linked with a progressive swing from a basically foraging economy which included the harvesting of some cultivated plants to one in which foraging was

Table 26. *Periodization of settlement in the Anasazi and Mogollon regions of south-west North America (after Willey)*

A.D.	ANASAZI	MOGOLLON	
	Pueblo V		
1700			
	Pueblo IV	5	
1300			
	Pueblo III		
1100			
	Pueblo II		1000
		4	
900			900
	Pueblo I	3	
700			
	Basketmaker III		600
		2	
400			400
	Basketmaker II	1	
0			
100 B.C.			

ancillary to the cultivation of a limited variety of preferred plants. The south-western people utilized a variety of plants and in the case of ones like amaranth, tansy and sunflower their precise status is difficult to define. There is no doubt whatever that maize and squash were introduced from the south as domesticated plants and that sedentary life in the south-west was firmly based on their cultivation.

In the Mogollon area it looks as though pottery appeared in the same context. The fact that further north it did not arrive before *c.* A.D. 400, until when reliance had to be placed on baskets for

228 North America. Early farmers at the time of the birth of Christ in the south-west and east in relation to Middle America and the Cape Dorset aspect of Paleo-Eskimo culture.

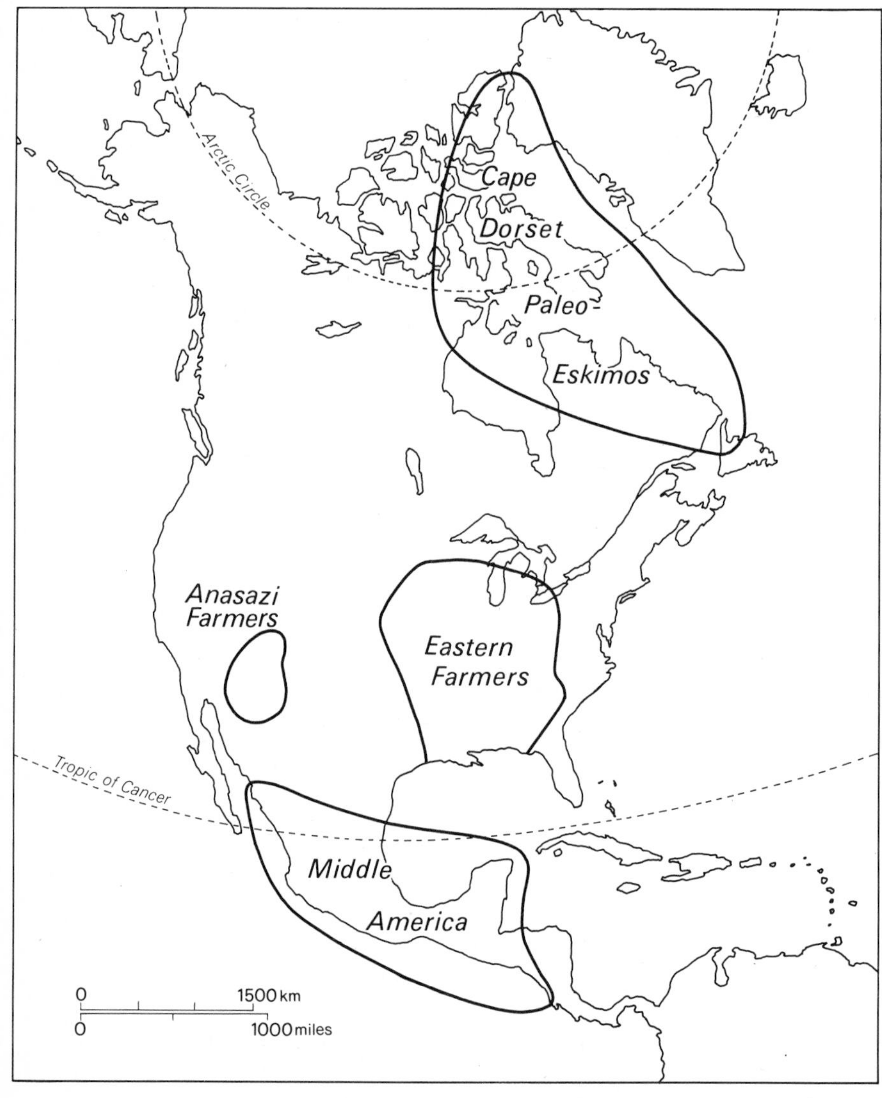

cooking as well as gathering, carrying and storing plant food, probably had little effect on daily life. The relations between their baskets and their pottery is sufficient to illustrate the cultural continuity between the Basketmaker and Pueblo phases. Pots and baskets were used side by side for most of the period. Both were built by the coil process and there is a clear affinity between the decorative designs woven into baskets and painted on pots. The Anasazi sequence gives evidence of a basic continuity. Maize and squash remained of key importance as cultivated plants but were joined from the south in Basketmaker III by peas and cotton. Foraging continued in respect of food plants and the fibres needed for basketry and the manufacture of sandals and clothing. The pursuit of hunting added another source of food as well as materials, including bone for the shredding tools and awls used in basketry and plaiting and the hides needed for cold-weather blankets and clothing.
229 The dart propelled by an atlatl was only gradually replaced as leading weapon by the bow, and arrows and darts alike continued to be armed with stone points finished by pressure flaking. The *mano* and *metate*, long ago evolved in Mexico and still in widespread use there, served throughout for grinding maize. Potting followed an essentially unbroken tradition, though one which permitted the
230 evolution of local styles. An example is the pottery made at Mimbres in south-west New Mexico between 1100 and 1250 and characterized by the liveliness of the stylized animals and humans depicted in black paint on a white slip. A certain evolution is displayed in architecture and settlement plans but this remained within well-defined social limits. Use continued to be made of the natural shelter of over-
231 hanging rocks right up to the time of the mis-called 'Cliff Palace' of Mesa Verde. The main development occurred in the artifical

229 Atlatl and spear showing mode of propulsion.

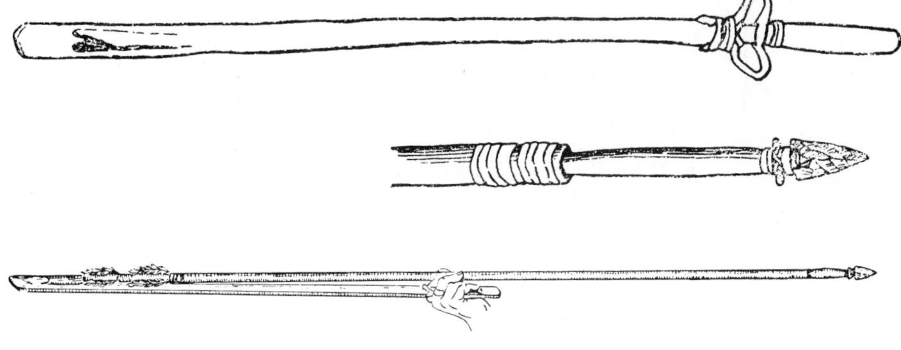

230 Anasazi painted pottery: (*left*) Pueblo I–II, Arizona–New Mexico border; (*right*) Pueblo II–III, Zuni, New Mexico.

231 'Cliff Palace', Mesa Verde, Colorado.

structures and their disposition. To begin with dwellings had their floors sunk into the subsoil on a round or rounded oblong plan and were made largely of timber and tree branches. The archaic pit-house continued in use in the form of *kivas* for initiation and other socio-religious rites down to modern times. Meanwhile cellular structures built above ground came into use for dwellings and stores. By Pueblo II the use of masonry gave added emphasis to the sedentary character of Pueblo economy. In the beginning villages of from twenty to fifty dwellings were normal, but in course of time there was a strong move in the direction of large apartment blocks combining dwellings and store houses commonly arranged in the form of arcs, like that of
232 Pueblo Bonito which comprised more than eight hundred rooms. By this time canals and dams were being constructed to ensure adequate supplies of food. Yet there is no evidence for hierarchy either of settlement or as between individuals. We are dealing with communities which to judge from modern analogy would have been organized on the lines of matriarchal clans. Evidence that objects were in some instances obtained from afar, for instance bracelets made from Pacific shells, are hardly in themselves evidence for long-distance trade on an organized pattern.

The impressive appearance of some pueblos should not obscure the fact that they were narrowly linked to the occasional patches of

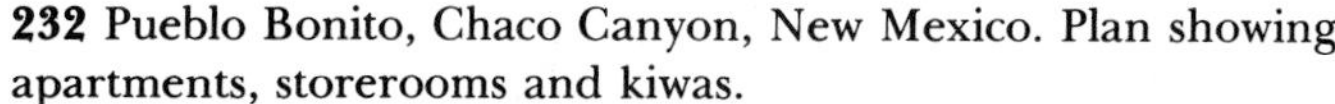

232 Pueblo Bonito, Chaco Canyon, New Mexico. Plan showing apartments, storerooms and kiwas.

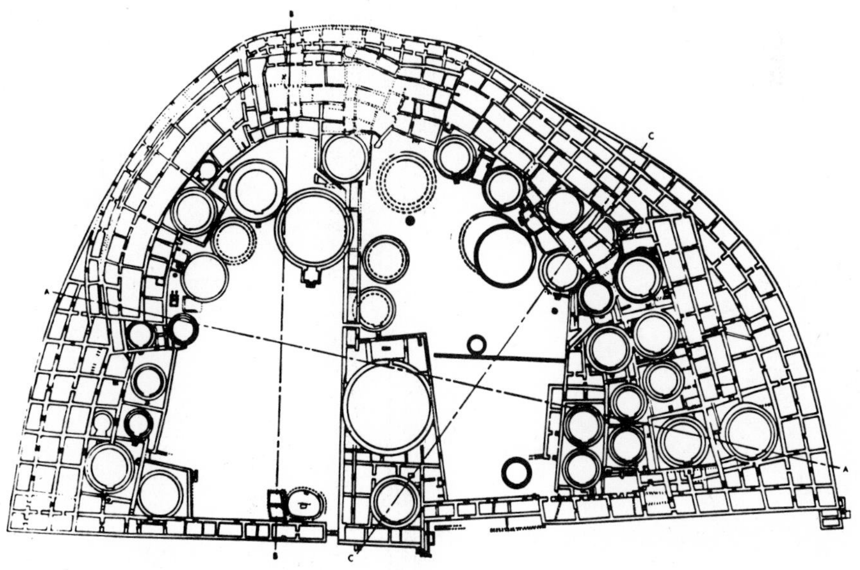

ground suited to maize-growing. In between were extensive tracts
233 of semi-desert territory fit only for transitory exploitation by hunter-forager bands. It could well be that the tightly structured plans of settlements like Pueblo Bonito reflect the defensive anxieties of cultivators in a sea of mobile hunter-foragers. It may also explain how Athapascan-speaking Indians, Navaho and various Apaches, were able to occupy so much territory, leaving the pueblos as so many islands. Yet the pueblos retained their vitality. The way the Pueblo Indians rose and destroyed the Catholic missions in 1680 is one sign of this. Another is the manner in which under the skilled and sympathetic guidance of United States agencies the indigenous crafts have revived. And over and above their basketry, textiles and pottery, the modern Pueblo Indians have contributed outstanding individual craftsmen like Maria the master potter of San Ildefonso. The Indians of the south-west illustrate a major theme of world history, that smallness in numbers does not prevent communities from contributing to the larger heritage of mankind.

East. By the beginning of the first millennium B.C. at least parts of
473, 475: the eastern United States experienced cultural developments com-
267–320 parable in some respects with the Early Formative stage of Middle

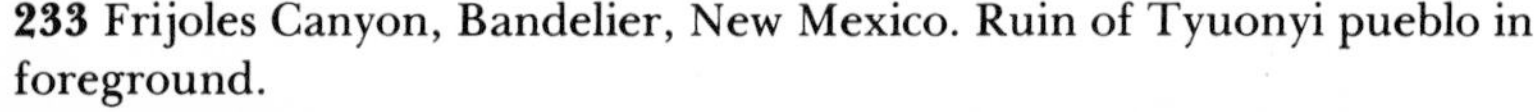

233 Frijoles Canyon, Bandelier, New Mexico. Ruin of Tyuonyi pueblo in foreground.

America. Yet there was a vital difference between the two regions. Whereas in Middle America the new developments led to the evolution of progressively more complex societies, culminating in certain instances in the growth of imperialist states, in eastern North America development was arrested at a much more elementary level. In Middle America the Spaniards encountered ceremonial centres and in some cases cities embellished with monumental structures and sculptural reliefs, whereas the British, Dutch and French explorers and settlers of eastern North America and the Spaniards in the south-east met with peoples warlike but relatively sparsely settled, possessed of a comparatively simple technology and whose social structure stopped well short of the organized state.

To a significant extent the inhabitants of the eastern parts of the sub-tropical and temperate zones of North America perpetuated the way of life evolved there during the Archaic phase of their prehistory. Animal and plant resources were sufficiently rich to supply their needs indefinitely within existing systems. There were no obvious forces making for change within the territory itself. Yet the archaeological record displays evidence for the construction since around 1000 B.C. of earthen monuments which imply a heavy expenditure of labour for no directly economic return and at the same time for an enlargement of the subsistence base. The appearance of maize and the form of the temple mounds constructed since around A.D. 700 suggest that the changes which defined a new phase in the prehistory of the region were precipitated by impulses from the south and explicitly from Mexico. On the other hand there is no suggestion that colonization took place or that a radically new way of life intruded. The Hopewellian and Mississippian culminations were each

Table 27. *Generalized sequence of eastern United States prehistory since* 1000 B.C. (*based on Haag & Willey*)

Dates	Periods	Cultural foci
A.D.		
	Temple Mound II	
1200		Mississippian of the lower middle Mississippi, Cumberland and Tennessee
	Temple Mound I	
700		
B.C.	Burial Mound II	Hopewellian of the upper middle Mississippi and Ohio basins
300		
	Burial Mound I	Adena of the Ohio basin
1000		

 in their own ways original manifestations of a distinct culture area.

The basis of subsistence continued to rest as during the Archaic phase substantially on hunting and foraging. On the other hand it was probably the accession of the more readily available products of plant domestication that permitted the more elaborate socio-cultural systems presently under review. Some of the most important cultigens were introduced, presumably from Middle America, notably beans, squash and maize. Others were indigenous. The process of establishing closer control of food plants was certainly proceeding during Archaic times. Firm evidence that the sunflower (*Helianthus annuus*) had been domesticated as early as *c.* 2000 B.C. is provided by seeds of larger size than those occurring in the wild from Archaic cave deposits in Kentucky and Missouri. It is likely also that Jerusalem artichoke (*Helianthus tuberosus*), marsh elder and seed-bearing plants

234 Extent of mound-building in eastern North America with Hopewell and Mississippi foci.

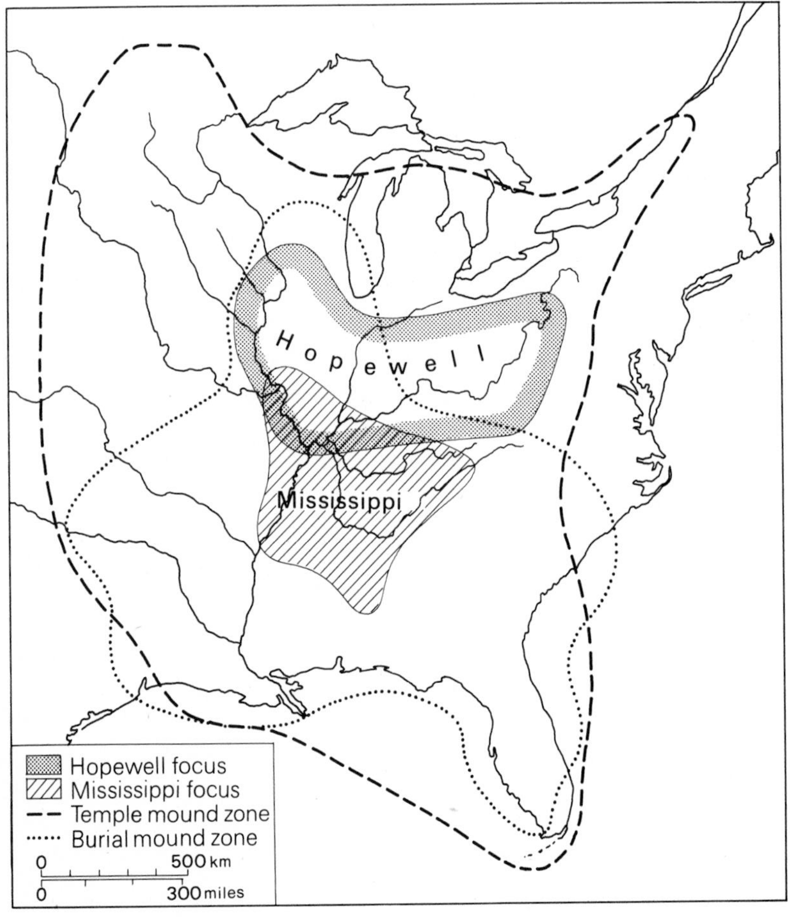

like goosefoot (*Chenopodium* sp.), pigweed (*Amaranthus* sp.) and knot-grass (*Polygonum* sp.) were also encouraged to grow in the immediate neighbourhood of the home base. There is still uncertainty when maize was first appropriated in this region. At the moment it looks as if it began to contribute significantly to the food base during Burial Mound II. Numerous corn cobs are known from Hopewell deposits. In due course the crop spread to the ecological limit set by a growing year of a hundred or more days. When the French colonists first reached the St Lawrence and the Great Lakes they found the Indians growing maize there. In the case of other plants of tropical origin, including beans and tobacco, local varieties better adapted to local conditions seem to have been domesticated.

Because pottery was once, mistakenly as we now realise, narrowly equated with the practice of agriculture, a good deal of interest has been attached to its first appearance in eastern North America. At the moment it seems that potting developed independently in both the tropical south-east and the temperate north-east. The fibre-tempered pottery which began to be made in Florida and Georgia *c.* 2000 B.C. shows no affinities with the pottery which had earlier appeared in Middle America. In the case of the grit-tempered cord
235 and fabric-impressed Woodland wares of the north-east comparisons have been drawn with pottery made over the circumpolar zone of Eurasia, but the 6,500 kilometre gap between Siberia and New York state is hardly consistent with a direct historical link. The adoption of pottery is interesting as a sign of growing sedentarism rather than of diffusion.

Notable new developments began already in Burial Mound I. The Adena population of the upper Ohio basin was dispersed in hamlets of two or three houses, but these were knit together into larger units by interchange and the discharge of common obligations. The most

235 Early Woodland pottery. Note the resemblance to baskets.

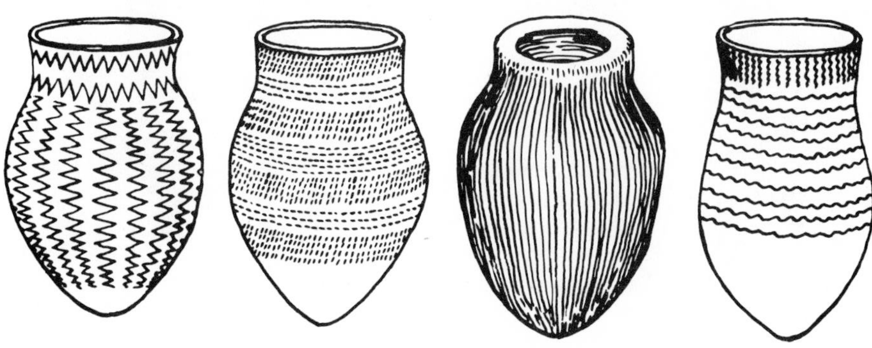

TEMPERATE ZONE

notable of these was the maintenance of ceremonial centres in the form of circular embankments up to a hundred metres in diameter with internal ditches and entrance causeways. Associated with these were conical burial mounds up to twenty metres high, which sometimes covered circular houses.

The trend towards a higher degree of integration and social interaction was only emphasized during the Hopewell phase. Once again the people lived in small dispersed units but were linked in larger units by sharing increasingly more intricate ceremonial observances and obligations. Hopewell earthworks were even larger than Adena ones and single embanked enclosures of rectangular, octagonal or circular form might extend over a much as a hundred acres. The burial mounds associated with them once again covered round dwelling structures and log-built tombs. The great intensity of the Hopewell manifestation is brought home by the wealth of grave goods, often ceremonially destroyed, and by the greater distances over which the raw materials from which they were made were obtained. Objects buried with the dead include profiles of human faces and hands, serpents, swastikas and animal claws cut out of mica from the Appalachians backed by copper from the region of the Great Lakes, caches of blades and dart heads made of obsidian from

236 Representations of eagles and other birds on Hopewell pot and copper sheet.

the Rockies or the south-west, conch shells from the Gulf, grizzly bear canines from the Rockies and heaps of freshwater pearls. Many of the artefacts display skill and aesthetic sensibility. Raptoral birds with
236 prominent beaks seem to have held a great fascination for the Hopewellians as they did for other peoples in many parts of the world: they are depicted in repoussé work on copper plaques, incised on pots and thrown into relief by oblique cord-impressions, and
237 skilfully carved on polished stone tobacco pipes. The artisans were fond of carving and polishing stone from which they made other forms of pipes, axeheads, atlatl weights and ear-spools. There are signs that the textiles made from plant fibres which survive as impressions on the corrosion surface of copper tools had been painted with designs. The degree of social interaction reflected in the wholesale and distant movement of raw materials makes it understandable that ceremonial activities most intensively practised in the core of the Hopewell culture nevertheless radiated over the whole territory between the prairies and the Allegheny mountains.

After a period of relapse when the intricate net-work broke down for a time, intensive ceremonial interaction picked up again during the second millennium A.D. to reach a renewed climax in the Mississipian florescence a little further south, one which culminated between the eleventh and fifteenth centuries and was already a thing of the past when the first European colonists entered North America. Charred remains of beans, maize and squash show that improved strains had been developed giving a greater return for the same input of labour. On this secure base more people were able to occupy the same sites for longer periods. Again they were able to build

237 Hopewell tobacco pipes of polished stone.

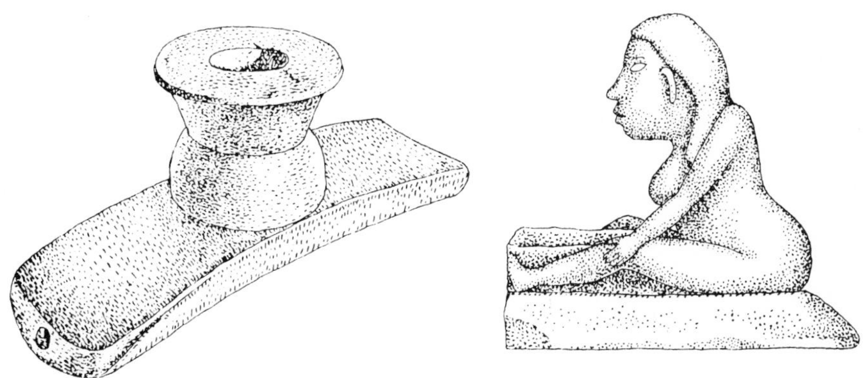

ceremonial structures of larger size and more elaborate form. Burial mounds continued to be raised but these were now overshadowed
238 by the rectangular flat-topped platforms, on which temples or chieftains' houses were erected, approached as in Middle America by external staircases. They were never as lofty as the masonry-clad pyramidal structures of Teotihuacan or Tikal but might still be of immense volume. Monk's Mound, Cahokia, in Illinois for example measured two hundred by three hundred metres at the base and

238 Plan of settlement and oblique view of stepped platforms of the Temple Mound I phase, Hiwassee Island, Tennessee.

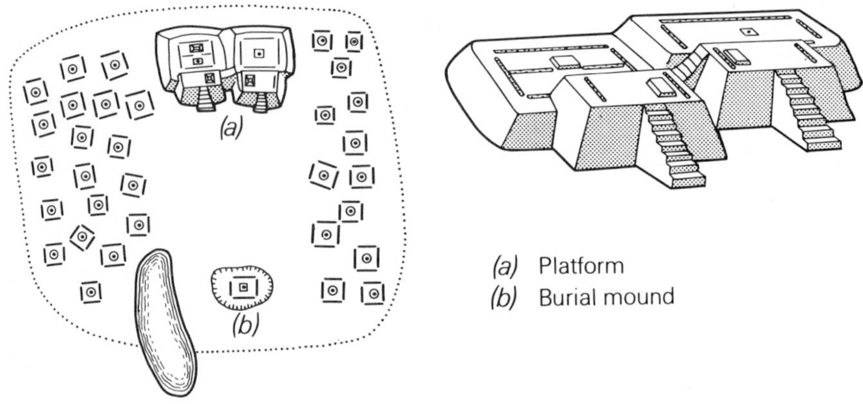

239 Symbols relating to the Southern Cult of Temple Mound II in south-east North America: (*lower*) feathered serpent; (*upper*) masked and feathered eagle dancer.

over thirty in height. Sometimes several mounds might be laid out flanking an open square or plaza. At Moundville, Alabama, there were as many as twenty dominated by one seventeen metres high and surrounded by rectangular houses with vertical timber walls set in slot trenches. Another form of ceremonial structure of this period was the effigy mound found rather commonly in Ohio and Wisconsin.
240 The serpent mound in Adams county, Ohio, was 4·5–6 metres across the bank and some 400 metres in length representing a formidable outlay of labour.

Although pottery was made in more sophisticated shapes and at the main centres tended to be painted rather than impressed by cord to bring out designs, there was no marked advance in technology over the Hopewell standard. On the other hand symbols displayed on copper plaques used for ornamenting headgear and garments, as well as being applied to shell and pottery, point to the prevalence
239 of a cult of southern aspect, featuring feathered serpents and eagle dancers, quite possibly mediated through the network of interaction which extended at this time as far as the Mexican highland. The representations of what appear to be dancers with eagle masks and feathered to suggest the birds are a vivid reminder that dances may sometimes last longer than the architectural embodiments of cults. Other symbols employed in this context were human hands marked with eyes and skulls accompanied by arm-bones.

North Woodland and Canadian Shield. East and north of the Ohio basin communities with a basically Archaic culture developed on simpler lines. Grave goods from cemeteries of the Meadowood culture of New York State, the St Lawrence zone of Quebec and the extreme

240 Serpent mound, Adams Co., Ohio.

east of Ontario lacked certain Archaic forms, notably polished stone atlatl weights and hollow-ground adzes, but this was balanced by the acquisition of Woodland pottery, tubular pottery pipes and large slate gorgets or pendants. Woodland pottery also came into use among the Point Peninsula and Saugeen groups occupying the territory between lakes Ontario, Huron and Erie. The occurrence of mounds with burials accompanied by exotic grave goods points to the influence of ideas radiating from the Ohio–Mississippi region.
482 On the other hand, the subsistence economy of the Great Lakes area continued on Archaic lines down to the middle of the first millennium A.D. Maize took a long time to adapt to the harsher climate and shorter growing season as it spread to its northern limits. When the immediate ancestors of the Iroquois-speaking tribes of southern Ontario at length acquired it they were able to settle in defended villages up to some ten acres in extent, but hunting and fishing continued to play significant roles in the economy even during the terminal phase of the Woodland culture (A.D. 900–1300). It was not until bean cultivation was added to that of maize to provide a balanced diet around A.D. 1400 that hunting and fishing reverted to subsidiary activities. When missionaries first encountered the Iroquois around 1615 they found them supporting relatively dense populations on the basis primarily of cultivation.

Meanwhile, the Archaic way of life persisted in all essentials in the forest zone of the Canadian Shield north of the Great Lakes. The Laurel culture associated with the ancestors of the Algonquian-speaking Indians retained most Archaic features apart from polished stone atlatl weights and hollow-ground adzes. Barbed bone harpoon-heads and points resembling those in use eight or nine millennia earlier in north-west America and for that matter in temperate Europe continued in use, as well as flaked stone side-notched pro-
479: 75–6 jectile heads and a variety of objects made of native copper, including fish-hooks, arrowheads, awls, chisels, bangles and beads. The most widespread acquisition from the south was the manufacture of coarse Woodland pottery with impressed decoration. The practice of building burial mounds was confined to the Minnesota border. The Algonquian Indians maintained basically the old way of life down to historic times, limited by the constraints on cultivation of beans and maize imposed by climate.

Arctic zone

The Arctic zone was the last in North America to be occupied by man. Although extending over 110° of longitude from Bering Strait to Labrador and Greenland, this is inhabited by less than sixty thousand Eskimos. Archaeological traces occur in the Elizabeth Islands and northernmost Greenland well beyond the northern limit of present Eskimo occupation, showing that in this part of the world there has
184, 489 actually been a contraction since prehistoric times. The archaeology of the far north poses many problems of a historical as well as of a merely technical kind. Among the former there is the question of the stage at which archaeological traces can be identified with Eskimo language and race, the sources of the prehistoric settlers and the manner of their spread, and above all the extent to which cultural changes and local efflorescences were due to ethnic movements, the diffusion of ideas or the outcome of mere social dynamics. From a technical point of view some of the problems are more apparent than real. Against the vast extent of the territory there is the consideration that settlement was to a significant degree adapted to coastal activities and that the same broad criteria have applied to the choice of site throughout the period of human occupation. This means that the evidence is less incomplete than might have been expected more especially since refrigeration of the soil has permitted the survival of an unusually large proportion of organic substances. It also means the local sequences are not too difficult to establish. The application of radiocarbon analysis, although still far too patchy, has made it possible to synchronize developments in geographically remote areas so that, although much remains to be done, far more is known about the prehistory of the region than might have been thought possible even a generation ago.

It needs to be emphasized that since race, language and culture are independent variables, connections between them need to be demonstrated rather than assumed. This is rarely possible. Racial affinities depend on adequate analysis of substantial bodies of well dated human skeletal material. This is not available for the earliest periods, the very ones at which the essential question is most at issue, and for some of the later phases for which ample material is available this has not always been adequately studied. In respect of language the position is even worse. Since the Eskimos were unable to write, no hard evidence about the language is available before contact with Europeans. It can only be said that there are signs that the Eskimo–Aleut language group emerged as distinctive and self-standing a

241 The Arctic showing prehistoric cultures and present limits of Eskimo settlement.

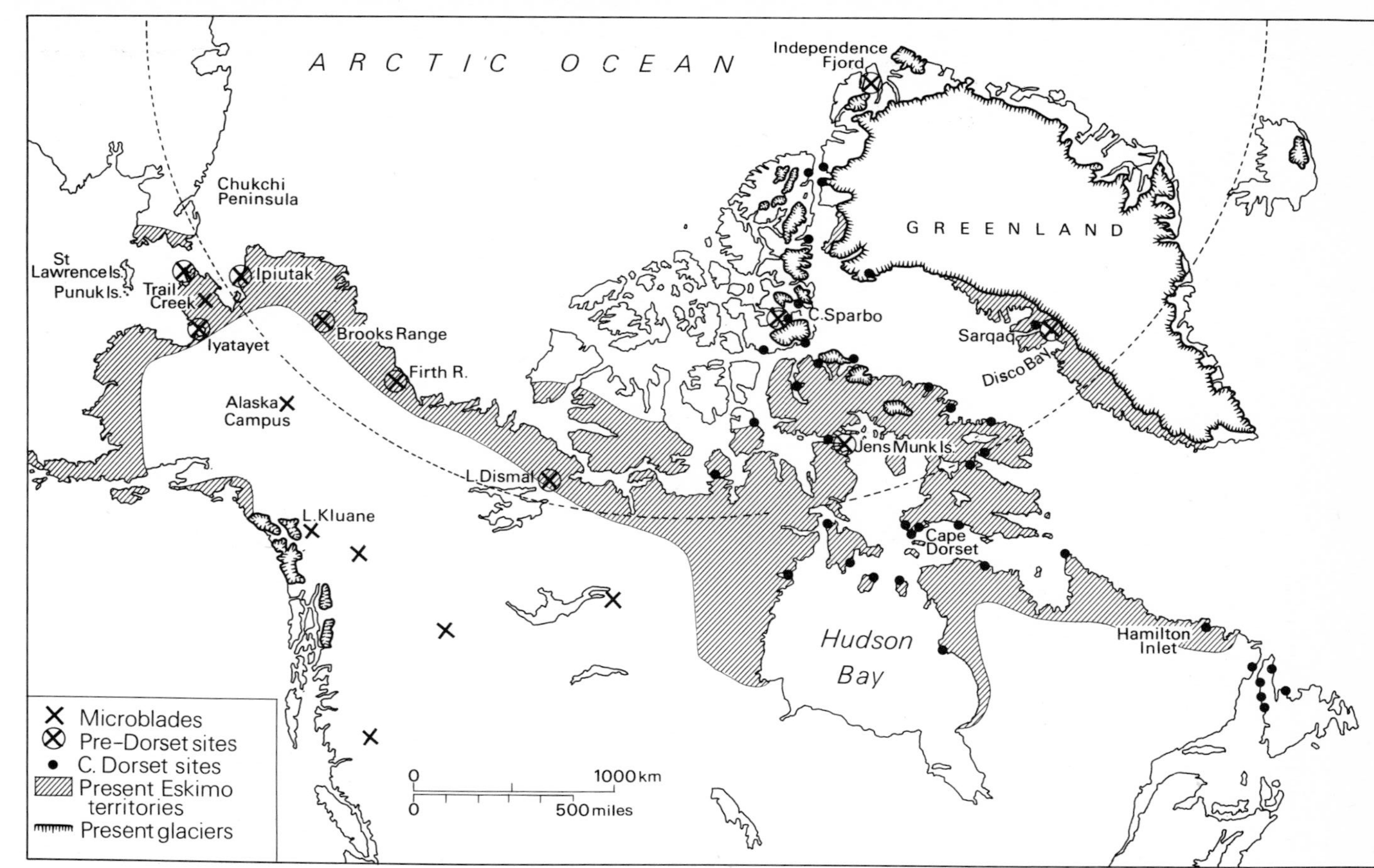

long time ago. In glottochronological terms Eskimo began to diverge from Aleut around three thousand years back. At the present time Eskimo speech preserves a remarkable degree of homogeneity over its whole expanse from Alaska to Greenland. How far back in time the rare congruence between race, speech and culture displayed in the Arctic can safely be projected may never be demonstrated. This need not prevent us from referring to those who first occupied the territories of the present central and eastern Eskimos as Paleo-Eskimo, if only by contrast with the Neo-Eskimo bearers of the Thule culture, immediate forebears of the existing population.

The Arctic tundra must originally have been penetrated from Alaska, the funnel through which men first effected entry into the New World, since a direct approach from the south was for long inhibited by the Laurentide ice-sheet. By the same token a full understanding of the impact of southern influences must wait on a much more complete knowledge of the timing of deglaciation. Some things are already becoming clear. It is apparent from the pollen analysis of lake deposits in central Canada that the process was as rapid in North America as it was in northern Europe. The contraction of ice-sheets was important in itself by making fresh land available for colonization and opening up new lines of movement. Hardly less important were the shifts in biozones that accompanied the rise of Neothermal temperature that was itself the immediate

Table 28. *Approximate synchronization of cultural manifestations between Bering Strait and Greenland*

	Bering Strait: Asiatic	N.W. Alaska	Arctic Canada and Greenland
A.D.	Recent	Recent	Recent
1700 ······			
	W. Thule	W. Thule	Thule
1000 ······	Punuk		
		Birnirk	
	Old Bering Sea		
		Ipiutak	Dorset
0 ······			
B.C.	Okvik		
		Norton	
		Choris	
1000 ······			Pre-Dorset
2000 ······		Old Whaling?	
		Denbigh	
8000 ······		Onion Portage	
		Trail Creek	

cause of deglaciation. This meant among other things that the vegetation which sustained the bison herds of the Plains moved decisively north. Their human predators followed suit, following in a reverse direction the corridor through which, millennia previously, the Paleo-Indians had passed on their way to inherit the New World.
455 Their trail is marked by the spread of Plano points across Alberta and British Columbia to the Yukon and Alaska to the very shores of Bering Strait. This southern contribution enriched not merely Alaska, but all those Arctic territories including Greenland orginally colonized from the west. Again, by a certain stage of Neothermal time geographical conditions would have permitted easy contact between the Eskimo population of northern Canada and Greenland with the Archaic people of the Canadian shield.

Microblade assemblages

Another element in the amalgam of Arctic culture derived from east Asia. This impulse is embodied most frequently in regular microblades and the conical or wedge-shaped cores from which these were struck. Bladelets of this kind were designed, as we know from sites where bone artefacts survive, to fit into grooves or slots of knives or weapon heads. This method of providing sharp edges for bone equipment is too highly specialized to have been invented independently in territories as contiguous as Eurasia and Alaska. The spatial and temporal distribution of slotted bone points and the associated flint technique argues strongly for their origins in the Old World. They occur over the whole extent of Eurasia from Norway to Japan and East Siberia and both in inner Siberia and the Ukraine they date back to the Late Pleistocene. In north America they appear first in the territory closest to Bering Strait and then only in early
242 Neothermal times. Flint bladelets occurred by *c.* 7000 B.C. with slotted
490 bone points at Trail Creek in Seward peninsula and without a bone
483 component in the bottom level (7) at Onion Portage on the Kobuk river dated to *c.* 6000 B.C. The distribution of bladelets and cores shows that the technique was widely adopted in the north-west.
492 During Neothermal times it spread through Alaska and the Yukon and ultimately reached the lower Fraser river in British Columbia by the first millennium B.C.

The fact that similar bladelets also feature in the earliest assemblages of stone artefacts not merely in Alaska but across the whole of the Arctic zone as far as Greenland argues that the main thrust of colonization was from west to east. In north-west Alaska itself bladelets, which were a key element in industries of the kind first *8: ch. 4; 489: 252–70* identified at Iyatayet on Cape Denbigh and at Onion Portage on the Kobuk river, have been dated in terms of radiocarbon to the third millennium B.C. Other components of Denbigh assemblages include scraping and cutting equipment and burins of angle and median type, a reminder of what must have been lost in the way of antler and bone artefacts. The Denbigh people were also skilled at making fine weapon armatures by a delicate bifacial technique, including leaf-shaped and hollow-based arrowheads of great delicacy, spear-heads and insets for slotted equipment. An imperfect fluted point from Iyatayet recalls prototypes on the North American Plains, but most analogies lie with Siberian manifestations, whether in Kamchatka, the upper Amur or Lake Baikal. The situation of Onion Portage at a habitual caribou crossing over the Kobuk river hints at

242 Artefacts from Denbigh and Trail Creek, Alaska.

the main source of animal protein and this is confirmed by the animal material from the site. Caribou also dominated at all levels in the Trail Creek caves, supplemented by fur-bearing animals, ptarmigan, water-birds and fish, probably salmon. The lowest level (7) at Onion Portage yielded the tips of numerous dog teeth broken off artificially, perhaps to prevent damage to the caribou skins needed for clothing and tents.

Central and eastern Paleo-eskimos

The key to the sequence of prehistoric occupation of Greenland and the territories north of Hudson Bay has been the investigation of locations well adapted to sea-hunting. The fact that such were frequently reoccupied at a time when sea levels were progressively falling as the land recovered from its former depression under the weight of the expanded Laurentide and Greenland ice-sheets means that encampments were spread out in temporal sequence. The
243 range of strandlines occupied by successive groups also gives a useful clue to their duration. Further precision can sometimes be gained from the radiocarbon dating of individual sites. The possibilities can
484: 137–8 be illustrated from Jens Munk island between Melville peninsula and Baffin island in the territory of the present Igloolik Eskimo:

Settlement phases	Beach levels	Radiocarbon ages
Thule	3 to 4–8 m	At 8 m A.D. 1350 ± 150
Dorset I–V	8–22 m	
Pre-Dorset	22–54 m	At 51 m 1750 ± 300 B.C.
		(after Meldgaard)

The designation Pre-Dorset arises from the circumstance that as in so many parts of the world phases of prehistoric settlement in the Arctic have been recognized in inverse order to their antiquity. The most important finds dating from the period before the Dorset phase, itself first distinguished in 1925, have come to light since 1953 at Sarqaq in the Disco Bay region of West Greenland, Independence Fjord in the extreme north-east and in the Igloolik region. Although these exhibit minor differences they share a number of features which link them to the west. These include the absence of ground slate tools and the smallness of lithic artefacts. Microlithic bladelets occur in the Igloolik region and north Greenland but not in the Disco Bay region. Bifacially flaked arrowheads of lanceolate and hollow-based form, spearheads and knives and not least burins are common to all three. Distinguishing features include the grinding of burins and the occurrence at Disco Bay and in the Igloolik area of small adzes with polished edges. Stone lamps appear only sparingly and at Independence not at all. This goes with the absence at this stage of semi-subterranean houses. The evidence of fossil pollen suggests that climate was notably warmer than it subsequently became during the Thule phase. Driftwood from Siberian forests would have kept the pioneers of Independence Fjord in firewood as well as providing props for the elliptical skin-tents resembling the Lapp *gamme* indicated on the ground by stones defining the outline, inner passage and hearth.

243 Dorset and Pre-Dorset house ruins in relation to sea-level, Jens Munk Island north of Melville Peninsula, Canada.

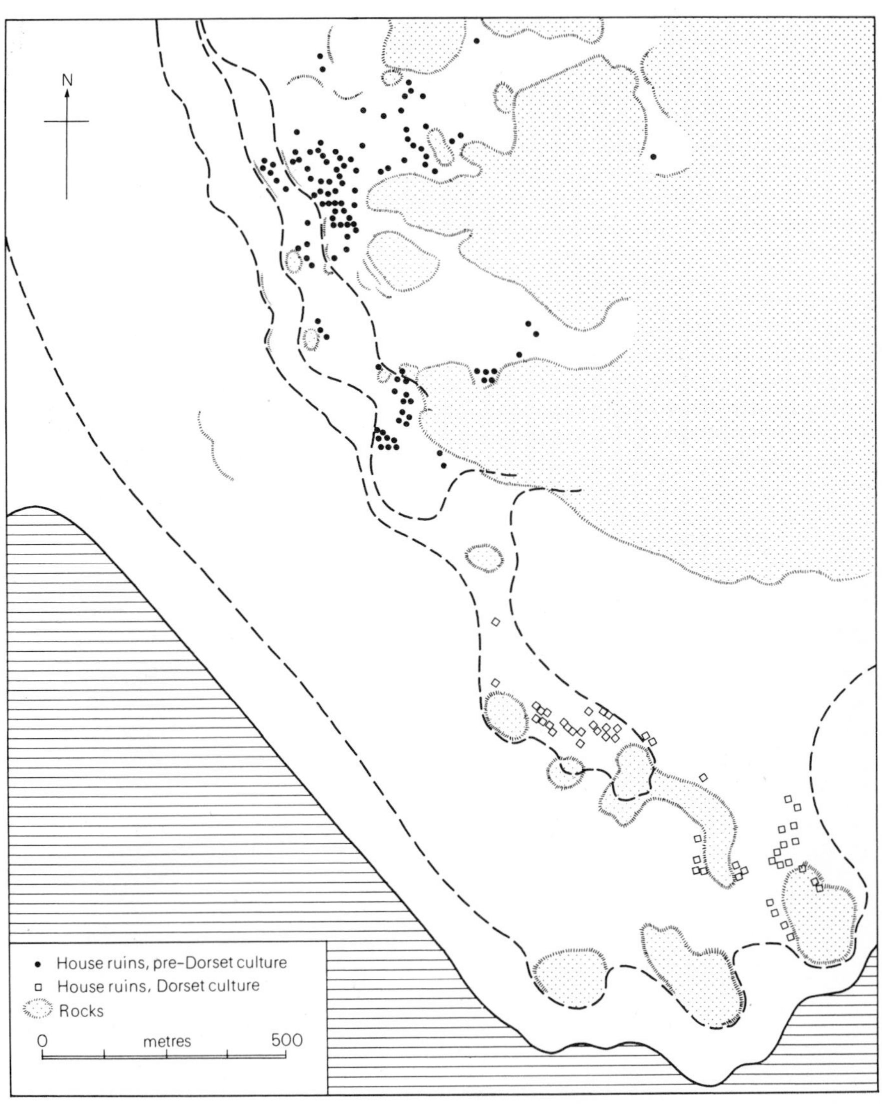

What attracted men to the tundra was doubtless what has held them there, namely the availability of abundant meat. Precise information about animals taken during Pre-Dorset times is scarce, but bones of musk ox at Independence suggest that these animals were followed as they crossed Robson channel from Ellesmere island while this was ice-fast. Once over, herds would certainly have found food and shelter in the deep valleys of Pearyland. The use of caribou antler for harpoon-heads by the pre-Dorset people at Kapuivak on Jens Munk island and in the second phase of occupation at Independence Fjord is a reminder that this animal also played its part. The evidence of these harpoon-heads and the coastal location of so many sites argues that sea mammals were hunted. Bone needles from Kapuivak point to skin clothing, an essential adaptation to an arctic environment and one which it is worth recording was first made in Eurasia already far back in the Late Pleistocene.

484: 42–5, The Dorset phase of settlement has been more adequately ex-
144–50 plored, although the most complete research has so far been published only in summary. This means among other things that the

244 Dorset artefacts from Abverdjar, Melville Peninsula, Canada.

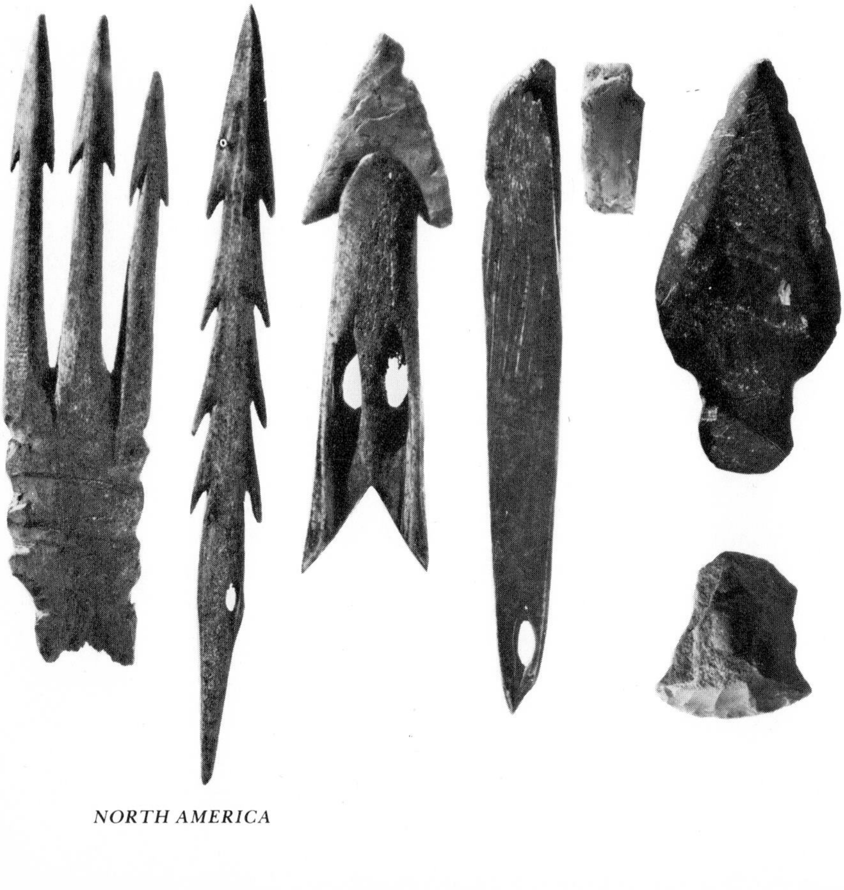

process of development over a span of some two thousand years can only be obscurely perceived. The environment remained much as before. It is only during the final stage that there are signs of the approach of the colder conditions to which the Neo-Eskimo hunters responded by developing an economy based to a significant extent on whaling. The economy of the Dorset people, while depending to some extent on hunting land fauna, including caribou, arctic foxes and arctic hares, together with bird catching, underwent a progressively more intensive adaptation to fishing and the hunting of marine animals, more especially seal, polar bear and walrus. Since they depended so much on marine resources it is hardly surprising that they should have spent at least much of the year as close as possible to the sea. The need for cooperation in their hunting and catching activities implies that several households must have lived together. This makes it less surprising that over two hundred Dorset houses should have been recognized at the Alarnerk site in Igloolik territory. On the other hand these occurred at varying levels between 8 and 22 metres above sea-level and there is no way of telling how many were occupied at once. The rectangular house floors at this site were sunk half a metre into the subsoil. They had benches for sitting and sleeping round three sides with a fireplace in the middle, but it was not until the closing phase that there is evidence for the cold trap in the form of an underground entrance passage used by the Neo-Eskimo.

244 Dorset material equipment has been recovered more completely than that of the Pre-Dorset period. The lithic industries display novel features but their small scale and general character show continuity. The microblade technique of ultimately Eurasiatic origin appears in assemblages as far as west Greenland and what is even more
487 significant on the coast of Labrador at sites like Ticoralak and East Pompey Island on Hamilton Inlet. The burin, a tool of special importance for cutting slots and grooves, continued to feature prominently and was now made more often than ever on broken bifacially flaked artefacts. On the other hand the application of grinding to the working edge, already noted in some pre-Dorset assemblages, is now applied to the whole burin facet. Convex scrapers served a continuing need among people who depended on skin clothing, but in the Dorset context the edge was commonly given an eared form that provided an expanded working edge and economized on material. A variety of knives, side-flakes and points continued to be made by bifacial flaking. Among novel forms were triangular points

with markedly concave base, of a kind used to tip toggle harpoon-heads, narrow tanged forms that were sometimes ground smooth and triangular bladed points with side notches to secure the binding. These last point to a contribution from the Amerindian Archaic adaptation to the south. This was also a potential source for the edge-polished adzes which continued in Dorset technology, as well perhaps for the ground slate equipment whose presence has been particularly remarked in the earliest Dorset phase. The open sockets of the toggle harpoon-heads used by the Paleo-Eskimos have even been derived by some from objects of the Archaic Old Copper industries of the Great Lakes region.

More is known of the organic component of Dorset technology than of the initial phase of settlement. In view of the availability of driftwood and of polished adzes it is hardly a surprise to find traces of wooden containers and figurines. No doubt also wood must have been shaped to make a variety of handles and shafts. Antler and bone served for a number of forms of toggle harpoon-heads, leister prongs and barbed points, as well as for the necessary and therefore persistent needles and needle-cases. The toggle harpoon-head inherited from pre-Dorset times is a significant pointer to seal-hunting.

Animal skeletal materials served as media for aesthetic expression, more especially during periods III–IV of the Dorset phase. This took the form of etching on bone, but above all of relief carving and

245 Dorset carvings in ivory from Abverdjar, Melville Peninsula, Canada.

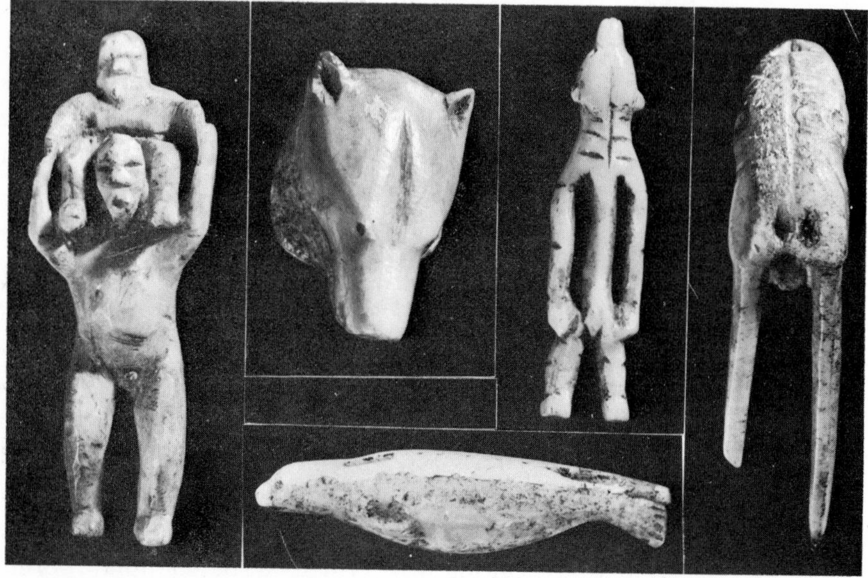

sculpture. Since animals were the main source of food and clothing as well as being the most stimulating element in the environment, it is not surprising that along with men they were the favourite
245 subjects. A point to note is that whereas whales, ptarmigan and owls were shown in simple naturalistic style, the animals on which the Dorset hunters mainly depended, namely seals, polar bear and walrus, were sometimes depicted more rigidly, a sign it may be of magical overtones. The linear designs suggestive of skeletal structure incised on the bodies of this last group point in the same direction. Human figures might be stylized, but heads carved in relief on caribou antler depict the Eskimo physical type with some fidelity and carvings in the round of naked men holding their infants aloft must have recaptured a scene common enough among people who habitually discarded their skin garments on coming indoors.

Western Paleo-Eskimos

The Bering Strait region, embracing the coasts of north-west Alaska, St Lawrence and adjacent islands and the Chukchi peninsula, was the focus of a highly successful economy based to a significant extent on marine hunting. This northern maritime tradition found aesthetic expression in lively and diverse ornamentation of artefacts, more particularly those connected with hunting, in personal ornaments and in three-dimensional carving.

On the coast of north-west Alaska three successive phases of the northern maritime tradition have been recognized. In the first of these, named after Choris peninsula and dating from the earlier part of the first millennium B.C., caribou, which in later phases played only a very minor role, accounted for around two-thirds of the mammalian bones. A possible explanation, which finds some support in the exceptionally small size of most of the caribou bones, is that the Choris people combined reindeer herding with maritime hunting. What is certain is that in their coastal activities they concentrated on seals. The same applies to the Norton and Ipiutak people, though we now find increasing evidence for hunting the walrus, which was absent from Choris and accounted for 6 per cent and 12 per cent respectively in the Norton and Ipiutak phases. In respect of whales only small-toothed species were hunted, notably the white whale, which at the Iyatayet Norton site accounted for the same proportion of bones as walrus. No attempt was made to hunt the larger whales on which Neo-Eskimo economy depended to some degree. Paleo-Eskimo seal hunters evidently lived in groups large enough to carry on cooperative hunting, though how many of the eight hundred houses strung out along beaches at differing levels at Ipiutak were inhabited at once is unknown. Individual houses were of rounded square plan approached by short entrance passages. Those at Ipiutak were provided with benches for sitting or sleeping round three sides with a fireplace near the centre.

Artefacts of ground slate which was to play such a key role in Neo-Eskimo equipment was still relatively unimportant, though the Norton people made extensive use of it for knives. The great majority of lithic artefacts were made by flaking, and certain forms, including
246 side blades and points for inserting into arrow- and harpoon-heads were shaped by a skilled bifacial technique. Other uses of bifacially-flaked points probably included spearheads and it is certain that the Ipiutak people used bows since a wooden specimen nearly two metres long has survived. Flaked stone equipment designed for cutting, perforating and scraping was used to fabricate a variety of objects made of antler or bone, as well as to cope with meat and skins. Among the most vital of these were different forms of harpoon-head, mostly made from caribou antler and including varieties of the toggle type and some of the barbed pronged variety. Pottery found on Choris and Norton, but not on Ipiutak sites, has been decorated by linear and chequer impressions recalling wares from the Lena

246 Ipiutak projectile heads, Alaska.

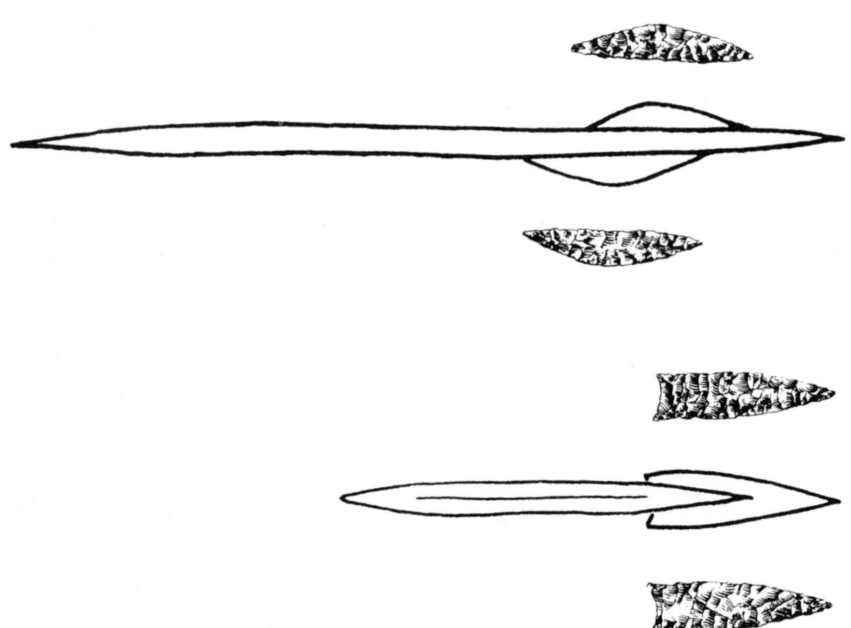

Valley and elsewhere in Siberia and presumably introduced to Alaska
from west of Bering Strait.

The culmination of Paleo-Eskimo culture centred on Bering Strait
was reached during the first millennium A.D. when the Ipiutak style
491, 495, 496 flourished on the Alaskan side and the Okvik and Old Bering Sea
on the coast of the Chukchi peninsula of eastern Siberia and on
486 Lawrence island. The potentialities of this region rested on exceptional abundance of marine mammals in demand by more advanced economies. The indigenous people could draw upon teeming sources of animal protein, heating-oil, skin-clothing, and bone and ivory for artefacts. Certain of these latter provided commodities of rare market value, notably walrus ivory and walrus hide which cut in continuous strips provided rope of exceptional strength. There is no proof that these materials were exported. On the other hand the
247 number of bones show that the walrus was hunted with outstanding vigour and sculptural representations leave no doubt of its importance to the Okvik and Ipiutak people. Again, there are many cultural borrowings from inner Asia or north China which can most easily be accounted for in terms of traffic. These include wrought iron,

247 Aspects of Old Behring Sea amulet carved from walrus ivory, Ekven cemetery, Chukchi peninsula.

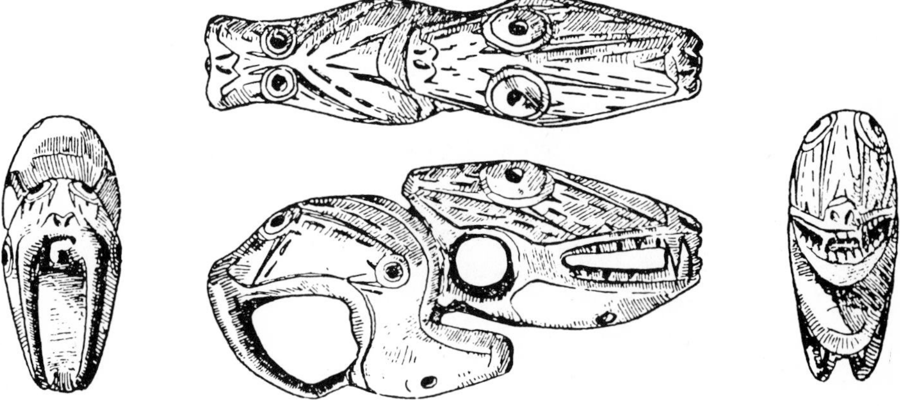

248 Ipiutak engraving tool.

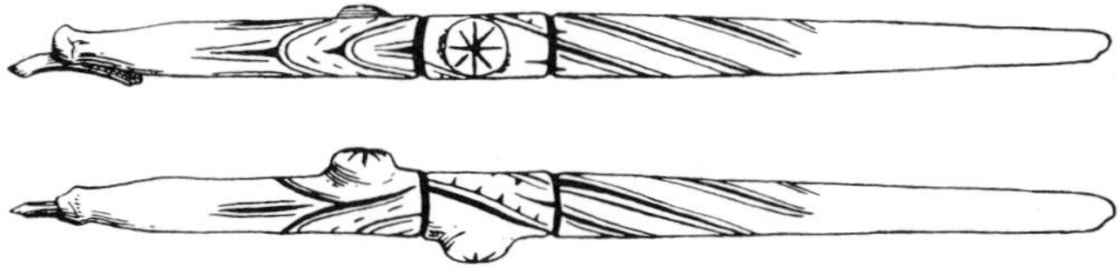

known to have been made in these territories by the middle of the first millennium B.C. In an Eskimo context this was used to tip
248 engraving tools of the kind needed to trace the fine, often double lines defining the curvilinear designs on such things as harpoon-heads
249 and the winged objects that may have served to stabilize darts. Iron must also have been used for the compasses used to make the regular circles incorporated in designs of the Ipiutak and Old Bering styles. The vitality of the maritime hunting cultures of the earlier part of the first millennium A.D. is further displayed in sculptures which not only recall the Asiatic animal style in general but also on occasion reveal stylistic features, such as the pear-shaped bosses on animal
250 flanks or the motive of the bear's head seen between front paws, which point specifically to inner Asia or China. Certain bizarre spiral pendants of bone have even been compared with the metal hangings on shaman costumes.

249 Ivory winged object used for steadying projectiles in flight. Old Behring Sea culture.

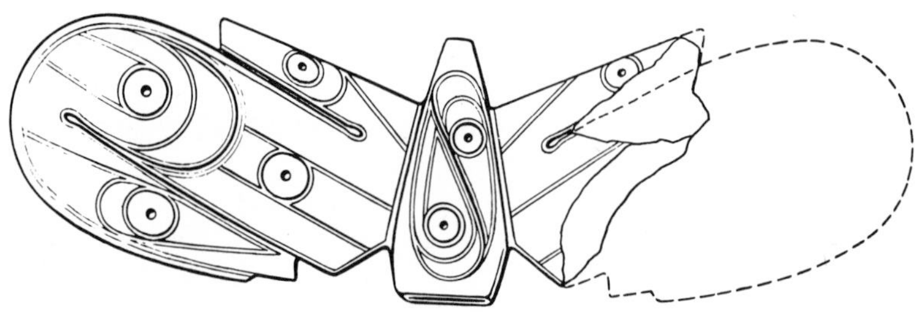

250 Ipiutak (*upper two*) and Scytho-Siberian animal carvings.

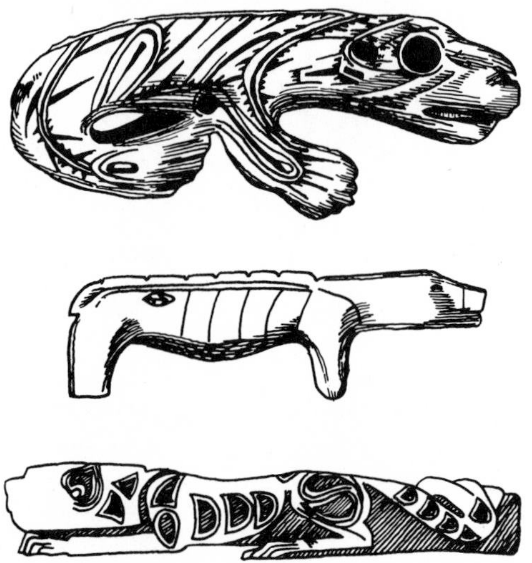

Asiatic influence persisted during the Punuk–Birnirk phase of settlement, for instance in sinew-backed bows and armour made up of bone plates on the pattern of the iron suits from Protohistoric tombs in Japan. The dog-drawn sledge, as opposed to ones drawn by hand, documented both for Punuk island and the Birnirk settlement at Barrow Point in north Alaska, was an Asiatic introduction of immense significance in facilitating movement during seasons of snow cover. Ingenious bone goggles were devised to overcome the glare
251 encountered in snow travel. Houses were now commonly rectangular in plan and might be paved with flat stone slabs. A greater emphasis on whale-hunting provided material additional to driftwood and stones for building the superstructure. As one way of countering low temperatures houses were approached by long narrow passages which might be set a foot or so lower to trap some of the cold. Another was the widespread use of blubber lamps for which increased supplies of fat were derived from whales. Punuk and Birnirk artefacts were already beginning to display the more sober and uniform aspect of the succeeding Thule inventory. Skilled flaking techniques were progressively replaced by the grinding and polishing of slate for knives and projectile heads. Antler and bone equipment assumed a greater uniformity in part because the limits may have

251 Plan of Western Thule house, Cape Krusenstern, Alaska.

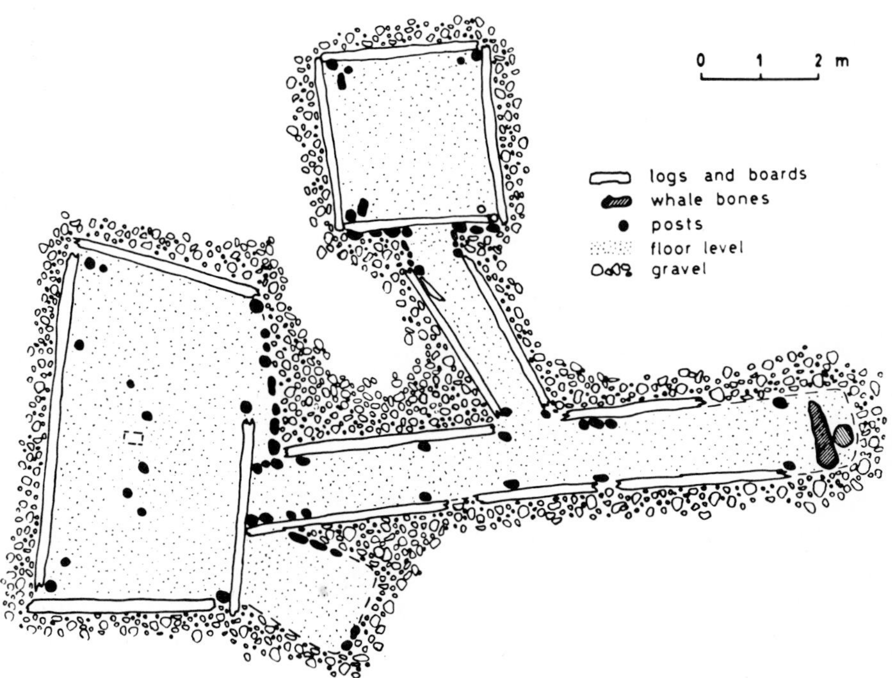

been reached in adjusting to the Arctic environment and in part because of the ubiquitous use of the bow-drill. The decoration of hunting equipment was simplified or even dropped and carving survived only in conventional figurines.

The Thule cultural pattern, originating from the Birnirk of Alaska, but named after the locality in north-west Greenland, was
493 the first to spread more or less uniformly across the whole Arctic territory from Alaska to Greenland. Although based partly on adjustment to a common environment, this was surely promoted by the ease of movement bestowed by skin boats and dog-drawn sledges, the means by which influences apparently flowed back again to Alaska from the east. The original easterly spread left Alaska around A.D. 900 and reached the Inglefield Land area of north-west Greenland soon after A.D. 1100. It is a testimony to ease of movement in the Arctic that contact was established with the Norse settlement 1,500 km to the south-east so rapidly that during the twelfth and thirteenth centuries a distinct Inugsuk pattern developed with Upernivik as a centre. In the archaeological record this was marked among other things by harpoon-heads with closed sockets and coopered wooden containers held together by baleen strips.

The contrast between the fate of the Eskimos and Europeans in Greenland illustrates with great clarity the importance of ecological adaptation as a factor in survival. Greenland, first discovered by Europeans in a ship off course from Iceland, was colonized from that
494 island in A.D. 986. At its peak the Greenland settlement amounted to some three thousand souls distributed among two hundred and eighty farms and ministered to by a bishop from Norway with a cathedral at Gardar and no less than sixteen churches. Yet its viability rested on its links with Norway in the form both of provisions like malt, cereals and altar wine and of personal reinforcement, not to mention moral support. When these weakened and ultimately broke down through a combination of dynastic problems and a southward deflection of trade under the growing control of Hanseatic merchants, the colony was placed in a most precarious situation. To make matters worse the increasingly isolated colonists had to face a decrease in temperature and an advance in the ice margin which, though minor in absolute terms, were enough to imperil the hay crops on which their subsistence was based. There is no sign that they made any serious attempt to adapt by developing a catching economy similar to that which had long sustained the Paleo-Eskimos. They remained prisoners of their own culture, as we are reminded

by their pathetic attempts to keep up with European fashions in their cloth garments. By contrast the conditions which defeated the Norse favoured the Unugsuk Eskimos. Although the Norse were in stadial terms more 'advanced' they were less fitted to survive under Arctic conditions than the more 'primitive' Eskimos. Spreading south the Eskimos first annihilated the western settlement of Godthaab Fjord around 1350–60 and then by *c.* 1500 the eastern settlement of Julianehaab. Finally, passing round the southern tip, they traversed Crown Prince Christian Land and amalgamated with the remnants of the ancient Eskimo settlement of north-east Greenland, where they survived until the mid-nineteenth century. When Europeans once again established a foothold in Greenland in 1721 they were only able to maintain themselves as a Danish dependency. As for the Eskimos, their main perils have been disease and cultural dislocation. Understanding treatment has recently helped them to relate to a cultural environment conditioned by modern technology and a cash nexus. The graphic art and some of the better carvings now emerging from the Canadian Arctic show that some at least have managed to adapt to their new social and economic environment with something of their fathers' success in respect of one of the most extreme physical environments encountered by man.

10

South America

During prehistoric times South America was intimately bound up with North and Middle America, while at the same time it had already begun to display its own individual character. One explanation for the measure of convergence displayed by the prehistory of the two continents, apart from biological communities and the fact that they were joined physically by the Isthmus of Panama, may be sought in their common ethnic basis. By comparison with the Old World the New was settled only at an advanced stage of human evolution. The first immigrants not only brought with them common genetic endowments, but also a common heritage of culture. The converse is equally true that a major cause of the diversity observable today both as between the two Americas and regionally within each is due to the varying character of the ethnic and cultural groups which intruded during and since the Colonial Period. Among the traits displayed by archaeological finds over the Americas one could mention the prevalence of netting and plaiting techniques, the widespread use of darts tipped by bifacially-flaked stone points and propelled by atlatls, various subtle similarities of style and symbolism in art and such negative features as the absence of the plough or of the use of the wheel for transport. Yet cultural divergencies had already begun to manifest themselves as far back as the Paleo-Indian settlement.

Over continents spanning so broad a range of environments it is hardly surprising that the degree of divergence should have increased as cultural responses grew more complex. At a time when ecological explanations are meeting with wide acceptance it is worth recalling that in choosing between the alternatives offered by most environments men are more or less strongly influenced by their cultural predispositions. Thus cultural differences are likely to prove not merely self-perpetuating but self-enhancing. To balance this it should be remembered that a growth in diversity tended to stimulate interchange.

Despite the basic underlying common elements noted at the beginning of this chapter, the complex and sophisticated civilizations encountered by Cortes in Mexico and Pizarro in the Andes differed profoundly in form and style as well as being separated by nearly twenty degrees of latitude. This was due in part to the varying biological endowments of the two territories but in part also to the exercise of different options. Whereas for instance maize emerged early in Middle and later in North America as the leading cultivated plant, in South America it had to compete not always successfully with other staple crops. The earliest plant to be cultivated in the coastal belt of the Andean zone was the lima bean (*Phaseolus lunatus*). In the highland basins the earliest crops included quinoa grain (*Chenopodium quinoa*) and a number of root crops, notably potato (*Solanum* sp.), oca (*Oxalis tuberosa*) and arracacha (*Arracaccia xanthorrhiza*). Again, in territories bordering the Amazonian tropic rainforest, notably parts of Bolivia and eastern Venezuela, the staple crop was the root of manioc (*Manihot esculenta*). Maize first appeared in coastal Peru around 1900–1600 B.C., possibly in a form domesticated in the highlands, but it did not become a significant source of food until the local type has been crossed with a strain introduced from Middle America in the ninth century B.C. Maize in this form was grown as high as 3,000 m in the fertile basins of the Andean highlands along with beans and the indigenous domesticate, the potato. Yet it failed to compete with, still less displace manioc in territories where this was the established staple. It is interesting to note that whereas the *metate* and *mano*, the apparatus on which maize is traditionally ground, abound in northern Venezuela, as in others of the territories intermediate between Middle America and the Andean zone, the clay riddle still used for preparing meal from the manioc root prevails on archaeological sites in the eastern part of the country bordering Amazonia.

A factor common to the New World as a whole is that domesticated animals contributed extremely little to the supply of animal protein. It was because this had to obtained almost entirely by hunting that projectile points played so pervasive a role throughout the prehistoric period in both continents. Animal domestication was nevertheless a distinguishing mark of the Andean as opposed to the Middle American zone. Guinea pigs seem to have been bred for food in the

coastal zone. In the highlands llamas and alpacas were domesticated
252 from native camelids. The former not only provided meat, but served as a beast of burden as well as yielding valuable wool. Since it could only carry up to 45 kg and journey 16 or 20 km a day, the llama, though useful in distributing wares in the mountainous terrain of the Andes, was of limited use as a draught animal. The lack of powerful animals and the failure to develop the wheel for traction meant that the stones used in monumental structures had all to be hauled by well-disciplined teams of men, a reminder of the degree of social cohesion attained in certain parts of South America during later prehistoric times.

The first settlers

The pattern of finds of bifacially-flaked stone points shows that the early intruders into South America traversed the Panama isthmus, fanned out over the intermediate zone from Venezuela to Ecuador, skirted Amazonia to south-west Brazil and pressed south through Argentina to the Strait of Magellan. The absence of bison herds probably explains why the early hunters of South America were less specialized than those in the north. Where animal bones have survived they point to a more generalized quest for animal protein.

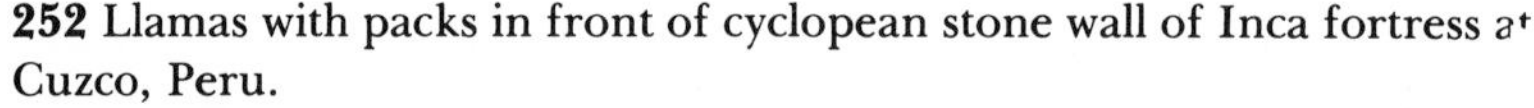

252 Llamas with packs in front of cyclopean stone wall of Inca fortress at Cuzco, Peru.

Thus the lake basin at Laguna de Tagua Tagua, central Chile, shows that towards the end of the Pleistocene (GX 1205: 9430±320 B.C.) deer, mastodon and extinct horse were being taken for food as well as rodents, birds, frogs and fish. The people who camped in Fell's and Palli Aike caves evidently hunted camelids as well as deer, extinct horse and sloth. High up in the Andes bones from the Lauricocha caves indicate a greater reliance on camelids, a family long since extinct in North America, but which in the south provided in the llama and the alpaca the two most important animal domesticates of the New World. The disposition of sites in the Andean zone suggests seasonal transhumance between the coastal tracts where the desert vegetation provided grazing during the summer and autumn, the

253 South American Paleo-Indian localities.

time of sea fogs, and the highlands where precipitation fell mainly during the winter. No doubt it was in the course of maintaining close touch with food animals that opportunities came to tame and domesticate certain species. Movements between coast and highlands, founded on the grazing needs of animals, ensured a close contact between cultural developments which persisted even during the period of settled life based on agriculture.

The bifacially flaked projectile points which help to define the activity of hunting in the archaeological record fall into two main classes. The leaf-shaped points from sites as widely separated as El Jobo in Venezuela, El Inga in Ecuador, Lauricocha in the Andean highlands and Ayampitin in the Argentine conform in some cases to the prototypical form found widely in North America as well as over extensive tracts of the Old World. On the other hand the
254 fish-tailed points which accompany leaf-shaped ones at El Inga and occur from the beginning of the Magellan sequence at Fell's Cave in the far south are absent from North America and represent a South American innovation that spread no further north than Panama and Nicaragua.

254 South American projectile points of fish-tail form.

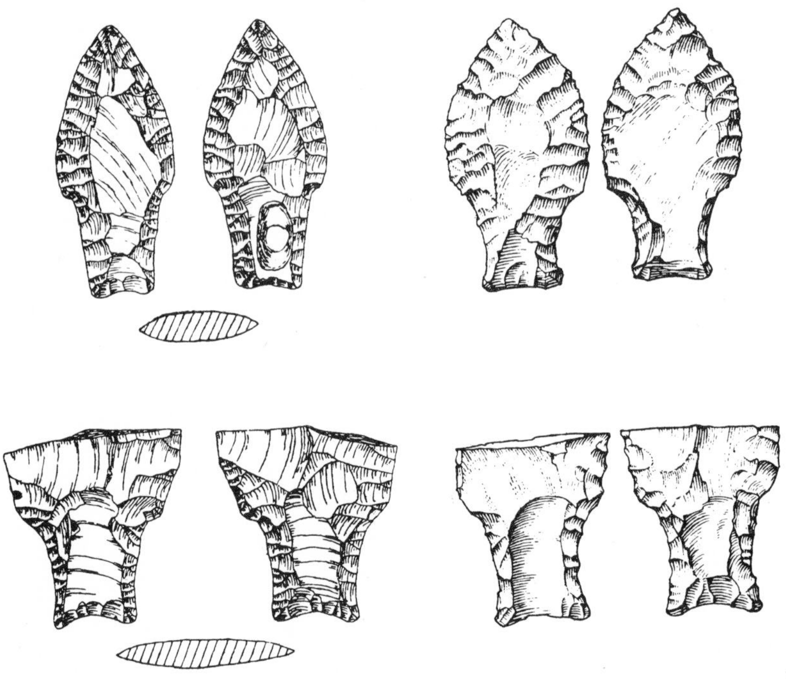

3, 500–1, 507: vol. 2

Preceramic

As we have seen, the movements of hunting bands following game animals as they moved from the coasts up the slopes of the Andes to reach the highest pastures from one season to another set a rhythm which ensured the fullest utilization of the natural resources of the entire Andean region. Although as plant cultivation and settled life grew in importance there was a certain pressure towards cultural differentiation, the varying resources of coasts and highland ensured that interchange between them was maintained. The sequences of deposits in the Lauricocha caves and elsewhere certainly document the occupation of the highland zone during early Neothermal times, but the arid conditions prevailing in the coastal strip

255 The Andean area.

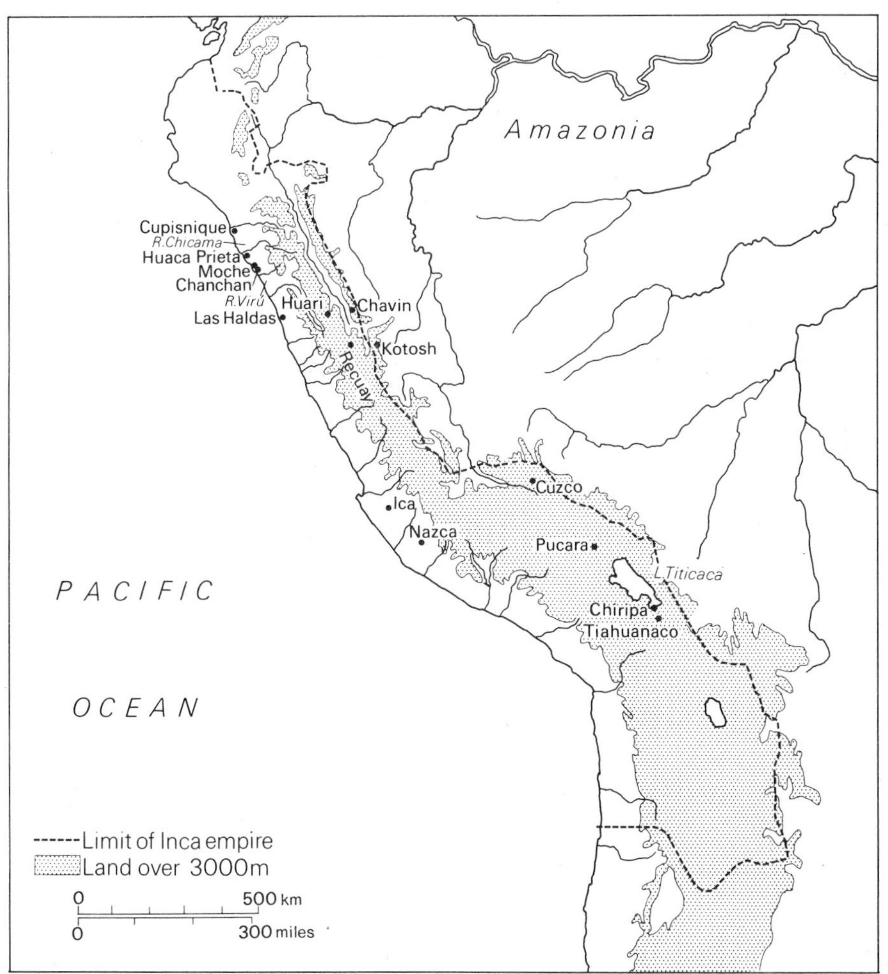

mean that thanks to the survival of organic materials and residues our information is much more complete. Although the soil was potentially fertile plants could only flourish there during the season of sea fog except in the valleys of the numerous rivers that flowed down from the Andes to the Pacific which was itself an important source of food. Excavations at Huaca Prieta in the Chicama Valley have thrown particularly welcome light on coastal settlement. The people occupied one-roomed dwellings which had evidently been roofed by whale bones as well as timber. The contents of the enveloping midden show that sea-urchins and shell-fish were gathered on the foreshore, fish were caught in nets weighted by stone sinkers and supported on gourd floats and porpoises were either hunted or scavenged. Vegetable food may all the same have been of major if not chief importance. A variety of fruits, seeds and tubers were foraged. What was even more significant for the future is that the inhabitants of Huaca Prieta had also learned to cultivate. Domestication preceded potting in Peru as in Middle America and for that matter in south-west Asia. On the other hand the species of plant domesticated varied in different parts of the New World. Maize was

Table 29. *Andean chronology of later prehistoric times (after Willey)*

Dates	Horizons	N., N.C. Coast	S. Coast	N. Highland	L. Titicaca basin
B.C.					
1550					
	LATE		INCA REALM		
1450					
	LATE INTERMEDIATE	CHIMU	INCA	Local styles	
1000					
	MIDDLE	Huari influence		HUARI	TIAHUANACO
600					
A.D.	EARLY INTERMEDIATE	MOCHE	NAZCA	RECUAY	PUCARA
200					
	EARLY	CUPISNIQUE	Chavin influence	CHAVIN	CHIRIPA (Late)
900					
	INITIAL	LAS HALDAS	—	KOTOSH	CHIRIPA (Early)
1800					
	PRECERAMIC VI	HUACA PRIETA			
2500					
	PRECERAMIC I–V				

absent at this stage in the south, but lima beans and pepper were grown as well as squash. It also looks as if the preceramic Peruvians were the first to domesticate cotton (*Gossypium* sp.) which only later found its way to Mexico and parts of North America. The coast-dwellers knotted nets and made mats and baskets plaited from reeds
256 by the twining method. Their fine cotton textiles have sometimes survived in a remarkable condition. Stone tools from Huaca Prieta included flakes and elementary pebble tools, but other coastal sites have yielded projectile heads and atlatls which confirm the importance of hunting.

Formative or Initial and Early

A notable advance in social life was represented by the building both in the coastal and highland zones of substantial ceremonial structures apparently half a millennium earlier than in Middle America. Indeed at Kotosh on the upper Huallaga river there is evidence that the first phase of the temple had been built already during the late Archaic preceramic phase. In each period the central chamber was provided with a low stone bench. Las Haldas in the coastal zone was even more impressive in scale. Whereas during the preceramic stage the site had been of a humble domestic order, it

256 Textile from the coastal tract of Peru.

was now transformed. Platform mounds faced with basalt blocks set in mortar and disposed around plazas now extended over as much as 640×185 metres. A change of such magnitude suggests an alteration in the economic base. One way of rapidly increasing the resources of the arid but potentially rich coastal zone would have been to divert water from the rivers for irrigation. Even quite elementary works could have made a decisive difference. Up in the highlands the humble potato may well have been the key to growth. In both areas the adoption of potting is a further indication of a more sedentary habit.

The most notable feature of the Early horizon (900–200 B.C.) was an art-style named after the highland site of Chavin Huantar. The name site was marked by a frequently reconstructed complex of stone platforms which evidently served as the foundations for buildings. The platforms themselves were honeycombed with galleries and chambers and had originally been embellished with stone sculptures and clay reliefs, as well as by carved stelae. Distinctive features of the Chavin style which dominated the northern part of Peru and of which the Cupisnique was only a local aspect, included a preoccupation with

257 Chavin de Huantar, Peru, stone reliefs: (*upper*) feline with serpent attributes; (*lower*) serpent with feline attributes.

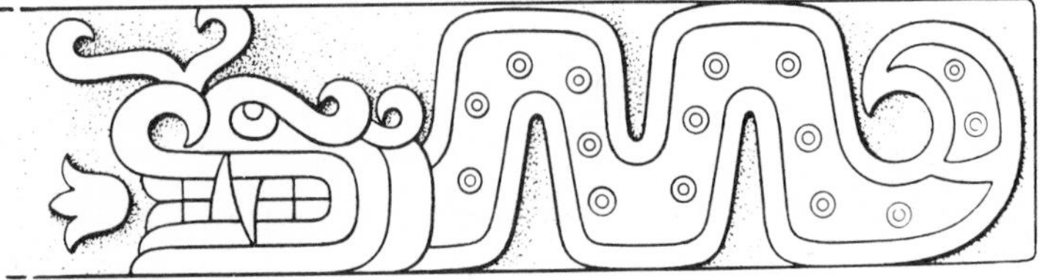

jaguars, serpents and eagles. Attributes of these animals and of human forms were intermixed in a fantastic manner to produce
257 intricate flowing designs. Although these were in themselves unique some of them recall in the most general fashion representations in the Shang art of north China. Chavin art was peculiarly adapted to and in all probability developed from the practice of stone relief sculpture. Apart from its use in the embellishment of buildings, it was applied to hammered gold, notably in Colombia, and more generally to the decoration of pottery. The view based on general analogies that the Chavin style was derived from the Olmec of Middle America in no longer in fashion. The jaguar after all is equally at home in middle and south America. More positively the Olmec and Chavin styles are individual and distinct. Yet contact between the two areas must be accepted if Middle American strains of maize in fact reached the Andean area and it may not be an entire coincidence that this should have happened around 900 B.C.

Classic or Early Intermediate

The Classic phase began in the Andean area several centuries before its counterpart in Middle America, but was yet in some respects the more advanced. Although several distinct manifestations have been recognized, the one which developed in the north coastal territory of the Andean zone may serve as an example. The Moche culture (*c.* A.D. 200–700) developed first in the Moche and Chicama valleys, but soon encompassed four others in addition. The focus of this realm was defined by monumental structures. These included a huge oblong terraced structure of sub-pyramidal form, built of adobe bricks and extending over an area of 228 by 136 metres, and a terraced platform supporting traces of a palatial structure, its walls painted with mythical scenes in Moche style. Although these have been dubbed respectively Temples of the Sun and Moon, a more plausible explanation of the latter is that it was intended to house the hierarchs who presided over the temple and indeed the realm of Moche. Traces of formidable canals traversing the arid Santa Valley suggest that this realm was sustained to a significant extent by irrigation.

Although the Andeans never adopted either hieroglyphic writing or an elaborate calendar, their technology was in some fields more precocious. For instance, whereas the Middle Americans made only sparing and tardy use of metal for tools, copper, already worked alongside gold for ornaments by the Chavin people, was employed

by the Moche population of the north coast of Peru early in the Christian era. The Classic period in the Andean zone witnessed such outstanding achievements that it has sometimes earned the designation Mastercraftsman. An exceptionally high standard was reached by the pottery of the Moche and contemporary groups. The thin-walled red ceremonial ware, often made in two-piece moulds, had plugged-in stirrup-shaped handles, displayed exceptional vir-
258 tuosity in modelling and was painted in red on a white slip. The diversity and naturalism of this pottery make it an invaluable source of information about many aspects of daily life. Among other things it tells about personal ornaments and clothing, disease, penal treatment, warfare, music-making and dancing, not to mention architecture, the deportment of rulers and mythology. Cotton and wool textiles were also outstanding. Tapestry, brocades and gauzes were turned out to fine standards. This was due in part to the high standard in the selection and spinning of fibres and in part to exceptional dexterity in weaving. Belt looms were used but a main role was played by the hands. The effect was enhanced by the use of vegetable dyes, indigo, red and yellow to orange-brown. Marked regional variation served still further to increase the richness of the crafts.

Postclassic or Middle, Late Intermediate and Late

Tiahuanaco and Huari. The several realms comprising the Andean area during the opening half of the first millennium A.D. invited the prospect of a struggle for hegemony. The Postclassic era witnessed several attempts to impose this, culminating in the success of the Incas. During the Middle stage of Andean prehistory a new cultural focus appeared at Tiahuanaco immediately south of Lake Titicaca in western Bolivia. This city had already attained some importance during the preceding era. In part no doubt this was due to the facilities for water transport and the cultivation of chinampa beds of the kind which sustained the Aztec capital of Tenochtitlan at the time of the Spanish conquest of Mexico. A feature of Postclassic architecture at Tiahuanaco was a gateway cut out of a huge monolithic block. A large relief carving over the doorway consisted of an
259 anthropomorphic figure with a jaguar jaw and a serpent head-dress holding a sceptre or staff in either hand. Flanking this Gateway God were friezes of repetitive winged figures on a smaller scale but also bearing staves. The Gateway God motive, which had suggestive antecedants in Chavin iconography, featured alongside eagle and

258 Pot in Moche style showing jaguar attacking man.

259 'Gateway God' symbol over monolithic gate at Tiahuanaco, Bolivia, and painted on vase from Peruvian coast.

jaguar designs in the repertoire of ceramic decorators and serves as a readily identifiable indicator of the Tiahuanaco style. To the south its impact was so strong as to suggest actual conquest of north-west Bolivia and as far south as the Atacama desert of northern Chile. Its spread over the rest of south Bolivia and the north-west of Argentina can reasonably be attributed to the influence of a more advanced over a more elementary culture.

It was influences from Tiahuanaco that stimulated the growth of a distinct focus of cultural and political importance based on the city of Huari in the central highlands of Peru. The rulers of Huari in turn expanded their influence and power over much of the territory north of lake Titicaca. In the north-Peruvian coastal zone this expansion was marked by the construction of rectangular enclosures built of adobe in valleys formerly dominated by the Moche culture. Although the Huari empire collapsed two hundred years or so before the end of the first millennium, its cultural influence persisted.

Chimu. The final emergence of urban as distinct from ceremonial centres defined the Late Intermediate phase of Andean prehistory and anticipated many of the features of the Inca state. The Chimu civilization which most clearly illustrates the new stage extended over some 800 kilometres of the north coastal plain. It included in a single system many river valleys and there is evidence that some of these were linked by inter-valley irrigation systems. It is likely that a road system and a network of defence posts also dates from this time. The capital city of Chanchan, situated in the midst of Chimu territory in the Moche valley covered an area of approximately 20 square
260 kilometres. Its most notable feature apart from its sheer extent was the fact that it incorporated ten or more rectangular enclosures averaging some 200×400 metres and each defended or at least defined by walls up to 12 metres high. This agglomeration of enclosures aptly symbolizes the subjection to a single urban community of a number of distinct groups. The inhabitants of Chanchan were no longer associated only by kinship or the practice of particular callings. They were citizens. As such they required administration and government. Outstandingly rich burials, not concentrated in a particular quarter but distributed among the various enclosures, may be the graves of such officials. The grave furnishings also bear witness to a skill in craftsmanship which must reflect a degree of specialization. As one example of technological advance at this time one should mention the beginning of tin-bronze metallurgy.

Inca. In the highlands broken topography and multiple sources of water made for the development of many small states. From among these the Incas of the Cuzco valley managed by their superior powers of organization and warlike qualities to rise to dominance. Under strong leaders they acquired their empire rapidly and organized it effectively. Between *c.* 1438 and 1460 they conquered most of the Peruvian highlands under their ruler Pachacuti. His son Topa Inca (1471–93) acquired much of Ecuador, the state of Chimu and later the southern coast of Peru, the highlands of Bolivia, northern Argentine and Chile north of the Maule river. The conquest of the remainder of Ecuador under the rule of Huayna Capac (1493–1527) rounded off the Inca empire which as it happened reached its peak only a short time before the arrival of the Spanish conquerors. During its brief heyday the Inca Empire was held together by a highly stratified social structure, the sanctions of religion and military force. A divine emperor was aided by an aristocracy related to him

260 Chanchan, the Chimu capital. Oblique air view showing one of ten walled enclosures.

by blood, by a priestly hierarchy and by officials who managed the extensive realm apparently without the aid of writing. At the cost of personal freedom, a concept which has after all only appeared late and in a confined area of world history, the citizens enjoyed security. Forced labour was exacted for agriculture, mining, road-making and
261 the army. Formidable terrains were harnessed by terraced agriculture and made to support cities, centres of administration and defence. An extensive system of narrow but well-engineered roads equipped at intervals with rest- and store-houses permitted runners and trains of llamas to carry orders and goods between the coastal areas and the upland basins set in sometimes precipitous highlands. The authority of the ruler and the psychic well-being of the people were ensured by religious observance. The lord of creation and of the heavenly bodies was worshipped in temples built of stone and decked with gold. The reality of religion was further impressed by calls for substantial sacrifice, on normal occasions involving such basic

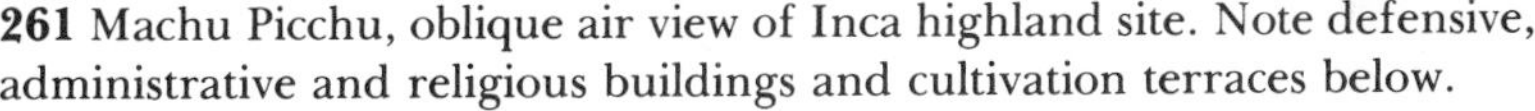

261 Machu Picchu, oblique air view of Inca highland site. Note defensive, administrative and religious buildings and cultivation terraces below.

necessities as maize, beer or llamas, but on the illness or death of the ruler calling for the very lives of women or children.

Like other empires that of the Incas had structural weaknesses. The excessive concentration of power in the hands of the living ruler, combined with the fact that having many wives he was likely to have several potential heirs, meant that crises were probable at the end of each reign. As ill-luck would have it the Spaniards under Pizarro arrived precisely during such a crisis of succession. Atahuallpa had no sooner revolted with success against the new emperor, his half-brother Huascar, than he was himself seized by Pizarro (1532). The crisis of succession may have made things easier for the Spaniards, but it was the weakness of Inca technology combined with a lack of immunity to European infections that proved fatal to the native inhabitants of Peru. Although they were ahead of the rest of the New World in respect of bronze metallurgy, their lack of iron, but still more of gunpowder, was decisive. Like that of the Aztecs the empire of the Incas was cut off at the height of its glory. In their own environment the Incas were supreme. Confronted by a superior technology and representatives of a politically more effective civilization who at the same time introduced lethal diseases they were unable to retain their independence.

Intermediate zone

The rather lowly and parochial developments attained in the extensive and varied territories which separate Middle America from the Andean highlands help to confirm the substantial independence of the two most notable foci of Amerindian cultural achievement. The territory, which stretches from Ecuador to Colombia and Venezuela with a northward extension through the isthmus of Panama, never attained anything like the level of social sophistication which so astounded the Spaniards at Cuzco and Tenochtitlan. Yet archaeology shows that the several regions comprising this territory contributed in their own ways to the overall pattern of New World culture. Again, the intermediate zone offers an important clue to one of the basic problems of New World archaeology, that is precisely how interchanges were apparently effected between the Middle American and Andean centres. We know that at some time cotton cultivation for instance spread north and that improved strains of maize, possibly accompanied by elements of the Olmec style, moved in the opposite direction early in the first millennium B.C. There is a strong suggestion that they travelled by sea.

The antiquity of coastal settlement in South America had already been emphasized in respect of Peru. There the survival of organic residues made it possible to demonstrate that plants were being domesticated long before pottery came into use around 1800 B.C. Further north on the Caribbean coast of Colombia and the Pacific coast of Ecuador, on the contrary, pottery was taken into use as early as *c.* 3000 B.C., that is about seven centuries earlier than in Middle America, among people who still depended exclusively on hunting, fishing and foraging. The shell mounds of Puerto Hormiga which began to form at this time yielded remains of small animals like birds, reptiles and rodents, as well as freshwater and especially estuarine fish and the stone grinding equipment that went with the preparation of plant food. If such resources were hardly exciting, at least they had the merit of being reliable. This meant that relatively stable settlement was possible and it is interesting that the middens show signs of having been levelled to provide platforms or floors. In such a sedentary context it is no surprise to find evidence of pottery in the form of fibre-tempered bowls ornamented on occasion by incised grooves and dentate shell impressions.

503 The pottery from Valdivia and other sites on the coast of Ecuador was characteristically grey in colour, sometimes had a red slip and might be ornamented by incised or punctuate designs. Analogies in the ornament on Valdivia pottery and on the Jōmon ware from Japan have led some scholars to think in terms of a trans-Pacific spread, which on account of the high Japanese dates for pottery must be presumed to have moved from Asia to the New World. The antiquity of pottery on the Caribbean coast suggests a more economical explanation, namely that potting was invented in many places where for one reason or another a sedentary life was possible. In any case the value of analogies between elementary motifs selected from ceramic repertoires separated by the Pacific Ocean is dubious. The possibility of trans-Pacific contacts cannot be entirely ruled out, though it has certainly not yet been proved. It is known from a study of fish-bones from Jōmon middens that fishermen ventured to distant fishing grounds at certain seasons. If most Japanese craft caught in the West Wind Drift and carried across the north Pacific would have been swept back east off the south Californian coast, some might have been carried along the isthmus coast by the North-west Monsoon Drift. In this case they would have hit precisely the Pacific coast of Ecuador. The recovery of mainland pottery on the Galapagos Islands some six hundred miles west of South America is a reminder from the

American side of the range of early boats. In this connection, the presence of deep-sea fish in the Ecuadoran middens argues for the use of boats on the open sea. To judge from pottery representations of boats made in Gallinazo and Moche wares, and from wooden centre-boards and steering sweeps from later burials in the same area it is evident that vessels resembling the prowed balsa rafts still in use off the Peruvian coast appeared at a relatively early period. Whatever the truth of this matter, the genesis of Valdivian pottery is hardly to be accounted of much importance at a time when interest is focused on such topics as ecological adaptation and developmental process.

Maize evidently reached the Ecuadoran coast during the Formative stage of the region between 1500 and 500 B.C., but settlement remained at the village level and there was no sign of any substantial advance in technology. Pottery vessels might now be painted in several colours, and the potters also made figurines, whistles, stamps and spindle-whorls. Copper was used for such small things as finger-rings, fish-hooks and eyed needles, but these were hammered, never cast. The use of shell, as well as polished stone, for adzes from Ecuador to Venezuela is of special interest since shell adzes are known from several early sites in the Greater Antilles and Florida. The peculiar distribution of the various components of the fauna of the Antilles has been plausibly explained by supposing that the animals were dispersed involuntarily on natural rafts borne on strong northward currents issuing from the mouths of the Magdalena and
505 Orinoco rivers. It is reasonable to suggest that the islands may have been colonized by man in the first instance through fishing craft being carried by the same currents.

During the thousand years which intervened between the end of the Formative period in the Intermediate area and the arrival of the Spaniards social structures underwent only limited changes. Petty chieftains occupied small townships at the centre of networks of village settlements and marked their superior status in death by carved stelae and elaborate tombs and in life by jewellery of gold and other metals. The burial chambers of San Agustín in the highlands of south Ecuador were covered by mounds and decorated inside by brightly painted designs. The tombs of chieftains were further identified by stelae carved with figures that might combine the
262 attributes of men and jaguars. Their patronage called into being specialized metallurgical craftsmen in copper as well as gold and silver. In Ecuador, but above all in Colombia where supplies of the

metal were richer, gold-smiths employed the lost wax method as well as practising hammering, soldering and annealing. Luxury objects in gold, some of the outstanding examples of which come from
504 Tairona in the Santa Marta region of Colombia, included flasks and
263 bottles, masks and jewellery, notably pendants depicting human forms of outstanding aesthetic power. The still fragmented nature of society in the Late period of the Intermediate area is reflected in the marked individuality of style of analogous artefacts from the various cultural groups, a point well made by comparing with the Tairona pendant figures ones made from stone or pottery from the
264 Valencia culture of Venezuela. The local diversity of cultural expres-
506 sion during the final stages in the prehistory of the Intermediate zone contrasts markedly with the degree of conformity prevailing in

262 Stela carved with figure combining human and jaguar attributes, San Agustin, Colombia.

the more advanced polities of the Andean zone of Middle America at the same time.

Marginal territories

N. Chile and Argentina

Over much the greater part of South America the Indians were living at the time of the Portuguese and Spanish conquest and settlement at an even more modest level than that prevailing in the Intermediate zone. In the south Andes cultures of an Archaic pattern prevailed until the middle of the first millennium B.C. with an emphasis on fishing and the hunting of sea-mammals on the coast and on the hunting of deer and guanaco, a kind of llama, in the interior highlands. Pottery and farming were adopted during the Early Ceramic period (500 B.C. to A.D. 600). In the northern part of the territory the influence of the Tiahuanaco culture centred on the south Titicaca area of Bolivia was strongly felt. The appearance of fortified towns during the Late Ceramic (A.D. 1000–1450) suggests the existence by this time of petty chiefdoms but none of these achieved prominence before being subject to the influence of Inca civilization. East of the Andes, pottery appeared first in Uraguay and adjacent parts of

263 Cast gold pendant in Tairona style, Colombia.

Argentina about the time of the birth of Christ, but in the south of Buenos Aires province it did not arrive till the middle of the first millennium and further south still, in north Patagonia, not until the latter half. In the extreme south of the continent, as we shall see, the hunter-fisher economy maintained its superiority down to modern times.

East Brazil

East Brazil was another country in which the manufacture of pottery was not adopted until the first millennium B.C. and then to begin with only in the coastal zone. The region was first colonized by hunting bands at the transition from Late Pleistocene to Neothermal times. By *c.* 5000 B.C. there is evidence from the shell mounds or sambaqui sites that intensive exploitation of coastal resources had begun. Finds from the middens include edge-ground and later polished-stone axes which may have been used in boat-making. Indications that life afforded leisure for inessentials is provided by stone palettes shaped and polished in the form of birds, fish and mammals and bearing on one face a shallow hollow perhaps intended for grinding pigment. What economic changes, if any, accompanied the introduction of

264 Pottery figure in Valencia style, Venezuela.

Periperi pottery, comprising simple bowl forms without decoration, is unknown. We are little better informed about the communities who made Taquara pottery during the latter half of the first millennium A.D. except that they sometimes lived in pit-houses, decorated their handmade pottery with punctate and impressed ornament and built low burial mounds, groups of which they sometimes enclosed in low banks. The first firm clue to subsistence dates from early in the second millennium when impressed and rusticated pottery was supplemented by polychrome painted Tupiguarani ware. The consistent occurrence of this ware in low-lying forested landscapes suggests that the people were engaged in slash and burn agriculture. This is confirmed by the occurrence of manioc riddles and it is interesting to note that Tupiguarani ware is paralleled in Amazonia where this crop was first domesticated. The Indians continued to produce handmade pottery during the Portuguese period, decorating it with punctate and rusticated ornament but borrowing flat bases and shoulder lugs from the Europeans.

Amazon basin

Since the low-lying areas of the Amazon basin are covered by stoneless silts, the early inhabitants had to depend as far as possible on equipment made from organic materials. The apparent absence of typologically archaic lithic assemblages does not therefore preclude settlement at an early period. The fact remains that the earliest evidence available to archaeologists comprises pottery decorated in a Zoned Hachure style with deeply incised geometric patterns including step frets. Pottery of this style is known from the upper courses of tributaries of the Amazon, the Napo in Ecuador and the Ucayali in Peru. Zoned Hachure ware from Tutishcainyo on the Ucayali has been assigned to the earlier half of the second millennium B.C. on the basis of typological analogies with other sites in Peru. Since occurrences on the Amazon and on Marajo Island at the estuary date to the first millennium it looks as though this pottery came in from the highlands and moved downstream. Food refuse from Ponta do Jauari just above the junction with the Tapajos suggests that the inhabitants of the lower Amazon at this time hunted tapir, bush pig, turtle and alligator as well as catching fish. Rubbing stones suggest the use of plant food, but it was not until Incised Rim ware had come into use (*c.* A.D. 400–900) that the first evidence for manioc in the form of riddles is available. An indication that the basin may have been penetrated also from the estuary is given by the appearance during the first half of the second millennium of polychrome pottery closely resembling the Tupiguarani ware of East Brazil. It was during this time that monumental structures first appeared in the shape of building platforms and burial mounds that might be as broad as 30 m, as long as 255 m and as high as 10 m, a testimony to effective food-production, but not necessarily to a stratified society.

The equatorial rain forest of the Amazon basin has sheltered down to modern times communities of Indians whose way of life would have been deemed Neolithic by archaeologists excavating their abandoned settlements. Their economy depends primarily on slash and burn agriculture involving clearance of forest and undergrowth by axe and fire and a persistent struggle against vegetation encroaching on the cultivated plots. The natural fertility compounded by the potash from burning timber makes the soil highly productive for two or three years, but the regime involves the frequent clearance and taking into cultivation of new ground. The most important crop is manioc, a plant indigenous to the area, which responded to domestication by growing substantially larger roots. Subsidiary cultigens include sweet potato, yams and pumpkins. Maize was introduced from outside and although handicapped by excessive moisture is widely cultivated, perhaps in part for reasons of prestige. Plants are used for a variety of other purposes. Coca and tobacco serve for narcotics, the qualities of rubber latex are exploited to make such things as balls and syringes, and fibres are utilized for basketry and the netting for hammocks and for fishing. In addition a number of poisons are secured for use in hunting and fishing. Animal protein is obtained in part through hunting bush pig, sloth and tapir with poison-tipped wooden spears and traps. Monkeys and birds are secured by the use of the blow-gun and poisoned darts. Fishing is pursued with varying resolution by different groups using trident-spears, hooks made from palm spines or bone, and nets.

People live in communities of between fifty and two hundred persons, each housed as a rule in a single communal building having a roof thatched with palm leaves extending almost to the ground and supported on timber posts up to thirty feet tall. Since settlements are changed at fairly frequent intervals in the course of shifting agriculture houses are not repaired but abandoned in favour of new ones. Although for most purposes self-sufficient, such communities are exogamous and it could well be that the presence of pots with exotic decoration is due to the introduction of foreign wives rather than to barter. On the other hand it is certain that materials not available locally can only have been obtained from a distance, notably salt and the grooved and polished stone axe-blades without which forest clearance and the preparation of house-posts and dug-out boats could hardly have been carried on. Since the forest is almost impassable contact must be achieved mainly by boat.

499, 502 *S. Patagonia and Tierra del Fuego*

The Tehuelche and the Ona who occupied Patagonia and all but the Pacific fringe of Tierra del Fuego during the historic period had no domestic animals other than the dogs used in hunting. They gathered plants but did not cultivate them. Their principal quarry was the guanaco and the ostrich-like rhea. For weapons they formerly depended mainly on the bow, but with the introduction of the horse early in the eighteenth century came to rely more on the bolas, a device comprising three stones linked by cords which could be hurled at the quarry. Although the pemmican made by combining dried and pulverized guanaco meat with rhea fat gave some security against the immediacy of dearth, the Pampean economy involved constant movement and prevented more than a rudimentary social structure. The Tehuelche bands were split into *tolderia* each comprising four or five families of about five persons. Since each band occupied around a hundred miles of coast and its hinterland, it follows that the density of population was a very low one. To judge from the succession of deposits starting with the third and fourth levels in the Palli Aike and Fell's caves on the Magellan Strait guanaco hunting appears to have been the backbone of Pampean economy already far back in the Neothermal. At this time the guanaco hunters still depended on lances with bifacially-flaked heads of triangular or square ended lanceolate forms, but grooved bolas stones were already in use as an ancillary weapon.

A discovery on Englefield Island in the Bay of Otway situated in the archipelago off the coast of southern Chile suggests that in the earlier part of Neothermal time the Pampean style of hunting-culture had reached the Pacific coast at the extreme tip of South America.
265 The bifacially-flaked projectile heads and grooved bolas stones compare with ones from Magellan III deposits. Bone equipment included awls, spatulae, single-barbed harpoon-heads of Magellan V type and bone points barbed down one edge. The last two of these featured
266 in the hunting equipment of the Yahgan canoe Indians encountered by European explorers of the Pacific archipelago off Tierra del Fuego. They spanned a major adaptation. In order to colonize this

rugged archipelago at the ultimate extremity of South America it was necessary to change from hunting on land to marine hunting from canoes. Prehistoric phases of an an economy based on shell-fish and marine birds, fish and mammals, are documented in middens strung along the Beagle Channel between Tierra del Fuego and the mainland. Two of the recurrent artefacts from these are knives made from chorro mussel shells and the single-barbed harpoon-heads

265 Early artefacts from Englefield Island, South Chile, and recent Yahgan harpoon.

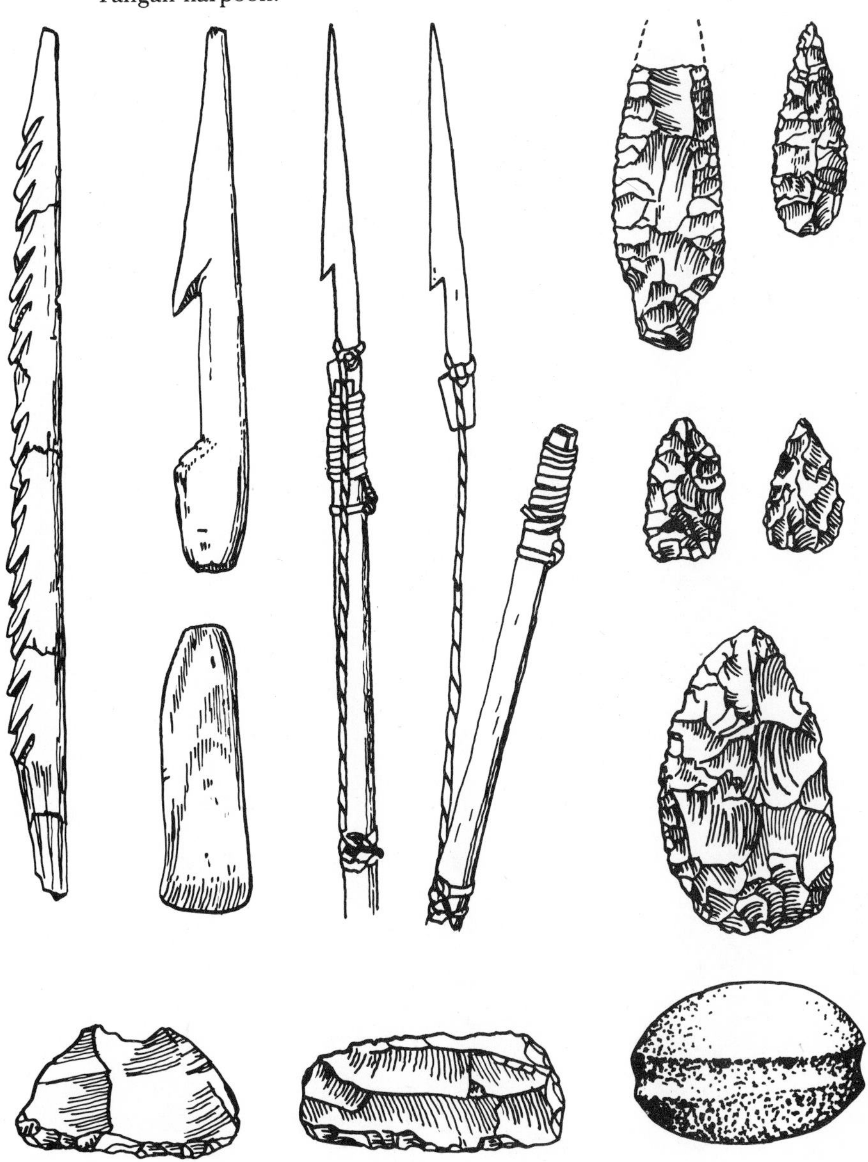

already noted as a link between early prehistoric and recent Fuegians.

Whether one agrees with Charles Darwin that these people were among the most miserable of men depends on one's point of view. At a biological level the Yahgans could claim some success. They not merely stood at the head of a food-chain at the time of their discovery by Europeans: archaeology shows that for thousands of years they had maintained a well-adjusted relationship to an environment

266 Yahgan Indian with spear mounted with barbed bone point.

which to a European even of Darwin's enterprise appeared forbidding. Moreover they did so with only the most meagre equipment. For instance neither they nor their prehistoric forbears had fish-hooks. This did not prevent them catching fish on baited lines by jerking them out of the sea, just as they caught cormorants by grabbing them in the hand as they roosted. Again, their basis of subsistence confined them to the society of small groups. For most of the year these were dispersed and restricted to only the scantiest possessions. In terms of human potential, at least as this is judged from a privileged position in a civilized society, their lives might appear wretched. Yet their compensations in personal relations, play and games, shamanistic rituals and mythology, however rudimentary, were arguably more intense and satisfying than the more diverse but superficial distractions of all but the upper levels of modern urban populations. One thing the Fuegians assuredly did not have and that was a future. Like so many heirs of the primitive societies of remote antiquity the Fuegians were only equipped to maintain and perpetuate their systems in isolation. Contact with peoples with a more potent culture was mortal. The land-based Ona sank from two thousand in the last quarter of the nineteenth century to less than a hundred by the mid-nineteen twenties and the canoe Yahgan from between two thousand five hundred and three thousand during the third quarter to two hundred by the end of the nineteenth century and less than forty by 1933.

11

Australia and Oceania

Australia

Ecological context of early immigrations and settlement

In respect of geological time Australia might be counted a peninsula of south-east Asia, the source of all its native plants and animals, yet the very facts of biogeography show that it was effectively cut off as an island continent at a period remote in terms of human prehistory. The native flora of Australia recalls that of the Secondary era and the fauna includes in monotremes and marsupials the most primitive of the three sub-classes into which the mammals are divided. These backward forms of life survived because their competitors were effectively kept at bay by sea breaks. Even at the peaks of glaciation, when ocean levels stood so much lower than they do today that the Indonesian islands were joined to the Asian mainland by the Sunda shelf, the deep channels between Borneo and Lombok formed barriers to the migration of animals and plants. It is true that some Asiatic species managed to traverse this Wallace line, but there is no evidence that any jumped the gap defined by Weber between the Celebes and the Moluccas.

One explanation for the effectiveness of these breaks may be found in the flow of ocean currents. Whereas in the western hemisphere the strong westward drift of the north equatorial currents played an active part in the involuntary transport of plants, animals and men from the estuaries of Venezuela to the West Indian islands, in the case of Australia and south-east Asia the same westward drift played a negative or inhibiting role. With ocean levels as they exist today currents flow from east to west between New Guinea and Australia and again between the main Indonesian islands until deflected north by the Asian mainland. During the mainland period currents presumably also flowed west, though then passing north of New Guinea and joining that which still flows north along the Wallace divide.

For man to have broken through the barrier, accompanied at least at a late stage by his dogs, his movement must, it would seem, have been intentional rather than accidental. The drive of organisms to explore their environment is after all a commonplace of ethology. In the case of man it is something to which all prehistory testifies, not least that of the New World, Australia and the Pacific. To reach
525 Australia must at any time have involved the use of sea-going craft. In the early stages at least it is a reasonable hypothesis that sea-passages were most liable to be undertaken when the gaps were at their narrowest, more especially when it is remembered that they had often to be made in the teeth of contrary currents. The earlier man's arrival in Australia is held to be, the more primitive the craft might be expected to have been and the more likely it is that man arrived during a mainland phase. The converse also follows that until modern times communication is likely to have been at its most tenuous, if not entirely suspended, during periods of high ocean levels.

A main clue to fluctuations in the accessibility of Australia to early man lies in the growth and retreat of the Pleistocene ice-sheets, since it was the water locked up in and released by these that determined the eustatic fall and rise of ocean levels. During the last interglacial between 100,000 and 65,000 years ago ocean levels rose at times even above those at which they stand today. Access was easier during the last glaciation, but only noticeably so during its colder phases, that is during the Early and Main Würm, to use designations taken from
54: fig. 12 the Swiss Alpine sequence. On the basis of Emiliani's correlations with palaeoclimatic curves derived from ocean cores these date respectively from *c.* 65,000 to 50,000 B.P. and from *c.* 30,000 to 12,000 B.P. When samples from known depths below modern sea-levels are precisely dated by radiocarbon these sometimes reveal local anomalies which in turn throw light on other factors, notably upward or downward warping of individual land-masses. Making all allowance for local anomalies a reasonably convincing picture now exists for the course of geographical change following on the contraction of the Main Würm glaciation. The rise of ocean levels and the growing isolation of the continent since 16,000 B.P. is well documented from the Great Australian Bight. More observations are needed before the most favourable periods for migration for south-east Asia can be accurately defined.

Systematic application of radiocarbon dating has already made

it certain that much of Australia was colonized during the Main Würm (or Late Wisconsin) period. Although, when aggregated, finds of artefacts, hearths and human skeletal material dating from the Late Pleistocene are impressive, they are not yet sufficiently numerous to define the course of the immigration in detail. The fact that the sequence at Lake Mungo began some few thousand years earlier than the oldest find yet dated from the New Guinea province of Greater Australia, that from Kosipe in the Papuan Highlands, is an anomaly which further research will doubtless rectify. The interesting point is that such early dates should have been obtained from so far south. The present pattern of dates argues that the more desirable parts of the continent were filled up rather rapidly, something which accords well with the theoretical rate at which population can increase in the absence of constraints. Assuming an initial group of only twenty-five persons, not unreasonable in view of the common
511 size of early social groups, Birdsell concluded that on the basis of an aboriginal generation of sixteen years the continent would have

267 Radiocarbon dates for Late Pleistocene Settlement in Australia.

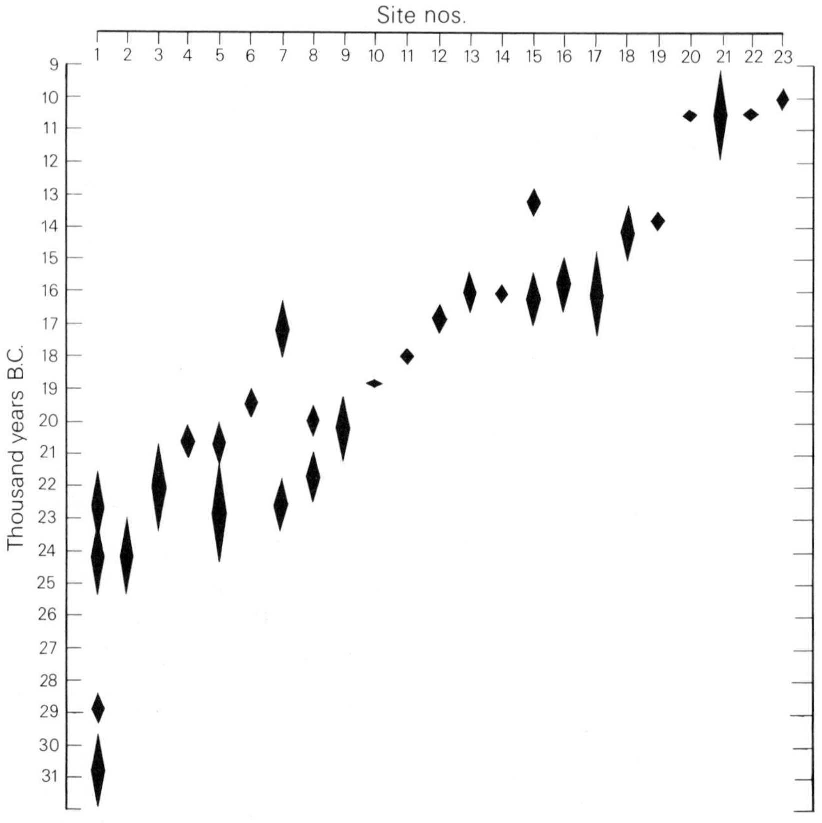

filled up to the level existing at the beginning of the colonial period, when the total is commonly set at three hundred thousand, within little more than two thousand years.

Comparatively few hard facts are yet established about the course
544 of environmental change since Australia was first occupied by man. One of the few topics about which much is known from local observation is the course of the marine transgression which insulated Tasmania from the mainland by the Bass Strait probably between 12,000 and 13,000 years ago and formed the Torres Strait separating New Guinea from Queensland perhaps as recently as 6,500–8,000 years ago. One of the incidental outcomes of this transgression is that traces of coastal settlement began to be flooded over and so lost to

Table 30. *Radiocarbon dates for Pleistocene Australia* (*see Fig. 267*)

Locality	Data	Ref. No.	B.C.
1. L. Mungo	Cremation burial	ANU 618b	22,760 ± *c.* 1,200
	Occupation	ANU 375b	24,300 ± 1,120
	Occupation	ANU 680	28,830 ± 520
	Occupation	ANU 331	30,800 ± 1,250
2. L. Yantara	Hearth	GaK 2121	24,250 ± 1,100
3. L. Leaghur	Shell midden	ANU 372a	22,070 ± 1,300
4. L. Arumpo	Shell midden	N 1664	20,650 ± 430
5. Malangangerr, Oenpelli	Ground axes	GaK 629	20,750 ± 700
	Ground axes	ANU 77a	22,850 ± 1,600
6. Nawamoyn, Oenpelli	Ground axes	ANU 51	19,500 ± 380
7. Devil's Lair	Occupation	SUA 33	17,300 ± 900
	Occupation	SUA 31	22,650 ± 800
8. Koonalda	Rock art	ANU 245	19,950 ± 450
	Rock art	ANU 244	21,750 ± 850
9. King's Table	Occupation	SUA 158	20,290 ± 1,000
10. Burrill Lake	Rock shelter	ANU 137	18,810 ± 80
11. Lindner Site	Occupation	SUA 237	17,950 ± 280
12. Kenniff Cave	Early occupation	ANU 345	16,850 ± 480
13. Keilor	Occupation of terrace	NZ 207	16,050 ± 500
14. Malakunanja	Occupation	SUA 265	16,090 ± 320
15. L. Victoria	Midden	GaK 2525	13,350 ± 500
	Hearth	GaK 2514	16,250 ± 800
16. Clogg's Cave	Early occupation	ANU 840	15,770 ± 840
17. Miriwun	Occupation	ANU 1008	16,030 ± *c.* 1,200
18. Seton, Kangaroo Is.	Fauna, bone tools	ANU 1221	14,150 ± 1,000
19. Bass Pt.	Open site	ANU 536	13,830 ± 300
20. Noola Shelter	Occupation	V 35	10,600 ± 185
21. L. Tandou	Midden	ANU 705	10,400 ± 170
	Cremation burial	ANU 703	10,580 ± 1,500
22. Lyre Bird Dell	Occupation	SUA 15	10,600 ± 145
23. Walls Cave	Earliest occupation	GaK 3448	10,050 ± 350
Addendum			
Not shown. Cave Bay, Hunter Is.	Charcoal	ANU 1361	18,550 ± 600

archaeology from the time when it began around 18,000 years ago. In respect of the biosphere, easy generalizations involving the shift of climatic zones are no longer acceptable. As a working hypothesis it is perhaps wisest to assume in default of evidence to the contrary that the broad picture was much the same during at least the latter part of prehistory as it is today. The main constraint on population in Australia has always been and still is not merely the mean average but the reliability of rainfall, though it may be emphasized that economies based on hunting and foraging were more elastic in this respect than ones involving permanent residence. It is interesting to note that the earliest radiocarbon dates are concentrated in the zone of heaviest and most reliable rainfall in northern, eastern, south-eastern and extreme south-western Australia. There is no present evidence that the arid interior, comprising nearly two fifths of the continent, in which rainfall was low (under 250 mm) and uncertain, ever carried more than a sparse population. In between were territories still risky for farmers or even graziers, but relatively favourable for people living by hunting and foraging.

Any discussion of the Australian biosphere should take account of the extent that it has been affected by human activities. The clearance of native vegetation and the destruction of native animals proceeded apace as the zone of settlement advanced during the colonial period. There can hardly be any doubt that the process began, though at a much slower rate, during prehistoric times, not merely through predation, but probably much more effectively
524 through the use of fire throughout the period of human occupation. This must have affected vegetation most directly, but by giving advantage to the hunter and modifying the ecology it is likely also to have made its impact on animal life. Although this did not happen until quite late, the introduction of the dog is also likely to have advantaged the hunter at the expense of his prey. A question still to be resolved is whether the extinction of the Australian megafauna, including the giant marsupials, the largest of which, *Diprotodon*, was the size of a large rhinoceros, the large wombat *Phascolomys* and a number of large flightless birds, was directly or indirectly due to man. All that need be said at the moment is that no specimens of these particular animals have been certainly dated to the period of human occupation, still less numbered among his prey.

535, 536, 555 Although impresive additions have recently been made to the still meagre record of fossil man in Australia, many of these are still in course of detailed study and the dating of most of the earlier finds is problematic. Yet it is already clear that the available fossils fall into
269 two main morphological groups. Of these the Talgai group, which
556 also includes a burial from Mossgiel and upwards of forty from Kow Swamp near Cohuna, although clearly sapient, retains a number of
537 archaic features. The large mandibles and palates, broad prognathic

268 Key prehistoric sites in Australia.

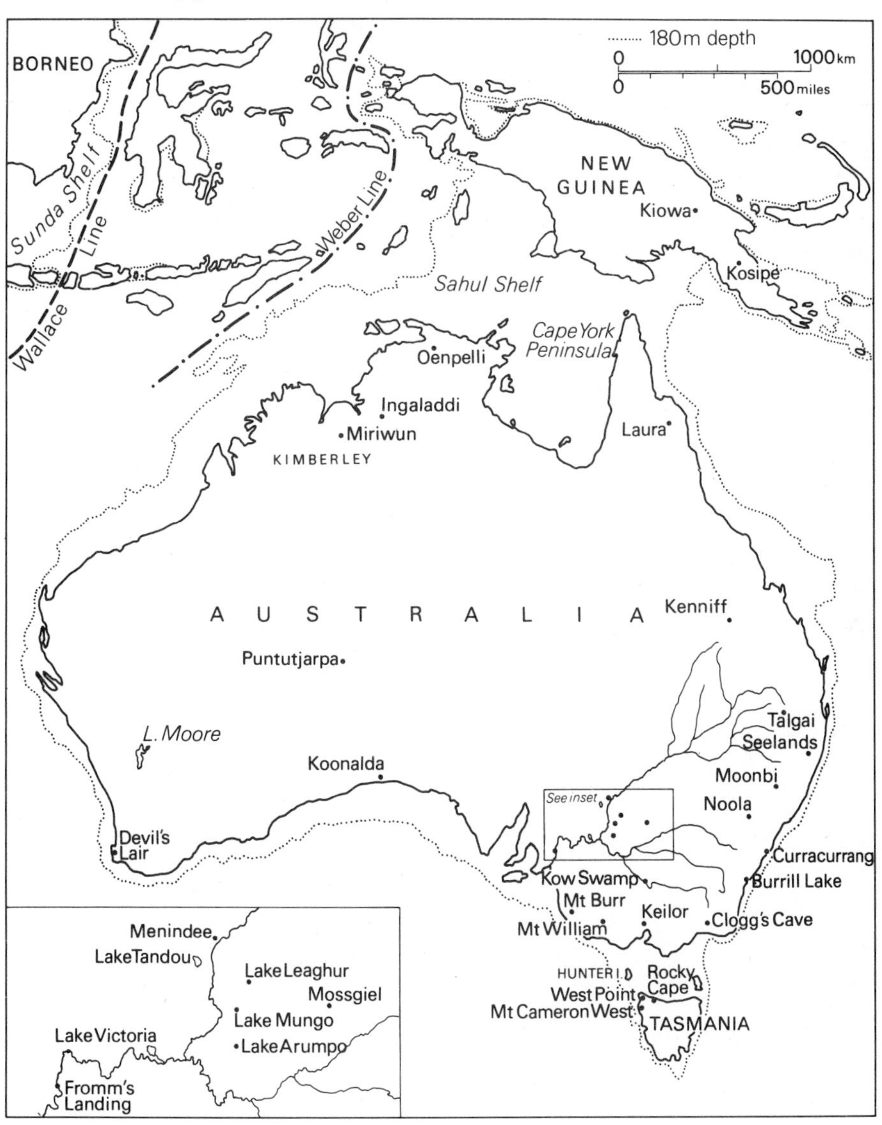

faces, thick and rather low cranial vaults, receding frontal bones and prominent brow ridges are all features shared with the fossils of *Homo sapiens Soloensis* from Ngandong in the Solo Valley, Java, a Late Pleistocene form which retains certain features present in fossils of the eastern group of *Homo erectus* recovered from Middle Pleistocene deposits in the same island. Carbonate still adhering to the cranium from Talgai dates from around 8900 B.C., but this only provides a minimum age for the fossil itself. Of the Mossgiel burial it is simply known that it is older than *c.* 2850 B.C. The most promising body of material is that from Kow Swamp, one fossil from which is firmly dated in terms of radiocarbon to 8120±250 B.C.

The Keilor type, also known from the nearby site of Green Gully and from Lake Mungo, differs in presenting what to a European is a more modern look. The frontal bone is fuller and more rounded, the vault better filled, the brow ridge less prominent, the palate and teeth are smaller and there is an absence of prognathism. In all these
429 respects it compares closely with the skulls from Wadjak in Java generally assigned to the early Holocene.

Perhaps it is only by chance that the few dates at present available point to the more modern type being the earlier of the two. Neither the Keilor cranium nor the Green Gully burial can be dated precisely, but radiocarbon analyses of the bones suggest that the former dates from around 11,000 and the latter 4,500 B.C. The surprise comes with the age of the cremated remains of a woman from an eroded dune

269 Outlines of fossil crania from Australia showing contrasts in the area of the forehead between the Talgai and Keilor groups.

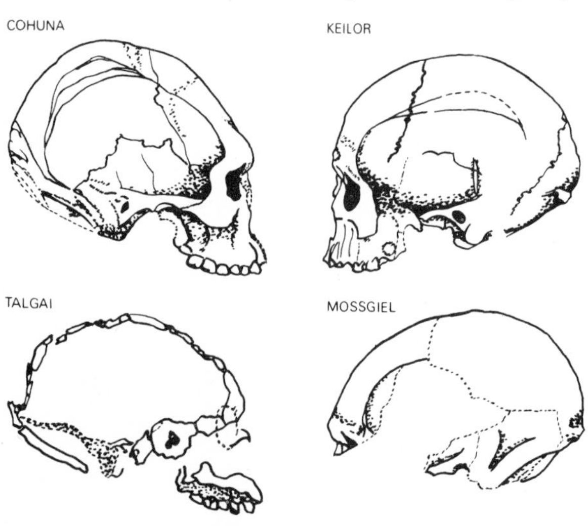

on the shore of the extinct Lake Mungo. Radiocarbon analysis of the
512, 513 bone collagen and from charcoal from a hearth at a level only 15
cm higher up yields dates which overlap 23,550±100 B.C. Whatever
problems the Mungo burial raises, it shows plainly that fully sapient
humans reached Australia during the Late-glacial mainland period.
Another point of outstanding interest is that whatever future discoveries have to say in respect of the first appearance of the Talgai
type, it is certain that the archaic form represented at Kow Swamp
was still flourishing in the Cohuna region as late as around ten
thousand years ago.

The arrival of man in a sapient form more than thirty thousand years ago in terms of radiocarbon is now an established fact. The question remains whether the original settlers were reinforced during prehistoric times by new immigrants. To reason for renewed contact with Indonesia from the mere fact that new forms and techniques of stone-working to appear late in the Australian Stone Age present analogies to finds from Indonesia is to prejudge the very question at issue, whether cultural evolution proceeded on parallel lines or whether observed similarities are to be explained in terms of cultural contact. One body of evidence not open to this circular reasoning is that provided by the occurrence of dog in prehistoric Australia, since it is a fair assumption that *Canis familiaris*, by definition a human domesticate, was brought to Australia by man. Dogs can hardly have been introduced by the first settlers since they had not by then been brought into existence. In any case the distribution of dogs, above all their absence from both Tasmania and New Guinea, argues that they did not arrive until after the insulation of each of these territories from continental Australia. Since New Guinea was not cut off until between eight and six thousand five
hundred years ago, this sets an upper limit to the time of arrival.
526 To judge from what happened in Tasmania at the beginning of
the nineteenth century, when the aborigines are known to have appropriated dogs for hunting in packs within two years of the first introduction of these animals, it seems likely that dogs would have overrun the continent soon after their first arrival. The reported occurrence of dog from about five thousand years ago at Mt Burr in South Australia may well be confirmed. On the other hand the
earliest occurrence stratigraphically established beyond doubt is the
270 skeleton in a good state of preservation from a level in the well-defined
546: 498–507 sequence at Fromm's Landing on the Lower Murray river which
dates from the end of the second millennium B.C.

The existence of two contrasting physical types in the fossil record highlights a main theme of Australian prehistory, namely the extent to which the people and their culture were the outcome of a single or multiple spread. In respect of the physical population there are many gaps in the evidence. The fossil record, although greatly increased during the last few years, is still very defective in respect of accurately dated material sufficient in bulk for modern analysis. Even in respect of the recent aboriginal population precise information about the range of variability in different parts of the continent leaves much to be desired. If the formulation of hypotheses like Birdsell's three waves (Negritoid/Tasmanoid, Caucasoid/Murrayian and Australoid/Carpentarian) serves no other purpose than to stimulate the recovery and study of more data, something which in respect of fossil material is most likely to come from archaeological excavations, it will not have been in vain. Meanwhile those who adhere to the idea that for example the Tasmanians were the outcome of genetic variation from a common south Australian prototype during the eleven or twelve millennia since the island was cut off from the mainland, are entitled to feel that they have a more economical explanation for two of Birdsell's groups. The archaeological data meanwhile suggest that certain cultural elements which may or may not have been accompanied by ethnic movement reached Australia at a fairly advanced stage of Neothermal time.

270 Skeleton of dog from Fromm's landing 6, Lower Murray river.

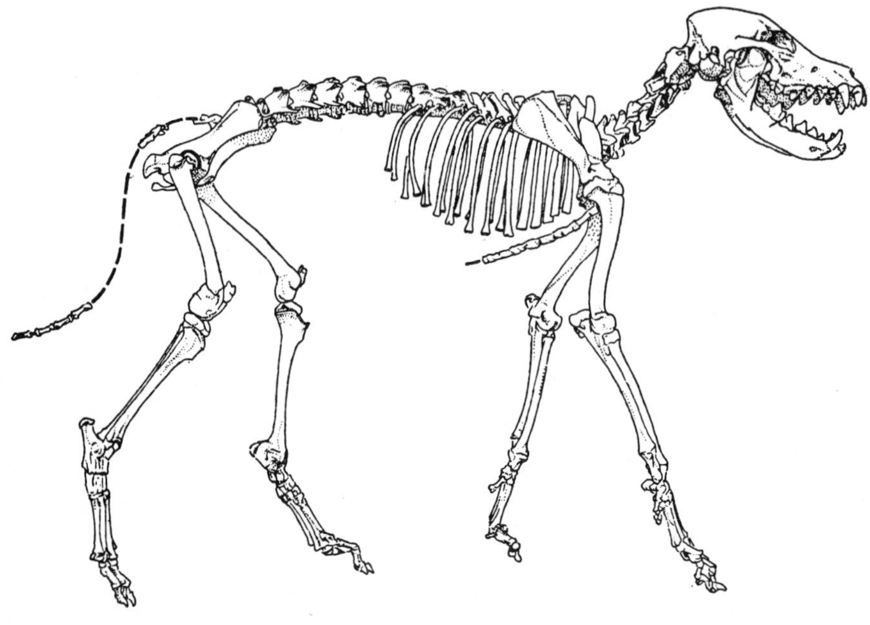

15, 534, 541, ***Earlier Stone Age.*** The stone industries, which in Australia as else-
543 where form the most persistent thread of archaeological evidence surviving from the whole range of human prehistory, fall into two main categories. The earlier is elementary and generalized in character, occurs over the whole of the territory occupied by man in Australia and Tasmania and superficially at least displays no clear cut change in the course of its long history. The industrial tradition brought in by the early immigrants was first noticeably enriched by
548 new forms and techniques, including points, backed blades and burins, around five thousand years ago. The extent to which the later phase of the Australian Stone Age was the product of external stimuli is still open to research. Of the arrival of new traits derived immediately from proximate parts of Indonesia there can be little doubt. It has already been noted that the dog was introduced about this time by man. It is significant that neither the dog nor the new lithic forms appeared in Tasmania during the prehistoric period. If backed blades and other forms were the outcome of indigenous development there seems no good reason why they should not have emerged in Tasmania as well as on the mainland. Again, it is suggestive that certain of the novel forms are known from proximate parts of Indonesia, one reason why Australian prehistorians have

271 Kenniff Cave, Queensland: section showing deposits from two main phases of occupation with a break between *c.* 3000–8000 B.C.

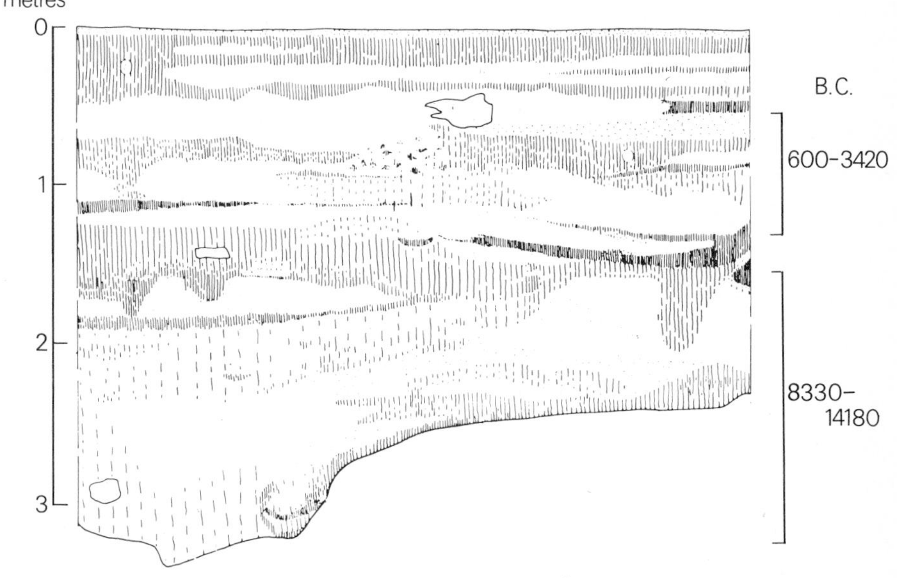

been attracted to the region. This is not to say that indigenous development contributed nothing to the later phase of the Stone Age of continental Australia. It may well prove that the effect of external contact was to stimulate local inventiveness as much as to promote the immediate adoption of new techniques. The existence of succes-
545 sive phases was suggested in the first instance by stratigraphic
271 sequences, the most important of which was that observed at Kenniff

272 Stone implements from the earlier phase of the Australian Stone Age: (1–4) scraping equipment, Lake Mungo, New South Wales; (5) horsehoof core, Port Augusta, South Australia; (6) uniface pebble tool, Kangaroo Island, South Australia.

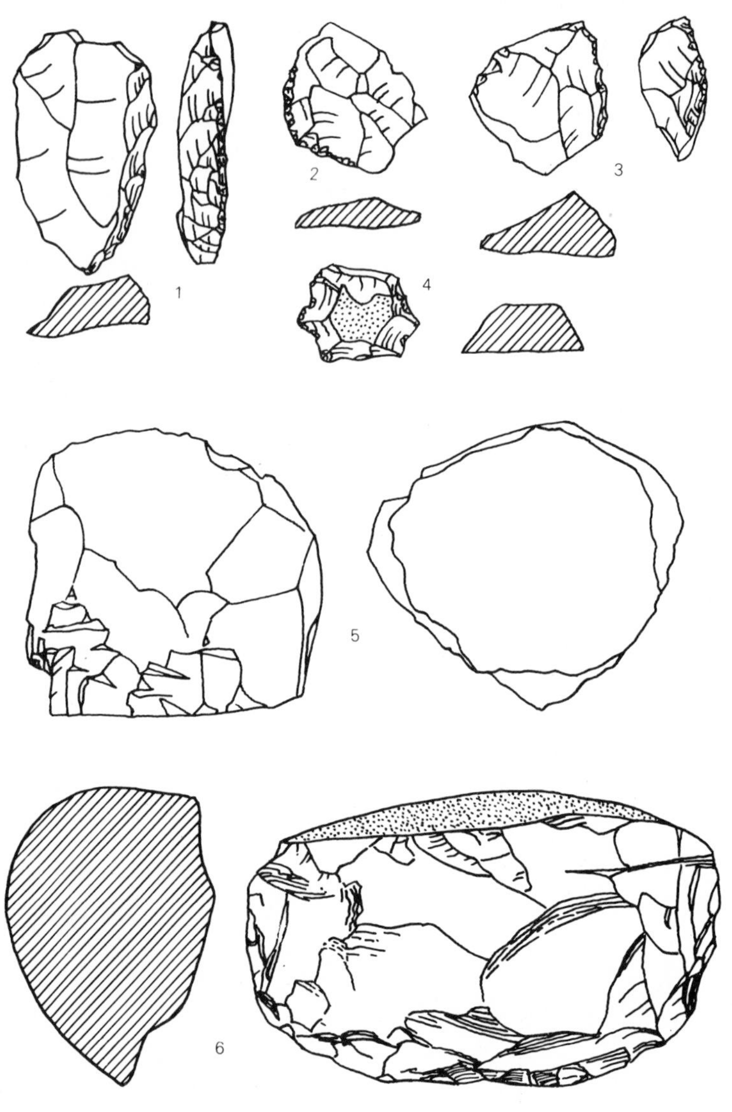

Cave in southern Queensland. Radiocarbon dating has confirmed the
543: 287–91 sequence and greatly extended the chronological range of the early
phase.

Although closer metrical and statistical studies may well reveal
temporal changes not evident from inspection, the degree of homogeneity of early assemblages from different parts of Australia and
Tasmania argues that they reflect the general character of those
272 introduced by the Late Pleistocene immigrants. The commonest tools
are scrapers, sometimes made on thin flakes trimmed to a convex
edge but sometimes steeply flaked on thick flakes to form convex
edges, concavities or spurs. Another frequent component of early
assemblages is the horseshoe core with the working edge trimmed
by secondary flaking. Bipolar cores (*outils écaillés*) occurred in the
516, 562 early assemblage from Devil's Lair, West Australia, and pebble tools
with a working edge struck from one face appeared in an early level
529 at Burrill Lake, New South Wales, as well as east of the mountain
divide at Curracurrang, below later Stone Age levels. Stone axes with
560 ground edges like those from apparently early contexts in north
Australia, for instance near Oenpelli, Arnhem Land, disprove the
earlier notion that the early industries were exclusively hand-held.

273 Bone artefacts from the earlier Stone Age, Australia: (1–3) Devil's Lair, West Australia; (4) Lake Mungo, New South Wales; (5) Cave Bay Cave, Hunter Island, Tasmania.

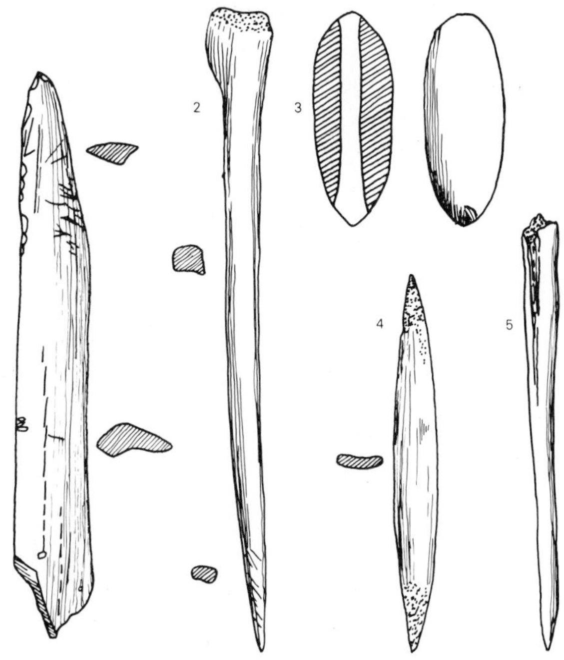

So, again, does the appearance of what seem to be traces of the resin used in hafting on the tang of a pointed limestone flake from
273 Devil's Lair. It is also plain that the early Australians made bone tools of kinds which in Europe first appeared in Upper Palaeolithic assemblages. Pointed bodkins made from portions of macropod fibulae are known from Devil's Lair and from Cave Bay Cave on Hunter Island, at present off the north coast of Tasmania, both dating from a period of low ocean levels. A double pointed piece from Lake Mungo and a bead from Devil's Lair carefully perforated along its main axis further extend the range.

Later Stone Age. The later phase of Australian prehistory saw a striking change in the character of stone artefacts. On the whole they tend to be smaller in size, display a wider range of techniques and assume a greater variety of forms. Moreover some of these have the restricted distributions one might expect of forms more finely adapted to circumstances. Thus of the two new forms, each displaying a technique not previously found in Australia, the Pirri point occupies the middle zone from Northern Territory to South Australia, covering also much of the interior of New South Wales and Queensland, whereas backed blades are more or less restricted to the south with strong concentrations in Victoria and New South
274 Wales east of the Great Divide. Pirri points of symmetrical leaf form range from 1 to 7·5 cm in length. Although sometimes associated with bifacially flaked points, they are themselves plano-convex in section, the lower face retaining the primary flake surface, the upper convex one more or less completely invaded by shallow pressure flaking.

274 Pirri (1–3) and bifacial (4–5) points, Australia: (1–3) South Australia; (4) Ingaladdi, Northern Territory; (5) Kimberley, West Australia.

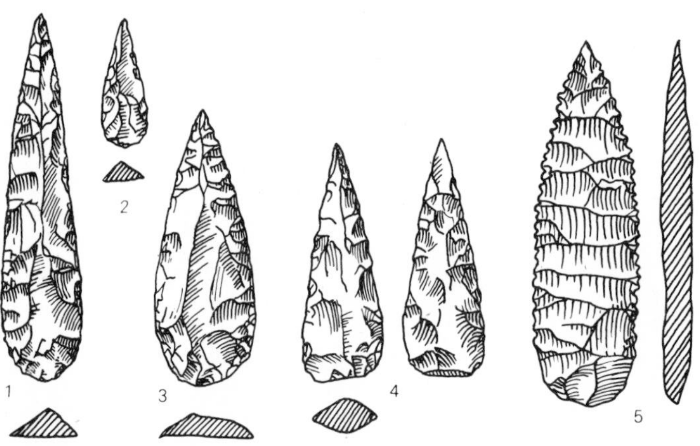

Their regularity and the thinning at one end argue that they served to tip projectiles, presumably some form of spear. Backed bladelets occur in two forms, points trimmed steeply up the whole or much
275 of one edge (Bondi points) and more or less geometric microliths of crescentic, triangular or trapezoid forms. Objects as small as these must have been mounted in some way. Since they have not been observed in use and indeed, if charcoal dates from superficial deposits are discounted, ceased to be made about a thousand years ago, they can hardly be interpreted directly from ethnographic data. On the other hand they cannot be interpreted, as in northern Europe, as arrow-tips or barbs, since the bow was unknown to the recent aborigines and is unlikely to have been discarded. More probably they were used to barb spearheads and fell out of use when these began to be carved wholly out of wood.

Other elements of the extensive components of lithic technology played a more or less vital part in the life of the aborigines down to modern times. The most elaborate stone artefact made by the aborigines was the type of bifacially flaked spearhead associated with the Kimberley Plateau of North West Australia. These must have been inferior as spearheads to the stouter bifacial points from which they probably stemmed. Clearly they ministered primarily to prestige and it is significant that they circulated in the ceremonial exchange network as far as the Gulf of Carpentaria to the east and Alice Springs to the south.

276 Edge-ground stone axes, which had already appeared in the

275 Backed bladelets, New South Wales: (1–4) Bondi points; (5–15) microliths.

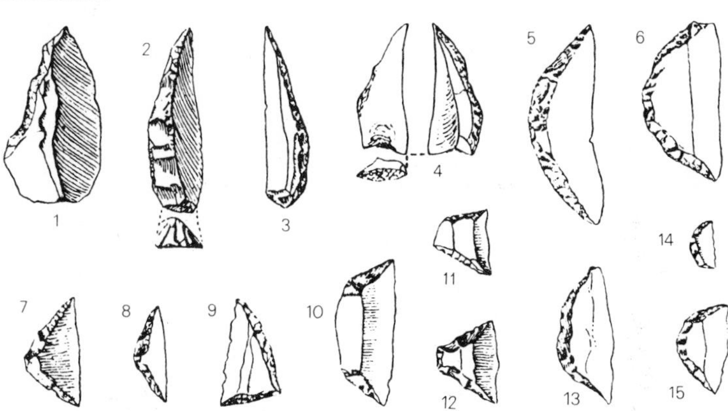

tropical north well back in the Pleistocene, were taken into use over much of the more populated parts of Australia during the Later Stone Age. Since they were still current in modern times plenty is known about the way they were manufactured, hafted and used. Recent specimens are commonly secured by resin like that obtainable from *Spinifex* grass to handles made from split branches looped round the head. Hafted specimens were already depicted in rock-paintings at Kenniff Cave. Modern aborigines used their axes for many different purposes, felling trees, shaping wooden artefacts, removing slabs of bark for canoes, dismembering large animals, cutting opossums out of tree trunks and extracting honey and grubs from branches. To judge from the debris found at the stone quarry
277 sites, including those at Lancefield, Mount William, on the outskirts of Melbourne which were worked by Billi-Billeri of the Wurrunjera tribe until his death in 1846, the blades were roughed out at the point of use. One sign of this is in the presence of axe-grinding
531 grooves immediately above the Seelands rock-shelter in the coast

276 Polished stone axehead with handle, Victoria.

277 Stone axe quarry and axe flaking site; Mount William, near Lancefield, Victoria.

zone of northern New South Wales, the deposits in which contained axe fragments associated with a backed blade industry. Another tool which continued to fill an important role down to modern times is
278 the scraper adze or *tula* blade. Mounted at the end of a stout handle
554 this tool was used for shaping wooden equipment and, set at the base of a spear-thrower, for cutting and delicate finishing and maintenance work.

The continuance of so many Later Stone Age artefacts down to

278 Wooden spear-thrower and scraper adze (*tula*): (*left*) spear-thrower or woomera with designs referring to creek-beds associated with totemic ancestors; (*upper right*) scraper adze blade mounted in spinifex resin on woomera; (*lower right*) scraper adze blades (*tula*) in different stages of wear.

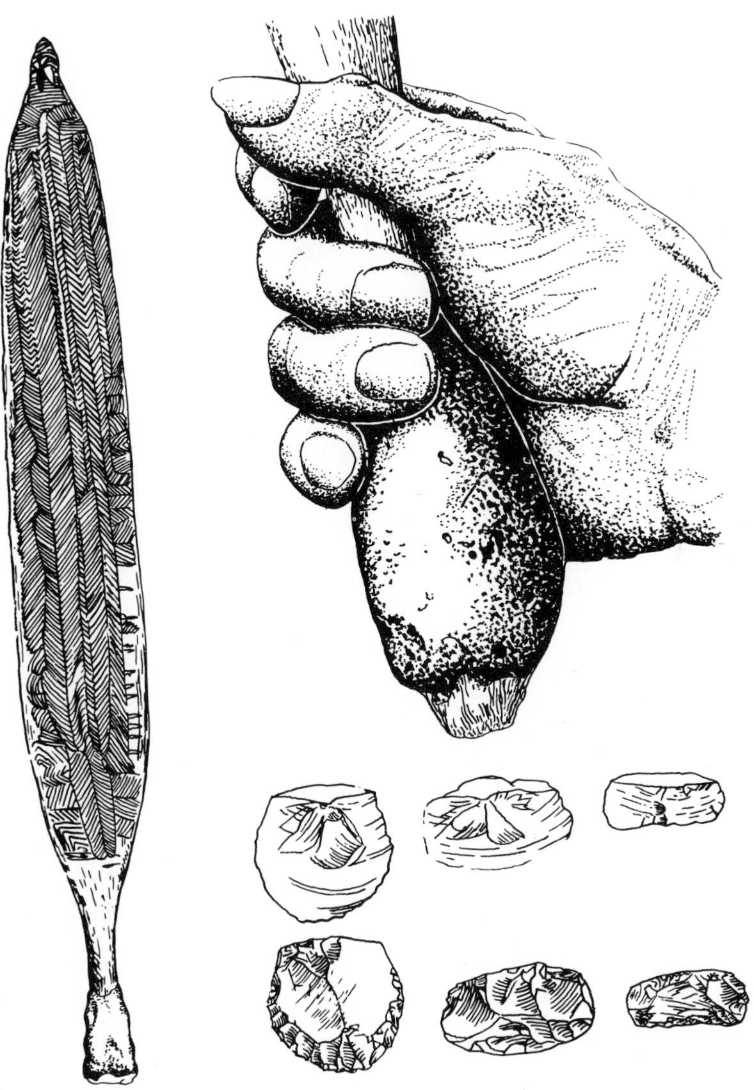

the present or recent past is not only valuable for informing us about the mounting and use of these particular forms. It gives us a right to suppose that other aspects of technology and, still more important, other aspects of aboriginal life reflect the prehistoric past. Again, thanks to ethnology, defective though this was in many ways, we have a unique chance of studying a phase of social development, usually represented by the vestigia of archaeology, through the eyes of direct observers. It has of course to be recognized that the earliest ethnologists were limited by prevailing conventions, and conversely that by the time more sophisticated observers were in the field aboriginal culture survived only in a more or less degraded form. Even so something can still be learned from illustrators, some of whom were there early enough to delineate artefacts from the final stages of Australian prehistory. One has only to compare drawings
508 of aboriginal life on the Lower Murray river published by Angas in 1847 with the data recovered by archaeology from rock-shelters like Fromm's Landing or Devon Downs in the same locality to see how attenuated our vision of Later Stone Age equipment would have been had we been restricted to the data obtained from excavation.
279 It is evident from the wealth of wooden gear, basketry, network and

279 Aboriginal artefacts used on the Lower Murray river in the eighteen forties.

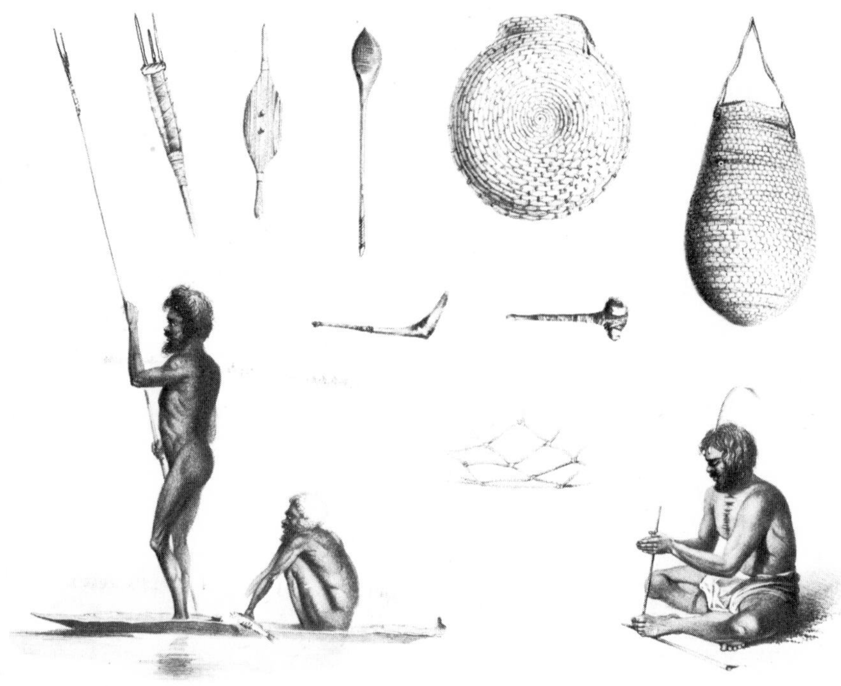

bark that the aborigines made ingenious use of a variety of materials other than stone.

Subsistence

Anthropologists agree that the recent aborigines depended entirely on foraging and catching. In doing so they displayed skill and understanding at least equal in some respects to that needed for agriculture at an elementary level. The fact remains that although in a figurative sense they could be held to 'farm' their environment – for instance through the extensive use of fire and the careful scheduling of activities to maximize returns – they neither cultivated the soil nor maintained domestic live-stock. They had no stored resources in the form of harvested crops, dairy products or meat on the hoof immediately at hand. On the contrary they had to rely on what they could obtain for more or less immediate consumption. Although there was scope for the kind of dietary discrimination observed by anthropologists, this was limited to the animals and plants immediately available. While plants contributed more and as a rule far more than animals to the diet of recent aborigines, almost the only data yet to hand from archaeological sources relates to the animal component and even so is extremely partial and local. One of the best records is that from rock-shelters on the Lower Murray river dating from the last five thousand years. The ancestors of the aborigines sketched by Angas left bones of the following mammals
546: 497 behind in the Fromm's Landing shelter no. 2:

Kangaroo	(*Macropus*)
Rat Kangaroo	(*Bettongia* & *Potorous*)
Wallaby	(*Wallabia* & *Thylogale*)
Wombat	(*Wombatus*)
Bandicoot	(*Perameles*)
Possum	(*Pseudocheirus* & *Trichosurus*)
Phascogale	(*Antechinus*)
Native Rat	(*Rattus*)
Eastern swamp rat	(*Rattus lutreolus*)
Tiger cat	(*Dasyurops maculatus*)
Tasmanian Devil	(*Sarcophilus*)

In addition they took two species of lizard as well as goanna, fish, crayfish, tortoise, emu eggs, birds and varieties of bivalve and univalve molluscs. Although not all species occur consistently throughout the section in the available sample, there is no significant trend throughout the section and several species, notably of kangaroo, rat-kangaroo, wallaby and rat, occur in each or nearly all the

eleven prehistoric layers. In this respect it is worth noting that the much smaller sample from Mungo Lake dating from around thirty thousand years ago included varieties of rat kangaroo, wallaby and wombat, as well as emu eggs, birds and mollusca. Throughout prehistory the aborigines seem to have been omnivorous while making the most of exceptional opportunities afforded by locality
527 and season. Middens at Rocky Cape and West Point, northern Tasmania, show that as far back as eight thousand years the aborigines were culling seals and catching parrot fish, the latter a resource which apparently was no longer being tapped at the time of the first colonial contact. Shell fish were gathered from inland waters but more especially round the coasts of Australia and Tasmania, basically as a stand-by resouce readily at hand and valuable in particular for filling gaps in the irregular supply of animal protein derived from hunting.

Little has yet been done to recover traces of the vegetative component of prehistoric diet in Australia, which observations of recent
530 aborigines suggests was of predominant importance. Observers are agreed that knowledge of plant resources was comprehensive and exact. According to Tindale the inhabitants of Bentinck Island, Queensland, only 16×21 kilometres in extent, named about 300 out
552 of an estimated 350 plant species. Donald Thomson's ecological study

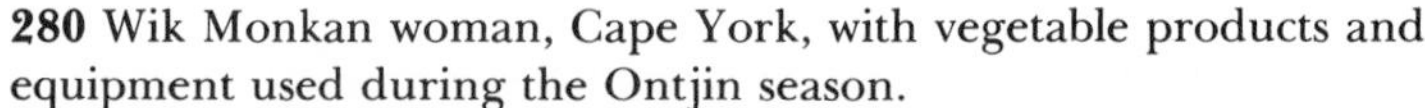
280 Wik Monkan woman, Cape York, with vegetable products and equipment used during the Ontjin season.

of the Wik Monkan of Cape York has brought out very clearly the way these people scheduled their food quest in the light of a precise knowledge of the maturation of each of a large number of plant and animal species. Further he has shown how the settlement pattern and social activities of these people were intermeshed with the cycle of seasonal change. So it was in every part of Australia. The people transmitted a wealth of knowledge about animals and plants relevant to their use in the food quest and systematically utilized this in organizing their hunting and foraging activities. Everywhere the seasonal rhythm involved movement, but the degree of this was attuned to ecological circumstances, the most important of which was
540 the density of rainfall. In the desert interior, where vegetation was sparse and brittle, movements between waterholes were frequent, whereas in territories with richer animal and plant resources, like the tropical north or the well-forested south-east, groups were able to set up camp at certain seasons for quite lengthy periods. The need to be mobile was a powerful constraint in several areas of aboriginal life. It meant that apart from natural rock-shelters, where these were available, the people had to make do with windbreaks formed from a few branches or at most with the kind of dome-shaped hut made
281 from bark sheets laid over a frame of branches erected during the rainy season in the tropical north. It also limited material possessions since equipment must needs be carried. The same applied to infants,

281 Wik Monkan dwellings, Cape York: (*upper*) windbreak and hearth for nuclear family; (*lower*) communal house for wet season.

a fact which of itself limited the numbers allowed to survive and so exerted a close control on population.

Population and social grouping

Although the population of Australia at the arrival of the first
511 Europeans cannot be accurately assessed, it was certainly low. The maximum prehistoric population of a continent only barely smaller than the United States without Alaska is commonly assumed to have been around 300,000, which gives a mean density of the order of one inhabitant to each twenty-five square kilometres. Disparities in rainfall and food resources meant a wide variation as between different zones. Whereas for instance among the Walbiri tribe of the central desert each family unit of fifteen people needed some 1,360 square kilometres of territory, similar units occupying the Riverina zone in the south-east occupied between 116 and 777. People in a position to exploit coastal and maritime resources were able to live at notably higher densities. On the west coast of Cape York a family needed only 77 square kilometres. Further, if the estimates formed by Governor Phillip are accepted at their face value, the Botany Bay area was settled so much more densely that a family group could support itself on no more than 7·7 square kilometres of land with the adjacent shore and sea.

The largest social grouping to which an individual was conscious of belonging was the tribe, comprising on the average about a thousand members. Daily life on the other hand was attuned to the minimal group, the family comprising a man, his wife or wives, their offspring and aged relatives. Greater or large aggregations of family units were able to establish close day to day contact only during brief periods when food was sufficiently plentiful in particular localities. Larger gatherings of this kind were of great importance socially. It was for instance in the context of large temporary gatherings that exogamous marriages were contracted and the young admitted through initiation ceremonies to the status of adulthood. Again, it was in the context of such larger groupings that people acquired a sense of corporate identity. Yet many of the basic features of aboriginal society are to be explained in terms of the smallness of the social group. Specialization of function stopped short at the differentiation between the sexes. Men confined themselves in the main to hunting and exploits, whereas women concentrated on the family and on foraging activities. The lack of craft specialization, apart from its direct impact, worked against progressive technological change as did the fact that the groups were too small to offer much in the way of alternatives. Over and above this, social codes and belief systems were so to speak imprinted on the young at times of heightened awareness when large numbers were temporarily together.

Tangible evidence of the role played by larger social groupings even at the level of technology survives most unambiguously in the archaeological record in the form of artefacts distributed at varying distances from their place of production. For instance axes made from greywacke from the Devonian Baldwin formation of northern New South Wales are spread over an eighty kilometre radius of their source. Although distributions of this kind are sometimes spoken of as indicating trade, it seems more appropriate in the context of aboriginal culture to interpret them as evidence for a form of gift
553 exchange. Thomson's study of the ceremonial gift exchange cycle in Arnhem Land has shown how gifts, including bundles of stone blades manufactured at the Nillipidje quarry, served to reinforce the sense of mutual obligation owed one another by the inhabitants of an extensive social territory, while at the same time serving an economic purpose by distributing local products. Exchanges of this kind help to show that, although existing for most of the time in tiny mobile groups, the aborigines were in reality enmeshed in a web of obligations and at the same time received support from other segments of the higher social group. Over and above traffic within social territories there was interaction between the inhabitants of different
510 territories. This again is documented by actual archaeological finds. Isolated greywacke axes of the kind just mentioned are known from the coastal tract some 160 kilometres to the east and in the west as far afield as the confluence of the Darling and Karoo rivers, a distance of some 580 kilometres. Carefully shaped oval pieces of baler shell (*Melo diadema*) and pearly oyster shell, obtained respectively from the inland waters of Cape York and the Kimberley coast, spread even more widely by way of the exchange network. West of a line between Adelaide and Cape York they cover between them the entire continent except only for the extreme south-west.

Psychic needs

509, 517, 521, All who have studied the aborigines in depth and at first hand have
551 been impressed by the emotional satisfaction they derive from ceremonial and ritual activities. It would be wrong to contrast this richness with what might at first appear a poor existence at a material

level. For one thing their economic systems operated satisfactorily enough on their own terms. For the individual hunter-forager the daily round was more varied and in many ways more interesting than that of many peasants or factory workers. But above all their economic and social routines were fully integrated with their ceremonial life. Religion permeated all. Everything they did or saw related to the dream-time when the totemic ancestors shaped the world. Apart from the emotional support it offered to people who for much of the year moved over extensive and sometimes desolate territories in isolated family groups, the traditional lore acquired at initiation often had its value in terms of biological survival. The need to memorize landmarks and waterholes associated with and sometimes embodying mythological beings had special value in the arid and sometimes featureless interior. The veneration of totems had the cumulative effect of making for the survival of species valuable to man. Again, the complex regulation of exogamous marriage prevented the ill-effects of inbreeding, just as ceremonial gift-exchange served to link groups which rarely came into physical contact as well as securing the more even distribution of scarce resources which in more complex societies could only be achieved by trade.

Much of the ceremonial life observed by anthropologists was enacted in words, gestures and dance. Even when expressed in graphic symbols these were most often applied to ephemeral media such as the human body, the ground surface, sheets of bark or the surface of wooden shields. Engravings deeply cut into the wood of tree trunks, like those found near ceremonial bora grounds or associated with burials, had a life of at most a few centuries. The only traces likely to survive from prehistoric antiquity were rock-paintings and, most durable of all, rock-engravings. The prehistoric antiquity of rock-engravings is now certain. Deeply engraved slabs from Ingaladdi, Northern Territory, came from a level dated by radiocarbon to early in the fifth millennium B.C. and for good measure were stratified well below a Later Stone Age industry. The occurrence of
282 rocks engraved with circular and other designs at Mt Cameron in
Tasmania is even more suggestive since the island was cut off from
the continent something like twelve thousand years ago. An even
more conclusive indication of the antiquity of rock art in Australia
563 is its occurrence on the walls of the Koonalda Cave on the Nullarbar
Plain in South Australia, in contexts dating back to twenty thousand
283 years or so. The Koonalda works included meandering grooves made

by the bare fingers on soft rock surfaces apparently in darkness and closely paralleled in the palaeolithic art of Europe, not least at Altamira. The best organized work is a grid formed by sets of more or less parallel lines engraved at right angles to one another.

By contrast it remains uncertain when rock-paintings were first made in Australia. It is known that ochre was used already eighteen thousand years ago by the people who occupied Kenniff Cave, the Miriwun Rock-shelter, East Kimberley, and Clogg's Cave, Victoria, but ochre is a material used for a wide range of ceremonial purposes.
284 Rock-paintings frequently overlook deposits containing Later Stone Age industries, notably at Kenniff Cave, at Laura, Queensland, and at Jacky's Creek, New England, but this is no proof that they were themselves of the same antiquity. Particular interest attaches to a
285 painting at Moonbi, New England, resembling that at Jacky's Creek in style, since it shows what appear to be dancing figures and what

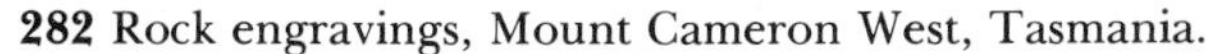

282 Rock engravings, Mount Cameron West, Tasmania.

283 Late Pleistocene art at Koonalda, South Australia: (*upper*) markings on soft clay made by finger-tips; (*lower*) incised grid.

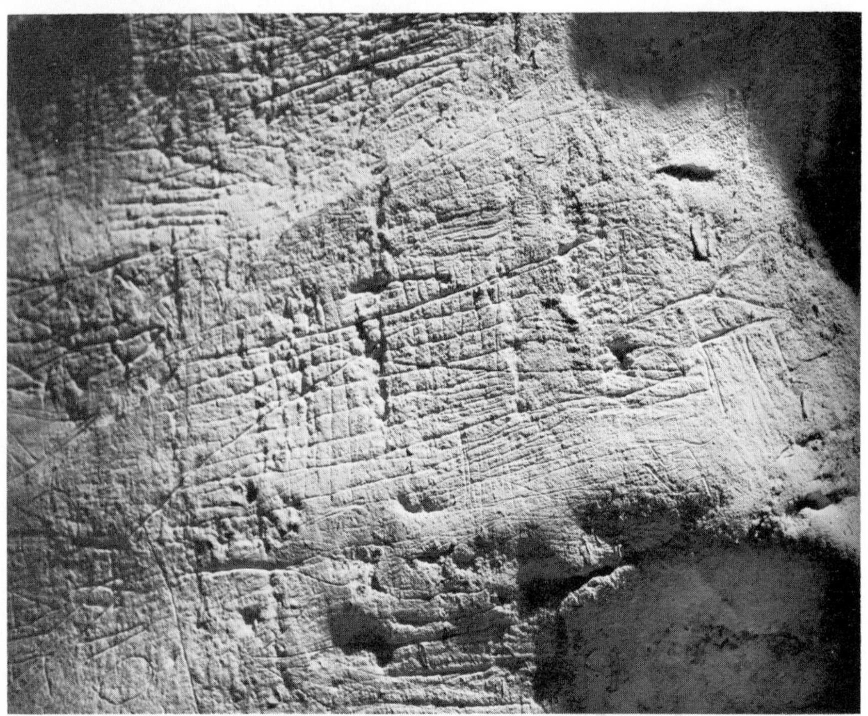

may be circles and a linear feature like those visible at the Samford bora or ceremonial ground near Brisbane. Rock-painting was certainly practised far more widely than rock-engraving during recent times. That is not to say that modern paintings are mere survivals from a past tradition. The X-ray figures of Arnhem Land for example may well reflect exotic influence just as scenes depicting droving mirror the impact of colonial settlement.

Monumental structures are so generally linked with societies based on some form of husbandry that it may come as something of a

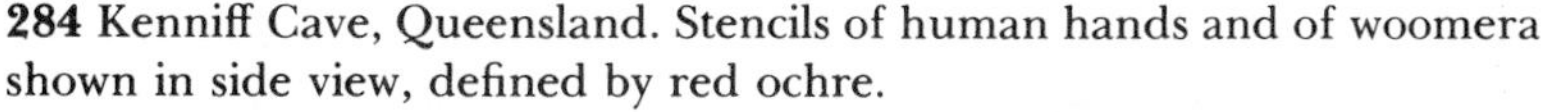

284 Kenniff Cave, Queensland. Stencils of human hands and of woomera shown in side view, defined by red ochre.

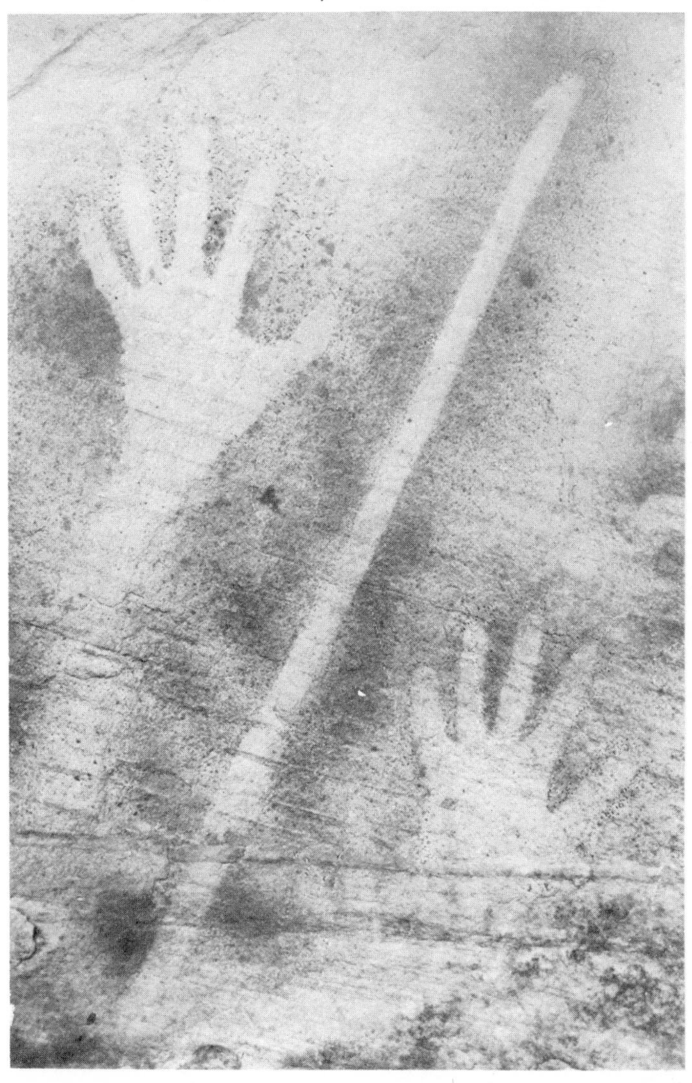

surprise to find them in the context of aboriginal Australia. Two
classes of stone structure are known in a territory extending right
across the continent, namely rock-piles consisting of heaps of small
rocks and alignments built of stone uprights. Rock-piles which occur
both in small groups and set in lines are associated in the minds of
recent aborigines with ceremonies designed to ensure the replenish-
ment of living species and as in themselves actual embodiments
of totemic ancestors. Stone alignments were more ambitious in scale.
286 They might be straight or terminate in loops or spirals and extend
521: ch. 6 over 60 m in length. On the other hand they differ from megalithic
monuments in that although single structures might comprise more
than four hundred uprights these did not as a rule exceed 60 cm in
height. In other words they could, given enough time, have been
erected by very few people or even by one determined man in
contrast with the organized group enterprise presupposed by megalithic monuments in Europe. Although in the aboriginal mind they
were associated with ancestral beings and presumably played a part
in ceremonial activities, it is not impossible that by deflecting animals
near waterholes they may at the same time have served a directly
economic purpose.

The aborigines also built earthworks, though again not ones that
presuppose any substantial concentration of manpower. These include avenues and low circular banks associated with ceremonial bora
grounds and also burial mounds, both categories of monument
associated with carved trees. The oval burial mound observed by
547 John Oxley in 1817 while exploring the Lachlan river, New South

285 Red ochre painting at Moonbi, New England, showing what may be a group of dancing figures on a *bora* ground with circles and linear feature.

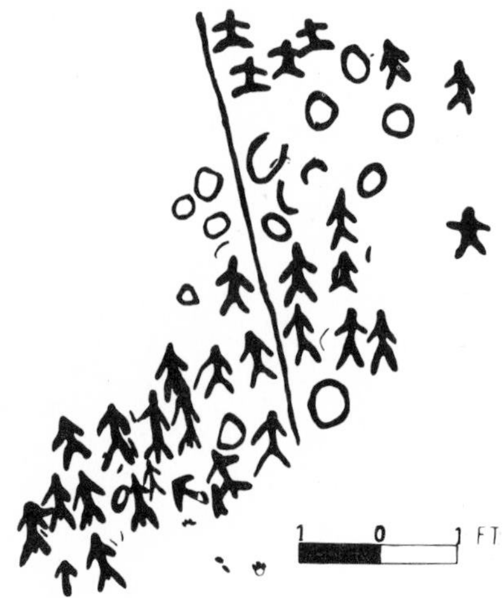

286 Stone alignment with spiral termination, Lake Moore, West Australia.

287 Burial mound within circular bank facing arc-shaped seats, Lachlan River, New South Wales 1817. Note tree carvings.

Wales, was newly constructed and when opened was found to cover a body heaped over with bark, grass and timber beams. The mound stood like the tump of a British disc barrow in the midst of a flat zone defined by a low circular bank. In this case however one
287 segment was left incomplete and fronted by three parallel arc-shaped banks. If we adopt the hypothesis that these were banks intended to seat those taking part in the burial ritual, this has interesting social implications, since the total length of the banks was 41 m, enough to seat around ninety people. This at least implies a substantial gathering, equivalent to perhaps six family groups or, if confined to initiated males, the greater part of an entire tribe. How far back in prehistory these categories of monument extend has still to be established.

The antiquity of careful burial itself went far back into the Late Pleistocene. Kow Swamp for example produced some forty inhumations and at Green Gulley, near Keilor, there was evidence for delayed inhumation, the bones recovered from primary burials being subsequently laid out in order, though not in this case confined to a
538 single individual. More surprising is the early use of cremation. The idea that this rite was used by the early settlers was first suggested by its appearance in Tasmania at the West Point midden. Definite proof has recently been supplied by the occurrence at Lake Mungo of the cremated remains of a young woman dated directly by radiocarbon to the twenty-third millenium B.C.

Retrospect

Why was it that the Australian aborigines having arrived at least thirty thousand years ago should have achieved so little in terms of world prehistory? In about half the time available to the Australians the Amerindian inhabitants of the New World attained a wide spectrum of cultural achievement ranging from specialized catching economies adapted to extreme Arctic conditions to the highly developed polities of the tropical zone. Why did Australia remain so sparsely inhabited by peoples whose experiences were restricted to a single span in the great bridge of human history? The explanation can hardly lie in the sphere of physical anthropology. The human fossils from Australia, though varying in genetic endowment, were invariably of sapient character. Nor, again, could their cultural endowment be termed primitive. Their lithic technology was admittedly elementary to begin with but it is significant that from an early stage bone artefacts were made, if only of a simple kind. What is perhaps even more relevant is that the early Australians shared up to a certain point in the full range of psychic expression indulged in by their contemporaries in Europe, North Africa and Asia. They wore personal ornaments, practised a symbolic art and displayed at least three rituals in the disposal of their dead.

To the exasperated white colonists of the early nineteenth century, short of food and of a basic infrastructure of settled life, the steadfast refusal of the aborigines to learn the elements of agriculture was a continuing affront. To such apostles, and in their own eyes at least, exemplars of progress the aborigines appeared so idle and unappreciative of the need for disciplined labour as almost to forfeit the right to be considered human. Yet as we have seen anthropological study of aboriginal societies even in the debased condition in which they existed when first subjected to scientific analysis presents a strikingly different picture. Studied objectively aborigines living in their own communities were seen to operate systems which provided them with adequate food and, apart from infant mortality, with a decent life expectancy, systems above all which provided emotional satisfaction on a scale that many more 'advanced' societies might well envy. In a sense the perfection of their ecological, social and ideological adjustment was their ultimate undoing. In the course of some thirty thousand years, during the last half of which the continent had been effectively isolated by the Neothermal rise of ocean levels, the Australians had perfected economic systems which functioned so smoothly and were so pervasively reinforced by social satisfactions and religious beliefs and ceremonials that they were proof against the minor infiltrations of the last five thousand years. Such technical and aesthetic innovations as could easily be accommodated were accepted, but in all important ways the people continued on their ineffable course until disaster overtook them. Isolation had enabled the aborigines to retain ways of life of absorbing interest to the western prehistorian, but had deprived them of the ability to adjust to the cataclysmic impact of European settlement.

Oceania

New Guinea

567 Although New Guinea formed part of the Greater Australian continent when man first crossed the Wallace Line, it has belonged geographically and culturally to Melanesia since ocean levels rose and insulated it from the mainland. Melanesia, extending as far east as

 New Caledonia and Fiji, has a special claim on the attention of prehistorians as the funnel through which economies and technologies emanating to a large extent from south-east Asia were mediated over the Polynesian islands. Racially the Melanesians were mixed. If the Negroid element is visually dominant through dark pigmentation and woolly hair, there is as might only be expected a strong Australoid component in their physical make up. In addition there is evidence for a later coastal infusion of Mongoloid stock. As skilled gardeners capable of supporting comparatively dense settled populations the Melanesians contrasted notably with the Australian aborigines. Their cultures were not merely differently based. They displayed a remarkable diversity. It was the presence of hundreds of different cultures finding rich expression in art, social arrangements and values that attracted Haddon to the Torres Straits, Malinowski to the Trobriand Islands and many later anthropologists to the New Guinea highlands as these were opened up under the impact of the Second World War. If this diversity reminds us of the limitations of economics and technology as determinants, it does not alter the fact that they imposed constraints. It is with seeking to reconstruct these contraints as they operated in prehistoric times that the archaeologist is in the first instance concerned.

288 Polished stone adze in use, Sepik district of Papua, New Guinea, 1964.

When the Melanesians first came into view at the close of their
prehistory they were skilled gardeners, relying primarily on the
569 cultivation of root crops, used bows and arrows for hunting and still
288 depended on polished stone axes as their main tools for felling trees
and shaping wood for boats and houses. Food was plentiful, but diet
was seldom well balanced and diseases due to protein deficiency were
common. Fish and meat provided only a minute proportion of food
570 by weight and a relatively minor one in respect of protein. Pigs were
the main source of meat. Although they found much of their food foraging, they were fed on leaves and waste from cultivated crops when returning to their stalls at the end of the day. Again, if the sows normally bore their litters in the bush, the young were cherished by the women and sometimes even fed at the breast. Another sign of their domestic status is that boars were commonly castrated so as to make them more manageable. Yet they were kept primarily for ceremonial and prestigious purposes rather than as a source of food. In fact pigs were rarely eaten save at festivals like the *tée* held after years of preparation. On such occasions prestige was acquired in proportion to the numbers exchanged along with other valuables. Festivals of this kind played a number of roles. Socially they were valuable for settling conflicts and strengthening relations and economically they not only stimulated production to provide the surplus needed for acquiring prestige, but also served the valuable purpose of ensuring the more even distribution of locally scarce commodities including shell and the stone axes which played a key role in technology.

The overwhelming proportion of food stuffs was obtained by vegeculture. Much the most important crop since anthropologists have studied these people has been the sweet potato (*Ipomaea batatas*), but how early this crop was established in the region has yet to be determined. Some think it was introduced during the first millennium, that is before the Spanish colonial period, others that it was brought by the Spaniards from the New World not earlier than the sixteenth century. Other root crops that presumably played the key role before the arrival of the sweet potato were the yams (*Dioscorea* spp.) and taro (*Colocasia esculenta*), both of Asian origin and like the sweet potato propagated by planting the discarded stalk. Yams might reach 18 kg in weight and because of their ability to keep for some time were important as symbols of wealth. Subsidiary crops often grown in yam gardens included banana or plantain (*Musa* sp.) and sugar cane (*Saccharum officinarum*), both of indigenous origin. The

mountainous nature of New Guinea and other Melanesian islands meant that there was considerable local variation in the relative importance of these and other crops as well as in the techniques of husbandry. Two main regimes have been observed in action at the same time, shifting cultivation with areas temporarily cleared by slash and burn and the continuous working of garden plots. In the latter mounds of earth were heaped over piles of vegetable mulch defined by drainage ditches and often fenced to prevent depredations by
289 pigs. The commonest implements were wooden digging-sticks and narrow spades used for building up the mounds.

There are many signs that this particular kind of horticulture had been practised with little change in the New Guinea highlands for
564, 568, 571–2 some thousands of years. Actual traces of gardens and even paddle-shaped wooden spades found buried under peat have been dated

289 Paddle shaped wooden spade in use for breaking up a sweet potato bed, New Guinea.

to the fourth millenium by radiocarbon analysis and substantially earlier dates have been assigned to drainage ditches. Pig bones dating from about 3000 B.C. from Kiowa and Kafiavana are significant because these animals must have been introduced to New Guinea by man and as we have seen they formed an integral part of the Melanesian horticultural economy. Again, pollen analysis suggests that the surrounding slopes were extensively cleared already during the fourth millennium perhaps for slash and burn cultivation.

Of the earlier and presumably much longer phases of New Guinea prehistory extremely little is certainly known. Since the island formed part of the Greater Australian continent during the time of low ocean levels it might be expected to have shared the same cultural traditions during the Late Pleistocene. A hint of this is suggested by the archaeological material from the lower levels in the rock-shelters of
565 Kiowa and Yuku in the east and west highlands, which in the former goes back to the ninth millennium B.C. (Y 1366: 8,400±140 B.C.). In addition to simple bone forms this comprised stone pebble tools, flakes and convex and concave flake scrapers. This basic industrial tradition persisted in later deposits in which it was successively enriched by polished axes of lenticular and quadrangular section. The radiocarbon date for the lenticular axe layer from Kiowa (Y 1371: 2890±140 B.C.) suggests that this form came in at the same
290 time as fully developed horticulture. At both sites waisted tools resembling hoe-blades and often ground at the edge were present in the same layers as polished axes. There are signs that they originally appeared earlier, perhaps much earlier. In the Juku section
574 they came in before polished axes and at Kosipe they appeared apparently at the same level as charcoals of Late Pleistocene age

290 Stone waisted tools, New Guinea.

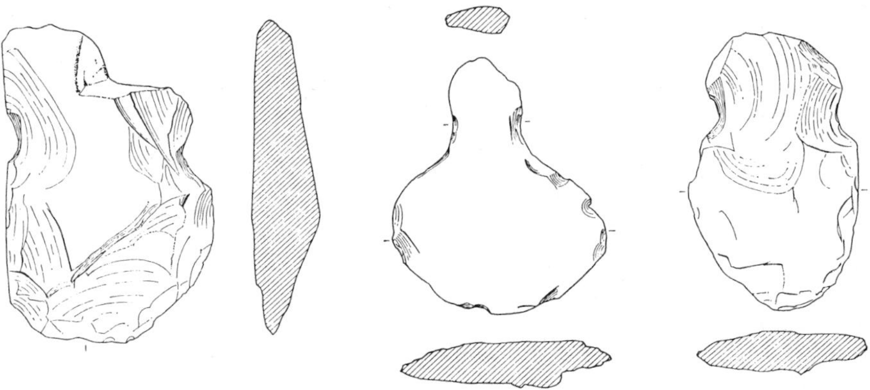

(ANU 191: 24,920±590 B.C.), though it is fair to point out that at the latter the shallow section lacked stratigraphic control by artificial features. Similar tools are known from south-east Asia, a region which was almost certainly an early focus of vegeculture. There is a strong possibility that at the very least New Guinea was strongly receptive to the spread of horticulture from south-east Asia and that this may have begun earlier than can yet be proved.

Polynesia: the smaller islands

Although the voyages of the *Kon-tiki* have amply demonstrated the capacity of quite simple craft to cross the Pacific and Heyerdal's discovery of Peruvian pottery on the Galapagos Islands between twelve and thirteen hundred kilometers to the east have shown that voyages must have been made in their direction, there are many reasons for thinking that the Polynesian islands were peopled from the west. There is no suggestion that the Amerindians contributed in any way to the ethnic make-up of the Polynesians. The incidence of disease points in the same direction. Venereal disease which originated in South America was apparently unknown in Polynesia until introduced by Europeans. Conversely leprosy, encountered in Polynesia by early European visitors, was absent from the New World until Europeans brought it there. Similarly with languages: there can be no question that the relationships of the Polynesian languages, like those of Melanesia and Indonesia, rest with Thai, Kadai and Li (Formosan). The same story is told by the plants and animals bred by the Polynesians for food. Except for the sweet potato, which as

Table 31. *Some Pacific radiocarbon determinations*

Marianas	Chalan Piao, Saipan Is.: midden	C669	1529±200 B.C.
New Hebrides	Tana	UCLA 734	420± 90 B.C.
New Caledonia	Foue Peninsula: midden	M 341	850±350 B.C.
Fiji	Viti Levu: midden	M 351	50±500 B.C.
Samoa	Vailele: village	NZ 363	±120
Hawaii	Puu Alii: dune site	GrN 2225	A.D. 290± 60
Marquesas	Ha'atuatua Bay, Nuku Hiva:		
	burial	1 AMNH 43	130±150 B.C.
	fire lens, house	1 AMNH 48	A.D. 40±180
Easter	Ahu Tepeu: burial	M 732	A.D. 310±250
	Poike: oven	K 502	A.D. 380±100
Society Is.	Afareaitu	GaK 218	A.D. 1010±90
New Zealand	Wairau, S.I.		
	oven	Y 204	A.D. 1010±110
	midden	NZ 50	A.D. 1100± 50
	Coramandel Peninsula, N. Is.:		
	midden	NZ 358	A.D. 1140± 50

291 Polynesia showing extent of Lapita ware and of Polynesian tanged adzes.

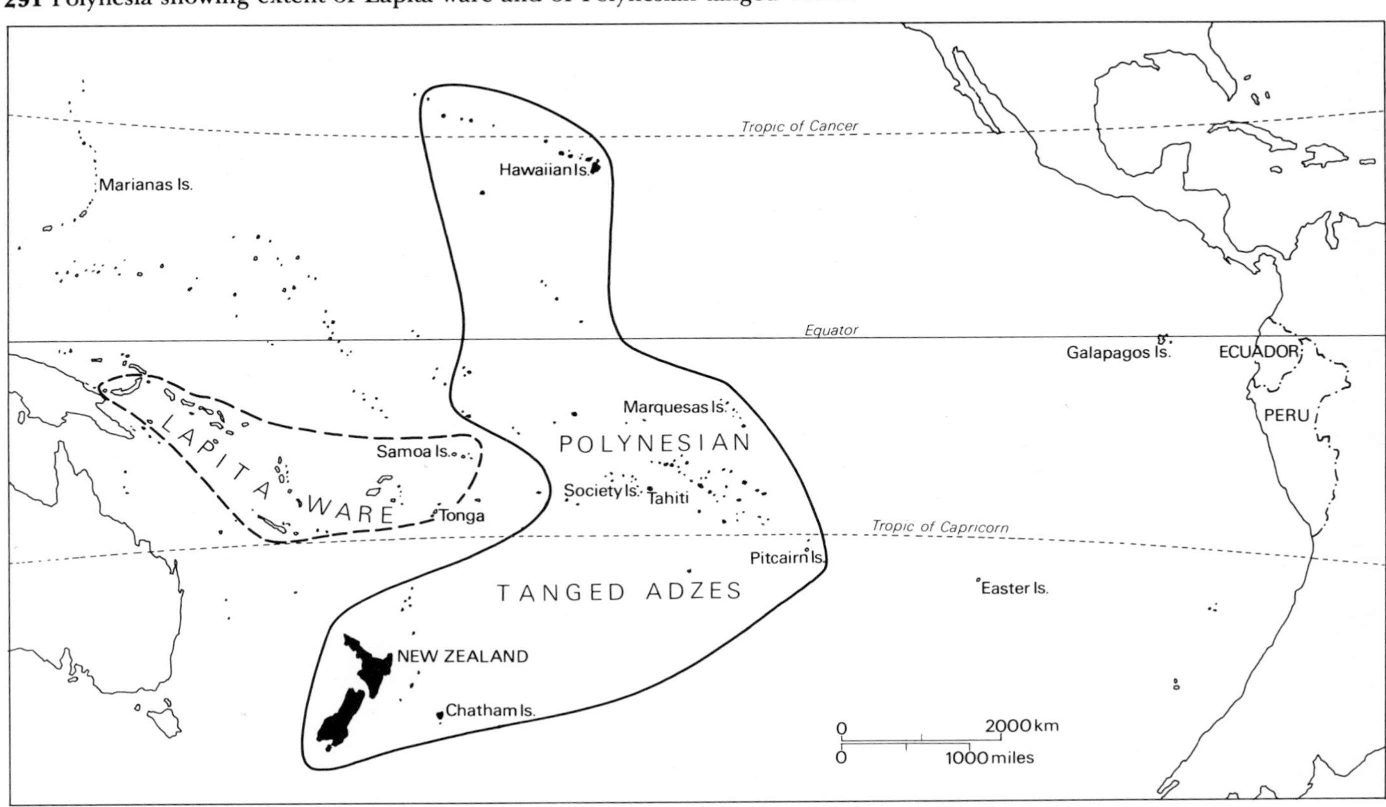

we have seen came from the New World, all the plants cultivated by the Polynesians and nearly all the weeds of cultivation originated in Asia and can only have been brought from there by man. Likewise the only domesticated animals, pig, dog and jungle cock, all came from south-east Asia. They must have been carried thence over great tracts of the Pacific Ocean together with the domesticated plants on which men and their pigs mainly fed.

590, 592, 601, 609 The colonization of Polynesia, the last extensive area other than Antarctica to be appropriated by man, began from the western margin of the Pacific. To judge from the radiocarbon date from Cholan Piao on Saipan the Marianas were occupied during the first half of the second millennium B.C. by people who made round-sectioned polished stone adzes, shell bracelets, fish-hooks and adzes and a distinctive red ware, but there is no evidence that these islands played any significant role in the peopling of the Pacific. Linguistic as well as archaeological evidence points to east Melanesia and the west Polynesian islands of Samoa and Tonga as the crucial area. A useful marker is provided by Lapita ware named after a site on the
589, 595 coasts of New Caledonia. This pottery was tempered by sand and shell and the vessels built up by coils and slabs. Most of it was plain,

292 Lapita ware from Watom Island, Melanesia.

comprising bowls and ovoid pots with well-defined rims. Decoration was as a rule confined to the upper part of flat-based and sometimes shouldered bowls. Designs, including triangles, crescents and meanders, were impressed by dentate stamps and sometimes picked out
292 by white infill. The distribution of Lapita ware is noticeably maritime. It is known from the coasts of Santa Cruz and New Britain to the north-west of New Caledonia and to the east from the New Hebrides, Fiji, Tonga and Samoa, where it is found with polished stone adzes of lenticular section, shell adzes, knives and bracelets and, locally, obsidian blades. This very distinctive ware has been dated to the first millennium B.C., but it apparently ceased to be made about the birth of Christ. In Melanesia it was succeeded by the quite different pottery with appliqué and incised decoration that continued down to modern times. On Samoa and Tonga decorated Lapita pottery gave way around 300 B.C. to plain ware and this in turn lapsed about A.D. 300. It is interesting that plain ware occurred at Ha'atuatua on the remote Marquesas Islands, which appear to have been settled since about the birth of Christ. With this exception pottery was unknown in east Polynesia before European contact and even in the Marquesas soon passed out of use. This is hardly surprising since effective natural containers in the form of coconut shells and gourds were readily available.

The voyage to the Marquesas was followed around the end of the first century A.D. by ones to the Hawaiian islands. The even more remote Easter Island was reached perhaps as early as the end of the
602 fourth century. The idea popularized by Sharp that the Polynesian islanders arrived at landfalls by a series of navigational accidents is hardly probable if we accept that the direction of movement was from west to east, that is in the face of the prevailing winds. Contingencies of weather may have played a part from time to time in the discovery of tiny islands scattered widely over great ocean spaces, but can hardly account for the main process of colonization. Effective colonization depended on the transport of women as well as men, not to mention the key food plants and domestic animals, something which presupposes purposive planning. Again, there is plenty of evidence, quite apart from their own oral traditions, that the peoples of Oceania were skilled navigators. The Tongans were able to describe the positions of islands between 800 and 1,600 kms distant to Captain Cook, and the Spanish explorers and conquerors of Tahiti about the same time were impressed by the Polynesians' ability to navigate by the stars and recognize minor variations of wind and

weather. In navigation, as in measurement, time-keeping, technology or applied ecology the achievements of early man are too often underrated by those who tend to equate knowledge and the capacity to think with the ability to read and write.

The Polynesians brought with them most of their important food
plants and all their domestic animals. The former included most of
the plants of south-east Asian origin grown in Melanesia and west
Oceania and it is significant that the earliest Marquesans were using
adzes of Melanesian type. Naturally there was wide variation in the
614 relative importance of different cultivars in the different island
environments. On coral atolls, which seem on the whole to have been
settled late, coconut flourished in the strand environment and was
often the staple crop with breadfruit and taro playing only minor
roles. On some volcanic islands taro was the staple with coconut and
bread-fruit of secondary and banana, sugar and yam only of minor
importance. On the Marquesas, on the other hand, breadfruit was
the staple with coconut and banana contributing significantly and
sugar, taro and yam only to a minor degree. As in Melanesia the only
plant food of New World origin, the sweet potato, was a relatively
late addition. All of the Melanesian domestic animals were carried
into Polynesia, where they were only eaten as a rule at ceremonial
feasts. Like food plants they were unevenly distributed. Chicken was
the only one to reach Easter Island and only dog came to New
Zealand during the pre-colonial period. Chicken as well as pig were
brought to the Marquesas and dog as well to Hawaii. The only
significant sources of animal protein in the normal way were birds
293 and above all fish. Composite fishhooks used for trolling bonito are
576 widely known from Polynesia, from Micronesia to Hawaii, from the
Solomon Islands to Tuamotu and south to New Zealand. They vary
substantially only in their raw materials, the barbless point made from
bone, mother of pearl or tortoise shell and the long shank of mother
of pearl or, in the case of New Zealand, of wood backed with an
abalone shell veneer. A distinctive form of barbless fishhook cut
from a single piece has a similarly wide distribution. Fish played so
important a part in diet that one may hazard the notion that voyages
were undertaken in quest of fish as much as of new land. The

293 Polynesian trolling and bait hooks.

uniformity of fishing and other gear, although explicable to some degree in terms of a common origin, most probably reflects continuing traffic by canoe over the Polynesian world.

582 Among the other artefacts which help to define East Polynesia were
294 varieties of polished stone adzes shaped with a tang for stable hafting. These tools had an additional importance to the Polynesians because of their role in shaping the canoes without which the colonization of remote islands would hardly have been possible. The absence of any of the varieties of this form of adze from Easter Island, colonized in all probability once and for all in the fifth century, reflects the isolation of this remote island and suggests that the new form did not emerge until later in the first millennium. Among other features of this central Pacific region defined in the archaeological record may be mentioned the ornaments based on sharks' teeth worn by those who carried tanged adzes and Polynesian fish-hooks to New Zealand and the Chatham islands towards the end of the millennium.

The societies to which the Polynesian voyagers belonged were chiefdoms. At the time of European contact the chiefs, themselves lineal descendants of founding canoe parties, were sanctified by taboos, accorded ceremonial deference marked by insignia and endowed with a monopoly of certain forms of consumption. From an

294 Tanged stone adzes of East Polynesian form.

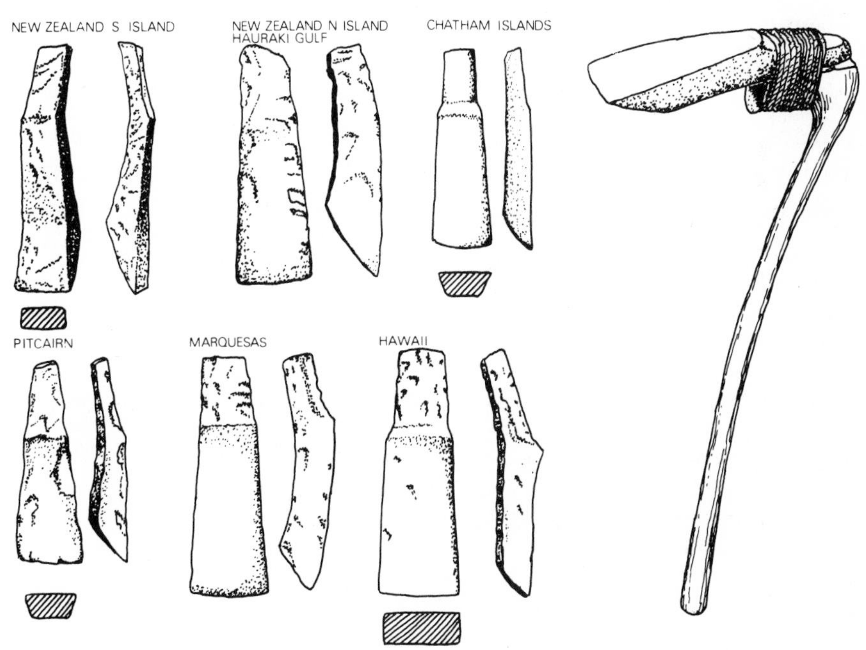

economic and social point of view they performed complementary functions. On the one hand their prestige enabled them to control crafts and the production of foods. On the other they acquired prestige not so much by owning as by redistributing wealth. By controlling social resources they were able to concentrate production, increase the surplus for redistribution and so enhance their prestige. The process was not merely self-perpetuating but self-enhancing. The existence of chiefdoms everywhere had the effect not merely of increasing production and the level of material well-being, but at the same time of speeding the tempo and enhancing the richness of social life in all its various facets.

On the comparatively small islands of Polynesia the scope for gaining prestige by undertaking elaborate agricultural works were
585 limited. Outlets reflected in the archaeological record include the building of monumental stone structures, the carving of stone sculptures, some of gigantic size, and the encouragement of craftsmen to produce artefacts of an elaboration going far beyond what was necessary for purely technological reasons.

295 Monumental structures of stone are known from many of the
610 islands. These include the *marae* of Tahiti and analogous structures on the Marquesas and on Easter Island. The Marquesan ones were centered on ceremonial plazas (*tohua*), oblong terraces that might be several hundred feet long and a hundred broad, around which were grouped temples, shrines and shelters for onlookers. The temples resembled large-scale houses and were built at one end of platforms. At the peak of their development, probably after A.D. 1400, stone images up to 2 to 2·5 metres in height and typically goggle-eyed with flaring nostrils, protruding tongue and short flexed arms were set both on the platforms and in the temples themselves. Other crafts

295 Tahitian *marae*.

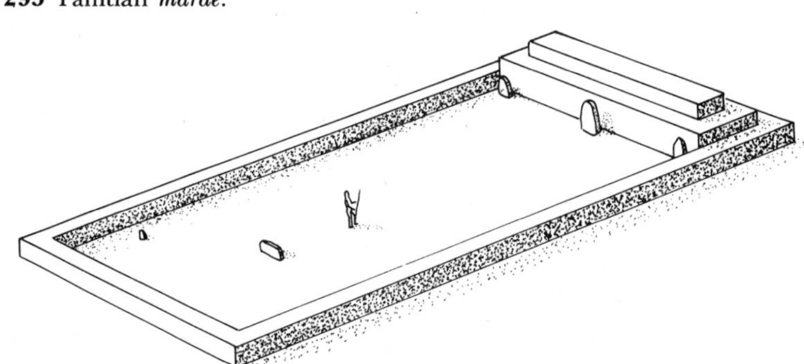

to benefit from chiefly patronage and quest for prestige included boat-builders, wood-carvers and tatooers.

584, 600 An analogous situation existed on Easter Island where the best known structures were oblong platforms (*ahu*) incorporating burials
296 and dominated by stone statues set on a raised area at one end. The statues differed from those in the Marquesas both in style and scale. The largest was some 19 metres tall and weighed about forty tonnes. The figures were cut from solid tufa in a recumbent position and it is interesting that they were not endowed with eyes until they were erected in place. The careful shaping of the stone slabs used to encase the platforms at a site like Ahu Vinapu recalls the finish of masonry at Inca sites in Peru, but hardly less so Mycenaean sites in Greece. The *ahu* themselves, the style of the sculptures and smaller artefacts of Easter Island on the other hand remain obstinately east Polynesian.

New Zealand

Although New Zealand prehistory lasted scarcely a thousand years it is of exceptional interest both on its own account and because of

296 Stone statues at Tano Raraku, Easter Island. The standing figure is Dr K. P. Emory.

the variety of sources for its understanding. Ecologically it displays the marginal intrusion into large temperate islands of an economy shaped by the inhabitants of small tropical islands scattered over the ocean spaces of Polynesia. From a technical standpoint it offers the prospect of combining insights derived from archaeology, Maori tradition, the accounts, illustrations and collections of early British and French explorers able to observe the final phases of New Zealand prehistory during the closing decades of the eighteenth and the opening ones of the nineteenth century, and not least Raymond Firth's exceptionally full analysis of recent Maori economy and society seen from the vantage of scientific anthropology.

579 If the first attempts at synthesis relied too uncritically on Maori tradition, they at least gave direction to the more systematic attack on New Zealand prehistory mounted in large measure by academics trained in prehistoric archaeology. To begin with two main cultures
588 were recognized. In terms of artefacts the Archaic culture was defined above all by east Polynesian forms of tanged stone adze, fish-hooks and ornaments, and the Classic Maori by specifically New Zealand forms of four-sided adze-blade, stone clubs, ornamented combs and nephrite ornaments. In respect of subsistence the Archaic culture was linked in both islands with the hunting of the now extinct moa, and the Classic Maori was seen in North but only marginally in South Island as associated with the cultivation of introduced food plants. The most prominent aspect of Classic Maori culture was the defended site or *pa* of which between four and six thousand instances are known, all but a few concentrated in North Island.

Archaeology confirms the east Polynesian origin of the Maori and it is at least likely that the stories of Kupe chasing a giant octopus and of Toi'te'huatai pursuing grandsons blown away from Tahiti in a canoe-race preserve memories of accidental discoveries, even if colonization can only have been effected by planned expeditions. The Classic Maori culture was confidently identified with a mass immigration in a fleet of canoes from a legendary Hawaiki. The credibility of this two-fold sequence was in turn held to receive support from chronology. The traditional date for the Fleet was mid-fourteenth century. Counting the generations back would place Kupe's exploit in the middle of the ninth century. This was well matched by the earliest date for the moa-hunter site of Wairau Bar (Y 204: A.D. 1010±110).

The recent school of New Zealand prehistorians regards the correspondence between archaeology and tradition as to a large extent illusory. In particular the identification of Classic Maori culture with a mass intrusion, let alone with the legendary Fleet, has been strongly challenged. The geographical context of the Fleet tradition is unproven and may well lie in New Zealand itself. A prime concern of archaeology in a territory so large and variously endowed is to seek explanations for cultural change first in indigenous terms. The only undoubted new addition to the resources available to the earliest settlers was the sweet potato (*kumara*), a plant which was certainly

297 New Zealand in prehistory.

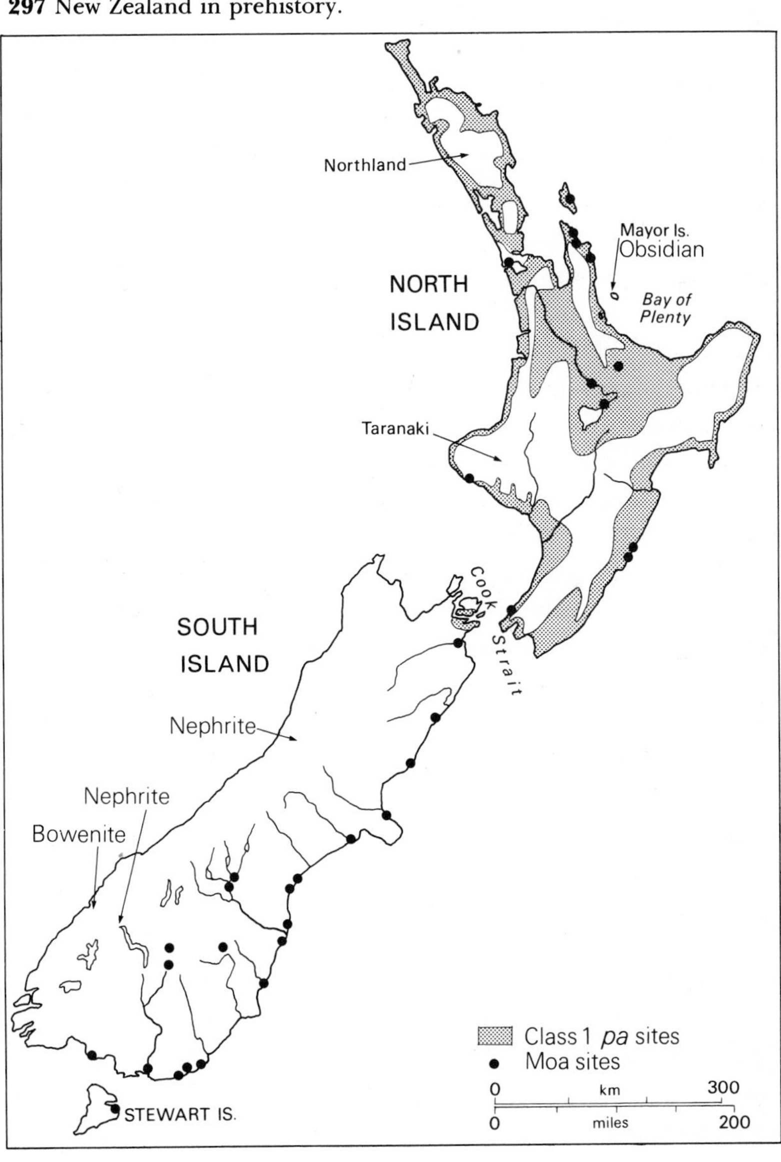

domesticated in the New World and one which played a key role in the genesis or at least in the development of Classic Maori culture.

Apart from being so much larger than the other Polynesian islands, New Zealand was remote from the main lines of trans-Pacific movement and lay wholly within the temperate zone. The size of the country provided many opportunities, but its situation set limits to the food resources available in different parts of the country. The indigenous sources exploited by the first immigrants were considerable and with some exceptions continued to serve the Maori down
598 to recent times. The rhizome of the bracken fern (*Pteridium esculentum*) was so popular at the time the Maori came under observation that in chewing it the people were seen at times to wear their teeth down to stumps. Other native plants to serve as food included the leafheads of the cabbage tree (*Cordyline australia*), bullrush roots and sundry berries. The vegetation of the country was also rich in materials of industrial value. The giant kauri, the totara and other trees provided timber for canoes, houses, defensive stockades and platforms, as well as smaller things like paddles, spears, clubs and boxes for keeping the bird feathers used for hair ornaments, not to mention a perfect medium for decorative and symbolic carving. New Zealand flax (*Phormium tenax*) was another plant of industrial value. It yielded a fibre useful for lashing adze-heads to their shafts and forming other things such as twined cloaks.

When the pioneers first arrived they were the first mammals, apart from seals, to appear in New Zealand. On the other hand, the new land was rich in birds, fish, crustacea and shell-fish. As the first mammalian predators in the country the original colonists found
581 exceptionally rewarding victims in varieties of moa, large ostrich-like birds unable to fly but carrying useful quantities of edible flesh. The species most commonly represented in middens, *Euryapterax gravis*, reached a height of up to 1·5 or 2 metres and the giant *Dinornis maximus* represented at the Papatowi site at the mouth of the Tahakopa river was twice this size. Whether the moa was primarily adapted to grasslands, forests or forest margins is still debated. Many midden finds have been made in coastal localities, mostly on the south and east coasts of the South Island, but sporadically also in the North Island. On the other hand as the map shows a number of finds have been made in the interior of both the main islands. At coastal localities like Wairau Bar and the mouth of the Rakaia river, as well as rarely in the interior, moa bones occurred with blades that could well have been used in butchery. Furthermore remains of Moa have

been found with signs of cooking in the form of hearths and stonelined ovens. Despite their relative defencelessness and the fact that, as we know from examples placed with human burials, their eggs were stolen, it seems that moa survived in Canterbury until the fifteenth and in Otago up to the sixteenth century. There can hardly be any doubt that man was the main factor in their ultimate extinction, partly through their direct slaughter and partly through modifying their plant environment mainly by fire.

The pattern of settlement shows very plainly that Archaic and for
575 that matter Classic Maori populations depended to a significant
596 extent on coastal resources. The occurrence of seal bones in Archaic
middens argues for the seasonal culling of these animals, and whale-
bones may point to the scavenging of stranded specimens. The
importance of fish is reflected in the ubiquity of composite and
single-piece fish-hooks, which were probably plied most frequently
when fish were shoaling in in-shore currents. Although there is no
proof that the nets, traps and weirs seen in use among recent Maori
were employed by the Archaic fishermen, analogy with other parts
of the world suggests that they most probably were. In addition to
fishing at sea, the later Maori also caught the eels and whitebait that
penetrated rivers in due season. Crayfish were another attraction
603 and midden deposits testify to the consumption of shell-fish in some
bulk, an invaluable standby in case of need. New Zealand was also
well provided with smaller birds. Among those known to have been
snared by the Maori are parrots, parakeets, pigeon and flightless
birds like the kiwi and weka of the interior and in the extreme south,
notably on Steward Island, the sooty shearwater or mutton bird of
coastal localities. The most effective exploitation of these and other
resources could only have been achieved by scheduling the quest of
food and raw materials on a seasonal basis. Some insight can be
586 gained from Raymond Firth's study of recent Maori economy, but
the situation as it developed in different parts of the country during
the course of prehistory can only be recovered by bioarcheological
studies. A beginning has been made, but much patient work remains
to be done before a reliable picture emerges. One of the main
factors contributing to the variegated pattern of economic prehistory
in New Zealand has been the differing local impact of introduced
species. The only animals to accompany the pioneers, dogs and rats,
were eaten from beginning to end of Maori prehistory. The dog
also provided some useful raw materials. The skins were prized for
making cloaks and the teeth for making the points of composite

fish-hooks. The impact of domesticated plants was greater and at the same time more local. This makes the difficulty of identifying their cultivation in the archaeological record the more tantalizing. One certain thing is that New Zealand spanned and in some instances lay beyond the climatically determined limits for the successful cultivation of these crops by means of the available technology. Neither banana, breadfruit nor coconut were established by the Maori in any part of their country. Yams, taro and gourds could be cultivated only in North Island. It is fair to assume that food plants of such value in east Polynesia would have been cultivated in the new homeland from the beginning. Even allowing for the common occurrence of indigenous plant resources the establishment of cultivated plants must progressively have increased the demographic potential of North as opposed to South Island. The need to tend gardens must also have promoted differences in the patterns of settlement. On the other hand taro and yams were near the limit of their zone of cultivation in North Island and could be grown only in favoured localities. They provided a basis, if a weak one, for horticulture in New Zealand.

The decisive factor, which underlay many changes associated with the transition to Classic Maori culture, was the introduction of the sweet potato (*kumara*). Provided that care was taken to protect the tubers from frost and store them during the winter within a narrow range of temperature (58°–60° F) and humidity (85–90%), it was possible to keep them for winter eating and for propagation in the following year. It was this capability of lasting through the winter, coupled with its heavy yield, that made *kumara* a crop of such great social and political as well as merely economic significance. The introduction of *kumara* may well have stimulated the growth of population at a pace more rapid than could easily be met within the limits of prevailing technology by commensurate increases in food
583 supply. It is in the context of competition for the limited areas of land suited to the cultivation of *kumara* that we ought to view the rise and intensification of warfare witnessed in the archaeological record most prominently by the appearance of defended sites (*pa*)
298 and the elaboration of hand weapons including the stone club (*patu*) itself one of the accepted fossils of Classic Maori culture. Support is lent to this hypothesis by the close geographical correlation between the distribution of *pa* and the extent of territory amenable to the cultivation of the sweet potato. There mere fact that *kumara* could be successfully stored made it a highly relevant form of booty in an

era of land-hunger. Again, once the crop was lifted the warriors were free and well-provided to raid their neighbours. From a dietary point of view warfare had another advantage. The extinction of the moa meant that apart from birds, dogs and rats the only source of red meat available to the Maori was the flesh of their enemies. If competition for *kumara*-ground was the prime cause of conflict, early records of the attitude of the Maori themselves leave little doubt that an appetite for human flesh was another. A point that bears emphasis
613 is that whatever its underlying cause warfare became a key institution of Classic Maori society, an outlet for emotional satisfaction, scope for the leadership of chiefs and a powerful factor in maintaining group solidarity.

604 The best estimates for the total Maori population at the time of Captain Cook's arrival range from one to two hundred thousand with an emphasis nearer the lower than the higher figure. The great majority of the population at this time lived on the North Island, a disparity which is closely linked with the extent of horticulture and in particular of the sweet potato. So long as moa were available in plenty, the initial population must have built up rapidly to its optimum level. It may still be doubted whether the total population ever exceeded some ten thousand during the life of the Archaic

298 Maori clubs (*patu*) of stone, wood and bone, brought back from Captain Cook's first expedition.

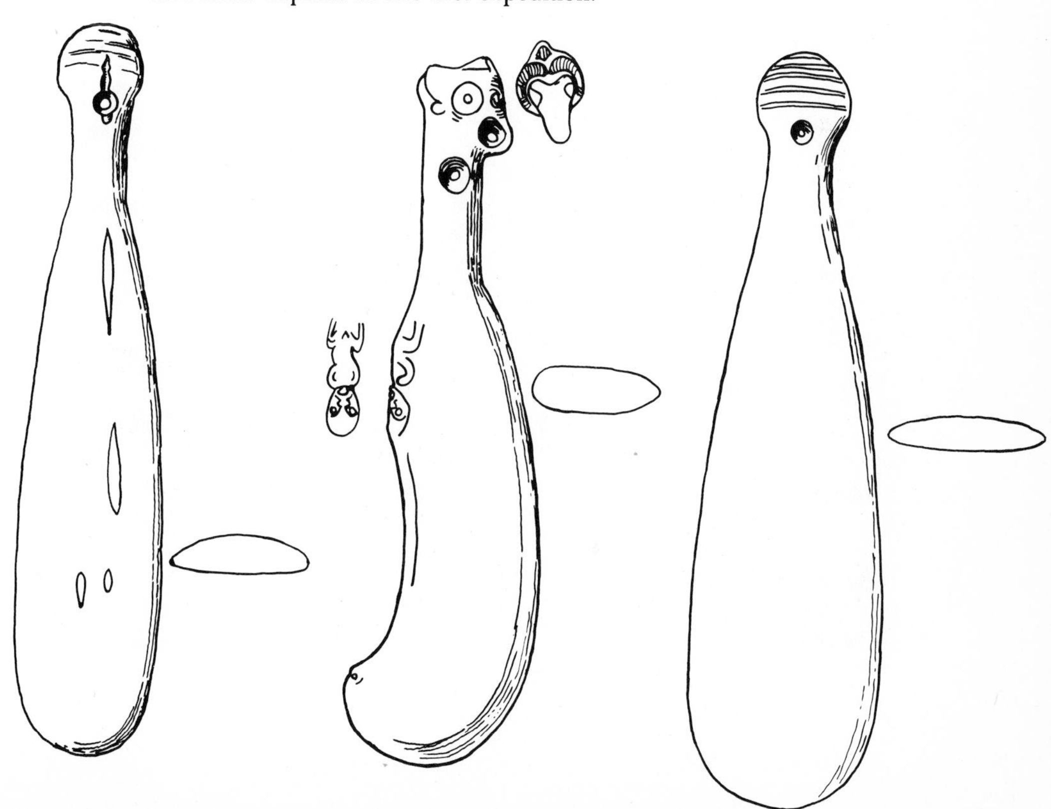

culture. Research on Archaic settlements is too rudimentary to allow objective assessment. Even at so extensive a site as Wairau Bar there is no way of determining the size of social group that settled at this locality at any moment of time. The evidence is at least consistent with the notion of repeated seasonal encampments of a group occupying three or four huts and corresponding in size to the extended family or *whanau* of recent Maori society.

There are indications that seasonal activities and to some degree seasonal residence were still important during the dominance of Classic Maori even on North Island and we know that the *whanau* was the basic economic unit of recent Maori society owning and exploiting such resources as eel weirs, canoes, rat-trapping rights and *kumara* plots. On the other hand horticulture, introduced at an early stage in respect of taro and yams in North Island, but greatly increased in importance with the introduction of the sweet potato, must have increased the trend towards sedentary settlement. The introduction of *kumara* in particular led to the need for concentration. Wherever they were at other times of the year, the *whanau* converged at harvest time on centres where their collective wealth could best be defended. It is significant that all but a few of the

299 Otatara *pa* (Class 1), Hawkes Bay, New Zealand.

estimated four to six thousand defended sites or *pa* are concentrated on North Island with only a few on the south of Cook Strait.

577, 594 Three main classes of *pa* are recognized:

299 Class I – comprises aggregations of platforms artificially scooped out of sometimes steep slopes

Class II – comprises sites commonly on narrow ridges cut off at the vulnerable end by a bank and ditch

300 Class III – comprises sites fully enclosed by bank, ditch and timber palisades.

Radiocarbon dates argue that Classes II and III were each being constructed by the fifteenth century, suggesting that the difference between them is primarily a matter of topography. One of the few instances of sequence is that noted at the site of Kumara-Kaiamo, north Taranaki, where a Class I *pa* was superseded by one of Class III. Apart from an inland conclave in the Rotorua-Taipo and Auckland regions, Class I *pa* sites are crowded into the coastal zone. Although this in part reflects the attraction of the coast in respect of fish and shell-fish, it coincides at the same time and at least as significantly with the areas of relatively low frost-incidence best

300 Reconstruction of wooden palisade and defences Otakanini, Pa, Kaipara Harbour, New Zealand.

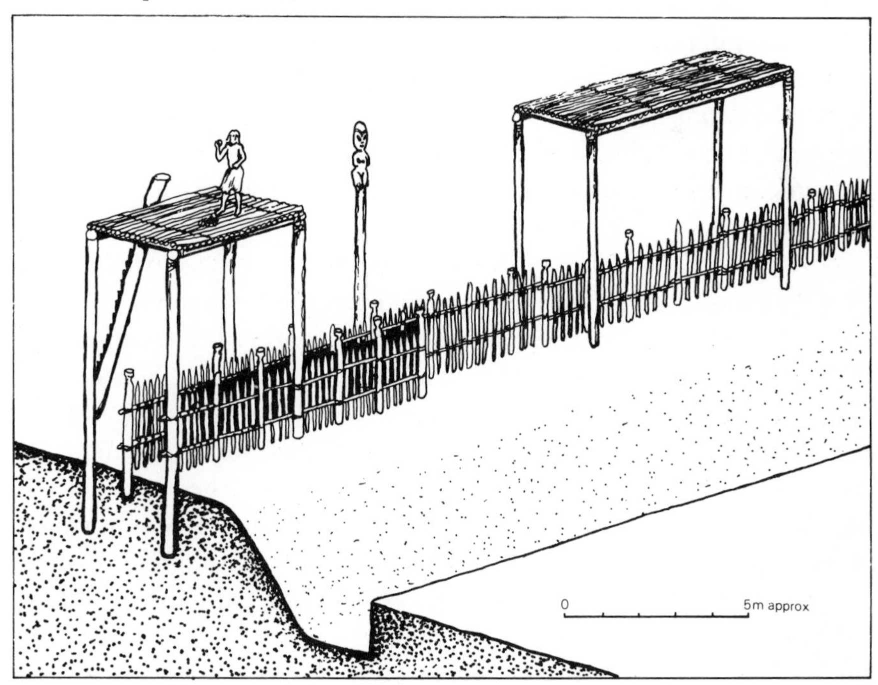

adapted to the growth and storage of sweet potato. It is significant that *pa* of Classes II and III reflecting an increased anxiety for defence were even more restricted, being confined to the coastal zones of west Northland, either coast of Taranaki and the Bay of Plenty. To some extent the large differences in scale between different sites reflect local conditions. Where topography was cramped or extreme, successive periods of use would be superimposed,
299 whereas the 48 hectares of terraces at Otatara, Hawkes Bay may have resulted from successive occupation of contiguous zones. Signs that some *pa* were continuously occupied are by no means inconsistent with the absence of individuals or even complete *whanau* on seasonal activities.

If when a denser cluster of early dates become available it should turn out to conform to a pattern focusing on the fifteenth century, two alternatives would present themselves. Either the sweet potato must have reached New Zealand from Ecuador or Peru independently of the Spaniards or it would have to be accepted that the *pa* developed initially independently of the sweet potato. A decisive way of checking the age of the introduction of the sweet potato to New Zealand would be to date traces of the tubers themselves. In default of this the storage pits offer possibilities, since botanical opinion inclines to the view that these were constructed for sweet potato tubers. How far one can be sure that they were never constructed for other purposes is another question. Again, the dating of large excavated hollows from material incorporated in their secondary infill offers many sources of error. Can we be sure for instance how the mid-fourteenth charcoal (NZ: A.D. 1351±78) from a disused storage-pit under the Otakanini *pa* relates to the construction of that pit?

When Maori first came under European observation their mode of warfare resembled that of the other peoples at a similar level of social development. Active hostilities were geared to the subsistence cycle and campaigns were brief. The *hapu*, intermediate between the extended family and the tribe, may well indeed have assumed the form it did because of the intensifying competition for land which motivated Maori society during the Classic phase. The *hapu*, mustering anything from one to four hundred adult males, was normally based at harvest time, if not the year round, on a single or a small group of defended sites. Although *hapu* might combine to defend tribal land, each was as a rule fighting as a unit under its own chief. Campaigns made up for brevity by excitement. Apart from the

possibility of winning or losing land or stores of *kumara*, defeat could mean being eaten by the victor or at least enslavement. One way of achieving surprise was to approach by sea, a tactic made easier by
578 the location of many *pa*. This helps to explain the attention paid to the construction and decoration of the war canoe. Although formidable to look at, this was no more than a dug out with upper strakes
301 lashed into position. By using straight kauri trunks up to 18 metres long and dovetailing extra sections at one or both ends it was possible to build vessels 24 or more metres in length. Boats of this kind were propelled by paddle-men ranged on either side, aided on occasion by a small triangular sail set upright on its apex. Since a
302 single canoe might carry up to a hundred and fifty men and Captain Cook and other early explorers observed fleets of numerous vessels, their utility for mounting large scale surprise attack may well be imagined. On the other hand their capacity for carrying supplies was limited and it may be supposed that they were intended mainly for sudden raids of brief duration.

Although Maori society was formed of basically self-supporting and seasonally bellicose communities, a well-developed network of exchange existed involving some of the smaller as well as the two main islands. It is true that keenly sought-after substances like nephrite were sometimes seized forcibly by raiding canoe parties, but by and large the process of redistribution was a peaceful one. To judge from the recent past, exchange was by no means limited to materials likely to survive in the archaeological record. There was even traffic in foodstuffs. Crayfish passed from the coast and birds from the forest. Mutton-birds from Stewart Island in the extreme south reached North Island as delicacies. The traffic best documented by archaeo-

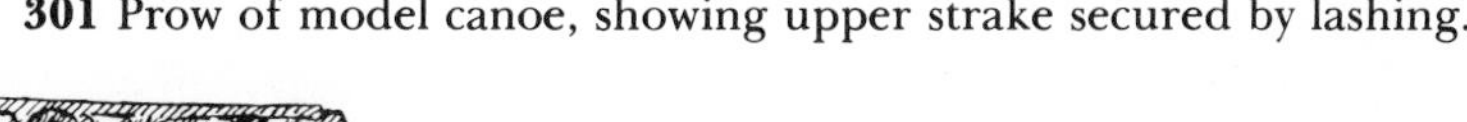

301 Prow of model canoe, showing upper strake secured by lashing.

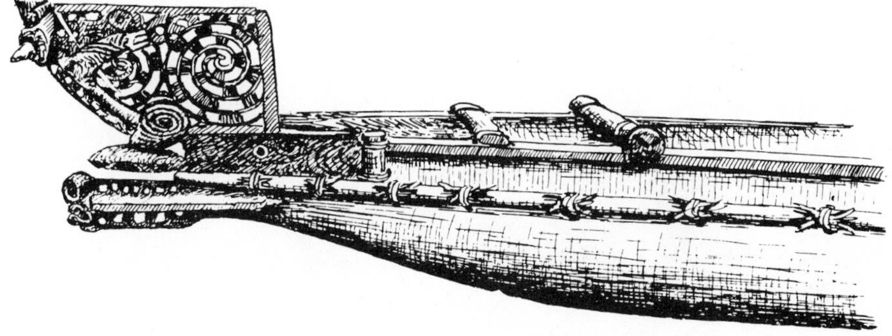

logy relates to lithic materials. The obsidian from Mayor Island
in the Bay of Plenty found its way to sites with moa bones over
both the main islands even in competitition with local sources. The
586: 388; 608; materials most keenly sought by the Classic Maori were nephrite and
612 translucent serpentine or bowenite, occurring in the form of pebbles
from riverbeds and strands in Westland and Southland. These were
prized for their comparative rarity, their extreme hardness, but
also for their appearance and feel when polished. Large quantities
of these fine greenstones found their way to the more densely
populated North Island where they were used notably for adze-
303 and chisel-blades, *mere* clubs, lobe-shaped ear pendants and *hei-tiki*
pendants. Much traffic must have gone by sea but in the interior it
had as a rule to be carried by foot along river courses or the crests
of ridges.

Although we know something of the religious dimension of recent Maori life as expressed in mythology and rituals little or no information has survived from prehistoric times. That nothing comparable to the stone-built *marae* of Polynesia exists in New Zealand is less surprising when it is remembered that these had not developed in any part of Oceania before the country was first settled. By the same token it undermines the notion that New Zealand was reinforced from Polynesia later in its history.

302 Maori war canoe as seen by Captain Cook.

303 Classic Maori *hei tiki* pendant made of nephrite.

In respect of art the Maori displayed many features common to
the Polynesian islanders. Like them they tattooed their faces and
304 bodies by means of finely toothed chisels dipped in pigment. They
painted human figures, dogs, seals, birds, fish and canoes on the
611 walls of many hundreds of shallow rock-shelters in the limestone
formations of New Zealand. They shaped some of the hardest stones,
including nephrite, by means of friction to produce anthropoid
pendants (*hei-tiki*) and decorative butts for clubs (*patu*). Above all they
enhanced by carving the importance of a broad range of their most
significant wooden artefacts, notably handles for their nephrite
adzes, feather boxes, the main uprights and weather-boarding of
their houses and storehouses and many of the appurtenances of their
war canoes, including their prows, stern-boards, paddles and bailers.
The carvers, like their colleagues the tattooers, luxuriated in spiral
designs, but no less pervasively in anthropoid forms both in relief
and as full sculptures. The Maori carvers employed a number of
305 conventions common to Polynesia, including representations with
587 protruding tongues and limbs angular and shortened. A device
sometimes employed by the Maori to enhance the eyes and sometimes
ears of anthropomorphic figures was to inset paua shell. In pointed
contrast with the Australian aborigines, the Maori have been able to
retain elements of their native culture and at the same time come
to terms with European civilization. Wood carving in traditional
Maori style for instance still flourishes in the plural society of modern
New Zealand.

304 Maori dried head with tattooed spirals and nephrite ear pendant.

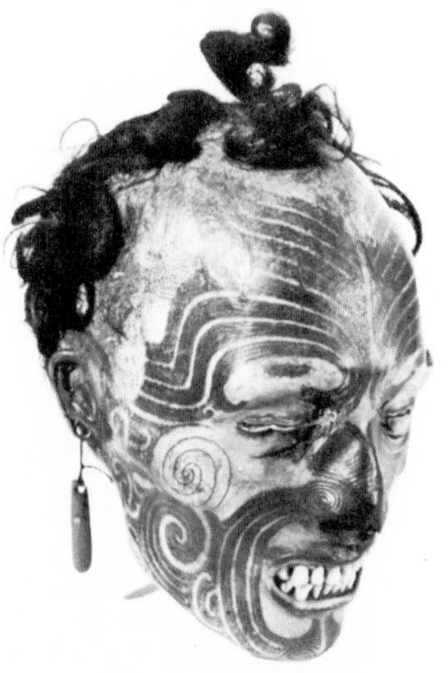

305 Wooden house panel carved with spirals and ancestor figure with protruding tongue.

FURTHER READING

Note. The following list of references is intended to give the reader access to published sources. To obtain additional references, more particularly to the earlier literature, it will be necessary to use the bibliographies provided in many of the books and articles cited. In general I have provided more references for regions still incompletely studied. For the better-known territories comprehensive books are often available.

PREFACE

Radiocarbon chronology

Since the second edition of W. F. Libby's pioneer work *Radiocarbon Dating* (Chicago, 1955), many determinations have been made in different parts of the world. Some have been published in successive supplements of *Radiocarbon.* Others have been published in articles or monographs concerned with specific areas or periods. Important studies have been devoted to the question of synchronizing radiocarbon and solar dates. A few key publications are listed:

1 Agrawal, D. P., Kusumgar, S. & Pant, R. K. 'Radiocarbon and Indian archaeology', *Physics News,* vo. 6, no. 4 (Dec. 1975), 1–10

2 Allibone, T. E. *et al.* (ed.). *The Impact of the Natural Sciences on Archaeology.* British Academy, 1970

3 Barnard, N. *The First Radiocarbon Dates from China.* Monographs on Far Eastern History: 8. A.N.U., Canberra, 1972

4 Brandtner, F. J. 'More on Upper Palaeolithic archaeology', *Current Archaeology* II (1961), 427–54

5 Dolukhanov, P. M. & Timofeev, V. I. *Absolute Chronology of the European Neolithic (According to the Radiocarbon Method)* Includes full tables and bibliography. Academy of Sciences, Moscow, 1972

6 Ehrich, R. W. *Chronologies in Old World Archaeology.* Chicago, 1965

7 Haynes, C. V. 'Carbon-14 dates and early man in the New World'. *Proc. 6th Int. Conf. Radiocarbon and Tritium Dating* (Pullman, 1965), 145–64.

8 Huxtable, J., Aitken, M. J., Hedges, J. W. & Renfrew, A. C. 'Dating a settlement pattern by thermoluminescence: the burnt mounds of Orkney', *Archaeometry* 18 (1976), 5–17

9 Libby, W. F. 'Radiocarbon dating' in Allibone, T. E., 1970, 1–10

10 Movius, H. L. 'Radiocarbon dates and Upper Palaeolithic archaeology in central and western Europe', *Current Archaeology I* (1960), 355–91
11 Mulvaney, D. J. *The Prehistory of Australia*, 287–91. Pelican, 1975
12 Neustupný, E. 'Absolute chronology of the Neolithic and Aenolithic periods in central and south-east Europe II', *Archaeologické Rozhledy* XXI (1969), 788–810
13 Neustrupný, E. 'A new epoch in radiocarbon dating', *Antiquity* XLIV (1970), 38–45
14 Olsson, I. (ed.). 'Radiocarbon variations and absolute chronology', *Proc. XII Nobel Symposium at Uppsala, 1969.* Stockholm, 1970
15 Ralph, E. K., Michael, H. N. & Han, M. C. 'Radiocarbon dates and reality', *Nasca Newsletter*, vol. 9, no. 1, 1–20. Philadelphia, 1973

Recent approaches to prehistory

16 Aitken, M. J. *Physics and Archaeology.* Oxford, 1976
17 Brothwell, D. & Higgs, E. (ed.). *Science in Archaeology. A Survey of Progress and Research.* Rev. ed. London, 1969
18 Chang, K. C. *Rethinking Archaeology.* New York, 1967
19 Clark, G. *Prehistory since Childe.* First Gordon Childe Memorial Lecture. Institute of Archaeology, London, 1976
20 Clark, G. & Hutchinson, J. (ed.) *The Early History of Agriculture.* (*Phil. Trans. Roy. Soc.* B, vol. 275, no. 936, pp. 1–213). Royal Society, London, 1976
21 Clarke, D. L. *Analytical Archaeology.* London, 1968
22 Clarke, D. L. (ed.) *Models in Archaeology.* London, 1972
23 Coles, J. M. *Archaeology and Experiment.* London, 1973
24 Doran, J. E. & Hodson, F. R. *Mathematics and Computers in Archaeology.* Edinburgh University Press, 1975
25 Hester, T. R. & Heizer, R. *Bibliography of Archaeology,* I: *Experiments, Lithic Technology and Petrography.* Addison-Wesley Modules in Anthropology, no. 29. Reading, Mass. 1973
26 Higgs, E. S. (ed.) *Papers in Economic Prehistory.* Cambridge, 1972
27 Higgs, E. S. (ed.). *Palaeoeconomy.* Cambridge, 1975
28 Hodson, F. R., Kendall, D. G. & Tăutu, P. *Mathematics in the Archaeological and Historical Sciences.* Edinburgh University Press, 1971
29 Kendall, D. G. *et al.* (ed.). *The Place of Astronomy in the Ancient World.* British Academy, London, 1974
30 Leone, M. P. (ed.) *Contemporary Archaeology.* S. Illinois University Press, 1972
31 Marshack, A. *The Roots of Civilization.* New York, 1972
32 Renfrew, C. *Social Archaeology.* Inaugural Lecture, Southampton University, 1975
33 Sieveking, G. de G., Longworth, I. H. and Wilson, K. E. (eds). *Problems in Economic and Social Archaeology.* London, 1976
34 Ucko, P. J. & Dimbleby, G. W. (ed.). *The Domestication and Exploitation of Plants and Animals.* London, 1969

CHAPTER 1. EARLY PREHISTORY

Animal behaviour

35 Hayes, C. *The Ape in Our House.* London, 1952
36 Jay, P. C. (ed.). *Primate Studies in Adaptation and Variability.* New York, 1968
37 Köhler, W. *The Mentality of Apes.* London, 1952
38 Lawick-Goodall, J. von. *My Friends the Wild Chimpanzees.* Washington, 1967
39 Schaller, G. *The Year of the Gorilla.* London, 1965
40 Schultz, A. H. *The Life of Primates.* London, 1969
41 Thorpe, W. H. *Learning and Instinct in Animals.* Cambridge, 1956
42 Washburn, S. L. (ed.) *Social Life of Early Man.* London, 1962
43 Yerkes, R. M. *Chimpanzees. A Laboratory Colony.* New Haven, 1943

Human palaeontology

44 Boule, M. & Vallois, H. V. *Les Hommes Fossiles.* 3rd ed. Paris, 1946
45 Butzer, K. W. & Isaac, H. Ll. (eds.). *After the Australopithecines.* The Hague, 1976
46 Campbell, B. G. *Human Evolution: an Introduction to Man's Adaptations.* London, 1966
47 Clark, W. le G. *The Fossil Evidence for Human Evolution.* 2nd ed. Chicago, 1964
48 Clark, W. le G. *The Antecedents of Man.* Edinburgh, 1959
49 Howell, F. C. 'The age of the Australopithecines of southern Africa', *Am. J. Phys. Anthrop.* XIII (1955), 635–62
50 Howells, W. *The Evolution of the Genus Homo.* Addison-Wesley Module, Reading, Mass., 1973
51 Isaac, G. & McCown, E. R. (ed.). *Human Origins: Louis Leakey and the East African Evidence.* Benjamin, California, 1976
52 Koenigswald, G. H. R. Von (ed.). *Hundert Jahre Neanderthaler.* New York, 1958
53 Oakley, K. P. 'Swanscombe Man', *Proc. Geol. Assoc.* LXIII (1952), 271–300
54 Oakley, K. P. *Frameworks for Dating Fossil Man.* London, 1969
55 Ovey, C. D. (ed.) *The Swanscombe Skull: a Survey of Research on a Pleistocene Site.* London, 1964
56 Tobias, P. V. *Olduvai Gorge.* Vol. II. *The cranium and maxillary dentition of Australopithecus (Zinjanthropus) boisei.* Cambridge, 1967
57 Weidenreich, F. 'The skull of *Sinanthropus pekinensis*', *Palaeontologia Sinica,* no. 127. Pekin, 1943

Quaternary environment

58 Butzer, K. W. *Environment and Archaeology.* Chicago, 1964
59 Deevey, E. S. 'Biogeography of the Pleistocene', *Bull. Geol. Soc. Amer.* LX (1949), 1315–416
60 Flint, R. F. *Glacial Geology and the Pleistocene Epoch.* 4th reprint. New York, 1953
61 Godwin, H. *The History of the British Flora.* 2nd ed. Cambridge, 1976
62 Zeuner, F. E. *The Pleistocene Period, its Climate, Chronology and Faunal Successions.* London, 1959

Palaeolithic archaeology
Most references are listed under their appropriate area headings and several are included under 'Human palaeontology'. General texts not otherwise listed include:

63 Bordes, F. *The Old Stone Age*. London, 1968
64 Burkitt, M. *The Old Stone Age*. 3rd ed. Cambridge, 1955
65 Coles, J. M. & Higgs, E. S. *Time, Man and Stone*. London, 1968
66 Feustel, R. *Technik der Steinzeit*. Weimar, 1973
67 Movius, H. L. 'The Mousterian Cave of Teshik-Tash, South-eastern Uzbekistan, Central Asia', *Am. School of Prehistoric Research Bull.* XVII (1953), 11–71.
68 Oakley, K. P. *Man the Tool-maker*. 4th ed. London, 1958

CHAPTER 2. BEGINNINGS OF CIVILIZATION IN SOUTH-WEST ASIA

General

69 Baly, D. & Tushingham, A. D. *Atlas of the Biblical World*. New York, 1971
71 Braidwood, R. J. & L. 'The earliest village communities of south-western Asia', *J. World History* I (1953), 278–310
70 Braidwood, R. J. 'Prehistoric investigations in southwestern Asia', *Proc. American Philosophical Society* 116 (1972), 310–20
72 Childe, V. G. *New Light on the Most Ancient East*. 4th ed. London, 1952
73 Fairservis, W. A. *The Threshold of Civilization*. New York, 1975
74 Frankfort, H. *The Birth of Civilization in the Near East*. London, 1951
75 Frankfort, H. *Art and Architecture of the Ancient Orient*. London, 1958
76 Garrod, D. A. E. & Clark, J. G. D. 'Primitive man in Egypt, Western Asia and Europe', *Cambridge Ancient History*, vol. I, pt. 1, pp. 70–121. Cambridge, 1970
77 Harlan, J. R. & Zohary, D. 'Distribution of wild wheats and barley', *Science* 153 (1966), 1074–8
78 Lloyd, S. *Mounds of the Near East*. Edinburgh, 1963
79 Renfrew, C., Dixon, J. E. & Cann, J. R. 'Obsidian and early cultural contact in the Near East', *Proc. Prehist. Soc.* XXXII (1966), 30–72
80 Singh, P. *The Neolithic Cultures of Western Asia*. London, 1974

Anatolia

81 Blegen, C. W. *Troy*. 4 vols. Princeton, 1950–8
82 Bostianci, E. Y. 'Researches on the Mediterranean coast of Anatolia', *Anatolia* IV (1959), 129–78
83 Braidwood, R. J., Çambel, H. *et al.* 'Beginnings of Village-farming communities in Southeastern Turkey', *Proc. Nat. Acad. Sci. USA* 68 (1971), 1236–40
84 French, D. W. 'Excavations at Can Hasan', *Anatolian Studies* XII (1962), 27–40; XIII, 29–42; XIV, 125–34; XV, 87–94
85 Garstang, J. *Prehistoric Mersin*. Oxford, 1953
86 Gurney, O. R. *The Hittites*. London, 1952
87 Koşay, H. Z. *Les Fouilles d'Alaca Hüyük; Rapport préliminaire 1937–39*. Ankara, 1951
88 Lloyd, S. *Early Highland Peoples of Anatolia*. London, 1967
89 Lloyd, S. & Mellaart, J. *Beycesultan*. 2 vols. London, 1962–4

90 Mellaart, J. 'Excavations at Haçilar', *Anatolian Studies* VIII (1958), 127–56: IX, 51–66; X, 83–104; XI, 39–76
91 Mellaart, J. *The Chalcolithic and Early Bronze Ages in the Near East and Anatolia.* Beist, 1966
92 Mellaart, J. *Çatal Hüyük. A Neolithic Town in Anatolia.* London, 1967
93 Mellink, M. J. 'Anatolia: old and new perspectives', *Proc. Am. Phil. Soc.* CX (1966), 110–29
94 Ogzuç, T. *Kultepe-Kaniš.* Ankara, 1959

Iran and Turkemenia

95 Contenau, G. & Ghirshman, R. *Fouilles de Tepe Giyan.* Paris, 1935
96 Coon, C. S. *Cave Excavations in Iran 1949.* University of Pennsylvania Museum, 1951
97 Engami, N. & Masuda, S. *The Excavations at Tall-i-Bakun 1956.* Tokyo, 1962
98 Ghirshman, R. *Fouilles de Sialk.* 2 vols. Paris, 1938–9
99 Hole, F. & Flannery, K. 'The prehistory of southwestern Iran: a preliminary report', *Proc. Prehist. Soc.* XXXIII (1967), 147–206
100 Lamberg Karlovsky, C. C. 'Urban interaction on the Iranian plateau: excavations at Tepe Yahya 1967–73', *Proc. Brit. Acad.* LIX (1973), 7–43
101 McBurney, C. B. M. 'The Cave of Ali Teppeh and the Epi-Palaeolithic in N.E. Iran', *Proc. Prehist. Soc.* XXXIV (1968), 385–413
102 McCown, D. *The Comparative Stratigraphy of Early Iran.* Chicago, 1942
103 Masson, V. M. 'The first farmers in Turkmenia', *Antiquity* XXXV (1961), 203–13
104 Meldgaard, J., Mortensen, P. & Thrane, H. 'Excavations at Tepe Guran, Luristan', *Acta Archaeologia* XXXIV (1963), 97–133
105 Mortensen, P. 'Additional remarks on the chronology of early village communities in the Zagros area', *Sumer* XX (1964), 28–36
106 Porada, E. *Ancient Iran. The Art of Pre-Islamic Times.* London, 1965
107 Pumpelly, R. *Explorations in Turkestan. Expedition of 1904.* Washington, 1908
108 Schmidt, E. F. *Excavations at Tepe Hissar, Damghan, 1931–1933.* Pennsylvania, 1937

Iraq

109 Adams, R. M. *Land Behind Baghdad.* Chicago, 1965
110 Braidwood, R. V. & Howe, B. *Prehistoric Investigations in Iraqi Kurdistan.* Chicago, 1960
111 Flannery, K. V. 'The ecology of early food production in Mesopotamia', *Science* 147 (1965), 1247–56
112 Hall, H. R. & Woolley, L. *Ur Excavations I: al'Ubaid.* London, 1927
113 Kramer, S. N. *The Sumerians.* Chicago, 1963
114 Lloyd, S., Safer, F. & Braidwood, R. J. 'Tell Hassuna', *J. Near Eastern Studies* IV (1945), 255–89
115 Mallowan, M. E. L. *Twenty-five years of Mesopotamian Discovery.* 2nd ed. London, 1959
116 Mallowan, M. E. L. & Rose, J. C. *Prehistoric Assyria: The Excavations at Tell Arpachiyah.* Oxford, 1935
117 Mortensen, P. *Tell Shimshara. The Hassuna Period.* Det kgl. Danske Vidensk. Selsk. Hist.-Fil. Skr. 5, 3. Copenhagen, 1970

118 Oates, D. and J. 'Early irrigation agriculture in Mesopotamia', *Problems in Economic and Social Archaeology* (ed. Sieveking *et al.*), 109–35. London, 1976

119 Oates, J. 'Choga Mami, 1967–68. A Preliminary Report', *Iraq* XXXI (1969), 115–52

120 Oppenheim, A. L. *Ancient Mesopotamia. Portrait of a Dead Civilization.* Chicago, 1964

121 Perkins, A. L. *The Comparative Archaeology of Early Mesopotamia.* Chicago, 1949

122 Schmidt, H. *Tell Halaf*, Bd. I. Berlin, 1943

123 Solecki, R. S. 'Prehistory in Shanidar Valley, Northern Iraq', *Science* 139 (1963), 179–93

124 Speiser, E. A. *Excavations at Tepe Gawra*, vol. I. Philadelphia, 1935

125 Tobler, A. J. *Excavations at Tepe Gawra*, vol. II. Philadelphia, 1950

126 Turnbull, P. F. & Reed, C. A. 'The fauna from the Terminal Pleistocene of Palegawra Cave, a Zarzian occupation site in northeastern Iraq', *Fieldiana Anthropology*, vol. 63, no. 3, 81–146. Chicago, 1974

127 Woolley, L. *Ur Excavations II: The Royal Cemetery.* London, 1934

128 Wright, H. E. 'Natural Environment of Early Food Production North of Mesopotamia', *Science*, 161 (1968), 334–9

Levant: Israel to Syria

129 Albright, W. F. *The Archaeology of Palestine.* 5th ed. London, 1960

130 Anati, E. *Palestine before the Hebrews.* London, 1963

131 Bar-Yosef, O. & Goren, N. 'Natufian remains in Hayonim Cave', *Paléorient* 1 (1973), 49–68

132 Garrod, D. A. E. 'The Natufian Culture: the life and economy of a Mesolithic people in the Near East', *Proc. Brit. Acad.* XLIII (1957), 211–27

133 Garrod, D. A. E. & Bate, D. M. *The Stone Age of Mount Carmel*, vol. I. Oxford, 1937

134 Harden, D. B. *The Phoenicians.* London, 1962

135 Kenyon, K. M. *Digging up Jericho.* London, 1957

136 Kenyon, K. M. *Archaeology in the Holy Land.* London, 1970

137 Kirkbride, F. 'Five seasons at the Pre-pottery Neolithic village of Beidha in Jordan', *Palestine Exploration Quart.* 98 (1966), 8–66

138 Moore, A. M. T. 'The excavation of Tell Abu Hureyra in Syria: a preliminary report', *Proc. Prehist. Soc.* XLI (1975), 50–77

139 Mortensen, P. 'A preliminary study of the chipped stone industry from Beidha', *Acta Arch.* XLI, 1–54. Copenhagen, 1970

140 Neuville, R. 'Le Paléolithique et le Mésolithique du Désert de Judée', *Arch. de l'Inst. Pal. Hum.* no. 24. Paris, 1951

141 Perrot, J. 'Le Mésolithique de Palestine...', *Antiquity and Survival* II (1957), 90–110

142 Perrot, J. 'Le gisement Natoufien de Mallaha (Eynam), Israël', *L'Anthropologie* 70, 437–83, Paris, 1966

143 Rust, A. *Die Höhlenfunde von Jabrud (Syrien).* Neumünster, 1950

144 Schaeffer, C. F. A. *Ugaritica*, vols. I–III. Paris 1939, 1949 and 1956

145 Stekelis, M. & Yizraely, T. 'Excavations at Nahal Oren. Preliminary report', *Israel Explor. J.* XIII (1963), 1–12

146 Stubbings, F. H. *Mycenaean Pottery from the Levant.* Cambridge, 1951

CHAPTERS 3 AND 4. FOUNDATIONS OF EUROPEAN CIVILIZATION

General

147 Böhm, J. & de Laet, S. J. (ed.). *L'Europe à la fin de l'âge de la pierre.* Prague, 1961

148 Boardman, J., Brown, M. A. & Powell, T. G. E. *The European Community in Later Prehistory. Studies in Honour of C. F. C. Hawkes.* London, 1971

149 Bruce-Mitford, R. (ed.). *Recent Archaeological Excavations in Europe.* London, 1975

150 Childe, V. G. *The Dawn of European Civilization.* 6th ed. London, 1957

151 Childe, V. G. *The Prehistory of European Society.* Pelican, London, 1958

152 Clark, J. G. D. *Prehistoric Europe: the Economic Basis.* London, 1952, 1971

153 Déchelette, J. *Manuel d'archéologie préhistorique,* I–III. Paris, 1924–7

154 Graziosi, P. *L'Arte dell'Antica Eta della Pietra.* Florence, 1956

155 Hawkes, C. F. C. *The Prehistoric Foundations of Europe to the Mycenaean Age.* London, 1940

156 Leroi-Gourhan, A. *Préhistoire de l'art occidental.* Paris, 1965

157 Piggott, S. *Ancient Europe.* Edinburgh, 1965

158 Previté-Orton, C. W. *The Shorter Cambridge Medieval History.* Cambridge, 1952

159 Sandars, N. K. *Prehistoric Art in Europe.* London, 1968

Eastern Europe and the U.S.S.R.

160 Bader, O. N. *La Caverne Kapovaïa.* Moscow, 1965

161 Berciu, D. *Contributee la Problemele Neoliticului in Rominia in Lumina Noilor Cercetari.* Bucharest, 1961

162 Boriskovskii, P. I. *Palaeolithic of the Ukraine.* Mat. Issled. po Arkh. S.S.R., no. 40. Moscow, 1953

163 Brjussov, A. J. *Geschichte der neolithischen Stämme im europäischen Teil der USSR.* Berlin, 1952

164 Chernish, O. P. *The Paleolithic site Molodova V.* Kiev. 1961

165 Gábori, M. *Les civilisations du paléolithique moyen entre les Alpes et l'Oural. Esquisse historique.* Budapest, 1976

166 Gaul, J. H. *The Neolithic Period in Bulgaria.* Am. School of Prehist. Res. Bull. XVI. Harvard, 1948

167 Gimbutas, M. *The Prehistory of Eastern Europe.* Am. School of Prehist. Res. Bull. XX. Harvard, 1956

168 Golomshtok, E. A. The Old Stone Age in European Russia. *Trans. Am. Phil. Soc.* N.S. XXIX, 2. Philadelphia, 1938

169 Hensel, W. *Ur- und Frühgeschichte Polens.* Berlin, 1974

170 Ivanova, I. K. 'Étude géologique des gisements paléolithiques de l'U.R.S.S.', *L'Anthropologie,* t. 73, 1–48. Paris, 1969

171 Klima, B. 'Übersicht über die jüngsten paläolithischen Forschungen in Mähren', *Quartär* IX (1957), 85–130

172 Klima, B. *Dolní Věstonice.* Prague, 1963

173 McBurney, C. B. M. *Early Man in the Soviet Union. The Implications of some Recent Discoveries.* Reckitt Lecture, British Academy, 1976

174 Milojčič, V. *Chronologie der jüngeren Steinzeit Mittel- und Südosteuropas.* Berlin, 1949

175 Minns, E. H. *Scythians and Greeks.* Cambridge, 1913

176 Minns, E. H. *The Art of the Northern Nomads.* The British Academy, London, 1942

177 Mongait, A. *Archaeology in the U.S.S.R.* Pelican, London, 1961
178 Parker, W. H. *An Historical Geography of Russia.* London, 1968
179 Pidoplichko, I. G. *Late Palaeolithic Dwellings of Mammoth Bones in the Ukraine.* Kiev. 1969
180 Piggott, S. 'The earliest wheeled vehicles and the Caucasian evidence', *Proc. Prehist. Soc.* XXXIV (1968), 266–318
181 Renfrew, C. 'The autonomy of the East European Copper Age', *Proc. Prehist. Soc.* XXXV, 12–47. Cambridge, 1969
182 Rostovtzeff, M. *Iranians and Greeks in South Russia.* Oxford, 1922
183 Rudenko, S. I. *Frozen tombs of Siberia: the Pazyryk burials of Iron-age Horsemen.* London, 1970
184 Sulimirski, T. *Prehistoric Russia.* London, 1970
185 Vértes, L. *Die Höhle von Istállóskö.* Acta Arch. Hung. v. Budapest, 1955
186 Vulpe, R. *Izvoare. Sapaturile din 1936–48.* Bucharest, 1957
187 Wiślański, T. (ed.). *The Neolithic in Poland.* Warsaw, 1970

Greece

188 Blegen, C. W. *et al. The Palace of Nestor at Pylos in Western Messenia.* 3 vols. Princeton, 1966–73
189 Chadwick, John. *The Mycenaean World.* Cambridge, 1976
190 Desborough, V. R. d'A. *The Greek Dark Ages.* London, 1972
191 Dow, S. & Chadwick, J. 'The linear scripts and the tablets as historical documents', *Cambridge Ancient History,* vol. II, pt. 1, pp. 582–626. Cambridge, 1973
192 Dunbabin, T. J. *The Western Greeks,* Oxford, 1948
193 Evans, Sir A. *The Palace of Minos,* I–IV. London, 1921–8
194 Evans, J. D. 'Excavations in the Neolithic Settlement of Knossos, 1957–60, Pts. I–II', *Ann. Brit. School Arch. Athens* LIX (1964), 132–240; LXIII (1968), 239–76
195 Evans, J. D. & Renfrew, C. *Excavations at Saliagos near Antiparos.* British School Athens Suppl. Vol. 5. 1968
196 Heurtley, W. A. *Prehistoric Macedonia.* Cambridge, 1939
197 Higgs, E. S. 'The climate, environment and industries of Stone Age Greece', *Proc. Prehist. Soc.* XXX (1964), 199–244; XXXII (1966), 1–29; XXXIII (1967), 1–29
198 Hutchinson, R. W. *Prehistoric Crete.* London, 1962
199 Karo, G. *Die Schachtgräber von Mykenai.* Munich, 1930
200 Long, C. R. *The Ayia Triadha Sarcophagus.* Göteborg, 1974
201 Mylonas, G. E. *Mycenae and the Mycenaean Age.* Princeton, 1966
202 Nandris, J. 'The development and relationship of the earlier Greek Neolithic', *Man,* vol. 5, no. 2, 192–213. London, 1970
203 Nilsson, M. P. *The Minoan–Mycenaean Religion and Its Survival in Greek Religion.* 2nd ed. Lund, 1950
204 Pendlebury, J. D. S. *The Archaeology of Crete.* London, 1939
205 Renfrew, C. 'Cycladic metallurgy and the Aegean Early Bronze Age', *Am. J. Archaeology,* 71 (1967), 1–26
206 Renfrew, C. *The Emergence of Civilization. The Cyclades and the Aegean in the Third Millennium B.C.* London, 1972
207 Rodden, R. J. 'Excavations at the Early Neolithic site at Nea Nikomedeia', *Proc. Prehist. Soc.* XXVII (1961), 245–67
208 Simpson, H. Hope. *A Gazetteer and Atlas of Mycenaean Sites.* Institute of Classical Studies, London, Bull. Suppl. No. 16, 1965

209 Snodgrass, A. M. *The Dark Age of Greece, an archaeological survey of the eleventh to the eighth centuries B.C.* Edinburgh, 1971
210 Taylour, Lord W. *Mycenaean Pottery in Italy and Adjacent Areas.* Cambridge, 1958
211 Taylour, Lord W. *The Myceneans.* London, 1964
212 Theocharis, D. P. *The Dawn of Thessalian Prehistory.* Volos, 1967
213 Theocharis, D. P. *Neolithic Greece.* National Bank of Greece, Athens, 1973
214 Wace, A. J. B. & Stubbings, F. H. *A Companion to Homer.* London, 1962
215 Wace, A. J. B. & Thompson, M. S. *Prehistoric Thessaly.* Cambridge, 1912
216 Warren, P. *Myrtos. An Early Bronze Age Settlement in Crete.* British School Athens, Suppl. vol. 7, 1972
217 Weinberg, S. S. 'The Stone Age in the Aegean', *Cambridge Ancient History,* vol. I, pt. 1, pp. 557–618. Cambridge, 1970

Northern Europe

218 Althin, C.-A. *Studien zu den bronzezeitlichen Felszeichnungen von Skåne.* Lund, 1945
219 Arbman, H. *The Vikings.* Ancient Peoples and Places. London, 1961
220 Becker, C.-J. *Mosefundne lerkar fra Yngre Stenalder.* Copenhagen, 1948
221 Brøndsted, J. *Denmarks Oldtid,* I–III. Copenhagen, 1957–9
222 Clark, G. *The Earlier Stone Age Settlement of Scandinavia.* Cambridge, 1975
223 Eggers, H. J. *Der römische Import im Freien Germanien.* Berlin, 1951
224 Foote, P. & Wilson, D. M. *The Viking Achievement.* London, 1970
225 Gjessing, G. *Norges Steinalder.* Oslo, 1945
226 Hagen, A. *Norway.* Ancient Peoples and Places. London, 1967
227 Holmqvist, W. *Germanic Art.* Stockholm, 1955
228 Jones, G. *A History of the Vikings.* Oxford, 1975
229 Kivikoski, E. *Finlands Forhistoria.* Helsingfors, 1964
230 Klindt-Jensen, O. *Bornholm i Folkevandringstiden.* Copenhagen, 1957
231 Malmer, M. P. *Jungneolithische Studien.* Lund, 1962
232 Rust, A. *Das altsteinzeitliche Rentier jägerlager Meiendorf.* Neumünster, 1937
233 Rust, A. *Die alt- und mittelsteinzeitlichen Funde von Stellmoor.* Neumunster, 1943
234 Stenberger, M. *Det forntida Sverige.* Stockholm, 1964
235 Todd, M. *The Northern Barbarians 100 B.C.–A.D. 300.* London, 1975

Western Europe

236 Allen, D. F. 'The Belgic dynasties of Britain and their coins', *Archaeologia* XC (1944), 1–46
237 Almagro, M. & Arribas, A. *El Poblado y la Necrópolis Megaliticos de los Millares.* Madrid, 1963
239 Arnal, J. & Burnez, C. 'Die Struktur des französischen Neolithikums...', *Ber. Röm-Germ. Komm.* (1956–7), 1–90
240 Atkinson, R. J. C. *Stonehenge.* London, 1956
241 Bailloud, G. & Mieg de Boofzheim, P. *Les Civilizations néolithiques de la France,* Paris, 1955
242 Bloch, R. *The Etruscans.* Ancient Peoples and Places. London, 1958
243 Brailsford, J. *Early Celtic Masterpieces from Britain in the British Museum.* London, 1975
244 Brea, L. B. *Gli scavi nella caverna delle Arene Candide.* Pt. 1. *Gli strati con ceramiche.* Bordighera, 1946

245 Bruce-Mitford, R. *The Sutton Hoo Ship-burial. A Handbook.* 2nd ed. British Museum, 1972
245* Bruce-Mitford, R. *The Sutton Hoo Ship-burial,* vol. 1. British Museum, 1975
246 Buttler, W. *Der Donauländische und der westische Kulturkreis der jüngeren Steinzeit.* Berlin, 1938
247 Childe, V. G. *Prehistoric Communities of the British Isles.* Edinburgh, 1940
248 Clark, J. G. D. *et al. Excavations at Star Carr.* Cambridge, 1954
249 Clarke, D. L. *Beaker Pottery of Great Britain and Ireland,* vols. I–II. Cambridge, 1970
250 Daniel, G. E. *The Megalith Builders of Western Europe.* London, 1958
251 Daniel, G. & Evans, J. D. 'The Western Mediterranean', *Cambridge Ancient History,* vol. II, pt 2, pp. 713–72. Cambridge, 1975
252 Dehn, W. 'Die Heuneberg beim Talhof...', *Fundber. aus Schwaben* XIV (1957), 78–99. Stuttgart
253 de Valéra, R. 'The court cairns of Ireland', *Proc. Roy. Irish Acad.* 60 C (1959–60), 9–140
254 Duval, P.-M. & Hawkes, C. (ed.). *Celtic Art in Ancient Europe. Five Protohistoric Centuries.* Seminar Press, London, 1976
255 Escalon de Fonton, M. 'Origine et développement des civilisations néolithiques Méditerranéennes en Europe occidentale', *Palaeohistoria* XII, 209–47. Groningen, 1967
256 Evans, J. D. *The Prehistoric Antiquities of Malta; a Survey.* London, 1971
257 Guilaine, J. (ed.). *La Préhistoire française: civilisations néolithiques et protohistoriques.* Paris, 1976
258 Guyan, W. U. (ed.). *Das Pfahlbauproblem.* Basel, 1955
259 Hawkes, C. F. C. 'From Bronze Age to Iron Age...', *Proc. Prehist. Soc.* XIV (1948), 196–218
260 Hawkes, C. & S. (ed.). *Archaeology into History.* Vol. I. *Greeks, Celts and Romans.* London, 1973
261 Hencken, H. *Tarquinia, Villanovans and Early Etruscans,* vol. I, 2. Cambridge, Mass. 1968
262 Herity, M. *Irish Passage Graves.* Dublin, 1974
263 Jacobstahl, P. *Early Celtic Art.* Oxford, 1944
264 Joffroy, R. *Le Trésor de Vix.* Paris, 1954
265 Keiller, A. *Windmill Hill and Avebury.* Oxford, 1965
266 Kimmig, W. 'Zur Urnenfelderkultur in Südwesteuropa'. *Festschr. für Peter Goesseler,* 41–107. Stuttgart, 1954
267 Laming, W. *Lascaux, Paintings and Engravings.* London, 1959
268 Leisner, G. & V. *Die Megalithgräber der Iberischen Halbinsel,* vol. I, II. Madrid, 1943, 1959
269 Leroi-Gourhan, A. & Brezillon, M. 'L'habitation Magdalénienne, No. 1 de Pincevent près Montereau (Seine-et-Marne)', *Gallia* IX, fasc. 2, 263–371. Paris, 1966
270 Lumley, H. de (ed.). *La Préhistoire française: civilisations paléolithiques et mésolithiques.* Paris, 1976
271 Maluquer de Motes, J. 'Pueblas Celtas', *Historia de Espana,* vol. I, pt. 3, 5–194. Madrid, 1954
272 Modderman, P. J. R. 'Die bandkeramische Siedlung von Sittard', *Palaeohistoria* VI–VII, 33–120. Groningen, 1958–9

273 Modderman, P. J. R. 'Elsloo, a Neolithic farming community in the Netherlands', chap. IX in Bruce-Mitford (ed.) *Recent Archaeological Excavations in Europe*. London, 1975
274 Myres, J. N. L. *Anglo-Saxon Pottery and the Settlement of England*, Oxford, 1969
275 Navarro, J. M. de *A Survey of Research on an Early Phase of Celtic Culture*. British Academy, London, 1936
276 Navarro, J. M. de *The Finds from the Site of La Tène*. Vol. I. *Scabbards and the Swords from them*. London, 1972
277 Obermaier, H. *Fossil Man in Spain*. Oxford, 1925
278 Pericot y Garcia, L. *La España primitiva*. Barcelona, 1950
279 Pericot y Garcia, L. *La Ceuva de Parpalló*. Madrid, 1942
280 Piggott, S. *The Neolithic Cultures of the British Isles*. Cambridge, 1954
281 Pittioni, R. *Urgeschichte des Österreichischen Raumes*. Vienna, 1954
282 Radmilli, A. M. (ed.). *Piccola guida della Preistoria Italiana*. Florence, 1962
283 Stone, J. F. S. & Thomas, L. C. 'The use and distribution of faience in the Ancient East and Prehistoric Europe', *Proc. Prehist. Soc.* xxii (1945), 37–54
284 Van der Waals (ed.). *Neolithic Studies in Atlantic Europe*. Groningen, 1966
285 Wainwright, G. I. & Longworth, I. H. *Durrington Walls, Excavations 1966–68*. Soc. Antiq. London. Res. Rep. xxix. 1971
286 Waterbolk, H. T. 'Die bandkeramische Siedlung von Geleen', *Palaeohistoria* vi–vii, 121–61. Groningen, 1958–9
287 Wilson, D. M. *The Anglo-Saxons*. London, 1960

CHAPTER 5. THE AFRICAN ACHIEVEMENT

General

288 Bishop, W. W. & Clark, J. Desmond (ed.). *Background to Evolution in Africa*. Chicago, 1967
289 Clark, J. Desmond. *The Prehistory of Southern Africa*. London, 1959
290 Clark, J. Desmond. *The Prehistory of Africa*. London, 1970
291 Clark, J. Desmond. *The Atlas of African Prehistory* (ed.). Chicago, 1967
292 Davidson, B. *Africa in History*. London, 1974
293 Shaw, C. T. 'Early agriculture in Africa', *J. Hist. Soc. of Nigeria* vi (1972), 143–91

Stone Age

294 Arkell, A. J. *Early Khartoum*. Oxford, 1949
295 Arkell, A. J. *Shaheinab*. Oxford, 1953
296 Balout, L. *Préhistoire de l'Afrique du Nord*. Paris, 1955
297 Caton-Thompson, G. 'The Aterian Industry: its place and significance in the Palaeolithic world', *J. Roy. Anthrop. Inst.* 76 (1946), 87–130
298 Clark, J. D. *Kalambo Falls Prehistoric Site*, vols. i, ii. Cambridge, 1969, 1974
299 Hugo, H. J. (ed.). *Missions Berliet Ténéré-Tchad*. Paris, 1962
300 Leakey, L. S. B. *The Stone Age Cultures of Kenya Colony*. Cambridge, 1931
301 Leakey, L. S. B. *Olduvai Gorge, 1951–1961. A Preliminary Report on the Geology and Fauna*. Cambridge, 1965
302 Leakey, L. S. B. & M. D. *Excavations at the Njoro River Cave*. Oxford, 1950
303 Leakey, L. S. B. & M. D. *Olduvai Gorge, 1951–1961. Excavations in Beds I and II*. Cambridge, 1971
304 Leakey, M. D. 'Report on the excavations at Hyrax Hill...', *Trans. Roy. Soc. S. Africa*. xxx (1945), 271–409

305 Lowe, C. van Riet. *The Distribution of Prehistoric Rock Engravings and Paintings in South Africa.* Pretoria, 1956
306 McBurney, C. B. M. *The Stone Age of Northern Africa.* London, 1961
307 McBurney, C. B. M. *The Haua Fteah (Cyrenaica).* Cambridge, 1967
308 Mori, F. *Tadrart Acacus. Arte rupestre culture del Sahara preistorico.* Turin, 1965
309 Nenquin, J. *Contributions to the Study of the Prehistoric Cultures of Rwanda and Burundi.* Tervuren 1967
310 Sampson, C. G. *The Stone Age Archaeology of Southern Africa.* Dallas, Texas, 1974
311 Shaw, C. T. 'Excavations at Bosumpra Cave, Abetifi', *Proc. Prehist. Soc.* x (1944), 1–67
312 Summers, R. (ed.) *Prehistoric Rock Art of the Federation of Rhodesia and Nyasaland.* New York, 1961
313 Vaufrey, R. *L'Art rupestre nord-Africain.* Paris, 1939
314 Wendorf, F. *The Prehistory of Nubia.* S. Methodist University, Dallas, 1968

Ancient Egypt

315 Brunton, G. & Caton-Thompson, G. *The Badarian Civilization.* London, 1928
316 Caton-Thompson, G. *The Desert Fayum.* London, 1935
317 Edwards, I. E. S. *The Pyramids of Egypt.* Rev. ed. London, 1961
318 Emery, W. B. *Archaic Egypt.* London, 1961
319 Junker, W. B. 'Vorläufige Berichte über die Gräbung...auf der neolithischen Siedlung von Merimde-Benisalâme', *Anz. d. Akad. d. Wiss. Wien (Phil.-Hist. Kl.)* 1929–30, 1932 and 1940
320 Lucas, A. *Ancient Egyptian Materials and Industries.* 4th ed. Revised by J. R. Harris. London, 1962
321 Petrie, W. M. F. *The Royal Tombs of the First Dynasty,* pts. I and II. London., 1900–1
322 Quibell, J. E. & Green, F. W. *Hierakonpolis,* vols. I–II. London, 1900–2

Iron

323 Caton-Thompson, G. *The Zimbabwe Culture.* Oxford, 1931
324 Connah, H. *The Archaeology of Benin.* Oxford, 1975
325 Fagan, B. M. *Iron Age Cultures in Zambia,* 1 and 2. London, 1967–9
326 Evers, T. M. & Van den Berg, R. P. 'Ancient mining in southern Africa...', *J. South African Inst. of Mining and Metallurgy,* vol. 74, no. 6 (1974), 217–26
327 Fagg, B. 'The Nok terracottas in West African art-history', *Actes du 4 Congr. Pan-African,* II, 445–50. Tervuren, 1959
328 Robinson, K. R., Summers, R. & Whitty, A. *Zimbabwe Excavations, 1958.* Nat. Mus. S. Rhodesia, Occ. Papers, III, no. 23A. Causeway, Rhodesia, 1961
329 Shinnie, P. L. (ed.). *The African Iron Age.* Oxford, 1971
330 Willett, F. *Ife in the History of West African Sculpture.* London, 1961
331 Willett, F. *African Art. An Introduction.* London, 1971

CHAPTER 6. THE INDIAN SUB-CONTINENT

Introductory

332 Allchin, B. & R. *The Birth of Indian Civilization.* Pelican, London, 1968
333 Fairservis, W. A. *The Roots of Ancient India.* 2nd ed. Chicago, 1975
334 Piggott, S. *Prehistoric India.* Pelican, London, 1950
335 Sankalia, H. D. *Prehistory and Protohistory of India and Pakistan.* 2nd ed. Poona, 1974
336 Spate, O. H. K. & Learmonth, A. T. A. *India and Pakistan. A Regional Geography.* 3rd ed. London, 1967
337 Subbarao, B. *The Personality of India.* 2nd ed. Baroda, 1958
338 Thapar, R. *A History of India,* vol. I. Pelican, London, 1966

Site reports

339 Allchin, F. R. *Piklihāl Excavations.* Hyderabad, 1960
340 Allchin, F. R. *Utnūr Excavations.* Hyderabad, 1961
341 Allchin, F. R. *Neolithic Cattle-keepers of South India.* Cambridge, 1963
342 Casal, J. M. *Fouilles d'Amri.* Paris, 1964
343 Fairservis, W. A. 'Excavations in the Quetta Valley, West Pakistan', *Anthrop. Papers Am. Mus. of Nat. Hist.* XLV, pt. 2. New York, 1956
344 Lal, B. B. 'Excavations at Hastinapura and other explorations in the Upper Ganga and Sutlej Basins, 1950–2', *Ancient India,* nos. 10–11 (1954–5), 11–151
345 Mackay, E. J. H. *Further Excavations at Mohenjo-daro.* Delhi, 1958
346 Marshall, Sir John *et al. Mohenjo-daro and the Indus Civilization.* London, 1931
347 Misra, V. N. 'Bagor – a late mesolithic settlement in north-west India', *World Archaeology* 1973, 92–110
348 Murty, M. L. K. 'A Late Pleistocene Cave Site in Southern India', *Proc. Am. Phil. Soc.* 118 (1974), 196–230
349 Rao, S. R. 'Excavations at Rangpur and other explorations in Guzarat', *Ancient India* 18–19 (1962–3), 5–207
350 Sankalia, H. D., Deo, S. B., Ansari, Z. D. & Ehrhardt, S. *From History to Prehistory at Nevasa (1954–56).* Poona, 1960
351 Sankalia, H. D., Subbarao, B. & Deo, S. D. *The Excavations at Maheswar and Navdatoli 1952–3.* Poona, 1960
352 Vats, M. S. *Excavations at Harappa.* Delhi, 1940
353 Wainwright, G. J. *The Pleistocene Deposits of the Lower Narmada River.* Baroda, 1964

General

354 Agrawal, D. P. *The Copper Bronze Age in India.* New Delhi, 1971
355 Dales, G. F. 'Recent trends in the Pre- and Protohistoric archaeology of South Asia', *Proc. Am. Phil. Soc.* CX, 2 (1966), 130–9
356 Dani, A. H. *Prehistory and Protohistory of Eastern India.* Calcutta, 1960
357 Ghosh, A. 'The Indus Civilization: its origins, authors, extent and chronology', in Misra & Mate, 113–56
358 Goudie, A. S., Allchin, B. & Hegde, K. T. M. 'The former extensions of the Great Indian Sand Desert', *Geogr. J.* 139, pt. 2 (1973), 243–57
359 Hammond, N. (ed.) *South Asian Archaeology.* Proc. 1st Int. Congr. South Asian Archaeology, Cambridge, 1972

360 Lamberg-Karlovsky, C. C. 'Archaeology and metallurgical technology in Prehistoric Afghanistan, India and Pakistan', *Am. Anthrop.* vol. 69, no. 2 (1967), 145–62
361 Malik, S. C. *Indian Civilization. The Formative Period.* Simla, 1968
362 Misra, V. N. & Mate, M. S. (eds.). *Indian Prehistory: 1964.* Poona, 1965
363 Paterson, T. T. & Drummond, H. J. H. *Soan, the Palaeolithic of Pakistan,* Karachi, 1962
364 Singh, G., Josh, R. D., Chopra, S. K. & Singh, A. B. 'Late Quaternary history of vegetation and climate of the Rajasthan Desert, India', *Phil. Trans. Roy. Soc.* B, vol. 267, no. 889, 467–501. London, 1974
365 Thapar, B. K. 'Recent excavations in India', *Verh. d. Indologischen Arbeitstagung in Museum f. Indische Kunst, Berlin, 1971,* 25–46. Berlin, 1973
366 Wheeler, Sir R. E. M. *The Indus Civilization.* 3rd ed. Cambridge, 1968

CHAPTER 7. EAST ASIA

General

367 Movius, Hallam L. *The Lower Palaeolithic Cultures of Southern and Eastern Asia.* Trans. Amer. Phil. Soc. N.S. 38, pt 4, 329–420. Philadelphia, 1948

China

368 Andersson, J. G. *Children of the Yellow Earth.* London, 1934
369 Anon. *Historical Relics Unearthed in New China.* Foreign Languages Press, Peking, 1972
370 Anon. *Exhibition of Archaeological Finds of the People's Republic of China. Catalogue.* Wen Wu Press, Peking, 1973
371 Barnard, N. *The First Radiocarbon Dates from China.* Monograph on Far Eastern History: 8, School of Pacific Studies, A.N.U. Canberra, 1972
372 Bylin-Althin, M. 'The Sites of Chi' Chia P'ing and Lo Han T'ang in Kansu', *Bull. Museum Far Eastern Antiquities, Stockholm* no. 18 (1946), 383–498
373 Chang, Kwang-Chih. *The Archaeology of Ancient China.* Revised ed. New Haven, 1968
374 Chêng, Tê -K'un. *Archaeological Studies in Szechwan.* Cambridge, 1957
375 Chêng Tê-K'un. 'The origin and development of Shang Culture'. *Asia Major* VI (1957), 80–98
376 Chêng Tê-K'un. *Archaeology in China.* Vol. 1. *Prehistoric China.* Cambridge, 1958
377 Chêng Tê-K'un. *New Light on Prehistoric China.* Cambridge, 1966
378 Childe, V. G. 'The socketed celt in Upper Eurasia', *Ann. Rep. Inst. Arch. Lond. Univ.* 1953, 11, 25
379 Creel, H. G. *The Birth of China.* London, 1936
380 Finn, D. J. *Archaeological Finds on Lamma Island near Hong Kong.* Hong Kong, 1958
381 Karlgren, B. 'Some weapons and tools of the Yin Dynasty', *Bull. Museum Far Eastern Antiquities, Stockholm* 17 (1945), 101–45
382 Li Chi. *The Beginnings of Chinese Civilization.* Washington Univ. Press, 1951
383 Li Chi *et al.* 'Chêng-tzû-yai. A report of Excavations of the Proto-historic site at Ch'êng-tzû-yai, Li-ch'eng Hsien, Shantung', *Archaeologica Sinica* I. Nanking, 1934

384 Loehr, Max. 'Zur Ur- und Vorgeschichte Chinas', *Saeculum* III (1952), 15–55
385 Maglioni, R. 'Archaeology in South China', *J. East Asiatic Studies* II (1952), 1–20
386 Maringer, J. *Contribution to the Prehistory of Mongolia.* Stockholm, 1950
387 Nai, Hsia. 'Our Neolithic ancestors', *Archaeology* 1957, 181–7
388 Needham, J. *Science and Civilization in China.* Vol. I. *Introductory Orientations.* Cambridge, 1954
389 Nelson, N. C. 'The Dune Dwellers of the Gobi', *Natural History* XXVI (1926), 246–51
390 Pei, W. C. 'On a Mesolithic (?) industry in the Caves of Kwangsi', *Bull. Geol. Soc. China* XIV (1935), 383–412
391 Pei, W. C. 'A preliminary study on a new palaeolithic station known as Locality 15 within the Choukoutien region', *Bull. Geol. Soc. China* XIX, no. 2 (1939), 147–87
392 Rawson, J. & Ayers, J. *Chinese Jade through the Ages.* Victoria and Albert Museum Catalogue, 1975
393 Sung, Wen-hsun. *Changpinian. A Newly Discovered Preceramic Culture...on the East Coast of Taiwan.* Taipei, 1969
394 Teilhard de Chardin, P. *Early Man in China.* Peking, 1941
395 Tolstoy, P. 'Some Amerasian Pottery Traits in North Asian Prehistory', *Amer. Antiquity* XIX (1953–4), 25–39
396 Torii, R. & K. 'Etudes Archéologiques et Ethnologiques. Populations primitives de la Mongolie Orientale', *J. Coll. Sci. Univ. Tokyo*, XXXV, art. 4 (1914), 1–100
397 Watson, W. *Cultural Frontiers in Ancient East Asia.* Edinburgh, 1971
398 Willetts, W. *Foundations of Chinese Art.* London, 1965
399 Wu, G. D. *Prehistoric Pottery in China.* London, 1938

Japan

400 Befu, H. & Chard, C. S. 'Preceramic cultures in Japan', *American Anthropologist*, vol. 62. no. 5 (1960), 815–49
401 Gowland, W. 'The dolmens and burial mounds of Japan', *Archaeologia* LV (1897), 439–524
402 Groot, G. J. & Shinoto, Y. *The Shell Mound of Ubamaya.* Ichikawa City, 1952
403 Keally, C. T. 'The earliest cultures in Japan', *Monumenta Nipponica* XXVII (2) (1972), 143–47
404 Kidder, J. E. *Japan before Buddhism.* London, 1959
405 Kidder, J. E. & Esaka, T. *Jōmon Pottery.* Tokyo, 1968
406 Morlan, R. E. 'The Preceramic period of Hokkaido: an outline', *Arctic Anthropology*, vol. IV, no. 1 (1967), 164–220
407 Odda, S. & Keally, C. T. 'The Sengawa site', *Tokyo Archaeological Records*, no. 2, 1974
408 Sansom, G. *A History of Japan.* 3 vols. Stanford University Press, 1958–63
409 Sugihara, S. *The Stone Age Remains found at Iwajuku, Gumma Prefecture, Japan.* Faculty of Literature, Meiji University Archaeology Report, no. 1. Tokyo, 1956
410 Sugihara, S. & Tozawa, M. *Microlithic culture of Shirataki-Hattoridai, Hokkaido, Japan.* Faculty of Literature, Maiji University Archaeology Report no 5. Tokyo, 1975

411 Suzuki, M. 'Chronology of Prehistoric human activity in Kanto, Japan. Pt. 1: Framework for reconstructing prehistoric human activity in obsidian. Pt. 2: Time-space analysis of obsidian transportation', *J. Faculty of Science Univ. of Tokyo (Sect. V: Anthropology)*, IV (1973–4), pt. 3, 241–318, and pt. 4, 395–469
412 Tozawa, M. 'Preceramic industry with knife-blades of Sunagawa, Saitama Pref.', *Mem. Tokyo Archaeological Soc.* vol. 4 (1968), no. 1, 1–42

North-east Asia

413 Chard, C. S. *Northeast Asia in Prehistory*. University of Wisconsin, 1974
414 Michael, H. N. (ed.). *The Archaeology and Geomorphology of Northern Asia*. University of Toronto Press, 1964
415 Okladnikov, A. P. *Yakutia*. McGill-Queen's University Press, Montreal, 1970

South-east Asia

416 Anon. *The Legacy of Phra Ruang*. London, 1974
417 Bayard, D. T. 'Excavation at Non Nok Tha, Northeastern Thailand, 1968'. *Asian Perspectives* XIII (1972), 109–43
418 Boriskovskii, P. I. *Vietnam in primeval times*. Moscow, 1966. Engl. transl. in *Soviet Anthropology and Archaeology* 7
419 Fox, R. B. *The Tabon Caves. Archaeological explorations in Palawan Island, Philippines*. Manila, 1970
420 Glover, I. C. 'Late Stone Age traditions in south-east Asia', *South Asian Archaeology* (ed. N. Hammond). London, 1973
421 Goloubew, V. 'L'âge du bronze au Tonkin et dans le Nord-Annam, *Bull. de l'École Française d'Extrême-Orient* 29 (1929), 1–46
422 Gorman, C. F. 'The Hoabinhian and after: subsistence patterns in Southeast Asia during the late Pleistocene and early recent periods', *World Archaeology* 2 (1970), 300–20
423 Gorman, C. F. 'Excavations at Spirit Cave, North Thailand', *Asian Perspectives* XIII (1972), 79–107
424 Gorman, C. and Charoenwongsa, P. 'Ban Chiang: a mosaic of impressions from the first two years', *Expedition* (1976), 18, no. 4, 14–26
425 Groslier, B. P. *Indochina: Archaeologia Mundi*. London, 1966
426 Harrisson, T. 'The Prehistory of Borneo', *Asian Perspectives* XIII (1972), 17–46
427 Heekeren, H. R. van. *The Stone Age of Indonesia*. The Hague, 1956
428 Heekeren, H. R. van & Knuth, E. *Archaeological excavations in Thailand*. Vol. 1. *Sai-Yok*. Copenhagen, 1967
429 Koenigswald, G. H. R. Von. 'Das Pleistozän Javas', *Quartar*, Bd. 2 (1939), 28–53. Berlin.
430 Mansuy, H. & Colani, M. 'Néolithique inférieure (Basconien) et Néolithique superieur dans le Haut-Tonkin', *Mem. Serv. géol. Indochine*, XII, no. 3, 1925
431 Mulvaney, D. L. & Soejono, R. P. 'The Australian–Indonesian Archaeological expedition to Sulawesi', *Asian Perspectives* XIII (1972), 163–77
432 Oakley, K. P. 'Palaeolithic cultures in Asia' *Framework for Dating Fossil Man*, chap. 6, esp. pp. 246–60. London, 1969
433 Rawson, P. *The Art of Southeast Asia*. London, 1967

434 Saurin, E. & Carbonnel, J. P. 'Evolution préhistorique de la péninsule indochinoise d'après les données récentes', *Paléorient* (1974), vol. 2, 1, 135–65
435 Sieveking, G. de G. 'Excavations at Gua Cha, Kelantan 1954. Part I', *Federation Museums Journal (Malaya)* I–II (1954–5), 75–138
436 Solheim, W. G. 'Northern Thailand, southeast Asia, and world prehistory', *Asian Perspectives* XIII (1972), 145–62
437 Sørensen, P. *Archaeological Excavations in Thailand.* Vol. II. *Ban Kao.* Copenhagen, 1967
438 Watson, W. & Loofs, H. H. E. 'The Thai–British archaeological expedition: a preliminary report on the work of the first season 1965–1966', *J. of the Siam Society* LV (1967), 237–72

CHAPTERS 8–10. THE NEW WORLD

General

439 Bushnell, G. H. S. *The First Americans.* London, 1968
440 Hagen, V. W. von. *The Ancient Sun Kingdoms.* London, 1962
441 Jennings, J. D. & Norbeck, E. (ed.). *Prehistoric Man in the New World.* Chicago University Press, 1964
442 Katz, F. *The Ancient American Civilizations.* London, 1968
443 Kroeber, A. L. *Cultural and Natural Areas of Native North America.* Berkeley, 1939
444 Sanders, W. T. & Price, B. J. *Mesoamerica. The Evolution of a Civilization.* New York. 1968
445 Willey, G. R. *An Introduction to American Archaeology.* Vol. I: *North and Middle America.* Vol. 2: *South America.* New Jersey, 1966–71
446 Willey, G. R. & Sabloff, J. A. *A History of American Archaeology.* London, 1974

Paleo–Indian

447 Borden, C. E. *Origins and Development of Early Northwest Coast Culture to about 3000 B.C.* Archaeological Survey of Canada, Paper no. 45. Ottawa, 1975
448 Butler, B. R. *The Old Cordilleran Culture in the Pacific North-west.* Idaho State University Museum 1961
449 Frison, G. C. (ed.). *The Casper Site: a Hell Gap Bison kill on the High Plains.* New York, 1974
450 Green, F. E. 'The Clovis Blades; an important addition to the Llano complex', *Am. Antiquity* XXIX (1963), 145–65
451 Harington, C. R., Bonnichsen, R. & Morlan, R. E. 'Bones say man lived in Yukon 27000 years ago', *Canadian Geographical Journal,* vol. 91, nos. 1–2 (July–Aug. 1975), 42–8
452 Haynes, C. V. 'Fluted projectile points: their age and dispersion', *Science* CXLV (1964), 1408–13
453 MacDonald, G. F. *Debert. A Palaeo-Indian Site in Central Nova Scotia.* Anthropology Papers, no 16. National Museums of Canada, Ottawa, 1968
454 Wormington, H. M. *Ancient Man in North America.* Denver, 1957
455 Wormington, H. M. & Forbis, R. G. *An Introduction to the Archaeology of Alberta, Canada.* Denver, 1965

456 Williams, S. & Stolton, J. B. 'An outline of southeastern United States prehistory with particular emphasis on the Paleo–Indian era', in Wright & Frey (eds.), 669–83

Middle America

457 Bernal, I. *Mexico before Cortez: Art, History and Legend.* New York, 1963
458 Bernal, I. *The Olmec World.* University of California Press, 1976
459 Coe, M. D. *The Maya.* London, 1966
460 Coe, W. R. 'Tikal', *Expedition* VIII, no. 1 (1965). University of Pennsylvania
461 Drucker, P., Heizer, R. F. & Squier, R. J. *Excavations at La Venta, Tabasco, 1955.* Bur. Am. Ethno. Bull. 170. Washington, 1959
462 Flannery, K. V., Kirkby, A. T. V., Kirkby, M. J. & Williams, A. W. 'Farming systems and political growth in ancient Oaxaca', *Science* 158 (1967), 445–54
463 Hammond, N. (ed.). *Mesoamerican Archaeology: New Approaches.* London, 1974
464 Hammond, N. *Lubaantun. A Classic Maya Realm.* Peabody Mus. Mon. no. 2. Harvard, 1975
465 MacNeish, R. S. 'Preliminary archaeological investigations in the Sierra de Tamaulipas, Mexico', *Trans. Am. Phil. Soc.* XLVIII, pt 6. Philadelphia, 1958
466 MacNeish, R. S. *et al. The Prehistory of the Tehuacan Valley: Environment and Subsistence* (1967); *Non-ceramic artifacts* (1967); *Ceramics* (1970); *Chronology and irrigation* (1972). University of Texas Press, Austin
467 Morley, S. G. *The Ancient Maya.* 3rd ed. Stanford, 1956
468 Thompson, J. E. S. *Maya Hieroglyphic Writing: an Introduction.* Carnegie Inst. Publ. no. 589. Washington, 1950
469 Thompson, J. E. S. *The Rise and Fall of Maya Civilization.* University of Oklahoma, Norman, 1954
470 Thompson, J. E. S. *Maya History and Religion.* University of Oklahoma, Norman, 1970
471 Valliant, G. C. *The Aztecs of Mexico.* Penguin, London, 1951

Temperate North America

472 Drucker, P. *Cultures of the North Pacific Coast.* San Francisco, 1965
473 Griffin, J. B. (ed.). *The Archaeology of Eastern United States.* Chicago, 1952
474 Griffin, J. W. *et al. Investigations in Russell Cave, Alabama.* Nat. Parks Serv. Publ. on Archaeology, 13. Washington, 1974
475 Haag, W. G. (ed.). *Early Indian Farmers and Village Communities.* U.S. Nat. Parks Service, 1963
476 Heizer, R. F. & Krieger, A. D. 'The archaeology of Humboldt Cave, Churchill County, Nevada', *Univ. Cal. Publ. Am. Arch. and Ethn.* 47, 1–19, Berkeley, 1956
477 Jennings, J. D. *Danger Cave.* Utah, 1957
478 Kidder, A. V. (ed.). *An Introduction to the Study of Southwestern Archaeology.* Rev. ed. Yale Univ. Press, 1962
479 Quimby, G. I. *Indian Life in the Upper Great Lakes.* Univ. Chicago Press, 1969
480 Tuck, J. A. *Ancient People of Port au Choix. The Excavation of an Archaic Indian Cemetery in Newfoundland.* Newfoundland Social and Economic Studies No. 17. Memorial University of Newfoundland, 1976

481 Wright, H. E. & Frey, D. G. (ed.). *The Quaternary of the United States. A Review Volume for the VIIth Congress of the International Association for Quaternary Research.* Princeton, 1965
482 Wright, J. V. *Ontario Prehistory.* National Museum of Man, Ottawa, 1972

Arctic North America

483 Anderson, D. D. *Akmak. An Early Archaeological Assemblage from Onion Portage, Northwest Alaska.* Acta Arctica, fasc. xvi. Copenhagen, 1970
484 Bandi, H.-G. *Eskimo Prehistory.* University of Alsaka, 1964
485 Campbell, J. M. (ed.). *Prehistoric Cultural Relations between the Arctic and Temperate zones of North America.* Arctic Institute of North America Technical Paper no. 11. Montreal, 1962
486 Collins, H. B. *Archaeology of St Lawrence Island.* Smithsonian Miscellaneous Collections, vol. 96, no. 1, 1937
487 Fitzhugh, W. W. *Environmental Archaeology and Cultural Systems in Hamilton Inlet, Labrador.* Smithsonian Inst., Washington, 1972
488 Giddings, J. L. *The Archaeology of Cape Denbigh.* Brown University 1964
489 Giddings, J. L. *Ancient Men of the Arctic.* London, 1967
490 Larsen, H. *Trail Creek. Final Report on the Excavation of Two Caves on Seward Peninsula, Alaska.* Acta Arctica, fasc. xv. Copenhagen, 1968
491 Larsen, H. & Rainey, F. G. 'Ipiutak and the Arctic whale hunting culture', *Anthrop. Papers of the American Museum of Natural History* 42. New York, 1948
492 MacNeish, R. S. *Investigations in Southwest Yukon.* Peabody Foundation Archaeology. Andover, 1964
493 Mathiassen, T. *Archaeology of the Central Eskimos.* Copenhagen, 1927
494 Norlund, P. *Viking Settlers in Greenland.* Cambridge, 1936
495 Rainey, F. 'Eskimo Prehistory: the Okvik Site on the Punuk Islands', *Anthropological Papers of the Am. Mus. of Natural History* 37 (4). New York, 1941
496 Rainey, F. *The Ipiutak Culture: excavations at Point Hope. Alaska.* Addison-Wesley, Anthropology Module 8. Reading, Mass., 1971

South America

497 Bennett, W. C. *Ancient Arts of the Andes.* Mus. Mod. Art, New York, 1954
498 Bennett, W. C. & Bird, J. B. *Andean Culture History.* 2nd ed. Am. Mus. Nat. Hist. New York, 1964
499 Bird, J. B. 'The Archaeology of Patagonia' in Steward, J. H. (ed.). *Handbook of South American Indians* i, 17–24
500 Bushnell, G. H. S. *Peru.* 2nd ed. Ancient Peoples and Places. London, 1963
501 Lanning, E. P. *Peru before the Incas.* New Jersey, 1967
502 Lothrop, S. K. *The Indians of Tierra del Fuego.* New York, 1928
503 Meggers, B. J. *Ecuador.* Ancient Peoples and Places. London, 1966
504 Reichel-Dolmatoff, G. *Colombia.* Ancient Peoples and Places. London, 1965
505 Rouse, I. *The Entry of Man into the West Indies.* Yale University Press, 1970
506 Rouse, I. & Cruxent, J. M. *Venezuelan Archaeology.* Yale University Press, 1963
507 Steward, J. H. (ed.). *Handbook of South American Indians,* Vol. 1: *The Marginal Tribes.* Vol. 2: *The Andean Civilizations.* Bur. Amer. Ethn. Bull. 143. Washington, 1946

Australia

508 Angas, G. F. *South Australia Illustrated.* London, 1847
509 Berndt, R. M. (ed.). *Australian Aboriginal Art.* Sydney & New York, 1964
510 Binns, R. A. & McBryde, I. *A Petrological Analysis of Ground-edge Artefacts from Northern New South Wales.* Austr. Inst. of Aboriginal Studies, Canberra, 1972
511 Birdsell, J. B. 'Some population problems involving Pleistocene Man'. *Cold Spring Harbor Symposia on Quantitative Biology* 22 (1957), 47–70
512 Bowler, J. M., Jones, R., Allen, H. R. 8 Thorne, A. G. 'Pleisocene human remains from Australia: a living site and human cremation from Lake Mungo', *World Archaeology* 2 (1970), 39–60
513 Bowler, J. M., Thorne, A. G. & Polach, H. 'Pleistocene man in Australia: age and significance of the Mungo skeleton', *Nature,* 240 (1972), 48–50
514 Clark, C. M. H. *A History of Australia.* Melbourne & New York, 1962
515 Davidson, D. S. & McCarthy, E. D. 'The distribution and chronology of some important types of stone implements in Western Australia', *Anthropos* 52 (1957), 390–458. Vienna
516 Dorch, C. E. & Merrilees, D. 'Human occupation of Devil's Lair, W.A. during the Pleistocene', *Arch. and Phys. Anthrop. in Oceania* 8 (1973), 89–115
517 Edwards, R. & Ucko, P. J. 'Rock art in Australia', *Nature* 246 (1973), 274–7
518 Eyre, E. J. *Journal of Expeditions of Discovery into Central Australia...in the Years 1840–1* (2 vols.) London, 1845
519 Golson, J. 'Both sides of the Wallace Line: Australia, New Guinea and Asian Prehistory', *Arch. and Phys. Anthrop. in Oceania* 6 (1971), 124–44. Sydney
520 Gould, R. A. 'Puntutjarpa rockshelter', *Arch. and Phys. Anthr. in Oceania* 4 (1969), 229–37. Sydney
521 Gould, R. A. *Yiwara.* London, 1969
522 Gould, R. A. *Australian Archaeology in Ecological and Ethnographic Perspective.* Warner Modular Publication 7 (1973)
523 Hale, H. M. & Tindale, N. B. 'Notes on some human remains in the Lower Murray Valley, S.A.', *Rec. S. Aust. Mus.* 4 (1930), 145–219. Adelaide
524 Hallam, S. J. *Fire and Hearth. A Study of Aboriginal Usage and European Usurpation in South-western Australia.* Australian Institute of Aboriginal Studies, Canberra, 1975
525 Jones, R. M. 'The geographical background to the arrival of man in Australia and Tasmania', *Arch. and Phys. Anthrop. in Oceania* 3 (1968), 186–215
526 Jones, R. M. 'Tasmanian Aborigines and dogs', *Mankind* 7 (1970), 256–71
527 Jones, R. M. *Rocky Cape and the Problem of the Tasmanians.* University of Sydney, Ph.D. thesis, 1971
528 Jones, R. M. 'Emerging picture of Pleistocene Australia', *Nature* 246 (1973), 275–81
529 Lampert, R. J. *Burril Lake and Currarong.* A.N.U., Canberra, 1971
530 Lawrence, R. *Aboriginal Habitat and Economy.* Occasional Paper 6, Department of Geography, School of General Studies, A.N.U., Canberra, 1968

531 McBryde, I. *Aboriginal Prehistory in New England.* Sydney University Press, 1974

532 McCarthy, F. D. 'The Lapstone Creek excavation: two culture periods revealed in eastern New South Wales', *Rec. Aust. Mus.* 22 (1948), 1–34. Sydney

533 McCarthy, F. D. 'The Archeology of the Capertree Valley, N.S.W.', *Rec. Aust. Mus.* 26 (1964), 197–246. Sydney

534 McCarthy, F. D. *Australian Aboriginal Stone Implements.* Australian Museum, Sydney, 1967

535 Macintosh, N. W. G. 'The physical aspect of man in Australia' in Berndt (ed.), 1964, 29–70

536 Macintosh, N. W. G., 'Fossil man in Australia', *Aust. J. Science* 30 (1967), 86–98

537 Macintosh, N. W. G. & Larnach, S. L. 'The persistence of *Homo erectus* traits in Australian Aboriginal crania', *Arch. and Phys. Anthrop. in Oceania* 7 (1972), 1–7

538 Meehan, B. 'Cremation in Aboriginal Australia', *Mankind* 8 (1969), 104–9

539 Megaw, J. V. S. 'Excavations in the Royal National Park. . .', *Oceania* 35 (1965), 202–7

540 Meggitt, M. J. *The Desert People.* Sydney & Chicago, 1962

541 Mitchell, S. R. *Stone Age Craftsmen.* Melbourne & New York, 1949

542 Mountford, C. P. (ed.). *Records of the American–Australian Scientific Expedition to Arnhem Land,* 2 vols. Melbourne, 1956 and 1960

543 Mulvaney, D. J. *The Prehistory of Australia.* Rev. ed. Penguin Books, London, 1975

544 Mulvaney, D. J. & Golson, J. (ed.). *Aboriginal Man and Environment in Australia.* Australian National University, Canberra, 1971

545 Mulvaney, D. J. & Joyce, E. B. 'Archaeological and geomorphological investigations on Mt Moffat Station, Queensland', *Proc. Prehist. Soc.* xxxi (1965), 147–212

546 Mulvaney, D. J., Lawton, G. H. & Twindale, C. R. 'Archaeological excavation of rock shelter 6, Fromm's Landing, S.A.', *Proc. Roy. Soc. Vic.* 77 (1964), 479–516

547 Oxley, J. *Journals of Two Expeditions into the Interior of New South Wales.* London, 1820

548 Pearce, R. H. 'Uniformity of the Australian backed blade tradition', *Mankind* 9 (1973), 89–95

549 Roth, H. L. *The Aborigines of Tasmania.* Halifax, 1890

550 Sharp, A. *The Discovery of Australia.* Oxford & New York, 1963

551 Spencer, W. B. & Gillen, F. J. *The Native Tribes of Central Australia.* London, 1899

552 Thomson, D. F. 'The seasonal factor in human culture', *Proc. Prehist. Soc. V* (1939), 209–21

553 Thomson, D. F. *Economic Structure and the Exchange Cycle in Arnhem Land.* Melbourne, 1949

554 Thomson, D. F. 'Some wood and stone implements of the Bindibu Tribe of Central Western Australia', *Proc. Prehist. Soc.* xxx (1964), 400–22

555 Thorne, A. G. 'The racial affinities and origins of the Australian Aborigines', chap. 21 of Mulvaney & Golson (ed.), 1971

556 Thorne, A. G. & Macumber, P. G. 'Discoveries of Late Pleistocene man at Kow Swamp', *Nature* 238 (1972), 316–19

FURTHER READING

557 Tindale, N. B. 'Relationship of the extinct Kangaroo Island culture with cultures of Australia, Tasmania and Malaya', *Rec. S. Aust. Mus.* VI (1937), 39–60
558 Tindale, N. B. 'Archaeological site at Lake Menindee, N.S.W.', *Rec. S. Aust. Mus.* II (1955), 257–73
559 Tindale, N. B. *Aboriginal Tribes of Australia.* University of California Press, 1974
560 White, C. 'Early stone axes in Arnhem Land', *Antiquity* 41 (1967), 149–52
561 White, C. & Peterson, N. 'Ethnographic interpretation of the prehistory of western Arnhem Land', *Southwestern Journal of Anthropology* 25 (1969), 45–67
562 White, J. P. 'Fabricators, *outils écaillés* or scalar cores?', *Mankind* 6 (1968), 658–66
563 Wright, R. V. S. (ed.). *Archaeology of the Gallus Site, Koonalda Cave.* Australian Institute of Aboriginal Studies, Canberra, 1971

New Guinea

564 Brass, L. J. 'Stone Age agriculture in New Guinea', *Geogr. Rev.* XXXI (1941), 555–69
565 Bulmer, S. & R. 'The prehistory of the Australian New Guinea Highlands', *American Anthropologist* 66 (1964), 39–76
566 Chappell, J. 'Stone axe factories in the Highlands of East New Guinea', *Proc. Prehist. Soc.* XXXII (1966), 96–121
567 Golson, J. 'Both sides of the Wallace Line: Australia, New Guinea, and Asian Prehistory', *Archaeology and Physical Anthropology in Oceania* VI (1971), 124–44
568 Lerche, G. & Steensberg, A. 'Observations on spade-cultivation in the New Guinea Highlands', *Tools and Tillage* II (1973), 87–104
569 Malinowski, B. 'Stone implements in Eastern New Guinea', *Essays presented to C. G. Seligman* (ed. E. E. Evans-Pritchard). London, 1934
570 Malynicz, G. L. 'Pig keeping by the subsistence agriculturalists of the New Guinea Highlands', *Search* 1 (no. 5), 2014. Sydney, 1970
571 Powell, J. M. 'The history of agriculture in the New Guinea Highlands', *Search* 1 (no. 5), 199–200. Sydney, 1970
572 Waddell, E. *The Mound Builders. Agricultural Practices, Environment and Society in the Central Highlands of New Guinea.* University of Washington Press, Seattle, 1972
573 White, J. P. 'Ethno-archaeology in New Guinea', *Mankind* 6 (1967), 409–14
574 White, J. P., Crook, K. A. W. & Ruxton, B. P. 'Kosipe: a late Pleistocene site in the Papuan Highlands', *Proc. Prehist. Soc.* XXXVI (1970), 152–70

Polynesia

575 Ambrose, W. 'The unimportance of the inland plains in South Island prehistory', *Mankind* 6, no. 11 (1968), 585–93
576 Annell, B. 'Contribution to the history of fishing in the South Seas', *Studia Ethnographica Upsaliensia* IX (1955)
577 Bellwood, P. 'Excavations at Otakanini Pa., South Koipara Harbour', *J. Roy. Soc. N.Z.* vol. 2, no. 3 (1972), 259–91
578 Best, E. *The Maori Canoe.* Wellington, 1925
579 Buck, Sir P. *Vikings of the Sunrise.* Christchurch, 1964

580 Buist, A. G. *Archaeology in North Taranaki, New Zealand.* N.Z. Arch. Assoc. Monograph No. 3, Wellington, 1964
581 Duff, R. *The Moa-Hunter Period of Maori Culture.* 2nd ed. Wellington, 1956
582 Duff, R. 'Neolithic adzes of Eastern Polynesia' in Freeman & Geddes (eds.), 121–47
583 Duff, R. 'The evolution of Maori warfare in New Zealand', *N.Z. Arch. Assoc. Newsletter.* vol. 10, no. 3 (1967), 114–29
584 Emory, K. P. 'Easter Island's position in the prehistory of Polynesia', *J. Polynesia Soc.* 81 (1972), 57–69
585 Emory, K. P. 'A Re-examination of East Polynesian marae: many marae later' in Green & Kelly (eds.), 1970, 73–92
586 Firth, R. *Primitive Economics of the New Zealand Maori.* London, 1929
587 Freeman, J. D. & Geddes, W. R. (eds.). *Anthropology in the South Seas.* New Plymouth, N.Z., 1959
588 Golson, J. 'Culture change in Prehistoric New Zealand', in Freeman & Geddes (eds.), 29–74
589 Golson, J. 'Lapita ware and its transformations' in Green & Kelly, 1971. 67–76
590 Golson, J. 'The Pacific Islands and their prehistoric inhabitants', chap. 1 of *Man in the Pacific Islands* (ed. R. G. Ward), Oxford, 1972
591 Green, R. C. *A Review of the Prehistoric Sequence in the Auckland Province.* Auckland Archaeological Society, no. 1, 1963
592 Green, R. C. & Kelly, M. (eds.). *Studies in Oceanic Culture History.* Pacific Anthropology Records, Bishop Museum, Honolulu, vols. 1–2, 1970–1
593 Groube, L. M. *Settlement Patterns in New Zealand Prehistory.* Occasional Papers in Archaeology, no. 1. Anthropology Department, Otago University, 1965
594 Groube, L. M. 'The origin and development of earthwork fortifications in the Pacific' in Green & Kelly (eds.), 1970, 133–64
595 Groube, L. M. 'Tonga, Lapita pottery, and Polynesian origins', *J. Polynesian Soc.* 80 (1971), 278–316
596 Higham, C. 'The economic basis of the Foveaux Straits Maori in prehistory', *Problems in Economic and Social Archaeology* (ed. Sieveking *et al.*), 221–33. London, 1976
597 Lanning, E. P. 'South America as source for aspects of Polynesian cultures', in Green & Kelly (eds.), 1970, 175–82
598 Leach, H. M. *Subsistence Patterns in Prehistoric New Zealand,* Studies in Prehistoric Anthropology, vol. 2. Department of Anthropology, Otago University 1969
599 Lockerbie, L. 'From Moa-Hunter to Classic Maori in Southern New Zealand', in Freeman & Geddes (eds.). 75–110
600 Métraux, A. *Easter Island. A Stone-age Civilization of the Pacific.* London, 1957
601 Oliver, D. I. *The Pacific Islands.* Rev. ed. New York, 1961
602 Sharp, A. *Ancient Voyages in the Pacific.* London, 1957
603 Shawcross, W. 'An investigation of prehistoric diet and economy on a coastal site at Galatea Bay, New Zealand', *Proc. Prehist. Soc.* XXXIII (1967), 107–31
604 Shawcross, W. 'Ethnographic economics and the study of population in prehistoric New Zealand: viewed through archaeology', *Mankind* 7 (1970), 279–91

605 Simmons, D. R. *Little Papanui and Otago Prehistory.* Records of the Otago Museum, Anthropology, no. 4, 1967

606 Simmons, D. R. 'Man, moa and the forest', *Trans. Roy. Soc. N.Z.*, General, vol. 2, no. 7 (1968), 115–27

607 Sinoto, Y. H. 'An archaeologically based assessment of the Marquesas as a dispersal centre in East Polynesia', in Gréen & Kelly (eds.), 1970, 105–32

608 Skinner, H. D. 'New Zealand greenstone', *Trans. Roy. Soc. N.Z.* 65 (1935), 211–20

609 Suggs, R. C. *The Island Civilization of Polynesia.* New York, 1960

610 Suggs, R. C. *The Archaeology of Nuku Hiva, Marquesas Islands, French Polynesia.* New York, 1961

611 Trotter, M. M. 'Prehistoric rock shelter art in New Zealand', *Archaeology and Physical Anthropology in Oceania* VI (1971), 235–42

612 Turner, F. J. 'Geological investigation of the nephrites, serpentines and related greenstones used by the Maoris of Otago and South Canterbury', *Trans. Roy. Soc. N.Z.* 65 (1935), 187–210

613 Vayda, A. P. *Maori Warfare.* Wellington, New Zealand, 1960

614 Yen, D. E. 'The origins of Oceanic agriculture', *Archaeology and Physical Anthropology in Oceania* VIII (1973), 68–85

INDEX

Italic figures refer to illustrations